Thirteenth Edition

Hospitality

An Introduction

Robert A. Brymer
Florida State University

Kathryn Hashimoto
East Carolina University

 KENDALL/HUNT PUBLISHING COMPANY
4050 Westmark Drive Dubuque, Iowa 52002

Book Team

Chairman and Chief Executive Officer   Mark C. Falb
President and Chief Operating Office   Chad M. Chandlee
Vice President, Higher Education   David L. Tart
Director of National Book Program   Paul B. Carty
Editorial Development Manager   Georgia Botsford
Developmental Editor   Denise LaBudda
Assistant Vice President, Production Services   Christine E. O'Brien
Senior Production Editor   Mary Melloy
Permissions Editor   Elizabeth Roberts
Cover Designer   Heather Richman

Cover image © 2008, Morozova Tatyana, Shutterstock, Inc.
All Shutterstock images used under license from Shutterstock, Inc.

Copyright © 1977 by Robert A. Brymer
Copyright © 1979, 1981, 1984, 1988, 1991, 1995, 1998, 2000, 2002, 2004, 2007, 2009
  by Kendall/Hunt Publishing Company

ISBN 978-0-7575-5268-7 Student Edition
        978-0-7575-5698-2 Special Edition

All rights reserved. No part of this publication may be reproduced,
stored in a retrieval system, or transmitted, in any form or by any means,
electronic, mechanical, photocopying, recording, or otherwise,
without the prior written permission of the copyright owner.

Printed in the United States of America
10 9 8 7 6 5 4 3 2 1

Dedication

My personal dedication for this book is to my Mom, E. Ann Brymer. She is lovingly referred to in her extended family of ten grandchildren and two great-grandchildren—who are her pride and joy—as Grandma "Annie." She's been a caring, loving, selfless, supportive influence in all of our lives for over 60 years. While she lives a simple life, it is a happy life, and one that we've all depended on in multiple ways.

Annie is always available to listen, to offer words of wisdom crafted from many years experience, and we can count on her to tell us like she sees it. She will assist in any way she can and has been a role model in many ways for my wife and me, as we raised three incredible children often guided from her valuable insights. She has been there through thick and thin, no words can capture the significance of her steady, on-going involvement and what it's meant to our family. Whenever anything happens in our family, Annie is one of the first we call.

Annie always puts the people in her life ahead of herself. She embodies selflessness, and is generous in most every way, especially in the acceptance of people for who they are. We think of her with friends all around, because everyone wants to be her friend. She is often described as a "Sweet Lady," which may also explain her appetite for sweets in many shapes and sizes.

Life with her in our midst has been wonderful, without her our lives would have been dramatically different. Annie means grace—she has been and continues to be, a grace gift from God to her children, grandchildren, and great-grandchildren every day. We appreciate her every day and can't imagine life without her.

Robert A. Brymer

To the man who, after 33 years of marriage, is still my best friend and colleague.

Kathryn Hashimoto

Brief Contents

Contents

Preface

We believe that it is important to give students a well-rounded background in hospitality to pique their curiosity. But from there, it is equally important to identify as many career paths as possible, so that students can identify areas about which they want to learn. Many students come from other disciplines and say, "Oh, if I had known all these choices, I would have switched majors." It is up to us, to show them how vast the industry is, and how many choices and options they can have. We believe this book provides this focus.

There are many introduction to hospitality textbooks available. However, while this book explores many of the general topics common to traditional business and hospitality topics in the first three sections, this book is unique in that it also explores many different career paths. We wanted to discuss the common areas so that students could understand the context in which the industry is housed. However, the topics that make hospitality distinctive lie in the wide variety of options available in each grouping.

Hospitality: An Introduction is systematically organized for the introductory student. The book begins with a broad overview exploring how and why the industry developed into the different components. It is important to understand the realities and opportunities that students may not be aware of in hospitality so we wrote chapter three. From there, we wanted to get students involved in the industry and offered chapter four to learn what associations and rating programs everyone should be aware of and to inspire them to join so that they can begin their valuable networking and learn the applications of the theory from our classes. So that students can learn more about their particular areas of interest, we develop knowledge for gathering information in chapter five. There are so many fields that students have never thought of in terms of a career path. This chapter aids them in expanding their knowledge base by providing them with resources for gathering data. This first section gives them the overall knowledge they need to learn more about this exciting industry and understand the general scope.

The second section, *Hospitality Operations*, explores six of the general areas of business: operations management, human resources, marketing, law, accounting, and physical plant. Except for physical plant, these topics can be found in a business curriculum. However in this book, we explore the subjects that are similar yet different in the service industry. The third section, *Hospitality Business Structures*, gradually narrows the focus to include an introduction to different forms of organizations and management that are available. These five topics discuss the different business structures that are available in hospitality. While other industries also use these formats, hospitality abounds with them and has honed them to a fine science.

In the final section, *Hospitality Career Menu*, we review many specific career options available to prospective managers. The goal is to provide a survey approach to hospitality, while offering the information needed to help students proceed into more advanced courses and readings. In this edition, we have expanded the lodging section to provide more detailed chapters on the types of properties that are available. With the largest subject areas, lodging and F&B, we began with the usually generic discussion of operations. However, we then explored deeper to specific types and their special needs and career paths in separate chapters. The four lodging chapters balance out the five chapters in F&B.

In addition, we have grouped the career paths by subjects and created two new sections on tourism and specialized career paths. The section on tourism includes many of the topics that excite students like casinos, golf, meetings and events, and cruise lines. These types of business also can have lodging and F&B; however, they become amenities to the business rather than the opposite. Meetings and events draws many different types of people to locations for a dedicated purpose. However, each location hopes that this will introduce people to the region or destination and want to return. The last section delves into specialized career paths. Areas are important to the hospitality industry but not in the limelight. Design, international hospitality, real estate, and teaching are not for everyone but they are important areas that should be explored.

As you can see, this book has a vast amount of knowledge for students that both excites them and allows them to go deeper into the subjects that most interest them. Because we have a chapter on each topic, it allows students to have enough basic knowledge to know whether the world of hospitality is for them and most importantly, where they might fit in.

Acknowledgments

The thirteenth edition of this book is a collection of readings written by 44 authors representing 31 colleges and universities across the United States. These authors have written papers specifically for this book, and without their generous contributions the publication of this edition would not have been possible. They have truly created an outstanding edition, and we are very grateful for the special role each and every author played.

Donna Albano, *The Richard Stockton College of New Jersey*

Susan W. Arendt, *Iowa State University*

Brad Beran, *Johnson & Wales University, Charlotte*

Daniel Bernstein, *Seton Hill University*

Ernest P. Boger, *University of Maryland Eastern Shore*

Sherie Brezina, *Florida Gulf Coast University*

Ronald J. Cereola, *James Madison University*

Wanda M. Costen, *University of Tennessee*

Dan Crafts, *Missouri State University*

John C. Crotts, *College of Charleston*

Chris DeSessa, *Johnson & Wales University*

Dawn M. Fiihr, *Iowa State University*

Reginald Foucar-Szocki, *James Madison University*

Morgan W. Geddie, *California State University, Chico*

Susan Gregory, *Eastern Michigan University*

Christian E. Hardigree, *University of Nevada, Las Vegas*

Joe Hutchinson, *University of Central Florida*

Miyoung Jeong, *Iowa State University*

Heather Kaikini, *College of Charleston*

Keith Mandabach, *New Mexico State University*

Karl J. Mayer, *University of Nevada, Las Vegas*

Cynthia R. Mayo, *Delaware State University*

S. Denise McCurry, *MGM Mirage*

Robert A. McMullin, *East Stroudsburg University*

Richard J. Mills, Jr., *Robert Morris University*

Gail Myers, *Suite Harmony Corporation*

Ken Myers, *University of Minnesota Crookston*

Radesh Palakurthi, *Oklahoma State University*

Wally Rande, *Northern Arizona University*

B. J. Reed, *University of Wisconsin–Platteville*

David Rivera, Jr., *East Carolina University*

Denis P. Rudd, *Robert Morris University*

Chay Runnels, *Stephen F. Austin University*

Michael Scales, *The Richard Stockton College of New Jersey*

John M. Stefanelli, *University of Nevada, Las Vegas*

Nancy Swanger, *Washington State University*

Marcia Taylor, *East Carolina University*

Patrick T. Tierney, *San Francisco State University*

Mel Weber, *East Carolina University*

Michele L. Wehrle, *Community College of Allegheny County*

Burch Wilkes, *Pennsylvania State University*

John Wolper, *University of Findlay*

Paula Wolper, *University of Findlay*

Christopher Woodruff, *Lake Michigan College*

About the Authors

Robert A. Brymer

*R*obert A. Brymer, Ph.D., CHA, is the Director of the Dedman School of Hospitality, College of Business, at Florida State University, and the Cecil B. Day Professor of Lodging Management. He is nationally recognized in hotel management and education in the following ways.

- Ranked 18th in hospitality research influence and 20th in hospitality research productivity worldwide
- Certified Trainer in Stephen Covey's *7 Habits of Highly Effective People*
- Recognized in Harvard University's *Profiles in Business & Management: An International Directory of Scholars and Their Research*
- Appointed to the *White House Conference on Travel and Tourism*
- Stevenson Fletcher CHRIE Achievement Award
- Van Nostrand Reinhold CHRIE Research Award
- Elected a Fellow in the American Institute of Stress
- Florida State University Teaching Award
- Certified Hotel Administrator by the American Hotel & Lodging Association

Dr. Brymer has over 30 years of management, consulting, and education experience in the hotel industry. He has held management and supervisory positions with Hyatt Hotels, Westin Hotels, and Hospitality Management Corporation. In 2000, while on sabbatical from Florida State University, he worked for several months in daily operations at The Ritz-Carlton Hotel, in Sydney, Australia. His management seminars have been presented for more than 7000 managers in the hotel industry, including Four Seasons, Walt Disney World, Ritz-Carlton, Marriott, Hyatt, Hilton, Westin, Inter-Continental, and many five-star independent hotels and resorts.

Dr. Brymer earned his doctorate in Psychology from The University of Denver, where he specialized in executive and management psychology. He has an M.B.A. in Hotel, Restaurant, and Institutional Management from Michigan State University and a B.S.B.A. in Hotel and Restaurant Management from The University of Denver. He is one of the hotel industry's leading authorities in managerial and organizational psychology, and has conducted research in the areas of executive personality, leadership behavior, ethics, service excellence, and managerial stress.

Kathryn Hashimoto

*K*athryn Hashimoto, Ph.D. worked in resort operations for over 12 years developing strategic marketing plans and sales. After obtaining her M.B.A. in management and another in marketing, she realized that consumer behavior was an area she would like to focus on and went back to school for her M.S. in theoretical psychology. She began teaching marketing in colleges of business and realized that a Ph.D. was necessary. So she returned for a Ph.D. in marketing and then another Ph.D. in Curriculum and Instruction before moving into teaching marketing and service classes in hospitality programs.

Her areas of interest are in international consumer behavior especially in advertising, service management/training, and casinos. Currently, Dr. Hashimoto has seven textbooks and numerous presentations and articles on these topics. She can be reached at East Carolina University, hashimotok@ecu.edu.

Part 1

Hospitality Industry

Hospitality: An Introduction

1

Kathryn Hashimoto, East Carolina University
Robert A. Brymer, Florida State University

© 2008, JupiterImages Corporation.

≈ *Learning Objectives*

☑ An overview of the industry
☑ An overview of this book so that you will know what to expect

≈ *Chapter Outline*

The Service-Tourism-Hospitality Connection
Hospitality

≈ *Key Terms*

Service
Service experience
Service product
Moment of truth
Ambience or servicescape

This book is about one of the fastest growing industries in the world. It comes to you at a time when the wonderful world of hospitality has never been more exciting. Hospitality refers to those organizations that offer services like food, drink, lodging, and entertainment. However, in creating these service products, there are many fields that are incorporated. For example, people may not realize that sculptors are needed in food organizations to create ice and food sculptures for banquets and restaurants. Interior designers help create the fantasy of a casino's pirate fantasy or a Chinese restaurant's theme. Meeting planners can organize weddings at Disneyland or a meeting of the local bar association or a convention of ten thousand attendees. In addition, hospitality enterprises need many different types of skills from artists to public relations to accountants.

On a broader scale, they are part of the service industry. There are four areas where service is different from manufacturing. First, the service product is intangible. This means that, unlike a table that you can take back and exchange, a service once offered cannot be taken back. Once a guest meets and interacts with the employee—*the moment of truth*—the service experience is created for better or worse. Second and third, the service is inseparable from and variable by the provider. You, the provider, cannot totally separate yourself and your thoughts from how you behave with other people. In addition, as you change moods, the service that you deliver also changes from moment to moment because each employee the guest encounters creates the service experience. Finally, service cannot carry inventory. The service experience is created at the decisive moment and a good encounter cannot be carried until tomorrow. This means that we need special people who like people and truly want to help make the guests' experience the best possible. The authors in this book will introduce you to an industry that is a "people" business. Chapter after chapter will reaffirm that, in the world of hospitality, taking good care of the guest is the single most critical element for success.

Hospitality: An Introduction is systematically organized for the introductory student. The book begins with a broad overview exploring how and why the industry developed into the different components. It is important to understand the realities and opportunities that you may not be aware of in hospitality so we wrote Chapter 3. From there, we wanted to get you involved in the industry and of-fered Chapter 4 to learn what associations and rating programs you should be aware of and to inspire you to join so that you can begin your valuable networking and learn the applications of the theory from your classes. So that you can learn more about your particular areas of interest, we develop your knowledge for gathering information in Chapter 5. There are so many fields that students have never thought of in terms of a career path. This chapter aids you in expanding your knowledge base by providing you with resources for gathering data. This first section gives you the overall knowledge you need to learn more about this exciting industry and understand the general scope.

The second section, *Hospitality Operations*, explores six of the general areas of business; however, they explore the areas that are the same yet different in the service industry. The third section, *Hospitality Business Structures*, gradually narrows the focus to include an introduction to different forms of organizations and management that are available. In the final section, *Hospitality Career Menu*, we review many specific career options available to prospective managers. Please see Figure 1.1 for a graphic view of how the book is organized. The goal is to provide a survey approach to hospitality, while offering the information needed to help students proceed into more advanced courses and readings.

The Service-Tourism-Hospitality Connection

For a better understanding of where the industry fits in the economy, please refer to Figure 1.2. Starting at the top of that chart—The Economy—you will see that the economy is made up of agriculture, manufacturing, and service. They are three separate parts of the economy, yet each plays a role in the service part of the economy. In the past, agriculture and manufacturing contributed the most to the economy. Agriculture focuses on growing the food that is necessary for survival. Once that production process is stable and people have enough to eat, the economy moves on to manufacturing. Manufacturing helps build products that make life easier. We can evaluate these products with our five senses like touch or smell. As other countries have developed cheaper labor, American manufacturing has changed. Now the service sector is the most dominant contributor.

Figure 1.1 Organization of the Book

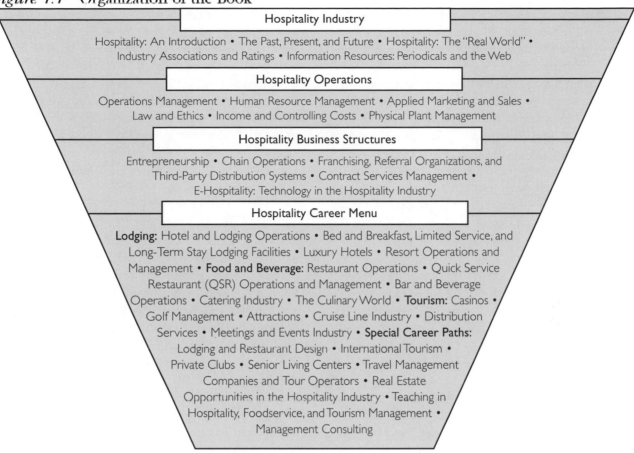

Figure 1.2 The Service-Tourism-Hospitality Connection

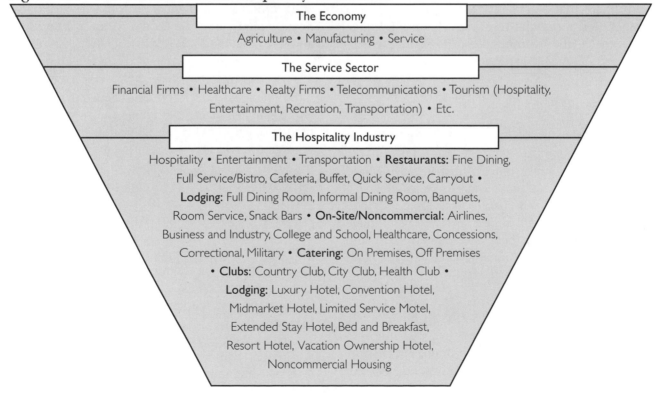

This shift of dominance from agriculture and manufacturing to service has required people to acquire different skills. In an agricultural economy, people were engaged in growing crops and getting them prepared for consumer consumption. Service played a very small role because most of the focus was on climates and crops. In a manufacturing economy, people were occupied with the process of creating a product and what machinery can be used to speed up the process. Service played a more important role because more people were involved in the process. In today's service economy, there is no tangible product—the product is mostly service—and the quality of that product rests in the mind of the guest. Therefore, people skills are critical to operations.

In a hotel, the room is the tangible product. However, in picking the hotel, the guest spends more money for the ambience and the service. By the same token, people go to a restaurant to eat, but the way they are treated is just as important. Think about your best experience in a restaurant. You enjoyed the food, of course. However, what if the server was rude? What would happen to your feeling about the restaurant experience? Herein lays the difficult and exciting part of this industry: forecasting the guests' service expectations. The skills necessary to survive in an agricultural economy and manufacturing economy are physical and mental. In the service economy, they are more interpersonal and intellectual. For many people, this is quite a change and a difficult transition. Figure 1.2 illustrates the relationship between the economy, service, and the hospitality industry.

Hospitality

The hospitality industry includes many different segments, as can be seen in Figures 1.1 and 1.2, including recreation, entertainment, travel, food service, lodging, and many others. We will devote a little more time in this chapter to lodging and food service, the two single largest sectors. Even though they are the largest, they are closely related and work hand-in-hand with many other vital segments of this vast industry.

Lodging

If you were to ask 10 people to give you an example of the lodging industry, you might get answers like: a resort in the Bahamas or Hawaii; a small inn in Vermont; a bed and breakfast in Cape May, New Jersey; a small exclusive converted castle in France; a roadside motel in Akron, Ohio; a 1200-room luxury hotel in New York; a 100-room budget motel in Fresno, California; an all suite hotel in Memphis; a mega hotel in Las Vegas; and an apartment hotel in London. All of these answers, although different in some ways, represent examples of the lodging industry. The common bond is that they all have sleeping rooms.

However, the amenities and quality of service will vary from concept to concept. A Motel 6 will give you a clean room with bed and bath, while a Marriott might provide you with additional amenities like a fitness center and a swimming pool. A resort will allow you to walk around the grounds and play golf or go to the spa and have a clean room with bed and bath. Some will have extensive food service with two or three restaurants with different cuisines and 24-hour room service. Some will have one restaurant that serves breakfast, lunch, and dinner. An apartment or residential hotel may provide the guests with a fully equipped kitchen. A bed and breakfast will serve only breakfast. Some will have no food service except for a vending machine with snacks and soft drinks. The profitability percentage of a sold guest room is usually higher than selling a meal. Therefore, many owners make the decision not to have food service in their properties because of the profitability picture and the difficulty of operating a food service facility. In some cases, lodging owners want to provide food service for their guests and will lease the food service facility.

Some lodging facilities will have five employees to service each room, while others will have two or more employees per room. The Peninsula Hotel in Hong Kong changes your linens and towels several times a day to provide the ultimate in service while other hotels will ask you to throw the towels on the floor only when you want them changed to protect the environment. If you think about how much water and soap it takes to wash all those sheets and towels, you can see that even using towels one more day before washing them can make a big difference in water usage. In places that regularly have droughts, like California, this is an important factor. It is amazing that there are over 50,000 lodging operations in the United States. What incredible opportunity.

The lodging industry is very broad and varied, with each segment requiring a different skill set. Can you imagine the amount of experience you

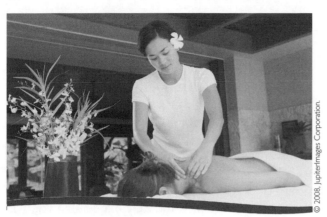

Amenities vary within the lodging industry. Some resorts include a spa.

© 2008, JupiterImages Corporation.

would need to run one of those mega properties in Las Vegas with 4,000 to 5,000 rooms? You would actually be running a medium sized corporation. You would need to have experience in all facets of hotel operations, excellent interpersonal and leadership skills, extensive food and beverage experience to run 12 to 24 different venues, plus excellent knowledge of the gaming industry. Obviously, to run a 100-room or less property without food and beverage would require much less experience than the Vegas property. Some managers of these properties have less than 5 years of experience in the lodging business.

The basic strategy in the lodging business is to sell rooms; that is pretty obvious. The challenge for marketing is to bring people in to buy rooms. Once the guest is at the property, a challenge might be to sell them the kind of room they desire at a price that represents value to the guest. Like quality, the guest, not the management of the property, determines value. A guest room is a perishable product. If it is not sold on any one night, that revenue is lost, so the challenge is to know how to sell that room based on the guests' expectation and their perception of value.

Food Service

This part of the hospitality industry is growing at a dramatic rate. The reason for this growth is that consumers are changing their eating habits. In the 1950s, the woman stayed at home and cooked for her husband and two children. The measure of her success as a wife and mother was her cooking abilities and how much time she labored in the kitchen. Going out to eat was only for special occasions. Now, there are varieties of households, ranging

from singles to one-parent families to couples with no kids to the two-parent family. In order to meet their economic needs, the adults in the family are working longer hours. Therefore, there is less time to spend buying groceries and preparing meals. As a result, more people are consuming meals away from their homes or are bringing prepared food home to eat. The increase in second-income families and the inadequate time to prepare meals is a significant factor in this trend.

However, this industry is far more than just food and service. For example, how many different reasons can you think of for going out to eat? Hunger, of course. However, what else? How about getting together with friends to socialize or impressing a special someone, or creating a romantic mood. Because there are so many different reasons for eating out, it makes sense that restaurants come in all types of price ranges and service qualities in order to meet the needs of their guests. For example, quick service restaurants cater to our frantic on-the-go lifestyle. Family restaurants attempt to keep kids occupied with activities like placemats that they can draw on while they wait for their food. At the upper end of the spectrum are restaurants that serve great food and deliver exceptional service. In each of these different venues, understanding the guests' needs and providing the kind of food and good service they want is important.

However, there is another aspect of any service environment: ambiance or servicescape. Ambiance is made up of the décor, the sound level, the lighting, the furniture, and the symphony of dining sounds created by both the diners themselves—their conversation and laughter—and the clanking of dishes and silverware. What type of ambiance do you like when going out to eat? When Windows on the World reopened in 1996, the president of Windows, Joe Baum, announced at the employee orientation, "We are not in the restaurant business; we are in the entertainment business because we are creating a unique experience." He took the notion of a dining experience to the next level. Windows on the World went on to become the highest volume restaurant in the United States. Unfortunately, that ended on September 11, 2001, when the industry and the world lost many good people.

The restaurant segment of the food service industry can be a trip around the world. In any major city, you can experience food from almost any country in the world. New taste sensations are created as chefs blend different cuisines to produce

When you go to a restaurant, the service is as important as the meal.

© 2008, JupiterImages Corporation.

what is called "fusion" cuisine. For example, the blending of the flavors from Chinese and French cuisine produces a new, unique taste. Creative themes and décor can enhance the eating experience by transporting the guest to any country in the world or make them feel like they are in the 18th or the 23rd century. The diversity of the restaurant segment is immense. As a customer, you can spend 5 dollars for dinner or you can spend 100 dollars for dinner. You can select from an assortment of 5 beverages or a selection of 1,000 varieties of wine. You can also experience an operation that is owned by an individual who has one restaurant and works at it all the time or a restaurant that is one of a thousand restaurants owned by a corporation, where the owners are never around. For the employee, both entrepreneurial properties and franchises have advantages and disadvantages.

In addition, the food service industry is made up of more than just restaurants. The non-commercial food service industry feeds students—elementary, secondary, and college—as well as patients and corporate employees. The challenge is to offer food they will eat and that is nutritious. In some college dining programs, a cafeteria is set aside just for vegetarians. That goes a long way to meet and exceed the expectations of the customer. There will be many students who will choose that university because they have a vegetarian cafeteria. Hospital food service is challenging in that meals must be suitable for all kinds of diets that are required by patients. Many institutional dining facilities (hospitals, schools, companies) have gone to branding. Branding is taking a known brand like McDonald's and opening that facility in a hospital or a school. This trend brings to the operation the name recognition and appeal that goes with it, as well as the standards of operation for that brand.

An often overlooked segment of the food service industry is the private club segment. Private clubs are owned and run by its members. Therefore, the focus is on satisfying the needs of a small group of people. You know these people because they come in regularly and they expect that you will know their names and their preferences for drinks and food. These operations can provide an exciting, interesting place to work, especially if the club has a large food service facility that serves a la carte and has catering for special events. In addition to the food service operation, a manager could end up managing the challenges of other activities like a golf course or tennis courts.

Probably the largest segment of this industry is the quick-service or fast food restaurants. As we mentioned earlier, quick service meets our needs for food when we are on the run. As you know, you can eat in or drive through, which affords a variety of eating options like eating at your desk or in the car on the way to classes. Quick-service restaurants are continually trying to reinvent themselves, but the eating public continues to go for that hamburger, fried chicken, and pizza.

Another subdivision of the food service business is found in special events and catering. Special events include food service at outdoor concerts, golf tournaments, tennis tournaments, and huge events like the Olympics. These events are intense and many times more difficult to operate because the dining tents and kitchens are normally temporary. During the Winter 2002 Olympics, the food service people were providing 100,000 meals per day. The dining tent in the Olympic Village housed 1,300 seats, a huge kitchen, and a full-service McDonald's. Working in stadiums and arenas is a unique challenge because they contain almost every segment of the food service industry: concession stands, private clubs, luxury skyboxes, a la carte restaurants, and catering for special events. As a free bonus, you get the excitement of watching a major sporting event. As you can see, food service has a broad variety of venues that will be explored in this book. Knowing about all these different types will allow you to decide whether this is the career path for you.

As you can see from our brief exploration of just food and lodging, there are many components of the hospitality industry that you may never have realized. In this book, you will find that there are even more opportunities for careers as we explore many segments. As a result, we have included sections on operations in tourism and specialized careers. In the tourism section, we explore companies that draw tourists to destinations on a regular basis like casinos, golf, and area attractions. On the other hand, meetings and events are more short-term attractors that draw people for a one time visit. However, we hope that tourists will enjoy the area enough to come back for the other local attractions.

Our last section in the book is what we call specialized career paths. They are topics that are close to the hospitality industry but not what we would call mainstream. However, we could not exist without them. If you are interested in designing or selecting sites, creating environments, both inside and outside, that makes people feel warm and friendly or excited, then this may be the career path for you. On the other hand, if you like to travel to see new places, then travel management companies and international hospitality may be something you would enjoy. Private clubs and senior living centers are specialized to cater to people who are regulars where outsiders are by invitation only. Finally, if you have a vast amount of experience, don't want the same work environment every day, and look for challenges, then management consulting is certainly an option. As you can see, there are many career choices in hospitality.

Summary

However, the bottom line in the hospitality business is managing the *moments of truth*. A moment of truth is any time the guest comes in contact with anything that represents the operation. The perception of that contact could be positive or negative. Those contacts could be the condition of the parking lot, the friendliness of the voice on the phone when the reservation was made, the cleanliness of the entranceway, the greeting by the front desk person or a hostess, the speediness of the elevator, and so on. In a one-night stay or the time it takes to enjoy a meal, the guest could experience 100 moments of truth. The greatest challenge in the industry is to manage those moments of truth so that they are positive for the guest who then wants to return and tell their friends how wonderful their encounter was. These happy memories create the desire in our guests and everyone who hears their stories to come and experience the adventure. Hospitality, tourism, and service are interwoven in this exciting worldwide industry.

Enjoy your exploration into the industry, companies, operations, and careers. Welcome!

≈ *Resources*

Internet Sites

Career Builder: hospitality.careerbuilder.com/
Hospitality Net: www.hospitalitynet.org
HCareers: www.hcareers.com/
Hospitality Online: www.hospitalityonline.com

Chapter 1
Review Questions

1. Why is the hospitality industry referred to as a "people" business?

2. What are the three separate parts of the economy described by the author? Define each.

3. Describe the major shift in the economy concerning the manufacturing industries and the service industries.

4. What is the product in a service economy?

5. Who judges the quality level of service?

6. What are the skills necessary to survive in the service economy?

7. Describe the various segments of the hospitality industry.

8. Describe the current trends in the food service industry. How and why are they changing?

9. List three to five factors which influence decisions concerning a meal away from home.

10. What is fusion cuisine?

11. What is a challenge of the non-commercial food industry?

12. Describe the different attributes of the private club segment of the hospitality industry.

13. What are the common menu choices of fast food restaurants?

14. What types of venues are likely to cater to or hold special events?

15. What makes working in stadiums and arenas a unique challenge?

16. Give six examples of different types of lodging.

17. What is the range of employees per guest room ratio? How does that vary within the lodging industry?

18. What are the different types of food services you will find in many hotels?

19. What type of lodging management skills would be needed to run a mega-property in Las Vegas?

20. What is meant by the concept that a guest room is perishable?

21. List five examples of "moments of truth" in a hospitality setting.

22. What is one of the greatest challenges related to managing moments of truth?

The Past, Present, and Future

2

Reginald Foucar-Szocki and Ronald J. Cereola
James Madison University

© Palis Michael, 2008, Shutterstock.

≈ *Learning Objectives*

☑ Describe the role of Ellsworth Statler in the evolution of the lodging industry
☑ Explain the culture of Marriott, Inc.
☑ Detail Escoffier's impact on the role of the chef
☑ Point out qualities of Julia Child, Ray Kroc, Colonel Sanders, and Walt Disney that influence our industry today
☑ Understand the changing role of the U.S. economy and the scope of the hospitality and tourism industry
☑ Begin to think outside the box of what the industry might look like when you are ready to retire at age 70

≈ *Chapter Outline*

Overview
Food: The Universal Language
2050: A Hospitality Odyssey

≈ *Key Terms*

Profit sharing plan
Condo-hotel
Scientific management
The Marriott Way
Democratization of travel
Environmental scanning
Franchise
Mega resort
Space tourism

$\mathcal{W}$elcome to a great learning experience, filled with new ideas, insights, and understandings about the wonderful world of hospitality. The focus of this chapter is to examine the past, present, and future of hospitality and tourism management. There are several ways we can explore the subject matter (1) prepare you to be a contestant who knows bits and pieces on "Jeopardy"; (2) drown you in facts and figures; or (3) provide a balance of people, places, and things that make your professors love the multi-faceted business of hospitality and tourism management. It should come as no surprise that Option 3 will be the direction of this chapter. We have selected a few of the colorful characters that shaped the business over the past century in order to present a snapshot of the present state of the industry and finish with what hospitality and tourism management might look like in 2050.

Overview

We will begin our tour of the lodging side of the industry with a gentleman called Ellsworth Statler, the most famous hotelier of the early 20th century, and then learn about how a simple nine-seat A&W root beer stand turned into Marriott, Inc. On the food side, one of the great visionaries was Augustine Escoffier who professionalized the role of chef/culinarian and created dishes that are still served a century later. Before Rachel Ray, Emeril, and Bobby Flay, there was Julia Child, who taught Americans how to cook. At the same time there was a milkshake mixer salesperson who founded McDonald's, a Colonel who had a recipe, and a man with a dream of a magical kingdom.

We'll continue our tour with the definitive hospitality and tourism event, the Olympic Games, and a passing of the torch from manufacturing to the service economy as the backbone of the U.S. economy. Lastly, we'll look at life after iPods, IMS, Facebook, the Travel Channel, and the Food Network to see what the field of hospitality and tourism management will look like in the future.

Again, there is no way to cover every person, place, and thing that makes our industry great. This is a simple snapshot; a single dimension model that we hope will be a springboard for future studies. We hope that after reading this book, you will turn our snapshot into a four dimensional interactive web-based model of hospitality and tourism.

Statler: The Light Bulb Goes On

In 1901, Buffalo, New York, was preparing to host 8 million people at the Pan American Exhibition. An entrepreneur named Ellsworth Statler started his fascination for hotels by building temporary structures for these guests. He opened his first permanent hotel in Buffalo in 1907, offering "a room with a bath for a dollar and a half."[1] His target market was the ordinary traveler. Value, guest satisfaction, and cleanliness were his priorities. Statler was fascinated with ways to make hotel operations more efficient and is credited with the idea of building bathrooms back to back, minimizing the expenses and allowing a private bathroom for each guest, something that was new and in stark contrast to the water closets (WCs) of European hotels. He would spend hours with housekeepers and engineers, looking at ways to make the hotel more efficient and thus more profitable.

On December 11, 1916, Ellsworth acquired the operating lease of the Hotel Pennsylvania in New York City for an annual sum of $1 million.[2] It was the largest hotel in the United States. More important than guest conveniences was his belief in his employees. Ellsworth Statler had a unique saying: "Life is service. The one who progresses is the one who gives his fellow human beings a little more, a little better service."[3] He was the first to give hotel staff a 6-day week, paid vacations, and free health care. He devised a profit sharing plan that matched a free stock share with each one purchased by employees.[4] It is easy to see why Ellsworth Statler is called "the hotel man of the half century" and the father of inn keeping science. On October 27, 1954, Conrad Hilton purchased the Statler chain for $111 million in what was then the largest real estate transaction in history.[5]

Marriott: Humble Beginnings

During the 1950s, another famous hotel line, Marriott, was in its infancy building on 25 years of success in food service operations. Today, this dynamic organization has more than 2,800 lodging properties employing 151,000 associates in the United States and 67 other countries and territories.[6] This company began in 1927 as a nine-seat A&W root beer stand in Washington, DC. J.W. Marriott, a devout member of the Church of Jesus Christ of Latter Day Saints, did missionary work in New York City and Washington, DC. In the spring of 1927 he moved back to Washington, DC, and opened up a nine-seat A&W root beer stand named the Hot Shoppe. His vision was simple: to treat all associates with respect and provide good customer value in a clean environment.

For 25 years Marriott scrupulously avoided putting his company in debt even while opening 45 restaurants in nine states. While the Hot Shoppes flourished, Marriott diversified his business interests by starting an airline catering business in 1937, "In-Flite Catering," serving Capital, Eastern, and American Airlines and signing a contract with the U.S. government to provide food service to the U.S. Treasury and with Miami International Airport. In the mid-1950s, Marriott landed its first institutional and school contracts, with Children's Hospital and American University, respectively.[7]

In 1956, the company moved into the hotel segment. The company's first hotel, the Twin Bridges Marriott, sat the foot of the 14th St. Bridge in Virginia, and was managed by Bill Marriott, J.W.'s son. By the time the senior Marriott turned the company over to Bill in 1964, he had built 120 Hot Shoppe restaurants, a dozen hotels, and had an $85 million a year business, all of which was virtually debt-free. In ensuing years, J.W. Marriott would often tell the same joke, "When I came to Washington in 1927, I owed $2,000, now in 1964 I owe $20 million. Is that progress?"[8]

Bill Marriott still leads the company today and is credited with creating the "Marriott Way." His management style incorporates concern for all associates, hands-on management, and an unrelenting commitment to customer service. This explains Marriott International's dominance of the hospitality industry. Bill Marriott embodies the industry's professionalism, compassion, commitment to ethics, and social responsibility.[9]

So what is the current statue of the lodging industry in the United States? The American Hotel & Lodging Association in their most recent projections suggests the following:[10]

- There are approximately 47,135 properties in the United Sates with more than 4.3 million guest rooms.
- In 2006 revenue totaled $133.4 billion in sales and generated over $26.6 billion in pre tax profits.
- The average room rate will near $97.78. The most recent data show 2005 was $90.88—up from $86.23 in 2004.

- The industry pays $177 billion in travel-related wages and salaries and employs 1.8 million hotel property workers.
- One of every eight Americans is employed either directly or indirectly because of people traveling to and within the United States.

Food: The Universal Language

The National Restaurant Association is based in Washington, DC, and its mission is to represent, educate, and promote a rapidly growing industry that consists of 935,000 restaurant and foodservice outlets and employs 12.8 million people. Today, this organization is the voice of the food service industry.[11]

However, before the industry had such a strong lobby, it was known for its cuisine. George Augustine Escoffier is the King of Chefs and the Chef of Kings. Born in 1846 near Nice, France, he revolutionized the culinary industry by simplifying cooking, kitchens, and reinventing the culinary profession. The hotel kitchens of the late 1800s and early 1900s were terrible places to work—long, grueling hours in poorly designed space with little air flow. It was commonplace for the cooks to cool off by drinking beer.[12] The limit was no more than three beers per hour. Alcoholism, swearing, and screaming were routine daily activities. Apprentices who wanted to learn the trade of cooking were particularly abused. The working conditions were not attractive, hazing was a right of passage. As a result, the industry was not attracting the best and the brightest.

Escoffier believed the best way to keep his palate as sensitive as possible was to avoid tobacco and alcohol. As a result, he created a nonalcoholic drink that contained barley, forbade cursing, and made all of his employees take an abstinence oath. He encouraged his staff to learn as much about their profession as they could. While this is the expectation today, it was a revolutionary concept in Escoffier's time.[13]

Escoffier created the kitchen brigade to increase efficiency. Rather than separating the kitchen as had been the practice, elements were logically organized and cleanliness became the cornerstone of kitchen practice. In the 1890s Escoffier partnered with Caesar Ritz and revolutionized European cuisine. At the turn of the century, Escoffier opened the Carlton Hotel in London, spending 20 years managing a team of 60 culinarians creating a la carte dining options. His first book, *Le Guide Culinaire* (1902), contained almost 5,000 recipes. To his credit, many of Escoffier's innovations are now standard in today's great food service operations.[14]

Just as Escoffier professionalized cooking, Julia Child personalized it. It is hard to imagine that people used to dine in restaurants only on special occasions. Today, half of all Americans purchase food to eat outside of the home every day.

Julia Child

Julia Child, 1913–2004, was 6'2," enjoyed puffing on cigars, and worked for the federal government in the Office of Strategic Services (now the CIA). In 1948, Child enrolled in the Le Cordon Bleu Cooking School in Paris, where she met Simone Beck and Louisette Bertholle. The three of them opened a cooking school in Paris to bring classic French cuisine to American expatriates which led to her popular cookbook, *Mastering the Art of French Cooking*. The theme of the book was that French cooking was not difficult if the cook had the correct skills and equipment.[15] In the early 1960s Child went to WGBH in Boston to promote her book. Instead of just talking about the book, she brought a hot plate, eggs, and a pan to show the audience how simple it was to prepare a French omelet. Shortly thereafter her show "The French Chef" became a staple of American television and her message was simple: "above all have a good time."[16] In 1981, with vintner Robert Mondavi and others, she co-founded the American Institute of Wine and Food in California to "advance the understanding, appreciation, and quality of wine and food."[17] Today, her kitchen is in the Smithsonian Museum, she was awarded the Presidential Medal of Freedom, and she is recognized by the French Ordre de Mérite Agricole, Order de Mérite Nationale, and the Confrérie de Ceres. Most importantly she opened the doors for today's culinary stars such as Rachel Ray, Emeril, Bobby Flay, Martha Stewart, Mario Batali, and Jamie Oliver. All one has to do is to look at the Food Network to see the impact of Julia Child on the world of gourmet cooking.

Ray Kroc Sold More than Mixers

In 1954, Dick and Mac McDonald of San Bernardino, California, ordered eight multi-mixers from Ray Kroc. They told him how their restaurant sold the cheapest burgers, fries, sodas, and milkshakes in town and people were standing in line to get their food. Kroc thought about how great it would be if McDonald's restaurants were all over the country with eight multi-mixers in each. Kroc strongly believed that people went to McDonald's to eat, not to dine. He formed a partnership with the McDonald brothers and slowly spread the Golden Arches across the country. In 1961 he purchased the exclusive rights to McDonald's for $2.7 million dollars.[18]

Kroc understood Fredrick Taylor's principles of scientific management. Fewer steps meant more customers could be served, and that meant more sales and more revenue. Every employee was told "if you have time to lean you have time to clean."[19] His values were quality, service, cleanliness, and value. He demonstrated that detailed planning, standardized practices, and tight controls can introduce a complicated operation to more than 119 countries.[20] Ray Kroc is the father of fast food, and his systems have been copied by restaurateurs around the world.

The Colonel Has a Recipe

In the 1930s, Harland Sanders made fried chicken dinners for people who passed by his service station in Corbin, Kentucky. Eventually, his popularity grew, and Sanders moved his enterprise to a motel and restaurant that seated 142 people. In the early 1950s, the Colonel perfected his method of pressure cooking chicken in 11 herbs and spices enhancing the flavor and allowing the chicken to be cooked much faster.[21] The Colonel devoted himself to the chicken franchising business by driving across the country, cooking batches of chicken for restaurant owners and their employees. If the people liked the food, he entered into a handshake agreement that stipulated that he would earn a nickel for each chicken the restaurant sold. By 1964, Colonel Sanders had more than 600 franchised outlets in the United States and Canada. That year, he sold his interest in the U.S. company for $2 million.[22]

Both Kroc and the Colonel were passionate about an idea and believed in their ability to take that idea from concept to product. This is as relevant today as it was 50 years ago. So what is the current state of the foodservice industry? The National Restaurant Association made the following predictions for 2007:[23]

- Sales: $537 billion
- Locations: 935,000—serving more than 70 billion meal and snack occasions
- Employees: 12.8 million—the industry is the largest employer after the federal government

The dining industry grows every year as people spend less time cooking and more time eating out.

- Restaurant-industry sales are forecast to equal 4% of the U.S. gross domestic product.
- Every dollar spent by consumers in restaurants generates an additional $2.34 for industries allied with the restaurant industry.
- The average household expenditure for food away from home in 2005 was $2,634, or $1,054 per person.
- The restaurant industry provides work for more than 9% of those employed in the United State and is expected to add 2 million jobs by 2017.
- Eating-and-drinking places employ more minority managers than any other industry.

Whether it is gourmet dining or fast food, the eating industry grows every year as people spend less time cooking and more time eating out.

A Man and His Mouse

During the fall of 1918, Walt Disney attempted to enlist for military service but was rejected because he was only 16 years old. Instead, Walt joined the Red Cross and was sent overseas to France, where he spent a year driving an ambulance and chauffeuring Red Cross officials. His ambulance was covered from stem to stern, not with stock camouflage, but with Disney cartoons.[24] In 1932, the production entitled *Flowers and Trees* (the first color cartoon) won Walt the first of his studio's Academy Awards. In 1937, he released *The Old Mill*, the first short subject to utilize the multi-plane camera technique. On December 21, 1937, *Snow White and the Seven Dwarfs*, the first full-length animated musical feature, premiered at the Cathay Theater in Los Angeles. The film produced at the unheard cost of

$1,499,000 during the depths of the Depression, the film is still considered one of the great feats of the motion picture industry.[25]

Walt Disney's dream of a clean, organized amusement park came true when Disneyland Park opened in 1955. Walt also became a television pioneer, beginning production in 1954, and presenting his daily *Mickey Mouse Club* and the first weekly full-color programming with his *Wonderful World of Color* in 1961. Walt Disney is a legend; his worldwide popularity was based upon the ideals of imagination, optimism, creation, and self-made success in the American tradition. He brought us closer to the future, while telling us of the past.[26]

Before we look at the future, one event is synonymous with our industry and ties together the past, present, and future.

Five Rings and So Much More

A foot race was held at Olympia in Western Peloponnese for the first time in 776 B.C.E. in honor of the Greek god Zeus. Coroebus, a cook from Elis, won the 210-yard race called the "stade." The victor was crowned with a wreath of wild olives and was granted special honors in his home city. This modest celebration, won by a hospitality employee, led to the modern Olympics.[27] There is no better example of what our industry is all about than the Olympics. Every 4 years, the international summer or winter games are held. This grand event showcases a city and region. Preparing a city to welcome visitors and athletes from more than 100 countries can be an overwhelming task. The pageantry of the opening ceremonies, the parade of athletes, the lighting of the Olympic Flame, and medal presentations are the easy part. We hospitality professionals know how to fit the pieces of the Olympic puzzle together. In short, the skills that are necessary to organize the Olympics are best learned in the hospitality and tourism area.

So you've met some of the founders of the hospitality business, examined the current volume of business and its economic impact, and seen how the Olympics are the ultimate example of hospitality and tourism management. As we conclude the chapter, we hope to share our thoughts about the future.

2050: A Hospitality Odyssey

If we could see the world of hospitality in 2050, we would immediately stop writing, access our brokerage accounts, and start buying shares in the Marriott and McDonald's of the future, so that our posterity would be able to live like Bill Gates. Although we cannot actually see the future, we can make some educated guesses based on what we know about the past and present.

Mega Resorts

It's 2008 and you're in Las Vegas after a 5½-hour flight on a cramped plane with way too little leg room. Here in one location, entire cities are re-created. You can dine on meals prepared by the world's greatest chefs and be entertained around the clock with non-stop music, theater, dance, and other performing arts. Hotels are among the most modern and the rooms are counted not in the hundreds, but in the thousands. You can shop in huge malls, ride roller coasters, and experience cutting edge IMAX, 4D motion simulation rides, swim and surf in wave pools, enjoy exclusive spa treatments, attend conferences and meetings, walk through museums, view great works of art by Picasso and Monet, and even get married, without ever leaving your hotel. Amazingly, there is not just one of these mega resorts, but dozens! This is the desert oasis called Las Vegas, today's mega resort.

You wonder about the early Spanish traders en route to Los Angeles who passed through this then unexplored Las Vegas Valley. They referred to the route through the valley as "jornada de muerte," the journey of death.[28] Could they have imagined that it would become the "City of Entertainment," the number one tourist destination in the world?[29] Despite Wall Street "pundits" periodic predictions of its demise due to overdevelopment, the city keeps prospering, building even bigger hotel resorts. Seventeen of the 20 largest hotels in the world are located in Las Vegas.[30] Each one of them is a destination in its own right. In recent years the Wynn Las Vegas opened, a $2.7 billion luxury hotel and destination resort.[31] The Wynn Las Vegas features 2,716 luxurious guest rooms and suites, an 111,000 square foot casino, an 18-hole golf course, 223,000 square feet of meeting space, a Ferrari and Maserati dealership, and 76,000 square feet of retail space. Among its 22 food and beverage outlets is the Alex Restaurant, internationally recognized by AAA as a Five Diamond restaurant offering fine French cuisine in a luxurious and opulent setting.[32]

It's 2010 and you have returned to the city to help plan the Hilton's newest property. It was a long flight but the food was better and your luggage arrived with you. The mega resorts are even larger, more elaborate, and more activity-inclusive. For some it's simply not enough to visit the city, they want to share in the unprecedented expansion of leisure and recreation that the future has presented. Partial, individual ownership in mega resort complexes has burgeoned since the early 2000s. Many "visitors" now own one or more units in the many hotel condominium resort complexes that have been built over the last 10 years around the Strip. Along with ownership comes access to the entertainment facilities, concierge services, fine dinning and beverage services as well as other upscale amenities.

In recent years, innovative chefs have flocked to the city, drawn by the money as well as the promise of fame. These young, highly trained culinary artists, armed with solid business credentials, are well equipped to operate successful restaurants. They follow in the footsteps of Todd English (Olives at Bellagio); Emeril Lagasse (Emeril's New Orleans Fish House at MGM Grand); Michael Mina (Aqua at Bellagio); Wolfgang Puck (Spago's, Chinois at the Forum Shops at Caesars); Julian Serrano (Picasso at Bellagio); and Joachim Splichal (Pinot Brasserie at the Venetian).[33] Each of these newcomers is determined to make their mark on the culinary world in a city that contains the largest concentration of famed chefs.

Ride in My Beautiful Machine

It's 2015 and you have flown into the Mohave Air & Space Port, America's first Inland Spaceport.[34] You just deplaned from the world's largest aircraft, the Airbus A380. It was quite the experience flying on an aircraft the size of a football field along with 500 other passengers. You were lucky enough to go below and work out in one of the small onboard gyms, then catch a few winks in your private sleeper compartment. You should have bought your 6-year-old son a souvenir from one of the onboard retail boutiques,[35] but maybe next time. Look, your luggage is actually at baggage claim before you are! You worried a bit about how they were going to serve all those passengers, as well as get them off the plane, but everything went very smoothly: "service with a smile." Wonder what they studied at college that enabled them to take care of all the detail? Tomorrow, 20 civilians will take the first sub-orbital tour in space. Back in 2001, Dennis Tito went to the International Space Station, but he paid $25.8 million. This group paid $200,000 to see the cobalt blue sky turn to mauve and indigo and finally black. The civilian space tourism industry started with the X-Prize, a $10 million reward offered to the first private company that succeeded in putting a person in space and then repeated the feat within two weeks.[36] On October 4, 2004, Spaceship One, designed by Burt Rutan, did just that. Almost immediately thereafter, Richard Branson announced the formation of Virgin Galactic Corporation (VGC), which would bring space tourism to the public.[37] Late in the fall of 2007, Branson partnered with Environmental Tectonics Corporation's National Aerospace Training and Research (NASTAR[SM]) to provide training and preparation for space travel.

New Atlantis, 2025

The 2000 mile trip went by rather quickly. Boeing's new 877 hypersonic aircraft travels at five times the speed of sound.[38] Hilton's Oceania 1 is part of New Atlantis, an artificial island floating in the Caribbean. The technology is based upon the old oil rig platforms now made obsolete by the new fusion energy sources. As soon as scientists figured out how to redirect the ocean storms, these floating islands became great leisure opportunities. Just in time too, as the global democratization of travel has started to stress traditional leisure travel destinations, especially the smaller islands. The concept of New Atlantis is the logical evolution of the cruise ship. The ships kept getting bigger and in 2006—Royal Caribbean launched the world's largest cruise ship, Freedom of the Seas, and a 3,634-guest ship with ice skating rinks, rock climbing walls, Broadway shows, surfing pools, and a host of other attractions.[39]

However, Royal had already placed an order for a new mega class ship to be delivered in 2009. Dubbed Project Genesis, it "costs around $1 billion, making it the most expensive ship ever ordered. It will be a 1,181-foot ship and will hold 5,400 passengers. The massive ships will be 43% larger than the current behemoth, Aker's 'Freedom of the Seas,' which will be the world's largest cruise ship when it is delivered to Royal Caribbean in April. The new ship should be delivered in late 2009."[40] From there it was just a short leap to the artificial leisure island. Among the first were the Palm Islands off the coast of Dubai, which were fully operational by 2010. Like New Atlantis, these islands sport luxury hotels, residential villas, unique water homes, shoreline apartments, marinas, theme parks and aquariums, casinos, restaurants, shopping malls, multiple golf courses and other sports facilities, health spas, cinemas, stadiums and theaters, and various diving sites on artificial reefs.[41] Also available on New Atlantis are fractional ownerships in residential vacation homes, modeled on the condo mega resort hotel complexes that appeared in Las Vegas in the early 2000s. Many include planned communities with assisted living facilities for today's active retirees.

A Room with a View, 2035

It's only been 20 years since you witnessed the launch of the first commercial space tourist and here you are in the new Hilton International Orbital Hotel. In 1964 Barron Hilton delivered a speech in which he envisioned hotels in space[42] and in 1999 Hilton International endorsed the concept of using spent space shuttle launch vehicles as the building blocks for a space hotel,[43] but it was your Virgin Galactic report that convinced the company. Today you are meeting here with top executives from all over the hospitality industry, a fitting location for the unveiling of plans for the Lunar I resorts.

Foodservice hasn't changed much and Escoffier would be pleased by the fact that every facility still needs an excellent chef. However, improved transportation technology, coupled with new techniques in food preservation and storage, has provided guests with a wider array of food choices and "fresh" means fresh. Kitchens are truly "clean rooms" and both facilities and workers are automatically sanitized by new lightwave technology. Cooking technology has made significant advances so that the food is prepared healthier and quicker, room service is no longer a 40 minute wait. Order-

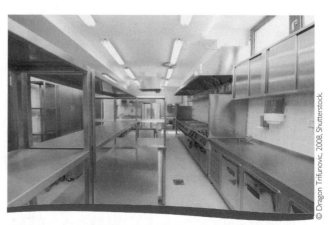

Kitchens are truly "clean rooms."

© Dragon Trifunovic, 2008, Shutterstock.

ing room service is completely automated. Guests simply use a menu touch tablet to place their order and, because of the advances in kitchen technology, specialty "off the menu" orders are no problem. After dinner you can take advantage of the equipment in your mini gym "closet."

Statler's bed and bath are still at the heart of the room but they too have evolved. The beds are equipped with "space age" foam mattresses that contour to your body and electronic sensors to monitor and induce deep restful REM sleep and noise canceling technology so that you are sure to awake refreshed. Standard bathrooms include the same lightwave sanitation devices used in the kitchen, voice-activated showers and wash basins to control flow and temperature, mini spas, and of course a flat panel multi purpose LCD monitor. Oh, and they also have variable environmental lighting make-up assistance (VELMA) that allows women to program of the kind of light they want when applying their cosmetics. Yes, the rooms back on Earth are quite different. Up here the rooms are still very much like the 1990s, but looking out the porthole at the home planet, the view is unbelievable!

Welcome to Hilton Galactic Resort I, 2050

You just alighted from the lunar shuttle and a sign in the spaceport says "Welcome to Galactic Resort I." The whole lunar leisure recreation complex would have been impossible without the strategic alliances with companies like Boeing Aerospace and Airbus, Virgin Galactic, Aramark, Disney, Universal, and MGM-Mirage. The high tech giants like Intel and IBM are well represented, as are a host of other private companies from around the world. It had been a true international effort, the epitome of business going global.

You sure traveled a lot over the course of your career, that's one of the perks of the hospitality business. This trip however is strictly for pleasure, here with your entire family to enjoy the semi-weightless recreational environment. In fact, it has been 6 months since you retired from the Hilton organization and this all-expense-paid trip is part of their recognition of your long time service, loyalty, and contributions that ensured that Hilton would remain a pioneer in the hospitality industry. Word is that a similar resort will be on Mars on 50 short years. You haven't walked too far when you spy the familiar Golden Arches and smile.

≈ Resources

Internet Sites

This is a complete one-stop Website for suppliers of products and services to the hospitality industry: http://www.hospitality-index.com/

The top 50 hotel companies: http://www.ahla.com/products_info_center_top50.asp

The top 25 Websites for restaurant professionals: http://www.restaurantreport.com/

The Nestle Library at Cornell University hosts hospitality links for most of the topics found in this book: http://www.hotel-school.cornell.edu/research/library/links/

This is a complete one-stop Website for information about the hospitality industry with emphasis on industry news, financial news, market reports, jobs, and allied associations to name just a few. http://www.hospitalitynet.org/news/index.html

An updated list of top food sites may be found at http://www.topfoodsites.com/

It is impossible to list every site or index available to you but by going to your favorite search engine and typing in the words in any of the chapters in this book you will find a wealth of information. Continued success on your journey!

≈ Endnotes

1. Dunn, Walter. (1972). *The History of Erie County*. Buffalo, NY: Buffalo and Erie County Historic Society.
2. Wikimedia Foundation at http://commons.wikimedia.org/wiki/Category:New_York_City_from_1900_to_1939
3. *Buffalo Historical Society Publications*, 30 (1), 2–4, 1930.
4. Conrad N. Hilton Collage at http://www.hrm.uh.edu/cnhc/ShowContent.asp?c=9297
5. Hilton World Wide at http://www.hiltonworldwide.com/en/ww/company_info/corporate_history.jhtml
6. Marriott.com at http://marriott.com/corporateinfo/culture/heritageTimeline.mi
7. Marriott.com at http://www.marriott.com/corporateinfo/culture/heritageTimeline.mi
8. Foucar-Szocki, R., Cereola, R. J., and Welpott, S. D. (2004). J.W. Marriott, Jr.: The Spirit to Serve. *Journal of Hospitality and Tourism Education*, 6–11.

9. Marriott, W. and Brown, K. (1989). *The Spirit to Serve*. Upper Saddle River, NJ: Prentice Hall.
10. American Hotel & Lodging Association at http://www.ahla.com/
11. National Restaurant Association at http://www.restaurant.org/research/ind_glance.cfm
12. Escoffier, A. at http://www.answers.com/topic/auguste-escoffier
13. Escoffier Society at http://www.escoffier-society.com/Bio.html
14. Escoffier, A. at http://en.wikipedia.org/wiki/Escoffier
15. Child, J., Beck, S., and Berholle, L. (2001). *Mastering the Art of French Cooking: 40th Anniversary Edition*, Vol. 1. New York: Knopf, Inc.
16. NPS Archives: Julia Child.
17. The American Institute of Wine and Food at www.aiwf.org/
18. Kroc, R. (1977). *Grinding It Out*. New York: Contemporary Books.
19. McDonalds.com at http://www.mcdonalds.com/corp/about/mcd_history_pg1/mcd_history_pg2.html
20. McDonald's Corporation at http://www.mcdonalds.ca/en/aboutus/faq.aspx
21. KFC Corporation at http://www.kfc.com/about/pressure.asp
22. Stream, C. (1974). *Life as I Have Known It Has Been Finger Lickin' Good*. Illinois: Carol Stream Productions.
23. National Restaurant Association at www.restaurant.org
24. Disney.com at http://www.justdisney.com/walt_disney/
25. Dirks, T. (1996). *Snow White and the Seven Dwarfs* (1937) at http://www.filmsite.org/snow.html
26. Smith, D. (2001). *The Quotable Walt Disney,* New York: Hyperion.
27. Maps of the World.com at http://www.mapsofworld.com/olympic-trivia/ancient-olympics.html/
28. City of Las Vegas at http://www.lasvegasnevada.gov/FactsStatistics/history.htm
29. Visit Las Vegas at http://www.lvcva.com/index.jsp
30. Chisholm, C. *Twenty Largest Hotels in the World* at http://hotels.about.com/cs/uniqueunusual/a/largesthotels_2.htm
31. Wynn Hotels Las Vegas at http://en.wikipedia.org/wiki/Wynn_Las_Vegas
32. Wynn Resorts *Overview* at http://phx.corporate-ir.net/phoenix.zhtml?c=132059&p=irol-IRHome
33. Restaurant Report at http://www.restaurantreport.com/features/ft_lasvegas.html
34. Mohave Airport and Spaceport at http://www.mojaveairport.com/
35. PBS. *Chasing the Sun Airbus A380* at http://www.pbs.org/kcet/chasingthesun/planes/a380.html
36. X Prize at http://www.xprizefoundation.com/about_us/default.asp
37. NASTAR Center. *ETC's NASTAR^SM Center to Provide Space Training for Virgin Galactic* at http://www.etcusa.com/corp/pressreleases/NR083007.htm
38. Boeing. *Boeing Joins X-432 Hypersonic Research Vehicle Team* at http://www.boeing.com/news/releases/2003/q4/nr_031120a.html
39. Garrison, L. *Royal Caribbean International Names New Ultra-Voyager Cruise Ship* at http://www.freedomoftheseas.com/
40. MSNBC. *Royal Caribbean Orders Largest Ever Cruise Ship* at http://www.luxist.com/2006/02/07/project-genesis-will-be-the-worlds-largest-cruiseship/
41. The Emirates Network. *The Palm* at http://realestate.theemiratesnetwork.com/developments/dubai/palm_islands.php
42. Hilton, B. (1967). *Hotels in Space* at http://www.spacefuture.com/archive/hotels_in_space.shtml
43. Whitehouse, D. (1999). *Hilton Backs Space Hotel Built From Shuttle Tanks* at http://www.gsreport.com/articles/art000116.html

≈ Contributors

Reginald Foucar-Szocki

James Madison University

foucarrf@jmu.edu

Dr. Reg Foucar-Szocki is the J.W. Marriott Professor in the Hospitality and Tourism Management program at James Madison University, Harrisonburg, Virginia, where he has taught since 1989. Reg believes the world is a special event and hospitality management is the centerpiece for success.

Ronald J. Cereola, JD, MBA

James Madison University

cereolrj@jmu.edu

Dr. Ronald J. Cereola is an Assistant Professor in the Hospitality and Tourism Management program at James Madison University, Harrisonburg, Virginia. He teaches Tourism, Hospitality Services Marketing, Hospitality Law and Entertainment Management.

Chapter 2
Review Questions

1. Using the text chapter, identify the core value, belief, or priority of Statler, Marriott, Escoffier, and Kroc.

2. Examine the similarities that exist among your responses to question #1. Why are they important?

3. List the basic amenities in Statler's early hotel rooms and do the same for your most recent stay at a hotel. What has changed and what remains the same?

4. Both Escoffier and Kroc were in the food service niche of the hospitality industry. In what way were their contributions similar?

5. Why is "environmental scanning" important for the hospitality industry?

6. After reading the authors' vision of "artificial islands" and space tourism, how realistic are these opportunities for the hospitality industry? What will be the technical, political, economic, and cultural challenges that will have to be overcome in order to achieve that vision?

Hospitality: The "Real World"

3

Michele L. Wehrle, Community College of Allegheny County

© Répási Lajos Attila, 2008, Shutterstock.

≈ Learning Objectives

☑ Explore positive and negative aspects of a hospitality career
☑ Understand skills and traits needed to become successful in the hospitality industry
☑ Develop an understanding of the size and scope of hospitality careers
☑ Develop resume building skills and interview strategies

≈ Chapter Outline

The Myths and the Realities
The Career: The Good and the Bad
The Skills and Qualities Needed for Success
The Money
The Career Pursuit
The Internship
Get "Real"—Take Control—Be Successful

≈ Key Terms

Career fair
Employment brand
Game show
Internship
Interview
Interviewee
Interviewer
Labor-intensive business
Myth
Relocation
Resume
Social networking
Student organizations
Organization's culture

*C*hoosing a career can be similar to being a game show contestant or part of a reality television series. Decisions about your future no doubt will involve competition against other players or job seekers while striving alone for a good outcome or high score. Will you win the "prize" for making the best career choice? Using popular reality television and game show formats, this chapter explores the size and scope of career opportunities within the hospitality industry. As a contestant (student), you need to answer questions to determine your career path.

Do you want to get paid to help people have fun? Do warm sunny beaches, majestic mountain views, or visiting far away places spark your interest? How about being around delicious food in exotic restaurant locations, working on a cruise ship, coordinating events for country clubs, or owning your own foodservice or lodging establishment?

Workers in the hospitality industry deal with people who are looking for a relaxing vacation or mini vacation—even if it's only going out to dinner at a local restaurant! The hospitality industry offers its employees a choice of working in the kind of climate they like best.

The Myths and the Realities

Are You Smarter Than a 5th Grader about the hospitality industry?

What do you know about the hospitality industry? Where do you see yourself in the future? Will you love your career and look forward to going to work each day? Will you like the people you work with? You may have preconceived notions about a career in the hospitality industry. *Do you know the difference between a myth and a reality about this industry or do you need to copy a 5th grader's answers?*

Myth: There is a shortage of job opportunities within the hospitality industry.

Reality: There is a shortage of qualified hospitality employees. There are *many* career choices and opportunities. The hospitality industry is the largest, fastest growing industry in the world. Globally, hospitality makes up 11% of the gross domestic product, 200 million jobs, 8% of total employment, and 5.5 million new jobs annually until 2010 (www. nra.org).

Myth: Anyone can become a successful hospitality manager.

Reality: The myth is that all you have to do to become a hospitality manager is sit behind a desk and give orders. A career in hospitality management is not suitable for every individual. The industry is people and service-oriented. A career in this field is rewarding for those seeking responsibility, opportunity for advancement, salary growth, and personal satisfaction. As a hospitality manager, you need to always try to meet and exceed your potential, treat others as you would want to be treated, work hard, learn from your mistakes, listen to your employees, and love your job. A college education and industry experiences are requirements for a successful hospitality career.

Myth: I will spend most of my time sitting at my desk.

Reality: A good manager is constantly on the floor working along side his/her employees and understanding what is going on during the day and night. Solving problems is a critical skill that takes wisdom, creativity, and information. The hospitality industry is too fast paced to sit at a desk. Every day brings a new set of guests and a new set of challenges. It takes a special person to rise to the challenge.

Myth: There is limited career advancement.

Reality: The potential for advancement is excellent for the capable individual who is willing to work hard. There is a critical need for people with general management skills to supervise all aspects of a hospitality property. The growth of the field has translated into exceptional opportunities for graduates. The hospitality field employment outlook is excellent for people from every race and ethnic background.

Myth: Starting salaries are low.

Reality: Starting salaries are competitive. Unlike many industries, hospitality has more flexible working hours and pay scales. You can work and get paid by the hour. There are even some supervisory roles with this capacity. Hotels work 24/7 so you can work on many different schedules so it does not interfere with your classes. And, after a few promotions, the compensation package is tremendous.

Myth: Graduating with a degree in hospitality is all I need to be successful.

Reality: A degree by itself is not enough! A college education combined with relevant work experience is! Many programs include work experiences as part of the curriculum. As you learn more about the industry through hands on knowledge, you appreciate and learn more in your classes because you understand why this material is important.

Myth: A job in the hospitality industry is boring

Reality: Hospitality employees have fun! Working alongside people you like, talking to new people all the time, and doing something you love. How can that be boring?

The Career: The Good and the Bad

Jeopardy

The hospitality industry has a long history of providing meaningful employment in a variety of career fields. According to the Council of Hotel, Restaurant, and Institutional Educators (CHRIE), the hospitality industry is comprised of four major career fields: food, lodging, tourism, and recreation. These areas include many diverse and exciting career opportunities. Examples of career opportunities include but are not limited to club management, foodservice, health care, parks, lodging, resorts, casinos, catering companies, conference centers, attractions management, marinas, prisons, colleges/universities, and school foodservice. Just quickly glance at the table of contents for this book to start your possibilities, and these are only the beginning.

The hospitality industry offers many advantages to employees but, just like any other industry, you face challenges. *Analyzing the categories of a hospitality career allows you to increase your knowledge of the industry's good and bad points, thus reducing mistakes that could cost you time and money. After reviewing the answers, you may be motivated to seek additional information and ask additional questions.*

The Good

Let's explore the "good points" of a career in the field.

1. Extensive list of career options
2. Creative opportunities
3. Varied work environment
4. Career growth
5. Social networking

Extensive List of Career Options

The hospitality industry offers an abundance of management opportunities. In lodging, you may choose a 500 room property or a 10 room bed and breakfast, an international franchise company or a local boutique hotel, a grand hotel or a camp ground. On the other hand, food service opportunities can include fine dining or a cafeteria, a privately owned catering company, a night club or an assisted living facility. When people want to be entertained or just recreate, hospitality includes final destination theme parks or city amusement parks, a metropolitan convention center, casinos, or museums. And always there is the shopping that everyone does. Hospitality career possibilities are endless. So, what do you want be when you grow up?

Creative Opportunities

Are you inventive? Do you have vision? Hospitality managers may design new products or remodel foodservice and lodging facilities. Managers may be asked to develop training programs or implement new marketing strategies. Even on a day-to-day basis, you need creativity to productively handle problem guests or motivate employees to do their best.

Varied Work Environment

If you desire a 9-to-5, 5 day a week career . . . please find the nearest exit, proceed straight to registration, and change your major! Hospitality careers are fast-paced and each day begins a new work environment. Power outages, severe weather, equipment failures, a bus load of guests, and staff shortages are some of the challenges that provide

No other industry can offer you the chance to work almost anywhere, with interesting work and people contact.

© Yiannis Papadimitrou, 2008, Shutterstock.

variety and excitement. Hospitality positions are not desk jobs. Quality customer service and meeting/exceeding guest satisfaction can not be obtained from merely hiding in your office. Hospitality employees should consider the entire facility as their "office" and seek the opportunity to interact with guests on a daily basis.

Career Growth

The hospitality industry is widely based. You can work almost anywhere in any setting, from a small country town to a metropolitan city, from a warm sunny beach to a deep powder ski resort, from a small bed and breakfast to a casino resort, from a small town in Kansas to a foreign country. Across the nation and around the world career opportunities abound for people of all ages, education levels, and backgrounds. No other industry can offer you the chance of working almost anywhere you choose, with interesting work, a chance for advancement, people contact, and stability of employment.

Social Networking

Surveys and statistics can not tell you all you want to know about a career. You need to spend time with people who perform the job you want. How do you network? You want to expand your base of contacts by attending career fair, and by joining alumni associations, student organizations, and professional organizations. Meeting people is a major advantage of your career. You will have the opportunity to meet people from all over the world and all walks of life including celebrities, political figures, wealthy clientele, top executives, professional athletes, and local community members. As in all businesses, the more people you know, the easier it is to find your dream job.

The Bad

All careers have advantages and challenges. The challenges or potential "bad points" of a career in hospitality include labor-intensive business, hours of work, and relocation. You may find the challenges to be to your advantage.

Labor-Intensive Business

Like all work environments, there is a downside that has to be put into perspective. So just how bad is it? There are three areas to be aware of in hospi-tality. First, the work can be very hands-on at times involving physical labor. This isn't all bad since, as a manager, it gives you better empathy and appreciation for the hard work of your employees. It is a way to keep you close to the customer, which is critical to understanding your business. If however, there is never any quiet time to plan and manage, this can be a major issue. In a labor intensive business, you can plan on being a "working" manager in this field at least in your formative years, if not always.

Hours of Work

The hospitality industry is open 365 days a year, 7 days a week, 24 hours a day. Most managers work 10–12 hour days and 60+ hours a week, weekends, and holidays. This is an industry where most people spend long hours on their feet and spend each day making complete strangers feel welcome and happy. These long hours can limit the time you have available for family, friends, and your social life. A common cliché is "employees in the hospitality industry work while others play." However, you can get your household chores done faster because you have off when everyone else is working. So the lines are shorter. In addition, you can recreate or go on vacation during low season when the rates are better and it is not so crowded.

Relocation

Relocation can be defined as the act of moving from one place to another for employment advancement. You may have to consider relocating several times since hospitality organizations have facilities in a variety of geographic locations. Larger chains may offer better opportunities than small, but relocation every several years is often necessary. A willingness to relocate often is essential for advancement. The decision is difficult: remain in your current area? Return home? Relocate? However, many people find relocation exciting and a benefit of a hospitality career. Also, if you want to travel and see new countries and cultures or just go back home after your training, large hotel and restaurant chains have sites worldwide. You can transfer or even be part of an exciting start up team.

The Skills and Qualities Needed for Success

American Idol

A desire to serve others is a strong characteristic of successful people. Wanting to give our guests a quality experience is an important trait. It comes down to something as simple as wanting to help. Whether it is giving them directions to an area attraction or clearing and cleaning a table so they can be seated in a restaurant, this type of activity must be a source of satisfaction for you. Liking to be with others and a desire to interact with them is something that is intrinsic to most positions in this business. Being friendly, sincere, and patient and a good listener are critical skill sets for anyone contemplating success in this field. Now, these skills take time and practice to develop and there will be days when they will be tested to the limit. However, *there are essential skills and qualities you will need in order to perform to the best your ability in front of the judges (employers) and the audience (guests).*

Skills and Qualities

1. conceptual skills (planning, problem solving, and decision making)
2. communication skills (verbal and non-verbal)
3. flexibility and diversity
4. leadership skills and qualities (supervising, team building, organization)

Enjoying interaction with people is essential to most positions in this business.

5. personality skills (outgoing, ethical, sense of humor, energetic, like to work with people, don't like to sit behind a desk, creative, problem solver, service oriented, ambitious)

The Money

Deal or No Deal

If you possess these skills and qualities, your earning potential can be limitless. *Don't be insulted by the banker's low offer, eliminate the low offers and strive to find the "lucky game case."* According to the National Restaurant Association (NRA), the table on the following page details potential earnings based on job positions within the hospitality industry.

Additionally, the American Hotel & Lodging Educational Institute (AH&LA) publishes information annually documenting compensation and benefits for the hospitality industry. The median salary compensation for management positions in the industry includes: Sales & Marketing Director—$80,400, Controller—$73,800, Senior Sales Manager—$56,000, Personnel/HR Director—$61,600, Sales Manager—$38,500. In addition to base salary, many jobs have a commission, shared gratuity, or bonus plan that pays up to 40% of salary as incentive compensation. Hospitality is an industry where pay for performance and career opportunities are especially strong. *Should you accept a position with a lower salary than you expected? The decision is up to you: Deal or No Deal?*

The Career Pursuit

The Amazing Race

There are several key questions that you will need to address for yourself. First, what segment of the industry is right for you and, secondly, who are the better employers in each sector? You may not be able to find answers to these questions until you have experienced a variety of employment settings. Start becoming a student of the industry now. Read various trade publications. Track different company performances and history during your time in school. Attend open houses and talks given by hospitality employers. Attend annual career conferences. Be sure to talk to employer representatives even if you are not looking for work at that time. It is a good skill to practice so you are comfortable with that format when it really counts. Definitely

Earning Potential in the Hospitality Industry

CAREER	AVERAGE ANNUAL EARNING POWER	REQUIRED EDUCATION	FOLLOW-UP CONTACT WEBSITE
President/Chief Executive Officer	$50,000–$350,000+	Bachelors/Masters Degree	www.nraef.org/hba/hba_career_ladder.asp
Owner	$35,000–$200,000+	Bachelors/Masters Degree	www.nraef.org/hba/hba_career_ladder.asp
Chief Financial Officer	$45,000–$200,000+	Bachelors/Masters Degree	www.nraef.org/hba/hba_career_ladder.asp
General Manager/Chief Operating Officer	$42,000–$200,000+	Bachelors/Masters Degree	www.nraef.org/hba/hba_career_ladder.asp
Director of Operations	$40,000–$150,000+	Bachelors/Masters Degree	www.nraef.org/hba/hba_career_ladder.asp
Regional Manager	$40,000–$100,000+	Bachelors Degree, Associate Degree, or On the job training	www.nraef.org/hba/hba_career_ladder.asp
Food and Beverage Director	$35,000–$85,000+	Bachelors Degree, Associate Degree, or On the job training	www.nraef.org/hba/hba_career_ladder.asp
Director of Purchasing	$35,000–$100,000+	Bachelors Degree, Associate Degree, or On the job training	www.nraef.org/hba/hba_career_ladder.asp
Director of Training	$35,000–$100,000+	Bachelors Degree, Associate Degree, or On the job training	www.nraef.org/hba/hba_career_ladder.asp
Unit Manager	$30,000–$70,000+	Bachelors Degree, Associate Degree, or On the job training	www.nraef.org/hba/hba_career_ladder.asp
Chef	$27,000–$60,000+	Associate Degree/On the job training	www.nraef.org/hba/hba_career_ladder.asp
Catering Manager	$30,000–$50,000+	Associate Degree/On the job training	www.nraef.org/hba/hba_career_ladder.asp
Kitchen Manager	$25,000–$45,000+	Associate Degree/On the job training	www.nraef.org/hba/hba_career_ladder.asp
Banquet Manager	$26,000–$45,000+	Associate Degree/On the job training	www.nraef.org/hba/hba_career_ladder.asp
Waiters and Waitresses	$6.50–$20.00+ per hour including tips	On the job training	www.nraef.org/hba/hba_career_ladder.asp
Cook	$6.30–$12.43+ per hour	On the job training	www.nraef.org/hba/hba_career_ladder.asp

Data from the National Restaurant Association, 2002.

take advantage of the resources your school offers, whether they are your advisor or the career services office. *A career in hospitality may take you on an adventure around the world leading you on a successful journey of personal and professional satisfaction.*

The Internship

The Apprentice

To gain experience, most colleges/universities require internships or work experiences as part of a hospitality student's major program of study. The first rule of thumb in this area is that some internships are good and some are bad, but you will always learn something from them. Obtain them through your career services office, your department, or on your own. Remember attending a school with a hospitality program gives you kind of a built-in employment brand for this industry. With the internet, your potential is limitless when it comes to obtaining an internship.

However, students need to avoid the trap of thinking their internship will be ideal and answer all of their questions. It won't be perfect; after all, it does take place in the real world. It may also create more questions for you than it answers. But you will learn from it and it will go on your resume. It can be a base upon which you can develop future job opportunities. You will observe various management styles in action, some that you will want to adopt, and many you will want to avoid. It may even bring a job offer for after school. This way you and the employer will be in a better position to make an informed decision about your suitability for the job and your fit within their organization's culture. *In reality, an internship is becoming an apprentice. You should strive to conquer your assignments, perform at your highest potential, and avoid being "fired."* Before you begin the search process for an internship, a well written resume is critical.

Get "Real"—Take Control—Be Successful

Survivor

Be the last one standing!! Outwit, outplay, and outlast your competition! How will you become the sole survivor? A well written resume, cover letter, interview strategies, and a thank you letter may grant you immunity.

The Resume

1 vs. 100

A resume is a written document that lists a person's personal and professional qualifications for a position. The purpose of a resume is to provide information to people about who you are and what skills you have. Because every individual is unique in their own way, there is room for individuality and creativity when writing a resume. In reality, it is your "personal advertisement."

Writing a resume during your first year of college helps you to answer questions about yourself. Documenting your career objective, your past and present education, and past and present work experiences enables you to see what you have accomplished and where you are going. It should be well-organized, concise, and written in a focused manner. A well written resume also aids you in obtaining scholarships, internships, and professional job positions. *Your resume may be 1 out of 100 resumes received for a single open position. Make sure all the information on your resume is accurate as one mistake may cause you to lose it all.* There

are certain headings and information that should be included in your resume:

1. Current contact information
2. Career objective
3. Education
4. Internship
5. Work experience(s)
6. Special skills and abilities
7. Awards and recognitions
8. References (people who are willing to speak with a potential employer about your personal and professional experiences. Make sure you ask them before putting their names as a reference. Make sure they will give you a positive recommendation. This includes faculty. Giving you a positive reference is not your right, but the reference's honest opinion of you.)

The Cover Letter

America's Got Talent

Included with your resume should be a cover letter. This letter introduces you to your potential employer. The content should include highlights of your personal and professional experiences (*talents*) and a request for an interview. Many potential employers will only review your resume, if your cover letter sparks their interest. *You do not want to get a big red "X" and be eliminated from the search. So, think carefully about what you are going to offer as your best skills and please check spelling.*

The Interview

Fear Factor

The goal of your resume and cover letter is to get you an interview with an employer of your choosing. An interview is defined as a formal meeting between two or more individuals. Interview etiquette includes dressing in a professional manner, introducing yourself, offering a firm handshake, maintaining eye contact, responding to questions, never saying anything negative, asking questions, smiling, and being enthusiastic. Enthusiasm is the single most important quality. Remember the saying "you only get one chance to make a first impression."

During an interview, the interviewer(s) asks the interviewee questions to determine their ability to meet the expectations of a position. Your answers say a lot about who you are. The Council of Hotel Restaurant Institutional Educators (CHRIE) offers the

Joe S. Student

Permanent Address	**Campus Address**
17 Apple Court	23 New Street
Pittsburgh, PA 15102	State College, PA 18423
(412) 555-1212	(814) 555-1212
jstudent@psu.edu	

OBJECTIVE To obtain a managerial level internship within the hospitality industry.

EDUCATION PENNSYLVANIA STATE UNIVERSITY   State College, PA
Bachelor of Science in Hospitality Management   May 20xx
Overall GPA 3.1/4.0
Course emphasis in Lodging Management
Minor: Mass Communication

COMMUNITY COLLEGE OF ALLEGHENY COUNTY   Pittsburgh, PA
Associate of Science   June 20xx
Hotel-Restaurant Management
Earned 75% of college expenses through work experience.

HONORS Pennsylvania State University Dean's List (three semesters)

EXPERIENCE **PITTSBURGH AIRPORT MARRIOTT**   Pittsburgh, PA
Front Desk Agent   April 20xx–Sept. 20xx
- Balanced check-in and check-out of multiple guests while responding to inquiries and needs of others. Achieved high customer satisfaction comments.
- Worked with various Hotel departments to make decisions and solve problems.

KENNYWOOD AMUSEMENT PARK   West Mifflin, PA
Event Coordinator/Trainer   June 19xx–May 20xx
- Part-time and seasonal employment providing customer service for various areas of tourist-oriented theme park.
- Served as relief shift leader for up to 20 employees.
- Trained new employees in guest relations and standard operating procedures for attractions.
- Received certificate of appreciation for one year of perfect attendance.
- Promoted within three months of hire.

PAYLESS SHOESOURCE   Pittsburgh, PA
Sales Associate   May 19xx–August 19xx
- Summer employment involving retail sales of shoes on a commission basis.
- Awarded bonus for highest monthly volume sales for August.
- Recommended merchandise recovery system reducing loss by $5,000 savings in the first quarter.

ACTIVITIES PSU Hospitality Association
Rho Alpha Tau Sorority, President and Vice President
Community Volunteer, Meals on Wheels
Weekend Youth Director

SKILLS Computer: Proficient in Microsoft Office (Word, Excel, Access, PowerPoint)
Working knowledge of HTML and Java
Language: Fluent in Spanish

Joe S. Student
17 Apple Court
Pittsburgh, PA 15102
412-555-1212

Ms. Lee Thomas
Hilton Hotel Corporation
Runway Road
Pittsburgh, PA 15102

Dear Ms. Thomas,

My unique mix of previous work experience and my status as a Pennsylvania State University hospitality student in my junior year studying hotel and restaurant management make me an ideal candidate for a summer internship with Hilton Hotel Corporation.

My experiences in sales and customer relationship management, combined with my courses in hospitality, have convinced me that hospitality marketing is a career option I would like to explore.

More importantly, an internship with Hilton Hotel Corporation would be mutually beneficial. Your company has an excellent reputation for customer satisfaction and I know that the combination of my experience, education, and motivation to excel will make me an asset to your marketing department.

I am sure that it would be worthwhile for us to meet. I will contact you within a week to arrange a meeting. Should you have any questions before that time, you may reach me via phone (412-555-1212) or via email (jstudent@psu.edu).

Thank you for your time and consideration.

Sincerely,

Joe S. Student

10 most common interview questions and suggestions how to answer the questions on their Website. Questions include:

- What are your weaknesses?
- Why should we hire you?
- Why do you want to work here?
- What are your goals?
- Why did you leave (are you leaving) your job?
- When were you most satisfied in your job?
- What can you do for us that other candidates can't?
- What are three positive things your last boss would say about you?
- What salary are you seeking?
- If you were an animal, which one would you be and why?

Today in many interviews, the employer wants to understand how you will perform on the job under certain circumstances. To get at this they will present you with a series of lifelike events that happen daily on the job and ask how you would respond to them. In some cases, you may have had actual experience in dealing with similar situations earlier in your work life and will be comfortable answering such inquiries. Other questions may represent your first exposure to a certain situation. "I don't know" is not an option. The key is to remain calm and think through how you would answer the question.

Remember, an interview is a two way street. The goal of both interviewer(s) and interviewee is to get enough information about each other to make an informed decision. Making a quality decision about going to work or not for a particular employer is just as important for you as it is for the employer as to whether they are going to hire you. You should develop a list of questions that you want answered prior to the interview. At some point toward the end of the interview, you may be asked if you have any questions for the employer. There is nothing wrong with pulling your list out at this point and reviewing it to see if there are any unanswered questions. There are different schools of thought about asking about salary in the initial interview. This shows the employer you are prepared and an active participant. Ideally, you should have some idea of the salary range for the position after the first interview. *During an interview, you will be challenged mentally and sometimes even physically. You must overcome your fears and not be afraid to answer questions and prove yourself to better and quicker than everyone else.* Send a thank you note to the interviewer. This is rarely done and can leave a lasting impression.

The Thank-You Letter
Identity

After completing an interview, it is important for you to write a thank you letter to the interviewer(s). This personalized, handwritten letter should be written and mailed the same day as your interview. *A well-written thank you letter can make you stand out from the other contestants, thus revealing your true identity.*

Summary
Dancing With the Stars

You are about to embark on a journey that can lead to a long term successful career in a dynamic and thriving industry. The hospitality industry is a very unique industry and it demands certain skill and qualities like strong interpersonal skills, attention to details, and the desire to be a problem solver. While the industry has different hours than most, it has many rewards to offer someone who is willing to work hard and "earn their stripes."

Your number one priority over the coming years is to be a student, a good student. This is both from an academic skills standpoint and from the standpoint of understanding this industry. Build your resume now while in school. Develop a variety of experiences that will help you land a great starting position when you finish your schooling. Definitely pursue one or two internship experiences to add to your portfolio. Utilize all the services of your school's career office and your department to assist you in the interviewing and the job acceptance process as you finish your studies. Be prepared to take the good work and study habits you developed during school with you into the hospitality industry so that you are ready to advance your career. Keep in mind that learning is not just in school, but for the rest of your career. *Aim high, pay attention to details, perform the steps correctly, don't miss a beat, and you too can be dancing with stars.*

17 Apple Court
Pittsburgh, PA 15102
412-555-1212

Ms. Lee Thomas
Hilton Hotel Corporation
Runway Road
Pittsburgh, PA 15120

Dear Ms. Thomas,

Thank you for taking the time to discuss the internship opportunities at Hilton Hotel Corporation with me. After meeting with you and observing the company's operations, I am further convinced that my background and skills coincide well with your needs.

I really appreciate that you took so much time to acquaint me with the company. It is no wonder that Hilton Hotel Corporation retains its employees for so long. I feel I could learn a great deal from you and would certainly enjoy working with you.

In addition to my qualifications and experience, I will bring excellent work habits and judgment to this position. With the countless demands on your time, I am sure that you require people who can be trusted to carry out their responsibilities with minimal supervision.

I look forward, Ms. Thomas, to hearing from you concerning your hiring decision. Again, thank you for your time and consideration.

Sincerely,

Joe S. Student

≈ *Resources*

Internet Sites

Council of Hotel, Restaurant, and Institutional Educators: www.chrie.org
American Hotel & Lodging Association: www.ahla.org
Hospitality Career Net: www.hospitalitycareernet.com
Hospitality Jobs Online: www.hospitalityonline.com
Hospitality Net: www.hospitalitynet.org
Hospitality Careers: www.hcareers.om
National Restaurant Association: www.restaurant.org
National Restaurant Association Education Foundation: www.nraef.org

≈ *Contributor*

Dr. Michele Wehrle is a full professor and program coordinator for the hotel-restaurant management program at the Community College of Allegheny County in Pittsburgh, PA, for more than 17 years. Michele earned her Bachelor's degree in HRIM from Indiana University of Pennsylvania, Master's degree in HRIM from Penn State University, and doctorate degree in foodservice and lodging management from Iowa State University. Dr. Wehrle can be reached at mwehrle@ccac.edu.

Chapter 3
Review Questions

1. Discuss several advantages and disadvantages of working in the hospitality industry.

2. List skills and qualities necessary to become a successful manager.

3. What are some common interview questions and how would you answer?

4. What are three questions you could ask a potential employer while being interviewed?

5. How would you go about securing an internship?

6. How can you research salary ranges of hospitality management positions?

7. What is the purpose of your resume?

8. Develop a resume, cover letter, and thank you letter for a position offered in your local newspaper.

Industry Associations and Ratings

4

Chay Runnels, Stephen F. Austin University

© Adam Gryko, 2008, Shutterstock.

≈ Learning Objectives

- ☑ Students will be able to identify and recognize major industry associations
- ☑ Students will be able to define the terms: *Industry association, by-laws, member benefits, rating services*
- ☑ Students will be able to understand the importance of industry associations and recognize leading industry associations in the hospitality and tourism fields
- ☑ Students will understand the rating systems of lodging and restaurants in the United States

≈ Chapter Outline

What Is an Industry Association?
Associations in the Food and Lodging Arena
Associations in the Travel and Tourism Arena
Finding a Place to Belong
Hotel and Restaurant Rating Systems

≈ Key Terms

By-laws
Hotel ratings system
Industry association
Member benefits
Mission statement
Networking
Restaurant ratings system

What Is an Industry Association?

*I*ndustry associations are professional organizations that assist members by providing opportunities for networking, education and training, recognition, and support within a given industry. Some associations are formed for the purpose of promoting a particular industry to the public. For example, originally the Automobile Association of America (AAA) was primarily dedicated to assisting members with their driving plans for vacations. The automobile was the up and coming transportation mode during the 1950s because it was economical to take the whole family for 2 weeks to see America and visit family in other states. AAA provided people with rated places to sleep and eat along with attractions that would keep the children in the back entertained when they said, "are we there yet?"

Other associations are formed to keep members informed about legislative issues that may impact their industry or business. The American Gaming Association (AGA) filled a need to act as liaison between the federal government and the casino industry. With the bad reputation of the gaming industry in the early 1900s, the casinos needed to have a voice in Washington to protect their interests against lobbyists supported by anti-gambling groups. The AGA helped turn around their image and get information to the people who were voting on the issues. In addition, the National Indian Gaming Association (NIGA) protected the Native American casinos from legislation that would chip away their rights as sovereign nations.

The hospitality industry has many associations that provide members with current information on industry trends while also keeping the general public aware of the industry through marketing and public relations efforts. The National Restaurant Association sends out periodicals each month to keep their members informed on what is happening in the industry. Then, to aid their members on learning what is new in the supply side, they have an annual trade show convention in Chicago in May. This is the largest restaurant show in the country and is designed to allow suppliers to show off their newest product lines, to give workshops on different trends, and to allow industry people to network. The American Hotel & Lodging Association (AH&LA) is also one of the largest in hospitality since it caters to businesses that allow people a place to rest overnight. Members benefit from product and service discounts, training opportunities, in-depth research and information, and a voice in Washington. Typically, in November, their trade show and convention occurs at the Javits Center in New York City.

While these two are the largest and broadest associations, there are also many smaller associations that cater to the different segments. Hospitality Sales and Marketing Association International (HSMAI) organizes marketers while Professional Convention Management Association (PCMA) informs the convention segment of industry. National Society of Minorities in Hospitality (NSMH) segments by diversity and multiculturalism and the International Hotel & Restaurant Association (IH&RA) combines countries into a global network. To find associations that are relevant to your interests, there is a set of books, called the *Encyclopedia of Associations*, in your library. Every association is listed by name, address, purpose, contact information, number of members, and areas of specialization. One of the volumes is searchable by topics. So, it is easy to find an association that suits your particular needs and interests.

Associations in the hospitality field may be organized on several different levels. Associations may be created to meet the needs of individuals, businesses, and organizations in a certain geographic area. Many communities and cities have specific industry-associations for lodging, foodservice, and tourism related organizations. For example, there is the New Orleans Restaurant Association, which is a branch of the National Restaurant Association. This allows members to network and organize projects that are necessary for their city. After 9-11, the New Orleans Restaurant Association began a media campaign to set aside one night to take someone out to dinner to create awareness that restaurants were failing without customers and tourists. An industry association could be an organization formed by bed and breakfast owners in a community or region. The American Bed and Breakfast Association (ABBA) is a national organization to improve marketing efforts. However, there are also organizations like the California Association of Bed and Breakfast Inns or the Bed and Breakfast Association of Virginia. States also have hospitality and tourism associations that serve the needs of members on a state-wide level.[1] *(See Industry Association Profile)*

Large national associations may include not only individual and business members, but also colleges and universities, affiliated industry partners, ven-

Business Profile
TEXAS TRAVEL INDUSTRY ASSOCIATION[2]

Mission: To unify and develop industry leadership that will support and influence the growth of Texas travel and tourism.

Membership: 774 members including attractions, convention and visitor's bureaus, chambers of commerce, historical and cultural sites, educational institutions, eco-tourism providers, hotels and guest ranchers, sports organizations, and transportation companies.

Structure: Governed by an executive committee, a board of directors, and president and CEO Paul Serff. TTIA has 3 councils, 11 committees, and 3 task forces that allow members to focus various aspects of the travel and tourism industry in Texas.

Programs: TTIA works with lobbyists to address legislative issues facing the travel and tourism industry in Texas. The organization also develops marketing programs and projects to promote the travel industry in the state. Every year, TTIA sponsors the Texas Travel Summit—a statewide conference that brings together tourism professionals and industry partners—and also hosts an annual Travel Fair for travel counselors and AAA representatives that allows attractions to share information about their destinations. With other state agency partners and ClearChannel radio, TTIA developed the "Rediscover Texas" campaign aimed at promoting Texas destinations during National Tourism Week each May. The organization also develops other marketing and promotional opportunities for members and industry leaders.

Publications: TTIA members receive a monthly newsletter, *TTIA Explorer,* as well as a membership directory that includes an annual listing of all association members. The organization also hosts a Website with exclusive membership content and sends out regular email updates and briefings to members, especially during the legislative session.

Education: TTIA partnered with Junior Achievement to create a tourism module for 3rd and 4th grade students, awards scholarships to college students who are members of the organization, and also sponsors an internship program that allows members to post internship opportunities free of charge. In 2005, the organization launched the "Texas Education Vacation" program for educators that emphasizes place based learning and casts a new light on Texas' destinations.

Contact Information:
Paul Serff, President/CEO, 812 San Antonio, Austin, Texas 78701
Phone: 512-476-4472
Website: www.ttia.org

dors, institutional members, and student members. These large associations, like the *National Tour Association*, may have thousands of members. Finally, some industry associations are international. Membership in these global associations is often made up of smaller industry associations from around the world. Many international associations also have national, statewide, or local chapters. These chapters are smaller, affiliated groups that share the same or similar purpose as the "parent" association. The Council on Hotel, Restaurant, and Institutional Education (CHRIE) is an association of educational hospitality programs around the world. There are states that are grouped together by region in the United States and the International Federations that are part of CHRIE but also operate independently in their own countries. These different regional groups offer special programs to help their students develop research studies as well as networking opportunities.

Determining Member Needs

No matter what the size or scope of membership, almost all industry associations will have governing documents that will include a mission and/or vision, by-laws, and a board of directors or advisors that oversees the organization.

Industry associations will have a mission—a statement of purpose—that should concisely describe why the association was formed and for what purpose. You should be able to look at an association's mission statement and immediately understand the purpose and scope of the organization. The **mission statement** is developed by the membership or governing board of an organization and often serves as the guide for the activities of the association. Industry associations will also have by-laws that govern the membership, board of directors or advisors, and any paid staff that the organization may employ. **By-laws** are rules or laws that govern the association's actions and internal operations. By-laws are typically developed internally by an association and adopted by the membership. With the membership's approval, by-laws may be amended or changed to meet the needs of an association. A **vision statement** is typically an umbrella statement about where the organization sees itself in the context of the industry as a whole. Vision statements tend to be broader in scope than mission statements and may include goals that the association hopes to achieve in the future.

Governing documents like by-laws and mission and vision statements help associations run smoothly. Many smaller industry associations have volunteer or part-time staffs. These associations rely on boards of directors or advisors to guide the organization's activities. Larger industry associations may employee both full and part time staff members to assist the association's board and membership in the day-to-day activities of the organization.

Why Join an Industry Association?

Everyone always says "networking is important." And it is. But, what does it mean? How do you "network"? Some students believe that if they become president of the student chapter of the restaurant association that they don't have to do any more than have the name on their resume. However, networking is more than that. It is meeting someone for the first time, exchanging business cards, and getting to know them. Then it is time to follow up. Email them a week later to say what a pleasure it was to meet them and how you would like to learn more about what they do and their company. Call them and set up an appointment to talk. Afterward, send them another email thanking them for taking the time to talk to you. Make sure at the next meeting, you say hello. This is the process for getting to know someone. In this way, people learn who you are, but it is a gradual process, not a one shot deal. Then, once you become friends, you can ask for help finding a job or learning about opportunities in their company and they will spend the time to ask around. If you are a perfect stranger, why should anyone go out of their way to help? Networking is building relationships.

Why should you join an association? Let me give you a personal example. I used to teach in a large ski school for many years. I did my job and had a lot of fun. Then, it came time for me to look for more responsibility. I didn't know anyone outside of my ski school, so I bought a book of ski areas and sent out over 500 letters to people I didn't know. Well, I got back around 20 rejections and wasted a lot of time and effort but finally managed to get a job. I thought to myself, "there must be a better way." So, I joined a number of associations, then volunteered for some committees, and talked to people. People began to know who I was. Then, the next time I wanted a better position, I called 5 people and within 2 weeks, I had 6 interviews and one offer. What made the difference? Networking. My five friends were trusted by a lot of people and when they vouched for me, people listened. Networking takes time and effort but it makes life much easier when you need help. Associations provide the contacts but you must provide the energy.

Most industry associations provide excellent networking opportunities for members through educational seminars, annual meetings, conventions, and conferences. Many industry associations maintain Websites and are now providing email updates in addition to printed newsletters. Becoming a member of an industry association may also give you a competitive edge in your chosen hospitality career path. Some associations extend **member benefits** to employees whose companies have institutional memberships or are affiliated with the association on some level. Member benefits may include newsletters, updates, and educational opportunities.

While most industry associations charge annual dues, many are now offering reduced rates for student members, or serve as parent organizations for student chapters. By joining a student chapter or joining an organization as a student member, you can gain valuable experience in your given field. First you are meeting future colleagues who share your interests and if they are working now, they are potential information sources about jobs and companies. Second, most student chapters invite guest speakers from industry so you have the opportunity to meet a professional who cares about helping students, otherwise they wouldn't be there. Third, become a leader. Leaders must interface with industry to get speakers and outside resources for the chapter. This is an excellent way to show your interest, demonstrate your leadership abilities, and to network. Fourth, go to parent chapter meetings.

Every student chapter has at least one industry liaison who is interested in helping you. Take advantage of that friendship. Have them introduce you around at the meetings. Talk to people about what they do and what kind of company they work for. This allows you the opportunity to learn the industry, meet new friends, and develop contacts. People begin to recognize you as an interested, involved person, not just a student.

When you become a member of an industry association, you are joining a network of professionals. There are many leadership opportunities in industry associations. You may be a chapter officer or hold a statewide position within a larger national association. Some associations have both state and regional annual meetings in addition to larger national meetings. These meetings are opportunities for professionals in the hospitality field to learn about industry trends and share ideas with colleagues. Also, many associations offer certifications in several areas. While there are years of experience requirements, many associations will waive some years for someone obtaining a degree in the field. Working on a certification allows you to bond with others by studying together and to give you a competitive advantage by having a degree and a certificate from a reputable, national professional organization. The certificate gives you credibility from a practitioners' perspective and the degree provides you with the theoretical knowledge, internship experience, and many different perspectives on handling the same problem. It is the best of both worlds.

Associations in the Food and Lodging Arena

Because the hospitality industry is so diverse, many associations have been created to meet the needs of professionals in the different arenas. We will take a look at some of the major industry associations for professionals in food and lodging. Remember that many states have their own food and lodging industry associations.

Founded in 1919, the National Restaurant Association represents over 60,000 members and over 300,000 restaurant establishments. The organization offers memberships to restaurants, allied industries, educators and students and international companies and not-for-profit organizations. The National Restaurant Association promotes the restaurant industry and related career paths, promotes dining out, and is committed to food safety in the industry.

With over 65,000 members the American Dietetic Association (ADA) promotes healthy lifestyles grounded in good nutrition and well-being. The American Culinary Federation (ACF) is the nation's largest organization for professionals working in the culinary arts including chefs, bakers, and cooks. The ACF sponsors competitions, awards, and educational events for chefs, including a comprehensive certification program for chefs. Both the ADA and ACF have student membership categories. Other important food and nutrition related industry associations include the American Association of Wine and Food, the International Food Service Executives Association, and the Catering and Institutional Management Association.

Professional organizations are also an important part of the lodging industry. The American Hotel & Lodging Association (AH&LA) promotes the interests of hoteliers throughout the United States and internationally. The AHLA offers student memberships and extensive educational opportunities for members. Other lodging related organizations include the International Hotel Association, the International Executive Housekeeper's Association, and the Hospitality Sales and Marketing Association International. Each of these organizations sponsors conferences, conventions, and educational opportunities for those interested in the lodging industry.

Associations in the Travel and Tourism Arena

There are a number of associations in the travel and tourism arena that have been organized to serve the

The American Hotel & Lodging Association promotes the interests of hoteliers throughout the U.S. and internationally.

© Andy Z. 2008, Shutterstock.

needs of tourism professionals. Many of these associations also promote the industry externally—by encouraging people to travel and visit destinations. The Tourism Industry Association of America (TIA) works with partnering organizations to promote travel within and to the United States. Through press releases, advertisements, and other marketing efforts, TIA encourages travel throughout the country with its "See America" campaign.

The World Tourism Organization (UNWTO/OMT), is a specialized agency of the United Nations. The organization is a leading international organization in the field of tourism. According to the mission of the UNWTO, the organization "serves as a global forum for tourism policy issues and practical source of tourism know-how."[3] The organization also encourages sustainable and regional tourism worldwide and sponsors tourism related research internationally. Other tourism industry associations like Destination Marketing Association International (DMAI) (formerly known as International Association of Convention and Visitor's Bureaus) and the National Tour Association (NTA) provide services to members in a very specific segment of the industry. These organizations promote travel and tourism awareness and also encourage travel to the United States. The Club Managers Association of America, the Meeting Professionals International, and the American Association of Travel Agents also are leading tourism related industry associations that offer networking and educational opportunities to their members. The Travel and Tourism Research Association works with educators, tourism marketing professionals, and other industry associations to promote research in the field, provide networking opportunities, and career information.

Finding a Place to Belong

As you can see, there are many hospitality industry associations that have been organized to assist professionals in their chosen fields. Joining an industry association could:

- Help you develop your professional skills
- Foster a sense of belonging in a large and diverse industry
- Provide important networking opportunities
- Communicate information about issues, trends, and legislation affecting the industry

In addition to personal and professional development, many associations also recognize industry leaders and innovators and set standards within the hospitality profession. Some industry associations provide mentoring programs and scholarship opportunities for early and mid-career professionals. No matter what part of the industry you are interested in, there is an association for you.

Hotel and Restaurant Rating Systems

Just as industry association set standards for professionals in the hospitality field, **hotel and restaurant ratings systems** also set standards with definite criteria. While there are no government rating systems of the hotel or restaurant industry in the United States, the American Automobile Association (AAA) and Mobil Travel Guide both provide independent rating services for hotels and restaurants.[4] AAA and Mobil Travel Guide use professionally trained inspectors to evaluate and rate hotel and restaurant properties based on a system of standards and guidelines. The goal of the ratings system is to provide an indicator for excellence in hospitality. According to Shane O'Flaherty, Vice-President of Quality Assurance, Mobil Travel Guide, "the Mobil Five-Star Award indicates that a dining or lodging experience is one of the best in the country. These properties consistently provide an unparalleled level of service and quality that distinguishes them from their peers."[5]

While Mobil Travel Guide assigns stars to properties that meet certain criteria, the AAA uses a classification system that awards diamonds to qualifying properties. The Five Diamond award is the highest award bestowed upon a restaurant or hotel by AAA. The AAA inspects over 57,000 properties in the United States, Canada, Mexico, and the Carribean—less than one half of one percent of the evaluated properties receive the coveted Five Diamond award each year. In 2006, more restaurants were added to the list than hotels, bringing the number of Five Diamond ranked properties to 150. According to Michael Petrone, director of AAA Tourism Information Development and head of the AAA Diamond Ratings®, this reflects trends seen in the hospitality and tourism industry. It is not surprising to Petrone that "the greatest numbers of Five Diamond restaurants are in areas of high tourism. As a nation, we are becoming more enlightened diners. Consumer demand is resulting in an emerging trend for more high quality dining experiences in our travel and vacations."[6]

Do Ratings Matter?

As the use of the internet for trip and travel planning increases, more and more Websites use rating systems to help consumers make decisions on where to stay and where to dine. As previously mentioned, the AAA and Mobil Travel Guide are among the oldest and most respected evaluators of hotels and restaurants. Some travel agents continue to rely heavily on ratings, while others trust their own experience with properties—rated or unrated. When a hotel or restaurant loses a star or diamond or is downgraded from a higher category, it suggests that the service and product have been reduced. "When a hotel's been downgraded, we pay attention," says Walter Littlejohn, president of Teaneck, N.J.-based Great Vacations. "Then we start to look for properties in the same area that are newer or have higher ratings."[7]

How the Ratings System Works

Hotel and Restaurant inspectors evaluate properties based on a set of guidelines. The AAA Diamond Ratings System uses the following criteria for restaurants:

- One-diamond restaurants must meet basic standards for management, quality, and cleanliness. These restaurants tend to have limited service menus and offer food at an economical price.
- Two-diamond restaurants have expanded menus and feature upgraded service and atmosphere. These restaurants are family friendly and may have enhanced or themed décor.
- Three-diamond restaurants employ professional chefs and offer entry-level fine dining. They exhibit a degree of refinement and there is an emphasis on quality and service.

- Four-diamond restaurants are distinctive and are focused on fine-dining. Often expensive, these restaurants are for those seeking a high quality experience.
- Five-diamond properties are "world class" and leaders in innovative menu selection and fine service. These properties are distinctive and feature "haute cuisine" and impeccable service.

Summary

Industry associations are professional organizations that assist members by providing opportunities for networking, education and training, and support within a given industry. Associations in the hospitality field may be organized on several different levels: community, statewide, regional, national, or international. They may include only one segment of the industry or encompass the hospitality and tourism industry as a whole. Industry associations will have governing documents that will include a mission, and/or vision, by-laws, and a board of directors or advisors that oversees the organization. Hospitality and tourism industry associations are important because they provide a voice for the industry and also provide many benefits to members. Industry associations may also set standards and guidelines for the hospitality industry.

Just as industry association set standards for professionals in the hospitality field, hotel and restaurant ratings systems also set standards with definite criteria. While there are no government rating systems of the hotel or restaurant industry in the United States, the American Automobile Association (AAA) and Mobil Travel Guide both provide independent rating services for hotels and restaurants. While Mobil Travel Guide assigns stars to properties that meet certain criteria, the AAA uses a classification system that awards diamonds to qualifying properties. Both the AAA and Mobil Travel Guide use professional inspectors to determine what properties will receive star or diamond ratings. The highest awards given by both organizations are highly sought by world class hotels and restaurants.

≈ *Resources*

Internet Sites

The National Restaurant Association: http://www.restaurant.org
The American Hotel & Lodging Association: http://www.ahma.org
International Executive Housekeeper's Association: http://www.ieha.org
Hospitality Sales and Marketing Association International: http://www.hsmai.org
Meeting Professionals International: http://www.mpiweb.org
American Society of Travel Agents: http://www.astanet.com
Destination Marketing Association International: http://www.iacvb.org
Tourism Industry Association of America: http://www.tia.org
Travel and Tourism Research Association: http://www.ttra.org
American Automobile Association: http://www.aaa.com
Mobil Travel Guide: http://www.mobiltravelguide.com

≈ *Endnotes*

1. 2006 Hospitality Associations. (2005, December). *Lodging Hospitality*, 16–18.
2. Personal communication with Scott Owings, Director of Membership, Texas Travel Industry Association, February 21, 2006.
3. Mission Statement of the United Nations World Tourism Organization at http://www.unwto.org/aboutwto/index.php
4. Rowe, M. (2003). Lost in Translation. *Meetingsnet.com*, 34.
5. Mobil Travel Guide Announces the 2006 Mobil Five-Star and Four-Star Winners at http://rez.mobiltravelguide.com/mtg/template.jsp?id=20413
6. Graziani, J. (2006). AAA Names 13 New Five Diamond Lodgings, Restaurants for 2006 at http://www.aaanewsroom.net/Main/Default.asp?CategoryID=8&ArticleID=407
7. Webber, S. P. (2000, February). Stargazing. *Travel Agent*. 298 at Business Source Premier Database.

≈ *Contributor*

Chay Runnels

Chay Rees Runnels is a lecturer in the Hospitality Administration program at Stephen F. Austin State University in Nacogdoches, Texas. Her experience includes working with non-profit tourism industry associations and heritage tourism organizations.

Contact information: Chay Runnels, Department of Human Sciences, Stephen F. Austin State University, P. O. Box 13014, Nacogdoches, Texas 75962. E-mail: runnelsc@sfasu.edu

Chapter 4
Review Questions

1. What are some of the benefits to joining an industry association in the hospitality or tourism field?

2. How can you determine for what purpose an industry association is formed? What are some of the basic governing documents of an industry association?

3. Explain the process of rating a hotel or restaurant property. What are the oldest, most-respected rating organizations in the United States?

4. If a hotel or restaurant is down-graded in a rating system, travel agents may take notice. Do you think industry ratings matter? Why or why not?

Information Resources: Periodicals and the Web

5

Miyoung Jeong, Iowa State University

© 2008, JupiterImages Corporation.

≈ Learning Objectives

☑ To introduce students to different information resources available in the field of the hospitality and tourism industry for their efficient and effective information search
☑ To familiarize students with key hospitality and tourism publications
☑ To improve students' skills to search information through a variety of available resources

≈ Chapter Outline

Comprehensive Information Resources

≈ Key Terms

Information resources
Offline resources
Online resources
Periodicals
Journals

*T*hey say that knowledge is power. The more information you know, the better the decisions you can make. How do you get knowledge? Well, of course, one way is to go to school . . . take classes . . . graduate . . . get a diploma. However, what if you want more information, what do you do? Where do you go? Learning is an on-going process. We are constantly acquiring new information through conversations with friends, colleagues, bosses, and family. Television, computers, newspapers, and other media are alternative ways to learn new things. Joining associations and being involved in the community and industry is another way. Networking is about meeting new people in the industry and maintaining contact so that you can talk to friends and discover new information. You never know when you might need some help or when they might come to you with a tempting idea. In order to compete with others, we need the best information available and so this chapter is designed to help you know where to look.

The hospitality and tourism discipline is an applied science, with its various disciplinary concepts adapted mostly from general business, sociology, psychology, and food science. So, a broad knowledge base is important. Within all those different concepts, there is one that stands out, service. *Service* is the characteristic that makes it and its industry unique and differentiated from other disciplines and industries. As you will continually read throughout this book, service is the human interaction or that "moment of truth" when employee and guest come together. That is when we learn whether our employees have the right kind of information to do their job. As we strive to develop and improve our service quality, more information is needed.

The first step in understanding the true meaning of hospitality and tourism, one must have a direct working experience in related industries. Such direct industry experiences provide one with a rich source of real, subjective information about the discipline and industry as a whole. Thus, one's direct work experience becomes the *primary* source of information for understanding.

We can also gain primary information from talking with our colleagues and managers. What clothes should I wear to work? What information do I need to finish the project? What career path can I have with your company? When we ask a question and gain answers, this is called primary data gathering. Some call this research and it is. However, the word, research, tends to scare people

Networking is about meeting new people in the industry and maintaining contact to stay informed.

© 2008, JupiterImages Corporation.

with its reputation for difficult statistics. In fact, research is no more than trying to get information to solve a problem. You do "research" every day. You ask questions, gather information, and decide how to proceed—classic research process. Think about it. Should I get out of bed and go to class? After you filter through the data in your head, you make a decision. A quest for knowledge about a career path is a research process. What field should I plan my career in? This book is designed to give you the information to start answering this question.

However, one may often look for more information from various perspectives about the industry to expand his or her understanding of current industry trends and industry-specific management/operational issues. When you want to look outside your personal contacts, you might want to explore what important industry people think about a topic or what objective research has been done in this area. Such published information can be obtained from industry newsletters, trade journals or magazines, and research journals, and these are generally called *secondary* information resources. Secondary data reflect the fact that you did not gather this information to answer your personal question. Someone else had a similar question and so they gathered the data. You came along and used this information to help answer your research question. Therefore, you were the second person to use the data, and hence, secondary information resource. Keep in mind that depending on who gathered the data and how they gathered the information, the findings may be valid and reliable or they may not.

Example: The Center for Gambling Addiction finds that 80% of people who enter a casino will become addicted. Is this true? What questions should you ask about the Center before you accept their findings? Do they have a reason to want a certain outcome? If the researcher appears to be objective and unbiased, then the second questions is "are they funded by another organization?" Does this organization have a reason to want the data to say certain things? If they are a center for gambling addiction, they want and need to show gambling addiction as a threat, that's why they are in business. However, the research findings may be objective and reliable. Unless you ask questions, you won't know whether the information you have acquired is good or bad. Just because something is in print, does not make it correct or objective. This is a hard lesson to learn because it is very easy to accept printed words at face value.

A good place to start is at the library. Know what is available in your area. Walk through the stacks and see what information can be found. You may be surprised at what you see. The offline resources offer traditional ways of obtaining necessary information and they include printed materials such as newspapers, newsletters, magazines, and journals. Remember that not all journals, newspapers, magazines, and newsletters are online. There are many good resources that only come in paper. Especially, information on specialty topics may not be accessible to outsiders online so you may have to rely on paper bound sources. For example, while there is a lot written on gambling, how casinos are actually run is not online. These specialty journals cater only to the casino employees and are only available by subscription. A library may have these periodicals and newsletters available for you to read. In addition, the library has special databases that contain academic literature that maybe easier to find in the database for a preliminary search rather than on the Internet.

However, today, more and more offline resources are being relocated to Internet sites by either totally eliminating their offline formats or offering both printed and online forms of information. Adoption of the Internet as a platform of information offering like this will accelerate exponentially by dint of its easy accessibility, convenience, ease of use, and currency. Even if many online information providers offer information to readers free of charge in return for the reader's registration for a free newsletter subscription (e.g., hotel-online.com, restaurant_hospitality.com, etc.), other providers set restrictions on information release by requiring membership (e.g., Hospitality Financial Technology Professionals).

With the advent of the Internet as a main hub for information searches, information resources have been divided into largely two categories based on where the target information is placed: online and offline resources. As a major information resource in the hospitality and tourism area today, the Internet makes our lives much easier by offering ready access to countless information sources for one's education and career development. The online resources provide the information from various, specific Websites accessible on the Internet. For example, to gather information about emerging trends or issues in the lodging industry for the upcoming year, the hotel-online.com, a major hotel news Website, is available for access on the Internet.

To make effective and efficient use of both online and offline information resources, the hospitality and tourism industry can be divided into four areas according to industrial characteristics: travel, lodging, foodservice, and recreation.[1] The travel sector is defined based on how people travel from one place to other place, so called different methods of transportation. This sector includes the airline, cruise, train, coach, and automobile industries. For instance, people tend to use a train, a coach, or an automobile when they travel domestically or in a short distance. For international or long distance trips, the airline is a typical transportation people use, so is the cruise. However, the cruise is used for more leisure and pleasure trips on a sea.

The second sector, the lodging industry, includes two major sub industries: (1) hotels and motels and (2) meetings, conventions, and expositions. The lodging sector is defined based on a place where people can stay while traveling, a hotel or a motel, and what business functions they participate in, meetings, conventions, or expositions. Meetings are typically held in a hotel or a motel in its conference rooms because a small number of people attend the meetings with range of 50 to 300 people, while conventions or expositions are typically held in a destination's convention center due to their large scale and big groups of people attending, sometimes more than 500 participants.

Commercial restaurants and onsite foodservice operations are classified as the restaurant sector. The restaurant sector refers to places where people can eat out while they are away from home. Think about places you usually go for lunch or dinner such as McDonald's, Chili's Grill & Bar, Panera Bread, a college' dining center, or residence hall. The first three places fall under the commercial res-

The hospitality industry can be divided into the four areas of travel, lodging, foodservice, and recreation.

taurant and the last two under the onsite foodservice. The last sector, the recreation sector, consists of attractions, parks, and recreation. The recreation sector focuses on places where people can enjoy and activities that people can participate in. Such places as Niagara Falls, the Grand Canyon, and Disney World are excellent examples for attractions. There are many national, state, and local parks in the U.S. in which people can participate in a wide variety of recreational activities and games including fishing, scenic drives, weekend getaway, camping, and excursion. Yosemite National Park is one of the well-known parks in the world.

In this chapter, we will review sources of information by three categories: (1) a comprehensive information resource, *Hospitality and Tourism Index*, (2) periodicals such as magazines and journals, and (3) industry newsletters and glossary.

Comprehensive Information Resources

Hospitality and Tourism Index

Many universities and colleges in the United States have already subscribed to the *Hospitality and Tourism Index* (HTI), a comprehensive index for the hospitality and tourism industry. According to the EBSCO publishing Website,[2] the HTI is:

> ". . . a bibliographic database covering scholarly research and industry news relating to all areas of hospitality and tourism. This comprehensive index combines the records of three renowned collections: Cornell University's former *Hospitality* database, *Articles in Hospitality and Tourism* (AHT), formerly co-produced by the Universities of Surrey and Oxford Brookes, and the *Lodging, Restaurant & Tourism Index* (LRTI), formerly produced by Purdue University. Together, this collection contains more than 500,000 records from more than 500 titles, with coverage dating as far back as 1965. Sources are both domestic and international in range and scope, with material collected from countries and regions such as Canada, Australia, Europe, and Asia . . . Subject areas covered include the culinary arts, demographics and statistics, development and investment, food and beverage management, hospitality law, hotel management and administrative practices, leisure and business travel, market trends, technology, and more."

The EBSCO publishing company also provides users with a full-text HTI with additional costs. Key sources of this index include academic journals, market research/industry/country reports, magazine, trade publications, and more. A complete coverage list of the index is available on the EBSCO Website.[3] Figure 5.1 is a front page of the HTI on the Internet that can be used to search potential periodicals with keywords and to refine the search process by setting limits of the search such as date and type of publication and document. This index is believed to be a first place to start for searching information in the field of hospitality and tourism.

Periodicals

Periodicals refer to publications such as magazines, newspapers, and journals that are published in regular intervals, usually daily, weekly, monthly, or quarterly.[4] Many periodicals in the hospitality and tourism industry are published either in magazines or in journals. All magazines are related to industry-specific publications written by experts in the field such as in *Lodging, Hospitality Technology,* and *Travel Weekly.* Articles in these magazines focus on industry trends both national and international, current operational and management issues, industry outlook, and/or consumers' buying patterns, based on the expert's experience and opinions, or brief interviews or surveys with target markets. Whereas most journals are focused on reporting academic research done by educators and industry practitioners such as articles published in *Cornell Hotel and Restaurant Administration Quarterly* and *Journal of Foodservice Management and Education.* The academic research, differed from expert opinions, requires more scientific evidence and process by identifying clear research problems or hypotheses

Figure 5.1 Database of *Hospitality & Tourism Index*

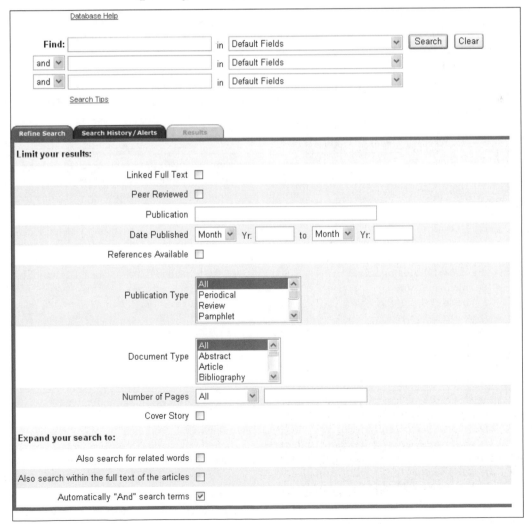

and providing valid results to the problems by analyzing collected data. Many of these publications have both online (their own Websites) and offline (hardcopy) platforms to disseminate information to potential readers. In this chapter, two types of periodicals (magazines and journals) are reviewed as classified by the industry sector and subject area.

Hospitality and Tourism Magazines

There are about 63 magazines in the hospitality and tourism area. Twenty three of the magazines relate to the foodservice sector, 23 to lodging, 10 to the hospitality sector in general (covering both lodging and foodservice), and 8 to the travel/recreation sector. As shown in Tables 5.1 and 5.2, most magazines across the sectors generally cover current issues and trends, industry news, and industry events for the focal business sector. However, such publications as *Wine Spectator, Cruise Industry News Quarterly, Air Transport World,* and *Hospitality Technology* concentrate on a specific product, service, and/or subject area. Therefore, magazines are grouped by their focal subject for a better use of magazines in one's research.

Table 5.1 List of Foodservice and Lodging Magazines and Their Main Coverage

INDUSTRY	TITLE OF MAGAZINE BY SUBJECT	COVERAGE AREA
Foodservice	Alcohol, beverage, and wine —*Beverage World* —*Cheers* —*Wine Spectator*	A comprehensive online listing of beverage products and services; wine ratings; daily wine picks; dining and travel; vintage charts; wine shops.
	Catering —*Caterer & Hotelkeeper* —*Catering Magazine* —*Catering Update*	A fresh, expert perspective and an independent view on the news, issues, and events; product information; contract catering to food, drink, and equipment.
	Equipment/supplies/recipes —*Chef Magazine* —*Cooking for Profit* —*Food Arts* —*Foodservice Equipment & Supplies*	New recipe; nutrition; up-to-date foodservice equipment; new energy-efficient technologies; foodservice facilities; equipment specifications.
	Onsite foodservice —*Food Management* —*Foodservice Director*	Current issues and events on noncommercial foodservice industry; food safety and layout/design; issues, ideas, and events in institutional foodservice organizations.
	Restaurants —*Efenbeonline* —*Foodservice & Hospitality* —*Nation's Restaurant News* —*Nightclub & Bar Magazine* —*Restaurant Business* —*Restaurant Hospitality* —*Restaurant Report* —*Restaurants & Institutions* —*Restaurants USA; Pizza Today*	Key issues and trends of the foodservice industry; new food and equipment products and trends; menu and recipe ideas; new technology; food safety; emerging new concepts; consumer attitudes and trends; labor and training; profiles of successful operations; buyer's guide to suppliers; franchise opportunities; community outreach.
	Clubs —*Club Management*	Club leadership; marketing; food and beverage; golf course; sport/fitness; technology; facilities.
Lodging	Hotels —*Crittenden Hotel/Lodging News* —*Hotel and Motel Management* —*Hotel Business; Hotel Resource* —*Hotelier; HotelOnline* —*Hotels; Lodging* —*Lodging Hospitality* —*Premier Hotels & Resorts*	Industry trends and issues on marketing, technology, operations, human resources, food and beverage, design and construction, legal, governmental affairs, finance; association news; suppliers; trade shows; hotel brands guide; employment opportunities; worldwide hotel project development; site selection; renovation.

(continued)

Table 5.1 List of Foodservice and Lodging Magazines and Their Main Coverage *(continued)*

INDUSTRY	TITLE OF MAGAZINE BY SUBJECT	COVERAGE AREA
Lodging (continued)	Housekeeping —*Executive Housekeeping Today* —*Room Chronicle*	Housekeeping issues and trends; training; management; operational strategies; energy savings; engineering; front office; guest services; housekeeping; people skills; reservations; risk management; complaint handling.
	Meetings/convention —*Association Meetings* —*Convention Forum* —*Meeting and Conventions* —*Meetings Net; Meeting News* —*Meeting Professionals International* —*Successful Meetings*	Issues and trends on the meetings and events industry; industry news; industry jobs; venue and supplier search database; events in five focused areas of association, corporate, insurance/financial, religious, and medical; destination-specific information about facilities, resources, local attractions, and events.
	Special lodging segments —*Cruise Industry News Quarterly* —*Green Hotelier* —*Vacation Ownership*	Cruise industry news and trends; cruise operations; ports and destinations; social and environmental issues and trends; sustainable travel and tourism operation; issues and trends on the vacation ownership industry; showcase; guide to vacation ownership.

Table 5.2 List of Hospitality and Travel/Recreation Magazines and Their Main Coverage

INDUSTRY	TITLE OF MAGAZINE BY SUBJECT	COVERAGE AREA
Hospitality	Hospitality —*Hospitality Interactive* —*Hospitality Matters* —*Hospitality Net* —*Hospitality News Resources* —*Hotel & Restaurant*	Industry news; association update; job opportunities and demands; marketplace; hotel schools; industry links; profiles of top chefs, restaurateurs, and hoteliers.
	Design —*Hospitality Design*	Hospitality design (hotels, resorts, restaurants, cruise ships, country clubs, night clubs, conference centers, spas, senior living facilities); other hospitality-oriented projects.
	Law —*Hospitality Law*	Hospitality legal cases; summaries of the latest court cases; employee policy development; practical ramifications of the latest cases; employment practices.
	Marketing/consulting —*HSMAI Marketing Review* —*HVS International Journal*	Issues and trends of hospitality sales and marketing; industry events; insights from HSMAI leaders; member education. Global consulting and services on the hotel, restaurant, timeshare, gaming, and leisure industries.
	Technology —*Hospitality Technology* —*Hospitality Upgrade*	Technology news and trends; industry solution; IT resources and research; software and hardware solutions; in-depth analyses by consultants; interviews with top industry executives; IT purchasing and maintenance.
Travel/ Recreation	Airline/Travel agent —*Air Transport World* —*Onboard Hospitality* —*Travel Agent*	Issues and trends on travel agents and airline operations, management, technology, safety and security, regulation, airport development, and air cargo; forum for news and views from the in-flight, cruise, and rail hospitality industry.
	Attractions —*Attractions Management*	Visitor attraction market; theme parks, museums; science centers; corporate brandlings.
	Travel —*Business Travel News* —*Canadian Travel Press* —*Travel Weekly* —*Travel & Leisure*	Current issues and trends on business travel; industry meetings and events; international business travel; trade news; global perspective through in-depth coverage of airline, car rental, cruise, destination, hotel, and tour operator; technology, economic, and governmental issues.

Hospitality and Tourism Journals

As briefly mentioned above, journals are slightly different from magazines in the ways that they have a relatively limited target audience, are more academic research-oriented, and do not always carry up-to-date articles due to a long lead-time for publication. However, articles in each journal tend to provide concrete conceptual frameworks for solving or analyzing real-world problems so that management can implement potential techniques or strategies borrowed from journal articles for its chronic operational issues. Journal articles often include sections for discussing how the study's procedures and results can be applied to actual managerial situations. Table 5.3 shows a comprehensive list of journals and their main coverage.

Table 5.3   List of Journals by Industry and Their Main Coverage

INDUSTRY/NAME OF JOURNAL	COVERAGE
Foodservice —*Journal of Child Nutrition & Management* —*Journal of Foodservice Management and Education* —*Journal of Nutrition Education & Behavior* —*Journal of Foodservice Business Research*	Child nutrition; school foodservice management; onsite foodservice industry; food behavior; sustainable dietary change; nutrition education; management and entrepreneurship; marketing, finance, and accounting; information systems and technology; legal matters; franchising; nutrition; food habits and food safety; global issues and cultural studies.
Hospitality —*Cornell Hotel and Restaurant Administration Quarterly* —*FIU Hospitality Review* —*International Journal of Contemporary Hospitality Management* —*International Journal of Hospitality Management* —*Journal of Applied Hospitality Management* —*UNLV Gaming Research & Review Journal*	Marketing; finance; human resources; international development; travel and tourism; more general management; innovative international academic thinking; practical examples of industry best practice; consumer behavior; business forecasting and applied economics; operational management; technological developments; national and international legislation; gaming laws and regulations.
Hospitality and Tourism —*Journal of Hospitality & Tourism Research* —*Journal of Hospitality and Leisure Marketing* —Journal of Hospitality and Tourism Education —*Scandinavian Journal of Hospitality & Tourism* —*Tourism & Hospitality Research* —*International Journal of Hospitality & Tourism Administration* —*International Journal of Tourism and Hospitality Research* —*Journal of Convention & Event Tourism* —*Journal of Human Resources in Hospitality and Tourism* —*Information Technology & Tourism* —*Journal of Teaching in Travel & Tourism* —*Journal of Vacation Marketing* —*Tourism Economics* —*Tourism Review International*	Strategic management; innovations in service strategies and customer satisfaction; lodging industry and human resources management; tourist decision-making and behavior; marketing and administration; legal issues; finance; cross-cultural and multicultural management issues; property management and hotel/restaurant development; research methodology; pricing hospitality and leisure products; econometric analysis of the price/demand function; empirical and conceptual research of issues; recruitment and retention; workforce diversity; the latest teaching developments; international travel and tourism course curriculum; teaching for excellence; perspectives on the changing directions of travel education; capital provision; economic appraisal; mathematical modeling; regional economic effects of tourism developments; international tourism data analysis; tourism promotion; cultural awareness; destination selection processes; destination marketing; general contractors and subcontractors.
Travel/Recreation —*Leisure Studies* —*Recreation* —*Tourism Culture & Communication* —*Tourism Recreation Research* —*Annals of Tourism Research* —*International Journal of Tourism Research* —*Journal of Sustainable Tourism* —*Journal of Tourism Studies* —*Tourism Geographies* —*Journal of Travel and Tourism Marketing* —*Journal of Travel Research*	Sociology; psychology; human geography; planning; economics; cultural attitudes toward the management of tourists with disabilities; gender aspects of tourism; sport tourism; age-specific tourism; recreational environments; ecology; economics; conservation development; regional planning and sociology; sustainable tourism; tourism product development; meeting services and conventions; tourist behavior and destination choice; marketing.

Table 5.4 **Free e-Newsletters by the Industry Sector**

INDUSTRY SECTOR	E-NEWSLETTER PROVIDERS
Foodservice	—*Beverage World:* http://www.beverageworld.com —*Food Arts:* http://www.winespectator.com/Wine/Free/FoodArts/FoodArts_Subscription/0,2613,,00.html —*Foodservice Equipment & Supplies:* http://www.foodservice411.com/fesmag/ —*Nation's Restaurant News:* http://www.nrn.com/ —*Nightclub & Bar Magazine:* http://www.nightclub.com/ —*Restaurant Business:* http://www.restaurantbiz.com/ —*Restaurant Hospitality:* http://www.restaurant-hospitality.com/ —*Restaurant Report:* http://www.restaurantreport.com/ —*Restaurants USA:* http://www.restaurant.org —*Wine Spectator:* http://www.winespectator.com/Wine/Home/
Lodging	—*Hotel Business:* http://www.hotelbusiness.com/main.asp —*Hotel Resource:* http://www.hotelresource.com/ —*HotelOnline:* http://www.hotel-online.com/index.html —*Hotels:* http://www.hotelsmag.com/ —*Lodging Hospitality:* http://www.lhonline.com/ —*Meeting and Conventions:* http://www.meetings-conventions.com/ —*Successful Meetings:* http://www.mimegasite.com/mimegasite/index.jsp
Hospitality	—*Hospitality Design:* http://www.hdmag.com/hospitalitydesign/index.jsp —*Hospitality Interactive:* http://www.hotelinteractive.com/ —*Hospitality News Resources:* http://www.hotelnewsresource.com/headlines.htm —*HVS International Journal:* http://www.hvsinternational.com/ —*Onboard Hospitality:* http://www.onboardhospitality.com/
Travel	—*Air Transport World:* http://www.atwonline.com/ —*Canadian Travel Press:* http://www.travelpress.com/ctp_kit/index.html —*Travel Agent:* http://www.travelagentcentral.com/travelagentcentral/

Industry e-Newsletters and Glossary Websites

All industry magazines reviewed in this chapter have their own Websites featuring additional information for readers. Approximately one third of these magazines provide free daily or, at least, weekly electronic newsletters to those who have submitted their email address to the publishing company. Subscription of e-newsletters is one of the best ways to help oneself keep up to date with the progress of the hospitality and tourism industry including industry outlooks, news, trends, and challenges. It is recommended that at least one e-newsletter in each industry sector be subscribed to stay informed of this complex and ever growing industry. Table 5.4 lists magazines by industry sector, along with their URL providing free daily or weekly newsletters.

Like many other disciplines, hospitality and tourism has developed its industry-specific terminologies. One needs to know main concepts and terms pertaining to this industry to understand the industry's issues and/or develop careers in this industry. There are eight glossary websites covering the industry in general and specific to areas:

- General hospitality and tourism glossary
  - Libra Hospitality: http://www.librahospitality.com/club/dictionary/
- Travel industry glossary
  - California Arts Council: http://www.cac.ca.gov/?id=252
- Restaurant industry glossary
  - Wikipedia: http://en.wikipedia.org/wiki/Category:Restaurant_terminology
- Hospitality law glossary
  - Hospitalitylawyer.com: http://www.hospitalitylawyer.com/?PageID=21
- Hospitality information technology glossary
  - SearchCRM.com: http://searchcrm.techtarget.com/gDefinition/0,294236,sid11_gci537805,00.html
- Accounting glossary
  - NYSSCPA.org: http://www.nysscpa.org/prof_library/guide.htm

- Internet marketing glossary
  - Marketingterms.com: http://www.market-ingterms.com/dictionary/

Summary

As a starting point to garner information about the hospitality and tourism industry, this chapter reviewed potential information resources available online as well as offline. Prior to visiting a specific journal or magazine website, one is recommended to browse the Hospitality and Tourism Index (HTI) first to identify recommended resources and read abstracts of articles so as to narrow down informa-tion search. When using the HTI, students should have a clear idea of what field and what subject they are in to search information; otherwise, results of each search are uncontrollable and unmanaged due to an excessive number of search results. Additionally, most industry magazines and research journals can be valuable resources to support students' coursework and career development. Therefore, subscribing to industry e-newsletters is highly recommended to keep abreast with industry trends and build a strong connection to the industry early on. Knowledge is power and knowing the sources of knowledge is a starting point.

≈ *Resources*

Internet Sites

Magazines

Air Transport World: http://www.atwonline.com/
Association Meetings: http://meetingsnet.com/associationmeetings/
Attractions Management: http://www.attractions.co.uk/
Beverage World: http://www.beverageworld.com
Business Travel News: http://www.btnonline.com/businesstravelnews/index.jsp
Canadian Travel Press: http://www.travelpress.com/ctp_kit/index.html
Caterer & Hotelkeeper: http://www.qssa.co.uk/reed/subcentre/default.asp?title=cho&promcode=1452
Catering Magazine: http://www.cateringmagazine.com/home/
Catering Update: http://www.cateringupdate.com/
Cheers: http://www.beveragenet.net/cheers/2005/0512%5Fchrs/
Chef Magazine: http://www.chefmagazine.com/
Club Management: http://www.club-mgmt.com/
Convention Forum: http://www.conventionforum.com/
Cooking for Profit: http://www.cookingforprofit.com/magfeatures.html
Crittenden Hotel/Lodging News: http://www.crittendenonline.com/
Cruise Industry News Quarterly: http://www.cruiseindustrynews.com/index.php?option=com_content&task=blogsection&id=4&Itemid=43
Efenbeonline: http://www.efenbeonline.com/index.asp
Executive Housekeeping Today: http://www.ieha.org/publications/editors_corner.html
Food Arts: http://www.winespectator.com/Wine/Free/FoodArts/FoodArts_Subscription/0,2613,,00.html
Food Management: http://www.food-management.com/
Foodservice & Hospitality: http://www.foodserviceworld.com/fsh
Foodservice Director: http://www.fsdmag.com/
Foodservice Equipment & Supplies: http://www.foodservice411.com/fesmag/
Green Hotelier: http://www.greenhotelier.com/
Hospitality Design: http://www.hdmag.com/hospitalitydesign/index.jsp
Hospitality Interactive: http://www.hotelinteractive.com/
Hospitality Law: http://www.shoplrp.com/product/p-7800.HOSP.html
Hospitality Matters: http://www.hospitalitymatters.co.uk/
Hospitality Net: http://www.hospitalitynet.org/index.html
Hospitality News Resources: http://www.hotelnewsresource.com/headlines.htm
Hospitality Technology: http://www.htmagazine.com/HT/index.shtml
Hospitality Upgrade: http://www.hospitalityupgrade.com/
Hotel & Restaurant: http://www.hotelandrestaurant.co.uk/
Hotel and Motel Management: http://www.hotelmotel.com/hotelmotel/
Hotel Business: http://www.hotelbusiness.com/main.asp
Hotel Resource: http://www.hotelresource.com/
Hotelier: http://www.foodserviceworld.com/hotelier/archives/septFour/septFour.shtml

HotelOnline: http://www.hotel-online.com/index.html
Hotels: http://www.hotelsmag.com/
HVS International Journal: http://www.hvsinternational.com/
Lodging: http://www.lodgingmagazine.com/
Lodging Hospitality: http://www.lhonline.com/
Meeting and Conventions: http://www.meetings-conventions.com/
Meeting News: http://www.meetingsnet.com/
Meetings Net: http://www.meetpie.com/registration/persistent/mee05_mit_subscription_free.asp
Nation's Restaurant News: http://www.nrn.com/
Nightclub & Bar Magazine: http://www.nightclub.com/
Onboard Hospitality: http://www.onboardhospitality.com/
Pizza Today: http://www.pizzatoday.com/
Premier Hotels & Resorts: http://www.premierhotels.com/premier/
Restaurant Business: http://www.restaurantbiz.com/
Restaurant Hospitality: http://www.restaurant-hospitality.com/
Restaurant Report: http://www.restaurantreport.com/
Restaurants and Institutions: http://www.foodservice411.com/rimag/
Restaurants USA: http://www.restaurant.org
Room Chronicle: http://www.roomschronicle.com/
Successful meetings: http://www.mimegasite.com/mimegasite/index.jsp
The Meeting Professionals International: http://www.mpiweb.org/cms/mpiweb/default.aspx
Travel & Leisure: http://www.travelandleisure.com/
Travel Agent: http://www.travelagentcentral.com/travelagentcentral/
Travel Weekly: http://www.travelweekly.com/
Vacation Ownership: http://www.vomagazine.com/
Wine Spectator: http://www.winespectator.com/Wine/Home/

Journals

Annals of Tourism Research: http://www.sciencedirect.com/science?_ob=JournalURL&_cdi=5855&_auth=y&_acct=C000050221&_version=1&_urlVersion=0&_userid=10&md5=e0c01093915f6542f4750140532315c7&chunk=xxx
Cornell Hotel and Restaurant Administration Quarterly: http://www.hotelschool.cornell.edu/publications/hraq/
FIU Hospitality Review: http://hospitality.fiu.edu/review/index.htm
Information Technology & Tourism: http://itt.ec3.at/
International Journal of Contemporary Hospitality Management: http://www.emeraldinsight.com/info/journals/ijchm/ijchm.jsp
International Journal of Hospitality & Tourism Administration: http://www.haworthpress.com/web/IJHTA/
International Journal of Hospitality Management: http://www.sciencedirect.com/science?_ob=JournalURL&_cdi=5927&_auth=y&_acct=C000050221&_version=1&_urlVersion=0&_userid=10&md5=39c3adc5ecc55a616cb22c83c4ce000b
International Journal of Tourism and Hospitality Research: http://www.anatoliajournal.com/index.htm
International Journal of Tourism Research: http://www.wiley.com/WileyCDA/WileyTitle/productCd-JTR.html
Journal of Applied Hospitality Management: http://www.robinson.gsu.edu/hospitality/jahm.html
Journal of Child Nutrition & Management: http://docs.schoolnutrition.org/newsroom/jcnm/
Journal of Convention & Event Tourism: http://www.haworthpress.com/store/TOC.asp?sid=76A1CPSPC0PG8JC19TH7QE3EQSBN8X0E&sku=J452
Journal of Foodservice Business Research: http://www.haworthpress.com/web/JFBR/
Journal of Foodservice Management and Education: http://www.fsmec.org/journal_current.html
Journal of Hospitality & Tourism Research: http://jht.sagepub.com/
Journal of Hospitality and Leisure Marketing: http://www.haworthpress.com/store/product.asp?sku=J150
Journal of Hospitality and Tourism Education: http://www.hlst.heacademy.ac.uk/Johlste/index.html
Journal of Human Resources in Hospitality and Tourism: http://www.haworthpress.com/web/JHRHT/
Journal of Nutrition Education & Behavior: http://www.jneb.org/
Journal of Sustainable Tourism: http://www.multilingual-matters.net/jost/
Journal of Teaching in Travel & Tourism: http://www.haworthpress.com/web/JTTT/
Journal of Tourism Studies: http://www.jcu.edu.au/fac1/public/business/jts/
Journal of Travel and Tourism Marketing: http://www.haworthpress.com/store/product.asp?sku=J073
Journal of Travel Research: http://jtr.sagepub.com/
Journal of Vacation Marketing: http://jvm.sagepub.com/
Leisure Studies: http://www.tandf.co.uk/journals/titles/02614367.asp
Scandinavian Journal of Hospitality & Tourism: http://www.tandf.co.uk/journals/titles/15022250.asp
Tourism & Hospitality Research: http://www.henrystewart.com/tourism_and_hospitality/
Tourism Culture & Communication: http://www.cognizantcommunication.com/filecabinet/Tourism_Culture/tcc.htm

Tourism Economics: http://www.ippublishing.com/general_tourism.htm
Tourism Geographies: http://www.tandf.co.uk/journals/routledge/14616688.html
Tourism Recreation Research: http://www.trrworld.org/
Tourism Review International: http://www.cognizantcommunication.com/filecabinet/Tri/tri.html
UNLV Gaming Research & Review Journal: http://hotel.unlv.edu/res_gamingJournal_main.html

Terminology Websites

Glossary of Tourism Terms http://app.stb.com.sg/asp/tou/tou08.asp
Hospitality Law Glossary http://www.hospitalitylawyer.com/?PageID=21
Glossary of Hospitality Terms http://www.librahospitality.com/club/dictionary/
Hospitality Information Technology Glossary http://searchcrm.techtarget.com/gDefinition/0,294236,sid11_gci537805,00.html
Travel Industry Terminology http://www.cac.ca.gov/?id=252
Restaurant terminology http://en.wikipedia.org/wiki/Category:Restaurant_terminology
Accounting terminology http://www.nysscpa.org/prof_library/guide.htm
Internet marketing terminology http://www.marketingterms.com/dictionary/

≈ *Endnotes*

1. Walker, J. R. (2004). Introduction. In *Introduction to Hospitality Management.* Upper Saddle River, NJ: Pearson Prentice Hall, 3–37.
2. EBSCO Publishing. (2006). *Hospitality & Index* at http://www.epnet.com/thisTopic.php?marketID=1&topicID=85
3. *Hospitality & Tourism Index* at http://www.epnet.com/thisTopic.php?marketID=1&topicID=85
4. *Glossary* at http://novaonline.nvcc.edu/eli/lbr105/glossary.htm

≈ *Contributor*

Miyoung Jeong, PhD, is an associate professor in the Hotel, Restaurant, and Institution Management (HRIM) program at Iowa State University. Corresponding email: mjeong@iastate.edu

Chapter 5
Review Questions

1. Why is it important to have both primary and secondary information resources?

2. What is the Hospitality & Tourism Index?

3. What are two different formats of information resources?

4. Describe similarities and differences between magazines and journals.

Part 2

Hospitality Operations

Operations Management

6

Richard Mills and Denis Rudd
Robert Morris University

© Kelly Young, 2008, Shutterstock.

≈ Learning Objectives

☑ Identify the importance of operations management
☑ Define the role of the manager in the hospitality and tourism industry
☑ Discuss the consequence of the recent materialization of management as a field of work and study
☑ Show how management is a set of balanced, problem-solving techniques rather than a group of inborn abilities and traits
☑ View planning as an organizational process that goes on at all levels
☑ Define and use key planning concepts used in this chapter
☑ Outline the general procedure of staff planning and identify and describe the major tools that are used in that process

≈ Chapter Outline

What Is Operations Management?
Basic Qualifications for a Successful Operations
    Manager
Levels of Management
Management Functions
Leadership and Directing in Hospitality and Tourism
    Management
Future Concerns for the Hospitality and Tourism
    Management

≈ Key Terms

Conceptual skills
Control
Empowering
Ethics
Interpersonal skills
Labor intensive
Leadership
Management
Moral development theory
Organizing
Planning
Staffing
Technical skills
Vision

What Is Operations Management?

Students considering a career in hospitality and tourism management must first, and foremost, identify the meaning of management and, second, identify the meaning of operations. It is equally important for them to understand the work of operations managers and supervisors. The word management has two meanings. First, management is a collective noun to identify those in charge of directing business affairs. Management is a group of persons or individuals who receive their authority and responsibility from ownership or a directive from organizations to oversee the entire operation. Managers use this authority, along with the resources that are supplied from the business, to produce a product or service that creates an operation. Second, management becomes a service. From the sale of a products and services, the operation itself becomes an additional product that engages management compensations, employee wages, and dividends paid to owners. Therefore, operations management becomes an act, the job that management does.

One distinguishes management and operations into categories of managing itself, consulting, or just doing routine operative tasks. Therefore, as a student, the first task at hand is to define what management *does*, and second, how these managerial tasks are learned, applied, and implemented. This defines the different operations that encompass the hospitality and tourism industry today. To be successful in the hospitality and tourism industry, it is imperative that students have a basic understanding of what management actually *performs* and why particular managerial styles, leadership skills, and personal qualities enhance the direction and overall outcome of any operation.

The Hospitality Managers' Role

There have been many definitions applied to the term management, but the one that seems to get directly to the point is: *Management is the process of getting tasks accomplished through people.* A manager is a person who is responsible for the work of others, deciding the tasks people should perform, and ultimately how they can accomplish these goals. Managers can accomplish their goals by acquiring skills and knowledge and passing these qualities on to employees.

Curtis and Manning[1] discuss how a manager can improve their skills and assign work more effectively.

- **Consider the availability of the employee's time and whether this is the ideal person to do the job.** If the employee's schedule is heavily loaded, explain the priorities of the job. It is important not to overwork the employee because the overworked employee does not know the priority of many assignments and the underworked employees are wasted or never developed.
- **Use work assignments as a means of developing people.** If a job does not have a deadline, an employee may be *tired* in the task.
- **Know exactly what you want to communicate before giving an order.** This eliminates confusion and encourages confidence in employees. If you are giving a speech to employees, practice it and be concise and clear. Write it down if it is complex to avoid confusion.
- **If many duties or steps are involved in an order, follow oral communication with a note and keep a copy.** Keeping records of important conferences, orders, and rules can be helpful to keep memos to a minimum as this practice encourages defensive behavior.
- **Ask rather than tell, but leave no doubt that you expect compliance.** This approach shows both courtesy and respect.
- **Use the correct language for the employee's training level.** Recognize that many people will not understand your words and terms as readily as you do.
- **Make assignments in a logical sequence, using clear and concise language.** Break up assignments into easily achieved goals so that everyone understands the process.
- **Be considerate but never apologetic when asking someone to do a job.**
- **Talk deliberately and authoritatively. Avoid shouting across a room or making an unnecessary show of power.**
- **Take responsibility for the orders you give.**
- **Give people the opportunity to ask questions and express opinions.**
- **Follow up to make sure assignments are being carried out properly and modify them if the situation warrants.**

Identifying *who management is* may be easier than defining *what management does*. The products of management are not easily recognizable. Part of the problem is that management products are not readily visible, such as a hamburger or an ironed table cloth, but management is responsible for both. The average employee may not see what management *does*, but management does produce. The production success of management is evident in a profitable business by the air of confidence, productivity, and motivation of its employees. Often, good management skills are observed in the failure of another business given equal resources. It is well recognized that the value of a business is based on its management talent as well as its physical assets.

Supervision, in a service business, is more complex than that in a factory and, for this reason, hospitality supervisors face a unique challenge. Manufactured products and labor are driven by volume and easily visible quality. Machines and its workers can see their progress and they perform the same tasks every day. As a result, the workers can be fatigued and dull working under these conditions. Service employees work under different conditions. The "product" of their work is not visible or measurable with our five senses. A satisfied guest is the goal of our employees. As a result, the work situation changes from guest to guest and changes with each individual guest. Because we are working with people, mundane tasks are always adapted to suit the new personality or problem a guest has. This keeps the supervisor on their toes because reactions to situations are unpredictable.

Managing Change

Management is a relatively modern institution and, ultimately, it must view the problems of work in an expanding and increasingly wealthy society. This new way of viewing employee productivity has become one of the strongest forces in the last 100 years. Because of the rapid development of technology and the service business, our view of the role of management has changed dramatically. Management responsibilities continue to adapt to the dynamic society in which it operates, and those who aspire to a career in management must be prepared to adjust to these changes.

Management styles change with the fluctuations in society. In colonial times, management was easy: do as I say or you are fired. Today's managers do not have the same set of goals that were evident in Colonial America or the sweatshops in the Industrial Revolution. These rules would be intolerable for today's managers housed in computer-age, air-conditioned, sanitary workplaces. There is a different set of rules for managing today's workers. We've learned that employees are more productive when they are happy and motivated so the role of management has changed to coaching and facilitating. . . .

Basic Qualifications for a Successful Operations Manager

Technical Skills

Technical skills involve having the knowledge of, and the ability to perform, a particular job or task. One requirement of a competent operations manager is that he/she thoroughly understands the specific, technical aspects of the operation of his/her unit or department.

Manning and Curtis[2] set forth three levels of managers: *Top managers* set forth the direction of the company by establishing the organization's goals, overall strategy, and operating policy. These individuals officially represent the organization to the external environment. However, in terms of knowledge, their technical skills are not as important as their conceptual ones. *Middle managers* are responsible for implementing the policies and the plans developed by top management. As a result, they breakdown the strategies and operating policies into smaller, measurable objectives that can be delegated to various departments. They also supervise and coordinate the activities of lower-level managers. Depending on the company's entrepreneurial spirit, middle managers can be sources of innovation when given the privilege. Again, middle managers are developing their conceptual skills while still maintaining their technical skills. *Front line managers* spend a large proportion of their time coordinating, facilitating, and supporting the work of front line employees. Because they are directly involved with the operation of a department, front line managers must possess the technical skills and specific know-how of the particular systems they supervise. As part of their responsibilities, they train and direct employees on a daily basis. This includes: developing standard operating procedures; using participative management principles; developing effective training; maintaining safety assurance; encouraging personnel to use efficient methods; and motivating men and women to do a better job by stimulating pride in their products and services.

For example, it would be difficult for an executive chef to supervise workers in a kitchen without knowledge of culinary arts and kitchen procedures. Similarly, a front office manager in a hotel needs to know the operation of the computer system at the front desk and the procedures for registering a guest. Therefore, while people who are front line managers need to have excellent technical skills, as one progresses up the managerial ladder, conceptual skills take primary importance.

Judgment

Judgment can be described as having "good sense." Individuals who hope to be qualified leaders must possess the ability to make sound and wise decisions. Sound thinking accompanies creative thinking, innovative brilliance, and invention. Change for the sake of change, can be detrimental unless it is balanced with common sense.

Being negative is never a substitute for judgment. If an individual approaches an idea with a negative history, the idea, no matter how creative, may be perceived as one that *will not work*. Enthusiasm and a positive attitude are important talents required of a leader whose judgment and decision-making activities will be tested daily.

Conceptual Skills

The organizational manager must have the ability to conceptualize the company or department as a whole and understand how the different parts work together. This involves technical skills utilized for problem solving, decision-making, planning, and organizing. Managers with conceptual skills are able to look at problems from a broad perspective and see them from different points of view. Conceptual skills are important at all levels of management, but they are essential for top managers who make decisions that can dramatically affect the future of the hotel or restaurant company.

Manning and Curtis[3] discuss conceptual skill as having knowledge about and being able to work with concepts and ideas. As a result, this includes the ability to think abstractly, implement long-range planning, create strategic decision making, and weigh ethical considerations in employee, customer, and government relations. Examples can include a labor relations vice president evaluating a proposed labor agreement or a company president deciding whether to support a community service project.

Interpersonal Skills

Interpersonal or human skills include a manager's ability to lead, motivate, and communicate with those around them. The ability to understand people and work well with them on an individual basis, and also in groups, is usually a developed skill since very few people are innately gifted. It requires focusing on active listening and observing body language. Some say that 70% of communication is through nonverbal behavior. For example, making eye contact with another individual or recognizing facial expression or hand movements are all useful when interacting with others. Another factor in interpersonal skills is being aware of cultural differences. With the diverse workforce of today, it is important to speak other languages as well as recognize that different ethnicities may have different reactions. For example, something as simple as eye gaze can change perceptions. Many cultures like Asians and Hispanics lower their eyes as a sign of respect to people with more status. A typical American might perceive this to be a sign of lying. Since all managers must deal directly with people, and in particular guests, interpersonal skills are essential at all levels of management.

Integrity and a Sense of Ethics

A person's level of morality is imperative and determines whether the leader is respected. Social psychologist Lawrence Kohlberg explains that each person makes ethical decisions according to three levels of moral development. Level I *Preconventional Morality:* This is very simple cultural norms of right and wrong behavior. The response is based on a black and white view of the world. Will I be harmed (punishment) or will I be helped (pleasure)? Level II *Conventional Morality:* This level of morality is characterized by group conformity and allegiance to authority. Morality at this stage is no longer a simple right and wrong but altered by the perception of what the group will think. This individual acts in order to meet the expectations of others and to please those in charge. Level III *Postconventional Morality* is the most advanced level of moral development. At this level, a person evaluates situations based on their own self defined moral principles. These standards may be influenced by levels 1 and 2, but actions are not solely based on right/wrong ideas or group ideals.

An organizational manager must have a set of principles or ethics to enhance interaction with others. Ethics should govern the general behavior of managers and guide them in making business decisions. The quality of one's integrity manifests itself in many ways, but the honesty and sincerity of an effective organizational manager must be unquestionable. This quality applies to *true leaders* and should not be compromised. Operational managers are responsible for the ethical treatment of five different groups of people: customers, employees, suppliers, owners, and the community at large. Ethical behavior means fair and consistent treatment toward members of each of these groups. A personal code of ethics is imperative for a qualified organizational manager to ensure truth, a lack of bias, consistency, and respect when interacting with others. Unethical behavior of a corporation through its managers can result in negative attitudes toward the business by the public. Many times, this results in a drop in profits because the community at large doesn't trust the managers or the products they create.

Levels of Management

It is agreed that all managers carry out the same functions; these functions become less important, relative to the others, as the manager moves up or down the organizational ladder. This shifting emphasis distinguishes the different levels of management. Although the line between the levels is often blurred, management is separated into three levels: *top management, middle management*, or *supervisory management*.

Top Management

Top management includes only a limited number of senior executives within the organization. In small properties, like an individually owned and operated enterprise, the owner-manager is the sole member of top management. But, in large corporations or organizations, members of top management usually have titles such as Chairman of the Board, Chief Executive Officer, Chief Operating Officer, President, or Executive Vice-President. Top managers determine the direction of the company by recognizing and identifying the basic mission and objectives of the company. They develop goals and established plans for the purpose of reaching the company's overall objectives or operational outcomes. Top managers possess conceptual skills and are responsible for strategic planning and decision making.

Middle Management

In middle management, the department heads, perhaps 2 to 20, are next highest in responsibility. Several titles are frequently used for middle managers in the hospitality industry: Regional Director, General Manager, Rooms Division Manager, and Food and Beverage Director. Although this group is larger in number than top management, there are still fewer middle managers than supervisory managers. Middle managers have relational skills and coordinate and plan implementation.

Supervisory Management

The line supervisor, who is the first manager up the managerial ladder and the last one down, is the most difficult to identify as management. Typical titles of supervisory managers are Front Office Manager, Executive Housekeeper, or Restaurant Manager. Supervisory managers implement the goals and plans of the organization by directing work of the line-level employees, who provide guests with products and services. They are closer to the operative employees than they are to other managers. In many instances, they have earned their promotions because of excellent operative skills. The ambiguity of who they are is reinforced by the lack of management title. This manager may be considered first-level management and demonstrate technical skills and implementation.

Different managers rely on different skills: the sales manager is expected to be more outgoing; a good server may become a host; a skillful bartender may be promoted to chief or head bartender; and a room attendant may become the floor inspector. Different managerial positions call on different elements of the personal and professional package that each individual brings to the position or job.

Management Functions

Planning

Planning is based upon the establishment of goals and objectives. Thus, the management must decide how to accomplish these goals. Planning is often referred to as the primary management function and the result of inadequate planning is chaos. Successful companies train at all management levels to assure successful goals.

Organizing

Managers must determine what activities are to be done and how employees are grouped to accomplish specific tasks. Reservations, housekeeping, or maintenance are examples of how groups of individuals are organized to perform a specific task. Additionally, at a higher level, many large hotel companies are divided into several divisions, according to the geographic location of their property or the product or service they provide.

Staffing

Staffing is the process employed to service guests at a lodging, food, or beverage, or tourism establishment. Managers involved with staffing have several responsibilities: they determine the number and type of employees needed; they recruit and select employees; and they develop and implement training programs. In addition, they must determine compensation and benefits received by employees.

Controlling

Controlling is the process of comparing the performance of employees in a workforce to the objectives and goals that have been set by the company. The purpose of any control system is to assure that the company is headed in the right direction and capable of making corrections when necessary. There are three distinct types of control: *preliminary controls*, take place before an event occurs, such as the planning of a major banquet; *concurrent controls* take place during an actual event, such as a server's responsibility; and *postactional controls* take place after an event has taken place, as when a general manager reviews a monthly "profit and loss" statement for a hotel.

Leadership and Directing in Hospitality and Tourism Management

Leadership Qualities

An organizational manager must instill and influence others for the purpose of channeling their activities toward assisting the hotel or restaurant's goals. Leadership can be viewed as having two separate components or elements: success and effectiveness. A successful leader demonstrates a quality that followers want to emulate; an effective leader instills a desire to follow in the same direction. Leadership may be defined in several ways. Often these qualities consist of the leader, the group, and the situation. Leadership is a *personal* and a *human* experience, as animals and computers cannot lead. Leadership is both an *art* and a *science* and is subjective in nature. There are fundamentals of leadership that can be learned and are based on research and observation. Leadership is *active*, as leaders must do something; leadership is one element of a three-part dynamic; the leader, the group, and the situation are always in *interaction* and tension with one another.

Organizational Success

Organizational success requires a leader to have many qualities, but perhaps of the most important is *vision*. Management author Peter Drucker once said, "The best way to predict the future is to create it." Drucker's difference begins with a vision for change; this creativity may be one of the most important ingredients a leader possesses. A vision alone will not assure success; there are five necessary components for organizational success: vision, skills, incentives, resources, and an action plan. When all five are present, organizational success is achieved. If any one is removed, the end result will change.

- Vision + Skills + Incentives + Resources + Action Plan = organizational success
- (remove vision) Skills + Incentives + Resources + Action Plan = Confusion
- Vision (remove skills) + Incentives + Resources + Action Plan = Anxiety
- Vision + Skills (remove incentives) + Resources + Action Plan = Gradual change
- Vision + Skills + Incentives (remove resources) + Action Plan = Frustration
- Vision + Skills + Incentives + Resources (remove action plan) = False Starts.

The word *vision* suggests a future orientation and implies a standard of excellence or virtuous condition and has the quality of uniqueness. Vision is an ideal image of what could and should be. The leader must ask three questions to test his or her vision: (1) Is this the best direction? (2) Are these the most productive goals to reach my projected end? (3) Is this the best time? Once the decision is made, the leader must share this vision and have it supported by others who are involved in the project. A leader must (1) take responsibility for initiating change; (2) create a vision and strategy for the organization; and (3) trust and support others.

Why People Follow the Leader

People enter an organization and perform their work for various reasons. They follow the leader of the organization for the purpose of being financially and socially successful. The most basic reason that people work is to provide themselves and their independents with food, shelter, and clothing. This is often identified as a *selfish* reason for working. In contrast, there is a more positive motive for *following the leader*. This is most evident when people seek work for societal goals. Making enough money to achieve both needs and wants supports the aspirations of the worker. Personal satisfaction is therefore necessary for individuals to pursue work. Through hard work and diligence, one is rewarded with independence, encouragement, praise, and recognition.

Followers must freely accept the efforts of the leader for leadership to occur. Followers must voluntarily align their will with that of the leader. A leader must manifest good qualities, without threats of discipline or punishment for followers to function within their own free will. It is only when followers make a true choice to follow the leader that true leadership occurs.

Future Concerns for the Hospitality and Tourism Management

Enthusiasm for the Industry

An enthusiasm for the industry is often identified as having the business "in their blood." For the purpose of developing a desire to work in this industry, it may be necessary to have a passion for the business. Leaders are the best "cheerleaders" for their organization and their people. They display enthusiasm or passion and instill it in others. They possess poise, stability, clear vision, and articulate speech. Their enthusiasm is often described as *infectious* and motivates workers that are in their presence.

Successful managers are confident that their abilities are up to the task of their actions and are able to gain the trust and support of workers. A

A successful manager must be enthusiastic and confident.

© 2008, JupiterImages.

manager must first be enthusiastic, with a passion for the position, and second the manager should be confident. It is obvious when these qualities are displayed; self confidence helps the manager adjust to the ever-changing direction of the industry.

Developing Your Own Style

We are impressed and often amazed with the ability of certain managers and their leadership style. All are unique, and top managers are uncommonly different; they are extraordinary people who can adjust from one role to another without losing momentum or hesitation in thought or action. The roles of managers may also reflect the styles of the managers. A leader possesses standards and values within the organizational culture. The manager is responsible for what happens in the organization in such areas as personnel choices, marketing, financial, and public affairs decisions. The manager is the chief tactician, strategist, spokesperson, negotiator, observer, and the one who ultimately represents the organization beyond whom decisions do not pass without a final determination.

Operations Management in the Future

There is an interrelated set of functions carried out by managers at all levels of the organization and, also, with the workers. Management is relatively new and has emerged as a field of study only in the last 100 years. As a separate practice, management grew up to meet the changing needs of society and eventually affect several areas including the hospitality industry.

Future events will transform the nature and structure of hotel operations, but one fact remains even in an environment of constant and rapid change. The future is in the hands of management; through a collective experience and wisdom, management must find solutions to meet the needs of an ever-changing society and industry. The managers will plan and implement strategies to deal with them successfully and introduce the new, while holding on to the best of the old.

Summary

Management is a profession with a body of knowledge gained through practical application of management principles. Excellent management means better individual operations and, therefore, a better and more efficient industry. The destiny of the industry is in the hands of competent, passionate managers with exemplary leadership skills and professionalism. Management must keep pace with the dynamics of the society.

≈ *Resources*

Internet Sites

Hospitality Operations Management–Hotel Lodging Operations HEI: www.heihotels.com/operations/leadership.cfm
Baldridge National Quality Program: http://www.quality.nist.gov/
Center for the Study of Work Teams: http://www.workteams.unt.edu/
Creative Learning: http://www.creativelearningcentre.com/default.asp

References

Brymer, R. A. (1997). *Hospitality & Tourism*. 11th ed. Dubuque, IA: Kendall/Hunt Publishing.
Fisher, W. P., Muller, C. C. (2005). *Four-Dimensional Leadership*. Upper Saddle River, NJ: Pearson Prentice Hall.
Manning, G., and Curtis, K. (2007). *The Art of Leadership*. New York: McGraw Hill.
Nykiel, R. A. (2005). *Hospitality Management Strategies*. Upper Saddle River, NJ: Pearson Prentice Hall.
Powers, T. F. (1979). *Introduction to Management in the Hospitality Industry*. 2nd ed. Hoboken, NJ: John Wiley & Sons.
Powers, T. and Barrows, C. W. (2006). *Management in the Hospitality Industry*. 8th ed. Hoboken, NJ: John Wiley & Sons.
Vallen, J. J., and Abbey, J. R. (1987). *The Art and Science of Hospitality Management*. East Lansing, MI: The Educational Institute of the American Hotel & Motel Association.

≈ *Endnotes*

1. Manning, G., and Curtis, K. *The Art of Leadership*. New York: McGraw Hill.
2. Ibid.
3. Ibid.

≈ *Contributors*

Dr. Richard J. Mills, Jr., has many years of both professional and academic experience. He is currently a certified sous Chef through the American Culinary Federation and has worked in the industry as a professional cook and chef for more than 12 years. He is presently teaching in the Hospitality and Tourism department at Robert Morris University, Moon Township, PA. In addition, Dr. Richard J. Mills, Jr., holds two master's degrees, an MLS and MA, and has taught, researched, and published. He implemented various courses at the undergraduate level in food production management and quantity food production at several colleges and universities. He received his Doctorate Degree in the Communication and Rhetorical Studies Department at Duquesne University in Pittsburgh, PA.

Denis P. Rudd, Ed.D., CHA, FMP, CTP
University Professor and Director of Hospitality and Tourism Management
Robert Morris University
VOICE: 412-262-8636; FAX: 412-262-8494; E-mail: rudd@robert-morris.edu

Denis P. Rudd, Ed.D., CHA, FMP, is the University Professor and Director of Hospitality and Tourism Management at Robert Morris University Pennsylvania at both the Coraopolis and Pittsburgh campuses. Dr. Rudd received his Bachelor's Degree in Finance and Commerce from Rider College, Lawerenceville, New Jersey, a Master's in Business Administration, a Master's in Education Counseling, Specialist in Higher Education Administration, and a Doctorate in Educational Counseling from the University of Nevada, Las Vegas.

In 1995 he accepted the position as Professor and Director of Hospitality and Tourism Management for Robert Morris College Coraopolis and Pittsburgh, Pensylvania. Dr. Rudd has recently published three texts entitled *Introduction to Casino Gaming, Club Operations*, and *Convention Technology*. In addition, Dr. Rudd has received certification as a CHA and FMP from the National Restaurant Association and the Educational Institute of the American Hotel & Lodging Association and PTC, from the International Meeting Planners Association. In 2005 Dr. Rudd was honored by being appointed the first University Professor of Robert Morris University.

Chapter 6
Review Questions

1. What is the author's definition of management?

2. What do managers do within operations?

3. What is the difference between management and operations?

4. How has management changed historically?

5. List the basic qualifications for a successful operations manager?

6. Define technical skills as a management function.

7. Define judgment as a management function.

8. Define conceptual skills as a management function.

9. Define interpersonal skills as a management function.

10. What five groups should managers be concerned with when ethics is applied?

11. What are the three traditional levels of management?

12. What are the primary duties of top management?

13. What are the primary duties of middle management?

14. What are the primary duties of supervisory management?

15. What are the four functions of operations management?

16. Define planning as a management function.

17. Define organizing as a management function.

18. Define staffing as a management function.

19. Define controlling as a management function.

20. List some basic leadership qualities that operations managers should be concerned with.

21. List some basic reasons why people follow. And what role does leadership play.

22. From the author's perspective why is enthusiasm for the industry important?

23. What is meant by developing your own style?

24. What are Kohlberg's three levels of moral behavior development?

25. What are some future concerns for operations managers?

26. What five key ingredients are needed for leaders with a vision?

Human Resource Management

Mel Weber, East Carolina University

7

© Stephen Coburn, 2008, Shutterstock.

≈ Learning Objectives

☑ To describe the functions of the human resource department
☑ To recognize the role any manager plays within human resource functions
☑ To describe the role legislation plays in human resource management
☑ To discuss the role human resources plays in guest satisfaction in the hospitality industry
☑ To develop a vocabulary of human resource terminology

≈ Chapter Outline

Human Resource Department Functions
Legislation
HR Is Involved in Every Supervisory
 or Management Position

≈ Key Terms

Americans with Disabilities Act of 1990
Civil Rights Act of 1964
Evaluation
Human resource management
Interviewing
Job analysis
Job descriptions
Job design
Job enlargement
Job enrichment
Job simplification
Job specifications
Merit pay
Progressive discipline policy
Recruiting
Selection
Team building
The training cycle
Turnover

*I*n today's business world, people are the key. Dealing with this people challenge is the human resource (HR) department. This is the department within the organization that handles the paperwork regarding selection, termination, legal mandates, benefits, training, and compensation. In the past, this department handled these responsibilities following policies formulated by top management. Today, HR managers no longer just follow policy. They are also responsible for formulating policy and assisting with strategic planning related to department functions. Although the HR department performs these functions, there is more to human resource management than paperwork. The reader must understand that HR goes beyond the functions of any department and is the responsibility of all supervisors/managers and every worker within the organization. Human Resource Management is concerned with the management and caring of the hospitality businesses' most important asset, the people who work for the organization.

J.W. Marriott, founder of the Marriott Corporation, is noted for saying that if a company takes care of the people who work for it then the people will take care of the company. This translates into a well-balanced 360° degree company/employee/customer relationship that can be evaluated at any of the three levels. To play a productive role in the organization HR must be involved in activities to enhance the ability of the company to meet the needs of the guest while satisfying the needs of the worker. As in every department, customer satisfaction is the bottom line. Simply stated, ***Human Resource Management is the process of how organizations treat their people in order to accomplish the goals and objectives of the firm.***

Human Resource Department Functions

Planning

As a management function, planning is one of the most important activities. This certainly is the case in the HR area. Like all strategic planning, managers must understand where they are. HR continually assesses needed skills and employees who have these abilities to maintain necessary competencies. Then, the HR department must not only attempt to predict future employment needs in terms of turnover, they must also look at future trends to assess additional skill needs or changing emphases to prepare the staff and assist the company in growth. Finally, the third step of any planning is to develop a stepwise progression and time table on reaching these changing objectives.

As a result, it can be seen that this is a dimension where the HR department cannot work in a vacuum. They must work with all departments to assess employment needs. In fact, if you want to meet people from all the different departments, HR is the hub. Additionally, they must be kept updated regarding industry shifts to enable them to assist the workforce in handling the ongoing changes. Moreover, they must remain competitive with wages in order to attract the best and the brightest to our industry.

Before an organization can determine how many people are needed to meet the demands of the business, planning functions are necessary to determine what work must be accomplished, how the work should be completed, and the skills necessary to complete the job. There are tools available to the HR professional to fulfill these tasks. The first is ***job analysis***. This is the information that focuses on what work needs to be accomplished. This analysis allows us to write job descriptions and job specifications. ***Job descriptions*** identify the tasks, responsibilities, and duties under which jobs are performed. Keeping a diary of daily activities is one way this can be accomplished. This allows for a more realistic assessment of tasks and abilities needed. It also allows HR to see how the job responsibilities change over time. Then summaries of the tasks and duties are listed and job descriptions and specifications created. ***Job specifications*** are the knowledge, skills, and abilities necessary to perform the position. Job descriptions and specifications are the basis for recruitment, selection, training/development, evaluating, compensation/benefits, and health/safety issues.

The task of determining how the job should be performed is the function of ***job design***. This looks at how the job is organized and how it can be planned to provide both productivity to the organization and the most job satisfaction to the employee. The most widely used techniques in job design are: (1) job simplification, (2) job enlargement, (3) job enrichment, (4) job rotation, and (5) team building. ***Job simplification*** is the process of determining the smallest components of the job and assessing how they fit into the whole job. It can be the case where the job responsibilities keep expanding to meet the needs of the department.

Therefore, this process can help break down the job to see how a division of labor can be accomplished. In other cases, where job sharing is an option, two people may need to examine job simplification to determine how they can subdivide the tasks. ***Job enlargement*** is the process of broadening the job by adding tasks. There are many reasons why adding tasks is necessary. One might be the process of changing a job from part-time to full-time status.

Job enrichment is the process of adding responsibilities to the job. To prevent the job from becoming boring, adding new responsibilities can give motivation to the employee who is looking for a challenge. It might also allow people to go back to school or travel to corporate for training. ***Job rotation*** is allowing the employee to work at different jobs. This technique requires employees to be cross-trained. This is good for the company because it allows additional people to be on hand in case you are short handed in another department. However, one of the issues with rotation is having more than one boss who is responsible for your schedule. If they don't communicate your schedule to each other, you could end up with a problem of having to be in two places at the same time or having double shifts. And finally, ***team building*** views employees as members of work groups, rather than as individuals.[1] When there are problems that need resolving, quite often a team of experts, that is people who work in that job or department, can be called together to brainstorm possible solutions. Sometimes they can be used to create policies or go across departments to offer larger alternatives.

Staffing

Once the organization determines the number and type of employment positions available, the task of staffing for these positions begins. This includes

A key element to staffing is finding the right employee for the job.

recruiting candidates for the positions and selecting the best person for the position. This must all be achieved within the guidelines set forth in both federal and state laws. Selection is not as easy as putting an ad in the paper and choosing a new employee from the stack of applications. For example, one hotel in New Orleans put a want ad in the newspaper and 300 people arrived at their doorstep. This is good you say? However, out of the 300, they could not find one person to hire. In some cases, applicants were on government subsidies and were required to apply for jobs as part of their duties in keeping their money coming. Others explained that after 2:00 in the afternoon or weekends or holidays, they could not work because they had to be with their children. Others could not read to fill out the application.

The key element is finding the right employee for the job. The labor market demonstrates fluctuations dependent on the economy at any given time. When the economy is tight, there are more applications; however, when the economy is booming, it is often difficult to find qualified personnel to fill the vacancies. We employ many entry-level employees in minimum wage jobs; this makes the challenge significantly greater for finding the right employee for every position. Given these variables, the current labor market conditions and shifting dynamics inherent in the labor force, a company today must go well beyond the traditional want ad and look for innovative ways to attract good employees. Many hospitality firms guest speak at nearby colleges and universities so that they can persuade students to apply. Some hotels have even formed alumni groups of employees to ask them how to reach students. One increasingly popular tool is the Internet, with many Websites available for the job seeker to research companies and pursue lists of jobs available. There are also services available to showcase the talents of the job seeker to any interested employer.

Once the company receives the individual's application, the task of interviewing begins. Many interviewing styles may be used; however, the overriding concern is to ensure fairness to the applicants and achieving the best match for the job. The interviewer must be sure they do not ask any questions that could be considered illegal or discriminatory in nature. Often one of the functions of the HR department is training the managers interviewing applicants in the proper methodology to conduct the interviews. One must also try to structure the interview in such a way that you can compare the candidates' qualifications without bias. Increasingly, behavioral or situational interviewing methods are used. These methods show greater validity (via statistical accumulation) in choosing the right person for the job. Other tools being used to help in the decision-making process are checking references and administering a number of pre-employment tests. Many organizations today are employing outside firms to administer appropriate personality and honesty tests in order to obtain unbiased information suitable to a particular job and or company. The goal of this process is to find employees that will enjoy their work and fit well into the organizational structure. Some firms have six interviews per applicant in order to assess the candidate's personality. After all, a favorite saying is "if the applicant doesn't smile during the interview, what makes you think they will smile on the job?"

Training and Development

Once the organization has selected the employee, the organization must train the new employee. New employee training introduces the corporate culture. It discusses the history of the company, its mission, and its priorities. This allows new employees to begin the assimilation process of identifying how they fit into this business. It is also used to introduce new employees to one another so that there is a social bond and a common experience everyone goes through. In Japan, some companies have departments climb Mt. Fuji at night so that they can share the sunrise together. This forms a bond between the participants. Other companies do wilderness or survival training. The hottest event, currently, is to cook together and serve a meal.

But the HR department is not only concerned with the new employees, they must continue to develop the tenured employees. To complete these tasks, the HR department may choose to use the training cycle.

1. Conduct a needs assessment—identify problems
2. Identify training objectives—goals of the program
3. Establish training criteria—benchmarks
4. Select trainees—new or tenured
5. Pretest trainees—establish a baseline of knowledge, skills, and abilities
6. Choose training methods—on the job or off the job

New employee training introduces the corporate culture and creates a social bond between participants.

7. Implement training
8. Evaluate training[2]

Evaluating training usually helps the HR department identify more needs, thus the cycle starts anew.

Turnover and Employee Loyalty

Failure to perform the recruiting, selection, and training/development processes adequately will often lead to unnecessary turnover. Turnover is the term used to describe the situation when an employee leaves and must be replaced. Turnover is an expensive occurrence, as the company must not only go through the entire recruitment and selection process once again, but it must also retrain a person for the position. Frequently, this ongoing training may produce negative effects of inefficiency until the new employee can achieve the expected level of productivity that the departed employee demonstrated.

Another expense to the organization is the time a manager needs to oversee this process. The replacement also takes a manager away from other responsibilities in situations where a manager performs all of the recruiting and selection duties. Previously, turnover was an accepted occurrence in the hospitality industry because there were always new bodies to fill the shoes of the departing employee. However, this is not always the case. In hospitality, the average turnover rate is around 60–70%. That means that one out of every three hired actually stays for more than six months. Therefore, more companies are emphasizing the need to select new hires wisely and to put programs in place to retain the existing employees. The new slogan is a job should be fun, fair, and interesting.

Retention programs can focus around activities such as softball leagues and opportunities for socialization. Still, it is widely believed that the best methods to enhance employee retention is an atmosphere of fair treatment, one where employees enjoy working, one where they feel they make a difference, and one where they are rewarded based on their own individual needs. Contrary to popular opinion, money is not the main reason for leaving a job, but it is the main excuse. Because employee satisfaction is an on going process, managers continually will need to monitor the climate as new generations come into the labor market. The tangible and intangible assets of the job are becoming increasingly important to successful retention programs coupled with creative packaging that either entices and/or satisfies the employee.

Evaluation

Employee evaluations take place after an employee has been selected, trained, and been on the job for a period of time. Evaluations have many organizational purposes. They can be used to determine if the employee requires more training, is in the best job for them, is ready for a promotion, and is entitled to incentive pay or any situation based on job performance. The best reason to evaluate an employee's performance is for official feedback. However, the employee should be receiving feedback concerning their performance on a regular basis. A significant reason for dissatisfaction with the job results from an employee not being aware of how they are doing on the job and this feedback must be completed in a timely fashion. This is just like a student's desire to know where they stand regarding a grade in any given class. Evaluations play a significant motivational effect on employees by encouraging the employee to improve on their performance based on the outcomes of the evaluation. The HR department's role in this process is one of providing the form, filing the evaluations for future reference, as well as training managers how best to complete the process. Evaluations are usually completed and administered by the employees' supervisor.

Employee evaluations also are used as backup documentation necessary if an employee is terminated based on performance. Although there are provisions for "employment at will" that allow an employer to terminate employment at the employer's discretion, most employers prefer to have a policy in place where an employee's performance is scrutinized, warnings are given, and an opportunity for retraining is provided before that termination takes place. This is also known as a ***progressive discipline policy***, where employees receive increasingly more stringent discipline for infractions. In this scenario, the evaluations serve as documentation if the former employee brings discrimination charges forward.

In many organizations, employee evaluations are the link between performance and pay raises. This makes it critical that the evaluations are performed in an impartial manner to ensure consistency regarding compensation across all areas of the organization. Merit pay is the approach of identifying employees who are performing at, or above, expected levels and providing them with increased wages. You must make every effort to evaluate the employee on the promised anniversary date, as it is one of the most contentious complaints employees levy against their supervisors. Failing to evaluate and process the appropriate paperwork is essential to maintaining a professional posture and image.

Compensation and Benefits

Employees receive compensation for the work that they do in three ways: (1) direct compensation (often referred to as base pay), (2) merit pay, and (3) benefits. The motivational effect of wages is often debated, but within the scope of this discussion, employers continually look for better methods of materially rewarding people for the work they perform. This acts as a catalyst for improved productivity and a better motivational tool. Each form of compensation is introduced as a motivational tool. Benefits are introduced in this fashion and are used to motivate or entice persons to work for their company. The predominant focus on wages today is that of merit pay, where only expected and above expected performance is rewarded above a base level.

One of the greatest challenges for the HR department today is finding and devising benefit packages that employees find attractive and that are affordable to the company. One of the most expensive components of any benefits package is health insurance. As the cost of health care continues to rise rapidly, it becomes increasingly more difficult for companies to find insurance carriers with reasonable premiums. Companies are looking for innovative methods to solve this dilemma and must be sensitive to both the needs of the employees and the profitability of the company. Each company must weigh the advantages and disadvantages of this move and proceed with the path that is best for the organization. HR professionals also look for a range of benefits that help employees meet personal goals and concerns. It should be duly noted, as in other HR areas, the overriding principle in compensation is one of fairness and equity.

Health and Safety

Organizations are obligated to provide employees with a safe and healthy work environment. Requiring them to work with unsafe equipment or in areas where hazards are not controlled is a highly questionable and often a costly practice. It is also the responsibility of managers to ensure that employees are safety conscious and maintain good health. Preventative safety is one of the best ways to avert an unsafe environment for the employee and often the customer. Both manager and the HR specialist are involved in health and safety practices in an organization. HR specialists coordinate programs, develop safety-reporting systems, and provide expertise on investigation, technical, research, and prevention methods. Managers must investigate, coach, monitor, and observe employees practicing safety in the functional areas of the operation. Communication and good record keeping is vital in this area as it is with any area of the business.

Legislation

Probably the largest responsibility of the human resource department is knowing the laws of employment. But not only do they need to know about the laws, they need to make sure that every member of the organization is aware of these laws. In managing their employees, organizations must comply with many laws, regulations, court decisions, and mandates arising from the social legislation, most notably after 1960. Personnel departments had to become much more professional and more concerned about the legal ramifications of policies and practices enacted by their organizations. All management and supervisory personnel must continually be updated and coached with regard to the legalities of the ever-changing fabric of our work environment.

Sweeping federal legislation that forever changed the standards for employment in the United States was passed under the Johnson administration. The act that provided the impetus for this change was the Civil Rights Act of 1964. This act prohibits discrimination on the basis of race, color, religion, sex, or national origin and has become the cornerstone piece of legislation protecting workers and their rights. See Table 7.1 for other legislation.

Table 7.1 Federal Legislation Affecting Employment Standards

LEGISLATION	IMPLICATION
Equal Pay Act of 1963	Men and women working for the same organization be paid the same rate for comparable jobs
Title VII of the Civil Rights Act of 1964	Bars discrimination on the basis of race, sex, religion, color, and national origin
Age Discrimination in Employment Act of 1967	Prohibits employment discrimination on the basis of age against people 40 years old or older
Vocational Rehabilitation Act of 1973	Required all employers holding federal contracts of $25,000 or more to employ "qualified" individuals with disabilities and to make reasonable accommodations as needed
Pregnancy Discrimination Act of 1978	Employers cannot stipulate the beginning and ending dates of a pregnant employee's maternity leave
Retirement Equity Act of 1984	Required companies to count all services since the age of 18 in determining vesting in retirement benefits
Immigration Reform and Control Act of 1986	Designed to regulate the employment of aliens in the U.S. by verifying citizenship status on all employees
Americans with Disabilities Act of 1990	Forbids discrimination against people with disabilities—expanded the list of included disabilities (see Act of 1973)
Family and Medical Leave Act of 1993	Required employers with 50 or more employees to offer 12 weeks of unpaid leave for a 12 month period for birth, adoption, care for an ill parent/spouse/child, or for medical treatment

Key governmental agencies generally impact many HR activities. The HR professional must be familiar with many of these agencies and their functions. Among the more important ones to be familiar with are the actions of the Equal Employment Opportunity Commission (EEOC); Occupational Safety, and Health Administration (OSHA); The Immigration and Naturalization Services; The Department of Labor (DOL); and the various state and city equal employment commissions and human or civil rights commissions. If the individual entrusted with the legalities of employment fails to maintain an awareness of current laws and regulations, either through an HR department or individual actions, organizations may find themselves faced with costly lawsuits and significant fines. Much of this can be avoided by constantly monitoring the legal environment, by complying with changes, and by careful management of employees.

HR Is Involved in Every Supervisory or Management Position

The human resource department works in concert with all management at every level. Typically, the HR department is known for hiring employees. An example of how the HR department works with everyone is that they may be responsible for recruiting prospective employees, performing initial interviews, completing reference checks, and completing the appropriate paperwork. However, the manager or supervisor of the department where this employee will work makes the final decision regarding the hiring of an individual. This is not the only area that must employ a combined effort and, from this, you can see that the HR department and all managers must work closely together to achieve the employment goals of the organization.

There are differences in the HR relationships between a small and a large organization. In a small organization, there is no formal HR department. Those responsibilities are relegated to the operational management or ownership. Here the organization's management staff is responsible for all of the HR functions along with all of the other management functions relegated to their duties. Managers in a unit of a multiunit chain find themselves responsible for the day-to-day functions; however, an HR department at corporate headquarters backs

them up. In the latter instance, the management staff must play a more active role in HR activities due to the distance from the corporate HR staff. Looking at this example more closely, we observe that the selection procedure, in this multiunit situation, finds the management responsible for all selection functions such as, recruiting, interviewing, completing reference checks, making the final decision, and completing the paperwork. The HR department at corporate office plays more of an advisory role and is responsible for the upkeep of the appropriate files and keeping unit managers aware of current accepted hiring practices as well as legal issues. As you can see from this example, it is critical that all management personnel have a thorough understanding of the functions involved in the management of human resources.

Summary

Much of what has been discussed in this brief overview of HR essentials is procedural in nature. Hospitality organizations are dynamic entities as are the individuals we seek to hire and to represent our organizations. Companies must be positioned to meet the needs of their employees every day. There can be no exception to this imperative. If your company does not provide and care for the employee, and consequently the customer, in meeting their expectations, then failure is eminent. Longitudinal studies indicate a direct relationship with a hospitality businesses failure with that of poor management. The numbers of annual failures are staggering with a clear majority of these failures pointing to poor management practices. There is always someone else out there who is able, willing, and ready to meet the challenges presented through the human resource functions.

The source of strength for successful companies is their ability to assess their surrounding and to adapt and change. In fact, a proactive posture generally accompanies these successful organizations. They are the industry leaders who remain in the forefront representing the most successful hospitality businesses in the world today. The future is very dynamic, and you have a wonderful opportunity to be a part of all the excitement and promise that is yet to come. Don't forget we are a people business and we must take care of all the people that work for and utilize our places of business.

≈ *Resources*

Internet Sites

The Society for Human Resource Management: www.shrm.org
The International Association for Human Resource Information: www.ihrim.org
Workforce Management: www.workforce.com
U.S. Department of Labor: www.dol.gov

≈ *Endnotes*

1. Woods, R.H. (2006). *Managing Hospitality Human Resources*, 4th ed. Lansing, MI: American Hotel and Lodging Association.
2. Ibid.

≈ *Contributor*

Dr. Mel Weber (weberm@ecu.edu) is an assistant professor in the Department of Hospitality Management in the College of Human Ecology at East Carolina University, Greenville, North Carolina.

Chapter 7
Review Questions

1. What is Human Resource Management?

2. Who typically does the actual hiring of employees?

3. Why should all managers have a fundamental knowledge of Human Resource Management?

4. Define the following:

   a. Job analysis

   b. Job description

   c. Job specifications

   d. Job design

5. What is the difference between job descriptions and job specifications?

6. What is the goal of the selection process?

7. Why do a growing number of companies today have you apply online?

8. Describe an effective recruiting tool that you have seen used in the hospitality industry.

9. What are the challenges of staffing?

10. Identify the training cycle.

11. Discuss the importance of the Civil Rights Act of 1964.

12. Please give five reasons for management to complete employee evaluations.

13. Why is it important for an employee to be evaluated on a timely basis?

14. What is a progressive discipline policy?

15. What are three different forms of compensation?

16. Describe a challenge that a company may face when designing benefits packages.

17. What is the Americans with Disabilities Act?

18. What role does a manager play with regards to health and safety?

19. Please list two ways a company can take care of their employees.

20. What methods can be used to help insure that management is selecting the right person for the position?

Applied Marketing and Sales

Heather Kaikini and John C. Crotts
College of Charleston

8

© Tan Kian Khoon, 2008, Shutterstock.

≈ Learning Objectives

☑ To develop a marketing framework
☑ To present marketing as an active relationship development process
☑ To link hospitality supply and demand to repeat patronage, account penetration, and long-term buyer-supplier relationships
☑ To provide students a realistic view of the knowledge and skills they will need

≈ Chapter Outline

Introduction to the Marketing of Hospitality Services
The Marketing Mix
Markets of Visitor Demand: Individual versus Group
Marketing for Transient Business
Group Sales
The Sales and Marketing Process
Future Trends

≈ Key Terms

AIDA
CRM
Distribution channels
DMC
Elasticity of demand
Look-to-book ratio
Macro environment
Micro environment
RFP
Rate integrity
SMERFE market segmentation
Supply and demand
S.W.O.T. analysis
The 4 P's of the marketing mix

Introduction to the Marketing of Hospitality Services

Consider for a moment: The association meeting planner who has just finished a successful convention; the restaurant patron who has dined again at his/her favorite bistro; the outbound tour operator who has just put together a line of tour products for a destination. At some point, all three of these customers were no more than a lead or prospect. In each case, the marketing and/or sales department of the convention hotel, restaurant, and the convention and visitors bureau did something right in gaining these persons' attention and winning their business.

In today's competitive environment, it takes more to be successful than to simply advertise that you are open for business. It takes sales to convert product attributes into benefits in the mind of the client. Make no mistake, the hospitality and tourism industry is competitive and clients have tremendous freedom of choice—with data readily accessible (and capitalized) from the internet. To create a level of awareness, interest, desire, and ultimately action (AIDA) in the consumer, it takes marketing professionals to probe and understand the client's needs and provide solutions that are better than the competition. The goal of all organizations is to supply a product that the customer demands—and then to exceed those expectations with an added value or service the customer does not anticipate. For example, hotels (who have supply) want to sell rooms and other services to guests (who provide demand) at rates that produce a profit. Doing it in such a way that creates satisfied loyal customers is the key to long-term profitability.

This chapter follows a framework that presents marketing as an active relationship development process that links hospitality supply and demand to create repeat patronage, account penetration, and ultimately long-term buyer-supplier relationships. This framework is designed to provide students a realistic view of the knowledge and skills they will need to master in order to be successful as hospitality marketing professionals. Your first job in hospitality sales and marketing will likely have little resemblance to your last and the framework provides a roadmap for your future. In today's harried business environment, the marketers should never overlook the important skills and knowledge areas that must be learned to grow and evolve.

In order to create a successful strategy or plan for the future, we need to be aware of activities in the local market and the industry as a whole that impacts a firm's abilities to successfully compete in the marketplace. With this awareness comes knowledge, which begets opportunity. We will address factors one might consider when establishing their strategies for a profitable return.

Marketing is a fundamental component of all hospitality and tourism organizations. Without the revenue generated from sales and marketing, firms would not be economically viable. In this chapter we draw our examples from the lodging industry. However, the marketing principles of market segmentation, promotion, pricing, and distribution can and are applied equally as well to all types of organizations.

The Marketing Mix

Owner/operators of hospitality and tourism enterprises must develop a marketing strategy to influence customers to buy their products and services. Only when customers begin to recognize the value of the product or service and begin buying it does the business hold opportunity for success. Therefore, without information the consumer cannot act; without a promotional strategy the marketer cannot sell. However, even a combined product and promotional approach is considered insufficient to succeed in today's competitive environment. Place and price of the offering must also be considered. One must recognize that a successful marketing mix, like a recipe, is a blending of several ingredients to reach and satisfy customers at a profit.

Owners and operators of hospitality and tourism enterprises must develop marketing strategies that reach and satisfy customers.

© 2008, JupiterImages Corporation.

The key to understanding the concept of the marketing mix is that it is a carefully developed reasoning process that is built solely around the customer. By understanding the customers' perspective, a manager can prepare a recipe for success (a mix of inducements to buy) that fits the needs and preferences of the target markets more than the competition. Elements the manager has to work with are commonly referred to as the 4-Ps: product, place, price, and promotion. We could also introduce an additional alternate of 5th P—people.

a. Design or offer a **product** (good or service) that customers need and want.

b. Offer the product in a **place** (location, channel of distribution) that is both convenient and available to consumers.

c. **Price** the product in terms of its value to the customer and the price of competitors' goods and services.

d. Communicate the offering to potential customers through appropriate and cost effective **promotion** activities (advertising, direct sales, and other forms of communication channels).

e. The **people** (staff) who make the experience truly memorable for the customer.

Markets of Visitor Demand: Individual versus Group

Would you prefer individual guests coming to your hotel, those who pay full price, but who leave possibly never to return? Or, would you be willing to offer a reduced price to a group of individuals? To attract individual consumers, the hotel or restaurant must understand many different reasons for people to come to the property. Some consumers are seeking value only, others convenience, others still seek amenities and an unforgettable experience. Therefore, it is more difficult to ensure guest satisfaction. On the other hand, organizational buyers make larger purchases in advance. For example, corporate travel agents (e.g., Carlson Wagonlit, American Express, among others) may prearrange all travel for a select company (e.g., IBM, Blackbaud, Hershey's, etc.). In doing so, the agents are able to negotiate discounted prices, specific room types, packaged activities, etc., because they have a large volume of business they are bringing to the hospitality establishment. Organizational buying is usually done by several people in the decision making

process and must be monitored for actual purchase (e.g., room night reservations) in the end by the sales team.

Among all hotel firms, a ratio exists of how much individual (transient) business the company receives as compared to group business. The elasticity of demand (whether an increase in price results in a decrease in demand) is significant to monitor. Traditionally, individual business travelers are an inelastic clientele—meaning that they will travel regardless of price—as compared to a vacationing family, who may cancel its annual trip due to increased costs (e.g., higher gas prices, plane fares) or a weakening economy. Important to note is that recent years have also introduced perceived risk of travel as a viable variable. Regardless, hotels wisely opt to diversify their client base to react to curves in demand in the market.

Marketing for Transient Business

Because potential guests are scattered within many different geographic areas, advertising and public relations are important. Advertising creates and controls one message and simultaneously conveys it to a large group of people. This may include print media like magazines or newspapers, television, radio, or billboards—also the e-medium (online) continues to gain momentum in the tourism industry. Public relations is similar except that the advertiser does not have control over the message. To remind potential guests about the property, sales promotions teams create items like golf shirts or key chains with the logo and name engraved on them, which keep the name visible in the short term. Quite often all of these are created together for a broader reach.

In recent years, online marketing has begun to emerge as a key component in the total communications package. However, while technology continues to infiltrate and indeed augment within our industry, certain segments still vastly benefit from tangible, traditional marketing pieces. Transient guests may appreciate the opportunity to pick up a brochure about the venue at their local visitors' center when they enter a new city. These guests may also wish to receive information in the mail prior to their visit. CDs are easy to update after completing renovations, changing menu options, adding recent photography, and are relatively cost-effective.

The swiftest change is the realm of e-marketing (electronic marketing). Currently, we are living in the "opt-in" world, whereby, in order for a marketer to contact you, you must check the box on the screen, answering that you would indeed like to take part. One of the challenges with e-marketing (from a business perspective) is that many individuals opt in initially but their spam filters are set too high and the marketing email does not come through. The other common challenge is that with the overabundance of email marketing in today's world, it is paramount for an organization to distinguish itself among the masses. However, email remains expedient, relatively inexpensive, and measurably effective as a marketing tool.

A hospitality organization, for example a cruise line, must first choose where it wants to market electronically: their corporate Website (i.e., Norwegian, Royal Caribbean, Crystal, etc.), travel agencies (i.e., American Express, Carlson Wagonlit), and/or third party online booking agents (i.e., Expedia, Orbitz, Priceline). When working with online intermediaries, often cruise lines will be bundled with rental cars, flights, and even onshore excursions or overnight stays. Additionally, the cruise line may choose to insert their advertisements in online newspapers and magazines (e.g., *NY Times, Travel and Leisure*) for maximum exposure. Certain ratios can be very effective tools in monitoring the success of online distribution channels as well as the competitive set. The look-to-book ratio (or the number of requests to a booking engine per reservation made) becomes essential when monitoring the effectiveness of online contributions.

Another tool for marketing to individual travelers (and groups as well) is that of public relations. In addition to positive features about the property appearing in newspapers, magazines, Websites, TV, and radio, public relations also includes industry outreach. Sponsorships, promotions, community involvement, and special events all help increase a property's visibility. In 2003, Holiday Inn ingeniously launched a major campaign allowing guests to bring in their previously stolen towels from HI hotels across the world, with a tale of what they were used for. The tales were included in a coffee table book, with profits going to the nonprofit "Give Kids the World." A positive, philanthropic spin on petty theft! Whether a grand opening, a special holiday promotional package, completion of renovations, or a special acclaim for the property, it is imperative to share the news with your feeder markets. Again, the primary goal is to keep your product and service foremost in mind to the client as well as cultivate the drive to purchase.

Targeting key groups of industry journalists is also a worthwhile venture. A new General Manager or Executive Chef for the hotel? A ghost story about one of the rooms around Halloween? Are you the only hotel with a Kosher kitchen in your area? Ideally, a master list of noted publication editors should be created. To gain further media exposure, hospitality organizations may opt to allow employees one day off to donate their time to a local charity, involve youth in a concert or choir on property, provide room night packages or meals for silent community auctions, or invite hospitality students from local schools to take a "behind-the-scenes" tour of your hotel. Finally, during low season, why not invite media to stay as guests at your hotel for basic operational costs? You may earn a complimentary article about your property and, at the very least, you put a few more "heads in beds."

Group Sales

Fundamental to many hospitality organizations are group sales departments. This department's sole responsibility is to solicit and book business from groups of (typically) 10 or more people, though this figure ranges upward for larger, convention properties. For example, some groups are very price sensitive. The SMERF market (social, military, educational, religious, fraternal) may be a major feeder depending on the location and type of the hospitality organization. Modifications in recent years have substituted medical for military and added an E on the end (SMERFE) for environmental. Traditionally, SMERFE clients may be unwilling to pay higher room rates but they can be good for business because they meet frequently, book both smaller and larger functions, and boast a vast network of referrals within the SMERFE market itself. SMERFE and association attendees may also bring their families with them for planned destination meetings, thereby spending more money in ancillary outlets (gift shops, restaurants, game rooms, etc.). The government segment works within established per diems. Government travelers have little rate flexibility, but may visit during low season and often utilize a large number of rooms. The tour and travel segment is also generally considered price-sensitive, but yields a large volume and steady business throughout the year. Additionally, this segment in particular may yield significant results for local attractions in your area, thereby building goodwill among industry practitioners and generating future revenues for your property.

Capturing profitable group business and cultivating an ongoing relationship is no small undertaking. One of the challenges of booking business is to maintain a sense of rate integrity. Rate integrity refers to the knowledge that your price is competitive with similar hotels and that guests perceive value. Remember, once rates are randomly lowered, it is next to impossible to raise them again and retain integrity in the market. Some clients will be purely rate focused. However, if rate integrity is maintained, the salesperson can have the negotiating edge. If the client persists in being offered a rate reduction, there are several alternatives: (1) shift the group's dates to a slower month; (2) move to slower nights of the week; (3) package more amenities, activities, food, and beverage so that the ancillary revenues will offset the discounted room rate; or (4) offer a multiple booking package. The ultimate goal is to increase sustainable market share in low demand periods and increase revenues (rooms and ancillary) and loyalty in high demand periods.

The Sales and Marketing Process

Two distinct types of marketing exist—direct and indirect. Direct sales implies that the sales force will have direct contact through personal interactions with prospective clients. This would also include direct marketing initiatives through various types of technology, including the Internet. Often a S.W.O.T. analysis (strengths, weaknesses—based on their internal organization and opportunities, threats—based on their external environment) is a useful tool when conducting research.

On the other hand, an indirect marketing team focuses their efforts on third party intermediaries who will be the contact for the end users. Examples of these wholesalers may include tour operators, independent meeting planners, or destination management companies (DMCs). The benefit to having strong relationships with DMCs, from a meeting planner's perspective, is that the DMC will have lists of local reputable suppliers. Therefore, marketing hotel sales teams often have strategic relationships with their local DMCs.

Indirect marketing teams focus efforts on companies, such as tour services, who provide end contact for customers.

Requests for Proposals (RFPs)

Another facet to the sales process is the request for proposals, or RFP for short. For example, imagine a planner has all the specifics about a meeting—name, date, alternate date, number of rooms, meals required, meeting space required, special events, budget, etc.—and she is considering three locations and only high end resorts. So, she writes an RFP and sends it via email (or possibly fax) to all of the four star hotels in St. John, Virgin Islands; Key Largo, FL; and Honolulu, HI. Those hotels in turn check the availability for sleeping rooms, meeting space, etc., and compile a package rate (encompassing all the requested experiences for the stay) and send it back to the client. The sales contact should always follow up to insure the client received the information and to see if there are questions. Additionally, the manager should request a history of the group pickup from previous meetings elsewhere. The group's history is a valuable tool to measure that the number of blocked rooms on the contract was nearly accurate to the number of rooms actually picked up by the client. Typically a 5–10% attrition rate is acceptable, depending on the property, but more will significantly and adversely affect the hotel's forecasted budget. At this time, the marketing representative may also offer to host the meeting planner for a site visit to the property, where he/she can experience firsthand the facilities, services, and ambiance.

Organizing a Marketing Team

Promotions need to be measurable. For every new print ad distributed, the marketing team should be able to track the resulting revenue derived. Reservationists ask each guest upon call-in what prompted them to think of that hotel. Alternately, if booked online, the advertisement may have a tracking number which individuals input before making a reservation. The direct sales force is responsible for making their weekly, monthly, quarterly, and annual quotas. Traditionally, these are determined by the budget, forecast, historical reports, sales manager, director of sales, and General Manager's inputs. Together, they determine what defines a SMART goal (specific, measurable, attainable, realistic, and timely). Sales teams can be divided by market segment, geographic regions, industries (i.e., pharmaceuticals, insurance, automotive, incentive houses, consulting firms, etc.) or size of groups.

Maximizing Technology

Technology has driven many positive changes in both direct and indirect marketing initiatives. One tool readily available to sales managers is sales management software system, such as Breeze, Delphi, or OPERA. These are tremendous tools which contain all the meeting space parameters, availability for conference rooms as well as sleeping rooms, clients' contact information, and even personal information (spouse's birthdays, last visit to the hotel, trace dates for recommended next date of contact, and what should be discussed, i.e., "contact David about coming out to the hotel for lunch so you can show him the renovated meeting space and talk about booking next year's meeting with us"). Smaller, independent properties may still function with paper function books and notecards to trace individuals for future contacts, as well as paper files, but even the few of these who remain tend to be moving toward paperless systems.

Distribution Channels

Distribution channels consist of manners through which travel providers advertise, sell, or confirm purchase of their products to clientele. For example, it would be logistically challenging and not cost-effective for a car rental agency to have physical sales offices in every city in the U.S. Instead, they have central reservation systems (CRSs) whereby clients can call a toll-free number to request more information. The local agency will then pay a commission to the national office and will provide transportation for the paying guest.

As is typical of the hotel industry, we have followed the lead of the airlines on many fronts. The airlines began to eliminate the use of travel agents directly in order to cut distribution costs and began offering online direct marketing and booking capacities to purchasers. Today, many airlines and hotels offer the "lowest price guaranteed" so that individuals will be sure to visit the host Website vs. booking through an intermediary (examples are Expedia, Orbitz, Priceline, etc.). Marketers know that reservations are booked through call centers, Websites, online travel agencies, and traditional travel agents, with direct Websites being the largest provider since 2004. E-commerce (the selling of goods and services via the internet) is thriving, though security is still a concern for many when required to release their confidential credit card information. However, an emerging generation of affluent, internet-savvy travelers is emerging rapidly. Yet, paperless ticketing is still being perfected as online travel searchers must continually wade through amateurish, uninformative, or outdated information as well as a maze of hyperlinks, constant pop-up ads, and dilemmas when flights and connections are missed. Ultimately, the number of travel distribution channels is vast and there are many opportunities for marketers.

Future Trends

With the continued globalization of our customers, we as marketers must continually adapt our targeting approaches to the current trend. As such, we must take into consideration gender, race, age, educational background, and economic status of our clients. Now, additionally, we must consider their sexual orientations, physical abilities, social status, and perhaps even religious or spiritual positioning. For example, we may not wish to target college fraternity groups to host their holiday formal parties on the same dates we are expecting to have groups of religious conservatives in house practicing prayer for many hours of the day. Pharmaceutical companies even often specify in their contract requests that they are unable to be "in house" at the same time as a competitor. A wise policy for all hoteliers to follow—consulting with prospective clients—prior to booking them simultaneously may avoid conflicts of interest. With DINKs (double income no kids), OPALs (older people with active lifestyles), and SITCOMs (single income two children one

Tourism Marketing National Campaign Profile
"INCREDIBLE INDIA"

"Before [the Incredible India campaign], India was being promoted differently in different countries, if at all. There weren't two or three distinct images. This campaign changed that."

– LAVANYA ANIRUDH, ACCOUNT DIRECTOR, OGILVY & MATHER (INDIA) IN 2004

"Namaste," beckons India. Welcome—and how gracious the welcome has been. According to data released ending 2005, India emerged as the fastest growing region for international tourist spending in Asia-Pacific, with tourists spending over USD $272 million in India, a 25% growth over 4th quarter 2004 (Department of Tourism, India). Much of this success can be directly attributed to the "Incredible India" campaign. For years, India had lagged behind China, Malaysia, Singapore, and Thailand in terms of number of tourists, results which were even more dismal when measured proportionately to GDP. A country with vast potential and a savvy marketing firm helped remedy that.

The "Incredible India" campaign began as a concentrated global marketing initiative meant to build awareness among tourists and highlight India's many riches, including ancient architecture, deep-rooted spirituality, flavorful cuisine, natural wonders, world-class tea plantations, heritage sites, famous hospitality, and eclectic sensuality. From the picturesque Himalayas to the iconic Taj Mahal and exotic beaches of Goa, virtually all types of travel are available in the country of 1.2 billion people. But how to broadcast this to the rest of the world . . . thus the inception of "Incredible India."

While many in the travel industry and tourists alike praised the campaign, others criticized it for overemphasizing the positives of India while glossing over the numerous challenges, including poor infrastructure (incomplete, outdated, or nonexistent road networks), lack of air connectivity and open skies agreement (since changed), power shortages, unsanitary conditions, poverty stricken rural areas, and insufficient upscale accommodations, among others. Those in the Tourism Ministry readily acknowledged that India, as a relatively young democracy, at only 60 years of age after liberation from Britain, had previously focused its finances, manpower, and intellectual efforts on other capital issues. These ranged from caste eradication to providing basic daily necessities—water, electricity—for its masses. However, with the economy growing at upward of 8% annually in recent years and the citing the opportunity to create jobs and contribute wealth to rural areas, the Indian government decided to make a collective effort to promote sustainable tourism.

The year 2002 was a watershed for India's tourism outreach. After several failed attempts by government to create a unified, professional national campaign, India finally harnessed its potential (with the assistance of Ogilvy and Mather, India). The Department of Tourism and government of India created a streamlined, stimulating ad campaign that showed off the rustic pleasures (e.g., elephant rides, desert camps, street vendors selling famous masala chai tea) as well as exotic grandeur (e.g., Incredible Taj! Hotels, Resorts, and Palaces). As of 2007, target markets included: Southeast Asia, Germany, Britain, France, Italy, and Australia, with the U.S. more concentrated on short-haul travel and where tourists were more concerned about devaluation of the dollar. Results to date suggest that tourists have grown more confident in "experimental" tourism, with a greater number venturing to India and when there, far beyond the traditional quest to the Taj Mahal in Agra. To date, major Indian metropolitan hotel occupancies hover at an estimated 80% occupancy annually (HVS International Research), as compared to an average 68% in the U.S. (PKF Consulting).

The 2006 WTTC report suggests that over the next 10 years, India's travel and tourism industry is expected to achieve annualized real growth of 7.9%, to bring in $28.4 billion in 2013. By then, the travel and tourism economy overall is expected to hit an annual $68.3 billion, yet India's share of the pie is still projected to be less than 2%. Much potential exists and, indeed, tourism in India is a bright beacon.

Ultimately, the terminology "Incredible India" could not be more apt. For the country and its contrasting visages, from cows and monkeys on the urban streets to the most intricate, ancient Kama Sutra carvings on the temples in Khajuraho, India is guaranteed to stir every tourist.

www.incredibleindia.org

mortgage), we must grow more savvy and sensitive as to who is our target market and who we wish it to be. In the U.S., the steadily growing number of Hispanics in management positions in the work-force will mean new adaptations and customizations to their specific needs (i.e., travel ads for vacation destinations in Spanish is one example). In East Asia, the emergence of travel for a growing number of female business executives has instigated customized butlers (female room servers only), smaller bathrobes and slippers for women, more fragrant toiletries, and even cocktail room service so women do not have to venture to a bar or lounge area alone if they so wish. After all, "We are all equal does not mean we are all the same" (Carmen Baker, VP Diversity, Carlson Hotels Worldwide).

As we have witnessed in the last decade, it will become even more imperative for companies to create strategic alliances with one another. High end (luxury) properties partner with Baccarat for crystal in their restaurants, Rolls-Royce for their transportation, Tiffany for their VIP gifts, Armani for their toiletries in the bathrooms. We will continue to see such liaising but soon with larger parties. Airlines and hospitality, car rental agencies, travel distributors, and real estate developers (such as Cendant who has now broken into these four divisions) will become industry behemoths, bundling packages for travelers at every turn. For independent operators, they will continue to align themselves with umbrella companies—e.g., Preferred Hotels and Resorts, Leading Hotels of the World, Small Luxury Hotels of the World, Relais and Chateaux, among others—many hospitality companies are aggressively seeking a global presence in today's world. While they may not all share a central reservation or even a referral system, these affiliated companies do subscribe to established standards for membership and court clientele with similar interests and lifestyles. Though outward alliances will be numerous in the years to come, diversification within individual companies and their product offerings

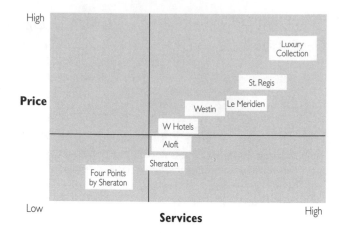

will morph as well. Hotel companies will continue to launch new brands within their portfolios in attempts to offer something for everyone, more clearly defining and recognizing the merits to niche markets. Starwood Hotels and Resorts, for example, has the brand tiering in the figure above.

By first accurately identifying a client base, they have then successfully launched and adapted new products (first W Hotels and now Aloft) customized to their target market, meeting with resounding success. India's tourism marketing campaign, "Incredible India," is a clearly defined campaign of branding at a national level.

Summary

Both challenging and rewarding, a career in hospitality sales and marketing continues to evolve. As with all successful managers, fulfillment and success are often derived through lifelong learning and exposures to new ideas. Ultimately, the goal is to produce the highest yield on investment for owners and, simultaneously, exceed customers' expectations. Research supports that buyers prefer to work with those sales and marketing individuals who are creative, genuine, knowledgeable, and perceptive in their professional liaising.

≈ *Resources*

Internet Sites

American Marketing Association: www.marketingpower.com
Direct Marketing Association: www.the-dma.org
Hospitality Sales and Marketing Association International: www.hsmai.org

≈ *Contributors*

Heather Kaikini was formerly an Instructor in the Department of Hospitality and Tourism Management at the College of Charleston, specializing in hotel and resort management. Prior to this position, she was in Sales and Marketing with the Biltmore Estate in Asheville, NC, representing the Biltmore House, Gardens, Winery, and Historic Farm Village as well as the renowned Inn on Biltmore. Prior to joining Biltmore, she was on the opening team as a Director of Sales and Marketing with a new Hilton brand hotel in the greater Chicago area. In the years preceding this, Heather nationally represented Starwood Hotels and Resorts, based out of Miami. Heather earned an MBA specialized in International Hospitality Management at IMHI (Insititut de Management Hotelier International), a joint program through Cornell University's Hotel School and Essec Business School in France. She currently resides in Mumbai, India.

John C. Crotts, PhD, is a Professor and Chair of the Hospitality and Tourism Management Program at the College of Charleston. Prior to this position, he lectured in the Advanced Business Programme on tourism subjects at Otago University, Dunedin, New Zealand, and was Director of the Center for Tourism Research and Development at the University of Florida. His research encompasses the areas of economic psychology, tourism marketing strategy, and management of cooperative alliances. Dr. Crotts received his PhD in Leisure Studies and Services from the University of Oregon. He also holds a Bachelor's degree in Sociology from Appalachian State University, a MS in Education from Mankato State University and an EdS in Adult Education from the Appalachian State University.

Chapter 8
Review Questions

1. What are the 4 Ps in the marketing mix? Explain how each contributes to a successful business model.

2. Who provides supply and who demand in the hospitality industry?

3. How does marketing to the individual transient guest differ from marketing to the group traveler?

4. Name the various market segments affiliated with group sales clients. Do all hotels target the same segments? Elaborate on your response.

5. Give an example of one common complaint a meeting or event planner might have concerning the sales-service delivery process. How might this be overcome?

6. With the growing presence of direct online booking of travel and reservations, how has the role of a DMC changed and why/why not is it beneficial to maintain strong professional connections with these individuals?

7. Imagine you are the proprietor of a highway economy hotel. Would you allocate a majority of your marketing funds for online distribution? If not, how would you promote your hotel? Explain your answer.

8. What is your understanding of "diversity" and how can it be interwoven into hospitality and tourism?

9. Describe the personal profile and skills necessary for a successful sales and marketing individual.

Law and Ethics

9

Christian E. Hardigree, University of Nevada, Las Vegas
S. Denise McCurry, MGM Mirage

© zimmytws, 2008, Shutterstock.

≈ Learning Objectives

☑ To have a working knowledge of the legal system and how it applies to the hospitality industry
☑ To be able to recognize what area of law would apply to specific fact scenarios
☑ To understand how the actions or inactions of employees and managers can create liability
☑ To have a working knowledge of employment laws that relate to hospitality
☑ To be able to recognize the ethical issues that arise in conjunction with the legal issues faced by a hospitality establishment

≈ Chapter Outline

Litigation in General: What Is the Process?
Areas of Law
Ethical Considerations

≈ Key Terms

Americans with Disabilities Act (ADA)
Appropriation
Cause of action
Copyright
Defamation
Defendant
Detour
Equal Pay Act (EPA)
Ethics
Fair Labor Standards Act (FLSA)
False light
Family Medical Leave Act (FMLA)
Frolic

Intrusion
Negligence
Patent
Plaintiff
Right of publicity
Risk management
Respondeat superior
Statute of limitations
Torts
Trademark
Trade secret
Unreasonable publication of private facts

The legal implications of the hospitality industry are virtually limitless. The law permeates every aspect of a hospitality organization, ranging from the formation of the organization, to the daily operations of food and beverage, to personal injuries on property, to the contracts formed with guests and others. It would be futile to attempt to cover every aspect of how the law applies to our industry. As you proceed through your educational experience, you will likely have an opportunity to take a course or two dedicated to hospitality law, which will likely go into much greater depth of the legal and ethical implications of our industry. This chapter serves as a mere introduction to the legal terms and concepts that you will encounter during your academic and work experience. We also pose ethical considerations that accompany many of the legal quandaries that you may face.

Litigation in General: What Is the Process?

Litigation is a scary process largely because most people do not understand it. Typically we think of law shows on television where the police investigate a crime, catch a suspect, and have a trial all within a 60 minute program. Such shows have taken artistic license in order to have an interesting and entertaining television program. Unfortunately, those shows only offer a miniscule glimpse into the litigation process, focusing primarily on the criminal realm. These shows are also "fast forwarded" in order to keep the audience entertained.

In reality, a case can take 4 to 7 years from the date of the injury until the date of trial, and even longer if the matter is appealed. Since full blown litigation can take so long, many cases are resolved by an agreed-upon settlement, the outcomes of which are generally kept confidential. Settled cases are virtually impossible to track due to the confidentiality. Settled cases also rarely involve any admission of liability by a party, instead noting that the liability issue is contested, but the matter is being settled to expedite the case. In order to predict the outcome of future cases, we are typically limited to a review of jury verdicts. And juries are notoriously fickle; for example, some regions of the country produce juries that give higher damage awards, some juries are more conservative than others, etc.

A large portion of the public perceives hospitality businesses as "cash-cows." There is also an ever-

growing sentiment that when someone is injured, it must be the landowners' "fault." When these two perceptions are combined, the hospitality industry becomes a target for people to make claims against and/or sue our businesses. Some people have legitimate claims for which they should be remunerated. However, an increasing number of incidents are either exaggerated and/or completely staged in an effort to extort money from the business. You may recall the "finger in the chili" case at Wendy's restaurant, where a woman fraudulently claimed that she bit into a human finger while eating. Wendy's estimated that they lost approximately $2.5 million in revenue due to bad publicity following that event.[1] While the woman and her husband (who obtained the finger) were ultimately sentenced to 9 and 12 years in prison, respectively, for their parts in the scam, the damage to the restaurant was already done.[2]

The Wendy's incident serves as a reminder to the hospitality industry that we are a target of unscrupulous people. As such, issues relating to retention of evidence become paramount. A scam similar to the Wendy's scam was attempted in 2004 when a woman and her son planted a dead mouse in the woman's vegetable soup. In that case, a forensic examination of the mouse revealed that it had died of a skull fracture, did not have any soup in its lungs, and had not been cooked.[3] Had the wait staff simply thrown the mouse away, the restaurant would not have been able to defend itself and prove the scam. This case illustrates how necessary it is for hospitality businesses to anticipate issues and to retain evidence in order to determine potential liability. In fact most jurisdictions will instruct a jury that the failure of a party to produce evidence on an issue within its own knowledge and control raises an inference that the concealed evidence would be unfavorable to that party. The parties to a lawsuit are required to retain evidence, even evidence that may prove their own liability, by the courts giving the aforementioned jury instruction they are forcing parties to act ethically or suffer an adverse jury instruction.

What Happens when a Claim Arises

Once someone is injured, whether in the form of personal injury, breach of contract, stolen property, etc., that person may have a "cause of action." The term "cause of action" simply refers to the legal theory under which the injured party believes that someone else should be held responsible for their injuries. Injuries are not always physical. A person can also be mentally injured, they may incur injury to their personal property or business, damage to their personal or business reputation, loss of future income, etc. If someone can demonstrate that they were damaged by the wrongful acts or omissions of another, then they can be compensated for those wrongful acts or omissions.

When a person is physically or mentally injured on your property, many times, the injured person will contact management in order to fill out an incident report or make a claim. Some hospitality facilities have Risk Management departments to handle these types of claims, while other facilities may simply have a high level manager. In some instances, the person claiming injury will simply go to a lawyer and then proceed with formal litigation, never contacting the business regarding their claims. There is no obligation that injured parties attempt to resolve the matter with the facility prior to proceeding to litigation. In some instances, the very first time that the business owner/operator learns of a claim is when they receive a copy of the lawsuit.

Each cause of action has a minimum timeframe during which it must be formally brought as litigation or the cause of action is lost. This is known as a "statute of limitations." The statute of limitations varies for each legal theory and may vary state by state. For example, if someone fell in your coffee shop because an employee spilled oil on the floor and did not clean it up, the cause of action would be negligence. In most states, the statute of limitations for negligence is 2 years. So the customer would have 2 years from the date of the initial fall in which to file their lawsuit, otherwise they lose the right to proceed. If children are involved, the statute of limitations for the injured child may not begin to accrue until the child reaches the age of majority (18 years old).

The statute of limitations is important because it tells the property owner/manager that they need to retain documents (i.e., incident reports, security reports, photographs, etc.), as well as other evidence (i.e., the dead mouse, videotapes of the incident, physical items involved, etc.) for a minimum period of time. For example, if someone was injured on January 1, 2008, and the statute of limitations for their possible claim was 2 years, then the documents relating to the incident should be maintained at least until January 1, 2010, plus 120 days. The in-

jured party has an additional 120 days from date of filing their claim to serve the complaint on the defendant (prudent business owners should retain the documents for another 6 months to a year, in case the lawsuit is delayed in being served upon the defendant). The fact that an incident occurs on the property owner's property is sufficient to give the owner notice of a potential claim.

Risk Management: To Have or Not to Have?

Rather than incurring the expense of hiring an on-staff attorney, or in-house counsel, many facilities simply create a claims department to handle claims made against the property. Sometimes the people in charge of the claims department have a legal background, perhaps even a law degree; but, more frequently, they are individuals who have simply worked in the business for many years in different departments. Many such claims departments, or Risk Management departments, are simply reactive to situations, as opposed to being proactive. Rather than conducting internal audits to identify problems and resolve them prior to injuries, these types of departments frequently just respond to claims and litigation. Even those companies that do conduct internal audits prior to an incident will undertake a cost/benefit analysis when assessing potential liability of a property. They assess whether the costs associated with fixing a hazard are too costly in comparison to the likelihood or risk of injury and/or lawsuit. For example, it may cost a restaurant $180,000 to fix cracks in the front walk area. A small restaurant may feel that the cost for fixing the cracks is too high given the minute risk that someone will trip and suffer injury. Sometimes facilities will simply ignore dangers, hoping that no one is injured and/or sues.

Those facilities that do engage in proactive risk assessment find that they can better quantify, assess, and manage risk, as well as improve the performance of their personnel. Certainly it makes sense to avoid situations that may create liability rather than simply reacting to lawsuits or claims after they have been filed. However, since it is difficult to quantify the savings to a facility, and the fact that Risk Management/claims departments are nonrevenue generating areas of an organization, they tend to be under-funded, under-staffed, and frequently under-appreciated.

Understanding the Difference between Civil and Criminal Law

There is a significant difference between civil law and criminal law. Civil litigation is usually initiated when the aggrieved party is seeking monetary damages for some wrongdoing; whereas the outcome of a criminal matter would be an individual charged with a crime and potentially incarcerated and/or placed on probation. The main difference between the two areas of law relates to the definition of the "Plaintiff." In civil hospitality cases, the plaintiff is generally an individual who seeks damages as a result of a claim that they have suffered a physical, mental, or monetary injury. In criminal cases, the plaintiff is the State that seeks to limit the freedom of the defendant. Most hospitality cases relate to civil litigation, largely stemming from contracts, torts, intellectual property, and employment law. While crimes do occur on our hospitality properties, the Risk Manager and employees are more likely to be witnesses in those cases, as opposed to defendants.

Let us look at some of the issues that are most commonly litigation in hospitality.

Areas of Law

There are various areas of law that you will come in contact with in the hospitality industry, in fact at times you may feel that the law, both statutory and case law, has invaded every aspect of the hospitality industry. Keep in mind that different states and jurisdictions may have variations on some of these concepts that differ from each other. This serves as a general introduction to the most common concepts you will encounter.

Employer Liability: Respondeat Superior

An employer can be held responsible or liable for the acts of its employees. In order to determine whether to hold an employer liable, the question is: Was the employee, at the time of the incident, *acting within the course and scope of their employment?* Another way to look at this is whether the actions, which caused the injury, arose out of or in the course of employment. For example, the hotel limousine driver is taking some hotel guests to the airport. He is speeding so that the guests can make their flight on time. The driver takes a corner too fast and the limousine flips over, injuring the guests.

Even though the limousine driver was speeding, he was still engaged in an act that was in furtherance of the employer's business interest and therefore acting within the course and scope of his employment.

Generally, an employer will not be held liable for the acts of an employee while traveling to and from work, this is known as the "going and coming rule." Although an exception exists when an employer sends an employee on a special errand that is undertaken outside of the usual working hours. For example, assume a bartender is asked to run to the grocery store for bar supplies and has a car accident on the way to the store. In that instance, the employer may be held liable to the injured person because the bartender was acting in furtherance of the employer's business interest. However, if the bartender was simply driving into work to start their shift and they had an accident, the employer would not be responsible for any injuries which resulted from the accident.

Traditionally, an employer will not be held liable for the actions of an employee that is in furtherance of that employee's private or individual interest. These independent acts of the employee fall into the legal categories of frolic (major deviations) and detour (minor deviations). Generally, the law holds an employer responsible for employees on a detour and only responsible if the employer has reason to know of the frolic. In either instance, the employer may be held liable for the individual actions of their employees.

Additionally, employers are not responsible for the acts of a competent, valid independent contractor. The primary difference between an independent contractor and an employee is the amount of control that the employer has over the daily job duties that each is required to perform. An employer may control the general type of work that an independent contract undertakes, but does not control the manner and method by which the independent contractor's work is accomplished.

For example, the Blue Note Hotel hires Pro-Tree, a tree trimming company, to perform an annual cleanup of the property. ProTree fails to properly trim all of the dead tree branches on the trees in the garden area. While tanning by the pool, a hotel guest is injured when she was hit on the head by a dead tree branch. ProTree is an independent contractor because the Blue Note does not direct its daily activities. Based upon ProTree's status as an independent contractor, the Blue Note should not be held liable for their omission.

Torts

Torts are a large classification of different types of civil wrongs that result in injury or damages to either people or property. Hotels and restaurants have a responsibility or duty to people on their property to keep the premises in a reasonably safe condition and to protect against physical dangers such as wet floors, construction, or spills or from harm or danger caused by other people such as employees, other guests, and even criminals. There are numerous tort theories under which one can be sued: assault, battery, false imprisonment, trespass to chattel, negligence, privacy torts, defamation, wrongful death, loss of consortium, retaliation, etc. It is important to have a basic understanding of some of these torts in order to protect yourself and your business.

Negligence

One of the most common torts is negligence. A cause of action for negligence occurs when a duty owed to someone on the property is breached, resulting in injury or damages to an individual. Hotels and restaurants owe a duty of reasonable care to their guests. A hotel or restaurant that has been sued for negligence can raise the defense that the injured party was to some extent responsible for their injury. This is called contributory negligence or comparative negligence. Individuals also have a duty to take reasonable precautions to protect themselves from harm or danger. An individual must act in a manner so as to protect themself in a similar fashion as someone of like age, intelligence, and experience would do under similar circumstances.

A person may sue a hotel for negligence if they believe they suffered an injury because the hotel did not uphold their duty.

For example, assume there is a wet substance that was spilled on the floor of a hotel lobby and a guest of the hotel, seeing the spill, chooses to walk through it, slips and falls and is injured. The hotel may have breached its duty of reasonable care by not cleaning up the spill quickly enough. However, the hotel guest contributed to his injury by failing to avoid the spill which he saw and attempted to traverse. In such cases, the guest has also failed to protect himself by taking reasonable precautions and thus his recovery may be limited, if not completely barred.

Defamation

A hospitality facility can also be held liable for the harm caused by the language of its managers and/or employees. An individual may be able to sue for defamation when a false statement is made about the individual and that statement is overheard or made to a third person resulting in damage to the reputation or business. To establish a defamation claim, the statement must be false so a defendant may use "truth" of the statement as a valid defense to the claim. For example employee A says to guest B, "You're a hooker!" If this statement was overheard by the business partner of guest B, and the business partner dissolves their partnership, then guest B can sue employee A (and most likely the employer) for damage to guest B's reputation. If, however, guest B was a prostitute, then guest B would have no claim because the statement was true.

Privacy Torts

Privacy is always a big issue, especially in hotels. Under the heading of privacy, there are actually five recognized causes of action: **intrusion, appropriation, right of publicity, the unreasonable publication of private facts,** and **false light**.

A cause of action for intrusion upon the seclusion of another requires that someone intentionally intrudes upon the solitude or the seclusion of another in a way that a reasonable person would find highly offensive. The individual who alleges that their right to privacy had been invaded must establish that they had a reasonable expectation of seclusion or solitude. For example, a dance revue show that is the feature attraction for Hotel A is being filmed for an upcoming television special. The performers in the show do not have a reasonable expectation of privacy while on stage. But if one of the cameramen filmed the dancers changing costumes in the changing room, the dancers would be able to sue for intrusion. Typically, the courts recognize an expectation of privacy in changing rooms, bathrooms, and bedrooms.

The use of the name or likeness of an ordinary, uncelebrated person without their permission for advertising or other commercial purpose is appropriation. For example, Todd takes a picture of Betsy and gives the photograph to his friend Bill who is the owner of Bill's Brew Pub. Bill uses Betsy's picture without her permission or knowledge to advertise for an upcoming ladies' night.

The right of publicity is essentially the same concept as appropriation, except that it protects the use of the name or likeness of a celebrity for commercial purposes. So a nightclub cannot legally use a photograph of Jennifer Aniston on their Web page unless they have obtained her permission to do so.

Intellectual Property

There are different types of intellectual property rights which can be obtained by businesses and individuals. These would include patents, copyrights, trademarks, and trade secrets. Intellectual property refers to creations of the mind: inventions, literary and artistic works, and symbols, names, images, and designs used in commerce.

A patent is the grant of a property right to an inventor issued by the United States Patent and Trademark Office. A patent enables its holder to exclude others from making, using, or offering for sale the invention.

A trademark is a word, name, symbol, or device that is used in trade with goods to indicate the source of the goods and to distinguish them from the goods of others. Trademark rights may be used to prevent others from using a confusingly similar mark, but it cannot be used to prevent others from making the same goods or from selling the same goods or services under a clearly different mark.

A copyright is a form of protection provided to the authors of "original works of authorship" including literary, dramatic, musical, and artistic works both published and unpublished. A copyright gives the owner the exclusive right to reproduce the work, to prepare derivative works, to distribute, perform, or display the work or copies of the work publicly. Keep in mind the copyright protects the form of expression rather than the subject matter. For example, the description of a hotel in a coffee table book could be copyrighted, but the copyright would only prevent others from copying the description not from writing a description of their own.

An example of a trade secret may be the identity of a customer of a hotel, casino, or restaurant. For example, casino host Joan leaves Casino A and takes employment at Casino B, taking the customer list with her. Casino A can then sue both Joan and Casino B for a violation of their trade secret.

Employment Law

Employment law is a vast area law that can be complex and tedious. This is an area of law that came about primarily to establish and protect the rights of employees. Some of the pivotal laws that have been enacted in this area are:

> Title VII of the Civil Rights Act of 1964 (Title VII)
> The Fair Labor Standards Act (FLSA)
> The Family Medical Leave Act (FMLA)
> The Age Discrimination in Employment Act (ADEA)
> The Pregnancy Act
> The Equal Pay Act (EPA)
> The Americans with Disabilities Act (ADA)
> The National Labor Relations Act (NLRA)

The 14th Amendment to the U.S. Constitution forms the basis for the Civil Rights Act and Title VII, laying the groundwork for basic equal rights in employment today. The Equal Protection Clause states that all people are entitled to equal protection under the law. Under Title VII it is illegal to discriminate against an individual in reference to any term, condition, or privilege of employment based upon their religion, race, color, sex, or national origin. Title VII prohibits both intentional discrimination and neutral job policies that disproportionably exclude minorities.

Fair Labor Standards Act

The Fair Labor Standards Act (FLSA) was first enacted by Congress in 1938. FLSA regulates the minimum compensation that an employee should be paid on an hourly basis, the maximum number of hours an employee should be required to work weekly, overtime pay, child labor, and record keeping.

Individual states can create laws that are more favorable to the employee than that under federal law. For example, in 2007, the minimum wage under FLSA was $6.15 an hour. However, as of January

1, 2008, in California the state's minimum wage was $8.00. Thus a business in California would have to comply with the state's minimum wage rather than the federal government's prevailing wage. The FLSA does not govern (1) vacation, holiday, severance, or sick pay; (2) meal or rest periods, holidays off, or vacations; (3) premium pay for weekend or holiday work; (4) pay raises or fringe benefits; (5) a discharge notice, reason for discharge, or immediate payment of final wages to terminated employees; and (6) pay stubs or W-2s.

Family Medical Leave Act

The Family Medical Leave Act (FMLA) was passed by Congress in 1991. The purpose behind FMLA was to balance work and family by allowing employees to take leave, as well as FMLA minimizing the potential for employers to discriminate against employees based upon gender. FMLA involves the entitlement to leave, the maintenance of health during leave, job restoration after leave, and it sets requirements for notice and or certification to get FMLA leave. In order for an employee to be eligible under FMLA he or she must have worked for the employer for 12 months, have worked 1,250 hours during the 12 months prior to the start of the FMLA leave, and work for an employer with 50 or more employees within a 75 mile radius.

An employer must grant an eligible employee up to a total of 12 work weeks of unpaid leave within a 12 month period. An eligible employee may only request leave under FMLA for the birth or adoption of a child, a serious medical condition for themselves or an immediate family member.

Equal Pay Act

The Equal Pay Act requires that men and women be given equal pay for equal work in the same establishment. The EPA does not require that the jobs be identical, but they must be substantially equal in job content, not job titles, to determine whether jobs are substantially equal. Pay differentials are permitted when they are based on seniority, merit, quantity, or quality of production, or a factor other than sex.

Keep in mind that on June 10, 1963, President John F. Kennedy signed the Equal Pay Act (EPA) into law. At the time, full-time working women were paid on average 59 cents to the dollar earned by their male counterparts, according to government data. Since 1963, the closing of the wage gap between men and women has been at a rate of less

An individual with a disability must be qualified to perform the essential functions of the job in order to be protected by the ADA.

than half a penny a year. As of 2006, women make approximately $.70 for each $1.00 made by men, with the disparity even greater for ethnic women.

Americans with Disabilities Act

Title I of the Americans with Disabilities Act prohibits employers with 15 or more employees from discriminating against qualified individuals with disabilities in job application procedures, hiring, firing, advancement, compensation, job training, and other terms, conditions, and privileges of employment. Under the ADA an individual with a disability is a person who:

1. Has a physical or mental impairment that substantially limits one or more major life activities;
2. Has a record of such an impairment; or
3. Is regarded as having such an impairment.

An individual with a disability must be qualified to perform the essential functions of the job, with or without reasonable accommodation, in order to be protected by the ADA. An employer is required to make a reasonable accommodation to qualified applicants or employee with a known disability so long as it would not impose an "undue hardship" on the operation of the employer's business. Reasonable accommodations may include:

- acquiring or modifying equipment or devices,
- job restructuring,
- part-time or modified work schedules,
- reassignment to a vacant position,
- adjusting or modifying examinations, training materials or policies,

- providing readers and interpreters, and
- making the workplace readily accessible to and usable by people with disabilities.

Business Formats

There are various types of business formats such as sole proprietorships, partnerships, and the various types of corporations. Prior to creating a business format, you should consult an attorney to determine the best format for your business. Briefly, let us look at the various formats.

Both sole proprietorships and partnerships have no separate existence from the owner of the business. A sole proprietorship essentially means that a person does business in their own name and there is only one owner. Whereas a partnership is two or more people doing business together, sharing in profits and losses. Neither sole proprietorships nor a partnerships limit the liability of the business owner(s) because neither is a separate entity apart from the owner(s). Thus, if a sole proprietorship or a partnership were to be sued, then the owner(s) of the business would be personally liable for any judgment or debt that is incurred by the business.

The lack of protection for the business owner(s) in a sole proprietorship and a partnership is one of the reasons why business owners prefer to form corporations. A corporation is a separate legal entity that has the same rights as an individual person. The primary advantage to forming a corporation is that the officers and stockholders of the corporation can avoid being held individually/personally liable for the action of their business.

Ethical Considerations

In addition to the legal implications of the various issues discussed above, a good manager must also balance these considerations with what is ethical. In 2005, the business world was rocked by corporate scandals such as Enron and Tyco. So what importance does a good hospitality executive place on the ethical considerations of their day-to-day tasks? Again, an entire book could be devoted to this arena, and you may have the opportunity to take an ethics course during your academic pursuits. Let us consider a few scenarios:

If you know your floor is uneven and sloping, only 1 of every 100,000 people will misstep or fall, and it will cost 15% of the annual profits to fix the floor, should you fix it? A risk manage-

ment analysis may indicate that the risk is not great in comparison with the cost of fixing it. But what about the ethical considerations involved?

As a purchasing agent, during the holidays, you receive a case of high-end champagne delivered to your home from one of the purveyors from whom you regularly submit orders. Since you use their company anyway, the champagne really isn't a "bribe," but could it be considered a "kickback"? Is it ethical to keep it? It may not be illegal, but what perception is created if the purchasing agent keeps it?

Applicable law only requires you to pay employees $6.15 an hour for their work. Fifty percent of your employees work in nontipped positions, and thus cannot easily supplement their income with tips. You know that it is difficult for a family to survive on such low hourly pay. You have an obligation to the company to keep your labor costs low. But should you consider paying the nontipped employees a higher wage? How do you balance your obligations to the stockholders and your obligations to the employees?

A guest of your hotel is injured when the headboard in her room falls off the wall and hits her on the head. You discover later that the headboard was too heavy for the wall and the hotel had not used enough screws to attach it to the wall. You know that there is an obligation to preserve all relevant evidence, but you are also aware that this evidence would be very damaging to the hotel. Do you throw the headboard away?

Summary

As we have seen, the law permeates every aspect of a hospitality organization. It is difficult in today's world to discern what is "legal" without having an attorney on hand to continuously ask questions, a luxury that most businesses do not have available. Rather than fear the unknown arena of litigation, a good manager must arm themselves with some basic knowledge of the law and the legal process. That same manager must also consider the ethical implications of their day-to-day decisions. Through trial and error (sometimes many errors), eventually a good manager will be able to manage in a proactive and ethical manner in order to create a safe and supportive hospitality environment.

≈ *Resources*

Internet Sites

The U.S. Equal Employment Opportunity Commission: www.eeoc.gov
The U.S. Department of Labor: www.dol.gov
American Bar Association: http://www.abanet.org/

≈ *Endnotes*

1. Retrieved from http://www.msnbc.msn.com/id/7594873 on December 22, 2005.
2. Retrieved from http://www.cbsnews.com/stories/2006/01/18/national/main1218315.shtml?CMP=OTC-RSSFeed&source=RSS&attr=HOME_1218315 on January 20, 2006.
3. Retrieved from http://home.hamptonroads.com/stories/story.cfm?story=71183&ran=107750 on December 22, 2005.

≈ *Contributors*

Christian E. Hardigree is the Associate Dean for Strategic Initiatives and an associate professor in the William F. Harrah College of Hotel Administration at the University of Nevada, Las Vegas. She teaches both graduate and undergraduate classes, including Hospitality Law, Laws of Innkeeping and Food Service, Labor Management Relations, Hospitality Employment Law, and Law and Liability in Sports and Leisure Studies. She is also a trial attorney for the law firm of Parnell & Associates, practicing primarily in the areas of premises liability, adequacy of security, products liability, and employment law. She is licensed to practice law in Nevada and Georgia. Dr. Hardigree conducts research and presents papers at various industry conferences relating to her areas of expertise. She is also available for private consulting and mediation/arbitration services. She can be reached at UNLV, William F. Harrah College of Hotel Administration, 4505 Maryland Parkway, Box 456014, Las Vegas, Nevada 89154. Her email address is Christian.Hardigree@unlv.edu.

S. Denise McCurry is the Vice President of Litigation and Risk Management for MGM Mirage. She also serves as an adjunct faculty member in the Harrah Hotel College at the University of Nevada, Las Vegas, teaching Hospitality Law and Employment Hospitality Law. In the past, she has served as an Alternate Judge for the City of Las Vegas Municipal Court. She is licensed to practice law in Nevada. Her email address is Denise_Mccurry@yahoo.com.

Chapter 9
Review Questions

1. Your hotel puts up a sign outside the ladies' bathroom that states "Wet Floor." The hotel does not barricade access to the bathroom. A hotel guest sees the sign, enters the bathroom, and slips and falls. Do you think your hotel should be responsible? Why or why not? What cause of action would the guest claim? What defense would you use?

2. You own a restaurant. One of your bartenders likes to flip the alcohol bottles while he is making drinks. On one occasion, the bottle slips and strikes a patron in the face, cutting her face. Do you think your restaurant should be liable? Why or why not?

3. A card dealer is dealing cards to gamblers at a blackjack table. One of the gamblers becomes irritated and calls the dealer a bad name. The dealer punches the gambler in the face, knocking him unconscious. Should the casino be liable for the dealer's actions? Why or why not? What if the dealer waited until after shift and attacked the gambler in the parking lot? Would that affect your analysis?

4. The hostess at the hotel café approaches a guest and states, "Your credit card was declined." The other guests at the table overhear this statement. Under what legal theory could the guest sue the hotel? What defense, if any, could the hotel use?

5. Your employee who you hired 3 months ago comes to you and tells you that he has cancer and needs time off work for chemotherapy. Can this employee take time off under the FMLA? Why or why not?

6. The marketing department at your hotel takes pictures of the employees to place on mailers that are sent to guests inviting them to the property. You picture see your picture on a mailer. Do you have a claim against the hotel? If yes, which cause of action would you claim? If no, why not?

Income and Controlling Costs

10

Daniel Bernstein, Seton Hill University

© 2008, JupiterImages Corporation.

≈ Learning Objectives

☑ To learn how income is evaluated in a hotel and restaurant
☑ To be able to calculate and use the ratios that are used for success in the hotel and restaurant industry
☑ To learn how to maximize income through selling
☑ To learn how to control costs in the hotel and restaurant industry

≈ Chapter Outline

Income in the Hotel Industry
Income in the Restaurant Industry
Maximizing Revenue through Selling
Controlling Costs in the Hotel Industry
Controlling Costs in the Restaurant Industry
Careers in Revenue and Cost Control in the
    Hospitality Industry

≈ Key Terms

AP (As purchased)
ADR (Average Daily Rate)
Cost control
Discounting
EP (Edible Portion)
Energy management
Food cost
Intangibility
Labor cost
Mom & Pop
Occupancy percentage
Perishability
POS (Point of Sale)
Portion control
Revenue
Top down approach
Units
Up-selling
Volume purchasing
Yield management

The two main ingredients in making a profit are increasing revenue and lowering cost. A company may often appear to be profitable because of the level of income. However, failure to control costs may actually cause the company to lose money and eventually go out of business. This chapter will introduce different types of income that exists in the hotel and restaurant industry and introduce possible alternatives to control costs. Because of the unique nature of this industry, different formulas for measuring hotel and restaurant income are used within this chapter.

Income in the Hotel Industry

It is important for students to understand that, in reality, most of the everyday tasks completed by managers are done for the financial wellbeing of the firm. Specifically, most hospitality managers increase shareholder value by decreasing expenses and increasing income. If the manager is not concerned with the success of the company, their employment will not last too long.

There are various means of measuring income, to assess how successful they are as managers. Before one measures their success, they must have a working knowledge of expectations. While hotel managers would like to sell out every room, every night, this is not always possible. Many factors can affect hotel occupancy, over which the hotel manager may have very little or no control. These factors are often external (outside) forces such as seasonality and competition. Certain seasons present more favorable weather conditions, which may increase occupancy. For example, Arizona, California, and Florida have high occupancy during the winter and lower occupancy in the summer when weather conditions are less favorable. Another factor that may affect occupancy is competition. New hotels in your market niche may compete for the same customers. These external factors may adversely affect hotel occupancy and, therefore, a manager must carefully plan to overcome these problems.

To aid in the strategic plan, three tools for measuring revenue are occupancy percentage, average daily rate, and yield management.

Occupancy percentage is a ratio relating the number of rooms sold to the number of rooms available. How does a hotel manager know if their hotel is running at an acceptable occupancy percentage? First, a hotel manager should be aware of national averages of occupancy percentages.

There are various resources for obtaining this data, such as the AHLA (American Hotel & Lodging Association). Secondly, your hotel company will have average occupancy percentages that they expect you to meet.

What if you work for an independent hotel, without any specific guidelines about expected occupancy percentages of your hotel? You will need to find out percentages of comparable hotels in your area. Another way of estimating occupancy percentage would be to look at a daily audit report. When comparing occupancy percentages from past records, it is important to know what to compare. If you want to know how well your hotel will do for December 15th this year, you may assume that you should look at December 15th of last year. But that would not be accurate. December 15th of this year and December 15th of last year were on different days of the week. Hotel occupancy percentages often fluctuate by days of the week. Some business hotels have higher occupancy percentages on weekends. Resort hotels tend to be the opposite, with high occupancy percentage on the weekends and lower occupancy percentage on weekdays. So, if you want to estimate how well your hotel will do for December 15th this year you should compare by the days of the week. If December 15th was on a Thursday this year, you would compare it to the third Thursday in December last year. The only time you would compare the same date from year to year would be holidays such as Christmas, which is always on December 25th, and New Years Day, which is always on January 1st. In this case, the day of the week is of little significance compared to the actual date.

ROOM (UNITS) FOR SALE

900 (Rooms available for sale) × 365 (days per year)
= 328,500 Rooms

OCCUPANCY PERCENTAGE
Number of rooms sold /
Number of rooms available for sale

670 (number of rooms sold) / 900 (rooms available for sale) = 74.44% (occupancy %)

(Always round off to the 100th place to insure accuracy, too much rounding off will change your answer)

For example, rounding off to 74% of 900 rooms sold would be 666 rooms sold. This would be inaccurate, as your statistics would indicate 4 less rooms sold. As you will read later in this chapter, if one statistic is off, other statistics will also be inaccurate.

Another calculation that the hotel manager should look at in reference to occupancy is how many guests are in each room. Most hotels charge more for double occupancy than for single. The reason is that hotels can incur additional costs like the use of another bed, length of time for a housekeeper to clean a room, free continental breakfasts, and happy hours. However, some hotels charge per room instead, though most hotels price by the number of guests in a hotel room.

DOUBLE OCCUPANCY

Number of Guests – Number of rooms sold /
Number of rooms occupied

1000 (number of guests) – 750 (number of rooms sold)
/ 750 (number of rooms occupied)

$$\frac{1000 - 750}{750} = 33.33\%$$

What this means is that 33.33% or 1/3 of the rooms occupied; 250 rooms had double occupancy and 66.66% (2/3) of the rooms had single occupancy, 500 rooms.

500 rooms × single occupancy (1)	=	500 guests
250 rooms × double occupancy (2)	=	500 guests
750 rooms		1000 guests

The second measurement of hotel revenue we will discuss is average daily rate, also known as ADR. The average daily rate is computed by dividing room revenue (income) by the number of rooms occupied. This formula is necessary when you sell rooms for more than one rate, which is often the case with most hotels. This is how we measure how well we are maximizing revenue (income) through double occupancy and through the selling of more expensive rooms. If your most expensive rooms are $250 per night and the lowest priced rooms are $100 per night and if average daily rate is barely above $100 per night, you are not maximizing your room revenue. You may be selling your least expensive rooms or not charging for double occupancy rates. This is lost income for the hotel, which will affect your hotel bottom line. A hotel can have high occupancy but a low average daily rate. Both are important in calculating how well your hotel is at selling rooms.

CALCULATING AVERAGE DAILY RATE*

$74,140 (room revenue) / 674 (rooms occupied)
= $110 (ADR)

*Rule of Thumb—In almost all cases, the ADR cannot be less than the minimum accepted room rate or greater than the maximum accepted room rate.

The $110 rate is simply the average price of rooms sold that night. It may very well mean that not a single room sold for $110 that night. In an extreme circumstance, a 900 room hotel may have their one most expensive room selling for $1,000 that night. If that was the only room they sold that night, the average daily rate would be $1,000. That would be impressive except that your occupancy percentage would be less than 1%, which would certainly not be impressive. Hotels want to maximize income potential by selling as many rooms as possible at as high a room rate as the market will allow.

The third and final measurement of hotel income we will discuss is yield management. Occupancy percentage and average daily rate combined are a utilization of yield management attempts to restrict occupancy. You might question why would we want to restrict occupancy? The answer is that we can restrict occupancy by holding out for a higher room rate. For example, due to seasonality, a hotel might change their rates January 1st, April 1st, July 1st, and September 1st. Any potential guest, who makes a reservation from April 1st through June 30th, will be restricted from making a reservation after June 30th, unless they are willing to pay the higher rate. Hotels that fail to adjust rates according to changing conditions will likely lose out in increasing income. It is often easy for anyone to estimate that hotel occupancy may seem high, but only the hotel manager will know if yield management principles were realized in attaining maximizing income for the hotel.

Income in the Restaurant Industry

Income concerns may be even more crucial in the restaurant industry than in the hotel industry because the restaurant business failure rate is very high. Over half of independent restaurants go out of business within the first 3 years of operation. Why do independent restaurants fail at a greater rate than chain restaurants? Independent restaurants cannot purchase in mass volume or afford to spend money on advertising. However, the initial purchase costs are lower for independent restaurants, which is why more try to enter the restaurant business.

There are various means of measuring income revenue. Prime cost is a term restaurants use for food and beverages expenses and payroll. They are referred to as prime costs, because these are your two largest expenses in the restaurant industry. If you cannot control your two largest expenses, smaller expenses that you controlled efficiently may not matter. Most restaurants fail financially because they cannot control their prime costs.

Labor costs, also referred to as payroll cost, consists of salaries and wages and employee benefits. Low labor costs may not be an indicator of efficient management. If, by controlling labor costs you are understaffed, customers will complain about poor service and not return. On the other hand, being overstaffed will likely result in having employees standing around doing very little. A good manager should be upset at seeing employees being paid to do nothing.

The best means for evaluating labor needs is to have a formula to determine how much labor you need based on the number of customers. Peak hours for breakfast may be 6:00 A.M. to 9:00 A.M., for lunch 11:00 A.M. to 2:00 P.M., and for dinner 5:00 P.M. to 9:00 P.M. A restaurant manager would increase staff service during those hours and reduce employee levels in between meals. Restaurants often have to estimate customer levels during different meals. When estimations are incorrect, a restaurant manager can control labor costs by sending some restaurant employees home. Most employees do not like coming into work just to be sent home. But this is a necessary tool in controlling labor costs in the restaurant industry.

Employee benefits are another concern in controlling labor costs. In the 1970s and 1980s it was unheard of for hourly workers in the restaurant industry to receive health benefits. In the 1980s, I was a hotel manager and did not receive health benefits. Today, most full-time hourly workers receive some type of health benefits. If your restaurant offers health benefits and another doesn't, your restaurant may be able to attract better quality workers. In order to control costs and avoid paying health benefits, a manager may choose to hire less full-time workers and more part-time workers.

Food cost includes the cost of food sold, given away, stolen, or wasted. Restaurant managers determine what food they need to purchase by buying food based on their recipes, menu, and customer demand. Recipes also assure that menu items are consistent in taste. Restaurant managers can adjust food costs by being creative about menu items. A leftover broiled chicken can become a chicken salad special tomorrow. Also, restaurant managers can determine the popularity of menu items from POS (point of sale) equipment, which determines the percentage of sales of each particular menu item. However, food can also be wasted by a failure to follow recipes or improper cooking of food. Another concern is employees who remove food from the restaurant. Restaurants that secure food well and have enough managers can lessen food theft. Another factor is employees who serve food to customers and purposely do not charge for the food. Food giveaways may also be accidental from servers who undercharge or forget to collect payment from customers.

Restaurant managers can measure how effective they are by measuring their food cost percentage. Most franchise restaurants will have established desired food cost percentages from the corporate office. Previously discussed concerns such as food given away, stolen, or wasted food, will make it more difficult to attain desired food cost percentage.

FOOD COST PERCENTAGE

Cost of food sold / Food Sales = Food Cost %

$30,000 (cost of food sold) / $100,000 (Food Sales) = 30% (Food Cost)

This formula determined that food cost was 30% of food sales. That means that $70,000 or 70% was profit out of this $100,000. Without the necessary labor, it will be difficult to produce revenue for the restaurant. If you do not manage food purchasing, food waste, food giveaways, and food theft, this will adversely affect the amount of incoming revenue. Controlling food cost will increase your revenue, which will increase your level of success as a restaurant manager.

© 2008, JupiterImages Corporation.

Restaurant managers must concern themselves with discounting when considering the perishability factor of food.

Maximizing Revenue through Selling

Most hotels and restaurants in this competitive environment must determine methods for maximizing revenue and gaining a competitive edge. Among the methods utilized by hotel and restaurant managers are discounting, up-selling, and the top down approach.

Discounting is a method of reducing an item from the regular price. A student might question how does one charge less and make more. Hotel managers must concern themselves with the perishability factor. A hotel room that has a rack rate of $100 returns zero dollars in revenue if the room doesn't sell that night. That is a loss of $100 in income revenue potential for that room. If that hotel room with a rack rate of $100 is discounted to $80, and it sells at $80, that is $80 in additional revenue for the hotel. It is better to get $80 for a hotel room than zero dollars. Each hotel room has a perishability factor of 24 hours or 1 day. For example if you do not sell Room 100 on December 30th, you can never sell that same product again for that time period. Yes, you can sell the same room the next day, but you can never sell Room 100 on December 30th after that date. It should be noted that hotel managers must set a specific amount to which they may discount no further. If a hotel room regularly sells for $100, there is a price that would be so low they would actually lose money from renting that room. Also, if a hotel attracts a certain clientele, severe discounting may attract a different type of clientele. Regular hotel guests may decide to stay elsewhere in the future.

Restaurant managers must concern themselves with discounting when considering the perishability factor of food. Food has a limited shelf life and must be used when it's fresh or must be discarded. Restaurants must develop methods of discounting menu items to encourage customers to purchase these items. Often customers walk into a restaurant not knowing what to order. Customers like to order a special menu item because they think they are getting a bargain. Instead of reducing the price of a menu item, they may charge the regular price but give a free dessert with the meal. Therefore, the discount is not with the meal, but with a free dessert. Discounting is used more often at lower priced restaurants and less at fine dining restaurants.

Up-selling is a technique that is used to get the consumer to purchase items that are more expensive. Quite often, it is simply a reminder question "For only $20 more, you can be upgraded to a pool-side room?" Up-selling is not selling more items; it is selling the same amount of items at a higher price per item. More profitable hotel rooms up-sell their most expensive rooms. Restaurants most profitable menu items are often the most expensive items with largest profit margin. So up-selling is in the best interest of the hotel or the restaurant.

In selling a hotel room, prospective customers come to a hotel or make a reservation by internet or phone. Your first priority is to sell rooms. Your next objective should be to maximize income by selling the features of the more expensive rooms. For example, in a more expensive hotel, rooms may be more deluxe or have a desirable location. This up-selling technique, if used effectively, should help to increase your ADR, which in turn maximizes revenue.

In restaurants, up-selling can be used for customers who are unsure of what they wish to order. An effective means is to recommend one of the more expensive items or purchasing in larger quantities to the customer. Fast food restaurants have done this in the past by asking customers if they wish to "Super Size" their order.

The top down approach is a method of attempting to sell the most expensive item first and then offering a less expensive item next, etc. In the restaurant industry, the top down approach is similar to up-selling and would consist of the restaurant server recommending items that are more expensive. They can further reinforce these recommendations by informing the customer, "This is my personal favorite" or "This is the chef's specialty."

Up-selling to a pool-side room will increase ADR and maximize revenue.

This increased check average and greater tips will likely lead to more satisfied servers. As a result, this will benefit the restaurant by reducing employee turnover, which, in turn, will maximize revenue by reducing employee recruitment costs. Discounting, up-selling, and the top down approach can all be effective tools in maximizing revenue in the hospitality industry.

Controlling Costs in the Hotel Industry

Cost control in the hotel industry is an important component in maximizing profits. Without proper cost control procedures, a hotel may appear to be successful financially in terms of room sales, but miss out on controlling expenses. Two means of controlling expenses are in the area of energy management and labor costs. Energy management in a hotel deals with heat, air conditioning, water usage, electric usage, and gas usage. Hotels can control heat and air conditioning by regulating minimum and maximum temperatures in individual guest rooms. Water usage can be regulated by use of low flow toilets and showerheads, which dispense less water. Also, sprinkler systems can be shut off outside when it is raining. Using lower wattage bulbs in guest rooms can control electric usage. Regulating temperatures based on changing weather conditions can control gas usage. If it is 60 degrees on a winter day in a cold climate, the heat can be lowered. Being aware of changing conditions can help to regulate energy costs.

Labor costs in the hotel industry are different than controlling labor costs in the restaurant industry. Hotels have less specific peak periods during a day, unlike restaurants, which have meal periods. Labor costs are more likely to be controlled by seasonality over long periods of time. If a hotel is operating at 90% occupancy during the summer and 50% occupancy during the winter, staffing should be adjusted accordingly. In a hotel that has low occupancy during a particular period, they can reduce the number of guest service agents at the front desk. Guest service agents can also handle reservations, reducing reservations staff. Housekeeping can be reduced by fewer full-time housekeepers and more part-time housekeepers.

Controlling Costs in the Restaurant Industry

Controlling food costs, as discussed earlier, is essential in the success of your restaurant. One means of controlling food costs is through volume purchasing. Restaurants can save money per pound or unit by purchasing in bulk. The supplier is willing to reduce the price so that they can keep repeat business. An astute steward (purchasing agent) should know, based on sales projections, how much food needs to be purchased. For example, a restaurant sells an average of 380 hamburgers a week and each hamburger is four ounces (380 hamburgers times 4 ounces equals 1,520 ounces); (1,520 ounces divided by 16 ounces in a pound equal 95 pounds of hamburger meat). So for the restaurant steward purchasing 100 pounds of hamburger meat would be a good amount to buy. You should always purchase slightly more than you need. As we talked about before, food is sometimes wasted, given away, or stolen. You do not want to cut it so close for the restaurant that you run out of supplies. Few things look as unprofessional as a restaurant that runs out of food.

Two additional concerns about volume purchasing are the perishability factor and the storage factor. While a restaurant may save money from volume, purchasing it must concern itself with the perishability factor. Saving money on purchasing volume will be offset if the food spoils and has to be discarded. A volume purchase for dry goods, canned goods, and frozen foods makes more sense because there is little or no concern about perishability of those food items. The second concern is storage since your volume purchasing will be limited by the size of your storage area. Larger restaurants with larger storage areas can be more profitable than smaller restaurants with smaller storage areas. Larger restaurants may sell the same exact item for the same price as a smaller restaurant, but the profit will be greater for the large restaurant due to volume purchasing.

Portion control is a very necessary component of cost control in the restaurant industry. If a restaurant does not use portion control, they will never know exactly how much profit margin they are making on each item. Portion control is not just about profit margins, it is also about uniformity. If you don't use portion controls individual menu items may look or taste different each time.

Two means of measuring portion control are as purchased (AP) and edible portion (EP). In the case of meat, such as sirloin steak, AP would mean what the steaks weighed when purchased. This is before waste of fat and bones are removed. The more the meat is cooked, the more it shrinks. The weight of the meat after waste is removed and it is cooked is known as EP, edible portion. If a recipe calls for 50 pounds of sirloin EP, you would need to know the yield factor before you decide how much to buy.

YIELD FACTOR

50 lbs / .72 yield percentage = 69.44 (quantity)
Quantity = 69.44 lbs rounded up to 70 lbs.

If we know the sirloin has a yield percentage of 72% or 28% waste, we would know based on this formula to purchase 70 pounds of sirloin steak AP to yield 50 pounds of sirloin steak EP.

These methods of cost control in the restaurant industry, volume purchasing, portion control, as purchased (AP), edible portion (EP), yield percentage, and costing are essential tools of a restaurant manager concerned with cost control.

Careers in Revenue and Cost Control in the Hospitality Industry

A majority of management and supervisory positions in the hotel and restaurant management industry involve revenue and cost control. We will explore the hotel positions first, then the restaurant industry.

Table 10.1 Key Hotel Management Positions in Revenue and Cost Control

TITLE	DEPARTMENT	REVENUE AND COST CONTROL DESCRIPTION	ADVANCEMENT OPPORTUNITIES
Executive Housekeeper	Housekeeping	In charge of all renovation and purchasing housekeeping supplies	Supervisor of more than one operation or corporate position
Catering Manager	Food and Beverage	Purchases and supervises the receipt and storage of food and beverage for the hotel	Director of Food and Beverage
Director of Food and Beverage	Food and Beverage	Oversees entire food and beverage operation	General Manager
Director of Sales	Sales	Sells convention facilities for meetings, banquets, and receptions; sells rooms to volume purchasers such as corporate travel directors of large companies	Resident Manager
Resident Manager	Administration	Takes over for manager in his or her absence; usually handles duties assigned by the manager	General Manager
General Manager	Administration	Supervises all activities with the hotel; responsible for the coordination of all departments	Managing Director
Food and Beverage Controller	Accounting	Controls food and costs through menu planning and pricing, purchasing decisions, storage issues	Assistant Controller

(continued)

Table 10.1 **Key Hotel Management Positions in Revenue and Cost Control** *(continued)*

TITLE	DEPARTMENT	REVENUE AND COST CONTROL DESCRIPTION	ADVANCEMENT OPPORTUNITY
Credit Manager	Accounting	Oversees accounts receivables from time of extension of credit until cash is collected	Assistant Controller
Assistant Controller	Accounting	Functions as office manager with responsibility for preparation of financial statements	Controller
Controller	Accounting	Acts as financial advisor to management in achieving profit objectives through detailed planning controlling costs and effectively managing hotel assets and liabilities	Area or Regional Controller

Table 10.2 **Key Restaurant Management Positions in Revenue and Cost Control**

TITLE	DEPARTMENT	DESCRIPTION	ADVANCEMENT OPPORTUNITY
Beverage Manager	Beverages	Orders for and stocks bar; maintains inventories of liquor and glassware	Food Production Manager
Cook or Sous Chef	Kitchen	Prepares and portions out all food served	Executive Chef
Executive Chef	Kitchen	Responsible for all quantity and quality food preparation supervision of sous chefs and cooks and menu recipe development	Assistant Manager
Purchasing Agent	Management	Orders receives inspects and stores all goods shipped by suppliers	Assistant Manager
Assistant Manager	Management	Performs specified supervisory duties under the managers' direction	Food Service Manager
Food Service Manager	Management	Responsible for profitability, efficiency, and quality of the entire food service operations	Multi Unit Regional Manager
Personnel Director	Management	Responsible for hiring and training of food service personnel and benefits	Regional Personnel Manager

Summary

In this chapter, we learned about income and cost control in the hospitality industry. Hotel and restaurant managers must utilize revenue and cost control in order to survive. In discussing revenue in the hotel, we learned about occupancy percentages, ADR, and yield management. In the restaurant industry, we learned about the prime costs of labor and food costs. In order to maximize revenue, we discussed selling through methods like discounting, up-selling, and top down. In our discussion on cost control, we learned about energy management and labor cost. For the restaurant industry, we also learned about controlling food costs through volume purchasing and portion control. Finally, we discussed the many rewarding and challenging opportunities in hospitality and tourism industry in revenue and cost control.

≈ *Resources*

Internet Sites

A Directory of Knowledge Manjagement Web Sites: www.knowledge-manager.com

American Hotel & Lodging Association (AH&LA): www.ahla.com click information center

A–Z topics/Business and Financial Management/Running your own business: www.restaurant.org/business/topics_financial.cfm

Council of Hotel, Restaurant & Institutional Educators (CHRIE) (Affiliation of hotel and restaurant educators): www.chrie.org

Financial Information Advertising: www.restaurant&results.org

Financial Management HQ—Financial Management: www.financialmanagementhq.com

Gecko Hospitality (Hospitality Financial): www.geckohospitality.web.aplus.net

Hospitality Careers: www.hcarres.net

Hospitality and Food Service Management: www.cccd.edu/hospitality/resources.htm

Hospitality Financial and Technology Professionals (HFTP): www.hftp.org

Hospitality net—in-depth decision support—Revenue Management: www.hospitalitynet.org

Hotel Resource: Hotel and hospitality industry resource: www.hotelresource.com

Hotel real estate: www.lodgingeconometrics.com

Microsystem Inc.—Fidelio—property management point of sale: www.micros.com

Profitable Hospitality: Resources and solutions for restaurants and hotels: www.profitablehospitality.com/links/index.htm

Restaurant Report: Top 50 food and hospitality industry web sites: www.restaurantreport.com/top100/index.htm

≈ *Endnotes*

Chatfield, R. and Dalbor, M. (2005). *Hospitality Financial Management*, Upper Saddle River, NJ: Prentice Hall, 10.

Council on Hotel, Restaurant and Institutional Education. (1993). *A Guide to College Programs in Hospitality and Tourism*, 3rd ed. New York: John J. Wiley & Sons, 13–14.

Dittmer, P. R. (2003). *Principles of Food, Beverage, and Labor cost controls*, 7th ed. New York: John J. Wiley & Sons, 9, 12, 549.

Vallen, G. K. and Vallen, J. J. (2005). *Check-In Check-Out, Managing Hotel Operations*. Upper Saddle River, NJ: Prentice Hall, 609.

≈ *Contributor*

Daniel Bernstein

Seton Hill University, Division of Social Sciences

Seton Hill Drive, Greensburg, PA 15601-1599

Email: Bernstein@setonhill.edu

Daniel Bernstein is currently in his fourth year as Program Director and Associate Professor of Hospitality Management at Seton Hill University. Daniel has over 15 years of teaching experience and holds the following degrees: EdD in Educational Administration from the University of South Dakota, MBA in Hospitality Industry from the University of New Haven, and a BA in English from Adelphi University. He has previous hospitality management experience as a restaurant owner, restaurant manager, hotel manager, hotel marketing director, hotel front desk manager, and as a consultant in the hotel and restaurant industry.

Chapter 10
Review Questions

1. An occupancy percentage measures the ratio of what two factors in determining the answer?

2. Why do hotels want to determine the difference between rooms occupied and double occupancy?

3. What is another term used in the industry for rooms?

4. How can a hotel have a high occupancy percentage and a low ADR (Average Daily Rate)?

5. What is the "Rule of Thumb" in determining if your ADR calculation is accurate?

6. How can controlling room rates and restricting occupancy be effective tools in yield management?

7. Why do you think the failure rate is higher for independent restaurants than franchise restaurants?

8. Why do more restaurants fail than hotels?

9. What are the two factors that make up prime cost in the restaurant industry?

10. How has labor cost changed over the last 20 years in relation to health benefits?

11. Why should restaurant managers not staff at the same levels throughout the day?

12. Name three methods of food cost incurred in which potential revenue is lost.

13. Hotels that are considered business hotels would likely discount their rates during what part of the week?

14. In up-selling a particular item in the hospitality industry, the seller must emphasize this characteristic of what they are selling?

15. The top down approach attempts to sell what priced hotel rooms first?

16. Name three areas within the hotel where effective energy management principles could be utilized to reduce energy costs.

17. Name the statistics in the hotel industry that may cause labor costs to vary.

18. Why would it not be cost effective to purchase food for a restaurant from a supermarket?

19. What are the incentives for restaurants to purchase larger quantities of various food items?

20. Why is the perishability factor important in the hotel industry?

21. Why should restaurants use portion control as a means of controlling costs?

22. What are three factors that reduces meat from AP form to EP?

23. Why is service an intangible?

24. Why is it important for hospitality managers to be able to visualize intangibles?

25. What are the job description responsibilities of a cook or sous chef?

Physical Plant Management

11

Robert A. McMullin, East Stroudsburg University

≈ Learning Objectives

- ☑ To be introduced to the importance of the physical plant
- ☑ To understand the value of curb appeal
- ☑ To understand the importance of communication between hospitality managers and independent contractors and corporate and property facility personnel with regards to property repairs will be covered
- ☑ To be exposed to human resources issues of the facilities department
- ☑ To understand the financial relationship between repairs and cost will be explored
- ☑ To be introduced to engineering systems, types of maintenance repairs, security, and the Americans with Disabilities Act
- ☑ To be able to develop the need and importance of facilities management and the relationship to guest satisfaction

≈ Chapter Outline

Manager Roles and Responsibilities
Engineering Systems
Maintenance
Security
Americans with Disabilities Act

≈ Key Terms

Alternating current (AC)
Americans with Disabilities Act (ADA)
Amperes
Capital projects
Contract maintenance
Curb appeal
Engineering systems
Furnishings, fixtures and equipment (FF&E)
Guestroom maintenance
Heating, ventilation and air conditioning (HVAC)
Life cycle costing
Property operation and maintenance (POM)
Refrigerant
Routine maintenance
Preventive maintenance (PM)

The hospitality industry and education places great emphasis on service, marketing, and profitability to be competitive. However, one salient facet of the industry that is often overlooked is the "curb appeal" or attractiveness of the physical operations. Potential guests like to see a picture of the facility before they make a decision and the traveling public can be fickle in choosing to patronize a hospitality entity. Quite often, they judge the quality of the potential experience based on what they think of the visual appeal. Along with the physical attractiveness of the facilities, physical operations can enhance guest satisfaction. How clean and well kept the property is also reflects on the perception of the guest. Therefore, learning and understanding the physical plant operations are imperative for hospitality management. The maintenance and design of a good working property can affect the service you deliver, or how your facility is marketed, ultimately having a great impact on profitability.

Primarily, the physical plant is comprised of landscaping, grounds, exterior and interior building structure, building systems, furnishings, fixtures, and equipment (FF&E). Landscaping and exterior appeal sets the tone of attractiveness of a hospitality facility. Many hospitality organizations spend great sums in marketing guests, but the greatest hook is visual appearance. Hospitality properties should have clean, bright, and well-lit signage to allure travelers along with attractive landscaping.

However, other elements of the physical plant that are experienced by guests include plumbing, electricity, heating, ventilation, and air conditioning (HVAC). Managers of hospitality properties need knowledge and experience in understanding the effects of the physical plant and the actual outcomes to guests if equipment fails. In addition, management needs to be able to communicate with contractors, maintenance, and/or engineering staff to effect proper repairs without jeopardizing the guests' stay.

Manager Roles and Responsibilities

The scope and depth of the knowledge a facility manager must have depends on the type of property and size. Budget and economy lodging operations have relatively small and simple physical plants, whereas convention, resort, and luxury properties may resemble small cities. Other hospitality enterprises like restaurants and country clubs may rely on the property's general manager's communications with independent contractors or corporate personnel to repair their facility. Therefore, depending on the facility, there are many different backgrounds a physical plant manager must have.

The role and responsibilities of the hospitality facility manager or maintenance engineer typically includes detailed knowledge about the following areas:

1. Systems and building design
2. Building and system operations
3. Guestroom furnishings and fixtures maintenance
4. Equipment maintenance and repair
5. Equipment selection and installation
6. Contract management
7. Utilities management
8. Waste management
9. Budget and cost control
10. Security and safety
11. Contractual and regulatory compliance
12. Parts inventory and control
13. Renovations, additions and restorations
14. Staff training
15. Emergency planning and response

The aforementioned responsibilities present challenges for many hospitality facilities managers or maintenance engineers. Each skill level varies depending on work experience and background. For example the facilities manager may have to work with various contractors when the property decides to renovate or restore its facility.

In many hospitality situations, the facilities manager will have some detailed technical background from contracting firms, trade or technical schools, or other similar related employment. Although a technical background in plumbing, electrical, or HVAC equipment is good, they may have little conceptual knowledge of the hospitality industry. This can create problems with communication as the different hospitality departments attempt to communicate their problems and facilities managers try to understand so that they can fix the problems. In some cases, it feels like each department is speaking a different language, and in some ways they are. This can place an additional burden on the management staff and lodging property because the facility management needs to work closely with the executive housekeeper, front office manager, and food and beverage manager. Bridging the communication gap is an important task for the general manager of a property because the property can lose its attractiveness.

In addition to working closely with other departments, the facilities manager must understand the financial relationship between maintenance, repair, and cost. For example, the facility manager needs to track energy costs while trying to find ways to decrease this expenditure. This position requires the need to analyze records, such as work orders, equipment data cards, equipment history records, architectural plans, and instruction and/or repair records. The facility manager needs to evaluate the cost of a repair while remaining committed to bring costs within a budget. In accounting terms, the actions of the facility manager is reported on the line item of the income statement called property operations and maintenance (POM). The challenge for the facility manager is to improve the quality of the physical plant while using minimal financial resources. Meanwhile the facility manager has to study the relationship of how equipment is used and consumption of energy usage from utility bills like electric, gas, and water. Therefore, the facility manager must work closely with the property controller, too. If the facility manager can maintain the same level of property efficiency while finding ways to reduce costs, this would have a positive effect on the hospitality property's financial statements. In addition, a clean, well-kept property is more attractive to potential guests, and there will be fewer problems. As a result, it will improve guest satisfaction.

Another significant financial responsibility of the facility manager is the evaluation of capital projects. These projects require a major cash outlay when either replacing or acquiring new equipment. The facilities manager along with other key hospitality management must judge the initial cost, durability, safety, and energy consumption of capital equipment. There are other accounting concerns like depreciation and tax implications. The process of judging the selecting and analysis of capital projects are called life cycle costing, which considers the following:

- Initial costs—for example, cost of the item itself including costs of installation, interconnection, and modification of supporting systems or equipment.
- Operating costs—for example, costs of energy or water to operate the equipment and supporting systems or those systems affected by the equipment; maintenance labor and supplies or contract maintenance services.
- Fixed costs—for example, insurance, depreciation, and/or property tax changes resulting from the equipment or system.
- Tax implication—for example, income taxes and tax credits such as investment, tax credits, and depreciation deductions.[1]

Engineering Systems

Management in the hospitality industry needs to understand the basic design and operations of the various engineering systems. This improves the communication between the facility manager and the rest of management. Having direct daily communication is imperative to relay any information on malfunctioning equipment so it can be repaired, while not disturbing the patrons or interrupting other management in completing their own tasks. The basic elements of the engineering systems include several areas.

Management should know the basic operations of water and wastewater systems, refrigeration systems, heating, ventilation and air-conditioning systems, or site power production, and safety and security systems, so he/she can intelligently explain what needs to be accomplished by the facilities management team.

Water and Wastewater Systems

Water supply is necessary for food and beverage and lodging establishments. Management should be familiar with the operation of backflow devices, which prevent water from re-entering a building. Other relevant systems include a storm sewer system for the disposal of rainwater and a sanitary sewer system for the removal of waste products. Another key system for restaurants is a grease separation or grease trap. Grease needs to be separated from wastewater to prevent water backup.

Refrigeration Systems

Hospitality managers should be knowledgeable about refrigeration systems. In the compressive refrigeration system, undesired heat is picked up in one place and carried to another place, where it is dumped or disposed. In many lodging establishments individual heating and air conditioning units are in each room. These are self-contained units that need to be maintained on a regular basis for guest comfort. Heat pumps work on a similar process except the unit is outside the room. This is a favorable way of heating and cooling for residential properties. The major components of the refrigeration cycle are:

1. Refrigerant, which is a fluid with a low boiling point that starts as a liquid, absorbs heat, and becomes a gas, and then is placed under pressure to become a liquid again.
2. The evaporation is the section of the circuit in which the refrigerant evaporates or boils to soak up heat.
3. An expansion value allows the refrigerant to soak up heat, allowing pressure to be lowered aiding the refrigeration cycle.
4. A compressor is a pump supplying the power to move the refrigerant through the system.[2]

Heating, Venting, and Air Conditioning Systems

Heating, ventilation, and air-conditioning (HVAC) systems provide levels of comfort based on heating, cooling, and humidity for guests, staff, and management. The key components of an HVAC system is pipes (hollow cylinder or tubular conveyance for a fluid or gas), ducts (any tubular passage through which a substance especially a fluid is conveyed), pumps (a machine or device for transferring a liquid or gas from a source or container through tubes or pipes to another container or receiver), thermostats (converts the temperature into a signal that is sent to the HVAC unit conditioning the space), and valves (devices that regulate the flow of gases, liquids, or loose materials through structures, such as piping or through apertures by opening, closing, or obstructing parts of passageways). Systems can be decentralized and operate as individual units or be centralized as one system working collectively.

Electrical Systems

Some hospitality properties operate an on-site power production, but most operations have electricity delivered by local utilities. In either case you should have a familiarity of electrical systems because you may experience brownouts (partial loss of electricity) or blackouts (total loss of electricity) that could disrupt your electrical service. Furthermore, management needs to understand electrical utility rates for cost control. Why should I be familiar with this? The utility is responsible for providing power at a correct voltage and frequency. The utility provides power through an electric meter that measures the rate and amount of power consumed, which generates the electric bill. The measure of the use of electrical energy is the watt. Amperes measure the rate of electrical flow through a device or appliance. The volt is the unit of electrical potential. Heating, ventilation and air conditioning (HVAC) systems should provide suitable temperature and humidity levels for guests, staff, and management. The HVAC system is an infrastructure of pipes, ducts, pumps, thermostats, valves, and pressure sensors. These systems can be decentralized and operated as individual units, or centralized as one system working collectively. Hospitality industry properties are supplied with alternating current (AC) from the local electric utility. If you do not have sufficient current your property may experience lights flickering or reduced illumination. Why do I need to know this? The goal of the facilities manager is to provide a suitable level of guest comfort but reduce electrical use.

Safety and Security Systems

Safety and security systems are another key responsibility of management. The entire management staff should be committed to a safe and secure environment in protecting guests, staff, and management. This can be accomplished by communicating safety and security needs at management staff meetings. There are far-reaching issues in the time, training, and financial investment of safety and security systems. One of the major concerns in this area is protecting people and assets. Guests should be made aware of their surroundings and encouraged to use all protective devices a room has installed. Most hospitality lodging establishments have two or three locks in each door. Guests should be informed that all should be used along with a door port viewer to prevent room invasions by potential criminals. Guests should be informed never to open doors to strangers and always contact the front office with any concerns.

Negligence in this area could result in legal situations. Hospitality management should know the operations of fire protection equipment, including detection, notification, suppression, and smoke control systems. In knowing these procedures, hospitality employees can aid in the deterrence of fire emergencies. Another key is security systems such as electronic lock systems, closed-circuit television, elevator controls, and exit alarms. These procedures aid in protecting the guests from unwanted intruders and safely evacuating the guests if an emergency arises. Procedures should be developed in case of emergencies. Each hospitality property should have plans for terrorists' acts, bomb scares, robberies, and extreme weather situations such as blizzards, hurricanes, tornadoes, and floods.

Maintenance

Regular Maintenance

Hospitality buildings are heavily used 24 hours of every day, seven days a week by guests, staff, and management. Each facility should have budgeted funds to reinvest in their property. Equipment will wear down, break down, and become obsolete. Management should have a tier plan to keep the property running efficiently.

- Routine maintenance is the general everyday duties of the facility staff, which requires relatively minimal skills or training. Examples of these duties include picking up litter, emptying trash cans, raking leaves, and shoveling snow.
- Preventive maintenance, sometimes referred to as PM, requires more advanced skills of the facility personnel. Examples of PM include inspections, lubrication, minor repairs or adjustments, and work order investigation.
- Guestroom maintenance is an activity applied to guestrooms of a lodging establishment. This is a form of prevention in ensuring guest comfort. Usually trained facilities personnel will remove several rooms a day from the rooms inventory and inspect them for the following:
  1. changing of filters in HVAC systems
  2. Test operation of TVs, electronic equipment, plumbing, and electrical equipment
  3. Ensure the guestroom is free of any maintenance issues.[3]

When a facilities manager plans, he/she must take into consideration scheduling regular maintenance, which requires advanced planning, significant amount of time to perform, specialized tools and equipment, and coordination of the departments affected. Each task should be assigned as part of each employee's schedule every day so that it does not get lost or forgotten when problems occur.

Funds must be budgeted for reinvestment because equipment wears down, breaks down and becomes obsolete.

Emergency Maintenance

Emergency and breakdown maintenance occurs when equipment fails based an unforeseen occurrence like flooding or thunderstorms. Hospitality properties cannot prevent equipment breakdown, but they can use preventative maintenance procedures to possibly keep breakdowns from occurring. Having contingency plans can aid when breakdown occurs. For example, when there is a power failure, backup electrical generators can keep the guests calm so that they can get to safety. Especially the day of a big banquet, the kitchen staff does not want to find out the refrigeration unit died, and everything is slowly defrosting without a backup refrigeration unit available. Or during a heat wave, guests and staff will not appreciate the facilities staff if there are no additional air-conditioning units when one fails. Therefore planning for common emergencies is necessary. With natural disasters like hurricanes, flooding, and snow, one cannot plan every detail. However, a disaster plan should be developed to prepare as carefully as possible. Many hotels and convention centers have been rethinking their disaster plans as the year of 2005 brought problems to all parts of the country. It is now becoming a major part of planning for all hospitality organizations.

Contract maintenance is necessary for certain equipment needs when repair and the skill level is beyond your facility staff. Some can be on retainer where they promise to handle emergencies as they happen for an annual fee, such as repair of refrigeration units where a repairman must come out. Cases for this type of contract might be washers and dryers for housekeeping or computer systems. Others contract for specific visits on a routine basis such as pest control. Some contractual arrangements can be available to assist in emergency or breakdown situations.

Security

Generally in the lodging industry we welcome guests to our properties and have them lower their guard, relax, and feel at home. However, it is not always possible to know when a person is a welcome guest or a pretender. Without security measures, strangers could go up the elevators and break into rooms or worse. Yet lodging facilities are a public building, and so guests need to be aware of safety measures as well. Many establishments provide "Traveler Safety Tips" on check-in or in the room.

However, in addition to the customer's awareness, equipment can be in place to increase security. For example, guestrooms should be equipped with phones to enable guests to place emergency phone calls. Many hotels put phones by the elevators or in hallways to make sure a guest can have access. The facilities staff should install guestroom doors that self-close and lock automatically. Doors should be equipped with deadbolts, view ports, security chains, or bars. Guestroom windows and sliding glass doors should be able to lock. Windows and sliding doors should only be able to open, but not wide enough for an intruder to enter. In many cases, a simple bar that fits into the floor track of the sliding glass doors ensures safety.

Guests should be encouraged to use in-room safes or safety boxes available at the front desk. This provides an extra level of security for guest valuables.

All lodging facilities should have a key control system for both manual and electronic keys. When keys are lost, stolen, or not returned the lock system should be evaluated. One approach to key control is referred to as the "five Rs."[4]

- Rationale—Criteria used to develop the keying schedule and to identify who will have various levels of access.
- Records—Involves guest information with regard to occupancy, status, and access.
- Retrieval—Actions by staff to recover keys from employees and guests.
- Rotation—Involves moving locks from room to room as a preventative security plan.

- Replacement—As keys are lost or locks compromised, replacement is necessary.

Historically older lodging properties with manual locks need to follow the aforementioned program. Even electronic locks have been comprised, which means the system should be evaluated from time to time.

Hospitality management and facility staff should work together to provide the highest means of safety and security to the guest and their own staff. This provides a safe environment for all.

Americans with Disabilities Act

An important consideration in the hospitality industry is the Americans with Disabilities Act (ADA) of 1990. This act spells out reasonable accommodations to make for people with disabilities. Most people think that the ADA is only for people with physical handicaps or sensory impairments. However, think about which other people could use some help. How about, your grandmother who is fine, but a ramp instead of steps would make it easier for her to gain entry into a building or a railing by the bathtub would make it easier to get out. Or, you break your leg and have a cast, wouldn't it be easier to use some of the wheelchair equipment? So this act requires a percentage of rooms to have special equipment, but many people have special circumstances when an ADA room would be appropriate.

© 2008, JupiterImages Corporation.

Electronic lock systems protect guests.

With vans that are equipped to allow wheelchair entry, wider parking spaces are needed to accommodate someone exiting from the side of the van. For people with hearing and visual impairment, this act covers emergency situations like visual and audible alarms like strobe lights. Additionally, many believe that complying with ADA standards is very expensive. However, many accommodations have simple inexpensive alternatives. Do you have two or three stairs but no ramp? Use a temporary metal ramp that can be folded and stored nearby and then put in place for the occasion. Some hospitality facilities will hire consultants to evaluate their facility to ensure their compliance with ADA laws.

Summary

The facilities staff is a critical department of a hospitality enterprise. The way the property looks, how it works, and the comfort of the guest is critical. Many of these factors will ensure repeat business and guest satisfaction. If measures are not taken to ensure guest comfort and safety, you may find yourself in financial and legal problems.

≈ *Resources*

Internet Sites

PM Engineer: www.pmengineer.com
International Facilities Management Assoc.: www.Ifma.com
FM Data: www.fmdata.com
Buildings Magazine: www.buildings.com
Burnham Boilers: www.burnham.com
American Solar Energy Society: www.ases.org
Green Globe 21: www.greenglobe21.com
National Fire Protection Association: www.nfpa.org
Water Web: www.waterweb.org
Water Online: www.wateronline.com
Electric Power Research Institute: www.epri.com
Air Conditioning and Refrigeration Institute: www.ari.org
Laundry Today: www.laundrytoday.com
Associated Landscape Contractors of America: www.alca.org
National Gardening Association: www.garden.org
American Institute of Architects: www.aia.org

Suggested Readings

American Hotel & Lodging Association (Producer). (1995). *Curb Appeal: Creating Great First Impressions* (Videotape). Available from the American Hotel & Lodging Association, P.O. Box 1240, 1407 S. Harrison Road, East Lansing, MI 48826-1240.

Borsenik, F. D., & Stutts, A. D. (1991). *The Management of Maintenance and Engineering Systems in the Hospitality Industry* (3rd ed.). New York: John Wiley & Sons.

Palmer, J. D. (1990). *Principles of Hospitality Engineering.* New York: Van Nostrand Reinhold.

Stipanuk, D. M. (2002). *Hospitality Facilities Management and Design* (2nd ed.). East Lansing, MI: Education Institute of the American Hotel and Lodging Association.

Usiewicz, R. A. (2004). Physical Plant Management and Security. In R. A. Brymer (ed.), *Hospitality & Tourism, An Introduction to the Industry* (11th ed., pp. 147–156). Dubuque, IA: Kendall/Hunt Publishing Company.

≈ *Endnotes*

1. Usiewicz, Ronald A., "Physical Plant Management and Security." (2004). In *Hospitality Tourism,* edited by Robert A. Brymer, 148–149. Dubuque, IA: Kendall/Hunt Publishing.
2. Stipanuk, David D., *Hospitality Facilities Management and Design,* 2nd ed. (2002). East Lansing, MI: Educational Institute of the American Hotel, Lodging Association, p. 231.
3. Ibid., p. 32.
4. Ibid., pp. 152–156.

≈ *Contributor*

rmcmullin@po-box.esu.edu

Dr. Robert A. McMullin, CHE, teaches hotel operations classes at East Stroudsburg University of Pennsylvania. Professor of Hotel, Restaurant & Tourism Management, East Stroudsburg University of Pennsylvania.

Chapter 11
Review Questions

1. Why is maintaining your hospitality facility so important?

2. What comprises the physical plant?

3. What is curb appeal? Discuss why this affects your properties image.

4. What are the responsibilities of the physical plant manager or maintenance engineer?

5. What is the relationship between the general manager and maintenance engineer with regard to the physical property?

6. What is the financial relationship between repair, guest satisfaction, and cost?

7. Name and discuss the engineering systems.

8. Name and define the three types of maintenance.

9. What is life cycle costing? Why is it important?

10. Why is security so important to a hospitality facility?

11. What is the importance of the Americans with Disabilities Act?

Part 3

Hospitality Business Structures

Entrepreneurship 12

Dan Crafts, Missouri State University

© Karin Lau, 2008, Shutterstock.

≈ Learning Objectives

☑ Explain entrepreneurship and its roles and contributions to the economic life of the hospitality and tourism industry

☑ To determine if you are ready to be an entrepreneur

☑ Describe entrepreneurial skills that will contribute to the hospitality entrepreneur's success

☑ Describe the techniques for assessing and developing opportunities in the hospitality and tourism industry

☑ Discuss how entrepreneurs generate and assess ideas for entrepreneurship in the hospitality industry

☑ Investigate the required resources and sources that may be used to evaluate and plan an entrepreneurial venture in the hospitality and tourism industry

☑ To review the development process for a venture plan for a hospitality and tourism business

☑ Explore career choices for entrepreneurship in the hospitality and tourism industry

≈ Chapter Outline

Characteristics of an Entrepreneur
The Entrepreneurial Process

≈ Key Terms

Adjusted gross income
Angel investor
Breakeven
Business plan
Cash flow
E-Generation
Entrepreneur
Entrepreneurial team
ESOP
Fixed expenses
Gross profit

Harvest the business
Independent business owner
IPO
Market share
Opportunity
Organization chart
Resources
Return on investment
Revenue forecast
SBA—Small Business Administration
SBIC—Small Business Investment Companies
Strategies
Third party liquor liability
Trend
U.S. Small Business Administration
Variable expense
Venture capitalist

Over the past two decades, the United States has seen an increase in entrepreneurial ventures that has set the standard for how business will be conducted for the new century and beyond. This new generation is often called the **E-Generation** not because they were raised on electronics, but because they are the equity generation. They are building their wealth through the development of their own businesses. If the sales of the top 16 entrepreneurial companies over the last 10 years were combined, they would be as large as the 10th largest country in the world.[1]

In 1970, the **U.S. Small Business Administration** reported that only 200,000 new companies had been created compared to today's 3.5 million new start ups of all kinds of businesses. In 1970, women were limited to small home operated businesses and typically employed less than one million people nationwide—representing less than 5 percent of all businesses. Today women represent almost 50 percent of all business owners and employee well over 20 million people.[2] You can read in newspapers and magazines about how women and minorities are starting and or reinventing businesses into very large multi-million dollar ventures.

Characteristics of an Entrepreneur

Entrepreneurs are willing to take action, to pursue opportunities that others typically view as too risky, nothing but problems and threats. These individuals exhibit behavior that is dynamic, risky, creative, and, definitely, growth oriented. The entrepreneur is willing to put part of their compensation at risk in return for the right to pursue entrepreneurial ideas and see their equity grow. The sky is the limit in terms of what the entrepreneur expects to achieve with the growth of their company and their return on investment. This requires that the entrepreneurs expand their business on a regular basis. An example of a successful hospitality entrepreneurial company would be Starbucks. The coffee company started small but grew to be quite a large operation with premium coffees, pastries, etc.

There are smaller entrepreneurial operations that are sometimes referred to as **independent owners**. A primary distinction of the independent company owners, such as the local coffee shop, prefers to operate with a more limited scope than Starbucks. They have purposefully decided on a smaller scale of operation. The local coffee shop owners will stay with the approach that has made them successful as an independent. Surely, the independent wants to see their business grow. However, same store sales growth might be more to their liking rather than seeing their company grow into a giant franchise machine with hundreds of outlets. It should be noted that even though a business owner has purposefully opted for a smaller scale operation many of the independent operators have a favorable outlook on larger companies. Lee Cohen, co-owner of the independent coffee house The Daily Grind stated, "I don't resent Starbucks, I learn from them." John Moorby, owner of the independent coffee house Uncommon Grounds stated, "I have a positive outlook on Starbucks. They are educating the public on what good coffee can be."[3]

Whether a business person is an entrepreneur whose company has experienced significant growth or an independent business owner working to manage a narrowly defined scope of business, they actually have more things in common than features that separate them. First, a lot of people who are working 40 hours a week already feel like they are maxed out. This is especially true for the almost 70 percent of U.S. workers who do not like their work. On the other hand, if a person is self-employed they put in very long days, which usually do not end until late into the night. Their weekends are spent planning and preparing for the next week. The 40 hour week becomes a distant memory. This is a fact of life that many aspiring entrepreneurs do not grasp until the reality sets in that their life is no longer their own.[4] They are beginning to understand that business ownership is not a job, it is a lifestyle. Walt Disney summed up the entrepreneurial spirit best when he said, "I don't make movies to make money. I make money to make movies."[5] Entrepreneurs simply like the chase and the challenge.

Gary Blankenship, owner of the Walnut Street Inn, sums up his thoughts of the work lifestyle at his inn:

To me being an innkeeper is an incredible way to immerse yourself in life. While opening your home to strangers you will be shocked and pleased, disappointed and thrilled, embarrassed and proud, defeated and motivated, but you will never be bored, lonely, or feel totally out of control. Why do I do it? Because serving the public has rewards greater than anything I have ever done. We soothe the soul of the tired business traveler. We allow romance to rekindle and burn bright again. We become close friends with perfect strangers, and then send them on their way, a little more content with their lives than when they checked in. Then we do it again."[6]

When you research all highly successful business owners they all share common traits. Entrepreneurs have an intense commitment and level of perseverance; they always see the cup as full—that's right, full (half full of air and half full of water). They have unquestioned integrity. They are also totally dissatisfied with the status quo and are trying to improve almost any business deal they encounter. Wally Amos of Famous Amos Chocolate Chip Cookies said, "You can do anything you want to do. The beginning is the most important part of the work."[7] Ray Kroc, founder of McDonald's, stated the principal reasons for his success were his ability (1) to react positively to challenges and learn from his mistakes, (2) to take personal initiative, and (3) to persevere with determination.[8]

J.W. Marriott did not start with a great idea or a brilliant strategy but with a simple desire to build something from the ground up—most important—and build it to last. From a very small single A&W Root Beer stand—hardly the invention of electricity or the personal computer—he developed a multi-billion dollar hotel empire. His basic belief he built his company on was there can be no distinction between a company's core values and the core values of its leadership. J.W. Marriott's core values are a commitment to continuous improvement and overcoming adversity, to keep a good old-fashioned dedication to hard work, and to having fun while doing it.[9]

Are You Ready To Be an Entrepreneur?

With small business, one must be prepared to evaluate their own feelings honestly about the demands of our industry along with being your own boss. Having a thorough understanding of the demands of entrepreneurship along with how and where you fit in to the industry will minimize the surprises when you put up your own sign for business.

Experienced entrepreneurs within the hospitality industry recommend that you ask yourself these ten questions if you want to own your own business:

- **How do you feel about people?** Successful entrepreneurs in the hospitality industry genuinely like being around and being of service to people. The appreciation and enjoyment of every guest you serve is what keeps them coming back. Repeat business is essential for a hospitality business to survive. This is first because it is most important.

- **Do you have the energy?** People who consider themselves dynamos will get winded operating a hospitality business. It is not only the quantity of energy, but the restructuring of when it must be expended. Weekends, evenings, and holidays are no longer time off. If you get some time off it will likely be a weekday and in the afternoon. At the same time, those spare moments when a guest is not demanding your attention are the times when you will make repairs, inventory, prepare advertising and promotional pieces, etc. The less you have in start up capital, the more you will have to do yourself, and the less leisure time you will have. Are you ready for that?

- **How do you feel about providing service to others?** We are talking about preparing a business plan and carrying out the act of providing your service and talents, resources, and support to other people. This is essentially the hospitality business, and you can tell how well it has been done the moment you enter a lodging operation, restaurant, or any other type of hospitality business.

- **How persistent are you?** This quality will be very important to you in every area of your life as an entrepreneur. It is being willing to keep trying something long after your energy is used up, long after your enthusiasm has waned, and certainly long after all other people have lost interest in helping you. The people who cannot make it as an entrepreneur are the ones who give up easily or divert attention from long, hard parts to do the easier more glamorous ones. It is going into the process with an awareness that changes happen slowly and wisdom is gained in the process.

- **What is your hands-on quotient?** A small business is definitely hands-on and requires many and varied skills from plumbing to cooking, to bookkeeping and gardening (curb appeal is essential). Being willing to jump in and actually get your hands dirty is often a basic necessity just to get the job done but also makes you knowledgeable and respected by those that have invested in your business.

- **What is your level of acceptance of other people?** All kinds of people will visit your business and almost all of them will place different demands on your business and will test your tolerance of people. Unmarried couples demanding quiet next to a married couple with children, mixed race couples, gay couples, demanding guests who come to your business alone and need special treatment because they travel for a living and this is the highlight of their day, older men with younger women and visa versa, the unsociable and the gossip. It is next to impossible to set limits on the type of people who you will and will not do business with in the hospitality industry. Be careful of starting an entrepreneurial activity if you are uncomfortable with serving people who are different from you.
- **How flexible are you?** If being in the center of *everything* happening at once sounds like fun to you, so will being an entrepreneur. If wearing different hats is your style, entrepreneurship is too. If you can shift gears quickly without stripping them, entrepreneurship is your career vehicle, and if you can break from a heated argument to gracefully serve the next guest with grace, then you have what it takes.
- **How do you feel about business?** Prospective entrepreneurs often express their interest in a business as something that would be fun to do or to escape from the corporate rat race and get back to a simple life. In fact, owning your own business brings a deluge of mundane problems and repetitive tasks. After the first year, some aspects of a hospitality business are considered boring. You will be tempted to make changes in your business just for excitement's sake. Enjoying the challenge of providing a great experience for each guest who comes to do business with you is crucial. You must take pleasure in seeing a plan executed smoothly over and over again. Thriving on total commitment to the needs of your business.
- **How well do you handle conflict?** The idyllic image of unhurried, pastoral calm is that of the guest—not the business owner. There is always some deadline to meet, something to be cleaned, food to be prepared, beds to be made, etc. You will have to handle disagreements with staff and guests, and it is disillusioning. Guest will refuse to pay for what you consider a masterpiece of your best efforts, demanding their money back. Some staff person will rearrange your carefully arranged lounge.
- **How is your sense of humor?** Being an entrepreneur is fun. You will make it that way. The longer you are in business, the less the disasters feel like your fault, and the more humorous the problems seem. Laughing at problems removes them from the anxious area in your stomach to a warmer place in your heart.

The successful entrepreneur has a business plan and has thoroughly researched the market segment of the hospitality industry they wish to enter. The idea is not a flight of fancy. A written research project can force the entrepreneur to hear and face all of the facts and thus minimize the risk of failure and increase the chance for an enjoyable predictable lifestyle change.

The Entrepreneurial Process

Simply put, the entrepreneurial process is a way of thinking, reasoning, and acting that is focused on opportunity. For an entrepreneur to succeed they must first go beyond an idea and determine if a good **business opportunity** exists. The opportunity must have a market with a customer base that can be defined and that will provide lasting growth. The entrepreneur must be able to determine the size of the market—current and potential. This will help them identify the profit margins the market will yield along with calculating realistic breakeven points before entering the market.

Resources such as finance, assets, and personnel must be available in addition to a well conceived business plan. Doing a lot with very little in the beginning of the process is a way of life for an entrepreneur. Determining what the capital requirement will be for the venture is a key activity. It is not only essential to determine whether an adequate return on investment can be made but also for the potential investor to determine how much of their capital they are willing to risk in the project. Will the requested amount of money solve the identified problem for an existing venture or achieve the goals associated with a new opportunity?

What has been proposed in the venture's business plan must be a good fit. The business plan is the document that will take a potential investor to a departure point where they will conduct their own investigation and determine the risk/return balance of the proposed project. Beyond the investigation of the opportunity, the potential investor will also scrutinize the abilities of the founder of the venture and the management team.

There is very little dispute among the experts that the **entrepreneurial team** is a key element when the scope of the opportunity is larger. It must be anchored by a leader who trains faster and better than the competition, deals with adversity, is dependable and honest, and builds an entrepreneurial culture. One of the most successful venture capitalist in the U.S., John Doerr, holds to a rule—he would prefer a Grade A entrepreneur and a team with a Grade B idea, over a Grade B team and a Grade A idea.[10] The leader must be able to time all three of these critical entrepreneurial dimensions—

opportunity, resources, and teams. Opportunity is a moving target, resources are limited, and the team must be carefully orchestrated to survive the venture's infancy and prosper.

Legal Issues and Business Structure Considerations

As you are intuitively aware, legal issues are a huge concern in today's business world and the hospitality industry is no exception. As a matter of fact, many would consider the hospitality industry a hotbed for legal issues. The following outline is intended to be a guide for discussion you should have with your attorney prior to forming a hospitality entrepreneurial business structure and proceeding with the development of a business plan.

Table 12.1 Legal Structure

Form of the business entity
  a. Options
      i.   Sole Proprietorship
      ii. S. Corporation
      iii. Limited Liability Corporation (LLC)
      iv. Others (Limited Partnership, C Corporation)
  b. Goals of Entity
      i.   Cost
      ii. Ease of formation
      iii. Flexibility in Form of Management
      iv. Operational Formalities
      v.   Taxation
      vi. LIMITED LIABILITY!
  c. Basic Elements of Each
      i.   Sole Proprietorship
          1. No cost (excludes costs not associated with any particular business from such as business licenses, etc.)
          2. Very easy to form—Do nothing!
          3. Flexibility of Management—You as the owner are king/queen!
          4. Operational formalities—None!
          5. Taxation—all expenses and revenues taxed directly to you the owner.
          It is all good up to this point . . .
          6. Limited Liability—NONE!
             (a) The owner is personally liable for all actions of the business.
             (b) Personal assets are exposed.
          7. Summary: Simple and inexpensive . . . but no limited liability, so in the end it may be very expensive for you.
      ii. Limited Liability Corporation (LLC)
          1. Cost
             (a) Fee with your state's Secretary of State (around \$100–\$150)
             (b) Attorney fee (optional)
          2. Ease of formation
             (a) Articles of Organization
                (i) One page document providing basic information to State (name, address, purpose, member or manager managed, etc.)

(continued)

Table 12.1 Legal Structure *(continued)*

Form of the business entity
(continued)

    (b) Operating Agreement
       (i) Organizational Structure
         (1) Purpose
         (2) Member or Manager Powers/Liabilities
         (3) Contributions
         (4) Distributions/Allocations
         (5) Meetings
         (6) Accounting
         (7) Addition of Members/Transfers
         (8) Dissolution
  3. Management Flexibility
    (a) As simple or complex as you want them to be.
    (b) Member Managed vs.
    (c) Manager Managed (day to day business) (members still have power to decide major business issues).
  4. Operational Formalities
    (a) As simple or as complex as you want them to be.
    (b) Formal annual meetings not required.
    (c) You determine notice requirements.
    (d) No annual reporting fees or requirements (like with corporations).
  5. Taxation
    (a) Taxed either as
      (i) Partnership—all income and expenses pass directly to members of LLC—no entity level taxation or
      (ii) S Corporation—pass through the entity, but may avoid Medicare and Social Security taxes
    (b) Discuss other differences with your CPA.
  6. Limited Liability
    (a) Liability limited to the assets of the company.
    (b) No personal liability. Personal; assets are shielded from creditors.
      (i) Careful . . . must keep separate books, bank accounts, all contracts in company name . . . no comingling of personal assets.
  7. Summary: Clearly the entity of choice for the last 15–20 years for small business. It is inexpensive to form and maintain, it is flexible, and it provides limited liability to its members.
 iii. S. Corporation
  1. Costs—initial cost is similar to the LLC
  2. Ease of formation
    (a) Must form a general business corporation, then file an S election form.
    (b) Due to corporate formality, there are more documents to prepare (minutes of meetings, consents, etc.)
    (c) Articles of Incorporation
    (d) Bylaws
  3. Management Flexibility
    (a) Not as flexible. Must have officers and board of directors.
  4. Operational Formalities
    (a) Must follow corporate formalities
      (i) Shareholder meetings, minutes, notice requirements, annual filings, annual fee, shareholder rights.
  5. Taxation
    (a) Taxed as a corporation (pass through entity if you make an S election).
  6. Limited Liability
    (a) Like an LLC, personal assets are protected. Only liable for capital contributed to the corporation.
  7. Summary: Not a bad option, requires more time to deal with administrative issues, higher costs to operate.

Table 12.1 Legal Structure *(continued)*

Name and Identification Issues	a. Entity name reserved at the time you form your LLC.
	 b. However, entity name may be different than operating name
	 c. Fictitious name registration (e.g., Your Name Enterprises)
	 d. Simple form to file with Secretary of State (along with filing fee—typically around $25–$30).
	 e. Provides baseline level of evidence that you should be able to use the name over someone else.
	 f. Trade name issues—highly specialized area of law.
	    i. Any name used to identify a business
	    ii. Protected
	       1. If its an inherently distinctive name (meaning protectable)
	       2. Descriptive (protectable only upon showing a secondary meaning).
	       3. Generic (not protectable)
	    iii. What is "Inherently Distinctive"?
	       1. Fanciful Marks (Kodak Photo Supplies)
	       2. Arbitrary Marks (Choice Hotels)
	       3. Suggestive Marks (McDonalds Arches)
	    iv. What is not inherently distinctive? (not protectable)
	       1. Descriptive marks—convey the idea of your product (Oat Nut Breads)
	    v. Why register (State and Federal)?
	       1. Constructive notice of ownership
	       2. Prime Facie evidence of validity of registration
	       3. Five (5) years after registration, becomes incontestable
	       4. Must be registered to file a federal action to enforce
	       5. Treble damagers and attorney fees
	 g. Domain Name Registration
	 h. In order to have a Website, you must purchase the right to use the desired web address. There are various companies that you can purchase/register a website with. The company that you use to design your Website will be able to assist you with that process.

Purchasing a Business or Property	a. Identify Possibilities
	    i. Possibly hire a business broker, real estate agent, and/or attorney.
	       1. How fees are calculated.
	       2. Exclusivity (with broker and real estate agents)
	 b. Letter of Intent—consider
	    i. General purpose—Put down on paper the parties in general understanding of major deal points that have been agreed to prior to formal contract execution.
	    ii. Executed in advance of formal contract
	    iii. Used to give parties some level of confidence that an agreement will be entered into by parties.
	    iv. Parties may or may not intend for the letter of intent to be bending—spell out intent of both parties . . . binding or not binding.
	    v. Sometimes used to invoke obligations or good faith negotiations.
	 c. Due Diligence (steps taken to determine if a business or property is the right choice from a business standpoint, cost, and legal. A phrase used to describe a business investigation. Commercial jargon for detailed analysis and risk review of an impending commercial transaction.)
	    A limited amount of due diligence is completed before the execution of the purchase agreement. Then the purchase agreement is typically conditioned upon the buyer completing its due diligence. Be sure and allow enough time to complete the process and make an informed decision.
	    Your primary objective of due diligence is:
	       1. Indentify strengths and weaknesses of targeted company.
	       2. Identify ways of improving the business after closing.
	       3. Identify liabilities of the company to exclude or assume (e.g., you may want to keep a marketing contract)
	       4. Tax and financing analysis
	       5. Understand the risk of the business (e.g., very high for a bar)

(continued)

Table 12.1 Legal Structure *(continued)*

**Purchasing a Business
or Property** *(continued)*

6. Decide on closing contingencies in your favor
7. Gets the buyer oriented for operating the business or perhaps integrate another business (bringing a catering business into your existing restaurant)

   d. Asset Purchase vs. Stock Purchase. Asset Purchase indicates you are buying the assets of the company but not liabilities. Purchasing the stock of the company indicates that you get the entire operation. You get the name, the assets, and the liabilities. There is no new entity formed. You just become the owner of the existing business. The seller prefers a stock sale, and of course, the buyer would prefer an asset purchase (not saddled with past liabilities).

     i. Structure of the Operations

        1. Separate Entities for Separate Functions Within the Business

          (a) Property Ownership

          (b) Food Functions

          (c) Catering

          (d) Wedding Planning

          (e) Gift Shop

          (f) Bar

            (i) May want consider forming separate entities for each separate function to shield each entity from liability of other functions. Intoxicated guest causes injury. Other entities of business would be protected from negligence in the bar. This is also important because customers will be able to contract separately with each entity for their various roles.

     ii. Applicable Law, Taxes, and Licensing

        1. Taxes

          (a) Federal and State tax identification numbers.

          (b) Filing requirements for your state's Department of Revenue.

          (c) Special taxes on hospitality business, e.g., tourism taxes, bed taxes, etc.

            (i) Local Business Licensing

            (ii) Safety and Sanitation Standards

The Business Plan

After the opportunity and resources for the venture have been identified, along with assembling a team with the diverse skills and backgrounds, it will be time to put together the **business plan**.

Investors will be looking closely at the characteristics of the team to assess whether they are a cohesive group with integrity, capable of developing and applying creative solutions to unforeseen challenges, able to respond positively to problems, and work cooperatively with the investor(s) during troubled times. As the business grows and develops, will this team be able to add value? Finally, the investor will be asking whether they should place their capital in the venture and go into business with this team. And, as J.W. Marriott would ask, "will we have fun?"[11]

Certainly, there will be varying views of the actual market. Not only that, but also the way in which the market should be approached. The reconciliation of these matters and the answers to the previous questions will determine whether the venture will be great, average, poor, or no venture at all. Without a well defined opportunity, adequate resources, and a cohesive team to run the right plays at the right time the business plan is not going to be successful.

The key to developing a successful business plan is to make sure it is a fit for the service industry in which we operate. A service business such as those found in the hospitality industry typically have

A successful business plan needs to have a well-defined opportunity, adequate resources and a cohesive team.

simple financial projections Usually, **fixed expenses** are equal to the total costs and the owner's objective is to make sure **sales revenue** exceeds **fixed expenses** while holding key **variable expense** ratios in line. Investors and lenders will look for proof that the plan's **revenue forecasts** can be met, since the business succeeds or fails based on that forecast.

The individual parts of a typical business plan are:

1. Executive Summary/Introduction

In many cases, this is the only section that will be read by a potential investor. In this section, you will explain the concept and the business approach that will be will applied. Discuss the opportunity and the strategies that will be employed to capture the opportunity. The target market will be described and show its forecasted levels of business over time. Tell the readers what makes the proposed business unique and what advantages it will have over the competition. Report to the prospective investor what is the projected value of the business if it were harvested in 5, 10, or 15 years. Outline the organization's team members and the strengths they bring to the venture.

2. The Industry, Company, and the Services/Products

Explain the details of the hospitality industry segment in which the company will operate; review the services and products the company will provide. Describe how the team expects to enter marketplace and illustrate projections for the company's growth.

3. Market Research and Plan

Identify the customers and guests the business will serve. Detail the size of the **target market** and its **trends**. Review what the competition is doing to maintain their share of the market. Explain what **share of the market** the planned venture will garner. The investor should have a clear picture of the **strategies** that will be implemented to market the business. The prices for product and service will be listed in this section.

4. The Economics of the Business

Show the venture's projected levels of gross **profit**, **adjusted gross income**, etc., based on a forecast of expenses, sales, and **return on investment**. Show the investor the projections of fixed and variable expenses as well as demonstrate how long it take the venture to **breakeven** and generate a positive **cash flow**.

5. Operating and Development Plans

Describe the business cycle in which the venture will operate, its geographic location, planned facilities (or planned renovations and improvements), special zoning (required for Bed and Breakfast operations), regulatory, or legal issues (liquor license).

6. The Team

Provide an **organizational chart** that illustrates the position of each team member within the organization along with an up-to-date resume of the key team members. Review the proposed compensation of each of the team members and the level of ownership each member has in the venture. Reveal other investors, officers of the corporation, and any supporting or professional advisors or services retained.

7. Critical Risks, Problems, and Assumptions

The team will need to describe any risk and consequences (**third party liquor liability**). Explain all assumptions about venture forecasts. If there is something typically considered as too risky (high rate of restaurant failures) then explain how the team will overcome this hurdle.

While this is going to expose the venture's weaknesses, it is important not to leave this section out of the plan. If the team is aware of inherent weaknesses of a venture then the potential investor probably knows it as well. There are only four perceptions that will result from leaving this section out and they are all bad: (1) the investor will think the team is naïve or stupid—or both, (2) the team is trying to hide something, (3) the team does not have enough expertise to recognize the weakness or the skill level to deal with it, and (4) presents a potential investor that falls into category three above. Even though in the short term this individual may invest in the project, he/she will not be effective business partners over the long term because they will not be able to give effective advice or share expertise in problem solving.

8. Financing the Venture

The entrepreneur will need to consider finances from the simple approach of getting as much financing as possible, as early in the project as possible and doing so without taking on a lot of unnecessary risk. The financing strategies executed for the venture should meet the entrepreneur's business and personal goals. Each of the financing options should be evaluated to determine if they meet the entrepreneur's particular needs. The team should avoid the temptation to take the money from a financing source simply because they are making the financing so easy to obtain. To accomplish this, the entrepreneur will need to develop a financing plan that answers several key questions. How much capital does the venture need? When is it needed? How long will the funding last? How is this process managed and by whom? Where and from whom can this money be raised?

Considering the last question from above raises three additional questions. When thinking about raising money for the business the team must ask: (1) Do we need outside capital? (2) Do we want outside investors? and (3) Who would invest? Regardless of the source from which the venture receives funding, one of the primary considerations is to determine how the investor will add value to the venture beyond the influx of money they have provided.

Regardless of your approach to raising capital, there are a few tips you should know. First of all, there are a lot of sources for capital and they should be qualified to ensure they are a fit for your company. Not all who are willing to invest will be good partners and the entrepreneur should be prepared to say no and stay focused on their best suited sources. The aspiring entrepreneur would also be wise not to divulge what other sources of venture capital they have access to. You should never meet with an associate or junior representative from a source of capital twice unless they bring a partner with them. In this case, the entrepreneur will likely be wasting their time and, in the worst case scenario, they would be giving away key pieces of information about their opportunity one meeting at a time. Stress your business concept in the executive summary. Stay away from a lot of number crunching and table/graph presentation—they don't matter. What matters to the investor are the long term value proposition and your business model that will support it. You should present as much information as you can that illustrates the demand for your business in the target market and specifically the market segment you have identified. Prepare very detailed resumes and current references for all of the key team members in your company.

As you move forward with qualified investors, you should align yourself with those who are as hungry as you are. Never say no to an offer price. You should make that decision together with your CPA and attorney. Do not stop promoting your idea until you actually see the money. Again, some unethical investors may actually be baiting the entrepreneur in an effort to gain more information about the business they have planned.

Make the process of obtaining capital a top priority. Throughout the process, be concise and straightforward in the answers you give about your proposed business—never lie. Don't even stretch tiny details that seemingly have no significance. They matter and when an investor catches wind of any sort of inconsistency in your presentation, they will terminate the negotiations immediately. In that regard, you should also know it is a small world and word travels fast.

This is going to be much more difficult that you originally imagined. Just remember you can do more and last much longer than you originally thought you could. Develop your plan and execute it.

9. Proposed Company Offering

Finally, the proposal spells out (1) how much financing is desired, (2) how the team will spend the money to move the venture forward, and (3) how it will bring in a return on investment that meets with the requirements of those who are providing the financing. The entrepreneur will indicate in this section what percent of the business the investor will hold after making their investment.

In order to orchestrate this process efficiently the entrepreneur will need to count on a financial advisor, typically a banker, to provide timely information. Making this decision is going to be one of the most important decisions that the entrepreneur will make. The banker should be evaluated based on their banking knowledge, a shared sense of urgency for the venture, knowledge of the business, willingness to share what they know, the financial stability of the bank, and a willingness to take a chance or work around a policy when the situation deems it necessary.

After the business is funded and has been operational for a period of time it will become necessary for the company to create new products and services and evolve to meet the changing demands of the target market. As the company evolves through these changes, the team will need to anticipate new rounds of financing as well as control the distribution of company ownership. In order for this to happen, the leadership of the business will need to be represented with a good balance between finance, marketing, and operations. If the team identifies opportunities that will allow the company to grow at a fast pace and beyond the capabilities of the current leadership team, then it may become necessary to bring in external expertise to facilitate the new opportunity.

If, on the other hand, the entrepreneur decides that a newly identified opportunity to accelerate the growth of the company is not within a framework that is suitable, then it may be time to **harvest the business**. The accumulation of wealth for an entrepreneur will become reality only if a great company is developed. In order for all of the pieces of the puzzle to be in place to bring a great company to a point at which it can be harvested requires that the entrepreneur start a business venture with the end in mind. Starting with the end in mind serves several purposes. It establishes the goals that must be achieved over the course of many years and creates a motivating force that keeps the entrepreneur going. The harvest may be what is necessary for the business to keep going. Being socially and economically responsible when doing so will allow employees of the business to keep their jobs. And with the harvest, a new venture is typically launched by the entrepreneur. It is more than just signing the bottom line and walking away. When planning the harvest the entrepreneur must be patient, have vision of what is next, be realistic in terms of valuation of the business, and seek outside advice from financial experts such as the banker who is already familiar with the business.

It is common to see entrepreneurs who have harvested their business to focus on assisting the next generation of entrepreneurs. The entrepreneurial system is too fragile to entrust it to just anyone. Therefore, the entrepreneur who has harvested their business must now turn their attention to the proposal of the new entrepreneur and make it better.

≈ *Resources*

Internet Sites

NOLO your legal companion: www.NOLO.com
Women who want to do business with government: www.womenbiz.gov
Business resource center for women: www.womenbiz

References

Pinson, L., and Jinnett, J. *Steps to Small Business Start-up.* NY: Dearborn Trade Pub.
Cohen, W. *Model Business Plan for Product Businesses.* NY: John Wiley & Sons.
McGarthy, T. *Business Plans that Win Venture Capital.* NY: John Wiley & Sons.

≈ *Endnotes*

1. Research Institute of Small and Emerging Businesses. *Human Capital Study.* Washington, D.C. 2004, 19.
2. U.S. Small Business Administration. Office of Women's Business Ownership. Report: Defining "Women-owned" Small Business. Federal Acquisition Regulation (FAR) 19.001. Washington, DC at http://www.smallbusiness.gov
3. Degroot, J., Independent Coffee Shops Hold Their Own vs. Chains at http://www.bizjournals.com/Albany/stories/2000/07/24/focus1.html
4. Bibby, N., Independent vs. Franchise Business Opportunity. *The Bibby Group Excellence in Franchising and Entrepreneurship Newsletter.* Shreveport, LA, 1–2.
5. Lammers, T., and Longsworth, A. (1991). *Guess Who? Ten Big Timers Launched from Scratch, Inc.* Boston, MA: Goldhirsch Group, Inc., 69.
6. Blankenship, G. (2006). *What It Takes To Be An Innkeeper.* Missouri State University and Bed and Breakfast Inns of Missouri Aspiring Innkeeper's Workshop Manual. Springfield, MO, 8.
7. Amos, W. (2006). Founder of Famous Amos Chocolate Chip Cookies Website. Wally's Wit and Wisdom Quote of the Week at http://www.wallyamos.com

8. Kroc, R. (1998). Ray Kroc—Big Wheels Turning: The Future of Business. *Time* at http://www.time.com/time/time100/builder/profile/kroc.html

9. Marriott, J.W., and Brown, K. (1997). *The Spirit to Serve: Marriott's Way.* New York: Harper Collins Publishers. See also http://www.yeartosuccess.com/google.cgi, http://www.hrm.uh.edu/?PageID=204, and http://www.wikipedia.org/wiki/J._Willard_Marriott

10. Doerr, J. (1997). *John Doerr's Start Up Manual.* New York: Fast Company, 84, at http://www.fastcompany.com

11. Ibid.

≈ *Contributor*

Dan Crafts
Missouri State University
901 S. National; PROF 440
Springfield, MO 65897
dancrafts@missouristate.edu

Dr. Dan Crafts is an Associate Professor and Acting Department Head of Hospitality and Restaurant Administration at Missouri State University. He has held multiunit management positions in the restaurant industry and the general manager position in the lodging business as well as owning and operating a full-service catering company. Recent entrepreneurial activities include hosting workshops for the past 7 years for aspiring hospitality business owners from across the United States. Dr. Crafts is a former recipient of a Moot Corp Entrepreneurial Fellowship at the University of Texas at Austin.

Chapter 12
Review Questions

1. How has the economy changed in the U.S. and around the world over the last 10–20 years? Why do you believe this to be so and where do you think we will go from here?

2. What can the entrepreneur do to get the odds of success on their side?

3. How would you describe the attributes of the most effective mangers you have worked for? The worst? Explain why you believe there are difference in the two styles.

4. Over time we have seen entrepreneurs come up with some very innovative ways of managing their resources. Why must the entrepreneur be so effective in this regard.

5. Why do you suppose Walt Disney said "I don't make movies to make money. I make movies to make movies"?

Chain Operations

13

Radesh Palakurthi, Oklahoma State University

© 2008, JupiterImages Corporation.

≈ Learning Objectives

☑ To learn the definition of a hospitality chain operation
☑ To understand the difference between a hospitality chain and a brand
☑ To know the different business models of hospitality chain operations
☑ To know the advantages and disadvantages of hospitality chain operations
☑ To know the big hospitality chains in the lodging and foodservice industries

≈ Chapter Outline

Structure and Business Models of Chain Operations
Advantages of Chain Operations
Disadvantages of Chain Operations
The Big Chains in Hospitality

≈ Key Terms

Brand
Business model
Business organization
Business structure
Chain advantages
Chain disadvantages
Chain operations
Franchise

Joan Tortza is a bright, young, enterprising undergraduate student in Hospitality Administration at a reputed national university. Ever since Joan started the program, she had harbored a passionate desire to start her own restaurant. With her excellent culinary abilities, people skills, and superior knowledge of management techniques (gained through hard work at school and internships), she was confident that she would be successful. During the end of her senior year, Joan put together a business plan for her proposed restaurant concept for the capstone class in strategic management. Joan's professor for the course was very impressed and offered an opportunity to present her plan to potential investors in the hospitality industry. Soon after graduating from school, Joan was making presentations to groups of investors that asked her pointed questions about the feasibility of her business plan.

Joan was eventually able to convince one local group of investors about the soundness of her proposed restaurant concept, and they agreed to convert one of their existing restaurant that was not performing up to standards into the concept proposed by Joan. After months of planning and renovation, the new restaurant opened with much fanfare. It was instantly a huge success, confirming that Joan's assessment for the need for such a restaurant concept was on the mark. In fact, the restaurant concept was so successful that the investors decided, with Joan's approval, to open a chain of additional restaurants using the same name and restaurant concept theme. Within a couple of years after graduation, Joan was overseeing four of her restaurants in the region. Needless to say, Joan was very happy with her success.

One fine day, a customer at one of her restaurants approached Joan to ask if she was interested in expanding her operations nationwide. Joan could not believe what she was hearing because the thought had crossed her mind. However, she was restrained by her original agreement with the investment group and also their relatively limited resources to expand rapidly nationwide. Additionally, the cash flow from her four restaurants was not high enough to expand rapidly in many markets simultaneously. If she decided to use only the profits from her restaurants to expand, the expansion would be very slow and other people with more money to invest could beat her to the market. The customer suggested that Joan consider the franchising route. In such a business model, many individuals or investors from across the country would make the capital investment to buy the land, build the restaurant, license Joan's restaurant name and logo, and agree to operate the new restaurants according to Joan's standards. In return, Joan would receive part of the new restaurants' sales as franchise fees and royalties, even though she had not made any additional investments. She could also charge them a management fee if they decided to allow Joan's employees to operate the restaurants. Although Joan was thrilled with the prospect of turning her four-restaurant concept into a national chain, she was immediately concerned with all the management issues that might crop up in the process. After all, the devil is in the details, isn't it? For example, Joan wondered if such rapid expansion would enable her to maintain control over the quality of the restaurant products that she now has. How about the fact that she now will have to deal with hundreds of investors (franchisees) from across the country, all with different personalities and financial goals? Will she be able to find an adequate number of employees with the required skills to run her restaurant concept nationwide? What about legal responsibilities of her company and the franchisees? Reflecting on such issues, Joan sat down to do some careful planning to set the course for the future of her company.

*T*he preceding vignette offers a scenario in developing chain operations. It describes one of the ways by which a hospitality chain operation can be created and the underpinning issues involved in growing it. The vignette also describes a chain operation without unfolding the specifics. The purpose of this chapter is to throw light on hotel and restaurant chain operations and discuss the nuances of structuring such chains.

A chain operation can simply be defined as a business under one management or ownership. More specifically, chain-operated hotels, restaurants, and other similar businesses are owned by the same company and offer similar goods and services, but are found in different geographic locations. Although there is no magic number in commerce that converts similar operations into a chain, generally, six similar type operations could be considered to be a chain. The scope of a chain operation could be regional, national, or international. A few examples of international hospitality chain operations include McDonald's Restaurants, Burger King Restaurants, Holiday Inn Hotels, and Marriott Hotels.

Structure and Business Models of Chain Operations

Although the concept of a chain operation is easy to understand, structurally it may become more complex with increasing size. The complexity comes from the ownership and management contracts that form the basis of the relationships between the unit operators and the corporate office. Additionally, the distinction between a chain and a brand confounds the issue. A brief description of each of the business models is described here.

Simple Form

In its simplest form, a chain can consist of a single owner/investor that has full equity stake in all the units owned by a company. In such a chain, the parent company fully owns and operates all the units in its chain. All the profits obtained by running the chain belongs to the parent company. All the employees of the unit operations are the employees of the parent company. For accounting purposes, the parent company may consolidate the sales and costs of all the unit operations to determine the total profit or loss for the parent company. Any marketing campaigns conducted would be at the expense of the parent company and would be performed for the benefit of all the unit operations. Usually, this type of structure is found in local or regional chain operations, and they constitute a large percentage of the smaller chains in hospitality. Figure 13.1 illustrates the simple form of structure of chain operations in hospitality.

Mixed Franchise Form

In this type of a chain, there is a mix of ownership with some units being owned and operated by the parent company (known as the franchisor) and the rest owned and operated by many other owners/investors (known as franchisees). Depending on the size of the chain, the number of franchisees can be large. The percentage of the total units owned that are franchised also determines the number of franchisees. Many of the franchisees may own multiple units through business partnership entities of their own. It is not uncommon for some of the franchisee partnerships to own more units than the parent company. The franchisor derives their revenues through multiple revenue streams:

- **Franchising Fees** (Franchise application fees and a flat fee as a percentage of gross sales)
- **Incentive Fees** (An additional fee based on the level of profitability of the unit operation)
- **Royalty Fees** (A fee for using the name, logo, and standard operating systems of the parent company)
- **Marketing Fees** (An additional fee to pay for marketing the entire chain through different campaigns)
- **Other Fees** (For project consulting, employee training, and inventory/supplies management)

It should be noted that although all such fees are reported as revenue for the franchisor, the gross sales of the non-company-owned (franchisors) units is not reported as revenue of the parent company. Although the fees charged by the parent company can

Figure 13.1 Simple Form of Chain Operations in Hospitality

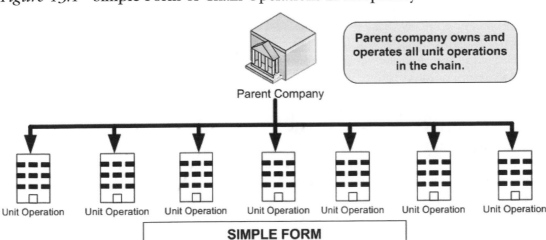

Figure 13.2 Mixed Franchise Form of Hospitality Chain Operations

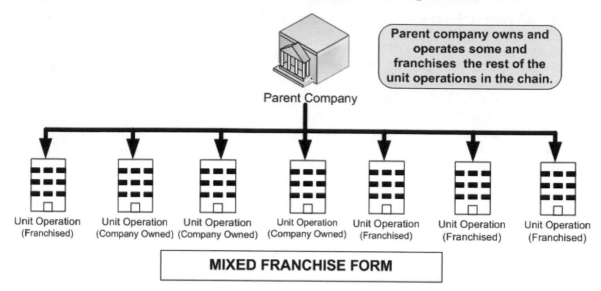

be a major part of the costs of a franchisor, the benefits derived can also be substantial. For example, the franchisor will not have to worry about the soundness or feasibility of the business concept because it is already a proven business model. Additionally, the operating systems are already laid out with clear plans for design, operations, and personnel management. Even though the marketing for the units is undertaken by the parent company (franchisor), the entire chain's brand name is emphasized rather than any individual unit. Figure 13.2 illustrates the structure of a mixed franchise form in hospitality.

Management/Franchise Form

When the parent-company (franchisor) also engages in offering professional management services for its non-company-owned (franchised) units, the company can be said to be using the management/franchise form of chain operations. The difference is that in this form, the parent company has an additional stream of revenue called "management fees" (i.e., fees that it charges the non-company-owned units for managing their operations). The parent company also charges the costs involved in running the units directly to the units. The employees of the unit operations that are managed but not owned by the parent company are the employees of the parent company (franchisor). Some management/franchise parent companies also help fund the investment projects of the franchisees such as opening a new unit or renovating an existing unit. All such functions may be conducted through a separate finan-

cial subsidiary of the parent company. Any profits obtained from such funding are retained by the parent company. Many such financing operations of the franchisors are currently more profitable than the franchise operations because of the low interest rates on loans. Many regional and national chain operations use this business model. A point to note in this model is that the franchisees may be free to hire any other professional operations management company rather than the parent company. In such a case, the unit will be owned by an investor and managed by an outside company that will operate the business strictly by the standards established by the parent company. The fee structure of the outside management company may be similar to that of the parent company. However, the outside management company may be operating many other operations that belong to other chains. In fact, the outside management company may also be either a partial or full business partner in some unit operations it manages. Figure 13.3 illustrates the management/franchise form of structure in hospitality.

Brand Management Form

When a mega-corporation owns multiple chain operations under the same parent umbrella structure, it prefers to refer to each of such chain operations as a brand rather than a chain to emphasize the importance of the distinctive brand image of each of the brands in its portfolio (see Figure 13.4). For example, Marriott International owns nine hotel chains (along with other related brands such as

Figure 13.3 **A Management/Franchise Form of Hospitality Chain Operations**

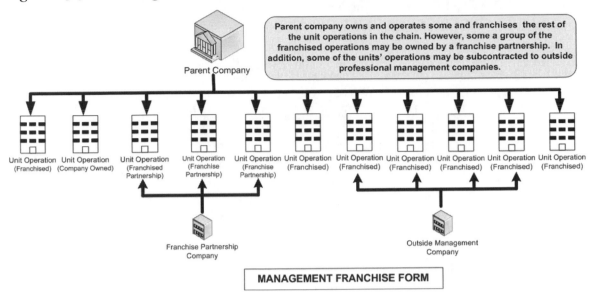

Figure 13.4 **The Mega-Corporation Form Structure of Hospitality Operations**

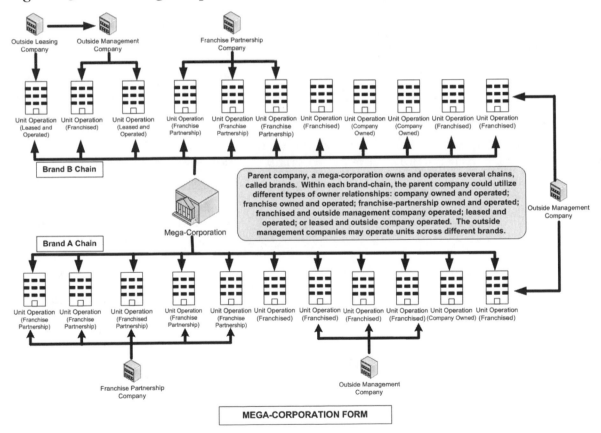

vacation clubs and time-share properties): Marriott Hotels & Resorts, JW Marriott Hotels & Resorts, Renaissance Hotels & Resorts, Courtyard by Marriott, Residence Inn by Marriott, Fairfield Inn by Marriott, Marriott Conference Centers, TownePlace Suites by Marriott, SpringHill Suites by Marriott, and The Ritz-Carlton Hotels. Each of the brands has a distinctive position and covers specific market segments of the lodging industry. For example, the JW Marriott Hotels & Resorts is an elegant and luxurious brand for business and leisure, whereas the Residence Inn by Marriott is designed to be a "home away from home" and caters to travelers who stay for an extended stay of five or more nights.[1] Each chain within the brand management form operates similarly to the management/franchise form in terms of the franchisor–franchisee relationships. The chain's units may be operated by the parent company directly, sole-owners as franchisees, partnership-owners as franchisees, or a management company as a third-party operator for a franchisee. The large size of the mega-corporation may also allow it to raise funds through the financial markets to make direct investments in real estate across the globe. In such a case, the parent corporation may buy land, build new establishments, or buy existing establishments and convert them into one of their brands. Such investments also allow the mega-corporation to offer the invested properties on a lease to third parties that may choose to operate the establishment or hire a professional management company to run it for them. The complexity of such relationships may be compounded when the mega-corporation chooses to enter into a joint venture or other similar partnership with a foreign entity to enter and expand in foreign countries. Figure 13.5 shows the partial portfolio of Marriott International.[2] It can be seen that the company owns, manages, leases,

and franchises its properties, although at a different level for each brand. The company uses different brand strategies for each chain within its portfolio. For example, although almost all units in the Fairfield Inn chain are franchised, none of the units are franchised in the Ritz-Carlton chain. Instead, all the Ritz-Carlton hotels are managed through full ownership or direct management contracts. This ensures full control of the quality of this upscale brand.

Similar to Marriott Corporation, other mega hotel chains also follow a strategy of their own in terms of managing and franchising their properties. Table 13.1 shows the top ten hotel franchisees and managers of hotel properties in the world. In the table it can be seen that all the major chains prefer to extensively franchise their hotels and manage them to a lesser extent. Some of the chains such as Cendant and Choice Hotels franchise all the hotels in their chain. On the other hand, the Tharandson Enterprise prefers to manage all the hotels in the company.

Advantages of Chain Operations

Hospitality chains operations have many advantages that can broadly be classified into the following categories.

Figure 13.5 **Partial Portfolio of Lodging Chain Operations of Marriott International**

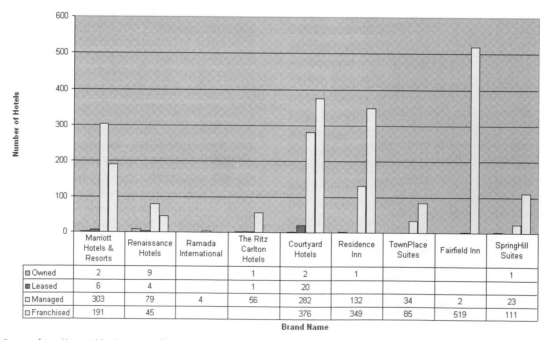

Partial Portfolio of Marriott International (At the End of 3rd Quarter, 2005)

	Marriott Hotels & Resorts	Renaissance Hotels	Ramada International	The Ritz Carlton Hotels	Courtyard Hotels	Residence Inn	TownPlace Suites	Fairfield Inn	SpringHill Suites
□ Owned	2	9		1	2	1			1
■ Leased	6	4		1	20				
□ Managed	303	79	4	56	282	132	34	2	23
□ Franchised	191	45			376	349	85	519	111

Brand Name

Source: http://www.Marriott.com; Company Reports

Table 13.1   Top Ten Franchisees and Managers of Hotel Chains

COMPANIES THAT FRANCHISE THE MOST HOTELS		
COMPANY	TOTAL FRANCHISED	TOTAL HOTELS
Cendant Corp.	6,396	6,396
Choice Hotels International	4,977	4,977
InterContinental Hotels Group	2,971	3,540
Hilton Hotels Corp.	1,900	2,259
Marriott International	1,658	2,632
Accor	949	3,973
Carlson Hospitality Worldwide	864	890
Global Hyatt Corp.	505	818
Starwood Hotels & Resorts	310	733
Worldwide Louvre Hotels (Societe du Louvre)	307	887

COMPANIES THAT MANAGE THE MOST HOTELS		
COMPANY	HOTELS MANAGED	TOTAL HOTELS
Marriott International	889	2,632
Extended Stay Hotels	654	654
Accor	535	3,973
InterContinental Hotels Group	403	3,540
Tharaldson Enterprises	360	360
Global Hyatt Corp.	316	818
Interstate Hotels & Resorts	306	306
Starwood Hotels & Resorts	283	733
Hilton Hotels Corp.	206	2,259
Worldwide Louvre Hotels (Societe du Louvre)	227	887

Source: HOTELS' Giants Survey, 2005.

Market Reach

How many times have we wished that one of our local favorite restaurants also traveled with us so we never have to miss the food we love? That is precisely the need that chain operations aim to fulfill by replicating a successful product in as many geographic regions as they can. In this way, chain operations have an advantage over single independent restaurants because they "reach" out to many markets with the same concept. Reaching new markets means increased sales and thereby increased profits (hopefully!).

Economies of Scale

Economies of scale refers to the cost advantages that a company can derive because of its large size. Because chain operations have multiple units, all products and supplies they buy are also multiples of the requirements of a single independent unit. Therefore, a chain operation will be able to negotiate better rates for its products and supplies from vendors compared to a single-owner unit. In addition, chain operations will also be able to derive cost savings through synergy. For example, a single-unit operation may have to have a different functional department (marketing & sales, finance, human resources, etc.) for running the operation, whereas in a chain, the same single functional department may manage many units in the chain. In other words, the chain operation could have the same departments (and staff) help run many units in the chain (say regionally). Therefore, the chain operation is able to spread the costs of such functional departments across many units compared to a single-unit operation and thereby reduce the overall unit cost of such functions for all units in its chain. Such synergies can only be derived in a chain operation.

Streamlined Operations

Chain operations often standardize the products and services offered to streamline their operations. The standardization also extends to operating procedures resulting in commonly understood requirements for managing all resources (people, finances, and equipment). Such standardization makes it easy for consolidation and reporting of performance across the chain. It also makes it easy to compare unit performance across the chain and assign accountability to individuals.

Marketing Power

The marketing power of chain operations comes from increased visibility gained through greater market reach. The greater visibility allows the chain to use mass media such as TV, radio, and newspapers for marketing purposes. It also allows the chain to embark on multiple marketing campaigns at the same time in different geographic regions. An added benefit of such campaigns is that successful campaigns in one geographic region can be repeated in other regions ensuring a more effective use of marketing dollars.

Service Options

Chain operations are often able to provide additional services both to the customers and the unit chain operations. Such services range from providing a reservations service to full-fledged consulting for running the operations. For the customers, the chain may provide a loyalty program to make sure they spend most of their product-related expenses with the chain. They may also have a full-fledged customer relationship management (CRM) program that keeps track of the customers' expenses and their likes and dislikes. For the unit chain operations, the parent company may offer preopening services, architectural and construction consulting services, employee training and certification services, operations and revenue management services, information technology consulting services, owners and franchisee services, and guest satisfaction survey services.

Access to Finances

The larger size of the chain operations may mean the company may have multiple options for raising money for growth. The cheapest way to fund growth may be through operational cash flows, which will be higher in chain operations compared to a single and independent operation. However, the chain may be able to borrow money from banks, savings and loans, and other financial institutions such as insurance companies. The chain may also be able to borrow money by issuing bonds on the stock market. All such funds raised can be used to fund operations, make capital investments for growth, or in turn be lent to the unit operations for

a fee and a reasonable interest rate. Such increased assess to finances means that a chain may be able to grow more rapidly than a non-chain operation.

Professional Management

Because of the enhanced legal requirements and the complexity of operations in a chain, many such companies are realizing that it is prudent to hire professionals such as students graduating from hospitality management programs. With professionalism and specialization comes a better understanding of company's operating needs. In that regard, chain operations are becoming incubators of good management practices in hospitality.

Disadvantages of Chain Operations

Depending on the perspective of the owner (or the parent company/franchisor) and the operator (or the franchises/management company), some of the advantages listed earlier can also be seen as drawbacks for managing hospitality chain operations. The disadvantages can broadly be listed under three categories as discussed in the following.

Operational Constraints

Although the parent company may want standardized operations throughout the chain to control costs and efficiency, it may put a lot of restrictions on the franchisees or owners that may want to vary in some small ways. For example, the ownership contracts may disallow independent marketing in the local areas by any unit operations without prior approval by the parent company. The type of marketing and the collateral used may also be restricted by the parent company. Such restrictions are only enforced to ensure a consistent image of the brand in the minds of the consumers in all geographic areas where the chain operates. In final analysis the power of the brand comes from maintaining the image of the brand, and hence, the parent company is often very stringent with their requirements. In fact, all chain operations have some form of quality-assurance program where they perform surprise inspections of their unit operations to ensure compliance with all company rules and regulations. Units that repeatedly violate the company requirements are dropped from the chain after proper notice.

Financial Strain

Another disadvantage of belonging to a chain operation may be the strain put on the financial resources of the company. Not only do unit operations have to contribute to the parent company through royalties, incentive, franchise, marketing, and other such fees, but they may also incur additional expenses if the parent company requires additional capital investments to comply with a new requirement they initiated across the chain. For example, if the parent company of a 300-hotel chain decides that the lighting in the guest bathrooms must be increased from 400 lumens to 500 lumens for better visibility and safety, each hotel may have to incur thousands of dollars in expenses to refit each guest bathroom in the hotel they operate. If one such hotel in the chain has 250 rooms, and it costs about $300 to make the lighting change in each bathroom including equipment, labor, and downtime costs, this particular hotel will have to spend $75,000 to meet the parent company's requirements. Extending the calculation, across the chain, it may cost up to $22.5 million to meet this new parent company requirement.

Legal Forces

The complex structure of most chain operations along with many types of owner–operator contracts and partnerships often plagues it with legal woes. Invariably a difference of opinion or perspective on the same issues may have no other recourse than the local courthouse. Consider again the example of the guest bathroom lighting enhancement requirement described earlier. This cost of improving the bathroom lighting at the unit level will have to come at the expense of the profit of the unit operations, and that is always a contentious issue between the parent company and the unit managers. The parent company may have a more holistic view of the costs associated because they believe that such an investment may pay off through lower guest accidents in the bathroom that may in turn reduce insurance costs and legal expenses. If the unit managers can be convinced of the justification of the costs, then the cost of making the lighting changes in the bathroom will be seen as an investment rather than an unjustified cost rained on them by the parent company. However, if the costs are seen as unjustified, the unit operations may first try to wield control by collective representation through unions or partnerships. If that fails, the parent company may have to deal with the issue in a court of law.

The Big Chains in Hospitality
Lodging

The increasing globalization of the hospitality industry is rapidly being reflected in the geographic profiles of large hospitality corporations, especially in the hotel industry. It is now commonplace for major hospitality corporations to consider the entire global market as their potential domain. Table 13.2 lists the number of countries each of the major hotel corporations operated in 2005. The top five companies operated in more than half the nations in the world.

In addition to the countries in which the hotel companies operate, the country in which the companies are based is also truly global in scope. Table 13.3 lists the top 15 hotel chains in the world in terms of number of rooms.[3] In the table, for example, the world's largest hotel company, InterContinental Hotels Group, is based in the United Kingdom, and Accor, the fourth largest, is based in France. Although many of the other larger chains are based in the United States, the ownership profile is changing rapidly with cross-national mergers and acquisitions such as the Hilton brand, which is now partly based in Herts, England, and in Beverly Hills, California, under two different ownership companies.

Table 13.2 **Top 15 Hotel Corporations Operating in Most Countries**

COMPANY NAME	NUMBER OF COUNTRIES
InterContinental Hotels Group	100
Accor	90
Starwood Hotels & Resorts	82
Best Western International	80
Hilton Group plc	78
Carlson Hospitality Worldwide	70
Marriott International	66
Le Meridien Hotels & Resorts	56
Golden Tulip Hospitality/THL	47
Cendant Corp.	44
Global Hyatt Corp.	43
Choice Hotels International	42
Rezidor SAS Hospitality	41
Club Mediterranee	40
TUI AG/TUI Hotels & Resorts	28

Source: HOTELS' Giants Survey, 2005

Table 13.3 Top 15 Hotel Chains in Terms of Number of Rooms (2005)

RANK 2004	RANK 2003	COMPANY HEADQUARTERS	ROOMS 2004	ROOMS 2003	HOTELS 2004	HOTELS 2003
1	1	**InterContinental Hotels Group** Windsor, Berkshire, England	534,202	536,318	3,540	3,520
2	2	**Cendant Corp.** Parsippany, N.J., USA	520,860	518,747	6,396	6,402
3	3	**Marriott International** Washington, D.C., USA	482,186	490,564	2,632	2,718
4	4	**Accor** Paris, France	463,427	453,403	3,973	3,894
5	5	**Choice Hotels International** Silver Spring, Md., USA	403,806	388,618	4,977	4,810
6	6	**Hilton Hotels Corp.** Beverly Hills, Calif., USA	358,408	348,483	2,259	2,173
7	7	**Best Western International** Phoenix, Ariz., USA	309,236	310,245	4,114	4,110
8	8	**Starwood Hotels & Resorts Worldwide** White Plains, N.Y., USA	230,667	229,247	733	738
9	11	**Global Hyatt Corp.** Chicago, Ill., USA	147,157	89,602	818	208
10	9	**Carlson Hospitality Worldwide** Minneapolis, Minn., USA	147,093	147,624	890	881
11	10	**Hilton Group plc** Watford, Herts, England	102,636	98,689	403	392

Source: HOTELS' Giants Survey, 2005

Foodservice

Unlike the hotel industry, the foodservice chains are currently dominated by American quick-service restaurants. Table 13.4 lists the top 12 foodservice chains in the world.[4] The top eight chains have substantial international operations with most of their growth actually coming from the overseas markets. It is interesting to note that although McDonald's Restaurants is still ranked first in terms of sales, the Subway Restaurants chain is the largest in terms of

Table 13.4 Top 12 Foodservice Chains in the World in 2005

2005 RANK	2004 RANK	CHAIN	SEGMENT	2004 SYSTEMWIDE SALES ($MIL)	2004 CHANGE IN SYSTEM SALES	NUMBER OF FRAN-CHISED UNITS	NUMBER OF COMPANY UNITS	TOTAL UNITS
1	1	McDonald's	Burger	$24,391.00	10.30%	10,989	2,684	13,673
2	3	Wendy's	Burger	$7,712.00	3.10%	4,605	1,328	5,933
3	2	Burger King	Burger	$7,700.00	−10.50%	6,982	642	7,624
4	5	Subway	Sandwich	$6,270.00	10.00%	17,909	1	17,910
5	4	Taco Bell	Mexican	$5,700.00	5.60%	4,590	1,281	5,871
6	6	Pizza Hut	Pizza/Pasta	$5,200.00	2.00%	5,790	1,729	7,519
7	7	KFC	Chicken	$5,000.00	2.00%	4,275	1,240	5,515
8	9	Starbucks	Snack	$4,804.10	38.30%	1,982	4,394	6,376
9	10	Dunkin' Donuts	Snack	$3,380.00	15.00%	4,418	0	4,418
10	8	Domino's Pizza	Pizza/Pasta	$3,173.20	5.70%	4,428	580	5,008
11	11	Arby's	Sandwich	$2,836.00	4.70%	3,100	235	3,335
12	12	Sonic Drive-In	Burger	$2,770.00	13.90%	2,374	542	2,916

Source: *QSR Magazine*: QSR 50 Survey, 2005

the number of units. It can also be seen that the more traditional quick-service concepts, such as Burger King and Wendy's, are either in mature or decline stage. Newer restaurant concepts such as Starbucks and Sonic Drive-In are rapidly growing. Not unlike the hotel industry, the foodservice industry also has a penchant for franchising, with some of the chains such as Subway and Dunkin' Donuts franchising almost all their restaurant.

Summary

In an increasingly competitive world, chain development strategy offers an opportunity for hospitality companies to take control of costs and harness their strengths. With the short time it now takes for the diffusion of innovation and migration of ideas across the world because of rapidly evolving telecommunication facilities, the world is swiftly shrinking and creating immense business opportunities for growth globally. As people around the world share the same information and ideas, they may also develop the same preferences for hospitality products and services. In such an environment, growing through the application of chain development strategy is prudent for business. Needless to say, the concept of hospitality chain operations will only get stronger in the future.

≈ *Resources*

Internet Sites

Hotel Chain

Marriott Corporation: http://www.marriott.com
Intercontinental Group: http://www.ichotelsgroup.com/
Accor: http://accor.com/gb/index.asp
Starwood Hotel & Resorts: http://www.starwoodhotels.com/
Best Western International: http://www.bestwestern.com/
Hilton Groups plc: http://hiltonworldwide.hilton.com/
Le Meridien Hotels & Resorts: http://www.lemeridien.com/
Carlson Hospitality Worldwide: http://www.carlson.com/
Golden Tulip Hospitality/THL: http://www.goldentulip.com/site/?ShowLanguage=EN
Cendant Corp.: http://cendant.com/
Global Hyatt Corp.: http://www.hyatt.com/hyatt/index.jsp
Choice Hotels International: http://www.choicehotels.com/
Rezidor SAS Hospitality: http://www.rezidorsas.com/
Club Mediterranee: http://www.clubmed.com/cgi-bin/clubmed55/clubmed/welcome.jsp
TUI AG/TUI Hotels & Resorts: http://www.tui-group.com/en/ir/group/

Foodservice Chain

McDonald's: http://www.mcdonalds.com/
Wendy's: http://www.wendys.com
Burger King: http://www.bk.com/
Subway: http://www.subway.com/subwayroot/index.aspx
Taco Bell: http://www.tacobell.com/
Pizza Hut: http://www.pizzahut.com/
KFC: http://www.kfc.com/
Starbucks: http://www.starbucks.com/
Dunkin' Donuts: http://dunkindonuts.com/
Domino's Pizza: http://www.dominos.com/Public-EN/
Arby's: http://www.arbys.com/
Sonic Drive-In: http://www.sonicdrivein.com/index.jsp

≈ *Endnotes*

1. *Marriott Hotel and Resorts Brand Factsheets*, 2005 at http://www.marriott.com
2. *Marriott International Annual Report*, 2005.
3. *HOTELS' Corporate 300 Report*, Giants Survey, July 2005.
4. *QSR 50 Survey*, 2005 at http://www.qsrmagazine.com/qsr50/charts/systemwide_sales.html

≈ *Contributor*

Radesh.Palakurthi@okstate.edu

Dr. Palakurthi is a professor and the coordinator of the master's program at the School of Hotel and Restaurant Administration at Oklahoma State University in Stillwater, OK. Dr. Palakurthi has a doctorate from Penn State University, MBA from San Jose State University, MS from Purdue University, and a BS from Florida International University. Dr. Palakurthi has previously taught at University of North Texas, San Jose State University, and The Wellington Institute of Technology in Petone, New Zealand.

Chapter 13
Review Questions

1. What is the definition of hospitality chain operations?

2. What is the difference between a hospitality chain and a hospitality brand?

3. What are the different business models used in hospitality chain operations?

4. Describe the differences between the different business models used in hospitality chain operations.

5. Describe the relationship between a franchisor and a franchisee in hospitality chain operations. When can the franchisors be more powerful than the franchisees?

6. What are the additional sources of revenue available to an owner in a mixed franchise form compared to a simple form?

7. How would you describe a megacorporation in hospitality? Explain how its operations are more complex than other forms of business models.

8. What are some of the advantages of hospitality chain operations?

9. What are some of the disadvantages of hospitality chain operations?

10. List the top ten hospitality chain operations in the lodging and foodservice industries.

Franchising, Referral Organizations, and Third-Party Distribution Systems

14

Susan Gregory, Eastern Michigan University

© Orkhan Aslanov, 2008, Shutterstock.

≈ Learning Objectives

☑ Describe the role of franchising in the hospitality industry
☑ Identify the benefits and constraints of franchising from the franchisor's and franchisee's perspective
☑ Explain the role of referral organizations and third-party distribution systems in the hospitality industry
☑ Identify the common elements found in franchising, referral organizations, and third-party distribution systems
☑ Discuss the trends impacting franchising, referral organizations, and third-party distribution systems in the hospitality industry

≈ Chapter Outline

Franchising in the Hospitality Organization
Referral Organizations
Third-Party Distribution Systems

≈ Key Terms

Franchise advisory board
Franchisee
Franchisor
Referral organization
Third-party distribution system

*I*n previous chapters you learned about independent, entrepreneurial, and chain operations. This chapter will add more options to the types of business structures that are available: franchises, referral organizations, and third-party distributions. These three structures are similar in that each business model offers a system or method of marketing a product or service under a trademark or brand name. Marketing can increase the amount of exposure a business would receive in the marketplace over what they would receive if they were on their own competing for guests. Marketing activities are direct in the case of franchisees and referral organizations and indirect through a middleman as in the system called third-party distribution.

Franchising in the Hospitality Organization

Franchise is a network of business relationships. It is a method of distributing goods and services that allows a franchisee the right to establish and operate a unit or units, and to use the franchisor's name and/or business system. These contractual rights require the franchisee to abide by all the standards and operational rules that are established by the franchisor. It's a proven way of doing business, and quickly creates a strategic marketing identity and image in the minds of customers for a new business. For the franchisee, being part of the network can also mean a shorter learning curve in a new business. An independent business person is not solely dependent on their own ideas and creativity. They don't have to "reinvent the wheel" because the marketing and operations expertise are already in place. If there are problems, the franchisor and other franchisees bring a wealth of knowledge and experience to the system.

In 2004 the U.S. Census Bureau estimates that 3.9 billion dollars in sales were generated by the top 200 franchise companies between their company owned units and franchisees. The largest franchise organization is McDonalds. The IFA (International Franchise Association) Website has a list of industries that offer franchises (www.franchise.org). In a time when America has lost their competitive edge in manufacturing, franchising has become a major export for the United States. In developing regions of the world, it has become a stabilizing force creating business ownership and personal wealth among the citizens. There has been over a 50% growth in the rapidly expanding economies in Asia and Eastern Europe since 1999. Since 2004, they have seen a 14% growth in the number of franchise units built. As a result, franchising is helping America balance their trade deficit.

Franchising is a method of growing a business that sells goods and services at multiple locations under a common name. Some hospitality businesses have used franchising as a means of expanding their brand name, creating broader name recognition, without operating the business themselves. A **franchisor** licenses their brand name, operating system, or even their marketing expertise to another business entity (individual or group). This allows people who are novices in the field to start a business without the expertise they should have to run a successful enterprise. They agree to follow the policies and rules set out in a franchise agreement. In some cases, the franchisor provides everything for the business, even management training. This allows someone to become a manager and be an owner quickly. The **franchisee** pays the franchisor an initial fee and then continuing fees (sometime called royalties or maintenance fees) over the course of the contract.

According to a survey conducted the Gallup Organization for the International Franchise Association (IFA),[1] 90% of franchise owners consider their franchise business to be successful or very successful. Franchise owners also indicated that they work hard for their money and made on average over $91,000 per year. These owners felt that owning the franchise was the key to their success.

Two Types of Franchises

There are two types of franchises, **product distribution** franchises and **business format**. A **product distribution franchisee** sells products or services that the franchisor manufactured. The most common product or services are: cars, soft drinks, gasoline, and insurance. These items usually require some preparation by the franchisee before they are sold. Travel agencies operate in this fashion, especially for cruises. A product distribution franchisee may represent several different franchisors and sell their products or services on an exclusive or semi-exclusive basis. The product distribution franchisor provides its trademark and logo to the franchisee but usually not a business operating system.

Business format franchising provides the trademark, logo, and the complete system for de-

Case Study
CHIPOTLE MEXICAN GRILL

As with many new franchise organizations they started as an independent and then began franchising their concept or they sold the concept to another organization that began to franchise the business. Such is the case of Chipotle Mexican Grill. Chipotle Mexican Grill started in Denver Colorado in 1992 by Steve Ells. This is a relatively new category of fast-casual dining restaurants. As an opportunity for McDonalds to expand their quick service restaurant business concept, in 1997 they became a minority investor in Chipotle and this grew to controlling interest in 2005. McDonalds grew the restaurant from the initial 14 to 480 by the end of 2005.

In the fall of 2005 Chipotle had an "Intial Public Offering" through the New York Stock Exchange to raise money for expansion. After this successful stock launch the McDonalds Corporation offered their shareholders the opportunity to acquire Chipotle shares at a discount. Now McDonald's Corporation has fully divested its investment in Chipotle Mexican Grill.

livering the product and or service and operating the business. Operations that use business format franchising range from restaurants (most common) and hotels to real estate services and tax preparation services. The franchisor provides a detailed system from physical appearance of the business, product and service standards, to policies and procedures that ensure consistency from one location and franchisee to another. The confidential operating and procedures manuals guide a franchisee in how to market their franchise; staff their venture from recruiting, hiring, training, to employee dress code; and order, prepare, and deliver their products and/or service. For instance, McDonalds provides all the manuals and created Hamburger University to train their managers. In addition, in order to maintain consistency, there may be a list of vendors that provide the approved food. No others are allowed. When the largest McDonalds was opened in Moscow, Russia, it took years of preparation for the opening. They had to provide seeds for the lettuce, tomatoes, and potatoes and then teach the Russian farmers how to grow them. Then, they did the same with the beef cattle and the bakers for the rolls, etc. All this was to maintain the same product consistency. Brand consistency in product and service provides the greatest business advantage for franchisor and franchisee.

Franchise agreements can be for a **single-unit** (sometimes called direct unit) or for multi-units. **Multi-unit** agreements allow a franchisee to purchase additional units, growing their business with a brand that they are familiar with, and thus lowering the financial risk for both the franchisee and franchisor. Multi-unit franchisees may have more leverage with the franchisor as they negotiate additional agreements and contract for services. **Area development** agreements grant the franchisee exclusive rights to a geographic area for opening up new locations within a specified time period. A **master franchisee** agreement is similar to an area development agreement with the addition of the ability to sell locations within a specified geographic area to persons or groups to open single-units franchises. A master franchisee becomes a franchisor to these single unit franchise owners.

Table 14.1 Franchising Fast Facts

- Over 1,500 franchise companies operating in the United States with more than 767,484 retail units.
- There are 622,272 business format franchising operations and 145,211 product distribution franchise organizations (2007).
- Business format franchising provides 7,787,454 jobs or more than four times the number of jobs in product distribution franchises.
- 80 industries use franchising to distribute goods and services to consumers.
- Between 2003 and 2005 over 900 new concepts began franchising.
- Average investment is less than $250,000 and range from as low as $10,000 to more than $1 million.
- Royalty or maintenance fees range from 3% to 6% of gross sales.
- Franchisors average slightly less than 100 units.
- Average length of contract is 10 years.
- When a property changes franchise affiliation it is referred to as re-flagging.

Table 14.2 Top 10 Types of Franchises

TOP 10 FRANCHISE COMPANIES (BY # OF UNITS)

1. McDonalds Corporation
2. 7-Eleven Inc.
3. Subway Sandwiches & Salads
4. H&R Block, Inc.
5. Burger King Corp.
6. Jani-King International Inc.
7. Taco Bell Corp.
8. RadioShack
9. Pizza Hut Inc.
10. Domino's Pizza LLC

TOP 10 FASTEST-GROWING FRANCHISES

1. Subway
2. Jan-Pro Franchising Int'l Inc.
3. Dunkin' Donuts
4. Coverall Cleaning Concepts
5. Jazzercise Inc.
6. Jackson Hewitt Tax Service
7. Re/Max Int'l Inc.
8. CleanNet USA Inc.
9. Bonus Building Care
10. Jani-King

Franchisor's Role

A franchisor can be a large public (McDonalds) or private company (Carlson Companies) located anywhere in the world (Accor—Paris, France, or Wendy's International—Dublin, Ohio, U.S.) and be a small start-up company (Rio Wraps—Detroit, Michigan) or a large conglomerate (Cendant Corporation—Parsippany, New Jersey, U.S.). The franchisor licenses the right to conduct business under their brand name. Brand recognition is one of the biggest advantages that franchisors have to sell to franchisees. A brand name communicates expectations to consumers and is closely controlled by the franchisor. Franchisors provide franchisees with support while exercising control over the way they operate under the brand. A consistent brand image is developed through the franchisor's marketing activities that are paid for by franchisees in the form of a marketing fee. Marketing fees are pooled together to provide advertising, public relations, and other activities that promote the brand name.

Franchisors also provide operating methods and procedures to franchisees in the form of technical and management training to maintain consistent quality of products and services. The franchisor owns the concept name and specifies how the franchisee deals with consumers. Product and service development is controlled by the franchisor to ensure that every franchise offers the same type and quality of products and services. The types of support provided by the franchisor vary from one organization to another and is outlined in the Uniform Franchise Offering Circular (UFOC). Franchisors like to say that "you are in business for yourself, but not by yourself."

There are several advantages and disadvantages to developing a franchise.

- Ability to grow business with minimum capital
- Do not have to manage each location, becomes responsibility of franchisee
- Franchisees are motivated to be profitable and in turn a portion is paid to franchisor
- Royalty or maintenance fees are less than what the franchisor could make if they operated the business
- Franchisees are independent operators and may have a different perspective on how the business should be operated or how they should comply with the contract
- Franchisees may not have the skills to profitably operate the business

Franchisee's Role

The franchisee agrees to operate under the franchisor's trademark or brand name, providing only approved products or services using franchisor's operating methods. The franchisee normally owns the land and building. The franchisee is responsible for securing capital for acquiring the physical assets and franchising fees and operating the business. Though a franchisor may provide access to capital for expansion or updating of existing franchise units over time. In addition, they are responsible for human resource activities like hiring, training, and compensating their employees.

There are several advantages and disadvantages to owning a franchise:

- Brand name recognition makes it easier to compete with established independent operators
- Access to training and operations manuals, site selection tools, and store design
- Quantity purchasing power when negotiating for equipment and supplies
- Research and development of new product and service offerings
- Loss of independence—must follow franchisor's policies and procedures

- Judged by management of other franchisees in system (reputation)
- Income expectations balanced with cost of franchising

Referral Organizations

Referral organizations are similar to franchise organizations in that they have the same name and provide similar core services. The typical referral organization is a nonprofit affiliation owned by members of independently owned and managed lodging operations. Typically, administrative expenses are covered by fees paid by its members. Rules, regulations, policies, and governance are determined by the voting members. Another difference is that referral organizations are comprised of member properties that are linked together for marketing purposes and therefore have fewer rules and regulations than franchise properties. The physical appearance of each member will be different, but they all provide similar products and have the same service standards.

Combining their marketing resources allows them to have a wider reach for advertising while creating a brand image. For example, The Luxury Romantic Collection by Great Hotels of The World is a small group of hotels that have joined together because they have a common image. So, guests select the image first and then decide which of the members has the best location for their romantic fantasy. Not only can they go to one website for information about each hotel, people can make reservations at the site as well. Everybody wins. Referrals allow independently owned businesses to compete more efficiently with franchise brands and still maintain their uniqueness.

The largest referral organization is Best Western International which is the world's largest hotel chain. They operate under a single brand name with 4,200 properties around the globe. Through referral organizations, members band together to market their business under a common trademark or brand. Their size allows them to leverage their combined purchasing power when buying products for quantity pricing and to share ideas for improved operating methods.

Referral organizations, such as Best Western International and Kampgrounds of America (KOA) maintain their individual property uniqueness found in their charm and local appeal while meeting global quality standards. Best Western International and KOA offer members the unique advantage of retaining their independence while providing the benefits of a full-service affiliation which includes marketing programs, training support, and purchasing power. A downside of this operating method is that travelers may be confused about different types of properties, differing quality and service levels, and wide range of rates. These are some of the challenges of all referral organizations.

Role of Franchising or Referral Organization Advisory Committee

All major franchise and referral organizations have some structured way of gathering information from members through a franchisee advisory board. Franchise advisory boards address issues of both the franchisor and franchisees or referral organization and its members. Franchisee advisory groups can be a valuable source of marketing, operations, and product/service development ideas. Changes in products and services, such as new menu roll-out, are discussed along with policies and procedures for their implementation. Often the best ideas come from operators. One of McDonalds' earlier franchisors, Jim Delligatti of Pittsburgh, Pennsylvania, invented the Big Mac in 1968 and another franchisor, Herb Peterson, developed the Egg McMuffin in 1973. Today, both of these sandwiches continue to be popular, profitable staples in the McDonalds product offerings.

Third-Party Distribution Systems

Third-party distribution systems act as middlemen between the buyer and supplier. In the hospitality industry this most often refers to Internet based companies that provide travel reservations such as "Travelocity.com," "Expedia.com," "Priceline.com," or "Hotwire.com." The third-party distribution company becomes a representative to the hospitality service provider. They do not own the products or services that they are selling; their role is to connect buyers with sellers. Some buy the product like blocks of rooms from the hotel for wholesale prices and then turn around and sell those rooms to the end user at discounted prices. Sometimes this results in a price war, with hotels competing for their own rooms. In New Orleans, hotels wanted to create a referral organization for only New Orleans properties to compete with these third-party distribution companies.

Third-party distribution systems can also operate reservation services on behalf of corporate, franchise, and independent lodging properties. For a fee or commission, these organizations provide reservations to the public. Examples of hospitality third-party distributors are "Expedia.com," "Orbitz.com," and "Travelocity.com." These Internet sites sell a variety of travel products and services: lodging, transportation (car rental, airline, train and bus tickets), and entertainment (theater, amusement parks). Think of these companies like a grocery store in that they advertise their Internet site to the general public. Once a customer visits the Internet site, each individual brand or property competes for the customers' business based on location, price, and amenities. Third-party distribution systems provide a means for independent or non-affiliated businesses to create brand awareness and compete with affiliated (corporate or franchise) properties. Affiliated properties have one more marketing tool for promoting their specific property in addition to brand system wide promotional activities.

Participating hospitality businesses provide a set number of rooms/tickets in a price range or established price. The third-party operator acts as a representative of the hotel and sells the room/ticket to the general public. The customer pays the third-party distributor and they in turn pay the lodging, transportation, or entertainment operator minus the commission.

Summary

Franchises, referral organization, and third-party distribution systems are other ways to manage your business. Each system operates differently giving the owners unique opportunities. Six of the top 10 largest franchisors are hospitality organizations.

Industry Spot Light
FREEDOM BOAT CLUB

This unique franchise operation provides boaters of all levels access to the water without the hassle of owning and maintaining a boat. There are 42 locations around the United States where, after booking online, club members can reserve the type of boat they want without having to worry about the upkeep, insurance, and maintenance. The Club concept is a private, members-only club that gives members unlimited access to a fleet of boats chosen by the members. With first-class boats and service, come indulge in the soothing boating lifestyle and see why Freedom Boat Club is the nation's leader in the boat club industry.

Chances are that you have visited one of these businesses and or worked for a hospitality franchised operation. Franchising offers many advantages to the owner/manager, employee, and customer: consistency in brand offerings, standardization of policies and procedures, and service standards. As a future hospitality professional you have many career options and employment choices. Owning a franchise is one way that you can go into business for yourself without doing everything yourself. On the other hand, if you operate a small business, perhaps referral organizations will give you marketing power without the necessity of merging with a large corporation. Finally, third-party distribution systems may give you a central reservation system and additional visibility to aid in obtaining more guests. Depending on what you need, each of these methods are possibilities when exploring your options.

≈ *Resources*

Internet Sites

Accor: www.accorhotels.com
Best Western: www.bestwestern.org
Cendant Corporation: www.cendant.com
International Franchise Association: www.franchise.org
KOA: www.koa.com
Rio Wraps Southwestern Grill: www.reowraps.com
Freedom Boat Club: www.Freedomboatclub.com

References

International Franchise Association. (2005). Franchise Development Super Session Series. Atlanta, Georgia, April 21–22.
Keup, E. (2004). *Franchise Bible: How to Buy a Franchise or Franchise Your Own Business*. (5th edition). Irving, CA: Entrepreneur Press.
Thomas, D., and Seid, M. (2000). *Franchising for Dummies*. Hungry Minds, Inc. New York, NY.
Top Franchise Companies. (2007). *Entrepreneur.com*

≈ *Endnotes*

1.   International Franchise Association. (2007). Industry facts, downloaded, August 24, 2007 at www.franchise.org

≈ *Contributor*

Susan Gregory

www.emich.edu/sts/hrm

Professor and Coordinator for the Hotel and Restaurant Management Program at Eastern Michigan University.

Chapter 14
Review Questions

1. What are some of the names of local hospitality franchise operations in your city?

2. Are there any local franchisors in your community or state?

3. What are the advantages for an independent business owner to join a franchise or referral organization?

4. As an employee, what are the advantages of working for a franchise operation (affiliated) over working for a nonaffiliated business and vise-versa?

5. As a consumer, describe how you have used a third-party distribution company.

6. What is the difference between a franchise and a referral system?

7. How can you find out what services a franchisor offers to its franchisees?

8. Why are franchise restaurants popular with consumers?

9. What are some unusual franchise opportunities related to your vocation and avocation?

Contract Services Management

Wanda M. Costen, University of Tennessee

15

© 2008, JupiterImages Corporation.

≈ Learning Objectives

☑ Understand the roles of owner and contractor
☑ Know the components of a management contract
☑ Understand the key criteria for selecting a hotel management contractor
☑ Be able to explain the roles of host, client, contractor, and self-operated
☑ Be able to describe the different segments of the on-site foodservice industry
☑ Know the key players in the on-site foodservice industry
☑ Understand the career opportunities available in contract services management

≈ Chapter Outline

Hotel Contract Management
Contract Foodservice Management

≈ Key Terms

Base fees
Board plan
Branding
Client
Contract services management
Host
Incentive fees
On-site foodservice management
Operator
Operator loan and equity contributions
Operator system reimbursable expenses
Owner
Self-operators
Term

*H*ave you ever thought about owning a lodging business but weren't sure you knew enough to make a profit? You may not realize it, but when you stay at a hotel or motel, sometimes the company that runs or operates the hotel is not the same company that *owns* the property. Similarly, when you eat in your university's dining facilities, there is often a separate organization providing the foodservice. After all, you wouldn't expect the university administrators to know all the details of how to feed all those students. The organization that manages lodging or foodservice operations for owners are called *operators*.

Over the years, real estate has been an attractive and lucrative investment. Many investment companies choose to purchase real estate, and subsequently build a lodging property on the land. These investment companies typically do not have the expertise necessary to operate a hotel or motel, but they believe that lodging would be a sound investment strategy. Therefore, they hire another organization to run the property. Likewise, most managers of businesses, universities, and hospitals know their own industries, but they have no desire to gain the knowledge and expertise necessary to feed employees or students. Since this is a secondary concern, they may not want to hire a department just to feed everyone. Therefore, they do not operate their own cafeterias. They, too, hire outside organizations to run their foodservice operations. The agreement between the owners and the operators is called a contract, and thus this segment of the hospitality industry is referred to as *contract services management*.

There are two types of operators: chain operators and independent contractors. Chain operators, as the name implies, are affiliated with major hotel chains like Marriott, Starwood, and Hilton. In recent years, there have been many mergers of these chains creating mega-brands. As a result of acquisitions, this group of major chains is becoming smaller each year. For example in July 2007, Blackstone Group purchased Hilton Hotels Corporation for $26 billion! Blackstone operates under the name brands of Wyndham, Extended Stay America, La Quinta, and Boca Resorts. They purchased Starwood that contains the following brands: Sheraton, Westin, W, Four Points, and St. Regis. All of these chain operators have name brand recognition, a history of successful performance, and efficient operating systems.

Independent contractors are not affiliated with any specific brand. They purchase brands and loca-

tions based on their assessment for compatibility with their objectives. For example, The Hotel Group manages 25 properties under brands like Double Tree, Sheraton, Crowne Plaza, Microtel, Best Western, Embassy Suites, and even Courtyard by Marriott.[1] Another independent contractor, Hostmark Hospitality Group, has managed over 250 hotel properties in 40 states, the Caribbean, Canada, and the Middle East since its founding in 1965. Currently it manages hotel properties under the names of Hilton, Radisson, Sheraton, and Embassy Suites.[2]

Hotel Contract Management

The concept of separating the ownership and operation of a lodging property fueled much of the capital needed to fund the expansive growth of the lodging industry in the 1970s and 1980s. Investors were able to purchase land all over the country, without having to be concerned with the challenges of running a lodging property. They simply bought great locations for hospitality ventures, and then turned them over to contract managers to ensure profitability. By the same token, successful management companies were able to grow their brand names and expand into new markets, without huge capital expenditures. It was a win-win situation for both parties.

The Contract Parties

Ultimately, there are three parties involved in hotel management contracts: operators, lenders, and owners. Each party has its own objectives or incen-

© 2008, JupiterImages Corporation.

The most significant recent change in contract negotiation is the increased involvement of lenders.

tives for entering into the contract. Operators desire an increase in both market presence and market share, maintaining control over the day-to-day management decisions, and long-term stability.[3] However, their knowledge about the industry and operations is no longer a monopoly as lenders and owners stay in the business longer and learn from their ventures.

The most significant change in the contract negotiating process over the past few years has been the more active involvement of lenders, and an increase in the power of the owners. Lenders are typically concerned with generating an adequate rate of return and protecting the investment. However, in recent years, as their knowledge about the process and success factors increases, lenders have become more involved in the negotiation of these contracts.

Owners are primarily interested in generating cash flow and ensuring that their capital investment appreciates or grows in value. As a result, owners have developed more knowledge about hotel operations as they acquire more properties and experience. In addition, there is an increase in the number of hotel operators (i.e., competition) which has shifted the bargaining power to the owners.

The Contract

Management contracts are comprised of several key provisions, which explain the contract. One key provision is operator loan and equity contributions. As a result of the increase in competition amongst operators, many are now choosing to make loan or equity contributions. In the past, operators were solely responsible for managing the hotel property, but today operators are willing to contribute funding, which demonstrates the operator's commitment to the success of the property.

All contracts include an initial term or length of the contract, and guidelines for renewing the contract. The length of the initial term for chain operators is approximately 8–10 years, with one or two 3–5 year renewals. Independent contractor initial terms are typically 1–3 years, with one or two 2-year renewals. Owners desire shorter terms, because they believe this will entice the operator to perform well in order for the contract to be renewed. Operators obviously prefer a longer contract term, because they want stability. Operators also argue that shorter termed contracts force them to focus on short-term goals instead of long-term strategy.[4]

Management fees, which have decreased in recent years, are paid to the operators. In general, basic management fees have been on the decline, and incentive fees have become more challenging for operators to achieve. These trends are a result of the increase in owner negotiating power and operator competition. Basic management fees for chain operators of full-service hotels average 2.25% of gross revenues without an operator equity contribution and 2.5% of gross revenues with an operator equity contribution. Independent contractors receive base fees of 1.5% and 2.5%, respectively.[5]

Incentive fees are now based upon cash flow after debt service or return on equity. Cash flow after debt service is the amount of cash that flows through the company after paying for its debts. Return on equity is the amount of profit a company makes with the money shareholders have invested. In the past, operator incentives were determined by gross operating profit, or the amount of revenue generated after the costs associated with the goods and services sold are removed. This shift indicates that owners expect operators to contribute to the bottom line profit of the venture, not just the revenue.

Another important area that must be addressed in the contract is operator system reimbursable expenses. The owner pays the operator for centralized services provided by the operator. For example, operators provide their own PMS systems, marketing, and advertising programs; centralized reservations systems; accounting and management information systems; purchasing services; as well as risk management and insurance. Owners pay these fees, because these systems are provided by the operator's corporation and the property benefits from them. For chain operators, these expenses range from 2 to 4% of gross revenues, while independent contractor expenses range from 0 to 1% of gross revenues.[6] Independent contractor fees are significant lower because they do not have an affiliation with a major hotel chain.

As with individual employee performance, operating companies must be held accountable for achieving certain outcomes. These performance standards are included in the contract. Typically, these performance provisions should be evaluated each year. Often the measures include year-to-year growth, based upon an initial 3–5 year gross operating profit projection. When the hotel first opens, an operator may have 1 or 2 years grace period before the performance criteria are fine-tuned. If the operator assumes control of an existing property, the operator usually has a 6-month grace period. When operators fall short of their projections due to changes in the economy or market, owners make allowances for lower than expected performance. If the operator simply does not meet the performance criteria, they are usually required to pay the owner the difference. Additionally, owners often include options for terminating a contract based upon continued poor performance.

The specific conditions under which a contract may be terminated by either party is a crucial component of every contract. Once again, there is a huge benefit to being a chain operator. In general, owners cannot terminate a contract with a chain operator at any time. However, after some period of time in the contract, owners may terminate the operator. Owners must pay operators a termination fee, which ranges from 2–4 times the management fee for chain operators, and 0.5–2 times the management fee for independent contractors.[7]

The final component of the contract is the degree of input the owner has in decision-making related to running the hotel. Owners are beginning to negotiate the right to have input on the annual budget and hiring the executive staff. In general, the executive staff (general manager, controller, directors of marketing, human resources, rooms, food and beverage, housekeeping, and engineering) is employees of the operating company. The hourly workers are employed by the owners.

It is important to note that as with all contracts, each provision or component is negotiated. A management contract is a written agreement between two organizations that outlines each party's responsibilities, and consequences for not fulfilling its obligations. As mentioned earlier, today owners have gained a slight advantage in negotiating, but major chain operators are still able to influence the provisions that matter most to them.

Choosing a Hotel Management Company

Given the large number of hotel operators today, it is important for owners to develop criteria for selecting a management company. Research shows that there are five key areas that should be examined and evaluated when choosing a company to operate a hotel. First, if the owner has other hotel properties, one should look at the operating performance of the current contracted companies. If the owner has no previous experience with other op-

erators, he/she should rely on feedback from clients with existing management contracts with potential operators. Next, the owner should try to determine how accessible the operating company's senior management is. How willing is the operator's senior management to meet with the owner and work through issues or discuss opportunities for growth? The owner should also try to get a feel for the overall integrity of the operating company. What is the operator's reputation in the industry? Does the operating company's organizational culture and values align with those of the owner's company? Finally, the owner should measure the marketing strength and penetration of the operator.[8]

Hotel owners and operators must work together to create a successful hotel that delivers or exceeds the level of customer service expected by its guests. The process of negotiating a management contract is one of give and take. Each party has its own goals, but must be flexible in order to create a mutually-beneficial contract. Today, owners have more bargaining power than operators, which is forcing the operators to invest in the property, and to meet increasingly challenging performance expectations. Additionally, this shift has resulted in lower base and incentive fees for operators, and more flexible terms for owners.

Contract Foodservice Management

The evolution of the term used to describe foodservice management contracts also explains the transition of this segment of the hospitality industry. Contract foodservice management was initially called institutional foodservice, because most contracts were with hospitals, industrial plants, and correctional facilities. The focus was on producing mass quantities of food that could be delivered quickly. Not surprisingly, quality was not a high priority. Today this segment of the foodservice industry is known as on-site foodservice management or managed services. The quality of food and service provided in business organizations, hospitals, schools, colleges and universities, and recreational facilities today often rivals that of top restaurants. The difference is that the foodservice is provided on-site (i.e., at the hospital, business organization, or recreational facility). Furthermore, today's providers of on-site foodservice now manage other services (copy centers, on-site childcare, company stores) as well.

This segment totals approximately $230 billion of the $800 billion global foodservice industry.[9]

The Players

In order to grasp the difference between on-site foodservice management and restaurants, one must first understand the terminology and the roles of the players. First, the *contractor* is the organization that provides the foodservice. The *host* is the organization that hires the contractor. The *client* is the person within the host organization that serves as the host organization's representative and is responsible for monitoring the contractor's performance. In a general sense, the term client is also used to refer to the entire host organization.

Some host organizations decide to operate their own foodservice instead of hiring an outside contractor. These organizations are *self-operated*. In these situations, the foodservice operation is a division of the host organization, and all of the managers and employees in the foodservice operation work for the host company. Many school districts operate their own foodservice organizations, but there is a trend toward outsourcing, that is hiring an outside firm to handle all the food operations. It is often difficult for organizations to operate two separate organizations profitably. Until 2001, the largest and most successful self-operated on-site foodservice organization was Motorola. Its Hospitality Group generated revenues in excess of $55 million in 2001.[10] However, the pressure to reduce costs, while maintaining quality and generating revenues became too challenging, and Motorola hired Compass Group North America to run its foodservice in September 2001.

On-Site Foodservice Management Companies

The largest on-site foodservice management company is Sodexho Alliance. Sodexho is based in France and is expected to generate $19 billion in revenue.[11] Sodexho operates in 80 countries and employs approximately 332,000 people.[12]

The next largest on-site foodservice management company is also a global company, Compass Group. This organization is based in Britain and is expected to generate revenue in excess of $10 billion in 2007.[13] Compass operates in 70 countries with over 400,000 employees.[14] Each of its businesses operates as separate entities under the fol-

Approximately 60–65% of college and university food service is managed by service companies.

lowing brands: Eurest, Bon Appetit, Restaurant Associates, Medirest, Morrison, Crothall, Chartwells, Scolarest, Levy Restaurants, ESS, and Canteen.[15]

The third largest on-site foodservice management company is ARAMARK Services, Inc., which is the only major player based in the U.S. In 2006, ARAMARK generated $11.6 billion in revenue.[16] It operates in 18 countries and employs 240,000 people.[17] As the numbers indicate, these companies manage the overwhelming majority of contracts in the on-site foodservice segment of the hospitality industry.

On-Site Foodservice Segments

The on-site foodservice industry is divided into market segments based upon where the foodservice is provided. The first market segment is business and industry.

Approximately 85–90% of this segment is operated by on-site managed services organizations.[18] In this market segment, on-site foodservice contractors operate dining facilities in corporate offices. These facilities include multiple food stations, often with different ethnic cuisines. Today the trend is toward exhibition cooking and meal replacement. Many on-site foodservice contractors prepare take-home meals for their customers. Customers can now eliminate a stop on the way home and this increases the revenue of the operation. The focus is on providing what the customers want and exceeding their expectations, while remaining profitable. Not surprisingly, these are the same goals of a free standing restaurant.

The education segment of the industry comprises K–12 schools, as well as colleges and universities. Approximately 60–65% of college and university foodservice is operated by managed services companies, while only 15–20% of K–12 foodservice is contracted out.[19] With the reductions in federal funding, the focus in K–12 schools is on reducing costs and increasing participation. Managed services providers are also offering on-site childcare (before and after-school programs). Moreover, occasionally the foodservice operator extends its services to adult daycare centers, preschools, and private schools that are nearby. Centralized production kitchens often allow the on-site foodservice contractor to serve these other organizations with little increase in costs.[20]

Foodservice operations on college and university campuses have two types of operations. One is the *board plan* and the other is termed *retail*. The board plan allows students to pre-purchase a set number of meals throughout the semester. These all-you-can-eat meals are typically offered in the campus dining halls. Retail operations resemble shopping mall food courts. Students transfer money to a debit card, which is used to purchase items in the food courts and kiosks around campus. Managed services providers use branding (which will be discussed later) to increase participation.

Healthcare is probably the most challenging segment of the on-site foodservice industry because it includes patient feeding in addition to operating on-site dining facilities. Not only are there nutrition and dietary concerns in this segment, but patient treatment has shifted from in-patient to outpatient services, and shorter hospital stays. This shift has resulted in lower foodservice revenue projections. Managed services companies have opted to offer additional services like housekeeping and facilities maintenance to offset these reductions. This shift might also explain why only 40–45% of this segment is managed by on-site foodservice companies.[21]

Recreation and leisure is the fastest growing segment of this industry, with 35-40% of the business being operated by managed services companies. This segment includes ball parks, stadiums, arenas, and national and state parks. Today's sports fan can find a wide variety of menu options ranging from clam chowder and garlic fries at AT&T Park in San Francisco to a Dodger Dog at Dodger Stadium in Los Angeles. Additionally, many of the top stadiums and arenas today have deluxe skyboxes, where gourmet meal packages are offered.[22]

Corrections or prison feeding is the final segment in this industry. Not surprisingly, only 10–15% of this industry is managed by on-site foodservice contractors.[23] Security is only one of the challenges in this segment. Prison foodservice production facilities were not built to accommodate the recent increase in the prison population, which presents many challenges for foodservice operators. Additionally, similar to K–12 schools and hospitals, the correctional nutrition requirements pose unique challenges in designing menus. Moreover, the workers in these facilities are inmates, which can present management challenges.

Branding

On-site foodservice management companies have realized the importance of branding for increasing revenues. In each segment, the dining facilities include national, regional, and corporate brands. Branding has shifted the ambiance of on-site dining from a cafeteria to a "market-style eatery."[24] National brands include fast food eateries like KFC and Pizza Hut, as well as Starbucks. Regional brands allow the management companies to bring in foods that are unique to the local area. Finally, each of the major on-site foodservice companies has developed their own in-house brands. For example, you might find a Coyote Jack's Grill next to a Burger King kiosk in a Compass account, or a Miso Noodle Bar next to a Quizno sub outlet in an ARAMARK account.

Career Opportunities

Like the restaurant industry in general, there are vast career opportunities in on-site foodservice management. In operations, a recent college graduate can expect to spend 2–3 months in a comprehensive training program, followed by an assignment as an Assistant Foodservice Manager at a particular location. Within 3–5 years, an Assistant Manager can move up to a Foodservice Director position (depending on the complexity of the operation). Most foodservice operators aspire to reach a District Manager position. This position oversees on-site foodservice operations within a specific geographic region and reports to a Regional Vice President. One of the primary benefits of a career in this segment is the hours. Typically, foodservice managers work during the hours of operation for their location. Thus, if a business and industry account operates Monday–Friday, 7:00 AM–6:00 PM, the management team typically provides breakfast and lunch, and does not have to work late nights and weekends. This structure allows those with a passion for the foodservice business to have a quality of life also.

Summary

Contract services management allows the ownership and operation of a hospitality venue to be separated. The owner and operator enter into a binding legal contract, which outlines the nature of the relationship and each party's responsibilities.

While hotel management contractors are facing increasing competition, which is impacting their bargaining power, on-site foodservice organizations are gathering up more of the market. This segment of the hospitality industry offers unique, challenging, and exciting career options, which provide options for hospitality majors.

≈ *Resources*

Internet Sites

Society for Foodservice Management: www.sfm-online.org
This site contains information about the on-site foodservice management segment of the hospitality industry.
American Hotel and Lodging Association: www.ahla.com
It is the premier website for the lodging industry. This site contains information on professional certifications, career opportunities, conferences, and more.
National Restaurant Association: www.restaurant.org
It is the premier website for the foodservice industry. This site contains information about professional certifications, career opportunities, current news, and more.
www.hotelresource.com
This Website provides a vast amount of resources and information about hotel management companies.
ARAMARK Corporation: www.aramark.com
Compass Group: www.compass-group.com
Sodexho Alliance: www.sodexho.com

≈ *Endnotes*

1. The Hotel Group Website. (2007). http://www.thehotelgroup.com/about_history.asp
2. Hostmark Hospitality Group. (2007). at http://www.hostmark.com
3. Eyster, J. (1993). The revolution in domestic hotel management contracts. *The Cornell HRA Quarterly,* (February), 16–26.
4. Eyster, J. (1997). Hotel management contracts in the U.S. *The Cornell HRA Quarterly,* (June), 21–33.
5. Ibid.
6. Ibid.
7. Ibid.
8. Rainsford, P. (1994). Selecting and monitoring hotel-management companies. *The Cornell HRA Quarterly,* (April), 30–35.
9. Reynolds, D. (2003). *On-site Foodservice Management: A Best Practices Approach.* Hoboken, NJ: John Wiley & Sons.
10. Ibid.
11. Sodexho Alliance. (2007). Sodexho profile at http://www.sodexho.com/group_en/the-group/profile/profile.asp
12. Ibid.
13. Compass Group. (2007). Interim Report at http://static.digitallook.com/digitalcorporate/cms/25/assets/COMPASS_INTERIM_2007.pdf
14. Compass Group. (2007). About Us at http://www.compass-group.com/aboutus/
15. Compass Group. (2007). Markets at http://www.compass-group.com/aboutus/markets.htm
16. ARAMARK Services, Inc. (2007). Company Snapshot at http://www.aramark.com/ContentTemplate.aspx?PostingID=369&ChannelID=203
17. ARAMARK Services, Inc. (2007). About Us at http://www.aramark.com/MainLanding.aspx?PostingID=336&ChannelID=187
18. Reynolds, D. (1999). Managed services companies: The new scorecard for on-site foodservice. *The Cornell HRA Quarterly,* (June), 64–73.
19. Ibid.
20. Ibid.
21. Ibid.
22. Ibid.
23. Ibid.
24. Ibid.

≈ *Contributor*

Dr. Wanda M. Costen, Assistant Professor
Department of Retail, Hospitality, and Tourism Management
University of Tennessee
1215 W. Cumberland Avenue
Knoxville, TN 37996-1911
Office: (865) 974-2909
Fax: (865) 974-5236
wcosten@utk.edu
Ph.D., Washington State University
MBA, Pepperdine University
BS, United States Military Academy

Chapter 15
Review Questions

1. Define contract management services.

2. What is a hotel management contract?

3. Describe three key provisions of a hotel management contract.

4. What are some of the challenges hotel management contractors face today?

5. What are the two terms used today to describe contract foodservice management?

6. Describe the market segments in the contract foodservice management industry.

7. Name the three key contract foodservice management companies.

8. What are some of the benefits of a career in contract foodservice management?

E-Hospitality: Technology in the Hospitality Industry

16

Wanda M. Costen, University of Tennessee

© Dmitriy Shironosov, 2008, Shutterstock.

≈ Learning Objectives

- ☑ To describe the different types of technology used in the hospitality industry
- ☑ To identify which technological applications are used in which segments of the industry
- ☑ To explain how technology usage affects a hospitality organization

≈ Chapter Outline

What Is E-Hospitality?
Technology and Consumer Behavior
Technology in Lodging
Technology in Foodservice
Technology in Conventions and Meeting Planning
Other Uses of Technology

≈ Key Terms

Back-office technology
Data management systems
Distribution channel
E-commerce
Front-office technology
Guest-related systems
Restaurant and banquet management systems
Smart phones
Third parties

$\mathcal{E}$ver since the advent of computers, the world of technology has been rapidly changing. Microchips keep getting smaller and smaller, and all the products that use them are shrinking as well. Luckily, along with the shrinking size comes the reduction in pricing making everything better and more affordable. This means that the average person can afford voice mail, e-mail, security systems, and computers. Not only can they buy these products and many more, but because of the size, they have become portable as well. People can get their voice and e-mail messages anywhere in the world. You can check the security of your house by accessing your house Web site. And, computers come in all sizes. Because people are using more technology, they expect high tech when they travel as well. Therefore, hotels and even restaurants offer wireless availability.

The dropping prices also allow businesses to use high-tech equipment to speed up operations, coordinate activities, and secure their properties. Hotels have programmed key cards and property management systems that allow a guest to turn the lights, TV, and heating/cooling systems off and on. Restaurants have systems to speed up ordering and check and credit card operations. Of course, the Internet has totally changed the way people shop, explore their options, and make reservations. This means that hospitality businesses need Web sites, online reservations, and property tours to accommodate this new way of attracting customers. As you can see, e-hospitality is growing faster than any other business.

What Is E-Hospitality?

Technology seems to be one of the most important components affecting business today. E-hospitality is the term used to reflect all aspects of technology in the hospitality industry. Technology encompasses everything from voice mail systems and electronic door locks to property management and menu engineering systems. Technology affects each segment and department of the hospitality industry. The purpose of this chapter is to expose you to the various types of technology used in different segments of the industry. It is important to understand the role of technology in the hospitality industry because research shows that technology positively influences organizational performance, employee productivity, and customer satisfaction.[1]

Unfortunately, the hospitality industry typically lags behind other industries in terms of adopting technology. This is usually because of the hospitality industry's slow response to information technology growth. Other industries have leveraged technology and increased efficiency and productivity. Leveraging technology is the process of using technology in ways that maximize its benefits. For example, most business managers have e-mail capability. Leveraging the use of this technology would include not only communicating using e-mail, but also attaching memos, policy changes, and new procedures. This process would reduce the amount of paper used in the organization, as well as the time it takes to implement changes to policies and procedures. Reducing implementation time increases the efficiency of the organization. Because many hospitality managers have little technological training, they are less comfortable adopting new technology.[2] Consequently, decision makers in the hospitality industry are only typically willing to invest in technology that is visible or has a direct impact on the bottom line. Visible technology falls into the "low end" of the technological spectrum. These applications are primarily clerical/administrative or operational and include computers, e-mail, fax machines, printers, and Internet access. Unfortunately, however, computer usage primarily duplicated the paper system that it replaced. For example, technology is not primarily used to allow the front office system to "talk to" the foodservice cost management system or the reservations system.

Technology and Consumer Behavior

According to the U.S. Department of Commerce, since the year 2000, more people are using the Internet to make purchases. See Table 16.1 for information on travel consumer behavior.

Consumers primarily use the Internet to find out information. Therefore, access to the company's Web site, quality of the content, and structure are the most important attributes that consumers use to evaluate a company's Web site. Access measures how easy it is for consumers to find a company's Web site. The quality of the content measures how current the information is and whether that information is readily understandable and useful to the consumer. The structure of the site is a measure of how the site is organized, including the usefulness of links and placement of important information. Additionally, information completeness and ease of use are the two characteristics that most influence

Table 16.1 Travel Planning on the Internet (in millions)[21]

	2000	2001	2002	2003	2004	2005
Online travelers	59.4	64.5	63.9	64.1	63.8	79.0
Online frequent travelers[a]	30.8	32.0	33.8	32.6	31.7	47.2

[a]The Travel Industry Association of America defines frequent travelers as those who make 5+ trips/year.

consumer behavior intentions. Information completion is whether consumers find the information they are seeking, and ease of use is how user-friendly the Web site is and whether consumers are able to conduct their desired transactions. When consumers are satisfied with the information they obtain from an organization's Web site, they are more likely to purchase that product.[3]

E-Commerce

E-commerce is the process of using the Internet to establish a distribution channel that allows companies to work with customers, suppliers, and partners.[4] A distribution channel is a way of getting a company's products or services to the consumer. E-commerce changes these relationships, as well as the flow of information. One way that e-commerce changes relationships is that the Internet allows people to retrieve the information they need when they need it.[5] Thus, consumers no longer have to contact a supplier to purchase an item. In the hospitality industry, this means that consumers can log onto the Internet and purchase a hotel room whenever they want, without the hassle of trying to find the telephone contact information for a reservation center. E-commerce influences the flow of information in that a consumer no longer has to interact directly with a company representative to get the information they need. Although the company does control the information that is posted on its Web site, how and when that information gets to the consumer is now at the consumer's fingertips.

Hospitality companies, and lodging properties in particular use multiple distribution channels, each with different rates, to sell their rooms. Hospitality companies sell their services through their own company Web sites, third-party Web sites, and company telephone reservations systems. The different rates are due to the costs associated with each channel. A third party often charges a fee for distribution, and there are obvious labor costs associated with a company's telephone reservations system. No one distribution channel consistently has

the lowest price, so consumers are likely to use the Internet to seek out the rates available from various providers that best suit their needs.[6] In 2005, many benchmark lodging properties noticed that 50 percent of their business was generated from the Internet.[7] A study of Internet use in the lodging industry indicated that hotel company Web sites received 75 percent of the market, while third parties (Travelocity, Orbitz, Expedia, etc.) received the other 25 percent. However, economic issues are forcing lodging companies to provide more inventory to third-party distributors. The Internet has given the consumer access to a wide assortment of lodging options, and therefore the hotel room is now a commodity. Each room that is priced similarly is seen as equivalent, regardless of the quality of the property. To distinguish its product, lodging companies now have to invest in customer-oriented amenities and offers of free services. These investments ultimately affect the bottom-line profit of the company and are quickly becoming the cost of doing business. As a result, hotel companies will most likely begin to rely more on third-party Web sites to sell their room inventory in the near future. Relying on third parties could potentially reduce the bottom-line profit of hotel companies because the company will no longer have exclusive control over room rates.

Technology in Lodging

Some of the greatest strides in technology in the hospitality industry have occurred in the lodging segment of the industry. In general, there are four types of information technology (IT) applications in the lodging industry:

1. Front office information technology applications include reservation management, room management, and guest accounting systems.
2. Back office technology includes human resources systems, financial reports, and inventory systems.

Consumers can log onto the Internet and make a hotel reservation whenever they want.

3. Restaurant and banquet management systems include cost control, menu and recipe management, beverage control, sales forecasting, and menu pricing.
4. Guest-related systems are those related to the call accounting system, energy management systems, guest-operated devices, and automated guest services like an automated wake-up call system.[8]

Technology can be used to increase employee productivity, reduce administrative and communication costs, enhance revenue, and increase guest services. The property management system is an example of how technology can increase guest services. Today's property management systems provide the front desk, room service, and other guest agents with a guest's name. This information gives the employee the opportunity to call the guest by name, thereby establishing a rapport with the guest. Technology geared toward employee productivity includes voice mail, interactive TV guides, and management e-mail. Interactive TV guides provide the customer the opportunity to check out of the hotel, which reduces the number of people with whom the front desk needs to interact. Ultimately this technology increases employee productivity. Internet bookings, teleconferencing, cell phone rentals, and ATMs are technology applications that generate additional revenue. Guest services technology includes in-room modems, in-room Internet access, and in-room fax machines.

Generally, the more upscale the lodging property, the greater the number of technological applications the property has adopted. Casino and convention hotels implement the most technology designed to enhance guest services (in-room Internet access and in-room modems and fax machines). Not surprisingly, convention hotels also implement significantly more technology that increases employee efficiency and enhances revenue. The most frequently adopted technological application in lodging companies is Internet bookings, followed by management e-mail systems and Internet access in hotel rooms.[9]

Technology has reached almost unbelievable heights in international hotels. In Dubai's Burj Al Arab, curtains, lighting, and heating in a guest room are voice controlled. The room even can sense when it is occupied! The latest lodging technology systems monitor and control smoke detectors, room entry, alarm systems, heating, air conditioning, television, and lighting all from a central location. Hallway sensors allow lights to be turned off unless someone enters the hallway. Motion sensors signal the system and turn on the lights as needed. This technology significantly reduces energy costs while maintaining safety. Today, some five-star lodging properties have interactive plasma TVs that not only allow the guest to check out without going to the front desk, but also order room service, schedule a spa treatment, or get a tee time.[10]

Technology in Foodservice

Technology in foodservice has typically been restricted to the back-of-the-house, but that is rapidly changing. The back-of-the-house is the term used to classify positions that have little or no guest contact. In foodservice these positions are located in the kitchen, such as chef/cook or dishwasher. Therefore, back-of-the-house foodservice technology refers to the technology that assists kitchen operations. Food and beverage cost control, recipe management, menu pricing, and sales forecasting are some of the types of technological systems currently in use in foodservice establishments. There is a new trend, however, in that cutting-edge foodservice operators are using their Web sites to facilitate online reservations and better serve their customers.

Pizza delivery restaurants seem to be taking the lead in on-site technology. When a customer calls into almost any national pizza delivery restaurant, the store is able to pull up pertinent information about the customer quickly. The data management system contains not only the name and address of the caller (retrieved by phone number), but also information about previous orders and delivery instructions. This same system is integrated with sales and marketing and allows the restaurant to send out direct mailers and promotional coupons to specific customers. For example, a store owner can run a query, download all the customers who have not ordered a pizza in the past 90 days, and send those customers a promotional advertisement.

Full-service, upscale restaurants are also using technology to enhance their customer service and guest experience. The Charlie Palmer Group uses an electronic wine list at its restaurants in Las Vegas, New York City, and Washington, D.C. The list, which contains 4,000 bottles, is presented on a personal data assistant (PDA) and given to the customer at the table. Each wine listing contains information on food and wine pairings, as well as background information about some of the wineries. This system has increased wine sales by 36 percent.[11]

In Atlanta, Nava uses wireless handheld terminals that allow cocktail servers to send drink orders immediately to the bar. By the time the cocktail servers get to the bar, the drink is ready! Additionally, this particular system sends each food order to the particular area in the kitchen. For example, each component of the order is sent to the grill, hot appetizers, or garde manger. These wireless handhelds can also be used to print out the guest check and scan credit cards at the table. According to the General Manager, John McDaniels, these wireless handheld terminals make the restaurant more efficient and more profitable.[12]

Smart phone technology is on the cutting edge of restaurant technology internationally. Smart phones are cell phones with PDA capabilities. In Asia and Europe, customers can use their smart phones to order and pay at some restaurants. This smart phone technology has huge implications for the restaurant industry, especially quick-service restaurants. Imagine going into a quick-service restaurant and beaming in your order while paying for it at the same time! This technology could help reduce labor and training costs, while simultaneously increasing customer satisfaction.[13]

Technology in Conventions and Meeting Planning

With the advent of teleconferencing, conventional wisdom suggested that technology would reduce the number of meetings held each year. To the contrary, technology has actually stimulated the need for technology shows and enhanced the demands of other shows. As a result, convention centers have needed to broaden their technological capabilities.

Fifty percent of the convention centers and convention and visitor bureaus (CVBs) that participated in a study in 1998 posted information for event planners and attendees online via their Web site. Approximately 60 percent provided Internet access to meeting planners and attendees in exhibit halls or meeting rooms and offered network setup. In terms of security, 45 percent of the participants used smart cards to limit access to secure areas of the convention center. Furthermore, 70 percent had teleconferencing capabilities, and 65 percent had videoconferencing capability.[14] This information means that convention center and CVB clients expect to have access to a variety of technological applications. In order to remain competitive, these organizations need to ensure that they can meet the needs of these technologically savvy clients.

In 2000, 70 percent of the major convention centers in the United States had T1 Internet connections capable of transferring 1.54 megabits of data per second. A large number of these centers also have T3 connections, which are **30** times *faster* than T1s! These connections allow exhibitors to use the Internet as part of their display in an exhibition hall. The Dallas Convention Center implemented the first wireless networking system in a convention center in 1997. Wireless systems provide Internet access without connecting a cable to a computer. According to the Technical Director, Cindy Coyle, this wireless system is actually cheaper than the wired communication systems offered by the local telecommunications provider.[15]

Other Uses of Technology

It seems clear that technology aids in sales and marketing, given the increased numbers of consumers booking travel online. Technology also influences other areas in hospitality companies. Many companies today use intranet systems to train employees and disseminate company information. An intranet system is similar to the Internet, only it is only accessible within the company by people granted access. Human resource departments have set up computers in the back-of-the-house to allow employees to access and update their benefits information.

With the success of Monster.com, e-recruiting is now revolutionizing the way companies find new employees. In 2000, 45 percent of the *Fortune* 500 companies used the Internet to actively recruit.[16] Using the Internet reduces the costs of advertising for open positions. Two of the most sophisticated Web sites for seeking a position in the hospitality industry in North America are Hcareers[17] and Hospitality Career Net.[18–19] See Figure 16.1 for a more thorough listing of online hospitality employment sites.

How Technology Adds Value to an Organization

In many manufacturing companies, technology is often adopted to reduce labor costs. By contrast, technology in the service industry is used to support, not replace, the employee. One of the challenges facing hospitality companies is how to train employees on the technology being implemented in the organization. Because a lot of the training in this industry occurs on the job, technological skills often are not shared in a systematic way.

One of the key reasons to adopt new technology is to increase bottom-line profit. Research shows that there is a positive relationship between IT and company performance and profit. Implementing IT systems cannot only reduce costs, but also increase productivity, revenues, and ultimately customer service. The effective use of technology can also create a sustainable competitive advantage and become a way for hospitality companies to differentiate themselves.

Summary

Although there is much discussion about the potential impact of technology on the hospitality industry, few companies are actually investing in technology designed to assist the organization in accomplishing its strategic goals and creating a sustainable competitive advantage. The most technologically developed segment of the hospitality industry is the lodging segment. However, a 1998 study revealed that almost 70 percent of the 4,520 lodging properties studied had adopted few or none of the existing technology available in the marketplace.[20] With a significant amount of the lodging customers coming from the business segment, lodging companies will have to adopt some of the customer-oriented technology available to meet or exceed their customers' expectations.

In the foodservice segment, technology designed to improve the efficiency of employees, who have face-to-face contact with guests, is still cost prohibitive. However, many restaurants interface with their food suppliers and order products online. Additionally, forecasting and cost control modules assist foodservice managers in obtaining more profit.

Many of the convention centers in the U.S.' largest cities are increasing their technological capabilities. Not only are technology shows on the rise, but many clients are now requesting advanced technological support. To drive business, convention centers will need to begin to invest in cutting-edge technology.

Overall, the hospitality industry is poised to take advantage of the benefits offered by technology. In the coming years, more hotel rooms will have wireless technology, and restaurant servers will be taking your order with a handheld!

Figure 9.1 **Hospitality Employment Websites**[22]

www.hotelresource.com—This site lists job openings in front office, food and beverage, maintenance, and hotel management.

www.hospitalityonline.com/jobs—This site lists lodging management and front line positions by location, company, and position.

www.hospitalityadventures.com—Contains U.S. and international positions listed by location, company type, or company name.

www.casinocareers.com—Information about career opportunities in the casino segment of the hospitality industry.

www.foodservice.com/jobs.htm—This site is the largest and most active Website for foodservice professionals.

www.e-hospitality.com—This site provides important information about the hospitality industry, as well as job listings, recruitment information, and salary information.

≈ *Resources*

Internet Sites

www.hospitalitynet.org: Contains current industry news and information, as well as job opportunities and hotel schools.

American Hotel and Lodging Association: www.ahla.com. This is the premier site for the lodging industry and contains information on professional certifications, career opportunities, conferences, and more.

National Restaurant Association: www.restaurant.org. This is the premier site for the foodservice industry and contains information about professional certifications, career opportunities, current news, and more.

Club Managers Association of America: www.cmaa.org. Here you will find important information about a career in club management.

Meeting Professionals International: www.mpiweb.org. It contains information about careers, educational programs, and the meeting planners' profession.

≈ *Endnotes*

1. Siguaw, J., Enz, C., and Namasivayam, K. (2000). Adoption of information technology in U.S. hotels: Strategically driven objectives. *Journal of Travel Research, 39,* 192–201.
2. Law, R. and Jogaratnam, G. (2005). A study of hotel information technology applications. *International Journal of Contemporary Hospitality Management, 17* (2), 170–180.
3. Jeong, M., Haemoon, O., and Gregoire, M. (2003). Conceptualizing web site quality and its consequences in the lodging industry. *International Journal of Hospitality Management, 22,* 161–175.
4. Garces, S., Gorgemans, S., Sanchez, A. M., and Perez, M. (2004). Implications of the Internet—an analysis of the Aragonese hospitality industry. *Tourism Management, 25,* 603–613.
5. Lee, S., Barker, S., and Kandampully, J. (2003). Technology, service quality, and customer loyalty in hotels: Australian managerial perspectives. *Managing Service Quality, 13* (5), 423–432.
6. O'Connor, P. and Murphy, J. (2004). Research on information technology in the hospitality industry. *International Journal of Hospitality Management, 23,* 473–484.
7. Rama, M. (2005, May 16). Third party web sites threaten brand loyalty, bottom lines. *Hotel and Motel Management,* 23.
8. Ham, S., Kim, W. G., and Jeong, S. (2005). Effect of information technology on performance in upscale hotels. *International Journal of Hospitality Management, 24,* 2005.
9. Siguaw, et. al., 2000.
10. Room for technology. (2002, May). *Hospitality Focus,* 15–16.
11. Gerst, V. (2004, May 1). Dining in the digital age. *Restaurants and Institutions, 114,* 56–58.
12. Gerst, 2004.
13. Allen, R. (2005, November 28). Call it a hunch, but industry should invest in smart-phone technology for ordering. *Nation Restaurant News, 39,* 21.
14. Kamp, A., and Petersen, D. (1998, October 19). Technology offerings play a major role in success. *Amusement Business, 110,* 26–28.
15. Chapman, B. (2000, September 1). Really wired. *Successful Meetings, 49,* 105–110.
16. Rushmore, S. (2000, June 1). 'E-' is for employment. *Hotels, 34,* 40.
17. www.hcareers.com
18. www.hospitalitycareernet.com
19. Rushmore, S., 2000.
20. Namasivayam, K., Enz, C., and Siguaw, J. (2000). How wired are we? The selection and use of new technology in U.S. hotels. *Cornell Hotel and Restaurant Quarterly, 41* (6), 40–48.
21. Adapted from Travel Industry of America. (2005). *Travelers' use of the Internet for travel planning.*
22. Adapted from Nagubandi, A. (2003, March 10). It's hospitality here. *The Hindu.* Retrieved on 20 January 2006 from http://global.factiva.com.proxy.lib.utk.edu:90/ha/default.aspx

≈ *Contributor*

wcosten@utk.edu

Wanda M. Costen earned her PhD in sociology from Washington State University. She also has an Executive MBA from Pepperdine University and her undergraduate degree is from the United States Military Academy at West Point. She is currently an assistant professor in the Retail, Hospitality, and Tourism Management Department at the University of Tennessee. Dr. Costen's research interests include racial and gender inequality in organizations, women and leadership, and strategic human resources. Her work has been published in Journal of Management Inquiry, Journal of Human Resources in Hospitality and Tourism, and Gaming Research and Review Journal. Dr. Costen has partnered with business organizations to help them develop diversity initiatives and training programs. She also has ten years of business management experience in sales, operations, and human resources.

Chapter 16
Review Questions

1. How does the hospitality industry compare to other industries in terms of adopting new technology?

2. What Web site characteristics influence a customer's decision to purchase something on the Internet?

3. How is e-commerce affecting the profitability of hotels?

4. What are the four types of technology used in the lodging industry?

5. What are some of the benefits of using a data management system in a restaurant?

6. How does technology impact the human resources function?

7. How does technology add value to a hospitality organization?

Part 4

Hospitality Career Menu

Special Career Paths

Hotel and Lodging Operations

17

Cynthia R. Mayo, Delaware State University

© Dino Ablakovic, 2008, Shutterstock.

≈ Learning Objectives

- ☑ Discuss factors that stimulated the development of hotel and lodging properties
- ☑ Identify the partners and classifications of hotel and lodging property
- ☑ Discuss key performance measures used by hotel and lodging managers
- ☑ Analyze the functions of each department and relate them to guest services
- ☑ Identify careers found in the hotel and lodging operations

≈ Chapter Outline

A Brief History

Assessing Guests Needs to Structure Required Products and Services

The Structure of the Hotel and Lodging Industry

Hotel and Lodging Departments

≈ Key Terms

American Hotel and Lodging Association
At-will employment
Average revenue
Benchmarking
Brands
Contract
Cost per room
Cross functioning teams
Diversity
Duty of care

Franchisor
Franchisee
Geographical locations
Hotelier
Investors
Job description
Job specification
Occupancy rate
Price levels
Property Management Systems (PMS)
Ratings
Revenue per available room
Room attendants
Service levels
Structures
Trade and travel
Travel agents
Trade association
Yield management

A Brief History

*H*otel and lodging operations have a long history. Generally, an atmosphere of friendliness and care existed throughout the decades. Early hospitality was based on the rules of common courtesy and rank order of guests. Lodging and meals were offered in the homes of private citizens who designed and offered accommodations for travelers which included a bed, food, and a place to exchange horses.[1] The advent of railroads stimulated the first grand hotels built in America, such as the Tremont House in Boston, the Astor House (1936) in New York, the Parker House (1936) in Boston, and the Palace House (1975) in San Francisco. During that period, the word "**hotelier**" was developed to refer to the keeper, owner, or manager. After 1908, many hotels were developed to meet the emerging needs of travelers. During the 1920s and 1930s, the number of hotels had grown to over 10,000, with one million rooms.

During the early 1900s, a typical hotel featured such amenities as steam heat, gas burners, electric call bells, baths, and closets. In 1904, the New York St. Regis Hotel provided individually controlled heating and cooling units in each guest room. When the Statler Hotel chain started in 1908, all of the guest rooms had private baths, full length mirrors, radio reception, and telephones. The hotel served as the model hotel for more than 40 years.[2]

Assessing Guests' Needs to Structure Required Products and Services

Quality service must be promoted by all hotel and lodging operation managers. **Quality** is not an accident. It comes as a result of high intention, sincere effort, intelligent direction, and skillful execution, done from a list of alternatives. Given what is promised, service expectations have proliferated in recent years. Guests' expectations are formed based on the hotel and lodging brand and impressions after staying at a property, as well as viewing the property on the Internet. Managers may be asked two basic questions to determine guests' expectations. What did you like best about your stay? What would make your stay more enjoyable? These questions can be asked through a formal system of evaluation and by managers "walking around" talking to guests. **Line level** employees (employees whose jobs are most often support roles and nonsupervisory) can also be asked about guests expectations because they provide the products and services to them.

Continuous assessments of guest services can be achieved through benchmarking and cross functioning teams. **Benchmarking** is a process of knowing what property managers do to deliver guests services and compare the service factors with their competitors. Studying available industry training materials, networking at professional conferences, and analyzing what others are doing to meet guests' expectations are also examples of benchmarking. What works well for one firm may also work with modifications for another firm. **Cross functioning teams** are groups of employees from various departments who work together to resolve operating problems.

The Structure of the Hotel and Lodging Industry

The structure of the hotel and lodging industry is mainly centered on **hotel owners, management companies, franchising,** and **ownership**. To understand the structure, one must understand who owns hotels and lodging facilities, who manages them, and who franchises them.

Many individuals and companies invest in hotels and other lodging products. Some **investors** are experienced in the ownership of hotels, while others are new to the business. An investor may own all or part of a hotel. Some individual investors take an active role in the management of the property, while others purchase the properties for investment purposes only. They have little or no experience in operating and managing a hotel. Therefore, they must rely on a management company to manage the day-to-day operations, based on some predefined goals. **Hotel management companies** are businesses that provide the day-to-day operations of properties. Management contracts may be written for 5, 10, or 15 years. The company receives a fee, a percentage of profits, ranging from 2 to 4.5 percent of gross revenues. In recent years, hotel contracts have become more popular because less capital is needed. In addition to providing operational standardized procedures, other resources are available: marketing, a centralized reservation system, and sales clout.[3] An **owner/operator** is a hotel investor who also manages the hotel or lodging property. The owner/operator may be extensively involved along with family members in the day-to-day operations of the facility. Usually with this type of set-up, the property may or may not be one of the national or international brands, such as Marriott, Hilton, or other such brands. **Franchising** is an arrangement where one party (**franchisor**) allows another party (the **franchisee**) to operate a business of a name brand product for a specified period of time for a fee. The brand's logo, trademarks, and operating systems are used exclusively. Franchising provides substantial benefits to the franchisee. Some include: a centralized reservation system, low fee charged by credit card companies, such as Visa and MasterCard, and national marketing and advertising. The franchisee must adhere to quality standards set by the brand.[4] A network is created of independent business owners sharing a brand name. According to the American Hotel and Lodging Association, hotel and lodging owners have many options to choose from in terms of managing a hotel property. There are a variety of ways hotels and lodging facilities can be owned and managed. They are:

- Single-unit property not affiliated with a brand. These single unit properties are usually historic properties that have been recently renovated. Or the properties may have a city name or some local name.
- Multi-unit properties affiliated with the same brand. The expectations and goals across operations are similar. Some hotel chains are now clustering two or three brands in one location. This allows them to use one general manager for all of the properties with assistants performing the day-to-day functions. This saves the company money, while meeting service goals.
- Multi-unit properties with different brands. Managing multi-unit properties means the owner must be able to satisfy the owner, operating under different brands and quality standards.
- Multi-unit properties operated by a management company or the brand. These services are offered to the hotel owner for a fee.
- Single or multi-unit properties owned by the brand. This set up is the most widely method in the United States. Many brand hotels hire and develop their own managers. One example is Marriott International.[5]

There are a variety of ways hotels and lodging facilities can be owned and operated.

Classifications of Hotel and Lodging Operations

Basic classifications and services offered will determine the extent of technical and managerial skills needed. The typical classifications are based on:

Geographical location: airport, downtown, highway, financial district, suburbia, others

Service levels: limited service, full service, convention, extended-stay, upscale, luxury

Price levels: low budget, budget, medium priced, upper scale, upscale, luxury

Rating: star ratings, ranging from one star to five stars (Mobil Travel Service); Diamond Rating, ranging from one diamond to five diamonds (AAA Travel)

Number of rooms: 50 rooms, 51–100 rooms, 101–150, 151–200, 201–250, 251–300, 301–350, 351–400, 401–500, 501–600, 601–1000, mega size hotels, such as The Opryland in Tennessee with 3,500+ rooms, MGM Grand with 5,500 rooms (largest hotel in terms of rooms in U.S.)[6]

The quality of facilities and the services assessment of properties are performed by two organizations: Mobil Travel Services and Automobile Association of America (AAA). The Mobil Travel Guide, a division of the Mobil Oil Corporation, uses the star rating system.[7] The most widely recognized system is the diamond rating issued by the American Automobile Association (AAA). These two classification systems offer brand hotel companies that operate internationally a uniform standard to which to ensure that their guests have comfortable experiences.

There are key performance measures that are used for hotel and lodging operations. They are: Average Daily Rate, Occupancy Rate, and Revenue per Available Room (REVPAR).

- The Average Daily Rate, computed as Total Revenue from Room Sales/Total number of Rooms Sold. If the revenue for a day was $45,000 and the hotel sold 200 rooms, then $45,000/200 = $225.00.
- Occupancy Rate, computed as total rooms sold/ total rooms available. If the hotel sells 200 rooms and they have 225 available, the occupancy rate is: 200/225 = 88%.
- Revenue per Available Room (REVPAR) is computed using the average daily rate and the occupancy rate: $225 × .88 = $198.00.[8]

Classifications within Brands

Using Marriott International, Hyatt, and Hilton's classifications of properties, brands are created. The classifications are based on lodging properties (brands) and the services provided. They include:

Marriott International

Full Service Lodging

Marriott Hotels, Resorts, and Suites include: **J.W. Marriott Hotels** is considered the most luxurious brand that carries the Marriott name. These hotels offer a higher level of personal service and amenities. Many of the upscale properties are offering spa packages to guests. **The Ritz Carlton Hotel** is the premier global luxury hotel brand owned by Marriott. The Ritz-Carlton has a worldwide symbol of prestige and distinction. The Ritz Carlton Hotels have won the Malcolm-Baldridge Award for 1992 and 1999.[9] It is the first and only award given to a hotel. **The Renaissance Hotels, Resorts and Suites** are considered as upscale, full-service lodging properties that provide a distinctive choice to travelers. **Marriott Conference Centers** offer a variety of conference packages.

Select Service Lodging

Courtyard by Marriott, Fairfield Inn, and **Ramada International** are included in this segment. Courtyard by Marriott was designed by and for business travelers. Services include a restaurant, lounge, meeting space, exercise room, and swimming pool. The Fairfield Inn is designed for the mid-tier business and leisure traveler. Clean and comfortable rooms, an exercise room, and enhanced amenities are included. Ramada International provides services for the international business traveler.

Extended-Stay Properties

Some of the extended-stay and corporate lodging include properties as **Residence Inn, TownePlace Suites, SpringHill Suites, Marriott Executive Apartments,** and **ExecuStay**. The Residence Inn is one of North America's top extended-stay brands, which provides a home-like atmosphere. Features include fully equipped kitchens, space for entertainment or meetings and ample work space, a swimming pool, and exercise room. Marriott Executive Apartment offers both the ambience and privacy of apartment living, while providing the convenience of hotel-like services and amenities. Most services are offered for 24 hours. ExecuStay by Marriott provides a corporate housing solution for the business traveler in need of a furnished apartment for 30 days or more.

Ownership Properties

Ownership resorts include **Marriott Vacation Club,** the **Ritz Carlton Club,** and **Horizons**. The Marriott Vacation Club International is a developer and operator of vacation ownership resorts. The resorts feature spacious one, two, and three bedroom villas, designed to provide high quality accommodations in a relaxed atmosphere. Each villa features a spacious living and dining area, master bedroom and bath, and a private balcony, kitchen, and laundry area. The Ritz Carlton Club is a collection of private residences in highly desirable resort destinations that are reserved for the exclusive use of members and their guests. Horizons, a Marriott Vacation Club offers value-priced resort communities that emphasize exciting, on-site recreation, planned activities, and entertainment for the entire family.[10]

The Global Hyatt Corporation

The Global Hyatt Corporation has specific brands similar to Marriott but offers distinct differences.

The Hyatt Corporation opened its first hotel on September 27, 1957. Hyatt's first property at Los Angeles International Airport was originally named the Hyatt House. The owner of Hyatt House was a local Entrepreneur, Hyatt R. von Dehn. Hyatt hotels expanded aggressively along the West Coast during the following years. In 1967, Hyatt opened the world's first atrium hotel in Atlanta, Georgia. The Hyatt name became worldwide. The hotel's 21-story atrium tower lobby and dramatic departure from traditional hotel architecture changed the course of the lodging industry. The challenge to hotel architects was no longer to eliminate extra space; rather, to create grand, wide-open public spaces. In 1996, the first international hotel opened, the Hyatt Regency Hong Kong, operated by a newly formed company called Hyatt International.

Full Service Upscale

Hyatt Regency hotels are Hyatt's core brand of hotels, offering guests opportunities to broaden their horizons and rejuvenate. Lobbies and rooms are designed to reflect the best of the local cultures, inventive food and beverage outlets, and exceptional technology. Meeting and fitness facilities are also available. **Grand Hyatt** and **Park Hyatt** brands were introduced in 1980 to further identify and market the diverse types of Hyatt properties worldwide. Grand Hyatt hotels serve culturally rich destinations that attract leisure and business travelers as well as large-scale meetings and conventions. The hotels, reflecting a grand scale and refinement, include features such as state-of-the-art technology, sophisticated business and leisure facilities, banquet and conference facilities of world-class standard, and specialized programs that cater to discriminating business and vacation guests. Park Hyatts are the company's smaller hotels.

Luxury hotels are designed to cater to the discriminating individual traveler seeking the privacy, personalized service, and elegance of a small European hotel. They offer a sense of sanctuary and luxury. In addition to state-of-the-art technology, Park Hyatts offer exceptional food and beverage facilities, intimate, understated surroundings, and 24-hour personalized service. The Hyatt Place is a new brand offered to guests. The brand features a signature bed, oversized sofa sleeper, and guests register through a kiosk located in the lobby. Guests may order hot breakfast entrees with Starbucks Specialty Coffee or eat the free continental breakfast provided.[11]

Hyatt Casino Hotels

Guests can choose from a sophisticated range of gaming titles, slot machines, and other popular games of chance. Each casino destination is unique and offers excellent restaurants, live entertainment, recreation venues, and shopping. Many of the casinos are located in wonderful resorts, complete with challenging sports facilities, recreation, and superb accommodations. Since the opening of the Hyatt Regency Maui in 1980, Hyatt has also become known as a leader in the creation and operation of dramatic luxury resorts as well.

Today, Hyatt specializes in deluxe hotels with meeting facilities and services for the business traveler. In many cities, Hyatt has made a significant contribution to revitalizing the area and stimulating business and population growth. Hyatt Hotels & Resorts have a reputation, not only for their physical distinctiveness, incorporating local art and design, but also for the amenities and services provided. These special services include Hyatt Gold Passport, Hyatt's renowned recognition and award program for the frequent traveler, Regency Club, a VIP concierge floor, complimentary morning newspaper, specialty restaurants, and custom catering.[12]

The Hilton Hotels

Conrad Hilton purchased his first hotel in Cisco, Texas, back in 1919. The first hotel to carry the Hilton name was built in Dallas in 1925. In 1943, Hilton became the first "coast-to-coast" hotel chain in the United States; and in 1949 opened its first hotel outside the U.S. in San Juan, Puerto Rico. Hilton went on the New York Stock Exchange in 1946, and Conrad Hilton purchased the Waldorf Astoria in 1949. Hilton has several world-renowned, marquee properties, some of which are: Hilton Athens, Hilton San Francisco, and Hilton New York. Hilton Hotel brands are the Doubletree, Embassy Suites, Homewood Suites, Hampton Inn and Suites, and Hilton Garden Inn.

The Upscale Properties

More than 60 years after Conrad Hilton opened his first hotel in Texas, his son, Barron, began another chapter in the innovative history of Hilton Hotels Corporation with the founding of Conrad Hotels in 1982. Conrad Hotels were established with the goal of operating a network of luxury hotels, resorts, and casinos in major business and leisure destinations worldwide. Since then, Conrad has earned a reputation for first class service and style as well as the highest standards of architecture, design, comfort, and cuisine. Such levels of excellence have allowed Conrad hotels to continue to receive numerous awards in prestigious leisure business travel publications around the world.

The Doubletree Hotels are uniquely-designed properties ranging from hotel, guest suites, and destination resorts to Doubletree Club hotels. Typical properties offer a full-service restaurant and lounge, room service, swimming pool, health club, complete meeting and banquet facilities, oversized guest rooms, and luxury amenities. This upscale, full-service hotel chain primarily serves major metropolitan areas and leisure destinations, with each unique property reflecting the local or regional environment in its design. From the signature homemade chocolate chip cookies to the deluxe amenities, Doubletree promises travelers a satisfying stay.

Suite Hotels

Embassy Suites Hotels are the nation's largest brand of upscale, all-suite hotels with more total suites than any of its competitors. Embassy Suites Hotels helped create the all-suite segment of the lodging industry and maintain the commanding presence in this segment in terms of system size, geographic distribution, brand-name recognition, and operating performance. Created in 1983, Embassy Suites Hotels serve as the pioneer in the all-suite concept and today is a marketshare leader worldwide.

Upscale Homewood Suites by Hilton is a national brand of upscale all-suite residential-style hotels targeting travelers who are on the road for a few days or more. Homewood Suites are designed to make guests feel at home, providing them with all the comforts, convenience, and privacy of home for the price of a traditional hotel room. **Homewood Suites** hotels feature such amenities as spacious one-bedroom, two-bedroom, and/or studio suites with fully-equipped kitchens, daily complimentary breakfast, and evening Manager's Reception (every Monday–Thursday) with hors d'oeuvres and beverages.

Mid-Price Properties

Hampton Inn Hotels offer value-minded travelers comfortable, well-equipped rooms. Guests will find that friendly service and many extra touches make every stay more enjoyable. A free breakfast bar and

a variety of beverages are offered. Local calls are always free and free in-room movie channels are provided. **Hilton Garden Inns** are positioned as the mid-priced brands targeted to today's growing segment of mid-market travelers. Focusing on what guests have said they want and need while traveling, Hilton Garden Inns offer quality accommodations, amenities, and services in a comfortable atmosphere designed for both the business and leisure traveler. From the welcoming Pavilion to the spacious work desk found in each and every guest room, to the Pavilion Pantry selling snacks and sundry items 24 hours a day, guests will feel "at home."

Other Brands

There are other lodging brands, which are classified as follows:

Budget	*Upscale/First Class*
Super 8	Holiday Inn Select
Motel 6	Doubletree
Shoney's Inn	Hyatt
HoJo Inn	Westin
Sleep Inn	
Thriftlodge	*Upper Scale/Luxury*
Fairfield Inn	Four Seasons
LaQuintin	Ritz Carlton
	Hyatt Regency
Mid-Price/Economy	Hyatt Grand
Comfort Inn and Suites	Independents, such as
Holiday Inn Express	the Jefferson Hotel
Sheraton Inn Four Points	Richmond, VA

Hotel and Lodging Departments

Hotel and lodging departments may be divided into two major components: Revenue Centers and Support Centers. The Revenue Centers are the centers that generate income. In order of predominance, rooms, food and beverage, telecommunications, and rentals receive money from services and products rendered. The Support Centers are those that provide the support for the Revenue Centers to earn income. The Support Centers include Marketing and Sales, Human Resources, Maintenance, Accounting, and Security and Safety. The departments are designed depending on the size and service levels of properties. Some properties may have two departments, with all the required functions listed under the two departments. Some properties may have a department for each function on the property. It depends on many factors. For the sake of this chapter, the aforementioned departments will be discussed.

The Rooms Division/Front Office

The Rooms' Division may consist of guest services, the housekeeping department, the accounting department, and security/loss prevention. Since selling rooms generates more than 60 percent of the hotel and lodging revenues, the rooms division may be operated in close concert with the Front Office. Check-in is the first step to selling a room, which is a perishable product. Therefore, the Front Office staff is usually the first guest encounter. Check-in requires the staff to use some form of technology to record guests' payment method and provide a room key. A Property Management System (PMS) is the technology used. The front office staff must know the Property Management System (PMS) well to process guests in a timely manner. Generally, a PMS provides:

- Who is scheduled to check-in the property.
- What they spend while they are there.
- The form of payment used upon departure. Each system depends on the needs of the properties. Franchised properties are usually required to use the brand's PMS.

More technology is used to increase the efficiency of guests checking-in. Check-in kiosks are growing in use in many hotels. Associates are available at the front desks also, but as kiosk use increases, the number of associates will decrease.

Guest Services

The Front Office is responsible for guest services that include welcoming guests, transportation, handling baggage, taking guest messages, delivering newspapers, management of safety deposit boxes, providing information to guests related to the city events, as well as handling concerns and disputes of guests.

Housekeeping Department

The Housekeeping Department is a critical component of providing clean, sanitized rooms for guests. A CLEAN ROOM is the number one request of hotel and lodging guests. Therefore, the housekeeping department must hire and train room attendants who are willing to meet the standards of cleaning

rooms in a timely manner, while serving as professional guest servers. The housekeeping department is also responsible for the cleanliness of the public areas, guest areas, and laundry areas.

The housekeeping department must interact with the rooms department daily. Rooms are assigned based on being cleaned and ready to receive guests. Rooms are assigned based on properly cleaned rooms that have been verified as clean and the status correctly reported to the front desk as "clean and vacant." This requires effective and open communications. Many mistakes can be made, thus making guests unhappy if planning, coordinating, and lines of communications are flawed. Each morning the housekeeping department receives a list of check outs and those who are expected to stay over. Currently room attendants clean from 13 to 20 rooms a day, depending on the type of property. If the property is a suite hotel, fewer rooms are required for cleaning by each attendant. The housekeeping coding system must be known by all persons in the department. Some typical terms used are:

- Clean and Vacant—The room is vacant, has been cleaned, and can be assigned to guests.
- Occupied—The room is registered to a guest.
- Stay-Over—The guest will stay in the room at least one more night.
- Check-out—The guest has departed.[13]

The housekeeping department must have an open and supportive role with all departments in the hotel. Managing a housekeeping department means that staff must be hired, trained, and developed to become proactive leaders determined to exceed guests' expectations. Room attendants must know what is expected of them. Each room attendant must be able to inspect his or her work and maintain a critical level of assessment in order to experience success.

Accounting

Rooms' revenue represents more than 60 percent of the total hotel and lodging revenue. Some accountability financial data include REVPAR, Occupancy, and Average Daily Rate. Yield management is a method used to match customer room purchase patterns and their demands to predict forecasts and maximize revenues.[14] In addition to the three previously mentioned items, **Cost Per Occupied Room** may be determined. Adequate funding is needed to maintain certain quality standards of providing amenities and services.

The accounting department also accounts for all monies received for operations. Analyses of income and expenses are conducted by the department. The analyses serve as a benchmark against standards and goals which have been set by administrators and managers.

Human Resources Department (HR)

The most important asset a hotel and lodging business has is the human resources. The business assets must be managed in order to realize the "best" possible service and productivity required. The human resources department serves as the key component in recruiting and selecting a productive workforce. The HR department's activities include recruitment, selection, orientation, training and development, developing compensation packages, monitoring the legal aspects of HR, providing safety, and health of employees. Maintaining diversity and employee relations on internal and external components of the industry are also required. The roles and responsibilities of HR present real challenges for the 21st century. The challenges become more intense as we realize that for the 21st century, ever-changing, dangerous conditions are emerging which requires more than the normal solutions.

Sales and Marketing Department

Sales and marketing of hotel and lodging are the systems designed and implemented to lure guests and, once they come, assure that they will return. It is better to keep loyal guests than to try to get new guests. Marketing then is a process of creating and sustaining productive relationships with desirable customers. The department managers must be creative and innovative to create brand identities for their market that are different from their competitors. The first step is to decide what the hotel and lodging service and products should be and what to offer to whom. Once this question is answered, the process of marketing involves setting prices, creating an awareness of services and products, making the site available and assessable, managing revenue, preparing and delivering delight, and "wow," retaining customers and measuring satisfaction and evaluating performance. If these steps are followed, a sales and marketing plan will be viable and relevant.[15]

Food and beverage services usually generate the second highest amount of revenue in a hotel and lodging business.

Food and Beverage Services

Food and beverage services usually generate the second highest amount of revenue in a hotel and lodging business. The range of services may extend from providing continental breakfasts to operating four or five various types of food and beverage services. Catering services may also be an option for the business. Each service offered depends on the facility, which may range from limited services to full-service venues.

Limited-service hotels typically offer breakfast in the lobby of the property. Some limited-service hotels offer continental breakfasts (juice, muffins, coffee, doughnuts, and other ready-to-eat items). Some limited-service property managers offer "made to order hot breakfast items" that may include omelets, bacon, sausage, grits, oatmeal, and other hot items.

Full-service hotels and lodging facilities may offer several menu choices provided by one or two in-house facilities. Full-scale hotels offer convention and banquet services and there may be two or three themed restaurants on the property. Full-scale properties typically accommodate the diverse needs of a wide range of guests in planning and implementing food and beverage operations.

Depending on the extensiveness of service, the number and types of managers are assigned. If the facility has only breakfast (limited service), one general manager may be assigned to direct the operation of the property and all of the components required. Typically, a person is employed part-time to come in and set-up and serve breakfast. Full-service properties hire specialized positions that may include chefs, directors and managers of food and beverage services, and directors and managers of convention services. Additional funds can be generated through room service offering food services 24/7 for hotel and lodging guests. Several measures are used to assess operations:

- **Guest Check Average** is the amount spent by a guest in a room service or dining room service order.
- **Contribution Margin** is the amount of revenue from food revenue after the cost of the food used to generate the revenue.

Safety and Security

Hotel and lodging managers "have a duty of care" to protect guests and their property. This need has heightened since 2001 and the threat of terrorism. Hotel and lodging owners must have systems in place, such as electronic door openers, that are programmed and disabled when guests check out. Other systems must be in place to assure the safety and security of guests. Surveillance and alarm systems must be in place to monitor entrances and exits to doors and other areas that may be vulnerable. Areas such as food and beverage cashier stations and front desks should have alarm systems tied to the police and fire stations.[16]

Summary

Careers in hotel and lodging management are unlimited. Due to the wide number and variety of hotel and lodging operations, the opportunities are phenomenal! Career choices include job titles such as: general manager, associate or assistant general manager, shift manager, director of sales and marketing, director of food and beverage services, director of human resources, sales manager, reservations manager, controller, front-office manager, restaurant manager, chief executive housekeeper, supervisor of catering, revenue manager, and director of guest services. This list is by no means exhaustive. Within each department supervisory jobs are available. It is a matter of assessing your interests, finding your niche, and developing into a productive leader. The level of service dictates the responsibilities of each manager. It is wise to learn all you can about the hotel and lodging industry, develop a passion for service, and be determined to become a productive, value-added employee. Keep learning, and as Bill Marriott says, "Success is never final."[17]

≈ *Resources*

Internet Sites

American Hotel and Lodging Association: www.ahla.com
Marriott International: www.marriott.org
Hotel related topics: www.hotel-online.com
Management of e-distribution channels: www.hedna.org
Training materials: www.ei-ahma.org
Professional Association for Hospitality Sales and Marketing: www.hsmai.org
Chamber of Commerce—Nationally: www.chamberofcommerce.com
Diamond Ratings: www.aaa.com
Hilton Hotels: www.hilton.com
Hyatt Hotels: www.hyatt.com
American Express—wholesale retail travel services: www.travelamericanexpress.com
Computerized contract management systems: www.act.com
Hospitality Educators Resource Organization: www.chrie.org
Summary results of individual properties: www.usfsi.com
Career opportunities in hotel management: www.hcareers.org
Team building organization: www.teambuilding.org
Resources related to legal aspects of hotel and lodging forms: www.hospitalitylawyer.com
Fair Labor Standard Laws: www.dot.gov/elaws/flsa.htm
Equal Employment Opportunity Commission: www.eeoc.gov
Immigration Reform and Control Act: www.usda.gov
Society for Human Resource Management: www.shrm.org
Requirements related to overtime pay and exempt employees: www.wagehour.dot.gov
Training Resources: www.hoteltraining.com
Hospitality Financial and Technology Professionals: www.htfp.org
Revenue management solutions: www.maximrms.com

Ideas for operation: www.ideas.com
Choice Hotels: www.choicehotels.com
Housekeepers' Association: www.ieha.org
Hotel Registry: www.americanhotel.com

≈ *Endnotes*

1. Noriega, P., and Mayo, C. (2005). *Contemporary Approaches to Hospitality and Tourism Management*. Hoboken, NJ: Wiley Publishers, 4.
2. Hayes, D., and Ninemeier, J. (2006). *Lodging Management*. Upper Saddle River, NJ: Prentice Hall, 4–15.
3. Walker, J. R. (2008). *Introduction to Hospitality and Tourism*. Hoboken, NJ: Wiley Publishers.
4. Ibid.
5. Rutherford, D., and O'Fallon, M. (2006). *Hotel Management Operations*, 4th ed. Hoboken, NJ: Wiley & Sons, 15.
6. Resource Guide for hospitality students. (2006). Dallas, Texas: NSMH Conference.
7. at http://www.hoteltravelcheck.com
8. Schmidgall, R. (2001). *Hospitality Industry Managerial Accounting*, 5th ed. Washington, DC: American Hotel and Lodging Association.
9. Ritz-Carlton, International at http://www.ritzcarlton.com
10. Noriega, P., and Mayo, C. (2005). *Contemporary Approaches to Hospitality and Tourism Management*. Hoboken, NJ: Wiley Publishers.
11. at http://www.hyatt.com
12. Hyatt Annual Report. (2000).
13. Hayes, D., and Ninemeier, J. (2006). *Lodging Management*, Upper Saddle River, NJ: Prentice Hall, 177–200.
14. Coltman, M., and Jagels, M. (2001). *Hospitality Management Accounting*. Hoboken, NJ: Wiley Publishers, 609.
15. Rutherford, D., and O'Fallon, M. (2006). *Hotel Management Operations*, 4th ed. Hoboken, NJ: Wiley & Sons, 308.
16. Ibid. 84.
17. Foucar-Szocki, R. F., Cereola, R., and Wetport, S. D. (2004). J.W. Marriott: "The Spirit to Serve," *Journal of Hospitality and Tourism Education*, *16*, 11.

≈ *Contributor*

Cynthia R. Mayo

Associate Director/Director of Hospitality and Tourism Management
Delaware State University
cmayo@desu.edu
www.crmdsc.com

Cynthia Mayo prepared for her career in hospitality and tourism management by receiving a Bachelor of Science degree and a Master of Business Administration degree from Hampton University, and a Master of Arts and Master of Education degrees in Economics and Education from Virginia State University. She received her Doctor of Philosophy degree from Virginia Polytechnic Institute and State University. She has worked as a middle and high school teacher, a food services supervisor, a director of food services, and she taught at Virginia State University for more than 13 years. She has worked in hotels, restaurants, and currently owns a catering business.

Dr. Mayo is the coauthor of several textbooks and she has published many articles related to competencies needed by hospitality graduates and leadership development. She resides in Glen Allen, VA, and is an active community volunteer.

Chapter 17
Review Questions

1. Explain the factors that contributed to the development of hotel and lodging operations in the United States.

2. Design a chart with the names and dates of the hotel and lodging companies that were termed the "first" to offer a service, technique, or product.

3. Explain the techniques of determining REVPAR, Occupancy, Average Daily Rate, and Yield Management.

4. Evaluate and summarize the duties of each department described in the chapter. Conduct research and determine requirements of departments not included in the chapter.

5. Visit three property's Websites and map out the products offered. Identify their brands and the key aspects of each brand. Describe what is being marketed.

6. Visit www.hcareers.org and write a summary of the careers available in hotel and lodging management.

7. Research using Internet sites to determine the number of hotel properties and rooms available today. Determine the average occupancy and average room rate. Determine the top five management companies in terms of revenue, property, and rooms.

8. Explain why all partners in the hotel and lodging industry must work together. Explain why diversity initiatives are important today.

9. Analyze and explain the types of ownership that can exist for hotel and lodging operations.

Bed and Breakfast, Limited-Service, and Long-Term Stay Lodging Facilities

18

Marcia Taylor, East Carolina University

© Cary Kalscheuer, 2008, Shutterstock.

≈ *Learning Objectives*

☑ Explain the difference between bed and breakfast, limited-service, and long-term stay lodging facilities
☑ Describe bed and breakfast, limited-service, and long-term stay lodging facilities
☑ Identify the different target markets for bed and breakfast, limited-service, and long-term stay lodging facilities
☑ Know the trends in the bed and breakfast, limited-service, and long-term stay lodging facilities

≈ *Chapter Outline*

Bed and Breakfast
Limited-Service
Long-Term Stay

≈ *Key Terms*

Bed and breakfast
Limited-service
Long-term stay

*I*n Chapter 17, you were introduced to the lodging industry. As you saw, this industry includes many different types of places to spend the night. This chapter introduces you to three special segments that tend to operate on the lower end of the price scale: Bed and Breakfast, Limited-Service/ Economy, and Extended Stay/Long-Term Stay lodging facilities.

Bed and Breakfast

Bed and Breakfasts, better known as B&Bs, offer an alternative lodging experience to the traditional and limited-service hotels. They pre-date hotels as a place to stay. Typically, it was the case that a person would offer a room in their house for a guest or traveler and then feed their visitor breakfast before they continued their travels. One of the origins of this practice was the development of a nicer room in the minister's house so that the Bishop or important dignitaries would have a place to stay when they visited. This practice was expected because the nicer house was usually provided by the church. In between visits from the Bishop, the minister could offer the room to travelers to make a little extra money.

In the 1970s, the United States experienced explosive growth. The opening of B&Bs in the U.S. was started by owners of attractive mansions and large family residencies to generate extra income. Owners would set aside bedrooms that were rented to overnight guests and serve breakfast in the family dining room or the kitchen. In the early years, B&Bs were considered an alternative to traditional lodging establishment for travelers who were cost conscious and willing to share bathroom facilities with the owner or other guests. On the other hand, with historical B&Bs, you can spend a night in the same room as George Washington or the same house as Lizzie Borden. However, in these houses, prices can rival most segments of the hotel industry with luxury accommodations and gourmet breakfasts.

Today, B&B facilities are found in all 50 states and in most countries around the world. In the 1980s there were less than 1,000 B&Bs in the United States catering to approximately one million guests. Currently, B&Bs are a major segment of the lodging industry. In 2006, it is estimated that the industry had grown to over 20,000 properties, catering to more than 40 million guests and accounted for over $2.6 billion dollars in sales annually. Occupancy in 2006 was reported at 43 percent, which represented a gain of 13 percent since 2002, but 20 percent behind the overall U.S. lodging industry (PAII. 2007) The low occupancy percentage is due to the seasonality of the business and low occupancy during the weekdays (most B&Bs are seasonal destinations). Weekends and holidays are the busiest at B&Bs.

Description

The name B&B was derived traditionally because of the offering of accommodation and breakfast for overnight guests. During the Depression, they were called boarding houses or guest houses. There is no one universal definition for B&B, but the segment is best described as lodging facilities with 2 to 12 rooms, which are either current or former private residences converted by the owner to accommodate guests, with breakfast service included in the price. They are usually independently owned and operated, with the owner and his/her family living on premises. However, some websites refer to three different categories of B&B facilities:

1. Bed and Breakfast—small lodging establishment in a private residence, with one to seven guest rooms.
2. Bed and Breakfast Inn—larger and more commercialized facilities with 8 to 15 rooms.
3. Bed and Breakfast Hotel—16 to 30 rooms and operates more like a hotel, but only serve breakfast.

Regardless of categories, the commonality is the serving of breakfast to the guests. The average B&B has nine guest rooms, but two-thirds have less than eight guest rooms, and one-third has fewer than four guest rooms.

Services

Once associated with small historic towns and historic mansions, B&Bs are also found in large Victorian single residencies, country inns, and old farmhouses. They are located in the mountains, by the shore, on farms, near educational institutions, and in urban areas. No two B&Bs are the same. Each room is decorated to match the architecture and era of the building, or to match a particular theme.

B&B guestrooms offer variation in size, attractive appointments, intimacy, in a relaxing home-away-from-home atmosphere. In our travels to Scotland, B&Bs gave us new insights into the culture. One of the appealing aspects of this venue was that

B&B facilities vary, but typically offer an intimate, relaxing atmosphere.

the tourism offices in each town offered reservation services. Each member of the staff had personally visited each B&B in their area so that they could tell you about the owner and facility from personal experience. This aided in selecting the right B&B for you and added a measure of comfort in knowing that this was a good, safe place to spend the night. The places ranged from a grand mansion where there was no personal contact with the owner to a cozy room where you sat in the living room with all the other guests and shared stories. They are smaller than regular hotels, personal in nature, have a quiet private atmosphere, and typically provide extraordinary personalized service—catering to needs of the individual guests.

One of the problems in the U.S. is that there is no creditable agency that screens B&Bs or maintains a list of acceptable quality houses. As a result, many people are reluctant just to reserve a room in a stranger's house without some outside references or word of mouth. On our Scotland adventures, one night we decided to stay in an unrated room because it was near the port where we were catching a ferry the next morning. When we walked into the house, the owner's lingerie was hanging in the entryway. As we walked up to the third floor, around a winding hallway, and into a corner room, our discomfort rose. The son reminded us of a movie ax murder we had just seen. When we went to dinner, we had a few drinks to calm our nerves. However, the anxiety mounted. So, we crept back to the house, took our bags, returned the key, and ran for the car. That night we slept in our only hotel for the trip. B&Bs are not considered very profitable and the delivery of personalized service and the owners'

ability to interact with the guests are very important to the success of the business. In addition, success is also dependent on the local market and word of mouth advertising. Only 7 percent of their business comes from the Internet.

Although breakfast is traditionally the only meal provided, at some B&Bs afternoon tea is served, and dinner is optional—served at the discretion of the owners. In some B&Bs in the Napa Valley of California, services are linked to the reason people come to the region—wine and food. As a result, you receive breakfast but then have snacks available throughout the day, complimentary wine tasting from 4–6 PM, and desserts after 7:00 PM. The addition of full scale, gourmet, or specialty restaurants, and cooking classes for their guests has become the main attraction to some B&Bs.

The amenities offered vary from property to property and may include private baths, in-room Jacuzzis, telephone, television, and fireplace. B&Bs that cater to the business traveler offer business centers with fax machines, high-speed Internet access, small meeting rooms, audio-visual equipment, and ergonomic chairs.

Target Market

Traditionally B&Bs cater to the leisure market, so occupancy is highest on the weekends and holidays. With more two income families, people do not have the time to take long vacations, but they still have the money. As a result, people travel just as much but the pattern has changed in America. Although many countries around the world take at least 2 weeks or a month off at one time, Americans have opted for 3–4 day vacations over the weekend or what is called extended weekends or "Get-Away-Weekends."

Another significant segment of the market is the elderly population. This age group tends to have more disposable income and the time to travel. The typical B&B guests are described as the older, affluent, well educated travelers, who seek shorter vacations relatively close to home. They are looking for variety in accommodation—not the location—and stay an average of 2 to 3.6 nights. The most popular destinations for B&B customers are the East Coast and California (see Table 18.1) with seven of the top ten best overall B&B in the U.S. on the East Coast (see Table 18.2).

Table 18.1 Top Ten U.S. Destinations for B&B

RANK	DESTINATION
1	Manhattan, NY
2	Charleston, SC
3	Boston, MA
4	San Francisco, CA
5	Key West, FL
6	Savannah, GA
7	Asheville, NC
8	Napa, CA
9	Santa Barbara, CA
10	New Orleans, LA

Source: BedandBreakfast.com

Table 18.2 Ten Best Overall B&B

RANK	BED & BREAKFAST AND LOCATION
1	A Storybrook Inn, Versailles, KY
2	High Pointe Inn, West Barnstable, MA
3	Inn at Harbour Ridge, Osage Beach, MO
4	Garden Gate Get-A-Way, Millerburg, OH
5	Sobotta Manor B&B, Mount Airy, NC
6	Terra Nova House, Grove City, PA
7	Bloomsbury Inn, Camden, SC
8	The Phillips-Yates-Snowden House, Charleston, NC
9	South Court Inn, Luray, VA
10	Woodstocker Inn, Woodstock, VT

Source: BedandBreakfast.com

Trends

Many people see operating a B&B as a simple venture that would bring in a little extra money to supplement their retirement incomes, after all, "mother" has been making beds and breakfast for the family for years and "dad" maintains the house and fixes things so how hard can it be to run a B&B? With the concerns for economic security, this appears to be a reasonable option and you can refuse reservations when you want to go travel or see the family. Some are entering the industry seeking a change of pace or to improve their standard of living, only to find it demanding, labor intensive, and time consuming. When the housing market was booming, many took advantage by selling their primary residences, moving to more remote or historic locations, and either converting their new residence to a B&B or purchasing an existing B&B business. With the increase in the number of B&Bs came an increase in competition. There is a move toward catering to the business market for meetings and the occasional business traveler, which helps the mid-week occupancy. Wedding groups are also a major market, because of the quaintness of some facilities, and the locations. In spite of the slumping housing economy, this segment of the lodging industry is expected to continue its growth, as more and more people look at the opening of properties as an investment opportunity to either enhance their income or seek a second career.

Limited-Service

The first limited-service hotels—Motel 6, Days Inn, and La Quinta—were built in the 1960s as an alternative to full-size hotels. They were able to offer low price by not having the amenities of the full-size hotels, such as restaurants, lobby, and meeting space. In addition, they used modular and prefabricated construction materials, which kept the building costs low. This made it more profitable at lower occupancy levels. Not only did this allow guests a less expensive alternative, but it also created a segment that was more affordable to purchase and hence more attractive to first time hotel buyers. The entry barriers to the economy segment are relatively low; less than $2 million, with minimal equity requirements, will develop a very nice 40- to 50-room economy property. As a result, in the late 1980s this segment experienced tremendous growth, which continued through most of the 1990s.

Description

Limited-service hotels, as the name implies, provide a limited number of services to the guests—a clean room, at a low price, in a secure environment. The idea is to meet only the basic needs of guests. Limited-service hotel size varies between 50–150 rooms, although some of the newer properties are larger, with 200 or more rooms. The size of the rooms are usually smaller than full-service hotels, but some limited-service hotels are suite hotels, and therefore offer more space than a traditional hotel.

The limited-service hotel category is divided into three different segments and offers three different levels of limited-service:

- Budget/economy, offers low priced, clean, and safe rooms in convenient locations. Amenities are limited to a continental breakfast. Examples of budget/economy hotels are Travelodge, Ramada Limited, Motel 6, and Econo Lodge.

- Midscale limited-service are priced higher than the economy level, and offer amenities just below a full-service hotel such as swimming pools, in-room coffee maker, iron and ironing boards, and hair-dryers. Examples of midscale limited-service hotels are Fairfield Inn and Springfield Suites by Marriott, Hilton Garden Inn, Holiday Inn Express, and Hampton Inn.

- Upscale limited-service without food and beverage, the highest priced segment in the category, offer a higher level of comfort and convenience similar to a full-serve hotel, such as upgraded décor and furnishing, hot breakfast and continental breakfast, and upgraded in-room amenities. Examples of the upscale limited-service, without food and beverage, are Marriott Towne Place Suites, Candlewood Suites, and Hawthorn Hotels and Suites.

Staffing is dependent of the number of rooms and the additional amenities. The role of the General Manager is usually dependent on the size of the property and the level of service. Figure 18.1 presents an organizational chart for a limited-service hotel, without food and beverage. It illustrates the different departments in a limited-service hotel.

Services

In the 1970s, the only amenities offered by many limited-service properties was a telephone, a bar of soap, and a television set with local channels. However, the concept of basic has changed. Are they only related to price/value, guest satisfaction, and market position? Or, do they revolve around minimum levels of amenities, service, and facilities? Although profitability and occupancy is the goal of both approaches, the former group additionally recognizes that average daily rate (ADR) plays a role in the room-revenue formula. As competition

Figure 18.1
Limited-Service Organization Chart

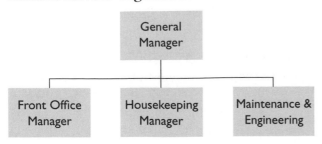

increased, more limited-services added amenities to enhance the guest perception of value like pools, hot tubs, and exercise rooms. In addition, complimentary breakfasts along with Internet access, fax machines, and copies are all part of the new "limited" service. These alter the costs, staffing, and land restrictions and as a result, room rates increase. Are these new rooms still considered to be limited-service?

Target Market

Originally developed for business travelers on a limited budget, today limited-service hotels cater to price sensitive business or vacationing families, government employees, tour groups, and the small group/meeting market. These demographic groups include the markets that most frequently are the last to feel the benefits of an economic recovery, and the first to be affected by a down turn in the economy.

The upscale limited-service without food and beverage hotels cater to the group/meeting market, providing almost everything that a full service hotel offers. Because there are no restaurants, they have a distinct advantage of providing whatever the customer requires, or the guest is free to bring their own food and beverage. Upscale limited-service hotels are usually located in central business districts, major urban centers, and airports. Groups find them to be a reasonably priced alternative, within walking distance to most attractions, restaurants, and convention centers.

The average length of stay at a limited-service hotel is 1–2 nights. This segment competes with full-service hotels by attracting guests with a combination of amenities and services.

Trends

Major growth in this lodging segment is predicted in the upscale and midscale without food and beverage segment along with increase in the average daily rates. The growth of the segment continues as more and more chains enter the market (see Table 18.3). As the numbers of hotels increase, so do the expectations of the guests. To meet this demand, hotel companies are increasing the amount of amenities and services provided. Full breakfasts with seasonally appropriate food and an attendant to help the guests were added by most hotels along with up-graded bedding and in room amenities. There is an increase in convention attendees who

Table 18.3 Top 10 Limited-Service Brands, 2007

RANK	BRAND	PARENT COMPANY	NUMBER OF ROOMS
1	Days Inn	Wyndham	149,926
2	Holiday Inn Express	InterContinental	140,206
3	Hampton Inn	Hilton	137,706
4	Super 8	Wyndham	124,584
5	Comfort Inn	Choice Hotels	110,525
6	Motel 6	Accor NA	87,877
7	LaQuinta	LQ Management	64,000
8	Econo Lodge	Choice Hotels	50,013
9	Fairfield Inn	Marriott	47,826
10	American Best Value	Vintage Hospitality	42,212

Source: Hotel & Motel Management

are choosing to stay at less expensive limited-service hotels instead of the convention hotel, adding to the demand in this segment. With the growth of this segment, most major chains have more than one brand in the limited-service segment (see Table 18.3). It is now considered the fastest growing segment of the lodging industry today with the largest number of rooms in the lodging industry.

Long-Term Stay

The concept emerged in 1995 as an alternative to the more traditional lodging for business and leisure travelers who need a place to stay for 7 or more days. Between 1995 and 2003, the number of rooms in the segment grew over 400 percent and is expected to grow another 20 percent by 2008. Occupancy averaged 72.5% in 2003, which was 12% higher than the overall lodging industry, and the number of rooms represents approximately 5% of the total hotel rooms in the U.S.

Description

Long-term stay hotels, also called extended-stay, are defined as a lodging facility where all guestrooms include a kitchenette and provide clean, comfortable, inexpensive rooms that meet the basic needs of the guests who need a place to stay for 7 or more days for business, leisure, or personal necessity. They are designed to offer a home-away-from-home atmosphere. The guests' rooms are apartment-style with living and dining area and a separate bedroom. The bedrooms, living, and dining areas are spacious and the kitchen is fully equipped with dishes and kitchenware. Rooms are rented by the day, week, or month and rates are much lower than traditional

hotels. The more nights a guest stays at the hotel, the lower the rates.

Long-term-stay hotels have higher occupancy, lower daily rates, longer average stay, lower expenses, and higher operating margin than transient hotels. Because guests stay longer, these hotels have lower operating expenses and higher gross operating profits due to fewer check-ins and check-outs and fewer housekeeping services. Because the average length of stay is approximately 14 days, these hotels do not experience low weekend occupancy. While a majority of the guests is long-term, they will however take bookings for one night.

Services

The guest is provided with services, amenities, and facilities that they want or need to facilitate a long-term stay in one location. Some of the services of a full service hotel are provided to attract the cost-conscious traveler. In addition, limited housekeeping services, grocery shopping services, business services, self-service laundry and valet, continental breakfast, manager's reception, and limited exercise and recreational facilities may be provided.

Target Market

The typical long-term stay guest is a business traveler on extended assignments, individuals relocating between jobs, corporate trainees, consultants, construction crews, occasional leisure travelers who are visiting relatives/friends, and families needing temporary housing.

Marketing is also different for this segment. They use direct mail, advertising on Internet sites such as rent.com and homebuyers.com, much like selling an apartment than a hotel room.

Trends

As competition grows in the segment, long-term stay hotels are building customer loyalty by adding more features for the business traveler to differentiate themselves from the competition. The trend is to bring feeling that is more homelike to the interior and exterior design. This is being accomplished by upgraded baths and kitchens, expanded fitness facilities, and updated amenities such as duvet covers and down pillows, granite counter tops, wood floors, and large plush terry towels.

Major Brands

The major brands for long-term stay are listed in Table 18.4. The major hotel companies have an entry in this market with some have more than one brand in this segment.

Table 18.4 **Example Long-Term Stay Brands**

BRAND	PARENT COMPANY	TYPE
Residence Inn	Marriott	Upscale
TownePlace Suites	Marriott	Upscale
Homewood Suites	Hilton	Upscale
Summerfield Suites	Hyatt	Upscale
Staybridge Suites	InterContinental	Upscale
Candlewood Suites	InterContinental	Upscale
Hawthorn Suites	Hyatt	Upscale
Homestead	Extended Stay Hotels	Midprice
Extended Stay America	Extended Stay Hotels	Midprice

Summary

While these three segments offer a different product, each is growing and expanding in marketshare. All offer free breakfast that 49% of leisure travelers and 53% of business travelers feel is extremely influential in their decisions when choosing a hotel. Due to this importance, other segments of the lodging industry are copying the successes of the B&B, limited-service, and long-term stay properties.

≈ Resources

Internet Sites

www.str-online.com
www.ahla.com
www.hsmai.org
www.iacvb.org
www.hotelsmag.com
www.abba.com

www.hotel-online.com
www.arccorp.com
www.iaapa.org
www.hotelmotel.com
www.hotelbusiness.com
www.paii.org

≈ References

Angelo, R. M., and Vladmir, A. (2007). *Hospitality Today: An Introduction,* 6th ed. Lansing, MI: Educational Institute.

Bair, J. (2007). More than breakfast. *Central Penn Business Journal, 23(33)*, 3, 17 at ABI/Inform Dateline Database.

Baker, M. (2007). Special report—BTN U.S. hotel chain survey. *Business Travel News* at http://www.btnonline.com

Bardi, J. A. (2006). *Hotel Front Office Management,* 4th ed. Hoboken, NJ: John Wiley & Sons.

Blank, D. (2002). Leisure travelers find welcome mats. Hotel and Motel Management at http://www.hotelmotel.com/hotelmotel/article/articleDetail.jsp?id=32199&searchString

Higley, J. (2007). Extended builds on history. Hotel and Motel Management at http://www.hotelmotel.com/hotelmotel/articlestandard/article/detail/467581

Higley, J. (2004). How much "limited" should be in limited-service? Hotel and Motel Management at http://www.hotelmotel.com/hotelmotel/content/contentDetail.jsp?id=106684

Higley, J. (2007). Hotel & Motel Management's 2007 limited-service-hotel-chain survey. Hotel and Motel Management at http://www.hotelmotel.com/hotelmotel/data/articlestandard/hotelmotel/052007/402126/article.pdf

Ismail, A. (2002). *Front Office Operations and Management.* Albany, NY: Delmar Thompson.

Kasavana, M. L., and Brooks, R. M. (2001). *Managing Front Office Operations,* 6th ed. Lansing MI: Educational Institute.

Kaufman, T. J., Weaver, P. A., and Poynter, J. (1996). Successful attributes of B&B operations. *The Cornell HRA Quarterly, 37(4),* 20–33.

Kelley, C. L., and Marquette, R. P. (1996). A tax primer for bed and breakfasts. *The Cornell HRA Quarterly, 37(4),* 34–42.

Lanier, P. (2000). Bed-and-breakfasts: A maturing industry. *The Cornell HRA Quarterly, 41(1),* 15.

Lanier, P., and Berman, J. (1993). Bed-and-breakfast inns come of age. *The Cornell HRA Quarterly, 34(2),* 15–23.

Ninemeier, J. D., and Perdue, J. (2008). *Discovery Hospitality and Tourism: The World's Greatest Industry,* 2nd ed. Upper Saddle River, NJ: Prentice Hall.

Poorani, A. A., and Sith D. R. (1995). Financial characteristics of bed-and-breakfast inns. *The Cornell HRA Quarterly, 36(5),* 57–63.

Professional Association of Innkeepers International. (2007). Bed and breakfast industry reports steady growth at http://www.paii.org/Press20%release.htm

Shaw, R. (2004). Limited service segments builds momentum. Hotel and Motel Management at http://www.hotelmotel.com/hotelmotel/content/contentDetail.jsp?id=92901

Sheridan, E. (2006). B&B and the bubble. *The Lane Report, 38* at ABI/Inform Dateline Database.

Skinner, M. (2002). Extended-stay hotels should be evaluated on the segment's operational characteristics. Hotel and Motel Management at http://www.hotelmotel.com/hotelmotel/content/contentDetail.jsp?id=20432

Stutts, A. T., and Wortman, J. F. (2006*). Hotel and Lodging Management,* 2nd ed. Hoboken, NJ: John Wiley & Sons.

Walker, J. R. (2007). *Introduction to Hospitality,* 3rd ed. Upper Saddle River, NJ: Prentice Hall.

Walsh, J. P. (2001). Making guests feel at home is marketing goal of extended-stay segment. Hotel and Motel Management at http://www.hotelmotel.com/hotelmotel/content/contentDetail.jsp?id=17729

Withiam, G. (1997). B&B fundamentally like hotels. *The Cornell HRA Quarterly, 38(6),* 13.

Zane, B. (1997). The B&B guests. *The Cornell HRA Quarterly, 38(4),* 69–75.

≈ *Contributor*

Marcia H. Taylor is an Assistant Professor at East Carolina University in the Department of Hospitality Management. She received a Ph.D. from Virginia Tech and has extensive hotel experience.

Chapter 18
Review Questions

1. Explain the difference between bed and breakfast, limited-service, and long-term stay facilities.

2. Describe bed and breakfast, limited-service, and long-term stay facilities.

3. Describe the different target markets for bed and breakfast, limited-service, and long-term stay facilities.

4. Identify the different trends in each of the segments.

Luxury Hotels

19

Morgan W. Geddie, California State University, Chico

© aida ricciardiello, 2008, Shutterstock.

≈ Learning Objectives

☑ Identify quality standards in the lodging industry
☑ Analyze the differences in hotel chains
☑ Comprehend what makes a luxury and ultra luxury hotel
☑ Identify luxury and ultra luxury hotel brands

≈ Chapter Outline

Quality
Luxury Hotel Companies
Ultra Luxury Hotels
Luxury Hotel Associations

≈ Key Terms

Auberge
Fairmont
Four Seasons
Jumeirah
Leading Hotels of the World, Ltd.
Luxury hotels
Luxury hotel associations
Mandarin Oriental
Orient-Express
Peninsula

Preferred hotels and resorts
Quality
Regent
Relais & Châteaux
Ritz-Carlton
Rosewood
St. Regis
Taj
Ultra luxury hotels
Waldorf-Astoria Collection

Luxury hotels are the ultimate lodging experience. They are beautiful properties with the highest level of service. The guest should feel pampered and leave wishing their home was this nice. However this high level of service and quality comes at a high price. A luxury hotel is often priced at twice as much as a deluxe hotel and can often cost over $1000.00 per night, and this is not the price for a suite. The luxury hotel plays to the guest that has high needs and high expectations. This population is growing as there are more dual-income households, with more discretionary income, who are well educated and well traveled. These fundamentals have caused the recent expansion of luxury hotels.

Quality

What makes a luxury hotel worth the premium price it demands? It would be difficult to justify the premium by saying that a luxury hotel is twice as nice as a deluxe hotel. Quality is not easily quantified and varies from one guest to the next. What one guest expects may be considered frivolous to the next. Quality can best be defined as details, details, details! Quality should be in the ambiance of hotel. It starts before one enters the building. Quality begins even before one sees the hotel. It begins with the first information a future guest receives on the hotel. The Website must exude luxury and printed material must be of the highest quality. All contact with the guest before arrival must be extremely professional.

From the moment a guest arrives on property, there must be a feeling of luxury. The grounds (if applicable) must be manicured and beautifully landscaped. The architecture of the building will often be impressive especially if it is in a nonurban setting. The appearance of each property must also be unique. Luxury hotels do not use a cookie cutter approach to construction.

The doorman and valet must be courteous and prompt when the guest arrives. Their uniforms should be professional, tailored, clean, and ageless as if new. These are the first employees the guest will see so it is important to make a good first impression.

The lobby should be a showcase for the finest products available. The woods should be exotic but not endangered. The carpets and rugs should be of the highest quality. The stone flooring should be beautiful and unique. The furnishings must be un-

marred and expensive. The textiles must be beautiful and make the guest want to touch and feel the quality. The artwork must be original and by well-known artists. The flowers must be extravagant and maintained on a daily basis.

The front desk must be well staffed by courteous, professional desk clerks with a desire to please. Many luxury hotels do not even have front desks. The guest may sit at a desk and be checked in by an attendant or simply greeted upon entering the hotel and led to their guest room where form of payment is confirmed.

The bell person plays an important role in welcoming the guest. The bell person should be a tour guide to the hotel and the guest room. He/she should orientate the guest of the services offered and where they can be found. Upon entering the guest room they should place the luggage on the stand and place hanging bags in the closet. The bell person should explain the features of the room and, before departing, fill the ice bucket for the guest and ask if there will anything else they will need.

Some of the finest luxury hotels have butlers who will see to the needs of the guest and even unpack the guest bags upon arrival and repack when it is time to depart. The butler will also press garments and polish shoes as well as arrange for cleaning.

Many luxury hotels offer a service where your bags are shipped overnight to the hotel so that they can be unpacked, pressed, and waiting for the guest's arrival. Another feature found in many luxury hotels is personalized stationery and business cards all with the hotel's address and phone number.

The guest room should be spacious and be filled with furnishings of the highest quality. The sheets should be of Egyptian cotton and have a high thread count. The beds should have layers of linens and feature an assortment of pillows as well as a pillow menu for any special requests. The room should feature the latest electronics.

The bathroom should be large with a separate shower and large tub as well as a water closet with a telephone. Two sinks are preferable and there should also be a makeup vanity with a comfortable stool. The towels should be plentiful, heavy, thick with tight loops, and oversized. The toiletries should be extensive, large and, expensive.

Room service must always be available, be extensive, and be able to do special requests. The presentation of room service must also be impressive and presented elegantly with fine china, silver, linen, and crystal.

The restaurants in the hotel must be among the finest restaurants in the area. The same should be true of catering. The hotel should be a natural selection for any event for a discerning clientele.

If the hotel offers a spa, it must be the best available. The offerings should be extensive and the staff well-trained. No matter what service a luxury hotel offers, it must be of the finest quality and staffed by the best.

Luxury Hotel Companies

There are many luxury hotel companies and several more are entering the market. The first names that often come to thought in luxury hotels are the Ritz-Carlton and the Four Seasons. Other luxury hotel brands include Fairmont, Regent, St. Regis, Mandarin Oriental, and Waldorf-Astoria.

Ritz-Carlton

The original brand was created by Cesar Ritz who is renowned for creating the ultimate in luxury for hotels. He was the first to incorporate private baths in each guest room, uniforms for waitstaff of white ties and aprons, morning suits for all staff, large bouquets of fresh flowers all around the public areas, a la carte dining, gourmet cuisine using methods from Auguste Escoffier, and intimate lobbies for a personalized experience. After his death in 1918, the only operating Ritz-Carlton was in Boston. The Ritz-Carlton Hotel Company was established in 1983 with the purchase of The Ritz-Carlton, Boston and the rights to the name Ritz-Carlton. The management company has grown from 1 hotel to 66 hotels worldwide (18,475 guest rooms) with plans for further expansion around the world. In April of 1995, Marriott International acquired a 49% interest in the Ritz-Carlton Hotel Company LLC.

Ritz-Carlton is the only hospitality company to have twice received the Malcolm Baldridge National Quality Award. The motto of the company is, "We are ladies and gentlemen serving ladies and gentlemen."[1]

Four Seasons

The Four Seasons distinguishing edge is service—service evolved over three decades of exclusive focus on luxury hospitality.

Today at Four Seasons, anticipating and satisfying those needs is second nature. Their guests trust them to deliver highly comprehensive, highly personalized service that feels completely intuitive. Consistently. Whenever and wherever they visit Four Seasons.

Four Seasons staff are chosen for their resourcefulness and dedication, and trained to be the best they can be. Their excellence is exemplified by multilingual concierge staff who are there to assist guests around the clock, with any detail: from changing travel arrangements to organizing business services, making dinner reservations, or securing last-minute theatre tickets.

Each property features the superb amenities their guests have come to expect; high-quality conveniences such as well-equipped fitness centers and spas, cuisine that transcends traditional hotel dining, and 24-hour in-room dining. It is the premier venue for business, family, or social gatherings. All invite travelers to make Four Seasons a part of their life at home, just as they do when traveling.[2]

Fairmont

If anything truly defines Fairmont Hotels & Resorts, it is the value they attach to lasting memories. Building upon a century of experience as hoteliers has endowed them with a rich tradition of hospitality. And genuine hospitality is achieved when engaging service and attention to detail elevates each stay into cherished memory.

Engaging Service

They know that even the best locations and offerings would be meaningless without outstanding guest service. Their skilled and motivated staff are equipped with the tools and the mindset to naturally deliver on this promise. Within a Fairmont experience, every guest is offered a warm welcome and is made to feel special, valued, and appreciated.

Unrivalled Presence

They transport their guests to extraordinary places steeped in unique architecture, expressive décor, and magnificent artistry. Fairmont locations don't just exude history; many are nothing less than regional landmarks. Fairmont's physical presence and character continues to inspire and excite guests.

Authentically Local

Fairmont's guests experience an authentic reflection of each destination's energy, culture, and history. One that extends from the solitude of a snow-wrapped peak or white sand beach, to up-tempo urban sounds of the world's most dynamic cities.

For more than a century, their grand collection of fabled castles, secluded lodges, storied meeting places, and modern retreats have hosted the rich and famous, kings and queens, Presidents and Prime Ministers, and stars of the stage and screen.

Many of their iconic properties have been integral in the development of cities, had an impact on the course of history, or even altered the social fabric. In fact, they are often deemed attractions in and of themselves.

Today, Fairmont is a growth organization. Throughout the United States, Canada, Bermuda, Barbados, Mexico, the United Kingdom, Monaco, Kenya, and United Arab Emirates one will find Fairmont Hotels & Resorts: the largest luxury hotel management company in North America.[3]

Regent

Regent introduced its first luxury hotel in 1970 with a focus on local culture, luxury for all the senses, and highly personalized service to create truly unique and memorable experiences for every guest. Regent's renowned service has continued to garner top accolades for the hotel group throughout the years. Now, with the recent alignment of Regent Hotels & Resorts with Regent Seven Seas Cruises, the hotel group is on a fast track to bring its ultra luxury experience to more locations. Regent plans to double its luxury portfolio over the next 2 years.

Memorable Experiences

Regent established its reputation on a commitment to exceptional, anticipatory guest service, attention to detail, and an uncompromising commitment to quality. Regent guests are greeted by name, but it is the unspoken details that make them feel truly welcome. Regent locations inspire awe, but it is the unseen that makes the hotels truly seductive. Guests are surrounded with architecture and design that is in keeping with each distinct locale, while providing the simple, familiar, and comfortable. The result is a hospitality experience that is richly personalized, genuine, and caring. It is The Regent Experience.

Regent opened its first hotel in Oahu, Hawaii, in 1970 as a joint venture between Mr. Robert H. Burns, who became chairman and chief executive officer of the company, and Tokyu Corporation of Japan.

The Regent offers luxury for all senses, highly personalized service and a focus on local culture.

From 1970 to 1979, the company opened and managed a number of prominent hotels, but gained truly international recognition in 1980 with the opening of The Regent Hong Kong, which brought a new dimension in amenities and service to hotels in the city and attracted attention throughout the world. It was in this way that the hotel innovatively combined the Eastern standard of service excellence with the Western standard of luxurious spaces.

In November 1997, Carlson Hospitality Worldwide, one of the major operating divisions of the global travel and hospitality industry conglomerate Carlson Companies, acquired Regent from Four Seasons Hotels and Resorts. Four Seasons continues to manage, under license from Regent Hotels & Resorts, Regent properties located in Singapore and Taipei.[4]

St. Regis

St. Regis prides itself on attention to the smallest details. An effortless arrival experience sets the tone of a spectacular visit—much like the welcome offered by a gracious friend at a fine private residence. Meticulous and discreet personal service is flawlessly delivered by carefully noting and recalling guest preferences from preceding visits.

According to St. Regis, the secret is their impeccable staff. As demanding as their criteria may be, their associates pride themselves in far exceeding the performance of customary duties. All embrace the authority to go to any lengths to ensure guests the utmost in comfort, down to the most minute detail.

St. Regis are unique refuges of timeless elegance, unwavering taste, and unrivaled care and courtesy that simply cannot be found elsewhere.

St. Regis is owned by Starwood Hotels and Resort.[4]

Mandarin Oriental

Mandarin Oriental Hotel Group is the award-winning owner and operator of some of the world's most prestigious hotels and resorts. In total, Mandarin Oriental now operates, or has under development, over 9,800 rooms in 22 countries with 16 hotels in Asia, 13 in The Americas, and 8 in Europe and North Africa.

The growth strategy of Mandarin Oriental is to progress towards operating 10,000 rooms in major business centers and key leisure destinations around the world.

Mandarin Oriental's Guiding Principles

Delighting Their Guests

They will strive to understand their client and guest needs by listening to their requirements and responding in a competent, accurate, and timely fashion. They are committed to exceeding guest expectations by surprising them with their ability to anticipate and fulfill their wishes.

Working Together as Colleagues

Mandarin Oriental emphasizes the sharing of responsibility, accountability, and recognition through a climate of teamwork. By working together as colleagues and by treating each other with mutual respect and trust, they all contribute to the Group's overall success more productively than if each worked alone.

Promoting a Climate of Enthusiasm

They are committed to everyone at Mandarin Oriental by providing a caring, motivating, and rewarding environment. As an industry leader, they are committed to bringing out the best in their people through effective training and meaningful career and personal development, and by encouraging individuality and initiative.

Being the Best

Mandarin Oriental strives to be the leader in the hotel industry and continually improves their products and services. They seek from their suppliers the highest quality products and services at the best value.

Playing by the Rules

They maintain integrity, fairness, and honesty in both internal and external relationships and will consistently live up to their commitments.

Acting with Responsibility

They actively participate in the improvement of the environment, just as they are responsible members of their communities and industry organizations.[5]

Waldorf-Astoria Collection

In 1932 Conrad N. Hilton wrote "The Greatest of Them All" onto a photograph of The Waldorf-Astoria in New York City. It was his dream to own this hotel and include it in his prestigious collection of hotels. In 1949 he realized his dream and extended his version of "the light and warmth of hospitality" to the legendary New York landmark. Today, the hotel is the inspiration for the distinctive hotels of The Waldorf-Astoria Collection where discovery and unique experiences are inherent in some of the most desirable destinations around the world.

Each celebrated property joining the Waldorf-Astoria Collection retains their name while adding The Waldorf-Astoria Collection designation as a mark of their exclusivity. Collection hotels include The Arizona Biltmore Resort & Spa, Grand Wailea Resort Hotel & Spa, La Quinta Resort & Club, Saudi Arabia's Qasr Al Sharq, and The Waldorf-Astoria, with plans for additional properties.[6]

Ultra Luxury Hotels

In recent years there have been a few hotel companies that have taken luxury hotels to the extreme. These hotels see to the whims of every guest and offer fabulous services and accommodations. These services come at a price that put them well above the price point for most travelers. These companies include: Auberge, Rosewood, Peninsula, Jumeirah, Taj, and Orient-Express.

Auberge

Auberge Resorts has established a timeless collection of exceptional properties, each with its own distinctive character that assures a memorable experience. All of the Auberge properties are characterized by a set of common elements: intimate, understated elegance, magnificent natural settings, inspired cuisine utilizing the very best regional in-

The Melisse Suite at the Auberge du Soleil in Napa Valley exemplifies the intimate, understated elegance and beautiful natural setting characteristic of all Auberge properties.

gredients, spa experiences to enhance one's well-being, and attentive yet unobtrusive service. In combination, these characteristics create resorts with prestige and strong financial returns.

Bringing industry expertise and a unique approach to resort development, management, and operations, Auberge Resorts has created some of the most recognizable and sought after hotels, resorts, and private clubs in the world. Among them are: Auberge du Soleil, Napa Valley; Esperanza, Cabo San Lucas; Calistoga Ranch, Napa Valley; The Inn at Palmetto Bluff, South Carolina; and Solage Calistoga, Calistoga, Napa Valley. Additional resorts are under development in: Santa Fe, New Mexico (2008); the Caribbean Island of St. Kitts (2010); and Sonoma Valley, California (2010).[7]

Rosewood

At Rosewood, they are devoted to creating hotels and resorts unlike any other in the world. Since 1979, they have bestowed each of their properties with one-of-a-kind ambiance and style. Whether located in the heart of one of the world's great cities or in the splendid isolation of a tropical isle, each is designed to enhance every aspect of a guest's expe-

rience, by reflecting the location's culture, history, and geography.

They believe that true world-class status is only achieved when a hotel or resort combines the traditions of its host community with exceptional service, a luxury product, and incredible attention to detail. This distinction has elevated the Rosewood Collection into the upper echelon of destinations for sophisticated travelers around the globe.

Competitive Advantage

Rosewood Hotels & Resorts operates a unique collection of properties offering luxurious accommodations, unparalleled quality, and personalized service. Each hotel features architectural details, elegant interiors, and innovative culinary concepts that reflect local character and culture. This design and operating philosophy is core to Rosewood's ability to create a uniquely authentic experience at each of its hotels and resorts.[8]

Peninsula

The Peninsula Hong Kong was opened in 1928 with the ambition to create the "finest hotel east of Suez." The hotel far exceeded this goal to become one of the premier luxury hotels in the world. The establishment of this hotel would eventually form the

The Peninsula hotel is famous for its service featuring Pages in crisp, white uniforms.

core and set the benchmark for what would become an internationally luxury hotel brand.

The hotel is famous for its service featuring Pages in crisp white uniforms. The other item that people think of when they speak of the Peninsula, Hong Kong, is the fleet of Rolls Royce limousines ferrying the guests to business meetings and shopping expeditions.

The global expansion of the brand from its roots in Hong Kong began in 1973 when The Peninsula Hotels was formed as the marketing division of Hong Kong, and Shanghai Hotels, Limited. The company also owns Quail Lodge Resort and Golf Club in Carmel, California.[9]

Courtesy of the Juneirah Hotel Group.

The goals of Jumeirah are to create hotels that offer a unique travel experience and are destinations in their own right.

Jumeirah

Jumeirah was founded in 1997 with an aim that was as clear in its simplicity as it was bold in its ambition; an aim to become a hospitality industry leader through establishing a world class portfolio of hotels.

The goals of Jumeirah are to have:

- Hotels that would not just aspire to the benchmarks set by the world's finest establishments, but actually redefine them.

- Hotels that would be destinations in their own right.
- Hotels that would offer a unique travel experience.

The hallmarks and guiding principles of Jumeirah employees are:

Hallmarks

- I will always smile and greet our guests before they greet me.
- My first response to a guest request will never be no.
- I will treat all colleagues with respect and integrity.

Guiding Principles

- Integrity—We act with honesty and sincerity in everything we do. We say what we mean, do what we say, and build confidence in our team.
- Teamwork—We work towards common goals through open communication, mutual support, and win-win attitudes. We respect our differences and build upon our strengths.
- Recognition—We ensure that people's individual needs and successes are supported and recognized.
- Innovation—We are open minded, challenging conventional thinking, improving our processes, and implementing new ideas faster than our competitors.
- Continuous Growth—We provide an environment where our colleagues and our business can flourish and grow.
- People Focus—We focus on our colleagues, customers, and business associates and they acknowledge us as preferred partners.[10]

Taj

For more than 100 years, they have acquainted guests with the living heritage of India—and a legendary experience in hospitality.

It began on December 16, 1903, when Jamshetji Nusserwanji Tata opened Taj's first hotel, the Taj Mahal Palace & Tower, Mumbai. This grand hotel epitomized a philosophy that still holds true today: provide impeccable service and unparalleled facilities so every stay is a memorable one.

A part of the Tata Group of companies, India's premier business house, Taj Hotels Resorts and Palaces comprises 57 hotels in 40 locations across India with an additional 18 international hotels in the

Maldives, Mauritius, Malaysia, Australia, UK, U.S., Bhutan, Sri Lanka, Africa, and the Middle East. Over the years, Taj has won international acclaim for its quality hotels and its excellence in dining, business facilities, interiors, and world-class, personalized service.

In India, Taj is recognized as the premier hospitality provider, spanning the length and breadth of the country, and gracing important industrial towns and cities, beautiful beaches, historical and pilgrim centers, and wildlife destinations.

An innovator in dining, Taj was the first to introduce Sichuan, Thai, Italian, Mexican, and Californian cuisine into the country. In 1972, it was the first to open a 24-hour coffee shop in India at Taj Mahal Palace & Tower, Mumbai. Today, each restaurant is reflective of that tradition, setting benchmarks for an outstanding culinary experience.[11]

Orient-Express

Orient-Express Hotels was founded in 1976 with the purchase of Hotel Cipriani in Venice, as the leisure division of Sea Containers Ltd and was later incorporated as Orient-Express Hotels Ltd. A Bermuda company.

Orient-Express Hotels seeks unique properties which have expansion potential. It owns or part-owns its properties because it believes that equity returns are greater than management fee incomes alone. Increases in property values allow the company to increase funding against those assets and thus fuel expansion. The unique nature of the assets insulates against competition.

The company avoids the use of a chain brand, so none of its properties is branded "Orient-Express" except the Venice Simplon-Orient-Express and its safari camps. The company believes that discriminating travelers will choose a famous individual property in preference to a chain brand.[12]

Luxury Hotel Associations

Hotel associations are marketing groups that hotels may join to gain name recognition. They provide a recognized brand, marketing campaigns, central reservation services, and a common Website for member hotels. Luxury hotel associations include: Preferred Hotels, Leading Hotels of the World, and Relais & Châteaux.

Preferred Hotels and Resorts

Preferred Hotels and Resorts is a global brand of independently owned luxury hotels and resorts and each provides the highest standards of quality and extraordinary service. Founded in 1968 as a referral service for the top guests of six independent hoteliers, the association has grown into its current status as a for-profit stock corporation representing more than 120 hotels worldwide.

To qualify as a preferred hotel or resort, each property must pass Preferred's award-winning Standards of Excellence®. This exhaustive quality assurance program, which includes an annual, unannounced inspection, ensures that only the best hotels are Preferred hotels.

The Preferred Standards of Excellence®: Ensuring Each and Every Stay Exceeds Your Expectation

Each Preferred hotel and resort conforms to Preferred's Standards of Excellence® program—marked by an unmatched 1,600 line item annual inspection process.

These unannounced inspections are performed every year by a licensed and independent quality assurance organization. Every detail that you would encounter during a typical stay is meticulously checked during the inspection: the cleanliness of the guest rooms from corner to corner, the dedication of the concierge to meet your special requests, and the commitment and care of the entire staff in anticipating your needs.

For a property to remain within Preferred, it must achieve an exemplary rating in all areas. As a result of this unique quality assurance program you will consistently receive the most attentive personal service and the most comfortable accommodations at all Preferred hotels and resorts.

Cornell University "Best Practices" Award

Cornell University, the American Express Travel Related Services, and the American Hotel Foundation honored Preferred Hotels and Resorts with the Best Practices Champion Award for its Standards of Excellence quality assurance program. Receipt of the best practices award confirms Preferred's unparalleled commitment to the complete and total fulfillment of Preferred guests' individual tastes, requirements, and expectations.[13]

Leading Hotels of the World

The Leading Hotels of the World, Ltd. is the prestigious luxury hospitality organization representing 430 of the world's finest hotels, resorts, and spas. Headquartered in New York City, the company maintains a network of 24 regional offices in key cities around the world.

Capitalizing on the strength of the Leading brand, the company introduced its first brand extension—The Leading Small Hotels of the World—in 1999. It also established several joint-venture companies: Leading Group Sales, Leading Quality Assurance, Leading Financial Services, Leading Interactive Reservations, The Leading Hotel Schools of the World, Leading Services and Products Network, The Leading Trust, Leading By Design, and Leading Insurance Services.

In 2005, the company launched Leading Spas of the World, the first global evaluation and certification program for the spa industry.

Each year, The Leading Hotels of the World, Ltd. publishes a directory of its member hotels, which is only one of the company's marketing endeavors. Additional services provided by the organization include extensive sales and promotional activities, advertising and public relations support, and an array of special programs for member hotels and their guests.[14]

Relais & Châteaux

The mission of the Association is to further the cultural and economic stature of its unique hotels and restaurants throughout the world by collectively promoting its members while recognizing their heritage and the soul and spirit of Relais & Châteaux. Services provided to member hotels include:

- An international guide published in 4 languages, which is also downloadable from the Internet.
- A Website, which can be accessed in 4 languages, 3 million page views, and 300,000 unique visitors per month, allows online reservation of Relais & Châteaux hotels and restaurants as well as the sale of gift certificates and special offers.
- An Intranet site, a true communication and information tool, intended for the members of the Association, accessible in 2 languages with a presentation of the Association and its services.

- Two e-mail addresses on a high security server with anti-virus features (anti-virus software updated several times a day).
- An international head office with a staff of 50 and 2 Relais & Châteaux Houses, the Association's embassies in Paris and New York.
- International promotion Offices in London, Berlin, Barcelona, and Tokyo.
- A guest loyalty tool: the Relais & Châteaux 5C Club.
- A marketing plan which encompasses:
  - Partnerships associating Relais & Châteaux with top brands
  - The promotion of the themes Golf and Spa
  - A customer database
  - E-marketing activities, in particular the Relais & Châteaux e-newsletter
- The Luxury Alliance, which associates Relais & Châteaux with the best brands in the travel industry, such as Leading Hotels of the World.
- A Quality Control department which monitors compliance with the Association's quality criteria.[15]

Summary

Whether it is a luxury hotel or an ultra luxury hotel, the overriding principle is quality and service. The guest must believe that what they are paying for their stay is worth every penny and preferably should leave feeling they got a good deal for their money. The sign of a good visit is when the guest books their next stay before departing. The hotel should become a second home for the guest and staff should become part of their extended family.

≈ *Resources*

Internet Sites

www.aubergeresorts.com
www.fairmont.com
www.fourseasons.com
www.jumeirah.com
www.leadinghotelsoftheworld.com
www.mandarinoriental.com
www.orientexpresshotels.com
www.peninsula.com
www.preferredhotels.com
www.regenthotels.com
www.relaischateaux.com
www.ritzcarlton.com
www.rosewoodhotels.com
www.tajhotels.com
www.waldorfastoriacollection.com

≈ *Endnotes*

1. The Ritz-Carlton. (2007) at http://www.ritzcarlton.com
2. Four Seasons Hotels and Resorts. (2007) at http://www.fourseasons.com
3. Fairmont Hotels and Resorts. (2007) at http://www.fairmont.com
4. Regent Hotels and Resorts. (2007) at http://www.regenthotels.com
5. Mandarin Oriental Hotel Group. (2007) at http://www.mandarinoriental.com
6. The Waldorf-Astoria Collection. (2007) at http://www.waldorfastoriacollection.com
7. Auberge Resorts. (2007) at http://www.aubergeresorts.com
8. Rosewood Hotels and Resorts. (2007) at http://www.rosewoodhotels.com
9. The Peninsula Hotels. (2007) at http://www.peninsula.com
10. Jumeirah. (2007) at http://www.jumeirah.com
11. Taj Hotels, Resorts and Palaces. (2007) at http://www.tajhotels.com
12. Orient-Express Hotel, Trains and Cruises. (2007) at http://www.orientexpresshotels.com
13. Preferred Hotels and Resorts. (2007) at http://www.preferredhotels.com
14. Leading Hotels of the World. (2007) at http://www.leadinghotelsoftheworld.com
15. Relais & Châteaux. (2007) at http://www.relaischateaux.com

≈ *Contributor*

Morgan Geddie is an Associate Professor of Resort and Lodging Management in the Department of Parks and Recreation Management at California State University, Chico. Professor Geddie received his doctorate from Oklahoma State University in Occupational and Adult Education with an emphasis in Human Resources Development. He also has an MBA with an emphasis in Marketing from the University of Central Oklahoma and a BS in Hotel and Restaurant Management from Oklahoma State University. Before joining the faculty at Chico State, he taught at the University of Houston, Oklahoma State University, Eastern Illinois University, and Arkansas Tech University. He also has several years of hotel experience in the New York City, New York, and Charlotte, North Carolina, markets. Professor Geddie specializes in the areas of Lodging and Cruise Line Management. He has published in many journals and trade magazines as well as being a featured speaker at several conferences.

Chapter 19
Review Questions

1. Define the market for luxury hotels and why is this market growing?

2. List quality standards found in luxury hotels.

3. What is the difference between a luxury and ultra luxury hotel?

4. Visit two Websites of luxury hotels and contrast them with the Websites of two ultra luxury hotels.

5. Do a web search on "Dubai." How would you classify the hotels of this destination?

6. What are luxury hotel associations? Best Western is another example of a hotel association. Using a web search, compare and contrast Best Western with Relais & Châteaux.

7. Regent also has cruise ships. Using a web search, compare the hotels and cruise ships of Regent. Are they a comparable product of equally high standards?

8. Marriott owns Ritz-Carlton, yet one never sees the name "Marriott" anywhere in a Ritz-Carlton. It is "Courtyard by Marriott" and "Residence Inn by Marriott" but it is not "Ritz-Carlton by Marriott." Why does Marriott not put its name on Ritz-Carlton?

Resort Operations and Management

20

Sherie Brezina, Florida Gulf Coast University

© Nataliya Peregudova, 2008, Shutterstock.

≈ Learning Objectives

☑ To understand how resorts are differentiated from traditional hotel properties
☑ To understand how resorts seek to satisfy resort guest needs
☑ To understand the variables that determine resort profits
☑ To understand the importance of spa amenities and other recreational activities in providing the resort experience to the guest

≈ Chapter Outline

Types of Resorts
The Resort Guest
Resort Characteristics
Resort versus Traditional Hotel Management
Resort Operations
Resort Economics

≈ Key Terms

Comfortable carrying capacity
Conversational currency
Destination resort
High season
Low season
Multi-use resorts
Non-destination resort
Recreational amenities

Residential resort lifestyle communities
Resort
Resort cruise ships
Resort hotel
Resort spa
Revenue per guest usage
Vacation ownership/Timeshare resorts/Condo hotels

In Roman times resorts typically centered around public baths for relaxation and social interaction. Early resorts in the United States were established around spas, often at seaside locations in the East. The first resort city was Atlantic City, NJ, touting sunshine and fresh air along the boardwalk and amusement pier. As transportation improved and more people had airline access and automobiles, warm winter resorts developed in places like California and Florida. By the 1960s the four season resort concept took hold, offering year round attractions, thereby minimizing the financial risk for owners of relying on one season a year for business. Historically, resort was a term used for a place or destination and resort hotels and inns developed in these areas to meet consumer demand. Most early resorts were either summer operations or winter ski resorts. Today, the term resort has expanded to include large self-contained lodging and recreational amenities compounds with many employees. As a result, resorts can be categorized according to:

- Location relative to the primary market—how far guests travel and by what means, car, airplane, or train
- Primary amenities, setting, and climate
- Mix of residential, lodging, and community properties[1]

The variety and complex nature of the food, beverage, lodging, and recreational amenities found at resorts demand sophisticated management practices to be successful.

Resorts are the fusing of traditional hospitality with recreational and leisure amenities. Therefore, resorts are a combination of three elements:

1. Housing/lodging, food, and beverage services that cater to people away from home
2. Recreational attraction that draw the guest
3. Activities that occupy guests during their stay[2]

Typically, resorts are associated with specific types of recreational amenities and are identified by an activity such as golf, tennis, skiing, mountain biking, fishing, health, wellness, and spa resorts. Premium facilities for sports, exercise, gaming, equestrian, and entertainment activities create unique reputations and images for resort destinations. These premium facilities become the attraction for people to travel to the destination. For example,

Pebble Beach Resort, CA, is a world-class golf resort. People travel from all over the world just to play at their golf course. At Pebble Beach, to book a specific tee time in advance of arrival, the person must also be registered as a guest of the hotel. This practice ensures that the entire resort benefits.

Resorts are often differentiated as destination or nondestination resorts. Destination resorts tend to be found in more remote locations around the world. The recreational amenities that the resort offers are the prime motivating factors for people to travel, often long distances to the selfcontained destination. Pinehurst Resort in the heart of the Sandhills of North Carolina is also a golf resort that draws people. While it has eight world-class golf courses, No. 2 is the most notable because it is the site of more championships that anywhere else in America. On the other hand, The Biltmore Estates in Asheville, NC, is an 8,000-acre self-sustaining estate created in 1895. People come to see the Biltmore mansion, but stay for the activities at the winery, stables, outdoor activities like white water rafting, and of course the food.

Nondestination resorts are usually found close to well-known natural or man-made attractions. The motivation to travel to the area is the attraction. The resort and its amenities are a secondary motivation factor, not the key consideration. Nondestination resorts are often frequented by visitors within a 2 or 3 hour drive, and often repeat visit several times a year. Resorts may fit both categories depending on where they are located and the nature of the recreational attraction. They appeal to residents in the nearby primary market and also to longer stay visitors that may come from as far away as overseas. British Columbia, Canada, is well known for their beautiful mountains and waters and, as a result, many resorts cater to the international visitors to the area. However, Whistler Resort has been named the number one ski resort in America, Britain, and Australia for several years in a row. Hawaii is another classic destination that people love to visit. As a result, many world-class resorts have been created to become destinations in their own right. For example, set on 880 oceanfront acres of the legendary North Shore, Turtle Bay **Resort** is the only true full-service luxury **resort** on the island of Oahu. And of course, no one can forget Disney Resorts in Orlando, FL.

Types of Resorts

Resort Hotels

Hotel resorts are the most common resort product. Resort hotels attract guests that are seeking relaxation and an array of recreational and leisure activities. These properties are also popular choices to host business meetings because the selfcontained environment provides everything needed for a successful meeting, including recreational activities with few outside distractions to pull the attendees away from the business meeting.

Resorts are found in all size categories from a few rooms or bungalows up to hundreds of rooms, suites, or housing units. Small resorts with 25–125 lodging units are often specialty "boutique" resorts catering to a small upscale market niche. Mid-size properties of 125–400 rooms are typically chains and located in mega resort areas offering more space and amenities than the traditional commercial brand hotel. Large resorts have more than 400 rooms and are often located in primary resort locations offering ski facilities, beach frontage, theme parks, gaming, spa, golf, or a combination of these amenities.[3] Many of the hotels in Las Vegas are called hotel resorts because of their large inventory of rooms, multiple restaurants, spas, theaters, entertainment, and of course gambling.

Vacation Ownership, Timeshare Resorts, and Condo Hotels

The fastest growing segment of the hotel and resort market is timeshares, also referred to as vacation ownership, vacation clubs, and condo hotels. Timesharing was introduced to the United States in the 1970s. The term timeshare is defined as "the right to accommodations at a vacation development for a specified period each year for a specified number of years or for perpetuity."[4] Owners of timeshares either purchase a time period, or fraction of a unit in the resort development by a lump sum payment, or financed over a number of years. Timeshare owners pay a yearly maintenance, management, and operation fee. Many timeshares allow the purchaser to exchange or trade the timeshare through exchange companies. Over time the timeshare option has evolved from a set week that was purchased, to the addition of floating week options and, most recently, the more flexible option of vacation club points, which are purchased and can be redeemed at resorts within the brand or a vacation time period.[5]

In the past few years, most major hotel companies have developed timeshares. Marriott, Hyatt, Hilton, and Disney are in the timeshare business. Having well known brands involved has helped to bolster consumer confidence in the timeshare product. The timeshare concept continues to evolve offering a wider range of products and choices for consumers.

Condo hotels have become very popular with major hotel brands over the past few years. The condo hotel has marketing appeal to the buyer as an investment and upscale vacation option, to the developer in securing investment funding upfront, and to lenders for minimizing investment risk. Condo hotels combine hotel style amenities such as public spaces, housekeeping, spa privileges, beach, golf, tennis, and skiing access with the lodging appeal of a condominium unit. The condo hotel touts all the comforts of home in a hotel resort atmosphere with none of the upkeep associated with owning a second home property. Structure and time options vary, however each unit is individually owned and the owner has a specified right to occupy the unit. When not in use by the owner the unit is part of the hotel's rental program and is booked and rented to guests who want to stay at the property.[6]

At many resorts, the distinction between hotel rooms, timeshare units, and condo hotels at the resort is becoming blurred. The consumer's expectation is that resort lodging includes the availability of units with full kitchens, separate bedrooms, bathrooms, living rooms, and patios. Management of resort timeshare units or condo hotels is particularly complex: the manager is often responsible to three or four stakeholders, the developer selling the units, the owner of the units, the owner of the hotel or shareholders, the timeshare association board which governs the timeshare community, and the guest who is renting the unit. As you can imagine, having multiple bosses can be very confusing when trying to meet everyone's needs and demands.

Current demographic and vacation trends suggest that the timeshare and condo hotel concept is filling a market need for people desiring a resort or second home experience. This consumer does not want the financial or maintenance responsibilities of year round ownership, since they only plan to spend a few weeks or long weekends on vacation. With the flex point system vacations are not restricted to one location and the desire to experience new places is appealing to many people. The United

States dominates the timeshare market worldwide. The outlook for continued robust growth in the resort timeshare industry and condo hotels is strong.

Residential Resort Lifestyle Communities—Second Home Developments

Fee simple, individually or family owned attached, detached, or multi-family homes are often found in resort second home development communities. These are best combined with primary and retiree residences to provide a mix of full- and part-time residents. These resort communities may be characterized by high rise condominiums on beach front locations, mid-rise low density residential communities near lakes or ski areas, single family developments with golf courses and a club house, or large planned communities with a variety of housing types and recreation activities. The recreational activities and amenities offered to the residents mimic those found in resort hotel destination developments. These communities often have a resort hotel and retail found in traditional resorts complete with concierge services to homeowners. For property owners, resort living becomes a lifestyle.

Multi-Use Resorts

Resorts often offer a combination of facilities, resort hotels, timeshare units, residential single- or multi-family homes. The recreational amenities are available to all owners and visitors to the resort. These structurally complex communities promote private club type exclusivity, state of the art recreational amenities, diverse food, and beverage and retail offerings with entertainment programming to guests renting out the affluent lifestyle. This type of resort requires skilled management at every level.

Resort Cruise Ships

Cruise ships are large floating resorts, with many of the same concerns as land based resorts. Sophisticated food, beverage, lodging, recreation, entertainment, and security are the expectation of the cruising guest. Many of the newer cruise ships are the size of a small city, with 5,000 or more people sailing at a time. New cruising products include timeshare cruising, with unit and package offerings modeled after the resort timeshare concept. Cruise ships compete with land based resorts offering amenities, entertainment, and vacation appeal, typically at very competitive pricing.

The Resort Guest

The fundamental needs that resorts seek to satisfy for guests are:

- Desire for change of pace, to get away from the familiar
- Desire to satisfy recreational needs while being entertained and stimulated
- Desire to travel to interesting places.[7]

The primary resort guest market in season is the leisure traveler seeking to vacation in a recreational and entertainment rich environment, in a relaxing atmosphere. Resort hotels often extend their season and fill the property in the months on either side of high season called the "shoulder season," with group business.

Resort Characteristics

The resort, particularly those referred to as mega resorts, offer more recreational activities and amenities than typical lodging properties. Location is critical to both destination and nondestination types of resorts. The surrounding scenery, environment, or close proximity to the regions natural or man-made attractions providing recreation offerings are the experiences that motivate people to travel and stay at resorts.

The time and money that guests spend at a resort is discretionary, meaning freely chosen. Because of this, resorts are impacted by demand elasticity to a much greater extent than traditional commercial hotel properties. This means management strategies must be always knowledgeable of economic, political, or social changes that may impact the resorts' projected revenues and expenses in the short and long term.[8]

Superior quality food and beverage choices, high service expectations, and a variety of recreation experiences and planned activities are anticipated by the resort guest. The foundation of modern day resorts are built on the provision of a wide variety of recreational and spa amenities that allow for a longer or year round resort operation.

Employees' need living arrangements and the resort must offer or make arrangements for housing in these often, high real estate value markets, in order to hire and maintain staff. In the United States and across the globe a common practice in areas where demand outstrips supply in the hospitality labor market during peak season is for resorts to

Resorts offer a variety of recreational activities.

recruit a number of their seasonal employees from outside the country and provide housing for them while they work for the resort.

Resorts versus Traditional Hotel Management

Resorts differ from traditional hotel properties in the following ways:

1. Resorts are typically self-contained. This means every need that the guest may have while on-site must be taken into consideration, planned for, and provided as needed. Basic needs such as laundry and maintenance must be done at the resort, rather than contracted out. Transportation, for employees and guests, must be provided. Shuttle service to and from the airport is important.
2. Attractive amenities are essential to the resorts success. Recreation and relaxation offerings are the reason people come to resorts. A good night's rest may be expected, but it is not the motivation to book a resort room. It is the extras that are available with the room that are important, the golf, tennis, skiing, spa services, man-made attractions, or a beautiful location to hike or swim.
3. Seasonality has a significant impact on resorts. High season is when demand peaks. Low season is when demand is low and resorts often struggle to attract guests. Most resorts are year round, having developed recreation attractions to bring business to the resort in the off-season. Though less and less common, some resorts only operate a few months of the year, around the primary recreation activity. For example, golf or snow ski resorts used to be one season and workers would migrate from location to location. People who taught skiing during November through March might relocate to South America or Australia to teach for the other 6 months of the year. The rest of the year the resort is closed or has very few people staffed to operate and manage it. This means that every new season, new employees must be hired and trained. Security during off-season is a concern.
4. The average length of stay is longer for resorts. Rooms are typically larger, with more closet or storage space to accommodate more luggage.
5. Resorts are spread out over a large land area to accommodate the variety of recreational amenities.
6. Resort guests have always been and continue to be consumers that are more sophisticated and have higher expectations of service and quality standards.
7. Resorts cater to repeat guests, annually or several times a year. Often the annual traditions and festivals attract and keep guests returning time after time to the resort. This must be incorporated with new offerings that keep the experience fresh for the guest.
8. The resort, especially those found in more remote locations, may be a primary employer in a community and, as such, the economic driver of the region's economy. The community's dependence on the resort for economic vitality, adds an additional consideration for the resort to be a conscientious community partner in making decisions to lay people off or close the resort during slow season. Many resorts do their best to make use of their full-time employees in the off-season by assigning them to maintenance detail in the off-season.
9. Resorts, especially those with timeshare units that can be sold prior to development, have a much quicker return on investment (ROI) for the project's investors in the resort than traditionally financed property.

Resort Operations

The staff and line positions found in the front of the house and back of the house in a typical hotel are also found in resorts. Resorts have a third position type: recreation personnel. Recreation and activity planning in a resort is a management concern and function. Recreation, social, and entertainment activities are planned 24/7 for guests. In the high season at large resorts, hundreds of planned activities must be coordinated, staffed, and managed each month. Skilled recreation oriented and trained staff are responsible for the running activities, guest relations, and guest services. If a resort has timeshare units for sale, a fourth position type may be added: timeshare sales. One size does not fit all for resorts, each property develops a particular structure that fits its mission and needs.[9]

Resort Economics

Four variables determine a resorts profit: capacity, length of season, amount of capital investment, and amount of revenue per guest per visit.[10] How well a resort maximizes these four variables determines the resort's economic success or failure.

Capacity

Capacity is determined by a number of factors. Physical and ecological capacities are determined by the limitations of the site. Comfortable carrying capacity is defined as "the maximum number of participants who can utilize the facility at any one time, without excessive crowding and without danger to the quality of the environment."[11] At a resort, safety for guests is the responsibility of management and it is considered in determining the carrying capacity maximum and minimum usage standards. Support facilities must be in place to contribute to full capacity at a resort. Support facilities at a resort include restrooms, food service, transportation, first aid, bars, lounges, and retail sales. Capacity is also determined by the design or footprint of the facility, number of available lodging units, meeting room, and banquet space and how many people they can hold for events and functions.

Length of Season

Weather and climate dictate what is considered "high season" depending on the nature of the recreational activity that drives guest demand. At most resorts in the U.S., across the country, high season is usually a 90–120 day period. Full capacity is the norm during season; it is in the off-season that a good marketing strategy can bring needed guests to the resort, extending the year to boost occupancy levels during shoulder season and the profitability of the resort.

Capital Investment

The amount of available money to develop the resort is important. The capital budget is specific to the design, site, and primary recreational activities the resort will offer. Millions and millions of dollars are typically needed in developing a large destination resort.

Revenue Per Guest Usage

The amount of revenue generated by each guest to the resort is a critical variable. This number is calculated by adding all total revenue during a specified time period, divided by the number of guest visits. The revenue comes from recreation amenities and activities, and all supporting services that the guest has purchased.[12]

Revenue-Generating Programs, Amenities, and Activities

People often pursue recreation to satisfy needs and wants important to them. Common reasons often cited for recreation participation are to: make new friends, belong to a group, experience competition, learn a new skill, share a talent or hobby, gain prestige, and get in shape.[13] The guest activity director and staff services are crucial to providing the guests with the benefits they seek while staying at a resort. Resorts often do best by recognizing guests as consumers of recreation products and services. Guest activity programming that is done well satisfies most of the needs and wants important to resort guests.[14]

In today's competitive marketplace the resort must perform at many levels. Guest activities and recreational amenities are not simply part of the supporting services available to the guest, but also must be revenue generating functions for the resort. Management at a resort is concerned that any space allocated to recreation offerings is also a producer of revenue for the resort. Golf, tennis, water-based recreation, skiing, and retail have traditionally generated revenues for resort operations. In the past few years, with people's concerns for health and wellness, spas have emerged as a lead revenue-generating amenity for resorts. Resorts and many hotels across the country are racing to benefit from this trend upgrading, enlarging spa space, and embracing stand-alone spa facilities, often bringing well-recognized branded spa companies on site. "A full service spa contains a full complement of facial devices, a comfortable facial bed or chair in each room, massage tables for a full body treatment, and a range of hydrotherapy treatment options."[15]

The three types of spas are:

1. "Resort spa: The resort spa is located at the property of a resort hotel with other sports and recreation activities are offered besides the spa program itself. Spa guests and hotel guests intermingle.
2. Amenity spa: Similar to a resort spa, the amenity spa is an added amenity to the hotel. The distinction is it is unimportant as a profit center when compared to the resort spa.
3. Destination spa: The destination spa is a hotel property targeted to the spa guest and program. Outside guests are not part of the program."[16]

The International Spa Association reports that spas are big business with revenues estimated in the billions annually. The U.S. has over 14,000 spas. The fastest 5-year growth rate for spas occurred in the hotel/resort segment. From 1999–2004 resort spas increased 300%. There are 1,345 resort spas in the U.S., making up 9 percent of the total spa market and employing over 77,000 full- and part-time employees. Thirty-seven percent of all resort guests utilize spa services. The average number of spa treatment rooms at a resort is 14, and the spa guest's bill averages $143.00 per spa visit. According to resort spa expert Mary Wisnom, "A well run resort spa should deliver twenty percent more to the resort's bottom line."[17]

Industry Trends

Resorts will continue to evolve to accommodate the changing vacation patterns of guests. Currently, shorter, long weekend vacation patterns have re-

Spas generate billions of dollars of revenue annually.

placed longer stays. Packaging is the key to providing the resort guest with a myriad of recreation and activity choices over relatively small time periods. As the baby boomer generation turns 60, the sheer magnitude of numbers of people will make this generation's needs and wants dominate the resort market's attention. Resort offerings and services have spawned resort residential communities offering all the amenities of a resort. This resort lifestyle is a growing trend with appeal to affluent baby boomers and the generation following them.

As resort customers embrace technology, they are demanding integrated voice, data, video, and information networks to be available, no matter how remote the destination or how relaxed the atmosphere. Staying connected is the new norm for current and future generations. This will require better technology management at resorts to provide strategic support to the whole operation at the destination. Use of new technological resources to manage guest and operational data seamlessly will be critical for resorts to remain competitive in the industry.[18]

Consumers are willing to pay more money than ever before for a powerful and truly positive emotional experience. They crave experiences that are more spiritual, educational and "feeling good" in nature. Eulogio Bordas refers to this notion as the Dream Society. For resorts, creating value is key to playing to the "it may be expensive, but it is worth it" mentality. Resort guests continue to like to take home "conversational currency," bragging rights to their latest resort experience.[19]

The economics of the industry suggest, that, as the resort market matures, consolidation will continue with a few industry players owning large numbers of resort properties. Independent resorts have the position of being unique, a desired characteristic; however, they will struggle to compete with the capital and marketing network the corporate owned resorts have available to develop and sell their properties.

Resorts are typically found in communities and locations with high real estate values compared to national averages, often out of the financial reach of resort staff. Affordable employee housing will continue to plague the resort industry. The resort industry will need to be creative to meet the challenges of recruiting, training, and keeping skilled employees.

Summary

As the resort market becomes more competitive, constant reevaluation by management of what services, experiences, and amenities guests are seeking is crucial to success. Rapidly changing lifestyles and needs are forcing operators to adapt to the sophisticated wants and needs of the resort guest, creating a fluid total resort experience.

≈ Resources

Internet Sites

International Resort Managers Association: www.resortmanagers.org/resort_links.htm
American Resort Development Association: www.arda.org
International Spa Association: www.experienceispa.com

≈ Endnotes

1. Mill, R. C. (2001). *Resort Management and Operation*. New York: John Wiley and Sons.
2. Schwanke, D., et al. (1997). *Resort Development Handbook*. Washington, DC: Urban Land Institute, 4.
3. Mill, R. C. (2001). *Resort Management and Operation*. New York: John Wiley and Sons, 15–16.
4. American Resort Development Association. (1997). *The United States Timeshare Industry: Overview and Economic Impact Analysis*. Washington, DC: American Resort Development Association, 5.
5. Ninemeier, J. D., and Perdue, J. (2008). *Discovering Hospitality and Tourism: The World's Greatest Industry*, 2nd ed. Upper Saddle River, NJ: Pearson Education, Inc., 170.
6. Baughman, M. A. (1999). New points system points industry in right direction. *Hotel and Motel Management*, (May), 22.
7. Mill, R. C. (2001). *Resort Management and Operation*. New York: John Wiley and Sons, 25.
8. Brymer, R. A. (2004). *Hospitality and Tourism*, 11th ed. Dubuque, IA: Kendall/Hunt Publishing Company, 337.
9. Ibid, 337.
10. Mill, R. C. (2001). *Resort Management and Operation*. New York: John Wiley and Sons, 296.
11. Phillips, P. L. (1986). *Developing with Recreational Amenities: Golf, Tennis, Skiing, Marinas*. Washington, DC: Urban Land Institute, 126.
12. Mill, R. C. (2001). *Resort Management and Operation*. New York: John Wiley and Sons, 297–298.
13. Farrell, P., and Lundegren, H. M. (1991). *The Process of Recreation Programming: Theory and Techniques,* 3rd ed. State College, PA: Venture Publishing, 43.
14. Mill, R. C. (2001). *Resort Management and Operation*. New York: John Wiley and Sons, 326.
15. Ibid, 417.
16. Ibid, 397.
17. Wisnom, M. (2007). "Spa 101," presentation, RCRA Annual Conference, Atlantis Resort, Nassau, Bahamas, November 2007.
18. Inge, J. (2003). Technology from an Investment Perspective. In: *Hotel Issues and Perspectives*, 3rd ed. Washington, DC: Educational Institute of the American Hotel & Lodging Association, 193.
19. Katz, L. (2006). Dream Theme: What Timeshare Europe Discovered. *Developments*, (February), 34–36.

≈ Contributor

Sherie Brezina, PhD, Director
Resort & Hospitality Management Division
Florida Gulf Coast University
10501 FGCU Boulevard South
Fort Myers, Florida 33965
Email: sbrezina@fgce.edu
Website: www.fgcu.edu or http://fgcu.edu/resort

Dr. Sherie Brezina is the founding Director of the Resort & Hospitality Management Division at Florida Gulf Coast University, in Fort Myers. The program curriculum focus is on resort management, blending traditional food, beverage, and lodging hospitality courses with recreation amenities management education. The program offers a PGA accredited Professional Golf Management Program Concentration, an Event Management Concentration, and a Spa Management Concentration option to majors.

Sherie Brezina received a BA and MA from the University of Florida and a PhD from Michigan State University, specializing in natural resource based tourism and the convention industry. She has held faculty positions at The University of New Haven and The University of West Florida. Prior to joining academia Dr. Brezina's work experience includes marketing management and budget analyst positions; feasibility and management consulting for convention centers, hotels, convention bureaus, and stadiums; and entry level positions in housekeeping and food and beverage operations with resorts, country clubs, and fast food businesses. Dr. Brezina teaches resort and hospitality courses at FGCU, works closely with the regions resort and club industry, and speaks on resort and tourism issues. She is an active member of numerous professional hospitality and tourism industry associations.

Chapter 20
Review Questions

1. What are the advantages of being a four season resort?

2. Explain the appeal of the timeshare or vacation ownership/club to the purchaser.

3. How has branding affiliation helped push timeshare or vacation club sales in the past few years?

4. Explain the meaning of resort lifestyle in second home development communities.

5. Why are cruise ships called "floating resorts"?

6. What fundamental needs are resort guests seeking?

7. List at least five common characteristics resort properties share.

8. How do resorts differ from traditional hotels?

9. What four variables determine resort profit? Briefly explain each variable.

10. Identify several trends that are impacting the resort industry.

Restaurant Operations

21

David Rivera, Jr., East Carolina University

© Josh Resnick, 2008, Shutterstock.

≈ Learning Objectives

- ☑ To better understand the restaurant industry
- ☑ To understand the different types of restaurant classifications
- ☑ To understand issues within the restaurant industry
- ☑ To understand the different types of operating practices of the restaurant industry
- ☑ To understand the importance of management functions
- ☑ To understand the need to control costs

≈ Chapter Outline

The Restaurant Industry, Classifications, and Types of Service
Restaurant Industry Issues
Restaurant Management Functions
Controlling Costs

≈ Key Terms

Casual dining restaurant
Coffee shop restaurant
Commercial foodservice
Dinner house restaurants
Noncommercial/institutional foodservice
Quick service restaurant (QSR)
Proactive management
Reactive management
Restaurant
Upscale restaurant

What did you eat last night for dinner? Did you cook it yourself? Or did you eat out? Perhaps you bought a fully cooked roasted chicken from the grocery store and brought it home. Any time a person buys food that they don't plan to cook themselves, the food industry is working. In this section, we will explore many different segments of the industry and still not touch on all the possible choices available.

The Restaurant Industry, Classifications, and Types of Service

There are many segments of the foodservice industry. The initial breakdown of the foodservice industry consists of commercial and noncommercial foodservice establishments. Businesses that are in the foodservice industry with the primary function of generating a profit are usually referred to as commercial foodservice establishments, while operations whose primary function is not to generate profits are referred to as noncommercial foodservice establishments. Often times noncommercial foodservice establishments are referred to as institutional foodservice operations. The institutional foodservice segment consists of healthcare, education, military, transportation, corrections, business, and remote settings. Associations that cater to this segment that you might be familiar with are the National Association of College and University Food Services and the American School Food Service Association. Now this initial separation might seem confusing. After all, why would you be in business if not to make money? Noncommercial food service is contracted by a host company that is not related to foodservice as its primary venture. For example, an insurance company might have an employee cafeteria as a corporate benefit. Many host companies subsidize foodservice therefore profitable foodservice is not a primary function. A breakdown of the foodservice industry segmentation may be seen in Figure 21.1.

Restaurants may be broken up into three basic categories: upscale, casual dining, and quick service restaurants. Upscale or fine dining restaurants are typically owned and operated by individuals and have fewer guests, but each guest pays a much higher average guest check. Expect to have white tablecloths, high quality alcohol brands, top quality meats and vegetables, and innovative recipes. In addition, the emphasis is on the presentation of the food and the ambiance. This operation is usually open for dinner only and is very formal in its types of service and food.

Casual dining restaurants offer a much more casual atmosphere than upscale restaurants. Casual dining restaurants offer a wide variety of cuisines and are typically very friendly to families looking for a nice dinner outside of the home. Most commonly, a casual dining restaurant can also be referred to as a "sit-down restaurant" because one sits for the waiter and table service. On the other hand, quick service restaurants (QSRs) are places where one orders food at a counter and then takes their food to a table. Quick service restaurants offer limited menus and are often referred to as fast food restaurants. These types of restaurants typically of-

Figure 21.1 Example of Foodservice Industry Breakdown

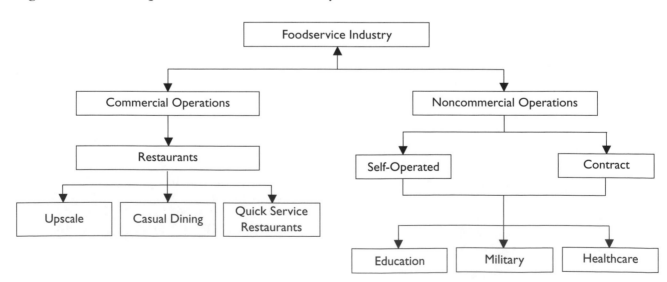

fer drive through windows to speed up the food delivery process. Average guest checks are typically lower than those at casual dining establishments and one of the main goals of a quick service restaurant is to serve many people in a very short period of time. Specialty QSRs may specialize in coffee or sandwiches such as Krispy Kreme Doughnut Shops or Mr. Goodcents submarine sandwich shops. More is written in a following chapter on this popular venue. Finally, foodservice may also be classified into many different categories outside of the restaurant industry. When looking at dining outside the home one may dine at a hotel/motel restaurant, country club restaurant, airport restaurant, cruise ship, within a museum or sporting event, or at a convenience store. When considering a career in foodservice there are many options that extend beyond the traditional restaurants with which many of us have become so familiar.

The classification of the restaurant profession is dependent on the type of service the operation desires. A rule of thumb is that the less formal the service, the faster the food is delivered. Therefore, QSRs create limited menus and develop assembly lines that allow for a quick turnover of customers. The key to their profitability is the volume of customers served. The higher the customer count, the more revenue generated. The more revenue that is generated leads to greater profitability. As a note, revenue is based totally on sales. Therefore, QSRs require a heavier flow of customer traffic through their doors.

On the other end of the spectrum, we have fine dining or luxury restaurants. This segment of the restaurant industry generally caters to those who demand excellence in service, ambience, and dining experience. Each detail of the operation must be overseen, as it is essential that nothing is overlooked. Of course, this argument may be said of each of the other previously mentioned segments. However, it is imperative in this restaurant segment that the type of service and menu meet or exceed customer expectations and enjoy an excellent recommendation in the form of word-of-mouth marketing from its clientele. These recommendations are crucial for this type of operation's long-term success. Simply put, the customer pays top dollar and expects top of the line service and products in an exceptional environment.

As an illustration to this point, a visit was made to a fine city club that will remain unnamed. Upon entering the club, you received a warm and personable greeting from the door person; one could feel their feet sink into the plush carpet. The foyer was elegant with richly decorated hand carved oak wood panels, staircase, and front desk area. The tile was marble and the chandeliers were made of exquisite imported crystal. The paintings that hung from the walls were original oils by well-known artists. The entire building was immaculate and service was outstanding. Upon entering the fragranced restrooms, one could not help but see the luxurious accouterments that were in place. For example, there were gold spigot faucets on marble sinks. More original oil paintings and other accent pieces were to be marveled by all who saw them. The linens were thick and fresh, laid out so everyone who entered would be assured of receiving a fresh towel. This entire experience was beyond compare until one looked at the soap dispenser. It was totally out of place. It was plastic and the 79-cent price tag was still on it that could be viewed by all. That one item destroyed the perception of exquisite surroundings and left the patrons wondering that, if this was done, where else were cost-saving measures occurring?

It is the attention to small details that make or break any restaurant operation: cleanliness, uniforms, plate presentations, personnel selection, floor and wall coverings, music selection, interior and exterior lighting, interior and exterior landscaping, purveyors, bar and food menus, and more. Each of these items must be specified clearly and concisely for operational uniformity and conformity. These

It is the attention to small details that make or break any restaurant operation.

become expected standards of operation for the restaurant unit or chain. Fine operations will deviate very little from established standards because their patrons expect quality and consistency in service, atmosphere, and product. To deliver that kind of quality and consistency every time requires vigilance by restaurant leadership.

Restaurant Industry Issues

Everyone has been in a restaurant. Many people believe that it is pretty easy to run a restaurant because there are waiters and cooks. In addition, while restaurants are great places to work in college because of the tips, you wouldn't want to make a career out of it. Some people have told me that "a restaurant would be a great thing to do when I retire. After all, I like to cook. And you only have to work from 5:00 P.M. until 9:00 P.M. because that's when the restaurant is open. So I would have plenty of time to do other things. How hard can it be?"

This public perception of running a restaurant is why many people open restaurants and many fail. Managing a restaurant is one of the hardest professions and requires the most dedicated people in operations. Contrary to popular opinion, depending on the type of restaurant operation, a kitchen crew can start at 8:00 A.M. or earlier getting ready for a 5:00 P.M. opening. There are perishable items that must be purchased each day and inventories to check in. Everything must be cleaned and cut to order. Broths, sauces, and soups have to be prepared early so that there is time for other last minute preps. An inventory of leftovers from last night and possible re-use must be determined. For example, baked potatoes last night can be mashed potatoes today or fried wedges. In Valencia, Spain, I was told that paella is only ordered at lunch time in restaurants. Paella takes a long time to prepare and cook so it is served fresh at lunch. Then according to my friends, if there are leftovers, it is reheated for dinner. Therefore "only tourists" order paella for dinner. So, as you can see from just a very brief list of things—and the list goes on for a long time—working and managing a restaurant is a very time consuming occupation. However, the National Restaurant Association estimates that 12.5 million people are currently employed in the restaurant industry.[1] The devastating effects of September 11, 2001 had negative implications to most of the hospitality industry; however, the restaurant segment continues to grow as more and more people are eating outside their homes.[2]

Therefore, the restaurant business is a challenging and unique profession. The challenges come from two main components: labor and perishable products. In the back of the house, people who work in the kitchen are usually skilled labor but there is room for entry level people to learn. Depending on the quality of foodservice, the skill level can be superior with graduates from the CIA (Culinary Institute of America) or the Cordon Bleu in France who train for years mastering their craft for taste and presentation to people who flip hamburgers. Blending the skill levels of different people can be a challenging experience. The front of the house waitstaff can be unskilled labor, depending on the level of service the restaurant desires. However, the higher the quality of the restaurant, the more skilled the waitstaff and the more training is required. Think how you would react if you wanted to impress your girlfriend by taking her to an upscale restaurant and the waitress sat down at the table and started jabbering away about her day.

The second concern is perishability of the food. For example, take something simple like lettuce. How much lettuce do you order? Think about what happens to lettuce that you bring home and cut up for dinner. What happens to it tomorrow? Wilted and brown spots do not allow the product to be served at its optimum nutritional value nor does it look appetizing. Would you want that served to you at a restaurant? Another consideration is the quality of a hamburger that has been reheated with a microwave? These are just some basic problems with handling food.

Why should you be concerned? It goes back to revenue management. Labor and perishable foods cause restaurateurs to seek out creative individuals that are motivated by their abilities to react to many different factors that cannot be planned in advance. The satisfaction of working in the restaurant industry comes from the inherent joy one receives when making others happy.

To be able to manage these different skill levels, there are two recognizable styles of leadership, proactive and reactive. Defining these terms are not difficult, practicing them is. Proactive leadership means that the one in charge forecasts what will happen. Forecasting can include, but is not limited to, the volume of business, safety and sanitation measures, or the ordering of food and supplies. As much as possible, managers try to anticipate guests' needs and plan accordingly. For example, when a waiting line begins to form, what can you do to plan for this expected occurrence to make the guest satisfied? There is more to proactive management than this brief overview. In essence, proactive management attempts to thwart any issues that may negatively impact the operation before such an occurrence takes place.

Reactive management is the opposite of proactive. A leader is forced to come to a reasonable conclusion that will avert a negative action and lessen its impact on the operation. For example, a customer falls in your restaurant and requires immediate attention to make sure the patron is made comfortable. They will also know that you are personally concerned about their welfare. This is also known as crisis management—the art of handling problems. It is in the nature of the restaurant business that reactive management skills are as important as proactive skills because of the two crucial items mentioned before. Careers are made or broken on how well your leadership style accommodates these two principles.

Restaurant Management Functions

The job of a restaurant manager is a tough one, but when done properly can be very fulfilling. The job of a manager within a restaurant involves the overseeing of several functions: planning, organizing, leading, and controlling various areas of the restaurant. These four categories of management may be broken down further and specifically applied to the most important area of the restaurant establishment, food. When given the privilege of running a restaurant a manager must control the food from the beginning to the very end.

Management in certain establishments may have little to no input when it comes to menu development; however, they have a lot of control of the food that goes into preparing quality menu items. The management process begins with the purchasing of products. After ensuring that procurement of products has been done properly, management must ensure that the food is received, stored, and issued to ensure that minimal food waste occurs. After the food has gone through that process, management must ensure that the proper production of the food is taking place and that the serving of the food is equal to the expectations of the guests. All of this must be done while ensuring that your employees are being given the proper training and developmental assistance to perform to the level of expectations of the guests.

The two greatest challenges of managing a restaurant are labor and perishable products.

Another key area for management in the foodservice industry, and one of the critical issues that face restaurant managers/leaders, is the selection of people that will impact their business operation in the near and distant future—especially the front line people that take care of the customers. Within the restaurant industry it is common that these are the least paid employees and yet have the most interaction with the customers. Therefore, the selection of these individuals is critical to the long-term success of the operation. When opening the Steak and Shake in Columbia, South Carolina, over 300 applications were accepted and interviews were conducted to secure about 50 full-time positions. This is because it takes time and planning to find the right person for the right job.

Controlling Costs

All management decisions can basically be placed in one of three categories: time, money and people costs. With managers being responsible for the financial success or failure of an establishment it is imperative that managers understand costs related to running the day to day operations of a foodservice establishment. Effective managers need to have efficient and effective time management skills. Managers are expected to have an understanding of all activities taking place in the foodservice establishment, and the only way that management can accomplish this is through the effective use and planning of their time. Having great time management skills also relates to the issues related to labor (people or human resource) costs. If a manager is able to hire efficient and effective people to help support them, then management is able to walk around and ensure the efficient and effective running of the business. However if a manager is surrounded by poor employees they may have issues in controlling both costs associated with time and human resources. Management of human resources involves the proper training and scheduling of employees so that they may have the tools necessary to achieve operational goals.

In dealing with foodservice one of the most important costs is food costs. Food costs are an area that a foodservice manager must have complete control of if they wish to achieve profitability goals. When dealing with food costs, managers must ensure that they not only know how to calculate and understand portion control, but that their human resources know and understand food costs and what affects it. Some of the things that affect food cost in a negative way that management must be aware of is improper training of food preparation employees, improper ordering of food products, quantity and quality control, and, one of the biggest contributors to increased food cost, theft.

Summary

The foodservice industry has become one of the fastest growing and most exciting areas of the hospitality industry. If one is looking for a career that will offer excitement and an opportunity to deliver great unforgettable experiences to customers, then a profession within the foodservice industry may be the career direction for you. The restaurant industry has various opportunities in many diverse areas for people with very different personalities and management styles. The level of expectation customers have of managers changes depending on which segment of the industry you choose. However the basic concepts and responsibilities of a restaurant manager are the same no matter which segment of the industry you choose. So being prepared is an essential component for management success in the foodservice industry.

≈ *Resources*

Internet Sites

The National Restaurant Association: www.restaurant.org
Nation's Restaurant News: www.nrn.com
Quick-Service and Fast-Casual Restaurant News and Information: www.qsrmagazine.com
Restaurant Supplies: www.restaurantsupplies.com
Food & Retail Industry: www.foodindustry.com

≈ *Endnotes*

1. National Restaurant Association. (2002). Forecast material at http://www.restaurant.org
2. Orilio, W. (2002). Hospitality bubble may have burst, but aim of operators still should be customers first. *Nation's Restaurant News, 36.*

≈ *Contributor*

David Rivera, Jr., worked in the foodservice business for over 10 years beginning with Little Caesars Pizza in Myrtle Beach, South Carolina. Subsequently he went on to work for Darden's Red Lobster, while earning his Bachelor's degree in Hotel, Tourism, and Restaurant Administration from the University of South Carolina. Upon graduation he took a position with Steak and Ale, while continuing his education from the University of South Carolina in their Master's in Hotel, Restaurant, and Tourism Management. While working on his Master's degree he moved from working with Steak and Ale to a position with Compass Group. After completing his Master's degree from the University of South Carolina, David took a position as an Opening Manager with Steak 'n Shake in their new markets in South Carolina. After being involved with opening restaurants for Steak 'n Shake, David decided to change careers and pursue a career in foodservice education.

David has been involved with foodservice education for over 8 years beginning with a stint as a graduate student instructor while attending the University of South Carolina. He continued teaching classes in foodservice management while earning his doctorate from Texas Tech University in Hospitality Administration. He is currently an Assistant Professor at East Carolina University where he teaches various classes on foodservice and diversity issues in management.

C h a p t e r 21
Review Questions

1. Why is it important to define proactive and reactive management techniques in the restaurant industry? What are the strengths of these concepts? Conversely, what are their weaknesses?

2. Identify the different classifications of restaurants. Why are there so many? Which are most attractive to you? Why?

3. Someone once said that the strength of a restaurant lies in the selection of its staff. Do you agree or disagree with this statement? Why?

4. How can a manager influence staff selection? Why is this a most critical task?

5. Construction of a new restaurant is costly. What can a manager do during construction that can offset future problems?

6. What are the most interesting aspects of a restaurant manager's position? What kind of individual attributes must an individual possess to have a successful restaurant management career?

Quick Service Restaurant (QSR) Operations and Management

22

© 2008, JupiterImages Corporation.

Nancy Swanger, Washington State University

≈ Learning Objectives

☑ Understand how the quick service restaurant (QSR) segment came to be and identify some of its key players
☑ Identify the QSR segment based on its characteristics
☑ Describe chain operations and their relationship to QSRs
☑ Explain the role of the QSR manager
☑ Discuss the trends and challenges of the QSR industry

≈ Chapter Outline

Introduction
Characteristics of QSRs
QSR Categories
Chain Operations
The Role of the Manager: A Personal Perspective
Trends and Challenges

≈ Key Terms

Chain
Check average
Co-branding
Fast casual
Franchise
Franchise fees
Franchisee
Franchiser
Quality, service, cleanliness, value (QSCV)
Quick service restaurant (QSR)
Royalties

Introduction

*A*s today's hospitality student, you have grown up with industry icons like McDonald's, Starbucks, Subway, and Jamba Juice being an integral part of everyday life. You have never known a life without fast food restaurants. Quick service restaurants (QSRs) and visits to them are so commonplace in today's society (the average QSR user makes 17.2 purchases each month[1]) that their existence is often taken for granted. However, nearly half of all adults in the United States have worked in the restaurant industry at some time during their lives.[2] Specifically, one of every eight Americans has worked at McDonald's.[3] This segment of the restaurant industry provides endless opportunities for the student serious about the hospitality business.

History

Quick service restaurants got started back in the 1930s and 1940s with White Castle, A & W, and Dairy Queen. However, it wasn't until the 1950s when Ray Kroc met the McDonald brothers that the face of the restaurant industry was changed forever. Kroc was not a restaurateur; he sold milkshake machines. In fact, he sold milkshake machines to the McDonald brothers for their fast food hamburger restaurant in San Bernardino, California. The fact that their concept often needed to produce up to 40 milkshakes at a time caught Kroc's eye and, because the brothers had no desire to expand, they sold Kroc the rights to the name and system they had developed.

In his early days with McDonald's, Ray Kroc established the standards of quality, service, cleanliness, and value (QSCV) that serve as the benchmarks for others in the quick service industry to this day. Because of his early jobs in sales, Kroc fully understood the importance of a first impression. He, himself, was always meticulously groomed and carried that standard forward with the employees of his own company. Today, McDonald's is one of the most recognized brands (along with Coca-Cola and Microsoft) in the world.[4]

Quality, service, cleanliness, and value have become synonymous with today's quick service restaurants. In a recent study of students on the campus of Michigan State University, the number one factor influencing which fast food restaurant they patronized was cleanliness. Friendliness, price, speed, consistency, menu variety, and location followed, in that order. Merely having QSCV guarantees a quick service restaurant operator nothing; however, lack of them almost surely guarantees failure. What separates the winning restaurants from the others is hospitality—the delivery of genuine, caring, personable service to the guests from each of the employees.

Characteristics of QSRs

Quick service restaurants are identified based on some common characteristics. They include limited menu, service style, size, location, and check average.

Limited Menu

QSR menus typically center on a common menu theme—pizza, tacos, burgers, sub sandwiches, chicken, etc. Although many chains have expanded menu offerings to attract a larger customer base, most can still be identified by their core menu. For example, Arby's has added chicken choices to its line; however, roast beef remains its signature product. Items are generally prepared in less than 5 minutes and use a few key ingredients in multiple combinations for the appearance of a broader menu.

Service Style

Customers inside the restaurant generally place their order at the counter prior to settling at a table or booth. The meal is usually paid for before it is prepared and eaten and is often picked up from the same counter where the order was placed. The restaurant business is very labor-intensive and, as a result, many operators have converted to self-service drink stations and condiment bars in an effort to reduce the number of employees required per shift.

Drive-thru windows provide a convenient way for customers to enjoy their favorite fastfood meals without ever leaving their cars. In the most recent report of the *QSR* Drive-Thru Time Study, Chick-fil-A led the list in order accuracy and Wendy's topped the chart for speed of service. The survey measured the following attributes: speed, order accuracy, menu board appearance, and speaker clarity.[5] The demand for convenience by customers has seen a modification of service style to include take-out and delivery options at many locations. Pizza has been delivered to the customer's door for years, but recently chains like KFC and Subway have experimented with delivery in certain areas of the country with success. The challenge with both take-out and delivery is in maintaining the quality of the product while in transit.

Size

The size of the QSR can vary; however, those including seating generally accommodate less than 100 patrons. Because of the need for speed and efficiency, unit layouts are designed to maximize productivity and reduce unnecessary steps for the employees. Operations can range from small, single employee carts or kiosks to large freestanding units with a drive-thru and inside seating, which may require double-digit numbers of employees per shift.

Location

As the number of people working continues to climb, the demand for convenience has also risen. Quick service restaurants locate where the consumers can access them easily. As America moved to the suburbs in the 1950s and 1960s, so did fast food. Units can be free standing, part of a strip mall, in a convenience store, inside the mall, at the airport, inside a grocery or department store—virtually anywhere traffic patterns have dictated a need. Because the reasons for choosing a quick service restaurant are not the same as those for choosing a special occasion or destination restaurant, location is key. The current trend favoring take-out food puts those restaurateurs with the most desirable locations in the best position to compete.

Check Average

Generally, prices in QSRs are lower than those found in full service restaurants and, as a result, quick service restaurants depend on high seat turnover to generate the necessary volume. In the late 1980s and early 1990s, Taco Bell turned the industry upside down with the introduction of its value menu. All items were less than $1 and many were priced at 49, 59, or 69 cents. To remain competitive, other quick service restaurants soon followed and value menus, meal deals, and daily specials remain a part of most major chains today. As a result, check average (Total Sales divided by Number of Guests/Transactions) can be pretty low (less than $5) in comparison to other segments of the foodservice industry.

QSR Categories

Quick service restaurants are classified, and sometimes compared, based on the category they represent. Those categories may include burgers, pizza/pasta, chicken, seafood, snacks, sandwiches, Mexican, and Asian.

The burger chains dominate the industry in market share and system-wide sales.[6] McDonald's is the leader in the burger category and in the QSR industry, as a whole. Based on 2006 sales, the top performers in this category, following McDonald's, include Burger King, Wendy's, Sonic Drive-In, and Dairy Queen.

Pizza Hut is the leader in the chain pizza/pasta category—followed by Domino's Pizza, Papa John's Pizza, Little Caesars Pizza, and CiCi's Pizza.

In the chain chicken category, KFC is the long-standing leader, with Chick-fil-A, Popeyes, Buffalo Wild Wings, and Church's Chicken following.

Chains in the seafood category, a smaller segment overall, include Long John Silver's and Captain D's Seafood.

Starbucks dominates the snack category, along with players such as Dunkin' Donuts, Baskin-Robbins, Cold Stone Creamery, and Jamba Juice.

Heading up the sandwich category is Subway, followed by Arby's, Panera Bread, and Quiznos Sub.

Mexican quick service restaurants are very popular and include the category-leading Taco Bell, Chipotle, Del Taco, and Baja Fresh Mexican Grill.

© 2008, JupiterImages Corporation.

The key to success in quick service operations is consistency.

A relatively new category for QSRs, Asian, continues to grow in popularity; however, the segment is still dominated by independent operators. Panda Express is far and away the category leader.

Chain Operations

The key to success in quick service operations is consistency—consistency of product, consistency of service, and consistency of facilities. One of the ways this is achieved is through tight controls established by the chain's corporate headquarters. Because the vast majority of quick service restaurants are part of a chain, a brief discussion of what that means follows here.

Defined

According to Jaffe (1995), a chain is defined as "any single restaurant concept with two or more units in operation under the same name that follow the same standard operating procedures."[7] Many of the chain operations franchise their business format. This allows the business owner (franchisee) to use the name, logo, recipes, system, products, and marketing of the particular chain (franchiser).

Advantages

One of the biggest advantages of being involved with a chain is that because the concept has been tested and proven, the risk of failure is greatly reduced. When nearly 40% of all new businesses fail within the first year and about 75% fail within the first 5 years of operation, buying into a system can be very beneficial. According to the U.S. Department of Commerce, less than 5% of franchised businesses fail within the first year.

Other advantages include help from the franchiser with site selection, design, and possibly financing. The purchasing power of a chain is greater than the purchasing power of a single operator, helping the franchisee to keep costs and quality under control. Systems of budgeting, inventory control, and accounting are generally available for immediate use by the new franchisee.

Disadvantages

While operators of QSRs enjoy many benefits being associated with a chain, there are some negative considerations, as well. First, there is not a lot of room for creativity and, second, decision-making opportunities are limited. While independent operators have complete freedom and autonomy, QSR operators are generally governed by the chain's corporate office.

Another disadvantage of being part of a chain is that the chain is only as strong as its weakest operator or its current place in the media. Wendy's "finger-in-the-chili" incident is a perfect example of how damaging negative press can be. A person claimed that they found part of a finger in their chili. Even though it was determined the entire story was a hoax (and arrests were made), the store involved, along with the entire chain, suffered through a period of declining sales from the unfavorable publicity.

Costs

The costs involved in franchising include the franchise fee (usually between $7,500 and $50,000), development costs (sometimes up to $1 million), royalties (usually between 3% and 8% of gross sales), and advertising fees (usually between 0.5% and 5% of gross sales).

Franchise Fee

The franchise fee is a sum of money paid to the franchiser for the rights to use their system. This fee includes training in the system and a copy of the company's Operations Manual. This manual includes all the information necessary for the franchisee to operate the business and its contents are invaluable to the new owner or manager. As part of the franchise agreement and included in the franchise fee, the parent company may also send an "opening team" (a group of employees trained in operations and new store openings) to assist the franchisee during the critical first days of operation. Once the restaurant is open, the franchiser may send people to inspect the store on a regular basis to make sure the franchisee is adhering to the chain's standards and offer any necessary support.

Development Costs

Development costs are those associated with the land, the building, the furnishings, and the equipment necessary for operation of the restaurant. There can be a huge variation in these costs, depending on the particular situation. For example, will the land be purchased or leased? What are the current land values or lease rates in the area? Is this a remodel of an existing building or a new structure created from the ground up? Is there a level of décor packages available from the franchiser based on price or is there a standard, one-price package required for all units? Is the required equipment very specialized and unique to the concept or is the equipment more generic and easily purchased? Although these considerations are by no means complete, you can see that many factors contribute to the development costs of the restaurant.

Royalties

Royalties are monies paid to the franchiser at regular intervals once the restaurant is open for business. Generally, the amount due is calculated as a percentage of gross sales for the period.

Advertising Fees

Monies for national and regional/area advertising are calculated and collected in the same manner as royalties. These fees are used to create and produce promotional materials and buy media, as examples, to help drive sales for the chain. Many times, each restaurant will also set aside an additional percentage of gross sales to support local store marketing efforts.

The Role of the Manager: A Personal Perspective

It can be argued that the unit manager is the most important factor in the success of a quick service restaurant. The following focuses on the three areas of the manager's position felt by the author to be most critical—their focus on selection, their role in training, and their influence on the environment.

Selection

One of the biggest challenges facing this industry is in finding quality employees. As mentioned earlier, this is a very labor-intensive business and finding enough people to fill all the available positions is almost impossible. Even with the tight labor market, it is imperative the unit manager be very selective about the employees. Managers must "Hire the smile and train the technical." A manager can teach a new employee how to make a sandwich or take an order, but he/she cannot teach the person how to smile and be nice to people.

Unit managers must be familiar with all legal and human resource issues involved in hiring; the process must be defined and implemented for each prospective employee. Having said that, it is important to remember that each new employee must "fit" with the other members of the staff. Because the success of the restaurant is based upon the efforts of the team, it is essential to keep the chemistry of the team in balance.

Standards of grooming and behavior must be addressed in the employee handbook and discussed during the interview and orientation sessions. The unit manager must "walk the talk" and always provide the example. Selecting the right people makes the manager's job much easier and sets the stage for building positive employee/guest relations.

Training

The time spent by the unit manager in the training of the employees is vital to the long-term success of the business. Too many times new employees come to work, it's busy, and they are left to flounder on their own or told to follow so-and-so and do what they do. The best training programs are structured in their content and are scheduled during non-peak times to allow for maximum attention to the trainee. Taking the time to teach the new employee right the first time saves the manager from having to go back and try to correct established bad habits.

Training is not a one-shot deal; effective managers are constantly coaching even their veteran staff members for improved performance. Winning managers are continually raising the bar for productivity and performance through on-going training and feedback.

Environment

It is the job of the manager to create an environment in which the employees feel motivated. A survey conducted by Rice found the unit manager to be the most critical element in employee satisfaction.[8] To help ensure employee satisfaction, it is important that the manager prove competency, show interest, and be sincere.

Prove Competency

Employees need to know the unit manager is on top of things. The manager doesn't necessarily have to be the best at every single position in the restaurant; however, they need to be good enough to hold their own and able to teach the position to others. Effective managers never ask an employee to do something that they are not willing or able to do themselves. One advantage to starting at the entry level and working up is the knowledge gained along the way about how the entire operation functions. Managers must demonstrate their ability.

Show Interest

Great managers get to know their employees as people. They build relationships with them that foster trust and loyalty. One way to do this is to spend some time with new employees on their first day doing a task where it is possible to chat while working. A good icebreaker question involves the employee telling the manager about their family. Usually, family is a topic people are comfortable with and it generally leads to other discussion topics such as interests or hobbies. During these informal visits, attempts are made to connect the new employee to others on the shift with whom they may have things in common. Great managers know their people.

Be Sincere

Managers with credibility avoid saying things to employees they don't mean. Employees know phony praise and false promises. Honesty and integrity are everything when it comes to managing people. Character leads by example.

Trends and Challenges

The past few years have fared well for quick service restaurants in comparison to some other segments of the hospitality industry. With rising gas prices and other pressures on the economy, the amount of disposable income in many households has been challenged. However, because we have become a nation that is used to dining away from home, we may have scaled back our choices but have continued to eat out. While fine dining and upscale eateries have shown limited or no growth in sales, the quick serve segment has been able to maintain and even show sales increases in many areas.

Events currently in the news that may have an impact on the industry include the use of irradiated and genetically modified foods, banning the use of latex gloves in certain states, minimum wage hikes, and state smoking bans. However, the emergence of the fast casual segment, an emphasis on nutritional offerings, "greening" of the industry, the rise of co-branding, and staffing may have the most profound effects on the QSR industry.

Fast Casual

Fast casual restaurants, those perceived to be a step above the traditional QSR but not quite a casual restaurant (due mainly to the service style), are growing in numbers of concepts and popularity. Players in the emerging fast casual arena include companies like Panera Bread, Chipotle, Qdoba Mexican Grill, and Buffalo Wild Wings. More upscale décor, prepared-to-order items using high-quality ingredients, and a pricier menu distinguish this segment of the QSR industry.

Nutritional Emphasis

To combat the negative press from obesity lawsuits, recently published childhood obesity rates, and Morgan Spurlock's documentary "Super Size Me," the QSR industry has begun to reevaluate some of its menu offerings. While some chains have created entirely new items that promote healthier eating (McDonald's Fruit and Walnut Salad), some have chosen to reposition items already on their core menu (Subway's "8 Under 6" campaign—8 sandwiches under 6 grams of fat). Whether employing either strategy the goal is to provide customers healthy choices, with the hope of growing—or, at the very least—maintaining sales volumes. The QSR industry, in general, targets 18–34 year old males; however, expanding menu choices may attract additional users from other target markets.

Greening of the Industry

The past few years have shown a growing movement toward greening of the hospitality industry across all segments, including quick service. Companies are looking for ways to reduce energy consumption, manage waste, design environmentally-friendly packaging, and construct more efficient buildings. While cost reduction may be driving some of the changes, customers interested in doing business with socially responsible companies also fuels the demand. In addition, some quick service restaurants are also looking for ways to support local farmers and incorporate sustainable agricultural practices into their operating philosophies.

Co-Branding

In an attempt to draw a larger share of the foodservice dollar, many QSRs are entering into co-branding agreements. These agreements are an arrangement between two or more concepts to operate at one location. One of the more common co-branding arrangements involves KFC and Taco Bell, as they have the same parent company (YUM! Brands). Patrons visit one location and have the choice of ordering from either or both menus with one transaction. Kitchens, signage, and menu boards have been retooled to accommodate both concepts and employees are trained to prepare and serve all food. Often times in a co-branding arrangement, the menus are a bit more limited than would be found at a traditional, one-concept-only location.

As KFC and McDonald's recently celebrated their 50th anniversaries, many quick service restaurants are making improvements they feel are necessary to enhance their own longevity. In addition to new menu items, those improvements include upgrades to facilities such as new designs, remodeling or rebuilding of older units, improved signage, enhanced technology, and updated décor options.

Staffing

The National Restaurant Association projects the restaurant industry, as a whole, will add 1.9 million jobs by 2016. Many QSRs are having a difficult time attracting people to fill current position vacancies; thus, who will fill the 1.9 million new positions? The QSR segment has traditionally drawn its workers from the 16–24 year old age group; however, that group, demographically, is shrinking in size. In addition, the QSR segment has suffered from an image problem—a reputation of providing minimum-wage, dead-end jobs—which compounds the problems of attracting new workers. Several studies in recent years cite staffing as the biggest challenge facing operators both now and in the future. Successful operators have incorporated a variety of strategies to recruit and retain employees including targeting older workers, offering referral bonuses, providing incentives and bonuses, using tuition reimbursement, and other creative methods.

Summary

What are the opportunities for you in quick service restaurants? As an industry segment, quick service restaurants did just under $149 billion in 2006.[9] The number of managers is forecasted to increase 12% from 2006–2016. These unit managers will earn between $25,000 and $50,000 and may be eligible for bonus compensation equal to an additional third of their base salary. This bonus is often centered on goals in relation to sales volume, food/beverage/labor costs, customer count/ticket average, and profit. What other industry allows young people in their 20's the chance to be responsible for hundreds of thousands of dollars (even millions of dollars) in assets and sales? The opportunities are endless—go out and be great!

≈ *Resources*

Internet Sites

National Restaurant Association: www.restaurant.org
QSR (online): www.qsrmagazine.com
Nation's Restaurant News (online): www.nrn.com
McDonald's: www.mcdonalds.com
Subway: www.subway.com
Starbucks: www.starbucks.com
Panera Bread: www.panerabread.com
Pizza Hut: www.pizzahut.com
Taco Bell: www.tacobell.com
Chipotle Mexican Grill: www.chipotle.com
Jamba Juice: www.jambajuice.com

≈ *Endnotes*

1. Sandelman and Associates Tracks Newsletter. (2006). Appetite for QSR grows in 2005 at http://www.sandelman.com/newsletter/200607
2. National Restaurant Association. (2007). Industry at a glance at http://www.restaurant.org/research/ind_glance.cfm
3. A&E Television Network. (1996). Ray Kroc: Fast Food McMillionaire. New York: New Video Group.
4. Cheskin Added Value. (2007). Global market bias: brand extendability at http://www.cheskin.com/view_articles.php?id=4
5. Consumer drive-thru preferences. *QSR Magazine* at http://www.qsrmagazine.com/reports/drive-thru_time_study

6. QSR 50. *QSR Magazine* at http://www.qsrmagazine.com/reports/qsr50/2007/charts/segments-2.phtml

7. Jaffe, W. (1995). Chain operations in the hospitality industry. In Brymer, R. *Hospitality Management: An Introduction to the Industry.* Dubuque, IA: Kendall/Hunt Publishing, 94–108.

8. Rice, G. (1997). Industry of choice: A report on foodservice employees. Chicago, IL: The Educational Foundation of the National Restaurant Association.

9. suite101.com. Top fast food countries at http://internationaltrade.suite101.com/article.cfm/top_fast_food_countries

≈ *Contributor*

Nancy Swanger, PhD, FMP
Washington State University, Todd Hall 475
Pullman, WA 99164-4742
509-335-2443
swanger@wsu.edu

Dr. Nancy Swanger is an Associate Professor at Washington State University, where she teaches the introductory and cost control classes. Nancy has over 30 years of restaurant experience as a coworker, manager, district manager, and owner. She and her husband have owned and operated Subway restaurants since 1988. Her research interests lie in the areas of quick serve restaurant operations and hospitality curriculum. Dr. Swanger received the Dean's Excellence Fellow Award in both 2004 and 2005 from Washington State University's College of Business and Economics. She also received the President's Award for Outstanding Teaching from Lewis-Clark State College in 1998 and the Associated Students of Lewis-Clark State College Outstanding Instructor Award in 1999.

Chapter 22
Review Questions

1. What is QSCV and why is it important for successful operations?

2. Choose a QSR in your area and explain how the operation compares to the characteristics presented in the chapter.

3. Define a chain and provide three examples of one.

4. Why can it be argued that the unit manager is the most important factor in the success of a QSR?

5. Of the trends and challenges facing the QSR industry, which do you feel is the most important and why?

Bar and Beverage Operations

23

Wally Rande, Northern Arizona University

© 2008, JupiterImages Corporation.

≈ Learning Objectives

☑ Define the term "bar" and describe the various components of a bar
☑ Describe the different types of bar customers and what they look for in a beverage operation
☑ Define "dram shop" and state how it impacts legal regulations in bars
☑ State the process of fermentation and distillation
☑ Name common fermented products found in bars
☑ Name common distilled products found in bars
☑ Describe the role that the various mixers play in drinks
☑ Describe the job outlook for the beverage industry
☑ Name the future beverage trends

≈ Chapter Outline

Bars and Beverage Management
Beverages
Career Opportunities in the Beverage Industry
Trends in the Beverage Industry

≈ Key Terms

Bar
Beverage cost ratio
Cost control
Distillation
Distilled beverage
Dram shop laws
DUI
Fermentation
Fermented beverage
Liqueur
Spirits
Wine

257

A bar is a counter or place where beverages, especially liquors, or light meals are served to customers.[1] A **bar** is a business that generally serves food as simple as peanuts and snacks and as elaborate as full meals, with an assortment of alcoholic beverages such as wine, beer, liquor, and mixed drinks, for consumption on the premises. Bars provide stools or chairs for the patrons along tables or raised counters. Some bars have entertainment on a stage, such as a live band. Bars that are part of hotels are sometimes called *hotel lounges*. Hotel can have an assortment of bars, such as pool bars, lobby bars, night clubs, etc.

The term "bar" is derived from the specialized counter on which drinks are served and is the name generally applied to the whole of the drinking establishment. The drinking establishment is made up of several components. The "back bar" is a set of shelves of glasses and bottles behind that counter. In some bars, the back bar is elaborately decorated with woodwork, etched glass, mirrors, and lights. When food is served elsewhere in the establishment, it may also be ordered and eaten at the bar.

Bars and Beverage Management

Types of Bars

There are many types of bars, which can be categorized according to the types of entertainment provided at the bar and by their clientele or customers. Bars categorized by the type of entertainment or activities offered at the bar include sports bars, where sports fans watch games on large-screen televisions, and dance bars, which have a modest-sized dance floor where patrons dance to live or recorded music. However, if a dance bar has a large dance floor and hires well-known professional DJs, it is usually considered to be nightclub or discothèque. Bars are often categorized by the clientele who come to the bar include: *biker bars*, which are bars frequented by motorcycle enthusiasts and, in some regions, motorcycle gang members; *police bars*, where off-duty law enforcement agents gather; and *singles' bars*, where (mostly) unmarried people of both genders can socialize and meet.

A bar's owners and managers typically choose establishment names, decor, drink menus, lighting, and other elements they can control so as to attract a certain clientele. However, bar operators have only limited influence over who patronizes their establishments and a bar envisioned for one demographic can become popular with another.

Types of Bar Customers

According to Katsigris and Thomas in their book, *The Bar and Beverage Book*, you can divide customers into several different groups according to their reason for choosing to drink in a public setting or bar[2]:

- ***Diners* at restaurants *where* drinks *are served.*** Although the food may be the primary focus at a restaurant, people often want to drink an alcoholic beverage, too. Restaurants that do a flourishing business without alcohol are the exception rather than the rule.

- ***Drop-in* customers *who are on their way elsewhere.*** They usually want refreshment, a quick pick-me-up, or a stress reliever after a day's work. In this case, the drink is the focus; the customer has one or two at most, and then is on the move again. People who are waiting to board a plane or a train or are meeting someone at the bar also belong to this group.

- ***Meet-and-go customers.*** These individuals are looking for a relationship connection, whether a date for the evening or a longer-term plan. They go to singles' bars or "meet bars" that are attractive to others like themselves. Today most singles' bars include dancing and very-late-night hours.

- **Entertainment seekers looking for relaxation, stimulation, or a change of pace.** They frequent bars, lounges, clubs, and restaurants where entertainment is offered, such as country-and-western music, games, and/or dancing. These individuals want to meet new people or keep up with social trends.

- **Sports fans.** Sports bars, featuring big-screen television viewing from every angle and special promotions for championship games, boxing matches, and so on, are very popular.

- **Regular *patrons of neighborhood* bars and *taverns.*** They are interested in enjoyment and relaxation, too, but their primary desire is for companionship: being with people whom they know and like, feeling comfortable, feeling that they belong.

Legal Considerations

Most of today's alcoholic regulations can be traced back to the repeal of Prohibition. Generally, liquor laws refer to any legislation dealing with the abolishment, restriction, or regulation of the sale, consumption, and manufacture of alcoholic beverages. The chief goals of these laws are to control the over-consumption of alcohol among citizens (which can often lead to an increase in crimes like drunk driving), the consumption of alcohol among minors, and the rising revenue for the government through taxation.

Most liquor laws are based on dram shop laws. According to law.com dictionary, **dram shop** law is (n.) a statute (Dram Shop Act) or case law in 38 states which makes a business which sells alcoholic drinks or a host who serves liquor to a drinker who is obviously intoxicated or close to it, strictly liable to anyone injured by the drunken patron or guest.[3]

The law holds establishments responsible for the dangerous actions of an intoxicated person when they have illegally sold liquor to that person. In addition to bars and liquor stores, these establishments can include restaurants, social clubs, and even private events where liquor is sold.

When Are Dram Shops Liable?

Generally, dram shops (bars) are liable when they have violated a law or regulation in the state where the liquor was served. While selling liquor to an obviously intoxicated customer represents the most common dram shop violation, the illegal sale of intoxicating beverages can take other forms, such as:

- Selling liquor without a license;
- Selling liquor after hours; or
- Selling liquor to a minor.

Liquor Liability Laws

Liquor liability laws describe circumstances when a person is financially liable for serving an alcoholic beverage to a visibly intoxicated person. The laws are also known as dram shop laws, referring to the 18th-century British practice of selling a dram (spoonful) of gin. Currently, liability laws vary by state. Some states hold a bar owner and bartender responsible for the harm caused by serving a drink to an intoxicated person. Liability is often part of a DUI (Driving Under the Influence) case and could be assigned to restaurants, liquor stores, clubs, and private events like home parties. That party could be liable if the intoxicated person commits a crime. Liability laws also apply to selling liquor without a license, selling it to minors, and selling alcohol after hours.

Federal Laws

Most laws that affect the daily operations of bar operation are governed by the state rather than the federal government. The federal government places an excise tax on alcoholic beverages that is paid for by bar in the price they pay for the beverages. Bar owners and beverage producers also pay an occupational tax to the federal government for the privilege of being in the beverage business. Federal taxes on alcoholic beverages generate billions of dollars for the U.S. treasury. Over half of the cost of a bottle of alcohol is taxes and fees paid to federal, state, and federal taxes.

Profit/Costing Issues

Alcoholic beverages are more profitable to sell than most food products in a food and beverage operation. The average mark-up of the average food item is around 3, meaning that the cost of the food item is multiplied by three to come up with the selling price resulting in a 33% food cost percentage. Beverage cost ratio is found by dividing beverage cost by beverage sales.[4] The average mark-up of most alcoholic beverage items is around 5, meaning that the cost of the beverage item is multiplied by five to come up with the selling price resulting in a 20% liquor cost percentage.

Different categories of beverages (beer, wine, mixed drinks, etc.) also may have different price mark-ups. Beer is sold two ways in food and beverage operations, by the bottle or can and on draft.

Bars serve an assortment of beverages; most are alcoholic.

Draft beer can cost almost half the amount per ounce than the same beer in a bottle or can. So bars can mark-up draft beer more than the same bottled or canned beer, making draft beer the most profitable alcoholic beverage sold in bars. Wine can be sold either by the bottle or by the glass. Wine sold by the glass is marked up more so is more profitable than selling it by the bottle.

Beverages

Bars serve an assortment of beverages; most being alcoholic. Bars also serve nonalcoholic drinks such as soft drinks, coffee, tea, and juices. Alcoholic beverages are made from the process of either fermentation and/or distillation. Alcohol is produced from sugar or from a product that can be changed into sugar. Once sugar is present, it can be transformed into alcohol by the natural process of fermentation.[5] Ethanol fermentation is the biological process by which sugars are converted into ethanol and carbon dioxide. Ethanol fermentation is responsible for the rising of bread dough, the production of ethanol in alcoholic beverages, and for much of the production of ethanol for use as fuel. Fermentation is responsible for the making of beer, wine, and sake.

A **distilled beverage** is a consumable liquid containing ethyl alcohol (ethanol) purified by distillation from a fermented substance such as fruit, vegetables, or grain. The word *spirits* generally refers to distilled beverages low in sugars and containing at least 40% alcohol by volume. The strength of the alcohol is designated by the percentage of alcohol or the proof, which is twice the percentage of alcohol. Distillation is a simple reduction. It concentrates and increases the alcohol content.[6] It is a process where a liquid containing alcohol from fermentation, such as beer or wine, is placed in a still. A still is a pot, with a heating source underneath, and a hood type attachment that collects the vapors and cools them to turn them back into a liquid. The liquid is heated to a temperature above the boiling point of alcohol (173°F) but below the boiling point of water (212°F). This causes the alcohol to vaporize (turn to gas) leaving the nonalcohol components behind. The process of distillation can be repeated multiple times to increase the percentage of alcohol and remove the "rough tasting" impurities. Common distilled spirits are vodka, gin, whiskey, tequila, etc.

Beer

Beer like many things we take for granted, is little understood. It is a much more complex drink than many realize.[7] It is a fermented alcoholic beverage made from water, malted barley, hops, and yeast. The percentage of alcohol ranges from 3–15%, but generally is around about 5%.

Wine

Great wines are made from great grapes, and the ultimate quality of a wine is determined in the vineyard as much as the winery.[8] Wine is a fermented alcoholic beverage made from fruits. By law, if the wine is made by any fruit other than grapes the fruit must be listed on the label. Most wine is produced by fermenting crushed grapes using various types of yeast, which consume the sugars, found in the grapes, and converts them into alcohol. Various varieties of grapes and strains of yeasts are used depending on the types of wine produced. The percentage of alcohol in wine ranges from 11–18%.

Other Fermented Beverages

While beer and wine make up the majority of fermented beverages, they are not the only ones. Sake, which is popular in Japan, translates to "the essence of the spirit of rice." Sake is considered a rice wine. Mead is one of first fermented beverages. It is a wine made from fermented honey water.

Spirits

Brandy, gin, rum, tequila, vodka, and whiskey are all types of spirits. Distilled beverages with added flavorings and relatively high sugar content such as Grand Marnier, Tia Maria, and American-style schnapps are generally referred to as liqueurs. Fortified wines are created by adding a distilled beverage, usually brandy, to a wine.

Nonalcoholic Beverages

Bars serve a number of nonalcoholic beverages in addition to the vast variety of alcoholic beverages. The nonalcoholic beverages can be consumed alone or in combination with one or more alcoholic beverages in a mixed drink. Some of the nonalcoholic beverages served in bars are carbonated beverages, juices, dairy products, coffee/caffeinated mixers, and premade mixers.

Carbonated beverages are very common mixers served in bars. The carbonation in the mixer adds a festive flair to drinks, while also increasing the absorption of the alcohol into the blood stream, potentially resulting in faster intoxication of the drinker. Common carbonated mixers are soda water, seltzer water, or sparkling water, cola drinks, ginger ale, lemon-lime soda, and tonic water.

Juices are flavorful additions to drinks. Bars have the option of purchasing fresh juices or canned. Some high-end bars squeeze their own juice for the highest quality product. Some juices add sweetness, others add a sour tang, and some add a sweet-tart sensation. Fruit juices are common additions to rum-based cocktails and are commonly served with vodka.

Dairy products add a smoothing effect to the feel of the drink to counteract the burn of the alcohol. They also turn the drinks opaque, usually enhancing and lightening the color of the drink. Most also add body to the drink due to the thick consistency of the product. Common examples of dairy products used as mixers in a bar are cream, half and half, ice cream, and milk.

Coffee/caffeinated beverages are gaining popularity as drink mixers. Coffee is the most common base of hot drinks that are popular in cold weather. Caffeinated "energy" drinks, such as Red Bull, have grown in popularity as a mixer. The caffeine helps counteract some of the depressant effects of the alcohol.

Premade mixers are used in most bars. They are great labor and time saving items allowing bars to cut down the steps in making drinks. Premade mixes contain all the ingredients for a particular drink premixed in containers. The only thing that needs to be added is the desired alcohol. Some common premade mixers are margarita mix, daiquiri mix, mudslide mix, and sour mix.

Career Opportunities in the Beverage Industry

According to the U.S. Department of Labor Career Guide to Industries, foodservice and drinking places may be the world's most widespread and familiar industry. These establishments include all types of restaurants, from casual fast-food eateries to formal, elegant dining establishments. The foodservices and drinking places industry comprises about 500,000 places of employment in large cities, small towns, and rural areas across the United States.

The beverage industry is dynamic and provides many and varied employment opportunities.

Job opportunities in foodservices and drinking places should be plentiful, because the large number of young and part-time workers in the industry will generate substantial replacement needs. As experienced workers find jobs in other, higher-paying establishments, seek full-time opportunities outside the industry, or stop working, a large number of job openings will be created for new entrants. Wage and salary jobs in foodservices and drinking places are expected to increase by 16% over the 2004–14 period, compared to 14% growth projected for wage and salary employment in all industries combined. Numerous job opportunities will be available for people with limited job skills, first-time job seekers, senior citizens, and those seeking part-time or alternative work schedules.[9]

There are plenty of career opportunities in the bar and beverage industry—management, hourly, and ownership. Jobs can be found in the vast variety of operations that serve alcohol, as well as with the companies that produce alcohol and distribute them to beverage operations. Companies such as brewers and wineries commonly look to the staff of beverage service operations for staff. Beverage operation staff's expertise in beverage service is beneficial to beverage producers and distributors.

Trends in the Beverage Industry

According to *Nightclub and Bar* magazine,[10] it's impossible to predict the actual future. Yet there is much to be gleaned of tomorrow's likely market conditions by simply studying a snapshot of today's on-premise beverage and spirits world, and then using a bit of creative and entrepreneurial imagination. Within this global sphere, there are a number of liquid developments to watch for their ability to influence the big picture of sales and profitability.

Here are some trends to watch:

1. **New Age of the Cocktail**

   The New Age of the Cocktail continues in full swing, bringing with it revenues unheard of in times past for bar, club, and lounge owners. The boom times that have seen the average price of and profit on a cocktail increase many fold likely will continue for at least another decade.

2. **Drinking Better, Not More**

   Across most of all spirits categories, patrons are drinking better spirits than ever before and doing so with more moderation. Shawn Starbuck Kelley of the Distilled Spirits Council of the United States says, "You can see it in the spirits statistics. Vodka, rum, tequila, and gin are where spirits and super-premiums are growing the most."

3. **The Price of Flavored Spirits Shall Rise Again**

   Flavored vodkas continue to increase in sales. The segment is awash with new product launches driving up the sales volume and driving down the price point. For example, vodka, the colorless, flavorless, spirit now is available in most any flavor imaginable.

4. **Capital "G" in Global**

   The spirits industry is one of the most global industries of them all, but there is a new dynamic at work that is putting a capital "G" in global spirits sales. Namely, it's the tendency of global travelers to impact sales and new launches back home based on spirits and cocktails they enjoyed on vacations and holidays.

5. **Hedge Your Bets**

   The vodka category is far and away the leading spirit in terms of global sales. But, Kentucky bourbons and Tennessee whiskeys are gaining respect worldwide. With small-batch, super-premium product launches from most if not all of the respected American bourbon and whiskey distilleries, from Jim Beam to Jack Daniel's to Evan Williams to Wild Turkey, this amber wave of spirits is destined to swell even more in the coming year.

6. **Getting Fresh and Muddling Through**

   When it comes to using fresh, authentic ingredients and labor-intensive methods such as muddling to mix cocktails, the exception is fast becoming the rule in bar, club, and lounge settings. "Bars are infusing flavors into vodkas and rums with different fresh ingredients. Customers are demanding better quality ingredients."

7. **Everybody's a Wise Guy**

   Consumers are more knowledgeable about the spirits and cocktails they choose to consume than ever before. As a result of this, bartenders and bar managers must have a higher education about the products they serve. Also, restaurants and bars can benefit from doing scotch and bourbon tastings in addition to beer and wine tasting to educate their consumers better.

Summary

The beverage industry is dynamic and provides many opportunities. The selling of alcoholic beverages is profitable but also heavily regulated and taxed by the federal, state, and local governments. Beverage operators must take care in the service of alcoholic beverages due to the intoxicating effect.

There are plenty of job opportunities in this industry as it continues to grow. Those seeking employment can work for the operations that serve beverages, the industry that produces the beverages as well as the businesses that distribute the products for the producers to the operations that sell it to consumers.

≈ Resources

Internet Sites

Responsible Alcohol Training Sites:

The Bar Code Program by the Educational Foundation of the National Restaurant Foundation:
http://foodserviceworkforcesolutions.com/content.asp?topicID=75&contentID=616

ServSafe Alcohol offered by the Educational Foundation of the National Restaurant Foundation Training for Intervention:
www.nraef.org/servsafe/alcohol/book/

TIPS (Procedures): http://www.gettips.com/index.shtml

A good source of information about the beverage industry: http://www.nightclub.com/

References

Thomas, K. A. (2007). *The Bar and Beverage Book*, 4th ed. Hoboken, NJ: John Wiley and Sons.

≈ Endnotes

1. Dictionary.com. (n.d.) at http://www.dictionary.com
2. Thomas, K. A. (2007). *The Bar and Beverage Book*, 4th ed. Hoboken, NJ: John Wiley and Son.
3. Law.com. (n.d.) at http://dictionary.law.com/default2.asp?typed=dram&type=1
4. Pavesic, D. V. (2005). *Fundamental Principles of Restaurant Cost Control*. Upper Saddle River, NJ: Prentice Hall.
5. Grossman, H. J. (1983). *Grossman's Guide to Wine, Beer, and Spirits*. Hoboken, NJ: John Wiley and Sons.
6. Schmid, A. W. (2004). *The Hospitality Manager's Guide to Wine, Beers, and Spirits*. Upper Saddle River, NJ: Peason Prentice Hall.
7. Glover, B. (2001). *The Complete Guide to Beer*. New York: Barnes and Noble Books.
8. Henderson, R. A. (2007). About Wine. Clifton Park, NY: Thompson Delmar Learning.
9. U.S. Department of Labor Career Guide to Industries. (n.d.) at http://www.bls.gov/oco/cg/home.htm
10. 7 spirit trends of tomorrow. (2006). *Nightclub and Bar Magazine*, (July), at http://www.nightclub.com/NCB_Magazine/NCB_July_2006/Spirit_Trends/

≈ Contributor

Wally Rande, wally.rande@nau.edu, is an Associate Professor at the School of Hotel and Restaurant Management of Northern Arizona University, where he has taught for 17 years. He has developed and teaches all of the bar and beverage classes at NAU. He teaches the bar and beverage management course, as well as the wine basics and beer course. He is developing a course on coffee, tea, and waters to supplement the school's curriculum. He is currently working on becoming a certified specialist of wine with the Society of Wine Educators.

Chapter 23
Review Questions

1. Name two types of bar customers and explain what they are looking for in a beverage operation.

2. What is the most common dram shop violation? Name two of the other common dram shop violations.

3. What is the common drink cost percentage in beverage operations?

4. Which came first: distillation or fermentation? Explain the process of both fermentation and distillation and why one has to occur before the other.

5. Name three common fermented alcoholic beverages.

6. Name three common distilled alcoholic beverages.

7. What is the difference between liqueurs and spirits?

8. What is the job outlook in the beverage industry?

Catering Industry

24

Susan W. Arendt and Dawn M. Fiihr, Iowa State University

© Lisa Eastman, 2008, Shutterstock.

≈ Learning Objectives

After reading this chapter, the student will be able to:

☑ Define catering
☑ Identify skills and traits needed to be a successful caterer
☑ Compare and contrast on-site and off-site catering
☑ Describe different catering locations
☑ Identify potential areas of concern for a caterer
☑ Recognize trends in catering
☑ Identify professional organizations related to the catering industry

≈ Chapter Outline

Introduction
Characteristics of a Successful Caterer
Types of Catering Operations
Catered Venues
Purposes of Catering
Concerns in Catering
Benefits and Challenges in Being a Caterer
Professional Organizations
Emerging Trends
Real-Life Examples
Career Path: Getting Started

≈ Key Terms

Caterer
Catering
Catering contract
Catering industry
Client
In-flight catering
Mobile catering
Off-site catering
On-site catering
Outsourcing

Introduction

*P*robably all of you have been introduced to the catering industry in some aspect of your life. Whether you attended a wedding where the food was catered, enjoyed a party with a catered menu, or ate a meal on an airplane, you have already experienced the catering industry. Catering is a growing segment of the hospitality industry with approximately 80,000 caterers in North America alone. In this chapter, you will be introduced to the catering industry, the different types of catering operations, and what it takes to be a caterer. Real-life catering examples are given and a mini case study will engage your critical thinking skills to solve a catering dilemma.

What is a caterer? What is catering? What is the catering industry? A definition of each term is provided below.

- *Caterer:* The person or people who provide food and services.
- *Catering:* The act of supplying and serving catered food. There are different degrees of catering from limited-service catering where food for an occasion is provided, to full-service catering where food and all food-related equipment, service, and even decorations and music are provided. Catering may be done on-site or off-site.
- *Catering Industry:* An area within the foodservice industry that cuts across many segments of the industry including independent caterers, restaurants, hotels, and clubs.

Characteristics of a Successful Caterer

A caterer must possess many characteristics to be successful. While food preparation is important, managing business aspects and fostering client relationships are just as important. Table 24.1 identifies several skills, knowledge, traits, and behaviors needed for successful caterers.

Planning is a major, essential skill for any caterer. All aspects of the catering event must be meticulously planned according to the nature and degree of the event. This may include menu planning and preparation only or may also include set-up and service of the meal. Organization skills assist with efficient and effective use of time and other

Table 24.1
Successful Caterer Characteristics

SKILLS AND KNOWLEDGE	TRAITS AND BEHAVIORS
• planning	• confident
• organizing	• flexible
• communicating	• efficient
• marketing	• dependable
• business skills	• detail-oriented
• cooking skills	• creative
• time management skills	• entrepreneurial
	• people-oriented
	• handle stress
	• leadership

resources—from an organized kitchen to an organized billing method. Both written and oral communication skills are needed to obtain business and keep business. Catering contracts are a form of written communication while face-to-face interactions with clients are an oral form of communication. Marketing food and services to attract the desired client base also is required. Business skills and knowledge, such as accounting, are needed to run a profitable catering business. Time management skills relate to timing of food preparation, transportation, and delivery.

Certain traits and behaviors also are essential in a caterer. Confidence will assist a caterer in both the marketing and sales aspect of the business. A caterer must have confidence in his/her abilities and convey this to the client when selling catering services and when things do not go as the client had expected. A caterer who is flexible will have a much easier time meeting the needs of clients and running a successful catering business. Flexibility is needed because clients change their minds, because employees get ill, and because accidents do happen. Efficiency is described as getting the most out of the resources utilized. Efficient caterers use their resources with care and concern. Human resources (employees) also are considered. Dependability is essential. A caterer often helps create an experience for their clients. The last thing a caterer wants the client or guests to remember is how long they had to wait to be served a meal because the caterer was late. The success of one event will sell future events for the caterer.

Great attention to detail is required. A missed serving utensil on a buffet line, a missed detail in the catering contract, or a missed turn on the drive to the service location can be costly to a caterer.

Creativity in menu development, room design and layout, and food display compliment a caterer's repertoire.

Leadership, along with an entrepreneurial sense, is needed to start, grow, and sustain a catering business. A caterer must enjoy working with and for a diverse group of people. Interacting with clients and exceeding client expectations are paramount to a successful catering business. Additionally, good working relationships with employees will help maintain an efficient and effective catering staff.

A good rule of thumb in the catering business is to expect the unexpected. Incidents such as limited water supply for handwashing at the site, not being able to locate an off-site event, or running short on food at an event can be extremely stressful. Therefore, in the catering business, the ability to handle and manage stress is essential.

Types of Catering Operations

The two primary types of catering are on-site and off-site (these are sometimes referred to as on-premise and off-premise). An additional type, mobile, also is addressed. The major differences between each type are where the food is prepared and where it is served.

On-Site Catering

On-site catering means the food is prepared at the same location it is served. Examples of on-site catering include hospitals, schools and universities, hotels, clubs, and attraction foodservice. Hospital foodservice departments have expanded services over the years to include catering for various meetings and events held at the hospital. These may include hospital board meetings, auxiliary functions, or fundraising events. School and universities may cater small items such as a platter of cookies for a teachers' meeting to larger functions such as athletic banquets. Larger hotels generally will have conference rooms utilized for wedding parties and meetings. Generally the mandate in these operations is for meals and foods to be purchased and catered through the hotel dining department. Attraction foodservices, including zoo restaurants and cafes or museum foodservice operations, often will cater on-site for special events. Other caterers own or lease a building and will do some catered events there.

Larger hotels typically have conference rooms utilized for wedding parties and meetings.

Off-Site Catering

Off-site catering is exciting as often locations are chosen because of their beauty or the fact that they can accommodate a large number of guests. Parks, open fields, private homes, or even parking lots may be utilized. However, these sites can provide challenges for a caterer due to limited electrical service, water sources, trash facilities, working spaces, and questionable security. If an event is held outside, pest control and weather conditions also may be of concern.

Restaurants may provide off-site catering as another source of revenue. Corporate meetings and social events provide the largest opportunities for off-site catering done by restaurants. Larger grocery stores and supermarkets offer limited catering services often providing food, beverages, and paper goods. Clients also can utilize supermarket floral departments for decorating purposes.

Off-site catering businesses can be home-based whereby the caterer produces all food and conducts business from their home. In contrast, an off-site catering business could instead be located in a leased or purchased space.

With off-site catering, caterers may choose to use their own equipment or the client's equipment. Some caterers transport steam tables (for hot holding of buffet items), utensils, guest tables, skirting, china, glassware, and flatware, all items needed for the event. Still others will provide only the food and utilize the equipment at the remote site. Of course, there are caterers that may be somewhere along this continuum and those that provide several options to clients. Still other caterers will transport food items in a variety of forms, raw and cooked. For example, a caterer doing an outside spring brunch buffet may bring most items prepared, but set up an omelet or pancake station to prepare the menu item in front of the customer. This enhances the overall customer experience but can certainly pose unique challenges for the caterer.

Labor utilized at off-site catering events also varies from caterer to caterer. Some will bring their own staff to set up, serve, and clean up. Others will provide food and minimal services while the client provides additional help needed for the event to run smoothly.

Mobile Units

Mobile catering utilizes a variety of movable units. Custom-built trucks are often used for some production and all service. These trucks contain heating and holding equipment. A large window will open on the side of the truck for customer access and some will have a picnic table attached on the back. Smaller mobile carts are used seasonally and may be manually pushed or motor operated. Street vendors often sell hot dogs, gyros, and other sandwiches from these units. The benefit of a mobile unit is the ability to sell from multiple locations so if sales are not stellar at one site, the caterer can move to a different spot. Many mobile caterers will target customers at construction sites or open-air markets due to limited competition and high customer traffic flow.

These three catering options are not distinct. A restaurant operation or other foodservice establishment may employ a dual catering strategy. They may offer both on-site and off-site catering to clients. Some caterers will have a small mobile unit that they use only seasonally but continue catering throughout the year either on or off premise.

Catered Venues

Generally when we think about catered events, special event celebrations and ceremonies come to mind (weddings, birthday parties, and corporate functions). Fundraising events may be extremely elaborate (see Real-Life Examples) and may rely on caterers. Private parties, whether in a client's home or at a different location, are other venues for catering. Catered meals may be contracted for meetings to allow meeting participants to eat at the meeting site, which generally takes less time and is more controlled than allowing participants to leave. Airlines also utilize catering to provide meals to passengers, referred to as in-flight catering. Food preparation for in-flight catering is said to resemble a food manufacturing plant as compared to a catering kitchen.

Case Study
OFF-SITE CATERING

Dawn is the manager of a foodservice unit within a large Midwest university dining services department. She and her staff are responsible for feeding 600 university students 3 meals a day while bringing in extra revenues through catering. There are other dining units within the university dining services department located across campus. The entire university dining system prepares over 15,000 meals a day for students and staff.

Recently Dawn received a catering request for an upcoming football game day—a picnic for 1,000 people at the football stadium located 1 mile from her unit. Hamburgers, hot dogs, potato salad, baked beans, and condiments are on the menu.

Game day arrives and the picnic menu items are loaded on the truck for transportation to the football stadium. The aroma of hot dogs, hamburgers, and baked beans waifs through the truck. Upon arrival, Dawn and two other dining service employees begin to unload the truck slightly ahead of schedule. However, a slight mishap occurs as the beans are being rolled down the truck ramp on a cart. The employee accidentally catches the cart's wheel on the edge of the ramp and spills all the beans. Picnic service is to begin in 40 minutes.

Questions:

- What are some factors Dawn should consider before deciding what to do?
- What are Dawn's options?
- What are the advantages and disadvantages of each option?

LSG SkyChefs and Gate Gourmet are two big name providers of in-flight catering. Gate Gourmet serves an average of 200,000,000 meals annually[1] while LSG SkyChefs tout service of 387,000,000 meals annually.[2]

Purposes of Catering

There are several reasons a preexisting foodservice establishment might decide to add catering to their service mix. Catering can help an establishment generate additional revenue and increase their client base. For a restaurant doing $1,000,000 in sales, the first year of catering can add an additional $200,000 in net profits.[3]

Zoos and museums are good examples of businesses that have started catering to fund other activities. A zoo restaurant may produce food for a wedding to be held at the zoo (likewise a museum might produce food for an event on-site). Monies generated through catering can be used to cover other expenses at the zoo or museum.

Outsourcing of foodservice can provide opportunities for caterers. Outsourcing occurs when an organization does not manage their own foodservice operations but rather "contracts it out." A factory or business may not have a foodservice operation on-site or may not view providing foodservice as a primary mission to their organization. To provide eating options to their hungry employees at lunchtime, a factory or business may contract with a local restaurant or hotel to cater food. This is a mutually beneficial relationship and allows the corporation to concentrate on their business priorities.

Concerns in Catering

The catering industry is susceptible to various threats, which can cause concern for the caterer. A discussion of five concerns follows: labor, finance, food safety, alcohol service, and government regulations.

Labor

Due to the fluctuating nature of catering, it is a struggle to find and keep regular staff. The greatest needs are generally on nights and weekends. Workers' schedules often fluctuate based on the catering events planned. One week may be extremely busy and the next may be slow. If catering is offered by a restaurant, staffing becomes a bit easier as regularly scheduled employees can be allocated to the catering event.

Finance

A caterer or catering business has financial concerns related to expenses and revenues. A caterer must be able to forecast expenses accurately to assure coverage of costs and still earn a profit. Expenses incurred by a caterer include insurance, rent, employee compensation, and food costs, to name a few. Appropriate pricing strategies are needed to guarantee a profit.

Collecting on client accounts to ensure revenues are realized is essential. A catering contract is the legal document between the caterer and client. The contract will specify when payment is due. Often the client will pay a deposit at the time they sign the contract. The deposit is generally a percentage of the total charges ranging from 10–50%.

A sample contract is illustrated in Figure 24.1. This contract includes information about the event set up, menu items, and estimated costs. The customer signature component at the bottom is essential. This document then serves as the record of "agreed upon details" by both the caterer and customer.

Food Safety and Food Defense

Food safety is defined as "a suitable product which when consumed orally either by human or animal does not cause health risk to consumer."[4] In comparison, food defense refers to protecting food from intentional contamination. Like all foodservice operators, caterers must be responsible for ensuring safe food. While catering may pose some unique challenges such as maintaining temperatures while transporting of food or holding temperatures on a buffet, these can be addressed. Good employee hygiene along with time and temperature monitoring are essential to prevent contamination of foods. For this reason, caterers will want to make certain that sufficient handwashing facilities are available for employees. Equipment for holding and maintaining adequate temperatures is a must. Additionally, time and temperature monitoring procedures need to be in place and enforced.

Food defense measures may include the following: (1) purchase food items from a reputable supplier, (2) check employees' background before hiring, and (3) keep food in a safe, secure place at all times (i.e., locked carts and locked refrigeration

Figure 24.1 Sample Catering Contract

ABC Catering CONTRACT					
Customer			**Event Information**		
Name: Address: Phone and Fax: Email: Preferred Payment: Account Number:			Event Date: Description: Guest Count: Contact Person/Phone: Contract Number: Event Salesperson:		
Location and Times					
Room:		Start Time:		End Time:	
Event Times:					
Menu Selections					
Description		Qty	Unit	Price	Total
Special Instructions			**Contract Estimate**		
			This is not a bill. Do not send payment at this time. A separate invoice will be sent later.		

Guarantees, Conformations and Cancellations

1. **Confirmation of Amount Ordered**—due by 12 P.M. three (3) full business days prior to event.
2. **Increased Amounts**—less than 72 business hours notice prior to the event may only be accommodated if items requested are available.
3. **Decreased Amounts/Cancellations**—less than 72 business hours notice prior to the event will be billed for cost of preparation that has occurred.

Customer Signature _____ Date _____

units).[5] Most importantly, caterers should have a monitoring system in place to assure intentional food tampering does not occur.

Alcohol Service

If alcohol is being provided and served by a caterer, additional concerns arise. Liquor license requirements, alcohol service legislation, and server age restrictions must be considered. Liquor license requirements vary by state; therefore, a caterer should seek out information specific to their state liquor license requirements. Legislation prohibits service of alcohol to underage persons and those that are intoxicated. Servers of legal age must be properly trained and understand alcohol regulations.

Additionally, a caterer needs adequate storage facilities and equipment for alcoholic beverage service. Items including glassware, portable bars, and cooling units are needed. A reliable inventory monitoring method should also be in place to record usage and detect any suspicious inventory activity (including theft).

Government Regulations

A caterer must learn and understand local and state requirements regarding zoning permits, occupational license, license to sell food, health permits, and taxation to name a few. Realizing that these vary from location to location and state to state, a caterer must take initiative to find out information specific to his/her city. Federal requirements including equal opportunity employment, unemployment, immigration requirement, and taxes related to employment must be considered dependent on the size of the operation.

Benefits and Challenges in Being a Caterer

As with any profession, there are benefits and challenges to being a caterer and working in the catering industry. Being a caterer allows involvement in multiple aspects of the hospitality industry. Working in a catering department of a large hotel will likely provide opportunities in foodservice, culinary arts, lodging, decoration, design, marketing, and sales. This said, other advantages are the variety of work, variety of potential settings in which work is done, and the variety of people (both employees and clients). Benefits also are noted for the caterer who starts his/her own business and possibly works from home. Being your own boss and freedom to set your own hours make this an appealing option for some. Catering is exciting and fun work as clients are often celebrating a joyous occasion. The caterer is provided the opportunity to "take part" in this excitement by providing memorable experiences for clients and their guests.

Fluctuations in the catering business may be considered one challenge. Holidays and wedding seasons are busiest for caterers while business generally slows down after the first part of the year. The financial risk involved in starting and maintaining a self-owned catering business is another challenge. As with many foodservice positions, catering can require long hours and great physical demands. Some find dealing with client complaints to be a challenge while others thrive on handling the day-to-day stress of catering.

Professional Organizations

The National Association of Catering Executives (NACE) promotes the catering profession while providing education and networking opportunities for its members. It is the oldest and largest catering professional organization with almost 3,000 members from the United States and Canada. Membership is available to students of junior and senior classification who are majoring in food and beverage. The NACE Website can be accessed at www.nace.net.

Another organization, the International Caterers Association (ICA), started in 1981 and is dedicated to providing education, mentoring, and service to professional caterers. Membership is available to students as well as caterers, chefs, event planners,

The catering industry is affected by food trends such as dessert buffets.

and bridal consultants. The ICA Website can be accessed at www.icacater.org.

Emerging Trends

The catering industry is affected by food and event planning trends as well as the ever-changing expectations of customers. Food trends include ethnic cuisines and Asian Fusion. Innovation with respect to presentation and service continues. Dessert buffets with a seated and served meal, individual tableside ordering, and "Retro Desserts" are current trends.[6] Dessert buffets with a seated, served meal allow guests to experience being served while given some freedom in dessert selection and reprieve from sitting. Individual tableside ordering is illustrated in the Pretty in Pink example below. Guests are given multiple menu options, which proves labor intensive for the caterer and staff. "Retro Desserts" include cherries jubilee and bananas foster that can be easily flamed, thus providing an exciting experience for guests. "Retro Desserts" are served from a station or from a rolled cart to allow guests to get an "up close" look.

Bite-sized portions, or small plates as they are sometimes called, have emerged in all aspects of the menu (from entrees to desserts). Small plates allow guests to mix and match different entrees or desserts.[7] A bite-sized dessert may be called a shot dessert as these are often served in a shot glass. Another bite-sized, small plate example is given in the Studio 1200 and the World's Largest Chef Table whereby bite-sized desserts were used to create a tic-tac-toe game representation.

Figure 24.2 Common Layouts for Business or Educational Events

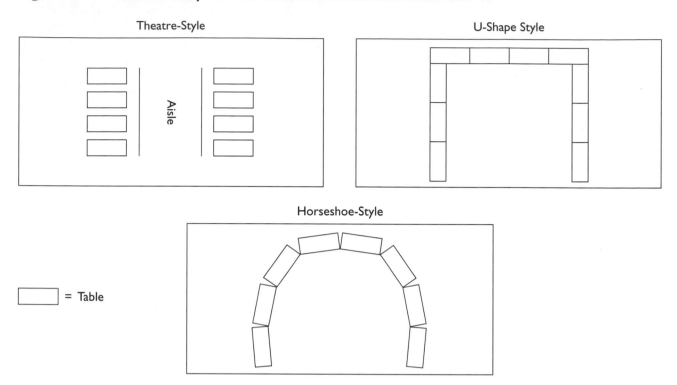

Catering is no longer just about the food. Customers now demand and expect one-stop shopping. Therefore, catering customers look to a caterer to "provide it all" including linens, entertainment, flowers, and tables. Three common table layouts for business or educational meetings are provided in Figure 24.2; however, the location, facilities, and customer's preference will dictate the layout used.

Real-Life Examples

Nordstrom's Miami Store Grand Opening: Pretty in Pink

To celebrate a new store opening in Miami, Nordstrom's hired Joy Wallace and her team (Joy Wallace Catering Production and Design) to cater the event, Pretty in Pink.[8] There were 1,500 guests in attendance. Menu options were elaborate including choices like petite tenderloin medallions crusted with fresh herbs and cracked pink peppercorns presented on a bed of caramelized onions; yellow-tail snapper fillets rubbed with cumin, black peppercorns, sugar, and kosher salt; and saffron breast of chicken sliced and presented on a bed of candied kumquats, lemon rinds, cinnamon, cilantro, caramelized shallots, and black olives. One station included an avocado bar where guests were served a pitted avocado and given choices of toppings like sour cream, capers, and crispy red tortilla strips. Guests enjoyed special treats including Jelly Bellies, red Gummy Bears, and Red Hots. To make certain guests had a memento of the occasion, the take-home treat was a carmeled apple, nutted, sprinkled, chocolate-chipped, and wrapped in a special cellophane bag with a Nordstrom's sticker.

Studio 1200 and the World's Largest Chef Table

Imagine receiving a DVD invitation in the mail. On this DVD is an Executive Chef explaining an adventure filled evening with exquisite food. You are one of the lucky 125 attendees. This is, in fact, how the Studio 1200 and the World's Largest Chef Table catering event began. The event was held outside near a lap pool. Tables were skirted in black and then covered with metal table tops to resemble a galvanized steel chef table found in a kitchen. Customized cutting boards were used as a charger and dishtowels were used as napkins. Table decorations included flowers, spices, dried pasta, spatulas, wooden spoons, and rolling pins elegantly arranged. Innovative menu items were bountiful with some of the more notable items being the lobster cannoli appetizer and sous vide style lamb loin flavored with Dijon mustard horseradish and whole fresh thyme. The dessert theme was tic-tac-toe whereby desserts were placed on a square plate resembling a tic-tac-toe board with chocolate swirl sticks used for the lines. The three bite-sized desserts were used: open-faced marshmallow with a coffee cream, warm liquid chocolate truffle, and roasted pineapple cobbler all arranged in a winning diagonal pattern on the tic-tac-toe board. This event won the NACE 2007 best catered on-premise event with a budget under $35,000.[9]

Career Path: Getting Started

While there are no educational requirements to become a caterer, there are academic courses and programs that can help a caterer succeed. Some aspiring caterers choose a culinary school or program to hone their cooking skills while others choose to study restaurant management, hospitality management, or business. Still others choose to go into catering after having extensive experience in the foodservice industry.

Recognize that starting a catering business will take money. Bode (2003)[10] gives these estimates for expenses and related costs:

* $1,000 can get you started if you plan to utilize your home kitchen. However, it may cost $100,000 or more to equip a professional kitchen.
* Revenues between $200,000 and $2,000,000 can yield $50,000–$1,000,000 pretax profit.

Still others note additional expenses related to transportation, noting that new refrigerated trucks cost $25,000 or more.[11]

If you choose to work for a hotel, restaurant, or other operation in catering, positions may include catering manager, catering coordinator, or conference and banquet manager. This allows you to work in the industry without assuming as much financial risk as you would if you were in business for yourself.

A student interested in catering should seek foodservice and catering work experiences or internships. Both NACE and ICA have student memberships offering valuable networking, mentoring, and educational opportunities. Also, check with your campus dining services provider. Many campus dining operations (whether self-operated or contract managed) have catering departments to cater campus events such as tailgates, weddings, and receptions.

Summary

The catering industry is dynamic and entails more than just providing food to clients. Caterers have many options available including whether to work independently or link with a larger organization. Caterers can be involved in providing limited services or providing a wide range of services including customizing menus, decorations, and entertainment. The opportunities are endless and the future for catering is bright.

≈ *Resources*

Internet Sites

www.nace.net
www.icacater.org

≈ *Endnotes*

1. Gategourmet at http://www.gategourmet.com
2. LSG Sky Chefs at http://www.lsgskychefs.com/en/about-us.html
3. Bode, S. (2003). *Successful Catering*. Ocala, FL: Atlantic Publishing Group.
4. FSIS at http://www.fsis.usda.gov/OPPDE/animalprod/presentations/residue/tsld003.htm
5. Powitz, R. (2006). Food defense for the small retail operation. *Food Safety Magazine* at http://www.extension.iastate.edu/foodsafety/biosecurity/FSMSanitarian120107.pdf
6. Hansen, B., and Thomas, C. (2005). *Off-Premise Catering Management*, 2nd ed. Hoboken, NJ: John Wiley and Sons.
7. Matthews, K. (2007). The big business of small plates at http://www.portfolio.com/culture-lifestyle/culture-inc/food-drink/2007/03/24/The-Big-Business-of-Small-Plates
8. ICA communicator cover story at http://www.icacater.org

9. Catered event of the year at http://www.nace.net/awards/cateredevent.html
10. Bode, S. (2003). *Successful Catering.* Ocala, FL: Atlantic Publishing Group.
11. Hansen, B., and Thomas, C. (2005). *Off-Premise Catering Management,* 2nd ed. Hoboken, NJ: John Wiley and Sons.

≈ *Contributors*

Susan W. Arendt

sarendt@iastate.edu

Susan W. Arendt is an Assistant Professor at Iowa State University where she teaches Human Resource Management and Foodservice Systems Management. Her research interests include food safety, leadership, and student learning.

Dawn M. Fiihr

dmfiihr@iastate.edu

Dawn Fiihr is an academic advisor at Iowa State University where she teaches Introduction to Hospitality Management. Ms. Fiihr previously worked in ISU Dining and has extensive experience in catering, retail, and quantity food production.

Chapter 24
Review Questions

1. What characteristics are needed to be a successful caterer? Why?

2. List three ways off-site catering and on-site catering are similar.

3. List three ways off-site catering and on-site catering are different.

4. List at least three catering locations and describe special considerations for those sites.

5. What are the benefits to a restaurant that adds catering services?

6. Identify four major concerns for caterers and why these are of concern to a caterer.

7. Identify three challenges for caterers and how a caterer might address these challenges.

8. Identify current catering trends and what impact they have on caterers and clients.

9. Identify two professional catering organizations.

The Culinary World

25

Keith Mandabach, New Mexico State University

© VR Photos, 2008, Shutterstock.

≈ Learning Objectives

☑ Identify what chefs do and describe at least three factors that might make a chef successful
☑ Identify different aspects of the culinary world
☑ Understand and discuss historical forces that contributed to our culinary world
☑ Describe at least six career culinary choices
☑ Explain six approaches and strategies for developing/creating a successful culinary career

≈ Chapter Outline

The Culinary World Is Growing
History of the Culinary Arts
Career Opportunities
Strategies to Build a Culinary Career

≈ Key Terms

The American Culinary Federation, Inc. (ACF)
Apprenticeship
Chef
Culinology®
On-site foodservice

What does it take to be a success in the culinary world and what do you do when you work as a chef?

*R*atings for television food networks and cooking shows featuring glamorous chefs appear to have increased interest in cooking or culinary careers. The programs certainly have piqued viewers' curiosity about becoming a chef and dedicating their life to the culinary world. Readers are cautioned that as glamorous as the shows make the chef appear, the individuals that star on television did not instantly become the famous "chef." They worked long hours, studied, and trained to reach the positions they are in today.

Successful chefs formally apprenticed, attended a culinary school or college, trained under qualified chefs, and/or any combination of the four. They certainly spent a great deal of time and effort mastering the basic culinary skills including knife skills and the correct methods to operate kitchen equipment. Each chef learned the correct methods of kitchen preparation including sautéing, frying, roasting, poaching, broiling, etc. In addition, these individuals understood and applied the principles of menu planning, recipe modification, food sanitation/safety, culinary human nutrition, and the science of cookery. Before one becomes a chef, one must be a cook, preferably a great one, and that is not always an easy task.

A great professional cook who aspires to become a chef must develop skills that supplement one's ability beyond simply following the steps outlined in a recipe. Cooking involves organic material (food products) with individual chemical and cellular structure (similar to the way each snowflake is unique) that also change over time. Complex factors also affect the process. These might include altitude, humidity, temperature, acidity, water chemistry, gauge or thickness of cooking pot or pan, regulation of cooking temperature, cooking techniques, and storage methods for the food. As one masters the art of preparation, one must utilize effective critical thinking skills to produce a tasty, attractive end product (something that people will enjoy eating).

A chef is also a business manager and thus one must develop one's leadership skills and master the use of the technological systems. Chefs utilize computer systems in menu planning, recipe development, marketing, purchasing, inventory control, cost control, scheduling management, accounting, and human relations. In our computer savvy world, the computer system is utilized in every facet of the operation. Knowledge of business skills is as important as the technical skills a chef possesses. No matter how well one cooks, if the restaurant is not profitable it will not stay in business. The chef must anticipate food trends and the public's changing tastes. Most importantly a chef must enjoy the work for chefs work long hours, holidays, and weekends. This requires a unique dedication to the profession and a passion for making people happy. To those whose hearts are in the profession, the rewards are fantastic. Chefs feed the world and it is an honored profession.

The Culinary World Is Growing

The culinary world will continue to grow and is a solid career choice. Within the U.S., the industry employs 12.8 million people today, and is expected to add 2 million new jobs in the next decade according to the National Restaurant Association's[1] Restaurant Industry Forecast. On a typical day in 2007, the restaurant industry will post average sales of nearly $1.5 billion. On an inflation adjusted base, restaurant industry sales are expected to increase 5% in 2007, which equal 4% of the U.S. gross domestic product.

History of the Culinary Arts

There is a long history of chefs and cooks whose lives were dedicated to improving the state of the culinary arts. Most traditional histories of cuisine have focused on the western world's contribution to the field and rightfully emphasize the influence of French cuisine on professional cookery. The French contribution is important because they codified western cuisine, developed standard cooking and baking techniques, and insisted on the finest quality ingredients including French wine. There have been many prominent French chefs. A few include Pierre Francois de La Varenne (1st French Cookbook), Jean-Anthelme Brillant-Savarin (book about the physiology of taste), Marie-Antoine Careme (the "Chef of Kings" was the father of Grande Cuisine), George Auguste Escoffier (wrote a cookbook that established standards of preparation for the world's chefs and developed the brigade system of kitchen management), Fernando Pont (clarified changes in cooking styles and taught his principles of cookery to the French from his classic restaurant the Pyramid), and Jacque Pepin (the ambassador of nouvelle cuisine who stressed method and technique in his writings). Each became legends in their own time because of their professional attitude and their contributions to their communities and nation. The French also developed a training system for the chef and the steward (procurer of the food for the chef) as well as establishing the chef as a professional who provided ethical leadership to all involved in the culinary world.

American Contributions

American culinary traditions up until the American Revolution were tied to England except for areas where Dutch (New York) or Germans (Pennsylvania) had settled. Americans ate quite well compared to the rest of the world. At times the early American diet may have been a bit bland and dominated by meat, but it was a definite improvement over what the majority of Europeans were eating. The most dedicated early American gourmet was Thomas Jefferson. He integrated the inside cookhouse into the design of Monticello. This integration produced warmer food because the food did not have to travel as far from the kitchen to the table. He also purchased one of the first cast iron ovens in America. He was one of the first Americans to make ice cream and hired the first French chef for the White House. Along with all of these culinary innovations Jefferson also cultivated grapes and made wine.

America was an emerging nation as was its culinary style. While European cuisine at this time was incorporating many of the new American foods into its meals, Americans learned fresh ways to merge old world and new world foods. America's greatest contribution to fine cuisine was cocoa and one cannot imagine life without chocolate. America's tomato, corn, potato, and chili pepper are also now part of the basics of the world's cuisine. Meats such as turkey and buffalo and a variety of fruits were also gifts from the new continent.

In addition, technological revolutions taking place throughout the world were having a major effect on the culinary world. The innovation of the stove in 1807, by an American in England, allowed for major improvements in the cooking process and for kitchens to be located within a hotel or restaurant. Improvements were made in food preservation by canning and vacuuming seasonal items making them available year round. Improvements in the transportation industry improved the portability of ice and made crude refrigeration possible. It became possible not only to transport food products quickly, but also to offer the products in a relatively healthy state in the market.

While these inventions would affect the processes of cooking and serving food, the transportation industry would have a greater influence by increasing demand for good food. Restaurants opened to serve the needs of residents and travelers. New York's Delmonico's was the first "in" American restaurant and it offered cuisine beyond the 19th century imagination. Ices and ice creams utilizing American fresh fruit were offered for the first time. They served foods in the French style with American adaptations. This was just one of many American restaurants whose food and service rivaled Parisian cuisine.

Global Cuisine— One World of Food

The culinary world is an ingredient of the economic and social development of the world's cultures. American professional cookery is an excellent example of how global and diverse our dining industry has become. Novice culinarians should realize that the ever changing cuisine is part of the world's industrial, trade, and transportation growth. It will continue to change. As the world has become global in perspective, the modern culinary world acceptance of foods from all cultures is essential for success.

Career Opportunities

There are a wide variety of career opportunities and places to work where a culinary professional will find satisfying work in five related industry career areas: commercial foodservice operations, culinology®, culinary education, on-site dining, and media chef. Each area has its own rewards and all are connected and require the acquisition of technical (cooking) and managerial skills. Commercial foodservice includes all forms of restaurants, hotels, clubs, bars, catering, sports venues, food markets, and ships. Most culinary careers begin in this discipline. Many of our premier chefs and restaurant owner's work in cutting edge independent establishments in this segment. The work is very intense because the public is demanding. Usually the owner and/or chef will be involved in everything from purchasing the freshest ingredients to production and service on the line. It is hard work and to be successful in this world, one must have the stamina and vision to satisfy the public with every plate that is served. Some dining companies also operate in these markets and, although it is a huge business, it is a small world. To get a job in this area, one must have a contact, friend, or find a way to get "in" because everyone wants to get a job in the "best" place. Networking and reputation are important in all areas of the culinary world.

Large national chains (Chili's, Red Lobster, Olive Garden, Bennigan's, etc.) provide career paths for aspiring culinary managers in casual dining. Instead of chefs, most companies have culinary or kitchen managers. Clear cut formulas are provided for management and for food service. Research teams in the head office develop proven recipes and the computer systems are usually state of the art. Quick service restaurants also offer financial rewards that many upscale facilities do not.

Culinary careers in hotels, clubs, and resorts are often very similar in the way they operate and it is not unusual for a chef to move from one area to the other. In this segment, the chef manages multiple leveled restaurants, catering, and room service. Because of the multiple venues a chef must manage, communication and the ability to see the entire operation are two keys to success. In addition, chefs are often required to play public relations roles with guests, members and the corporate officers. It is also important to understand the practicalities of budgeting and computer skills are must. Careers are often grown in this segment either through a corporation or mentor and if one makes solid contributions on the way up the ladder, career success is possible.

Catering is hard work, requires a certified inspected kitchen, and is a tough business to break into. The personal chef either works directly in a client home cooking all of the meals or serves a variety of clients by bringing in ready-made food. There is also increased demand for culinary classes and catering chefs and personal chefs have responded by offering fun cooking classes to the public. Food markets or what were once called grocery stores are one venue that is increasingly hiring culinary professionals. These establishments showcase their chefs and pastry chefs. They now offer "food to go" at the level of a fine dining restaurant quality. Bars and associated business traditionally provided only minimal foodservice but, with the growth of sports and gentlemen clubs, demand for culinary professionals has increased.

On-site or Noncommercial Foodservice

Commercial properties by their very nature require 24-7 attention and for this reason a popular career path is to move into the on-site dining segment.

Vignette
TIPS FROM SUCCESSFUL CHEFS

Chef Ronald Kuralt is Executive Chef and Dining Services Manager of Corporate Services in Columbus, GA, an on-site dining operation. Kuralt feels his work in on-site dining is a good fit for his talents. He utilizes his culinary leadership skills managing within the system provided by Sodexho. The position also offers many opportunities to showcase his culinary expertise and shine in special events and parties. Chef Kuralt chose this business because he enjoyed the hard work and the team effort it takes to serve great food.

- There is always going to be a need for trained culinary professionals.
- Work in the business, determine if you really love it, then go to a good culinary school.
- Remember school does not teach you everything you need to know about cooking and it certainly does not make one a chef.
- Develop a career plan focused on continuous learning.
- Job changes contribute to learning but do not change jobs too often.
- Working for a quality hotel company or chain allows one to move and learn and not have to quit a job.
- Build a network of contacts to promote your career.
- Learn how computerized systems help to complete your daily purchasing, scheduling, sanitation, and food production duties.
- The support of wives, significant others, as well as family support can be a major positive force in many chefs' careers.

Once labeled noncommercial or institutional, those working in this area might provide food to employees at an office building or manufacturing plant, manage the dining services of an educational facility, carefully supervise the food of health care operation, or integrate high quality foodservice in the life of a retirement community. In addition opportunities in on-site dining also include producing healthy food for those incarcerated in detention facilities, managing foodservice operations for the military, or coordinating events and food for a religious facility. This area also includes planning and delivery of food for sporting events including the Olympics, sports stadiums, recreational facilities, and camps.

Culinology®

For many who find their love of food and innovation challenged by the repetitive nature of commercial foodservice, on-site dining, or those who begin their culinary careers as food scientists, an alternative might be culinology®. This term describes those involved in a variety of capacities in food product development, production, manufacturing, marketing, and distribution. The term was coined in 1996 by the Research Chefs Association to describe research chefs and food scientists (technologists). However all those involved in the development and distribution of food product now fall under this umbrella of culinology®. The field embraces those involved in product, recipe, and menu development and innovation, food manufacturing, technology system (computer) development and application, purchasing, procurement, and media (television, newspapers, magazine, Internet).

Chef Educator

All chefs must teach and train their staffs and thus many at some time consider careers in education. For whatever reason, the number of culinary schools has more than doubled in the last 10 years. In addition to traditional private and community college culinary schools a variety of opportunities exist for chef educators. High school culinary arts programs hire experienced culinarians. Four-year universities are also expanding foodservice offerings, and public and private training programs addressing special needs are also growing.

Media Chef

The celebrity chefs featured on television programs and in the media are the most visible spokespersons for this growing field and their success has provided a growing opportunity in this area. Most are successful chefs who begin their media careers in culinary competitions, appearing on local news programs, online performances and blogs, performing in person demonstrations at stores, donating their time and culinary skills to charity events, or writing a cookbook for print or the internet. They are celebrities in their local areas and opportunities continue to expand. The American Culinary Federation has offered "how to" seminars on this topic at national and regional meetings and they are always well attended. In addition to having outstanding culinary skills, the media chef must understand the medium he or she is working in. Communication skills, performing skills, writing, and charismatic qualities are all important to media chef success.

Vignette
TIPS FROM SUCCESSFUL CHEFS

Chef Gary Needham has worked in every segment of the industry except on-site dining. He has been a pastry chef, bakery operator, line cook, sous chef, and chef at restaurants, hotels, and resorts. He has appeared on a variety of television programs, radio, and print. He also worked in research and was the chef owner of the award winning Silver Oak Bistro in Washington, NJ. Chef Gary likes to simplify his advice to aspiring culinarians:

- Find out if you love the business before you spend the money on school.
- Listen to your clientele, they will tell you where you are as a chef.
- Be true to who you are as a chef.
- Don't try to please everybody's palate: Just your own.
- Create a daily mantra for yourself. Mine is "Keep it fresh, keep it good."
- Enjoy cooking and talking to customers and staff—they are all your extended family.
- This business is hard work but very rewarding when you bring happiness into peoples' lives through a good meal.

Strategies to Build a Culinary Career

The Culinary World Is Hard Work

Getting started in a culinary career is a daunting prospect and aspiring culinarians might research the topic by reading stories and strategies in three great books: *Becoming A Chef*,[2] *If You Can't Stand The Heat*[3] and *So You Want to be a Chef: Your Guide to Culinary Careers*.[4] After your reading, the first step is to land an entry level position and find out if the career is right for you. The most common question students ask is, "What entry level position is the right one?" This is a difficult question to answer but similar to new cooks asking, "When will the cake be done?" With a cake one sticks a toothpick into the center of the cake. If it comes out clean, one knows it is done. In finding the right job, the job interview is the toothpick, if it does not come out clean, don't take the job.

Almost all entry positions require a variety of hours and one must accept the fact that weekends and holidays are normal workdays in the industry. Kitchens are also hot places to work and entry level positions will often have little of the glamour of higher level positions. Expect washing dishes, cleaning tasks, and uncertain schedules as your daily routine. But no matter how menial, the right entry level job is one that you are proud of and provides ample learning opportunities. Sanitation and safety are essential behaviors/skills in any kitchen. Follow the adage "clean as you go" not just in your work space but also in your personal appearance, and be careful to avoid accidents. Kitchens are energized workplaces and one must take care to behave appropriately and respect coworkers/ bosses, come to work on time, be ready to work,

Vignette
TIPS FROM SUCCESSFUL CHEFS

Chef E. J. Harvey, the chef/owner of the Seagrille, part owner of The Band of Thieves Restaurant and the Nantucket Chowder Company on Nantucket Island, MA, says his favorite parts of his day are the beginning and the end. His day usually starts the organizing and planning the food production for the day. He starts the bread dough and the mixing and baking the bread provides him with a real sense of love. Creating the stocks, then the finished soups and sauces for the operation, and getting the staff set up for the busy day's business is also a tranquil time. The end of the day provides time for reflection and satisfaction. Every day his team successfully serves large numbers of customers a wide array of food. His wife Robin is his partner and manages the front of the house of the restaurant. After it is over the spirit of camaraderie that is evident in his team makes the hard work worthwhile and he kicks back and reflects in the shadows of the day. Chef Harvey is also an avid runner who just completed his first Boston Marathon. He believes:

- The culinary profession is constantly changing.
- All students should work in the industry before attending culinary school.
- Develop a palate by tasting a wide variety of foods and do not prejudge a dish before you taste it.
- It is important to travel and experience different countries, cultures, and their cuisines because the word fusion cuisine is more than a word.
- Finally don't expect to graduate from school and be handed a top job.
- You must work hard, earn the respect of the people around you as well as keep your sense of humor.
- Be a professional and remember that manners are important.

Chef Harvey says that "My goal was always to become a chef and I never lost sight of it no matter how many gatherings, holidays, or family events I missed. But I never put my family off. We might have Thanksgiving dinner on Friday, but we always celebrated. I set out to be a successful chef and I carried that vision to my family and to the community. It would mean nothing to me to be successful if I did not have the respect of my community and the people around me most importantly my family. I have been blessed with a very supportive wife and children. Without them it might have been very easy to lose my focus and thus my success."

ask questions if you do not understand assignments, and master whatever tasks are assigned to you.

Culinary School, College, Apprenticeship, Certification

Many individuals might have taken a culinary job to earn money for school or to support their families and then decide to formally train to advance their careers. Educational choices include culinary schools, colleges, and formal apprenticeships. The American Culinary Federation has a list of accredited programs and has detailed standards that list skills that must be mastered for the program to grant a certificate or degree. Almost all of the programs require work experience that range from 400–1600 hours.

Students should carefully investigate their options and consider local community college programs in addition to the high profile culinary programs. The first public culinary school in the U.S. was founded in 1929 and America has a strong history of community or technical colleges offering certificate (800–1200 hours) and associate 2-year degree programs. Programs of this type have had great success at national culinary competitions.

2-Year Associate Degree and Certificate

The highest profile private culinary schools are the Culinary Institute of America (CIA), Johnson and Wales University, The Schools of Culinary Arts at the Art Institutes, and Le Cordon Bleu Schools and all have more than one campus. Other smaller quality private programs are the New England Culinary Institute and Kendall College. Whether large or small, public or private, the objectives of these programs are to provide high profile quality culinary education and all require internships. Some require work experience prior to enrolling. Costs at private schools are significantly higher than public programs and thus it is wise to have had experience in the industry prior to enrolling and investing big dollars in an education.

Certification and Accreditation

Some culinary schools are accredited by the college accrediting agencies and some are accredited by trade school agencies. Coursework from schools with trade school accreditation usually will not transfer to accredited academic degree programs, so it is wise to find out what kind of accrediting agency granted the diploma before enrolling. The American Culinary Federation (ACF) inspects and certifies culinary programs in the U.S. and a list is included on their Website. This is a voluntary program and schools that are trade school accredited can be certified as accredited by the ACF if they complete the standards required. In addition, Peterson's Guide to Culinary Schools publishes a list of culinary schools available both online and in print.

College 2- and 4-Year Management Programs

These are usually part of hotel and restaurant management 2-year or 4-year degree programs at community colleges or universities. Most emphasize foodservice or restaurant management and are both public and private. Almost all have a variety of cooking classes in the curriculum. Many students who advanced to college directly from high school complete a 4-year management degree, intern in culinary positions, and then go directly into culinary positions, culinary school, or apprenticeship programs after graduation. For those who have completed a 4-year degree and have experience in the industry, CIA Greystone has a specific program designed for 4-year graduates.

Bachelor 4-Year Culinary Arts Degrees

Currently there are over 20 accredited bachelor degree programs. Nicholls State, University Nevada Las Vegas, Walnut Hill College, the Art Institutes, CIA, Johnson and Wales, St. Louis University, Kendall College, and SUNY Cobleskill are a few of the best known programs. All offer intensive culinary degrees with the general education components that allow them to grant a bachelor degree. These programs were designed in response to industry demand and provide the quality of an intensive culinary degree with a stronger business and general education component.

Apprenticeship Programs

This method of training has historically been the world's standard culinary training method. The ACF apprentice program is modeled after the European system and was approved formally in 1971. Individuals work in establishments under approved chefs, attend educational sessions, and rotate through the varied work experiences for a 2 or 3 year period. The first step is to the ACF Website, find your local chapter, and contact the president or apprenticeship chair. Not all chapters have apprentices. The ACF

Website also lists which programs are involved in apprenticeships. Sometimes the apprenticeships utilize the local community college to provide the educational component and the chef at your school might also have information. The key to finding the right apprenticeship is finding the right chef and property. This is a systematic method of training. Apprentices are provided an overview of the industry, trained in sanitation and safety, and imitate chef demonstrations of basic knife cuts or cooking tasks. Eventually, the student or apprentice will complete the competencies required and complete the program. To graduate apprentices must successfully complete both written and hands-on tests and acquire the Certified Culinarian, or CC after their name, from the ACF.

Certification

This certified culinarian is part of the larger certification process. Because culinary education and skill development are lifelong processes, the ACF has a program in place to certify one's skill and experience. One is never certified as a chef upon graduating from school and must gain experience and skills. Many individuals with no formal culinary education have very successful careers and rise to positions as chefs. Whether one has a formal education or just on-the-job training, certification documents and one's culinary accomplishments provide potential employers a standard to measure a chef's professional competence. After documenting experience/skills, passing stringent exams and hands on tests, certification at a variety of professional levels is awarded from the ACF. An excellent strategy for building a culinary career would be to investigate skill requirements and strive to master skills and requirements for certification. The first step to achieving certification is to visit the ACF Website and reviewing the educational and experience requirements and tests necessary for certification at a variety of levels including: Certified Master Chef (CMC), Certified Master Pastry Chef (CMPC), Certified Executive Chef (CEC), Certified Executive Pastry Chef (CEPC), Certified Culinary Administrator (CCA), Certified Culinary Educator (CCE), Certified Chef de Cuisine (CCC), Personal Certified Executive Chef (PCEC), Certified Secondary Culinary Educator (CSCE), Certified Working Pastry Chef (CWPC), Certified Sous Chef (CSC), Personal Certified Chef (PCC), Certified Culinarian (CC), or Certified Pastry Culinarian (CPC). *The Soul of a Chef: The Journey Toward Perfection* by Michael Ruhlman[5] provides a fascinating description of the master chef certification exam and details the challenges chefs face when they attempt to reach the highest level.

Other Options

There are a variety of Websites for organizations that serve educational functions, networking opportunities, job sources, as well as social organizations. All stress the importance of improving the professional image of the culinarian. In addition to the ACF other organizations also provide opportunities to enhance your career. The National Restaurant Association (NRA) also has a certification program as does the International Food Service Executives Association (IFSEA). NRA holds the premier restaurant show in the world (currently in May in Chicago) and is the organization to join for restaurant chefs. IFSEA is primarily an on-site and military organization that provides outstanding support within their organizations. The Club Managers Association also provides excellent networking opportunities for its chefs. There are two personal chef organizations and the International Association of Culinary Professional offers support for personal and media chefs. In the culinology® field, the Research Chefs Association provides certification opportunities and networking. For educators, Foodservice Educators Network International (FENI), Center for Advancement of Foodservice Education (CAFÉ), the ACF, and International Council of Hotel, Restaurant, and Institutional Educators all provide support and certifications for culinary educators.

Summary

The culinary arts field is an exciting and growing career path. The history of the profession is tied to national and economic growth and has been heavily influenced by French and European chefs. Immigrant chefs, trained in Europe, were the dominant force in American cuisine. These professionals adapted American ingredients and began the process of blending the ethnic variety that was American into the food they served. They formed professional associations that promoted training in the culinary arts. Aspiring culinarians have a variety of career choices and educational paths. Before going to culinary school it is good idea to work in the industry and learn through on-the-job training. While the culinary world has long hours and hard work, the rewards are many for the right person.

≈ *Resources*

Internet Sites

Schools

The Art Institutes Schools of Culinary Arts (all campuses): http://www.artinstitutes.edu/culinary/
Culinary Institute of America: www.ciachef.edu
Culinary Institute of America at Greystone: http://www.ciachef.edu/california/
John Folse Culinary Institute: http://www.nicholls.edu/jfolse/
Johnson and Wales (all campuses): http://www.jwu.edu/
Kendall College Culinary: http://www.kendall.edu/Academics/CulinaryArts/tabid/70/Default.aspx
Le Cordon Bleu International (all campuses): http://www.cordonbleu.net/International/English/dp_main.cfm
Le Cordon Bleu USA: http://www.lecordonbleuschoolsusa.com/
New England Culinary Institute: http://www.neci.edu/home.html
Petersons Guide to Culinary Schools: http://www.petersons.com/culinary/

Networking and Support Organizations

American Culinary Federation (ACF)
800-624-9458
www.acfchefs.org

American Dietitic Association (ADA)
800-877-1600
www.eatright.org

Educational Institute of the American Hotel and
    Lodging Association
517-3724567
www.ei-ahla-org

American Institute of Wine and Food (AIWF)
800-274-2493
www.aiwf.org

American Personal Chef Association (APCA)
800-644-8389
www.personalchef.com

Asian Chefs Association
415-531-3599
http://www.acasf.com/

Assocation for Career and Technical Education (ACTE)
800-826-9972
www.acteonline.org

Black Culinarian Alliance (BCA)
800-308-8188
www.blackculinaries.com

Canadian Culinary Federation
905-773-4277
http://www.ccfcc.ca/en/

Club Managers Association of America (CMAA)
703-739-9500
www.cmaa.org

Confrerie de La Chaine des Rotisseurs
973-360-9200
www.chaineus.org

Foodservice Educators Network International (FENI)
312-849-2220
www.feni.org

Healthcare Foodservice Managers
212-297-2166
http://www.hfm.org/index.html

International Association of Culinary Professionals (IACP)
502-581-9786
www.iacp.com

International Caterers Association (ICA)
888-604-5844
www.icacater.org

International Food Service Executives Association (IFSEA)
702-838-8821
www.ifsea.com

National Association of College and University Food
    Services (NACUFS)
517-332-2494
www.nacufs.org

National Restaurant Association (NRA)
The National Restaurant Association Educational
    Foundation (NRAEF)
202-331-5900
www.restaurant.org

Research Chefs Association (RCA)
404-252-3663
www.culinology.com

School Nutrition Association (formerly the American School
    Food Service Association)
703-739-3900
www.schoolnutrition.org

Society for Foodservice Management (SFM)
502-583-3783
www.sfm-online.org

United States Personal Chef Association (USPCA)
800-995-2138
www.uspca.com

Women Chefs and Restaurateurs (WCR)
877-927-7787
www.womenchefs.org

Women's Foodservice Forum (WFF)
855-368-8008
www.womensfoodserviceforum.com

The World Association of Cooks Societies
http://www.wacs2000.org/index.php

References

Dornenburg, A., and Page, K. (2002). *Becoming a Chef.* Hoboken, NJ: John Wiley and Sons.

Gilsen, W. (2006). *Advanced Professional Cooking.* Hoboken, NJ: John Wiley and Sons.

Kim, K. (2006). National Restaurant Association announces record sales projected in year ahead for nation's largest private sector employer. *Nation Restaurant Association* at http://www.restaurant.org/pressroom/pressrelease.cfm?ID=979

National Restaurant Association. New Mexico Restaurant Association at http://www.restaurant.org/pdfs/research/state/newmexico.pdf

National Restaurant Association. *The Cornerstone Initiative* at http:///www.restaurant.org/cornerstone/index.html

Root, W., and Rochemont, R. (1976). *Eating in America.* New York: Morrow.

≈ *Endnotes*

1. National Restaurant Association. (2007). Industry research at http://www.restaurant.org/research/
2. Dornenburg, A., and Page, K. (2002). *Becoming a Chef.* Hoboken, NJ: John Wiley and Sons.
3. Davis, D. (1999). *If You Can Stand the Heat: Tales from Chefs and Restaurateurs.* New York: Penguin Putnum.
4. Brefere, L. M., Drummond, K. E., and Barnes, B. (2008). *So You Want to be a Chef: Your Guide to Culinary Careers.* New York: Wiley.
5. Ruhlman, M. (2001). *The Soul of a Chef: The Journey Toward Perfection.* New York: Penguin Putnam.

≈ *Contributor*

Dr. Mandabach is an award winning chef and educator who enjoys his students. He is a frequent speaker at chef and educator conferences in the U.S. and abroad and has written numerous articles on culinary education. He is an expert on the history of American Culinary Education and currently serves as the chairman of the American Culinary Federation Curriculum Review Committee.

Chapter 25
Review Questions

1. Describe at least three skills that make a chef successful.

2. What are three major contributions of French cuisine to the culinary world?

3. What forces are contributing to growth of today's global cuisine?

4. Describe two behaviors that will contribute to your success in your first job.

5. Please describe at least six areas of the culinary world where one might build a career.

6. List at least two formal approaches/strategies to improve your skills and knowledge and which approach you think would be best for your career.

7. Why is it important to get experience before beginning your culinary education?

8. What is certification and why is it important?

Casinos

Christopher Woodruff, Lake Michigan College

© Roman Rybaleov, 2008, Shutterstock.

≈ Learning Objectives

☑ To develop some objective facts about the casino industry
☑ To understand the differences between casinos and other hospitality organizations
☑ To comprehend the layers of a casino organizational structure
☑ To understand that casinos have different levels of service for different customers
☑ To explore all the different career opportunities casinos can offer

≈ Chapter Outline

Problem Gambling
Differences between Casino Operations and Traditional Hospitality Enterprises
Organizational Structure
Levels of Service
Career Opportunities

≈ Key Terms

Casino manager
Check (checks)
Chips
Comp(s)
Dealer
Drop
Eye (Eye in the sky)
Fill
Floor person
Handle
High roller
House
Low rollers

Marker
Pit
Pit manager
Security department
Shift manager
Slot attendants
Slot shift managers
Slot manager
Slots
Slot supervisor
Surveillance department
Table games
Win

*W*hy learn about casinos? Don't all hospitality operations run pretty much the same way? Well, not exactly. Certainly, a good manager can function in many environments. However, this industry has some differences that are important to understand. We'll begin externally by examining the impact of casinos on the surrounding communities and then examine the internal organizational and power structures. Have you heard the one about all guests are created equal? Not in a casino. Think you might want to work in one? Let's talk about the possibilities at the end of the chapter.

Casinos are a unique industry because their reputation has been less than socially acceptable. However, despite this perception, the American casino business has grown by leaps and bounds. The casino industry came of age in 2005 following the trends of manufacturing corporations and merged creating three out of the four largest gaming companies in the company: Harrah's Entertainment and Caesars, MGM Mirage and Mandalay Resort, and Penn National Gaming and Argosy.

When politicians see the amount of money generated by the gaming industry, everyone wants a piece of the action. As a result, legislators push to have gambling legalized. In the year 2007, more than 500 commercial casinos and 160 Indian casinos were in operation generating nearly 85 billion dollars in gross gaming revenue.[1] In addition, some form of casino gaming is allowed in 37 states across the country.[2] These casinos hired over 366,000 direct employees who earned more than $13.3 billion in wages.[3]

Table 26.2 **Total Commercial Casino versus Total Gaming**

	TOTAL COMMERCIAL CASINO	TOTAL GAMING
1995	$16.0	$45.1
1996	$17.1	$47.9
1997	$18.2	$50.9
1998	$19.7	$54.9
1999	$22.2	$58.2
2000	$24.3*	$61.4
2001	$25.7*	$63.3
2002	$26.5*	$68.6
2003	$27.02*	$72.9
2004	$28.93	$78.8
2005	$30.29	$83.7
2006	$32.42	Pending

Note: All amounts in billions
*Amount does not include deepwater cruise ships, cruises-to-nowhere, or noncasino devises
Sources: American Gaming Association, Christiansen Capital Advisors LLC

Table 26.1 **Top 20 U.S. Casino Markets by Annual Revenue**

Gross revenue is earnings before taxes, salaries, and expenses are paid—the equivalent of sales, not profit.

CASINO MARKET	2006 ANNUAL REVENUES
1. Las Vegas Strip	$6.689 billion
2. Atlantic City, NJ	$5.508 billion
3. Chicagoland, IN/IL	$2.595 billion
4. Connecticut	$1.734 billion
5. Detroit	$1.303 billion
6. Tunica/Lula, MS	$1.252 billion
7. St. Louis, MO/IL	$990.98 million
8. Reno/Sparks, NV	$939.50 million
9. Boulder Strip, NV	$929.70 million
10. Shreveport, LA	$847.18 million
11. Biloxi, MS	$845.20 million
12. Lawrenceburg/Rising Sun/ Elizabeth/Vevay, IN	$795.13 million
13. Kansas City, MO (includes St. Joseph)	$751.33 million
14. New Orleans, LA	$696.47 million
15. Lake Charles, LA	$656.85 million
16. Downtown Las Vegas, NV	$630.29 million
17. Laughlin, NV	$629.76 million
18. Black Hawk, CO	$554.48 million
19. Council Bluffs, IA	$477.96 million
20. Charles Town, WV	$448.23 million

Source: The Innovation Group (4/07)

Gaming can be an economic goldmine in other ways, as well. Typically, gambling establishments begin by developing an infrastructure to bring outsiders to the area. In fact the trend in casino developments moving toward increasing amenities with more restaurants, shopping complexes, spas, and world entertainment venues. In fact, over twice as many casino visitors say they come for the food, shows, and entertainment than for the gaming. This creates jobs for the locals and generates many different tax bases for the government. Then, to meet the needs of the visitors, the new tax revenues are used to improve the infrastructures that support the traffic. As the commercial base expands, new businesses open to support the growing number of tourists and locals. As a result, gaming is a very strong, economic development tool. Casino development creates an upward spiral that increases jobs, adds more taxes from businesses and tourists, and decreases taxes for the townspeople. When residents see the projected economic impact, the positive aspects of gaming are impressive.

However, as with any growth in tourism, this expansion comes with costs. The main problem is rooted in the business itself. Casinos generate millions of dollars a day in hard currency. For example, to convert the customers' paper money to chips and back again, the casinos have many areas called "cages." They act as mini-banks. On average, one cage may have 5 million dollars in cash. That does not even include all the money that is on the tables, in the slot machines, or on the patrons!

Think about being around that kind of money! Does it make you contemplate some different ideas? Everyone does. This brings about the negative aspects of the industry. It is perfectly normal to watch millions of dollars changing hands and think what it would be like to have some of it for your very own. Politicians, employees, customers, or local people are not exempt from this fantasy. Because of the enormous amount of money all in one place, organized crime has always been reputed to be a part of gambling. This resulted in bribery and graft in politicians and criminal activity like money laundering and illegal criminal operations, creating a negative image for gambling. However, as more respectable business people like Howard Hughes and Baron Hilton invested their money in these properties, casinos gained respectability. While the criminal background will always be part of the excitement of a casino, strict regulations on employees and owners, as well as the large business conglomerates, have helped to alter that reality.

There are two main problems for employees and players: wanting the casino's money and spending too much of their own. Some people want the cash they see in the casinos. If they cannot win it, stealing is another option. This is one of the perceived problems that many anti-gaming advocates use to deter people from voting for gaming. They assume that crime increases in the areas where casinos operate. This is simple logic. With any increase in population density, problems are going to arise. On the other hand, with some more thought, this becomes counterintuitive. Casino owners understand that this open display of cash is a temptation. Therefore, security and surveillance are a major part of any casino operation to deter people from thinking along these lines for too long. The casinos do not want big winners to get robbed because it is bad for business. People who do not feel secure are not going to come back. Reinforcing this premise are newer longitudinal studies that show crime increases during the introductory phases of casino development, but then the rates actually decrease over the long term.

Problem Gambling

The second aspect of the money problem revolves around the fact that some people get caught up in trying to win the jackpot and stay too long. A select few will become pathological gamblers. Problem gamblers tend to follow similar patterns. See table 26.3 for a list of traits for problem gamblers.

Table 26.3 **Ten Questions about Gambling Behavior**

1. You have often gambled longer than you had planned.
2. You have often gambled until your last dollar was gone.
3. Thoughts of gambling have caused you to lose sleep.
4. You have used your income or savings to gamble while letting bills go unpaid.
5. You have made repeated, unsuccessful attempts to stop gambling.
6. You have broken the law or considered breaking the law to finance your gambling.
7. You have borrowed money to finance your gambling.
8. You have felt depressed or suicidal because of your gambling losses.
9. You have been remorseful after gambling.
10. You have gambled to get money to meet your financial obligations.

If you or someone you know answers "Yes" to any of these questions, consider seeking assistance from a professional regarding this gambling behavior by calling the National Problem Gambling HelpLine Network (800.522.4700) toll free and confidential throughout the U.S.

Usually, problem gamblers win big early in their careers, and then they chase their losses. This means that if you lose, you double the bet to get the money back. This is a bad strategy and rapidly increases gambling debts. About 2 million, or 1%, of U.S. adults are estimated to meet the criteria for pathological gamblers per year. Another 4–8 million would be considered problem gamblers who do meet all the criteria for pathological gambling but meet one or more of the criteria and experience problems due to their gambling.[4] The key point to remember is that it all depends on how you define problem. Is it when you spend $10 more than you budgeted or is it when you steal to get money to gamble? On the whole, over 98% of the people who come to a casino will not suffer any ill effects from the experience.[5]

Because of the large amounts of money generated, gaming has inherent bonuses and risks. Understanding both sides of the issues is important for each person so that they can decide how they stand based on facts, not emotions.

Differences between Casino Operations and Traditional Hospitality Enterprises

Controlling the Money

With all these people spending their cash, the primary focus of casino management is to track the money. With $100 bills and $10,000 chips floating around the floor, controlling and securing the flow of cash is the name of the game. Computers, accounting departments, security, and surveillance are very important in this process. With all this money, there is a serious temptation to walk away with cash that is not yours. Therefore, the organizational structure is set up to accommodate the primary directive: track the money.

Accountants use computers to access credit information and verify customer accounts. Casino floor people can quickly determine credit lines for vouchers by searching the computer online or calling the credit department. Because money watching is the most important activity in the casino, accounting terminology is important. When casinos talk about profits, they describe them in terms of the process. For example, the "drop" is the total amount of cash plus the value of the markers (credit slips) the casino takes in. This is similar to gross revenues. However, the "handle" is the total amount of money that has continuously changed hands before it is actually won or lost. For example, a person can start with $5, then win $45, and lose $50. The casino counts it as a "handle" of $100. However, the casino "win" for this person would be "0." "Win" is comparable to net revenues.

Why is this important? This is part of tracking the money. The money has to be accounted for each time it changes hands. If a casino cannot follow the money trail, they may be losing cash without knowing it. To begin the process, patrons can play with dollars or they can exchange the dollars for chips. Chips are easier to use. For example, $10,000 converts instantly into a single chip. It's definitely less bulky to carry around the casino. Also, the casinos would like you to carry around the chips. It makes it easier for them to keep track of their money. Psychologically, the chips make sense for the casinos. When a person throws a chip onto the table, the gambler does not perceive it as "money." Spending chips operates on the same psychological principles as credit cards. Signing a piece of paper does not "feel" like spending money. On the other hand, handing over $100 bills to a clerk empties your wallet and you know you have spent your paycheck. The last step in tracking the money is when the customer leaves the casino. Gamblers must cash in their remaining chips because you cannot play in one casino with chips from another "house" (casino). This allows the casino to track the cash flow from the time it enters the casino to the final moment when the gambler leaves.

Following the money trail also means a big job for security and surveillance. The temptation to cheat the casino is particularly strong, and stealing is not just limited to the clients. Think of it. You are a dealer. In front of you could be stacks of chips worth $250,000 in different denominations. One chip, the size of a half dollar, is worth $5,000. Ok. You are an honest person and you have a code of ethics that says you do not steal from other people. Then you get in a car accident and need a car, but you haven't saved enough money to buy one. If you took just one chip . . . a small one . . . $5,000 . . . that's small money for a casino, and it would help you get back on your feet again. Would you be tempted? The assumption is that anyone would.

Therefore, the casino has two departments to watch everyone. This is the security and surveillance or "eye in the sky" department. The security people walk the casino floor and make sure everything is above board. Their surveillance counterparts are in an office above the gaming floor. They watch hundreds of cameras embedded in the ceiling of the casino. Every square inch of the casino can be watched, photographed, and recorded on videotape. Surveillance can zoom in to a table and read the face of a coin at that table. A call to security can have cheaters picked up on the floor. Anytime there is trouble, surveillance can rewind and view what happened on the casino floor. Also, there are customer safety people, who help protect the customers. As we said before, it is very tempting to palm a $50,000 chip, so security and surveillance people design procedures to minimize the risk.

Organizational Structure

In addition, because everyone is watching everyone else, the hierarchy of power in the casino comprises several layers to act as additional security. All levels of management are responsible for making sure no one under them is taking money that does not belong to them. Typically, there are two main divisions with many layers of management: table games and slots.

Table Games

They define table games as any game played on a table. This encompasses the most prevalent games like blackjack, baccarat (*bah-ka-ra*), roulette, and craps that are played against the house (casino). The front line personnel for the table games are the dealers, who are responsible for keeping the games moving and for making sure the games are played according to the rules. They also watch the games for players who cheat. For each two to four tables, there is a floor person, who looks for irregularities and handles most customer conflicts. Several floor people and their respective dealers work in an area called the "pit." The pit manager is the most senior gaming supervisor in the pit. This person is responsible for maintaining the record of customer activity and handling the financial accounting like fills, credits, and closing inventory. A fill is when a table needs more chips. Overlooking all the different pits is the shift manager. He/she does the scheduling, oversees the operations for a specific time, and supervises the floor and dealers. Finally, there is the casino manager. Status reports, radical changes in operations, suspicions of misconduct, personnel, and long term planning are the domains of the ca-

Slot machines account for 60–70 percent of the win in many casinos.

sino manager. Because of these layers, the games are well protected.

Slots

Traditionally, the table games were where the "real" gamblers played, usually men. However, casino operators realized that wives and girlfriends needed something to do while the men gambled. Otherwise, the women would get bored and insist that the men leave the games before they were ready to go. Slot machines were the perfect decoys. The women could sit, chat, and "pretend" to gamble in a ladylike fashion. These are games that include slots, video poker, and other computerized games. Because computers have revolutionized the industry, all the table games in the casino usually have a video equivalent. Instead of playing around a table with a dealer, the computer chip is the competition. This is less threatening for novices and it gives them a chance to practice the games. Some machines allow a person to play any table game at a single machine. The screens are user friendly and touch sensitized for game selection. The quarter slots are the most popular denomination. If you think that's not much . . . imagine four spins per minute . . . 240/hour . . . more than 1,000 in less than 5 hours . . . with three coins in a 25-cent machine, that's 75 cents per spin . . . in less than 5 hours, a person could wager $750 on a quarter slot machine. In the high stakes groupings, there are slots for $5, $25, $100, or $500. As it turns out, slots have become a bigger profit center than anyone could have imagined. In many casinos, slot machines account for 60–70 percent of the win. (Remember win? It does NOT refer to how much the gambler wins.) As casino managers realize this is a gold mine, more slots are added to the casino floor.

Slot departments have several layers of managers. On the floor, the slot attendants supervise an assigned area to cater to customer needs like change, payouts, and problems with the machines. Slot shift managers are in charge for a specific period and oversee slot personnel, verify major slot payoffs, and sign major jackpot slips. Finally, the slot manager handles slot operations, verifies authenticity of major payouts, looks for unusual variations in operations, and works on promotional programs. Each manager has the responsibility of making sure the patrons have gambling change and ensuring the safety and honesty of each machine.

The primary goal of casino management is to follow the money. With cash being the primary product of a casino, it is imperative that many layers of management be employed in order to ensure the honesty of everyone involved. More management positions are available as a result.

In any organization, the department that directly brings in revenues is considered a profit center. This means that they have more control in the everyday operations than other departments. In the hotel, the rooms division directly generates the money and, therefore, they are the most influential. What happens when a rooms division manager moves to a casino/hotel? Many casino operations use rooms and F&B as marketing tools or "comps." "Comps" are free items that players can receive as bonuses for playing at the casino. Therefore, in casino/hotels, the rooms division manager does not always have control over how many rooms are in inventory or what price the clients will pay. There must always be a block of rooms for "comping"; therefore, 100 percent occupancy is *NOT* optimal planning. The casinos like to have a certain percentage, say 10 percent of the room inventory available at all times. As a result, the power positions, types of responsibilities, and goals will change when a person moves from a traditional hotel to a casino/hotel.

Levels of Service

Comps

Depending on how much money you wager, the casino has different levels of service and rewards. Like other hospitality operations, casinos treat each patron according to their level of involvement. However, casinos offer a much wider variety of services for free ("comps"), and the level of service can be radically different. "Comps" are based on a special formula that each casino generates. To create the information, they have to track a player's "action" or amount of play. When a casino "tracks" a player, they watch and record information like length of time at the casino, amount of money wagered, how often they come, and credit line. Because this is a time consuming and labor intensive process, historically high rollers (people who bet large sums of money) were the only ones who received ratings and, therefore, "comps." However, with the age of computers, the casino generates player information quickly and easily. Therefore, they can track any individual for "comps." Although they rate each person individually, casinos can cat-

egorize levels of "comps" to three major groups of people.

Low Rollers

"Low rollers" are people who play the nickel, dime, and quarter slots. They only gamble small amounts of money. For example, bus programs were created to accommodate low rollers and can include round-trip bus fare, $20 in tokens for the slot machines, and a complimentary lunch at the buffet. While this might seem like an extravagance for the casinos, it pays off. On average, each person on the bus will leave approximately $40–$50 of their own money at the casino. This is the McDonald's principle. Price low, but sell volumes.

Middle Rollers

This relatively new category of player was added with the arrival of computers. Previously, casinos ignored these players because there were too many of them, and it was hard to find a way for the casino people to keep track of them all. Now, players can request that they be "tracked" at the casino's Players' Club. The casino immediately puts personal information into the computer and hands back a Player's Club Card. All a gambler has to do is insert the card into each slot machine he/she plays. Once inserted, the gambler's personal information file keeps track of play. It also keeps track of playing time, machines used, amount bet, etc. So no matter where the customer goes in the casino, management can follow their "action."

High Rollers

"High rollers" are people who gamble large amounts of money at the tables. At one casino in Las Vegas, there is a penthouse suite with 10,000 square feet of floor space, a butler, a swimming pool, Jacuzzi, and an optional chef. To expedite the high roller's request, there is a special casino person called a "host." The sole purpose of the host is to be available for a particular high roller while he/she is in town and make sure that everything is in order. "Instant gratification" is the name of the game. They will obtain anything for this guest on demand, no questions asked. Everything is "comped." In addition to free room and board, casinos invite high rollers on "junkets." These are special event parties where the casinos obtain top seats to heavyweight title fights, Super Bowl games, or professional golf tournaments. The casino will invite these high rollers to join them, free, provided that they spend a certain number of hours playing at the casino. So as you can see, they treat high rollers with a great deal of respect and lots of service. The levels of service can be met because they carefully track the money. Each patron is followed around the casino and the casino notes and documents each monetary action with employees and computers. The number of different managers and marketing people guarantee that each person will be treated to the level of their spending habits.

Career Opportunities

Do you think a career in a casino is for you? Well there are definitely plenty of options! As with other hospitality operations casino growth has made it possible for you to go worldwide seeking a career in the gaming industry. In fact, according to Bill Burton of casinocareers.com, casino gambling continues to expand around the world. There are now casinos in places such as Russia, South America, Macau, and other countries. The gaming business has truly become a global employer.

Industry Profile

Steve Kline is the Vice President of Food and Beverage for Four Winds Casino Resort in New Buffalo, Michigan. Steve was hired by Harrah's Lake Tahoe fresh out of the Culinary Institute of America and today is currently responsible for over 750 employees in the Food and Beverage department serving over 7000 meals a day to guests and employees.

1. What are the major daily activities of your job?

I am responsible for all aspects of the food and beverage department including menu development, employee training, and guest service. Another important aspect of my job is the constant reevaluation of our products and employees to streamline our operations. Ultimately my job is to make our guests happy and get them back out on the gaming floor.

2. What is the most satisfying part of your job?

By far people are the most satisfying part of my job. Seeing my employees can help to make a guest trip even better and to see them shine and do just this. To see them take a potentially troublesome situation and turn it around to a positive is very rewarding for me.

3. What is the most frustrating part of your job?

Well, along the same lines, it is very frustrating for me to see employees coming in with ability and talent but they don't see it in themselves and don't realize their own self worth. Many potentially great future leaders in our industry are not patient enough waiting for their careers to develop and leave the industry. Our employees touch people's lives every day and once you realize how important you are that will help in your career.

4. What makes casino foodservice different than stand alone dining?

Mainly two things. The first is that you can get all different aspects of food service in one place. We serve everything from grilled cheese sandwiches and soda, to lobster and fine wine. The second is how we are able to run our operation at a lower cost because of the casino, and then pass the savings on to our guests.

5. What is a trend you see in casino foodservice?

The trend is becoming that we are run more and more like retail restaurants with a stronger emphasis on the profit and loss (P&L) statement. While we still have some control over running at slightly higher costs, we are still responsible for making a profit and meeting financial goals.

6. What advice could you offer to students preparing for careers in hospitality management?

Stay positive and upbeat, and give 100% to your job in terms of heart, spirit, and abilities. We are always looking for people with passion for the industry and their job. We can train the skills, but if you come in with a positive, upbeat attitude this makes all the difference. We are looking for people who believe in themselves, and those who want to stand out and be recognized. You should try and strive to rise above the crowd so you will be recognized.

If you do not love what you do then get out of that job and move on to something else. Whether you roof houses or manage a restaurant if you are not passionate about your job you will never be truly happy.

While most all casinos have the normal hospitality positions that traditional hotels and restaurants have, there are a whole new set of jobs in casinos, such as casino credit, slot management, table game managers (pit bosses), surveillance, compliance, and auditing. There are also support services to casinos such as working for suppliers such as International Gaming Technology (IGT) who makes and develops slot machines, and jobs working for the gaming regulators.

Table 26.4 **Summary Employment Statistics**

The following are some statistics concerning employment in the commercial casino segment of the gaming industry:

- Commercial casinos provide direct employment for over 354,000 people and generate an additional 450,000 jobs in related businesses.
- During the past decade, the casino workforce has increased more than 79 percent, from 198,657 employees in 1990 to 354,921 in 2005.
- From 2004 to 2005, more than 5,000 new jobs were created in the commercial casino industry.
- Casino employees earned more than $12.6 billion in wages (including tips and benefits) in 2005, more than $1.7 billion more than in 2000.
- According to a 1996 economic impact study by Andersen, gaming industry employees earn higher average salaries than their counterparts in the motion picture industry, other amusement and recreation sectors, and the hotel/motel industry.

Source: www.americangaming.org

≈ *Resources*

Internet Sites

www.americangaming.org
www.casinocareers.com
www.fourwindscasino.com
www.foxwoods.com
www.gamingfloor.com/Associations.html
www.harrahs.com
www.hcareers.com
www.indiangaming.org
www.macauresorts.com
www.mgmmirage.com
www.michigan.gov/mgcb
www.ncalg.org
www.ncpgambling.org
www.state.nj.us/casinos
www.theborgata.com
www.wynnlasvegas.com

Summary

To evaluate this business effectively, one must understand two relationships: (1) the pros and cons of gaming as an industry and (2) the differences between the traditional hospitality operations and a casino driven one. Of course, this chapter has only dealt with the casino positions that are different from the traditional hospitality operations. There are still all the regular positions in marketing, accounting, human resources, etc. Because of the multiple layers of managers, there are many opportunities for people who want to be a part of this industry. The main thing to keep in mind when evaluating a career in gaming: money is the product. As a result, this makes it different from other hospitality operations. Knowledge about the industry is the first step to making good career choices.

≈ *Endnotes*

1. Gambling Operations by First Research, Inc. at http://www.marketresearch.com/browse.asp?categoryid=771
2. American Gaming Association. Casino Industry Fact Sheet at http://www.americangaming.org/industry/factsheets/general_info_detail.cfv@id=15
3. American Gaming Association. State of the States: survey of casino entertainment at http://www.americangaming.org/assets/files/aga_2007_sos.pdf
4. Nevada Council on Problem Gambling at http://www.ncpgambling.org/i4a/pages/Index.cfm?pageID=3315
5. Ibid.
6. Hashimoto, K., and Fenich, G. (2007). *Casino Dictionary*, 2nd ed. Upper Saddle River, NJ: Prentice Hall.
7. Hashimoto, K. (2008). *Casino Management, A Strategic Approach*. Upper Saddle River, NJ: Prentice Hall.

≈ *Contributor*

email: woodruff@lakemichigancollege.edu

Before teaching in hospitality at the college and university level, **Chris Woodruff** managed front office operations for city center and resort hotels and has 20 years of industry experience. His Master's thesis was titled "Land-Based Casino Patron's Views on Internet Gambling," and continues to research topics in casino operations. He is the full-time faculty member of the Hospitality Management program at Lake Michigan College.

Chapter 26
Review Questions:

1. Describe your opinion of casinos and their impact on society.

2. Why are legislators interested in gaming?

3. List at least five ways gaming can bring revenue to an area/state.

4. What is the history associated with crime and casinos? How is it different today?

5. What does the research show about crime in casino areas? How does this differ from perception?

6. What is the main problem for both employees and players in a casino?

7. What is meant by "chase your losses"? Is it an effective strategy?

8. What tools are used in casinos to control the money?

9. Define the following casino terms:

    a. Action

    b. Pit

    c. Fill

    d. House

    e. Handle

    f. Cage

    g. Drop

10. How do chips compare to credit cards?

11. How does a surveillance system work in the casino?

12. Who does the surveillance team watch?

13. Sketch the hierarchy of positions in the table games segment of a casino.

14. Compare and contrast the rooms division in a hotel with the rooms division in a casino.

15. What are the differences in people who are classified as:

    a. "Low rollers"

    b. "Middle rollers"

    c. "High rollers"

16. When, why, and to who is a casino manager likely to comp room nights?

17. What is the role of the "host" assigned to a high roller?

18. What is a "junket?"

19. How has the casino industry perfected the relationship between level of service given and the level of money spent by the consumer?

20. Could other hospitality segments benefit from this service to money-spent ratio? If so, which segment(s)? Give an example.

Internet Exercise

Go to casinocareers.com and search their Website for current jobs in casinos or related fields. Through your research of the site find five jobs that you might be interested in. Make sure they are from different companies, and have at least one from a foreign company. Be prepared in class to discuss why you chose the companies and jobs you picked.

Mini Case Study

Divide the class into two groups, with one being for the building of a new casino in your community, and one group opposed. Have each person in class go find two examples of how other casino openings had either a positive or negative impact on the communities they were in. Have the students be prepared to summarize their findings in class.

Classroom Activity

Divide the class into two groups. Have one group be in support of a new casino being built in the community, and one group opposed. Develop arguments pro and con and be ready to debate. Then have a mock public meeting with both groups presenting their arguments. The teacher will decide which group won the debate based on their presentations.

Golf Management

27

G. Burch Wilkes, Pennsylvania State University

© Jim Lopes, 2008, Shutterstock.

≈ Learning Objectives

- ☑ To learn trends in golf
- ☑ To learn about career opportunities in the golf industry
- ☑ To learn what factors motivate customers to play more
- ☑ To learn why people leave golf

≈ Chapter Outline

The Game of Golf
Economics
The Consumers
The Venues
The Business of Golf and Career Opportunities
Trends

≈ Key Terms

19th hole
Bag drop
Club manager
Foursome
Front nine
Golf superintendent
Starter
Tee time

The Game of Golf

*A*s an introduction to this chapter, we believe it is important to describe the common rituals of playing the game of golf.

With this common understanding of the culture of golf, it will be possible to introduce golf management and compare it to the more traditional hospitality professions.

Although most of us have seen some professionals play the game on TV, less than one in ten of us has actually experienced play at a golf club. We will use as our example a typical public course at which a fee for play is collected. This could be a resort course, for example, in Florida or the Carolinas or a course that is privately owned at which we can pay to play an 18-hole round of golf.

Prior to the date of play, we would have called to make a reservation, called a "tee time." Without a tee time, it is unlikely one would be able to play on many of the days at a great number of courses. The tee time would usually be made for four people, as the game is commonly played in what is known as "foursomes."

On the day of play and usually about an hour or so before the tee time, we would arrive at the golf course in our car. On arrival, we go to an area called the "bag drop." The bag drop allows outside assistants to help us unload the golf bags and clubs from our cars and put them onto golf cars or take them to a designated place if we are walking and carrying our clubs. Because so few clubs today have an option for the use of caddies to carry the clubs, we will not consider their use. On depositing the clubs and bags at the bag drop, we take our golf shoes and proceed to the "golf shop" to check in. The driver of the car must obviously take the car (unless of course the club provides valet services) to the parking area and then return to the golf shop.

At the golf shop, the assistant behind the counter checks us in and makes sure that our names match the reservation. The check-in process involves paying the daily fee and, if we are riding a golf car, the fee for the golf car as well. On payment, we are given a receipt and told that the receipt will be collected by the "starter." In the golf shop, there are all the accoutrements necessary to outfit us for the game. So if we need apparel, new golf clubs, a golf glove, or golf balls, we can purchase them in the golf shop. If there is enough time before the tee time, usually about a half hour is

what is needed, we may choose to practice in an area designated as the practice range and putting green.

To practice on the practice range, a quantity of range practice balls is needed. These balls are rented or provided without charge at the golf shop or at the practice range. If we just practice putting, range practice balls would not be needed. We would use the balls that would be used during our upcoming game.

Prior to moving to the practice range or putting green, we might visit the locker room to change from street shoes to golf shoes and to perhaps change clothes as well. Many clubs make lockers available to players. These lockers can be used to store street shoes and other personal belongings while on the golf course. Many clubs offer complimentary shoe shine service for street shoes while we are playing. Of course, a tip is expected by the person shining the shoes. There is often a locker-room attendant who sometimes serves as the shoe shine person, as well as a provider of towels for the shower and other bathroom amenities. This person expects a gratuity when we exit the locker room at the completion of the game, after perhaps showering and changing back to street shoes.

With golf shoes and proper dress, we proceed to practice at the range and on the putting green until a few minutes before our tee time, when we head to the starter's area. The starter checks that the receipts indicate payment has been made for that day and proceeds to give us instructions about the golf course. These instructions normally consist of rules of golf car use and special local rules of golf affecting the play of the game. The starter also tells us when we can move to the first tee and begin play.

As we play the game of 18 holes of golf, which usually takes about four to five hours in the United States, we may encounter a couple of additional people on the golf course. We often see a food and beverage attendant driving a modified golf car asking us if we would like to buy the products that are for sale. There is also, on most courses, a person employed as a course advisor. This person's job is to make sure that the play of the game proceeds at a pace that will allow everyone to enjoy themselves. This means that the course advisor "polices" the property and "hurries up" those who are taking too long to play the game.

After playing the first nine holes, or the so-called "front nine," we may choose to take a short break before starting play on the "back nine." During this break, food and drink are purchased and consumed. Often there is a facility placed at the convenience of the players called a halfway house. This is a small food and beverage establishment that services only players between each nine holes.

On completion of the game, we return our golf cars to a designated area where there are attendants to clean the clubs and take them back to the bag drop area. These attendants expect a tip as well.

Now we may visit the "19th hole" to rehash the game, settle our bets, have a liquid refreshment or two, and perhaps have a bite to eat. This activity takes place in a space that many clubs call the "grill room." This is an informal food service and bar area that can accept golf shoes as footwear. It is an area that usually allows smoking; card playing is often seen among the regulars. Often, there is another, more formal, dining room, where such casual attire would not be allowed.

Following the enjoyment of food and drink, we would return to the locker room. Perhaps we would shower and change clothes, change to street shoes, and depart the locker room. We would then return to the car, pick up our golf bags from the bag drop area, and return home.

From this description of a normal day of golf, it is obvious that there are a number of service encounters. Many of these encounters are similar to those in more traditional hospitality professions like food and beverage service or lodging service. We will go into greater detail a bit later in the chapter; however, let's get a sense of the game and the size of the golf industry.

Economics

A study commissioned by GOLF 20/20, the golf industry's initiative committed to growing interest and participation in the game, found that the golf economy in the United States accounted for over $62 billion worth of goods and services in the year 2000.[1] This includes the billions of dollars associated with annual golf travel, that is, lodging, transportation, food and beverage, and entertainment. The number of golf fans increased 36.4 percent since 1999, reaching 106 million people in 2004, thanks in part to Tiger Woods and an increase in media coverage; however, watching does not translate to doing.[2] According to a 2005 GOLF 20/20 industry report by Dr. Joe Beditz, the president of the National Golf Foundation (NGF), participation has grown from 36 million golfers in 2000 to 39 million golfers in 2004; however, rounds played during that time dropped from 518 million rounds in 2000 to just under 500 million in 2004. In line with a decrease in participation, course construction has significantly slowed in recent years. For several years, the building of new golf courses has exceeded one new golf course each day; however, it appears that supply is now catching up with demand. As reported at the 2005 GOLF 20/20 Conference, there were 398 new courses opened in 2000 and only 150 new courses opened in 2004. Additionally, we have seen an increase in course closings from 32 in 2001 to an estimated 80 in 2005.[3] However, even with the recent economic downturn, rounds appear to have stabilized, and gains in overall participants have been primarily due to junior golf initiatives. Consumers also continue to demonstrate a willingness to spend a sizable portion of their discretionary dollars to join an exclusive country club, play high-end resort properties, or purchase the latest equipment.

The Consumers

The 39 million U.S. golfers are a population overrepresented among higher income households, college graduates, white males, homeowners, and those occupying professional, managerial, and administrative positions. According to the National Golf Foundation (2001),[4] the average golfer is male, approximately 40 years old, has an annual household income of slightly over $68,000, and plays about 21 rounds each year. In addition, when we compare the participation rates of golfers to those engaging in other lifetime recreation activities, we find a marked difference with respect to age. Typi-

Many golfers enjoy the sport well into their 60s, 70s, and 80s.

© Lisa F. Young, 2008, Shutterstock.

cally, as individuals age, their tendency is to constrict both the number of leisure pursuits and also the frequency of participation.[5] Whether it's tennis, bowling, jogging, or using exercise equipment, individuals tend to give up these activities in their later years. For the most part, golfers remain with the sport well into their 60s, 70s, and 80s. Some may use larger grips on their clubs to accommodate arthritic conditions. Others may use a golf car to address issues of mobility or use a more flexible shaft or lighter equipment to compensate for a loss of strength or, perhaps, play from the forward tees to compensate for loss of distance.

From the mid-1980s through the 1990s, an additional 6.5 million citizens have joined the golfing community; this translates into a 33 percent increase. The NGF (2001)[6], in its *Trends in the Golf Industry—1986–1999,* noted that during the same period, women's participation only increased 11 percent, whereas juniors' growth rate increased by 43 percent to 2 million. The 1996 NGF trends report predicted significantly greater participation rates among boomers in the 30 to 39, 40 to 49, 50 to 59, and 60 to 64-year-old cohorts through the year 2010.[7] NGF also indicated the echo boomers will represent a significant increase among junior golfers, ages 12 to 17, and young adults, 18 to 29-year-olds. Boomers will also play more frequently and spend more money as they reach their pre-retirement/retirement years with greater discretionary income.

Two additional markets that continue to be untapped are women and minority participants. Although women have represented approximately 36 percent to 40 percent of all beginning golfers, their percentage among all golfers has dropped to approximately 19 percent. Those who stay with the game play fewer rounds than their male counterparts; however, their household income and expenditures on golf are very similar to men. Beginning in the 1980s, African-American golf participation began to grow at a significant rate. For example, the 315,000 African-Americans playing golf in 1980 represented only 2.4 percent of all African-Americans.[8] A more recent study by the National Golf Foundation (2001)[9] indicates there are currently 882,000 African-American golfers. This only represents less than 3 percent of the golfing community, but it does represent a 100 percent increase since 1991.

The Venues

By the end of 2001, there were over 17,000 courses throughout the United States. Approximately 71 percent are accessible by the public. This would include daily fee facilities/resorts (approximately 9,300) and municipal courses (approximately 2,700). The remaining 29 percent, nearly 5,000, are private, with nearly three-fourths of the private courses being owned by the membership (equity clubs).

The Business of Golf and Career Opportunities

When most of us think of golf, we think of it as a game, and we do not consider the supporting business organization necessary for us to enjoy the game. From the general manager or club manager to the attendant who drives the food and beverage cart around on the course, all have important service functions that are required for the golf operation to run smoothly and for the players to have an enjoyable experience.

As we discussed earlier, there are a number of different kinds of golf operations. Each type of operation would have an organizational structure necessary to meet the needs of that particular golf entity. Depending on the size of the operation, whether it is a private or public course, and the number of functions or amenities offered to the players, the organization will vary. Therefore, to talk meaningfully about the golfing operation, we will have to generalize a bit. The following positions represent a typical public golf resort operation. Many private clubs and municipal courses have fewer personnel.

Careers in the golf industry fall within three rather distinct tracks: the physical facility, club management and auxiliary services, and management of the game. The career track, which is more closely aligned with what we normally think of as the hospitality industry, involves the management of the club and its various services. The following organizational discussion represents only one of many organizational structures that exist. This one is used for illustrative purposes only and is not meant to indicate a preferred model.

Let's discuss the roles of these employees in delivering the golf experience. That is, what do these people do in their jobs to allow the players to enjoy the game of golf? Like any business or organization, if it is to function well, that is, to make a profit or be successful, all the employees must contribute positively by executing their jobs in the way they were intended to be executed. Each employee is critical to the success of the operation because all the operations are interrelated. As in most organizations, it is often the lowest-paid employee or the employee way down in the organizational structure who has the most contact with the customer and is often the reason why customers (golfers) do not return.

The General Manager or Club Manager

This individual is assigned management responsibility for the complete golf operation. We will abbreviate this role from now on as the GM. The GM is responsible for the bottom line of the operation. People who usually would report directly to the GM are the director of golf and the food and beverage manager. The golf superintendent would also report to the GM or to the director of golf, depending on the operation.

You can see that this person is the executive of the golf operation. It is this person's responsibility to plan so that the organizational goals are met. It is almost always the case that the GM is also responsible to a higher authority. Depending on the type of golf operation, that higher authority could be a board of directors, a corporate office, or a director of parks and recreation.

Traditionally, the career path to the GM has been through more customary hospitality roles like food and beverage manager. Recently, however, the path has become more varied. Directors of golf and club professionals are now moving into GM positions with greater frequency.[10] (See chapter 34, "Private Clubs," for a more detailed discussion of the club manager's position.)

The Director of Golf and Head Professional

Direct provision of golf services is an employment path leading to the position of head professional or director of golf. Among the 17,214 golf courses, approximately 56 percent are Professional Golfers' Association (PGA) affiliated courses. Those who complete the PGA's requirements for membership can, on average, expect a compensation package that is nearly twice that of the non-PGA member. The average 2004 compensation package for a PGA head professional was $68,447.

In terms of preparation for a career as a golf professional, individuals should consider another option, that of completing a four-year degree program in business or a closely related field, or possibly attend one of the colleges or universities offering a program in Professional Golf Management (PGM). The PGA of America has developed a program that provides each potential member with the most current training in the profession. While attending a PGA accredited college or university, each student is required to complete the PGA of America's Professional Golf Management (PGA/PGM) program. Integrated into the university curriculum, the availability of the PGA/PGM program essentially allows a student to fast-track to PGA membership, thereby reducing the time commitment by approximately three years. Upon graduation, students become members of the PGA of America. The PGA/PGM program is currently accredited at the following colleges or universities: Pennsylvania State University, Florida State University, North Carolina State University, Clemson University, New Mexico State University, Mississippi State University, Ferris State University, Arizona State University, Methodist College, Campbell University, Coastal Carolina University, University of Colorado (Colorado Springs), University of Nebraska (Lincoln), University of Nevada-Las Vegas, University of Idaho, Florida Gulf Coast University, and Sam Houston State University.

Golf Superintendent

For those interested in the golf course itself as the physical facility, their focus must be in agronomy, specifically turf management. With the millions of dollars invested in today's golf courses, formal university training through two- and four-year turf management programs is essential. Individuals interested in this career track should contact the Golf Course Superintendents of America to obtain a list of recognized college and university programs. The importance of a quality agronomy program cannot be overestimated. A recent reader survey of *Golf Digest* subscribers indicated that the golf course superintendent was the single most important employee. In addition, as reported at the 2005 GOLF 20/20 Conference, the two highest factors in motivating customers to play more golf are well-maintained greens and bunkers and well-maintained fairways and greens.[11] As we focus on increasing rounds of golf, it is essential for managers to have a well-maintained golf course.

The demand for golf-related housing is a driving force in golf course development.

The Food and Beverage Manager

This individual is responsible to the GM for all the food service operations at the club. This position is a bit more varied than that of a food and beverage manager in a restaurant, but it is certainly similar to the food and beverage manager in a hotel. A hotel with its variety of outlets and functions such as room service offers the complexity similar to that of the golf operation. There are many opportunities for a food and beverage manager in golf operations as the business of golf continues to grow.

Trends

One of the most significant trends in the golf industry is the importance for managers to lower the time commitment and raise the value of the golf experience. As reported in a segmentation study at the 2001 GOLF 20/20 Conference, the lack of time is the number one reason people tend to leave the game of golf, followed by family obligations. The golf course building boom of the 1990s has created a surplus of supply and a shortage of demand. The "if you build it, they will come" attitude no longer applies to the industry. Now more than ever, owners and managers need to focus on assessing customer needs and actively improve the pace of play through course advisors, easier pin placements, shorter tees on certain holes, and rewards for faster play. In addition, marketing golf as family-friendly and a way to strengthen relationships, as well as meet new friends, will help raise the value of their time investment.

The second significant trend involves the demand for golf-related housing developments. This is one section of the golf industry that continues to add significant supply. According to Robert H. Dedman, Jr., the Chairman of ClubCorp, Inc., the economics of the real estate profit potential and the ability for golf courses to help developers accelerate sales are a driving force in golf course development.[12]

Another trend that will continue to accelerate in the next five years will be the growth of management companies, such as ClubCorp, to be "one-stop solution providers" to manage golf and the club experiences for members and guests.[12] Mr. Jesse Holshouser, Chief Financial Officer of the PGA of America, also indicated at the April 1998 general meeting of the Philadelphia PGA Section that approximately 16 percent of all U.S. golf courses were owned and/or managed by management firms. He further indicated that some predict approximately one-half of all courses will fall under management companies within the next decade or two. Management companies such as Club Corporation of America, Marriott Golf, Troon Golf, Heritage Golf Group, Casper Golf, and others are both acquiring and managing golf courses in ever-greater numbers. How this will affect employment opportunities and public access has yet to be determined.

Another significant trend involves the information superhighway. Club managers and golf professionals are only now beginning to realize the significance of the Internet. Golfers are using Web sites not only to see how their favorite tour professional is doing, but also to make vacation plans, decide what courses to play, and perhaps purchase golf equipment. The challenge for those wishing to use the Internet is how they get people to their site. For example, using the Google search engine, this author in January 2006 typed in the term *golf*. The Google search engine identified 465,000,000 Web sites containing the term *golf*!

Summary

We have described the game, its economic impact, and its origins. You have read about the kinds of venues at which golf is played and the people that work to make it happen. The role and impact that each employee has in the golf experience is similar to that of the hospitality employee in the more traditional food and beverage or lodging roles. Each service encounter is important to the success of the operation. It is the intent of professional golf management to make every experience a great one so that we will continue to play the game and continue to provide revenue to those for whom that is important.

≈ *Resources*

Internet Sites

Golf Course Builders Association of America—A nonprofit trade association representing all segments of the golf course construction industry.
http://www.gcbaa.org/

Golf Press Association—A daily transaction golf newsletter, offered through e-mail, that keeps you abreast about equipment, events, players, etc.
http://www.golftransactions.com/aboutgpa.html

Golf Web—A Web site that covers or is linked to most aspects of golf, both as a sport and a business.
http://www.golfweb.com/

Ladies Professional Golf Association—As the official site of the LPGA, everything pertaining to the LPGA is provided—tour schedules, news releases, player standings, etc.
http://www.lpga.com/

Multicultural Golf Association of America, Inc.—The Multicultural Golf Association of America, founded in 1991, is the first national organization to promote opportunities for minorities in golf and is recognized as a leading authority on inner-city junior golf programs with the theme "Golf Is for Everyone."
http://www.mgaa.com/

National Golf Course Owners Association—Represents over 7,200 golf courses with over 5300 members.
http://www.ngcoa.org/

National Golf Foundation—Serves as the primary research wing of the golfing industry. The foundation provides a variety of business and consulting services, houses the largest reference library, and provides an excellent series of links to many aspects of golf.
http://www.ngf.org/

Off the Fringe—This newsletter offers an "unconventional perspective on the world of golf."
http://www.offthefringe.com/

PGA of America—In addition to member services, pgaonline offers current headlines and stories on all the professional tours, tour statistics, instruction, and other industry news.
http://www.pgaonline.com/

United States Golf Association—Serves as the national governing body for the game of golf. The USGA writes and interprets rules, conducts national championships, provides a handicap system, maintains equipment standards, funds turfgrass and environmental research, etc.
http://www.usga.org/

World Golf-Links Around the World—Eighty plus golf links ranging from a history of golf in France to the Association of Left Handed Golfers.
http://www.worldgolf.com/golflinks/golfpages.html

≈ *Endnotes*

1. SRI International. (2002, November). *U.S. golf economy measures $62 billion.* [On-line] http://www.golf2020.com:80/mediacenter/fullView.cfm?aid=70
2. Beckwith, R. (2004, June). *The golf 20/20 industry report for 2003.* Ponte Vedre, FL. The World Golf Foundation.
3. Beditz, J. (2005, November). *Rounds played changes.* GOLF 20/20 Conference Report. Ponte Vedre, FL, The World Golf Foundation.
4. National Golf Foundation. (2001). [Online] http://www.ngf.org/
5. Guadagnolo, F. (1997). Presentation at PGA merchandise show, Orlando, Florida.
6. National Golf Foundation and NFO World Group. (2001, November). *2001 segmentation research: An unprecedented undertaking.* [On-line] http://www.golf2020.com/reports_2001Segmentation.asp
7. National Golf Foundation. (1996, May–June). "A different look at what's up with golf's growth." *Golf Market Today,* 4.
8. Warnick, R. (1991, November 21). "On the green." *Black Issues in Higher Education,* 20.
9. National Golf Foundation and NFO World Group. (2001, November). 2001 segmentation research: An unprecedented undertaking. [On-line] http://www.golf2020.com/reports_2001Segmentation.asp
10. Gordon, J. (1996). "Making the General Manager Jump." *PGA Magazine* 77 (9), 24–31.
11. Last, J. (2005). *Avid golfer research.* GOLF 20/20 Conference Report, Ponte Vedre, FL, The World Golf Foundation.
12. Nakahara, K. (2005). "The supply side challenge." *PGA Magazine* (5), 28–47.

≈ *Contributor*

G. Burch Wilkes, IV, professor-in-charge, Professional Golf Management, Department of Recreation, Park and Tourism Management, The Pennsylvania State University, 201 Mateer Building, University Park, PA 16802
Phone: (814) 863-8987, Fax: (814) 863-8992, email: gbw104@psu.edu

Chapter 27
Review Questions

1. Explain the significance of a tee time.

2. Describe the check-in process for playing golf at a club from the point of entering the club for a tee time.

3. How long does it usually take to play 18 holes of golf?

4. Describe the roles of the:

   a. Starter

   b. F&B attendant

   c. Course ranger

5. What is a "grill room?"

6. What is the economic impact of golf?

7. What is the profile of the average golfer?

8. Where and when did golf begin as the game we know today?

9. What is the relationship between age and the continuation of playing golf?

10. What is the fastest-growing population of golfers?

11. What are golfing trends involving females and African-Americans?

12. What are three categories of golf courses?

13. What type of growth has been experienced in golf course development? In what sector of ownership/operation?

14. What are the three distinct tracks of golf industry careers?

15. Identify key responsibilities of the following positions:

    a.   General manager or club manager

    b.   Food and beverage manager

    c.   Director of golf/head professional

    d.   Golf superintendent

16. What is the impact of PGA membership on the compensation package of a head professional?

17. What are the requirements for PGA membership?

18. What type of academic background is required for a golf superintendent?

19. Discuss three significant trends in the golf industry.

20. Cite at least five of the most referenced golf Websites.

Attractions

28

Ronald J. Cereola and Reginald Foucar-Szocki,
James Madison University

© Elena Ray, 2008, Shutterstock.

≈ Learning Objectives

☑ Define an attraction
☑ Explain how attractions benefit local economies
☑ List the ways attractions are classified
☑ Describe the characteristics for each classification of attractions
☑ Classify examples of attractions according to their product offering or benefits they provide
☑ Apply your knowledge of why people travel and attractions to match and select appropriate attraction products

≈ Chapter Outline

What Are Attractions?
How Are Attractions Classified?
Culture and Heritage Attractions
Planned Play Environments
Industrial Attractions
Infrastructure

≈ Key Terms

Amusement parks
Attractions
Cultural tourism
Economic growth
Events
Gaming
Grand tour
Heritage tourism
Industrial attractions
Lifespan
Man-made attractions

Museum
Natural attractions
Nonprofit organization
Origin
Planned play environments
Secondary attraction
Shopping
Status
Theme parks
Topography
World's first national park

What Are Attractions?

Attractions Promote Travel to Destinations

Go to *Google.com,* type *"attractions"* in the search box, select the *image* function and click *search.* Look over the various pictures presented to you in the next few pages and you are likely to see pictures of Disney World and other theme parks such as Six Flags, natural environments such as Bryce Canyon and San Diego ocean beaches, cultural landmarks in the form of Scottish castles, adventure experiences on the Jurassic Coast Railway and Southern California hot-air balloon excursions. Venturing further into the web pages you will see pictures of assorted museums, mountains and lakes, themed mega resorts and hotels such as NYNY in Las Vegas, and even a few proverbial "biggest ball of twine" road side stops. Consider for a moment, the diversity of the items which appeared on your computer screen. What do they all have in common? They are places, activities, and experiences sought out by leisure travelers. Some are wildly popular, while others may be just interesting stops along their way to the final destination. They are in the vernacular of the hospitality industry "attractions." *Attractions are the places we visit and the things we do while we are traveling for leisure.*

Attractions Help Satisfy Needs

Attractions are the lifeblood of tourism. Families take vacations to theme parks, or the shores of Southern California to enjoy the ocean, the mountains of Vermont and New Hampshire for recreational skiing, and to Washington, D.C. to visit the capital monuments and museums. Attractions are an integral part of the need satisfaction that fuels the desire to travel. Whether the need is belongingness (family vacation in Disney), physiological (rest and recuperating at the shore), or self actualizing (visiting cultural and historical sites of Washington, D.C.), it is an attraction that the traveler will seek out to help fulfill that need. In short, attractions assist in satisfying the needs that motivate travel.

Attractions Are Economic Engines

They provide economic benefit to the region in which they are located. The money spent for the theme park admission may only be a small percentage of the leisure traveler's expenditure but then consider all the other amounts the traveler will spend on lodging, food and beverage, purchasing souvenirs, rental cars and other forms of transportation, guided tours, and ancillary activities as well as shopping in local stores and malls. These expenditures provide economic benefits such as employment for the local residents who in turn use their wages to generate additional economic activity. Without the attraction these jobs might not exist. In addition to providing employment, attractions also support local governments when they generate income, sales, and excise taxes. A visitor to Maui can visit Haleakala (ha-lee-ah-ka-la) an extinct volcano that rises through the clouds, over 10,000 feet above sea level. While the volcano is part of the National Park System local tourism entrepreneurs have flourished around the attraction. There are bike rental stores and guided tour packages starting on the mountain just outside the Park limits. (As of October 10, 2007, the National Park Service suspended bike tours within the park for 60 days while it investigated several fatal biking accidents.[1]) While guided tours are being limited by the Park Service, the more adventuresome can still purchase everything they need at one of the local shops and go it alone at their own pace. There are also guided excursions 3000 feet down into the crater itself either on foot or by horseback as well as helicopter and airplane tours, balloon rides, and ATV excursions all centered upon the volcano.

All of these activities are available through local businesses and generate economic benefits to the providers and their employees as well as to the community. The fees and taxes they generate circulate through the local economy. Without an attraction such as Haleakala none of these tourism business opportunities would exist nor would the economic benefits that they generate.[3]

How Are Attractions Classified?

The most common methods of classification are status (importance or interest to the traveler), origin, lifespan, ownership, profit orientation and product attributes.[4]

Status

Attractions are often broadly characterized as either *primary* or *secondary* attractions. A primary attraction is essentially the main reason a visitor travels to the destination and spends several days. As a result,

Vignette 1
LIVING IN ECO HARMONY

Economics and Ecotourism are not necessarily mutually exclusive. Attractions often provide local residents an improved quality of life through increased economic opportunities from business activities that support tourism. Often these business opportunities are criticized as occurring at the expense of the surrounding ecosystems. Companies such as Kauai Backcountry Adventures have learned to use the surrounding ecosystem as part of their business plan, while at the same time being sensitive to the impact on the land. The mission of Backcountry is to provide ecotourism activities that preserve the environment, history, and culture of Hawaii. To that end they offer zip line and tubing adventures to a broad range of individuals.

Visitors opting for a zip line adventure soar over the rainforest and traverse mountain sides while attached to a cable strung high above the forest floor. They are able to enjoy the awe and beauty of the rainforest with minimal intrusion upon the forest floor.

The less adventurous might try the tubing adventure down irrigation ditches and tunnels of a sugar plantation that were hand dug by the workers in the 1870s, all the while enjoying the majesty of Kauai's coastline, valleys, and mountains. The company restored the irrigation system covering over 17,000 acres of pristine land after sugaring ceased in late 2000.

Both the zip line and tubing adventures are accompanied by certified guides explaining the Island's history, culture, flora, and fauna.[2]

primary attractions are usually supported by extensive ancillary facilities: lodging, food and beverage, transportation, extensive retail, and other hospitality services. An excellent example of a primary attraction is Disney World in Orlando, Florida. Visitors, especially families, make the trip and stay for several days. They purchase multi-day passes to the Disney theme parks and may stay in one of the many Disney owned properties, eat at Disney food outlets, use the Disney transportation system, and shop for their needs at Disney retail outlets. Because Disney World has tremendous drawing power, significant non-Disney owned hospitality facilities have developed around the theme park and have contributed to the growth of the Orlando area in Florida.

In contrast, a secondary attraction is of lesser importance to the traveler and might be considered simply something nice to do while on the way to or in the area of the primary attraction. Again, using the Orlando area as an example, there are many secondary attractions like Gatorland which even advertises itself as the "best half day attraction minutes away from Sea World, Walt Disney World and Universal Studios."[5]

Origin

Attractions may be classified according to whether they are *natural* or *man-made*. Natural attractions are those that occur in nature without human intervention. They include mountains, coastlines, lakes, islands, forests, deserts, rain forests, and other landforms and seascapes. Man-made attractions owe their very existence to the intervention of humans. Examples of pure man-made attractions are theme parks, shopping centers, sports and entertainment facilities, festivals, casinos, and museums. Often, human intervention combines with nature to create a mixed origin attraction such as the Hoover Dam constructed on the Colorado River which created Lake Mead. The surrounding area, referred to as the Lake Mead National Recreation Area, is a premier inland water recreation area managed by National Park Service and encompasses over 1.5 million acres of land with 700 miles of shoreline. The area generates over 500 million dollars directly for the local economy and is within a day's drive of more then 23 million people from Los Angeles, California, to Phoenix, Arizona, making it one of the fastest growing tourism destinations in the country.[6] Some natural attractions are made more accessible by man-made attractions that are constructed on or about the natural formation, such as the rain forest cable tours available in Costa Rica and other parts of the world. In these locations various forms of cable transportation and other viewing facilities have been constructed to permit visitors access to the natural attraction that would otherwise be relatively inaccessible to the visitor. The excitement of traveling along the cable itself has become one of the "things to do" for visitors to the area.[7]

Lifespan or Time-Oriented

Attractions can be classified according to their lifespan or whether they are *relatively* permanent or temporary. Natural attractions such as lakes, mountains, and other landforms and seascapes are permanent attractions. However, permanent attractions can also be man-made such as an amusement park, a zoo, or a historical monument. Although these attractions can be demolished and moved they are relatively permanent in comparison to temporary attractions which are short lived or can be easily relocated. Examples of temporary attractions are concerts, conferences, trade shows, parades, award shows, certain sporting events like the Super Bowl, and festivals. Permanent attractions are sometimes referred to as *site* attractions while temporary attractions are referred to as *event* attractions.

Ownership and Purpose

Approximately 85% of all recreational land in the United States is under *public ownership* managed by the federal and state governments for the benefit of the public at large. The National Park Service, part of the Department of the Interior, manages the majority of federal lands under the auspices of the National Park System which includes parks, monuments, and preserves. The world's first national park—Yellowstone—was created in 1872, at which time Congress set aside more than one million acres as a public park for the benefit and enjoyment of the people.[8] This American invention marked the beginning of a worldwide movement that has subsequently spread to more than 100 countries and 1,200 national parks and conservation preserves. Today there are more than 388 units in the national park system encompassing more then 83 million acres.[9] These units are variously designated as national parks, monuments, preserves, lakeshores, seashores, wild and scenic rivers, trails, historic sites, military parks, battlefields, historical parks, recreation areas, memorials, and parkways. All represent some nationally significant aspect of the American natural or cultural heritage.

While the federal and state governments own and manage a significant portion of natural attractions, *private ownership* accounts for the overwhelming number of man-made attractions. Major corporations such as Disney, Universal, and Six Flags own and operate theme and amusement parks; MGM Mirage operates mega gaming resorts in Las Vegas, Nevada; and Simon Malls provide shopping opportunities throughout the United States.[10]

Closely aligned with ownership is the purpose for which attractions are operated, either as *nonprofit* or *profit seeking* entities. Generally, nonprofit entities that own man-made attractions, such as museums, or natural attractions, such as nature preserves, do not have tourism as their primary goal. Rather, their interest is that of preservation of the natural environment or a historical, cultural, or religious consequence. Profit seeking entities, on the other hand, are seeking to provide a return on investment to the private owners. There is a delicate balance for both types of owners. Profit seeking entities cannot engage in unrestrained use and development without fear of the public backlash resulting from spoiling the environment or encouraging unrestrained commercial development of the surrounding area. In addition, it would not be in the long term interest of the private owners to exhaust or physically depreciate the attraction through overuse thereby shortening its useful life. For nonprofits the balance is between their preservation goals and generating sufficient revenues to maintain the attraction, while at the same time permitting public access at an acceptable level. The National Park Service faces this very same dilemma. How do they provide the widest array of access to the public while at the same time avoiding the overcrowding that would destroy the natural beauty of the environment, which is the very reason visitors come to the parks.

Attractions: Product Attributes

We can also categorize attractions based upon what the attraction has to offer to the tourist as leisure activity. Common classifications include topography, culture and heritage, planned play environments, and events and entertainment.

Topography

The topography of an area is significant as an attraction and has an added benefit to the tourist in that scenery is free. Topography attractions consist of three areas of interest: *landforms, wildlife,* and *ecology.*[11]

Landforms such as beaches, mountain vistas, and deserts can all be visually appreciated free and in many instances be utilized for little or no dollar

Landforms such as beaches, mountain vistas and deserts can be enjoyed by tourists free of charge.

costs to the traveler. Often because climate is closely aligned with topography these attractions experience heavy seasonal demand. The beaches of Florida are in "high season" when the northern states are in their winter season while, despite their ability to make snow, the ski slopes of the West and New England are largely dependent on a snowy winter for a successful ski season. The challenge for these seasonal attractions is to manage the heavy demand during peak season and to create additional off season activities to create demand during slow times.[12] Each year thousands of individuals travel to California's Sequoia National Park[13] to take in the majesty of giant sequoia trees or to the California Redwood Coast[14] to view the giant redwoods.

In addition to scenic beauty, topography is closely tied to recreational activities as well as wild-life viewing and ecological activities. In recent years concern for the environment has created a heightened awareness of the effects of tourism on the natural environment.[16] Efforts to control access and the types of tourism activities centered on natural attractions have been implemented by federal and state governments in the United States as well as by their counterparts around the world.[17] At the same time this heightened awareness has created environmentally friendly or ecotourism opportunities centered on natural attractions. A prime example of this is the whale watching excursions that permit visitors to Maui, Hawaii, to see and hear the humpback whales during the annual migrations in December and January.

Culture and Heritage Attractions

Since the early days of mankind, travel has been closely linked to culture and heritage. The preservation for future generations, of artifacts and sites, in particular those associated with a peoples origins, religion, war, art, as well as science and myth, are common place among the world's cultures. Cultural attractions are very popular among travelers. In fact, most U.S. adult travelers attend a cultural activity or event while on a trip. Most often attended are performing arts events and/or museums.[18]

Museums

Visitors are attracted to museums out of both curiosity and for education. The Grand Tour, a root of modern tourism, was a long, arduous, albeit cultural journey through Paris, Venice, Florence, and Rome, and a capstone educational experience for the elite of the 16th century. Today a visitor can approximate the experience by visiting the plethora of museums around the world, such as The Metro-

Vignette 2
WALK THE SKY

The Glass Bridge of the Grand Canyon Skywalk located on Hualapai Indian Tribal land extends 65 feet over the edge of the Grand Canyon's West Rim. Since its opening on March 27, 2007, more than 200,000 visitors have paid the $25.00 fee to walk across the glass floor and peer 4000 feet into the abyss of the Canyon to the Colorado River below. The glass floor is designed to support the weight of 71 fully loaded Boeing 747s, withstand 100 mph winds and an 8.0 magnitude earthquake. Visitors are given shoe covers to prevent the highly polished glass floor from being scratched.[15]

politan Museum of Art[19] or The Museum of Natural History[20] both in New York, wherein many great works reside. In addition to exhibits, awaiting the visitor of museum attractions are programs and events which include lectures, performances, workshops, and films. Many have been designed for children, the tourist of tomorrow.[21]

Religious Attractions

Rivaling museums in their numbers and diversity are religious attractions primarily consisting of cathedrals and churches, temples, and mosques. There are also geographic areas which consist of entire cities and the surrounding locals of religious significance, such as the Holy Land in Jerusalem where many of the principal religious sites for Christianity, Judaism, and Islam converge; or the city of Mecca in Saudi Arabia, where millions of Muslims from around world make an annual pilgrimage. Modern tourism has its roots in religion. During the Middle Ages individuals made pilgrimages to visit religious sites and many of the same are still visited by tourists today. Much like travelers today, these pilgrims came from every strata of society.

Vignette 3
A VIRTUAL PILGRIMAGE

Take a virtual tour of Vatican City a tiny sovereign state within the city of Rome. It is the seat of the Roman Catholic Church, referred to as the Holy See. Every year it is visited by millions of tourists both Christian and nonChristian alike not only because of its religious significance, but because of the cultural aspects of its architecture as well as the great works of renowned masters such as Michelangelo, Botticelli, and Bernini. While there you can visit St. Peter's Basilica and the Sistine Chapel as well as the Vatican Museum.[22]

Historical Attractions

Often quoted, George Santayana, "Those who cannot learn from history are doomed to repeat it" is at the heart of historical attractions. They are the efforts to preserve the events of the past that demand remembrance. Primarily consisting of monuments and structures such as the Pyramids of Egypt, the Statute of Liberty, Tiananmen Square, or the Great Wall of China, they also encompass area attractions of his-

torical significance such as battlefields. A recent survey reveals that 41 percent of travelers say they visited a designated historic site such as a building, landmark, home, or monument during their trip. Three in 10 visited a designated historic community or town.[23] All too often, war provides tourism opportunities. American Civil War sites such as Gettysburg, Pennsylvania, are extremely popular and many Civil War attractions involve battlefield re-enactments (*events*) which heighten the visitors' understanding and appreciation of the historical significance as well as increasing visitor involvement.[24]

In addition to battlefields attractions there are numerous memorials in Washington, D.C. such as the Vietnam Veterans Memorial[25] whose principal exhibit is The Wall containing the names of the 58,249 men and women who gave their lives, visited by over 3 million people in 2004 as well as the Korean War Veterans Memorial.[26] Lest you start to believe that historical attractions are just about war there are numerous attractions celebrating historic ideas that changed the world and in particular America, many of which are found at the National Mall in Washington, D.C. There a tourist can visit the Thomas Jefferson Memorial, the Lincoln Memorial, the Washington Monument and the Franklin Delano Roosevelt Memorial.[27] In December 2005 the National Capital Planning Commission (NCPC) unanimously approved a preliminary design for the Martin Luther King, Jr., National Memorial to commemorate the life and work of Dr. Martin Luther King, Jr., and to honor his national and international contributions to world peace through nonviolent social change. The King Memorial site is a 4-acre plot on the northeast corner of the Tidal Basin and creates a visual "line of leadership" from the Lincoln Memorial, where Martin Luther King, Jr., gave his famous "I Have a Dream" speech, to the Jefferson Memorial.[28] Like museums many of these monuments also include programming and special events to enhance the experience of the visitor.

Planned Play Environments

Planned play environments provide recreation and entertainment and are a significant sector of the tourism market. The ancient Greeks and Romans traveled for both theater and sport.

Sporting Facilities

Sports, recreation, and travel go together. The array of sporting and recreational attractions available to the traveler is almost endless. Fishing, hunting, cycling, mountain climbing, hang gliding, horseback riding, boating, surfing, snorkeling, and scuba diving are but a few and for each there is a sporting attraction where one can engage in their desired recreational activity till their heart's content. Would you like to go fishing? Then try steelhead fishing in Northern British Columbia, Canada. Need a bit more excitement, try your hand (wings) at Lookout Mountain Flight Park in Georgia[29] where you can purchase a complete hang gliding instruction package that will have "most students flying the mountains in less than one week." The point is that no matter what your interest there is either a natural or man-made attraction drawing you to a destination where you can recreate.

Among the most popular sporting and recreational activities are skiing and golf. In 2003, approximately 10 million Americans spent 58 million days on the slopes of more then 500 ski resorts across the United States. About 10 percent of the United States population are snow sport enthusiasts, making the ski industry a multibillion dollar business. Twenty-five percent of all ski excursions are multi-day visits more then 500 miles from home. In the United States, the ski resorts of the Rocky Mountain West are the prime ski attractions accounting for approximately 30 percent of all lift tickets sold in the United States.[30]

If ski and snow sports are a bit too adventuresome, consider golf. There are over 25 million golfers in the United States. Reportedly, a golf facility is the only significant sports activity that will influence a meeting planner's choice of destination.[32] In a recent year, one in eight U.S. travelers played

The ski industry is a multibillion dollar business.

golf while on a trip of 100 miles or more away from home. Sixteen percent of travelers who played golf said that golf was the most important reason for taking the trip. Golf is a time to be among friends and a time to compete, to relax, and to do business; as well as to just enjoy the beauty of the natural surroundings.[33]

Vignette 5
GOLF'S HOME

Scotland is known worldwide as "the home of golf." Dutch sailors are thought to have introduced to Scotland "kolf" a game originally played by them with a stick and ball on the frozen canals in winter. It was transformed on the public links land becoming the game we know today.[34] Visitors have been coming to Scotland for golf holidays for over 100 years to play world famous championship golf courses such as The Old Course St Andrews, Royal Troon, Carnoustie, Muirfield, Turnberry, and Gleneagles.[35]

Vignette 4
ROCKY MOUNTAIN HIGH

SKI Magazine ranked the Vail owned ski resorts: Vail (#2,) Keystone (#11), and Heavenly (#17) among the top 20 ski resorts. The resorts and resort hotels derive revenue through a comprehensive offering of amenities, including lift ticket sales, ski and snowboard lesson packages, resort accommodations, retail and equipment rental outlets, dining venues, private club operations, and other recreational activities such as golf, tennis, horseback riding, fishing tours, float trips, and on-mountain activities centers.[31]

Theme and Amusement Parks

Theme and amusement parks are likely the most often recognizable attractions to the general public. Theme parks offer escape and replicate both real, as well as "unreal" places that may or may not exist beyond the gates. Amusement parks on the other hand have rides, games, and exhibitions. Today the distinction has been blurred as both tend to contain elements of each in their offering.

According to the Travel Industry Association of America approximately 1 in 10 (9%) trips includes a visit to a theme or amusement park, equating to over 92 million person-trips taken in the U.S. in 2002. Households visiting a "theme park" spend an average of $845 per trip, excluding transportation to their destination. On average, overnight theme park trips last 5.3 nights. A large share (55%) of household trips involving a visit to a theme park includes children under age 18.[36] As with many businesses of the 21st Century, theme parks and their product offerings have been driven by technology. Today's visitor demands an immersive, realistic, and intense experience. Universal's "Back to the Future: The Ride" in Orlando, Florida, in 1991 was one of the first to blend movie themes, IMAX technology, and computer-based motion simulation technology to meet that immersive, intense, and realistic requirement.[37] Since then, theme park and amusement attractions have become increasingly sophisticated. The Amazing Adventures of Spider-Man attraction at Universal incorporates 3-D technology and pyrotechnics into the experience.[38] Of course, not to be forgotten is the roller coaster, virtually defining the "thrill ride," having been around since the early 1900s.

Vignette 6
THE TALLEST FASTEST ROLLER COASTER ON EARTH

The 456-ft Kingda Ka ride at Six Flags Great Adventure park, a 1-hour drive from Philadelphia, will reach 128 mph on its 50.6-second journey. The 18 riders on Kingda Ka's four cars will feel weightless at some points as they are propelled to 128 mph in just 3.5 seconds before being shot vertically to 456 ft. After reaching the top they will plunge straight back down while turning in a 270-degree spiral before climbing a 129 ft-high hill and returning to the starting point. A chest harness with two locking devices will be used to secure passengers.[39] If fast isn't enough, you can see the tallest, longest, and biggest drops list at http://www.coastergrotto.com/fastest-roller-coasters.jsp.

Of course not every visitor to a theme park is looking for the intense experience of a thrill ride. Theme parks must continue to be family friendly by offering a wide spectrum of attractions, suitable for all ages and tastes. Universal's Seuss Landing[40] is a whimsical attraction that appeals to young and old alike and suitable for the less adventurous. In addition to diverse product offerings, modern theme and amusement parks need to be clean, visually appealing, and family friendly.

Gaming

The modern Las Vegas style casino resort has created a hybrid between gaming and entertainment. Moving along the Las Vegas Strip, one is presented with an Egyptian Pyramid, a Medieval Castle, New York City and the Statute of Liberty, the Eiffel Tower, ancient Rome, Venice, as well as an Arabian Oasis. All of which might be classified as an adult theme park given the numerous adult oriented attractions contained therein, of which gaming only happens to be one activity.

Table 28.1 Top 20 U.S. Casino Markets by Annual Revenue

Gross revenue is earnings before taxes, salaries, and expenses are paid—the equivalent of sales, not profit.

CASINO MARKET	2006 ANNUAL REVENUES
1. Las Vegas Strip	$6.689 billion
2. Atlantic City, NJ	$5.508 billion
3. Chicagoland, IN/IL	$2.595 billion
4. Connecticut	$1.734 billion
5. Detroit	$1.303 billion
6. Tunica/Lula, MS	$1.252 billion
7. St. Louis, MO/IL	$990.98 million
8. Reno/Sparks, NV	$939.50 million
9. Boulder Strip, NV	$929.70 million
10. Shreveport, LA	$847.18 million
11. Biloxi, MS	$845.20 million
12. Lawrenceburg/Rising Sun/ Elizabeth/Vevay, IN	$795.13 million
13. Kansas City, MO (includes St. Joseph)	$751.33 million
14. New Orleans, LA	$696.47 million
15. Lake Charles, LA	$656.85 million
16. Downtown Las Vegas, NV	$630.29 million
17. Laughlin, NV	$629.76 million
18. Black Hawk, CO	$554.48 million
19. Council Bluffs, IA	$477.96 million
20. Charles Town, WV	$448.23 million

Source: The Innovation Group (4/07)[41]

Shopping

Shopping is one of the most popular trip activities for U.S. adult travelers.[42] This should be no surprise for anyone who has visited Disney World in Orlando, Florida. As you stroll along Main Street in the Magic Kingdom and the other streets of the park, you are flanked on both sides by retail opportunities. It may be that part of the genius of Walt Disney was his disguising a retail mall within a theme park. Approximately 91 million people, or 63 percent of adult travelers in 2000, included shopping as an activity on a trip.[43] In a reverse of the Disney strategy, the West Edmonton Mall in Alberta, Canada, contains the Galaxyland Amusement park (the world's largest indoor theme park), the World Waterpark (the world's largest indoor water park), the Ice Palace, (a national Hockey League size ice arena), an exact replica of the Santa Maria (which is available for weddings and special functions), an 18 hole, par 46 miniature golf course, and the 354 room Fantasyland Hotel.[44] The West Edmonton Shopping Mall is listed in the Guinness Book of World Records as the "largest shopping center in the world." The Mall's web page refers to the center as an "entertainment and shopping center, Alberta's *number one* tourist *attraction*."[45]

Lest you think that the West Edmonton Mall is an anomaly consider the Mall of America located in Minnesota which, in addition to 520 stores, contains The Park at MOA™, which has 30 rides including the Timberlane Roller coaster, the Underwater Adventures® Aquarium, LEGO® Imagination Center, Dinosaur Walk Museum, A.C.E.S. Flight Simulation, and the NASCAR Silicon Motor Speedway. On the MOA Website you can plan your entire visit including air, hotel, and auto packages. The MOA even hosts meeting facilities at its Executive Meeting and Events Center.[46]

Events

Events are temporary attractions. Relative to permanent site attractions they are generally easier and less expensive to develop, although that may not always be the case in every instance, such as with the Olympics and other large scale events including the Super Bowl. Events include such activities as fairs and festivals, live entertainment offerings as in the performing arts, sports exhibitions, parades, pageants, and other celebratory gatherings such as New Year's Eve, "First Night" celebrations. In many instances events give birth to site attractions. The sporting facilities specially constructed for the Olympics live on as site attractions for future sport exhibitions.

Sporting events, both professional and intercollegiate, are significant attractions for travelers. Over 75 million U.S. adults attended an organized sports event as either a spectator or as a participant while on a trip of 50 miles or more, one-way, in the past 5 years.[50] One of the fastest growing sporting events is NASCAR stock car racing[51] NASCAR races are broadcast in over 150 countries. With 75 million fans it holds 17 of the top 20 attended sporting events in the United States.[52]

The performing arts have always been events that attract travelers. They include theater, dance, and music of all forms. Some destinations such as Branson, Missouri, and Monterey, California, are well associated with music festivals that serve as primary tourist attractions for the area. New York City's Broadway theater district is just one of the performing arts attractions the city offers to visitors.

Vignette 7
2008 OLYMPICS: SHOWCASING THE "NEW" CHINA

The 2008 Olympics is scheduled to be held in Beijing, China, from August 8 through August 24. The Olympic Games will generate enormous business opportunities and facilitate a major face-lift of the host city, Beijing. The city and surrounding areas are experiencing considerable economic growth in construction, building, and upgrading sports stadiums and other facilities; as well as up-scaling the various service industries, including hospitality services, that will accommodate the onslaught of visitors driven by the Olympic games.[47]

In addition to the massive construction projects underway, as part of its promise to prepare for the Olympic visitors, China has pledged to host "green games," by improving the environmental quality for visitors with a goal of making Beijing a pollution free city.[48]

It is estimated that a half million tourists will visit China during the Olympic Games and that approximately 5.6 billion U.S. dollars will be spent on tourism and related activities. Further, the exposure and increased cultural awareness spawned by the games will stimulate cultural tourism, entertainment, and development opportunities for China. In addition to the potential economic benefits of hosting the Olympics, there are the political objectives of legitimatizing government, as well as enhancing the national pride of its citizens.[49]

A legendary musical performance event was the 1969 Woodstock Festival and Concert, and though planned for 50,000 people it is believed to have been attended by over 500,000 individuals.[53]

The modern day epitome of an "event" is the Super Bowl which occurs annually at the end of January each year. The first Super Bowl was between the Green Bay Packers and the Kansas City Chiefs. Tickets cost only $12 and the game had less than 50% attendance. Today, ticket costs are measured in the thousands of dollars and are difficult to come by as the game is sold out. On average, 80 to 90 million Americans are tuned into the Super Bowl at any given moment. Cities compete to host the game in a selection bidding process similar to ones used by the Olympics and soccer's World Cup. Entertainment has become a major component of the event. A number of popular singers and musicians have performed during the pre-game ceremonies, the halftime show, or even just singing the national anthem of the United States. Among the notables have been Stevie Wonder, Paul McCartney, Aretha Franklin, The Rolling Stones (Super Bowl XL 2006), and of course the infamous "wardrobe malfunction" by Janet Jackson and Justin Timberlake in 2005.[54]

Industrial Attractions

Industrial attractions consist of operating concerns, manufacturing and agricultural, whose processes and products are of interest to visitors. For example, many manufacturing concerns provide tours of their facilities. Ethel M in the Las Vegas conducts free interactive tours where the visitor can watch them make chocolate confections. You can tour the kitchen, walk through the enrobing and molding rooms, then, finally, try a free sample. Of course your tour ends in their retail outlet.[55] The Boeing Everett factory tours are conducted to showcase The Boeing Company and the Everett product line, the 747, 767, and 777 aircraft. Visitors can see airplanes in various stages of flight test and manufacture. The facility also contains conference space for 250 people, special event space for groups of up to 700 people, as well as a 240-seat theater and a 125-seat restaurant and retail space. There is also an aviation education program for children K–12th grade.[56] Virtually every state has one or more factory tours that would qualify as industrial attractions. Some charge a fee but most are free. You can get a comprehensive listing, by state, of available factory tours on the web at Factory Tours USA.[57]

Wine tourism is experiencing steady growth.

Wine tourism is defined as visitation to vineyards, wineries, wine festivals, and wine shows for which grape wine tasting and/or the experiencing the attributes of a grape region are the prime motivating factors for visitors.[58] Wine tourism is experiencing steady growth edged along by the growing public interest in wines. The 2004 movie *Sideways* spurred the creation of wine tours mirroring the journey of the film's two main characters through Santa Barbara, California, wine country.[59] (Note how the movie is a convergence between culture and tourism.) Napa and Sonoma in California, both major wine producing areas in the United States, have flourishing wine tourism industries centering around vineyards and wine tasting attractions. The Beringer Vineyard is just one of many vineyards that provide tours and tasting to visitors.[60]

Infrastructure

While the infrastructure of a destination would not be considered an attraction, any discussion of attractions would be incomplete without some reference to infrastructure. In order for attractions to be viable tourism components they must be supported by roads, airports, and other transportation facilities; municipal services such as water, police, and fire protection; medical, power, and communication resources. In addition, there must also be hospitality services to serve the travelers' needs while away from home. Hospitality services consist of lodging, food, and beverage services. Integral among all of the infrastructure components and, in particular with hospitality services are people available to work in the various supporting functions. In order for an attraction to be successful the local employment base must be trained in the technical of skills of each area of service. Yet technical skills are not enough because the hospitality industry is a people industry. The workforce as well as the community at large must also have a "hospitable" mindset; that is, they must truly care about delivering a quality experience and being warm and friendly toward visitors. They must understand that their self interest, and that of the visitor, is inextricably intertwined in a unique partnership that creates both a high quality experience for the visitor, while at the same time providing a high standard of living for them.

Summary

In order for attractions to be viable tourism components they must be supported by the area's *infrastructure*; roads, airports, and other transportation facilities; municipal services such as water, police, and fire protection; medical, power, and communication; resources as well as *hospitality* services, lodging, food, and beverage facilities. In addition, the people of the area must have hospitality service skills and be open and amenable to the tourism industry and genuinely friendly to the visitor.

≈ Resources

Internet Sites

American Gaming Association: http://www.americangaming.org
American Museum of Natural History: http://www.amnh.org
Beringer: http://www.beringer.com
Civil War Traveler: http://www.civilwar-va.com/
Disney Theme Parks: http://disney.go.com/home/today/index.html
Google: http://www.google.com
Factory Tours USA: http://factorytoursusa.com
Gatorland: http://www.gatorland.com
Mall of America: http://www.mallofamerica.com
Martin Luther King National Memorial: http://www.mlkmemorial.org/
National Park Service: http://www.nps.gov
Maui Mountain Cruisers: http://www.mauimountaincruisers.com/
NASCAR: http://www.nascar.com
National Football League: http://nfl.com/
Olympic Movement: http://www.olympic.org/
Pacific Whale Foundation: http://www.pacificwhale.org
Travel Industry Association of America: http://www.tia.org
The Holy See: http://www.vatican.va/
Universal Theme Parks: http://www.universalorlando.com/

≈ Endnotes

1. Haleakala bike tours suspended at http://news.yahoo.com/s/ap_travel/20071008/ap_tr_ge/travel_brief_haleakala
2. Kauai Backcountry Adventures. (n.d.) at http://www.kauaibackcountry.com/index.html
3. Maui Mountain Cruisers at http://www.mauimountaincruisers.com
3a. National Park Service. NPS Haleakala at http://www.nps.gov/hale
4. Mill, R. C., and Morrison, A. M. (2002). *The Tourism System*. Dubuque, IA: Kendall Hunt.
5. Welcome to Gatorland at http://www.gatorland.com
6. National Park Service. Lake Mead National Recreation Area Strategic Plan 2001–2005 at http://www.nps.gov/applications/parks/lame/ppdocuments/ACFB12.doc
7. Hacienda Baru National Wildlife Refuge at http://www.haciendabaru.com/tours.htm
8. National Park Service. Yellowstone at http://www.ns.gov/yell
9. National Park Service. The National Park System Acreage at http://www.nps.gov/legacy/acreage.html
10. MGM-Mirage at http://www.mgmmirage.com
11. Goeldner, C. R., Ritchie, J. R., and McIntosh, R. W. (2000). *Tourism Principles, Practices, and Philosophies*. New York: John Wiley and Sons.
12. Middleton, V. T., and Clarke, J. (2001). *Marketing in Travel and Tourism*. Oxford: Butterworth Heinemann.
13. National Park Service. Sequoia and Kings Canyon at http://www.nps.gov/seki
14. California's Redwood Coast at http://www.redwoods.info
15. Walk the Sky: The glass bridge at Grand Canyon West at http://www.grandcanyonskywalk.com

16. Weaver, D. (2001). Criteria and Context. In: *Ecotourism*. Milton, Australia: John Wiley and Sons.
17. Weaver, D., and Lawton, L. (2002). *Tourism Management*. Milton, Australia: John Wiley and Sons.
18. Travel Industry Association of America. Cultural Events/Festivals at http://www.tia.org/pressmedia/domestic_a_to_z. html#c
19. The Metropolitan Museum of Art at http://www.metmuseum.org/home.asp
20. The American Museum of Natural History at http://www.amnh.org
21. The Metropolitan Museum of Art at http://www.metmuseum.org/home.asp
22. The Holy See at http://www.vatican.va
23. Travel Industry Association of America. Shopping at http://www.tia.org/pressmedia/domestic_a_to_z.html#s
24. You can explore the Civil War historic monuments and battlefield attractions of Virginia, North Carolina, South Carolina, Pennsylvania, West Virginia, and Washington, DC, at http://www.CivilWarTraveler.com
25. National Park Service. Vietnam Veterans Memorial at http:///www.nps.gov/vive
26. National Park Service. Korean War Veterans Memorial at http://www.nps.gov/kwvm
27. National Park Service. National Mall at http://www.nps.gov/nama
28. Build the Dream at http://www.mlkmemorial.org/site/c.hkIUL9MVJxE/b.1190591/k.B083/About_the_Memorial.htm
29. Lookout Mountain Flight Park at http://www.hanglide.com
30. Aron, A. A. (2004). Marketing the Thrill of Skiing, the Serenity of the Mountains, the Luxury of Travel. In: Dickinson, B., and Vladimir, A. *The Complete 21st Century Travel and Hospitality Marketing Handbook*. Upper Saddle River, NJ: Pearson Prentice Hall, 191–200.
31. Vail Resorts at http://www.vailresorts.com/Corp/index.aspx and http://www.vailresorts.com/Corp/awards-and-accolades. aspx
32. Cook, R., Yale, L., and Marqua, J. J. (2002). *Tourism: The Business of Travel*. Upper Saddle River, NJ: Pearson Prentice Hall.
33. Travel Industry Association of America. Golf and Tennis at http://www.tia.org/pressmedia/domestic_a_to_z.html#g
34. United States Golf Association. What is the origin of the word golf at http://www.usga.com/questions/faqs/usga_history. html
35. Scotland, the home of golf at http://golf.visitscotland.com
36. Travel Industry Association of America. Theme/Amusement Park Travel at http://www.tia.org/pressmedia/domestic_a_to_ z.html#t
37. Lounsberry, F. (2004). The Theme Park Perspective. In: Dickinson, B., and Vladimir, A. *The Complete 21st Century Travel and Hospitality Marketing Handbook*. Upper Saddle River, NJ: Pearson Prentice Hall, 191–200.
38. Universal Studios. The Amazing Adventures of Spiderman at http://www.univacations.com/themeparks/IOAspiderman. asp
39. Six Flags Theme Parks, Inc. Tallest Fastest Roller Coaster on Earth at http://www.sixflags.com/greatAdventure/rides/ Kingdaka.aspx
40. Universal Studios. Suess Landing at http://www.univacations.com/themeparks/IOAsuesslanding.asp
41. American Gambling Association. Industry Information Fact Sheets: Statistics Top 20 Casino Markets by Annual Revenue 2004 at http://www.americangaming.org/Industry/factsheets/statistics_detail.cfv?id=4
42. Cook, R. A., Yale, L., and Marqua, J. J. (2002). *Tourism: The Business of Travel*. Upper Saddle River, NJ: Pearson Prentice Hall.
43. Travel Industry Association of America. Shopping at http://www.tia.org/pressmedia/domestic_a_to_z.html#s
44. West Edmonton Mall at http://www.westedmall.com/about/wemtrivia.asp
45. West Edmonton Mall. Welcome to West Edmonton Mall's Website at http://www.westedmall.com/about/default.asp
46. Mall of America at http://www.mallofamerica.com/home.aspx
47. China says no to post Olympic Bubble. *People's Daily* at http://English.peopledaily.com.cn/200703/20/eng20070320_359415. html
48. China: Race to improve air quality for 2008 Olympics. *IPS* at http://ipsnews.net/news.asp?idnews=32097
49. Center for Chinese Studies. The Beijing Olympics 2008. *IPS* at http://ipsnews.net/news.asp?idnews=32097
50. Travel Industry Association of America. Profile of Travelers Who Attended Sports Events at http://www.tia.org/Pubs/pubs. asp?PublicationID=80
51. NASCAR at http://www.nascar.com
52. About NASCAR at http://www.nascar.com/guides/about/nascar
53. Woodstock Festival at http://en.wikipedia.org/wiki/Woodstock_festival
54. Super Bowl at http://en.wikipedia.org/wiki/Super_bowl
55. Ethel M. Chocolates. Factory Tour at http://www.ethelm.com/jump.jsp?itemID=117&itemType=CATEGORY
56. Boeing. About Us at http://www.boeing.com/companyoffices/aboutus/tours/index.html. You can find out more on Boeing's factory tours at http://gown.about.com/od/attractionsWA/a/futureofflight.htm
57. Factory tours USA at http://factorytourusa.com/index.asp
58. Hall, C. M., Johnson, G., Cambourne, B., Macionis, N., Mitchell, R., and Sharples, L. (2002). Wine Tourism: An Introduction. In: Hall, C. M., Sharples, L., Cambourne, B., and Macionis, N. Wine Tourism Around the World. Oxford: Butterworth Heinemann, 1–22.

59. Chiff.com. Sideways: The Virtual Wine Tour at http://www.chiff.com/a/sideways-wine-tour.htm
60. Beringer. Winery Tours at http://www.beringer.com/beringer/page/tours2.jsp

≈ *Contributors*

Ronald J. Cereola, JD, MBA

James Madison University

cereolrj@jmu.edu

Dr. Ronald J. Cereola is an Assistant Professor in the Hospitality & Tourism Management program at James Madison University, Harrisonburg, Virginia. He teaches Tourism, Hospitality Services Marketing, Hospitality Law, and Entertainment Management.

Reginald Foucar-Szocki

James Madison University

foucarrf@jmu.edu

Dr. Reg Foucar-Szocki is the JW Marriott Professor in the Hospitality & Tourism Management program at James Madison University, Harrisonburg, Virginia, where he has taught since 1989. Reg believes the world is a special event and hospitality management is the centerpiece for success.

Chapter 28
Review Questions

1. Define an attraction.

2. Explain how attractions benefit the community in which they are located. Provide an example.

3. For each of the following methods of classifying attractions indicate the characteristics of each classification and provide an example for each type.

   a. Status

   b. Origin

   c. Lifespan

   d. Ownership

4. What are the methods for classifying attractions by product attributes? Provide an example for each.

5. What is the relationship between an attraction, infrastructure, and hospitality services in the surrounding area?

6. Revisit questions #3 and #4 and provide examples not found in the chapter for each.

7. Using *Google.com,* search the Internet for an attraction (as per the chapter introduction) and select one of the search results. Classify your choice using as many of the classification techniques described in the chapter. Support your answer with a brief explanation for each.

Cruise Line Industry

29

Chris DeSessa, Johnson & Wales University

Courtesy of Carnival Cruise Lines.

≈ Learning Objectives

- ☑ Discuss three benefits of cruising
- ☑ Explain what is included in the cost of a cruise
- ☑ Name two possible disadvantages of cruising
- ☑ Generalize about cruise line clientele
- ☑ Name four factors that determine the cost of a cruise

≈ Chapter Outline

History of Cruising
The Ship Itself
Types of Cruise Lines
The Major Cruise Lines
Trends
Career Opportunities

≈ Key Terms

Berth	Gross registered tonnage
Bridge	Purser
Bow	Space ratio
Cabin	Stabilizer
CLIA	Stern
Deck plan	Tender
Flag of convenience	
Galley	

*W*elcome aboard to the wonderful world of cruising. The cruise industry is the fastest growing segment of the travel industry. More than 12 million people took a cruise vacation in 2007. Industry estimates are that one-half million more will cruise in 2008. The cruise industry's growth is also reflected in its expanding guest capacity. Nearly 40 new ships were built in the 1980s and during the 1990s, nearly 80 new ships debuted. By the end of 2007, 88 new ships will have been introduced since 2000. There are plans to build 28 new ships between 2009–2012 Since more huge ships are being built, the competition between cruise lines is very competitive. However, because 83 percent of U.S. adults have never taken a cruise vacation, there remains an enormous untapped market.

The number of Americans taking cruises continues to grow every year. The top states producing the most cruise passengers are Florida, California, Texas, Massachusetts, New York, and Pennsylvania. There are many reasons for the popularity of cruises. Historically, cruise ships were for people to sit in a deck chair and eat 24 hours a day. Now, you can book a fitness cruise with spa treatments, healthy dietary cuisine, and exercise programs for everyone. Cruise lines continue to build new ships with more shopping, health clubs, casinos, and restaurants. In addition, cruise companies have expanded their choice of itineraries to include more exotic ports of call and have introduced more innovative onboard facilities such as cyber-cafes, multiple themed restaurants and state-of-the-art meeting facilities to attract a more diverse clientele. So, for many, a cruise represents a vacation that allows one to do as little or as much as he/she wants.

Not all boats are large Carnival cruises that carry 3,000 people. Some are small boats that sleep four or six people, which can go up rivers to see places one cannot get to by any other means of transportation. For examples, you can go to Amsterdam and hop on a schooner for 4–6 people and stop to check out the tulip fields, historic cities, and museums from the water. Stopping at a cheese farm that can only be reached by canal is a tasty change of pace. You can watch as the captain pays tolls by putting the money in a wooden shoe that swings out from the tollbooth operator. There are actually stop lights at major intersections and you can watch as the crew dismantles the steering cabin to get under a short bridge. If you get bored, you can ride a bike along the canal paths. And then there are always the gourmet dinners with short educational sessions tasting different cheeses, ports, and wines. There is a cruise for every budget, age group, eating habit, and activity level. It is easy to see why a cruise is the choice for many vacationers. Americans love to cruise. They represent about 70% of the people who take cruise vacations. For many, a cruise represents both value and piece of mind. Unlike a land based vacation, the hassles of paying for meals and entertainment and deciding where to eat are eliminated. A cruise allows passengers to pack and unpack once. There is security in knowing that everything is taken care of and no money for necessities is needed once you are on the boat. On board the problem of carrying money is eliminated because on board one is part of the "cashless society" which allows the passenger to sign for extra expenses. You can relax and enjoy yourself. In addition, because there are a lot of people on the boat, you can meet new friends, have drinks, party, and know that you are steps away from your bed when it is over.

The price of the cruise includes one's accommodations, all meals and in-between snacks, entertainment, lectures, social functions, movies, and the use of a ship's facilities including entry into the casino and fitness centers. Sometimes the price also includes the price of flights to the ship and transfers (transportation between airport or hotel and the cruise port).

For many vacationers, a cruise represents both value and peace of mind.

Courtesy of Carnival Cruise Lines.

What is not included in the price of a cruise? Some people have the misconception that everything is included in the price. Therefore, it is important to clarify in advance what is not included. With a little common sense, most of these are obvious. Alcoholic beverages and gambling debts are not included. In addition, the following are not included in the price of a cruise: shopping, liquor, photos, health spas, Internet cafes, tipping (on some ships), phone calls, seasickness inoculations, and shore excursions.

History of Cruising

The concept of cruising has changed dramatically over the years. Not so long ago cruising was for the very rich or very poor. Cruise ships were divided into classes. Many of our ancestors came to America via cruise ship. Their experiences were less than joyful because they were in the part of the ship known as "steerage" which was little better than bare bones accommodations. They were housed at the bottom of the boat with no windows or air. Their recreation deck was the only place they could get sun. The movie *Titanic* with Leonardo DiCaprio portrayed what it was like in steerage. It also portrayed the problem if something happened to the ship but it did allow poor people to be able to cross the ocean. Of course the very rich could cross the oceans in elegance cruising in first class accommodations on such famous ships as the S.S. France, Queen Mary, and the ships of the White Star Line.

Many of the early cruises were for transportation. Before airplanes cruise ships were the main method of crossing from one continent to another. While the cruise could be luxurious, it was still basically walking around the deck, sitting in lounge chairs, and eating. So, up until the 1960s recreational cruising was considered a vacation option for senior citizens. That all changed with the creation of the hit television series, *The Love Boat*. Television viewers then saw cruising as a getaway to exotic ports such as Acapulco, where romance filled the air, and passengers were pampered with dinners with the captain and adventures with fellow passengers. The series portrayed passengers as young or young at heart, adventuresome, and available. Certainly, a more exciting image was created.

Activities

Another important event that changed the image of cruising was when Carnival Cruise Lines introduced the idea of a cruise ship as a destination in itself with its introduction of "The Fun Ships." The cruise ship itself was the focal point of activities with a myriad of scheduled fun activities from morning until night. The ships contained everything that a small city would have minus the crime. A passenger can do as little or as much as he/she wants on a cruise. Most ships have pools, basketball and volleyball courts, and jogging tracks. Or, people could go rock climbing, golfing, skating, or skeet shooting. You can even go surfing in a surfing pool. On the quieter side, one can go to nightclubs, libraries, or art and photo galleries. Typically a passenger will have an opportunity to attend a Broadway-type production before or after dinner. Another option could be to attend a first run movie in the ship's movie theatre.

The cruise lines have also introduced innovative onboard amenities and facilities, including cell phone access, Internet cafes and wireless fidelity (Wi-fi) zones, multi-room villas, and multiple themed restaurants. They could get a massage or facial at the spa or work out at a state of the art health club. Clients can take a tour of the galley (kitchen) or the bridge (area where the captain and crew navigate the ship). Or, as before, they could sit in a lounge chair and soak up the sun with occasional dips in the pool. These are all included in the price of a cruise.

The role of a cruise director is to ensure that clients have the opportunity to have a good time. Many activities are geared toward clients meeting each other: a typical cruise may have a single's party, grandmothers bragging party, dance lessons, trivia contests, passenger talent shows, scavenger hunts, and poolside games. Other activities are geared toward teens or younger children.

When a cruise ship is planning to enter a port, the cruise director may give a port talk on sights to see or places to shop. Cruise lines also offer shore excursions which are half-day or full day trips that can be bought on the cruise ship and are recommended by the cruise line. Sometimes these excursions can be previewed and bought ahead of time.

Oftentimes a cruise line will deliver an activity sheet to a passenger's cabin at night so that the client is aware of activities for the next day.

Figure 29.1 Funship—Carnival Cruises

35 Years of Fun

CARNIVAL IMAGINATION

On behalf of **Captain Vito Giacalone**, his officers, staff and crew, as well as Carnival Cruise Lines, Welcome Aboard the Beautiful "Funship"

Thursday, October 4th, 2007

Chief Engineer: Carlo Paiella / **Hotel Director:** Miles Willis / **Cruise Director:** Jaime deSouza
Sunrise 7:16am / Sunset 7:02pm

LIFEBOAT DRILL 3:30pm prior to sailing - MANDATORY FOR ALL GUESTS

Remember, the Imagination is a moving ship. Please be careful, watch your step and use the handrails.

GRAND BUFFET LUNCH
11:30am - 3:45pm .... Horizon Bar & Grill

TASTE OF NATIONS
Today's Theme" *Italian*"
11:30am - 3:45pm Lunch .... Horizon Bar & Grill
11:30am-6:00pm SunLovers .... Poolside Grill
(Service will be interrupted during the Boat Drill)

DINNER
For a full dinner service dining experience. Please join us in our main restaurants. Check your Sail & Sign card to find your place & time to dine. All three restaurants are Smoke Free Environments.

EARLY SEATING
5:45pm Spirit Dining Room .... Atlantic Deck, Aft
6:15pm Pride Dining Room .... Atlantic Deck, Fwd

LATE SEATING
8:00pm Spirit Dining Room .... Atlantic Deck, Aft
8:30pm Pride Dining Room .... Atlantic Deck, Fwd
Dress for this evening is Resort casual (No shorts or tank tops)

Maitre D's Wine Selections
White: Fume Blanc, Robert Mondavi, Napa Valley
Red: Cabernet Sauvignon, Wolf Blass, Australia

SUSHI BAR
5:00pm - 8:30pm .... Promenade Deck 9, Fwd

SEAVIEW BISTRO
We are pleased to offer an alternative dining venue with varied selections from the grill and the salad bar.
6:00pm - 9:30pm .... Horizon Bar & Grill

LATE NIGHT BISTRO
11:00pm - 1:00am........ Horizon Bar & Grill

PIZZERIA 24 Hours .... Horizon Bar & Grill

COFFEE & TEA 24 Hours .... Horizon Bar & Grill

ICE CREAM STATION 24 Hours Horizon Bar & Grill

The United States Public Health Service has determined that eating uncooked or partially cooked meat, poultry, fish, seafood or eggs may present a health risk to the consumer particularly those that may be more vulnerable.

BEVERAGE SERVICE
Sip on your favorite drink as you explore the IMAGINATION. You must be at least 21 years old to be served alcohol on board. Proper identification with birthdate is required.

Daily Specials
"Funship Special"

Dream Bar	11:30am - late	Promenade Deck
Pinnacle Club	11:30am - late	Promenade,Aft
Lido Pool Bar	11:30am - late	Lido Deck
Horizon Bar	11:30am - 1:00am......	Horizon Bar & Grill
Shangri La	9:30pm - late	Promenade Midship
Xanadu Lounge	8:00pm - late	Promenade Midship
Illusions Disco	10:30pm - late	Promenade Midship
Vittorio's Cafe	11:30am - 12:30am	Promenade Deck

FOUNTAIN FUN CARDS
For a small, one-time fee, you can enjoy unlimited soda for the entire cruise. See one of our friendly bartenders for details.

THE PINNACLE Fine Cigar Bar
Choose from Macanudos, Partagas, Cuban-seed and others. Enjoy your cigar with some of the many fine whiskies, wines, cognacs, martinis, gins, vodkas and liquors offered onboard. Promenade Deck Aft

CANDIES - CANDIES - CANDIES
Great selection at the Formalities Shop on Promenade

ATM MACHINES
The ATM Machines are located on the Promenade Deck in the Grand Atrium forward & Casino cash desk. The machine is open 24 hours.

ICE
Ice is available from your stateroom steward or you may call room service. You may also get ice from the Pool Bar, Lido Deck.

ROOM SERVICE
Room service is available 24hrs by calling 8000 from your cabin.

TOWELS & BATHROBES
A Carnival Beach towel will be supplied to you every day by your stateroom steward. Please leave the white towels in your stateroom. Remember to return the Carnival Beach towel to your steward or your Sail & Sign account will be billed. If you would like to purchase a Carnival Beach towel or Bathrobe as a souvenir, your stateroom steward will deliver a new one on request. In addition, Carnival Beach Towels will be available on the open deck from 9am - 6pm. Please remember to turn them in at the end of the day, or your Sail & Sign card will be charged.

INFIRMARY
Located on Deck 3 Forward. In case of an emergency please call 911.

SHARPS CONTAINERS
If you have a medical condition which requires the use of a hypodermic syringe, please advise your stateroom steward so they may provide you with a Sharps container to safely dispose of the needles. Thank you.

PHONE HOME
Call ANYWHERE in the world from your cabin. $6.99 per min. U.S. calls. $9.99 per min. International calls.

LAUNDRY
Laundry Machines available. Empress Fwd by Cabin E2 and Upper Aft by Cabin U164. Laundry soap and Fabric Softener available at the laundry.

SMOKING AREAS
Casino - Promenade Deck 9, Pinnacle Bar - Promenade Deck 9 Port Side, Lido Deck 10 Starboard Side Outside & Verandah Deck Afts. All other areas are smoke free. Thank you for your cooperation.

POOLS AND JACUZZIS
Lido main pool & Jacuzzis 12pm-10:30pm, Verandah aft Jacuzzi's 12pm-10:30pm, Spa Jacuzzi's 12pm-9pm, Verandah aft & Kid's Pool is closed today,
ADULTS ONLY - Funnel Deck 11 (21 & UP)

RENEWAL OF WEDDING VOWS
Renew your wedding vows with Captain Giacalone and relive your special day. Inquire at the Formality Shop, Promenade Deck Midship.

DRESS CODES (Important, Please read)
Formal Night this cruise will be tomorrow, your very first sea day. On this night, Formal or Business Attire will be required to enter the dining room. On all other nights, a dress code of Elegant Casual will apply. Please note, guests wearing shorts or tank tops will not be permitted in the dining room. Thank you for your understanding.

IMPORTANT
IT IS IMPORTANT TO NOTE THAT THE BEST DEFENSE AGAINST THE SPREAD OF ANY STOMACH VIRUS IS THE CONSTANT WASHING OF YOUR HANDS BEFORE EATING.

Carnival Colors

SHOPPING TALK

The Ultimate Team Challenge!

Are you ready to play?

Whenever you see the Carnival Colors logo next to an activity, it means you can earn points for your team by winning or perhaps just participating in that event. It's a lot of fun! Find out which team you are on (Red or Blue) in the dining room, tonight during dinner.

7:45pm - Dynasty Lounge - 8 Fwd
Join your Destination Shopping Specialist, Stephanie, for this informational meeting regarding the fantastic Shopping in our ports of call!
*How to have a fun & safe Vacation
*Best Steals & Deals - VIP Benefits & More
*Shopping Rewards Program
*Where and when to go ashore, and more!

SHORE EXCURSIONS
Shore Excursions: Want to book your tours early? Tour Desk opens today 12:30pm-3:30pm & 5:00pm - 6:30pm.
Travel Tips and Adventure Talk is currently being played on Channel 17 on your cabin television!

Carnival Cruise Lines Environmental Compliance Hotline For all concerns related to Carnival contact: I-305-406-5863 (International) 1-888-290-5105 (North America) or 4ENV (From your ship phone) Environmental Compliance Web Site www.carnivalcompliance.com Carnival Cruise Lines is proud to be at the forefront of Safety and Environmental Protection. You will never see any crewmember throw anything overboard, and to help continue protect YOUR oceans and seas, we ask guests to also refrain from doing so. You must never throw a lit cigarette overboard or flick hot ash overboard as this could blow back into the ship and start a fire.

Figure 29.1 Funship—Carnival Cruises *(continued)*

PHOTO GALLERY

Take home the best souvenirs of your entire cruise. Photos, albums, frames, everything you need. Including Digital , disposable and underwater cameras. Gallery opens 7pm-10:30pm - Empress Deck Check Our Daily Special!

FUN SHIP FILMS

You are the stars of Funship Films production of "The Voyage Video". When you see the camera this week, make sure you smile and wave! Some of you may be interviewed. Don't be shy, this is YOUR vacation captured on film! Be sure and pre-order your copy of the video at the Shore Excursion Desk or at the Photo Gallery, Empress Deck 7. Available on VHS or DVD. Also, be sure to pre order your Bridge and Engine Tour and Gourmet Cooking DVD's.

SHORE EXCURSIONS

Want to book your tours early? Tour Desk opens today 12:30pm-3:30pm and 5:00p - 6:30pm. Tours available on a first come, first serve basis. Some tours may sell out by tonight. Learn more about all of our tours by tuning into your Travel & Adventure Talk on Channel 17 on your cabin televisions.
Shore Excursion Desk, Empress Deck 7 Atrium

FORMALITY SHOP

Paint the town red on Formal Night in a rented tuxedo. While you're at it, order some flowers for your loved one. How about decorating your stateroom for that special occasion, or a bottle of bubbly as a night-cap in your suite. This and much more. .... Promenade Deck
1pm-6pm & 8:15pm-10:30pm.

SHOPPING ASHORE

The Shopping Ashore Talk will take place at 7:45pm in the Dynasty Lounge. Learn about Carnival's Recommended & Guaranteed Shopping Program, customs allowances & best buys ashore. We recommend at least one member of each stateroom attend. FREE diamond jewelry raffle! For additional and personal shopping ashore information, see Stephanie at the Desk on Promenade Deck, midship.
Desk Hour: 8:15pm - 9:15pm.......Promenade Deck

SHOPS ON BOARD

Open Approx 5:30pm - 10:30pm
Atlantic Deck 8 Fwd

FREE LIQUOR TASTING

Place your liquor order in tonight and enter our raffle at 10:00pm to win a 4 Bottle Gift Pack Free!

Also check out the Boutique on Promenade Deck Aft, where everything is just $10

CA$INO

Coinless Gaming Is Here!
EACH 1000 POINTS = $10 CASH BACK
It's Simple, Easy, and Safe! Insert Your Sail and Sign Card, and Let The Winning Begin!

Complimentary Gaming Lessons
6:30pm - 7:15pm

Texas Hold 'em is here!

Located in the Pinnacle Club Promenade

Casino Chips and coins may be purchased using Sail and Sign Card. A service charge of 3% applies for all Sail and Sign chip, coin and credit purchases.
You must be over 18 to enter the Casino

PARK WEST AT SEA

Tonight, come guess the price of Picasso and get the chance to meet your Art Director Dave before tomorrow's auction. It's your chance to preview all the work before you bid!
Atlantic Deck, 2pm - 11:00pm

CARNIVALGOLF.COM

Meet your golf professional in the lobby Empress Deck 7. Find out about Golf Excursions, Custom club fitting and golf lesson opportunities. .... Empress Deck 7
2:00 - 4:00 pm.

CELL PHONE SERVICE

BRAND NEW! Stay connected out at sea using your cellular phone. International roaming rates apply.
Motorola 2 Way Radios
Stay in touch with family and friends both on board and in port of call.

INTERNET - EMBARKATION SPECIAL

Purchase an Internet Time Plan TODAY and receive up to 10 additional minutes FREE! Also enter the raffle in the Internet Cafe for your chance to WIN up to 180 FREE minutes! Drop box is located at Empress Deck 7 Atrium. Winner will be posted at the Internet Cafe on the second night of the cruise. Now also offering WIRELESS access with your own laptop computer or rent one of ours! Visit Internet Café on Empress Deck (next to Information desk). Open 24 hours. Contact your Internet Manager Jacques for details.

IMPORTANT (Important, Please read)

IT IS IMPORTANT TO NOTE THAT THE BEST DEFENSE AGAINST THE SPREAD OF ANY STOMACH VIRUS IS THE CONSTANT WASHING OF YOUR HANDS BEFORE EATING.

MUSIC AND DANCING

Cool Calypso with "Island Sounds"
 2:00pm - 3:30pm & 4:45pm - 5:45pm ......Lido Deck
Cocktail Music with "Luis"
 5:15pm - 6:15pm & 8:30pm - 9:30pm .... Dream Bar
 7:15pm - 8:15pm ..... Pinnacle Club
Piano Bar Party with "Russell"
 8:00pm - 8:30pm & 9:30pm - 12:30pm .... Mirage
Karaoke Madness with "Kay"
 9:00pm - 10:00pm (All Ages) ....Xanadu Lounge
 10:00pm - 12:00am (18 & Up) ....
Party Music with "Flashy"
 9:30pm-1:00am ..... Dream Bar
Live Music with "Lifeline"
 10:00pm - 1:00am ..... Shangri La Lounge
Dance Music with "DJ Spice" ..... Illusions Dance Club
 10:30pm - Late (18 & Over) ....

ACTIVITIES

Ship's Tour
 2:45pm ..... Dynasty Lounge
Sailaway Party
 Live Music with "Island Sounds!" Enjoy great drink specials. Come and join us as we say goodbye to Miami!
 After sailing ..... Lido Deck
Trivia Fun
 Interactive quiztime with one fo your fun social hosts.
 8:15pm ..... Dynasty Lounge
Latin Dance Class
 Join one of your friendly Imagination dancers and learn a sultry move or two!
 8:45pm ..... Dynasty Lounge
Game Show Mania
 The bells, buzzers, whistles plus great prizes to win.
 9:15pm.

WELCOME ABOARD SHOW

Hosted by your Cruise Director JAIME
An evening of fun & entertainment!
Starring:
The Imagination Dancers
Vocals by:
Analyn Gepte
& Kendrix Singletary
Enjoy music from
BRETT BONNELL &
the Imagination Showband
followed by
The Hilarious Comedy of
Hank McGauley
10:30pm Dynasty Lounge
Do Not Miss This!

Get there early as we kindly ask that you do not save seats! The Dynasty Lounge is a nonsmoking lounge! Video taping/photography of tonight's star performer is prohibited. Thank you!

SPA CARNIVAL

SPA CARNIVAL WELCOMES YOU
Spa and Gym open 12:30 - 10:00pm
Sports deck 12 fwd call #2009
Early Bookings Special
Valid For Embarkation Day only
Cut Color Or Highlight & Blow dry $99
Travelers Tension $89
40 minute Back of the Body Massage
FREE Hair, Skin & Cellulite Consultations from 5:00pm to 9:00pm

Please don't forget to drop off your raffle tickets before 5:00pm
Cancellation policy applies

CAMP CARNIVAL

This welcome meeting is for parents and children. Your Youth Director, Kim, and her staff will explain how to sign up for baby sitting, available activities and where to find the Playroom & Teen Club. We look forward to seeing you there!
5:15pm Orientation Meeting (2-11yrs)..Xanadu Lounge
8:00pm Teen Orientation (12-14yrs)....Illusions Disco
8:30pm Welcome Aboard Party ......Illusions Disco

AIRBRUSH BODY ART

It's daring...it's crazy...it's FUN! Check out your NuEmage Air Brush Artist for the latest in temporary art and body jewel. 2:00pm-6:30pm & 8:00pm-10:00pm Lido Deck

24 HOUR VIDEO ARCADE

Fun for everyone! Located on Promenade Deck forward, next to the Casino!

JACKPOT CA$H BINGO

Play all 3 games on 1 card! Cards available as a Cash or Sail & Sign purchase. Get a great seat for the show and try your luck at $600!!!
9:45pm ..... Dynasty Lounge

Welcome Aboard the Fun Ship Carnival Imagination — MIAMI

Time	Event	Location
12:30pm	Tour Desk opens 'til 3:30pm	Empress Deck
1:00pm	Spa Tours	Sports Deck Fwd
	Formalities Shop 'til 6pm	Promenade
1:30pm	Ch ldrens Playroom opens	Atlantic Deck, Aft
2:00pm	Dining Room Inquiries	P-ide Dining Room
	Calypso Music	Lido Deck
	Art Gallery opens	Atlantic Deck
	Spa Show	Sports Deck Fwd
	Gof Inquiries 'til 4:00pm	Empress Deck
	Nu Emage Airbrush Body Art	Lido Deck
2:45pm	Ship Tour	Dynasty Lounge
3:30pm	Lifeboat Drill for all guests(approx.time)	
4:00pm	Imagination sets sail (approx.time)	
	After Boat Drill	
	Sail Away Party	Lido Deck
	Golf Swing Check	Verandah Deck aft
	Tour Desk open 'til 6:30pm	EmpressDeck
5:00pm	Spa Raffle	Spa Carnival, Deck 12 Fwd
	Consultations available	Spa Carnival
5:15pm	Camp Carnival Orientation	Xanadu Lounge
	Piano Music	Dream Bar
5:30pm	Gift Shops Open	Atlantic Forward
	Free Liquor Tasting	Atlantic Deck
6:00pm	Full Casino opens	Promenade Deck
	Golf Swing Clinic	Conference Room
6:30pm	Complimentary Gaming Lessons	Casino
7:00pm	Photo Gallery Opens	Empress Deck
	Golf Seminar	Mirage Bar Deck 8 Fwd
	Formalities Shop 'til 10:30pm	Library
	Friends of Bill W	Pinnacle
	Piano Music	Pinnacle
7:45pm	Shopping Ashore Talk	Dynasty Lounge
8:00pm	Piano Bar Party (til 8:30pm)	Mirage Piano Bar
	Nu Emage Airbrush Body Art	Lido Deck
8:15pm	Quiztime	Dynasty Lounge
	Destination Shopping Desk	Promenade Deck
8:30pm	Camp Carnival Party	Illusions Disco
	Piano Music	Dream Bar
	Friends of Dorothy	Pinnacle Lounge
8:45pm	Latin Dance Class	Dynasty Lounge
9:00pm	Karaoke Madness	Xanadu Lounge
	15-17 Gathering	Club O2
	Nu Emage Airbrush Body Art	Dynasty Lounge
9:15pm	Gamshow Mania!	
9:30pm	Piano Bar Party (til 12:30am)	Mirage Piano Bar
	Party Music	Dream Bar
9:45pm	Jackpot Bingo	Dynasty Lounge
10:00pm	Liquor Raffle (must be present)	Gift Shop
	Live Variety Music	Shangri La Lounge
	Mature Singles Party	Mirage Piano Bar
	Friends Of Dorothy	Dream Bar
	Gathering for all Dancers	Shangri La
	Not so Single Gathering	Xanadu Lounge
	Babysitting Available (fee applies)	Playroom
10:15pm	Dance Club opens for Adults	Illusions Disco
10:30pm	Welcome Aboard Show	Illusions
11:30pm	18-24 Singles Gathering	Empress Deck 7
	24 Hours Internet Cafe	Promenade Deck Fwd
	Videc Game Arcade	Promenade Deck Fwd

Figure 29.2 Carnival Cruise Itinerary

35 Years of Fun

Captain Vito Giacalone Welcomes you to

Calica, Mexico

Always stay on ship's time!

*Be careful using cell phone clocks as you will pick up local time...

Arrival to Calica: 1:00pm / Back On Board: 8:30pm / Ship Sets Sail: 9:00pm

Saturday, October 6th, 2007

Sunrise 7:38am / Sunset 7:31pm

Chief Engineer: Carlo Paiella / **Hotel Director:** Miles Willis / **Cruise Director:** Jaime deSouza

---

BREAKFAST
7:00am Continental Breakfast ...... Horizon Bar & Grill
8:00am-10:00am Open Seating Breakfast ...... Pride DR
8:00am-10:30am Lido Breakfast ...... Lido Deck
8:00am-12:00pm Breakfast ...... Horizon Grill, Poolside
OMELETS SERVED HERE

GRAND BUFFET LUNCH
12:00am - 2:30pm ...... Horizon Bar & Grill

TASTE OF NATIONS
Todays Theme : French
12:00am - 2:30pm Lunch ...... Horizon Bar & Grill
11:30am - 6:00pm Sun Lovers ...... Poolside Grill

DINNER
5:45pm Early Seating ...... Spirit Dining Room
6:15pm Early Seating ...... Pride Dining Room
8:00pm Late Seating ...... Spirit Dining Room
8:30pm Late Seating ...... Pride Dining Room
Dress for this evening is casual, no shorts or tank tops. Both Dining Rooms are Smoke-Free.

Maitre D's Wine Suggestions:
White: Sauvignon Blanc, Nobilo, New Zealand
Red: Chateauneuf-Du-Pape, Les Closiers, Rhone Valley
SEAVIEW BISTRO
6:00pm - 9:30pm ...... Horizon Bar & Grill

SUSHI BAR
5:00pm - 8:30pm ...... Promenade Deck 9 Fwd

LATE NIGHT BISTRO
11:30pm - late ...... Horizon Bar & Grill

Pizzeria 24 Hours ...... Horizon Bar & Grill

Coffee & Tea 24 Hours ...... Horizon Bar & Grill

Ice Cream station 24 Hours ...... Horizon Bar & Grill

The United States Public Health Service has determined that eating uncooked or partially cooked meat, poultry, fish, seafood or eggs may present a health risk to the consumer particularly those that may be more vulnerable.

BEVERAGE SERVICE
Sip your favorite drink as you explore the IMAGINATION.

Daily Specials
"Mexican Mama"

Early Morning Special
Bloody Mary/Screwdriver/Mimosa

Lido Pool Bar   9:00am - Late ...... Lido Deck
Dream Bar   10:00am - late ...... Promenade Deck
Pinnacle Club   3:00pm - Late ...... Promenade Deck
Horizon Bar   7:30am - 1:00am ...... Horizon Bar & Grill
Shangri la   9:00pm - Late ...... Promenade deck
Illusions Disco   10:30pm - late ...... Promenade Midship
Vittorio's Cafe   7:30am-1:00pm & 4:30pm-12:30am ..Deck 9

You must be at least 21 years old to be served alcohol on board. Proper I.D. Which birthdate is required.

THE PINNACLE FINE Cigar Bar
Choose from Macanudos, Partagas, Cuban-seed and others. Enjoy your cigar' with some of the many fine whiskies, wines, cognacs, martinis, gins, vodkas and liquors offered onboard Promenade Deck Aft.

CAMP CARNIVAL (SM)
Super Late Night Party (fees apply)
10:00pm-1:00am (6-8yrs) ...... Teen Club, Atlantic Aft

CLUB O₂ (SM) (15-17yrs)
9:00pm-Late ...... Club O₂
11:30pm Tropical Deck Party ...... Lido Deck
Check your Club O₂ Caper......Available at the Pursers.

PHONING HOME
You can call anywhere in the world direct from your cabin. NOTE: Calls made using credit or calling cards (1-800 calls) will be billed at the same rate as a direct call. Rates & dialing instructions are posted next to your phone.

LAUNDRY
Laundry Machines available. Empress Fwd by Cabin E2 and Upper Aft by Cabin U164. Laundry soap and Fabric Softener available at the laundry.

CARNIVAL SEAMILES PROGRAM
Earn FREE cruises on Carnival or any other cruise line. Apply on board today at the SeaMiles Hospitality Desk located on the Promenade Deck.

POOLS AND JACUZZIS
Lido Main Pool & Jacuzzis 8:00am-10:00pm
Lido Main Pool closed from 7pm - 8pm
for Camp Carnival Activity.
Verandah aft Pool & Jacuzzis 8:00am-10:30pm,
Kid's Pool 8:00am-6:00pm, Spa Jacuzzi's 8:00am-9:00pm
ADULTS ONLY - Funnel Deck 11 (21 & UP)

$$$$$$$$$$$$$$$$$$$$$$$$$$$$$$$$
Big Bucks Bingo
10:00pm in the Dynasty Lounge
Not to be missed!
Tonight's Jackpot:
$700!!!
$$$$$$$$$$$$$$$$$$$$$$$$$$$$$$$$

IMPORTANT PLEASE READ
IT IS IMPORTANT TO NOTE THAT THE BEST DEFENSE AGAINST THE SPREAD OF ANY STOMACH VIRUS IS THE CONSTANT WASHING OF YOUR HANDS BEFORE EATING.

Carnival Cruise Lines Environmental Compliance Hotline: For all concerns related to Carnival contact 1-305-406-5863 (International) 1-888-290-5105 (North America) or 4ENV (From your ship phone)/ Environmental Compliance Web Site www.carnivalcompliance.com Carnival Cruise Lines is proud to be at the forefront of Safety and Environmental Protection. You will never see any crewmember throw anything overboard, and to help continue protect YOUR oceans and seas, we ask guests to also refrain from doing so. You must never throw a lit cigarette overboard or flick hot ash overboard as this could blow back into the ship and start a fire.

SAME DAY LAUNDRY SERVICE
Tomorrow morning you have the opportunity to take advantage of our onboard laundry special. This is the perfect time to quickly have your swimsuit or undergarments washed and folded the same day! In your cabin you will find a Carnival logo bag and laundry form. Place your selected clothing for wash, drying and folding in the bag, complete & sign the laundry slip. The bag will then be collected by your Stateroom Steward or Stewardess by 9:30am tomorrow morning. Your freshly laundered and folded clothes will be returned to your stateroom by 7:00pm that evening. The special price for this limited service is just $15 per bag. This offer must be limited to 1 bag per stateroom.

INFIRMARY HOURS
The Infirmary will be open from 8:00am - 11:00am & 4pm - 7pm. In the case of an emergency please call 911.

RENEWAL OF WEDDING VOWS
Renew your wedding vows with Captain Giacalone and relive your special day. Inquire at the Formality Shop, Promenade Deck Midship.

LOOKING AHEAD TOMORROW
Join your Cruise Director Jaime for the important and informative debarkation talk tomorrow morning at 11:00am in the Dynasty Lounge. At least one family member should attend.

Festivale
FunShip Deck Party

Live Music from Island Sounds

Deck Party

Games start at 11:45pm

Great Music, Dancing,
Mexican Buffet
Main Pool Area, Lido Deck
Mexican Buffet starts at 11:30pm

Figure 29.2 Carnival Cruise Itinerary (continued)

CALICA MEXICO

Time	Activity	Location
6:00am	Gym Opens	Sports Deck
7:30am	Legs, Bums, and Tums Class	Aerobic Studio
8:00am	Spa Carnival® Opens	Sports Deck
	Pathway to Yoga ($10 fee)	Aerobic Studio
	Pool & Whirlpool Open	Sports Deck
9:00am	Slots open ('til arrival)	Casino
	Tour Desk ('til 11:00am)	Empress Deck
	Max & Master Art Sale	Art Gallery
	Photo Gallery ('til arrival)	Empress Deck
	Gift Shop 'til arrival	Atlantic Deck 8
	Body Cycle Spinning ($10 fee)	Aerobic Studio
10:00am	Good Morning Trivia	Dynasty Lounge
	Nu Emage Airbrush Body Art	Lido Deck
10:15am	Burn Fat Faster	Aerobic Studio
10:30am	**Bargain Bingo!**	**Dynasty Lounge**
10:45am	Watch Seminar & Raffle	Atlantic Deck
11:00am	**Battle of the Sexes Mini Putt Sun Deck 14 Fwd**	
12noon	Calypso Music	Lido Deck
1:00pm	**Approx arrival in Calica, Mexico**	
	Triva Challenge (unsupervised)	Dynasty Lounge
4:00pm	Basketball	Verandah Aft
5:00pm	Movie-Spiderman 2	Xanadu Lounge
7:00pm	Phizo Gallery opens	Empress Deck
	Max & Master Art Sale	Art Gallery
	Formality Shop 'til 10:30pm	Promenade
	Piano Music	Dream Bar
7:30pm		
8:30pm	**ALL ABOARD!**	
9:00pm	**Imagination sets sail for Miami**	
	Gift Shop Opens	Dynasty Lounge
	In The Bag Game	Dynasty Lounge
9:30pm	Match Game	Dynasty Lounge
	Casino Opens	Promenade Deck
	Watch Sale Starts	Gift Shop Deck 8
	Live Party Music	Shangri La Lounge
	Piano Party Music	Mirage Deck 8 Fwd
	Guitar Music	Dream Bar
	Club O₂ (15-17 yrs)	Club O₂
10:00pm	**$700 Bingo**	**Dynasty Lounge**
	Tropical Deck Party Under The Stars!	Lido
	Late Night Party (6-8 yrs)	Teen Club
	Baby-sitting Available (fees apply)	Playroom
	Nu Emage Airbrush Body Art	Dynasty Lounge
10:30pm	**Showtime**	**Illusions Disco**
	Dance Club (18 & up)	Atlantic Deck Fwd
	Watch Raffle	Lido Deck
11:45pm	Deck Party Activities	Promenade Deck Fwd
	24 Hours Video Arcade	Empress Deck 7

PHOTO GALLERY

All photos taken during the cruise will be available for purchase from the gallery, including last night's formal photographs.

Going to the beach! We've got waterproof and disposable cameras available at the gangway as you go ashore.

9:00am-arrival & 7:00pm-11:00pm ... Empress Deck

FUN SHIP FILMS

We captured YOU on film today in Calica! Be sure to visit the Shore Excursion Desk or the Photo Gallery to reserve your copy. Your last chance to pre-order your "Voyage" Videos at a reduced rate. Available on VHS or DVD. Also, be sure to pre order your Bridge and Engine Tour and Gourmet Cooking DVD's.

SHORE EXCURSIONS

HOT TOUR ADVENTURE PICKS

*Mayan Ruins of Tulum *ATV Adventure - *Caverns by Jeep & Beach Combo *ATV Jungle & Beach Adventure - Other tour choices are available. First come first served! The Information Desk on Empress Deck is open for last minute inquiries. Shore Tour Desk Open: 9:00am-11:00am

CARNIVALGOLF.COM

Golf at beautiful Iberostar Golf Club! Free food and beverages all day!

SHOPPING IN PLAYA DEL CARMEN

Welcome to Calica! Today is your last chance for Tax & Duty Free Shopping Ashore. Best buys include diamonds, tanzanite, designer timepieces, leather and traditional souvenirs. Pick up a shopping map at the gangway on Deck 3 forward

SHOPS ON BOARD

9:00am - Arrival
& After sailing - 11:00pm
Atlantic Deck 8 Fwd

INCH OF SILVER

TODAY only - The first 100 Guests to purchase 21 inches will receive 2 FREE Bracelets

SAVE UP TO 50% DIAMONDS TODAY

WATCH SALE 10-44% Off CITIZEN, SEIKO, FOSSIL & GUESS

WATCH RAFFLE 10:45AM & 10:30PM!

Tax & Duty Free Savings!

MUSIC AND DANCING

Relaxing Piano Music with "Luis" ... Dream Bar
7:30pm-9:30pm

Piano Party Music with "Russell" ... Dream Bar
9:30pm - 1:00am ... Mirage Piano Bar Deck 8 Fwd

Party Music with "Flashy" ... Dream Bar
9:30pm-12:30am

Live Party Music with "Lifeline" ... Shangri La Lounge
9:30pm - 1:00am

Live Caribbean Music with "Island Sounds" ... Lido Deck
Noon - 1:00pm & 10:00pm - Late

Dance Music with "DJ Spice" ... Illusions Disco
10:30pm - Late (18 & Over)

GOOD MORNING BARGAIN BINGO

Lots of CA$H to be given away before Showtime!
Cards available as a cash or Sail & Sign® purchase.
TRIPLE CARDS ONLY $10!!
10:30am ... Dynasty Lounge

$700 JACKPOT BINGO

Lots of CA$H to be given away before Showtime!
Cards available as a cash or Sail & Sign® purchase.
10:00pm ... Dynasty Lounge

SUPER SCRATCH LOTTO

Scratch Lotto tickets available in the Dynasty Lounge from one of your friendly Imagination Dancers at any bingo during your cruise. Win up to $1000 instantly!

VIDEO GAMES ARCADE

Open 24 Hours. Located Promenade Deck 9 Fwd outside the Casino.

CA$INO

The More You Play, The More We Pay!
1000 Points = $10 Instant Cash Reward!
Slots open 9:00am - Arrival
Full casino opens after we sail at 9:00pm

Insert your Sail & Sign Card each time you play any of our slots to earn points. Every 1000 OPC Points= $10 Instant Cash Award

DIAMOND CARIBBEAN STUD POKER

ROYAL FLUSH JACKPOT NOW OVER $125,000.00

VIDEO GAMES ARCADE OPEN 24 HOURS

Casino Chips and coins may be purchased using Sail and Sign Card.

You must be over 18 to enter the Casino

FORMALITY SHOP

How about surprising your loved one with a box of chocolates? Or maybe a bouquet of flowers. You can!
7:00pm- 10:30pm ... Promenade Deck

CELL PHONE SERVICE

BRAND NEW! Stay connected out at sea using your cellular phone. International roaming rates apply. Please turn off your cell phones during dinner and shows.

INTERNET CAFE

Internet HAPPY HOUR: 50% off of Time Charges today between 9am and 12nn. Offer does not include Activation Fees, Application Charges, or new Price Plan Purchases. Contact your Internet Manager Robert for details. Send an E-mail home! It's easy! Pre-Paid Internet Time Plans available from $ 0.40 /minute! Take advantage of our discounted Internet Time Plans and save as much as 47% off the pay as you go rate. Visit the Internet Café on Empress Deck (next to the Information desk). Open 24 hours... **(If you do not wish your child to have Internet access, please see the Internet Manager to deactivate their account)**

PARK WEST AT SEA

Max and Master SALE for one day only our entire collection of Max and Master works are going on SALE. Join your art directors in the art gallery to view works by Peter Max, Picasso, Dali, Chagall, Miro and Rembrandt. Receive a FREE work of art just for attending. Don't miss this special event. See you there!
9:00am - 12:00pm & 7:00pm - 10:00pm ...... Atlantic Deck

Showtime!

A night of great entertainment with your Cruise Director Jaime

Featuring
Direct from Argentina
The Amazing
Fire Gauchos
&
The Hilarious Comedy of
Roman Murray

10:30pm
One show only
Dynasty Lounge

Technical Team - Vinay, Chris & Rusty
The Dynasty Lounge is a smoke-free environment!

"FUN SHIP" ACTIVITIES

Mini Golf Putting Greens Open (Unsupervised) ... Sun Deck 14 Fwd

Good Morning Trivia
Come tweak your brains for a little morning fun to get you ready for your day!
10:00am ... Dynasty Lounge

Battle of the Sexes Mini Putt
Join your host for some major Putt Putt on the greens!
11:00 am ... Sun Deck 14 Fwd

Big Screen Movie - Spiderman 2
5:00pm ... Xanadu Lounge

In the Bag
Fill a bag full of stuff and join us in the lounge for fun. You never know what we'll ask for!
9:00pm ... Dynasty Lounge

Match Game
Just like the TV Show you watched growing up!
9:30pm ... Dynasty Lounge

Airbrush Body Art
It's daring...it's FUN! See your NuEmage Air Brush Artist for the latest in temporary art.
10:00am-1:00pm & 10:00pm-12:30am Lido Deck

SPA CARNIVAL ®

Spa and salon opens 8:00am - 8:00pm
Gym opens 6:00am - 8:00pm
Phone 2009 Deck 12 Fwd

FREE SEMINAR
10:15am Burn Fat Faster studio, Deck 12 fwd

Spa taster combo   Only $99
25 min. back neck & shoulder massage 25 min Hydrating facial or Foot & ankle massage.

ONITHERMIE SUPER DETOX $129
Lose 1-8 in 50 inches Firm, Tone, Cellulite, IBS, Excellent for Men And Women

*Stay on Ship's time!

Make sure you save your Sail & Sign Card & Photo I.D. Your Shopping Map, & Carnival Caper. Stay on ship's time! In case of emergency: Aviomar Agency 011-52 987 872-3779 or 011-52 987 876-0507 *Souvenir weapons such as decorative knives, swords and spears will not be allowed on board the ship. *Liquor will be collected at the gangway for safe keeping & returned to your stateroom at the end of the cruise. *No fruits, vegetables, or food is allowed ashore.

The Ship Itself

Ships come in various sizes. The modern cruise ship can be the height of a 10-story building and cover the space of 3 football fields. Currently the world's largest ship, Royal Caribbean International's *Freedom of the Seas,* and her new sister ship *Liberty of the Seas,* can accommodate 4,370 vacationers. Royal Caribbean International has plans to build a ship that can accommodate 6,400 passengers by 2009. Some clients prefer large ships because of the many amenities. Others prefer the intimacy of a smaller ship. The size of a cruise ship is registered in gross tonnage (GRT). Some large ships cannot pull into ports so passengers must be ferried to shore. A tender is a smaller boat that will ferry passengers from the larger ship to shore. Some of the tenders can hold more than 400 passengers.

Cruise passengers do not want to wait in long lines for service, so clients enjoy ships with plenty of room. The spaciousness of cruise ships is measured by dividing the tonnage by the number of passengers. This is referred to as the space ratio and represents a rough approximation of how much space there is on a ship. The left side of the ship facing forward is the port while the right side is the starboard. The front of the ship is referred to as the bow of the ship. The rear of the ship is referred to as the stern.

Cabins

Throughout your trip you will rest and relax in your cabin sometimes called a stateroom. The cost of a cruise also depends on the location, size, and special amenities of your cabin. Cabins that have a porthole or window are referred to as outside or exterior cabins. These are more expensive. Some cabins have a porch or veranda to enjoy the scenery. Inside or interior cabins do not have a porthole or window. Inside cabins do have access to natural light. Beds on a cruise ship are referred to as berths. One can decide between king, queen, and twin. Many cabins have bunk bed type accommodations, which are referred to as upper/lower berths, which are perfect for accommodating children on a cruise.

On modern ships all passenger cabins are above the water line. Only the crew's quarters are below the water line. Other considerations that may affect the choice of a cabin may be proximity to elevators, stairs, and public areas and the propensity for seasickness. Like any hotel, when an elevator or stairs is next door, it is very noisy all day and all night as people constantly are on the move.

A deck plan is a chart that displays the location of cabins and public rooms.

With larger ships, you have a choice of levels of floors, depending on how close to the activities one wants to be. Each deck on a ship is identified by a name or letter. Normally the higher the deck, the more expensive the cabin. Also cabins in the middle of the ship (amidship) are more expensive. These are more preferable to passengers who are prone to seasickness since there is less ship movement in the middle of a ship. Modern day cruise ships have wing-like projections called stabilizers that are used in rough seas.

Figure 29.3 Deck Plan and Ship Profile

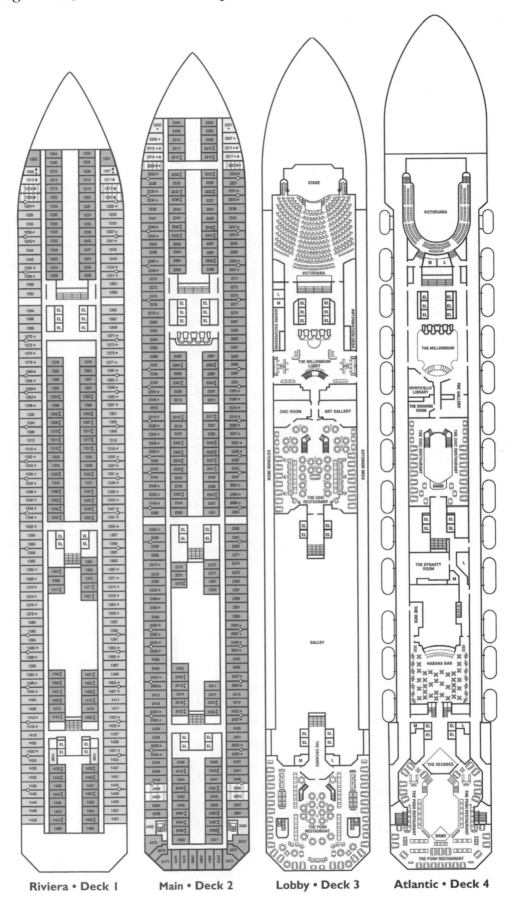

Riviera • Deck 1   **Main • Deck 2**   **Lobby • Deck 3**   **Atlantic • Deck 4**

Figure 29.3 Deck Plan and Ship Profile *(continued)*

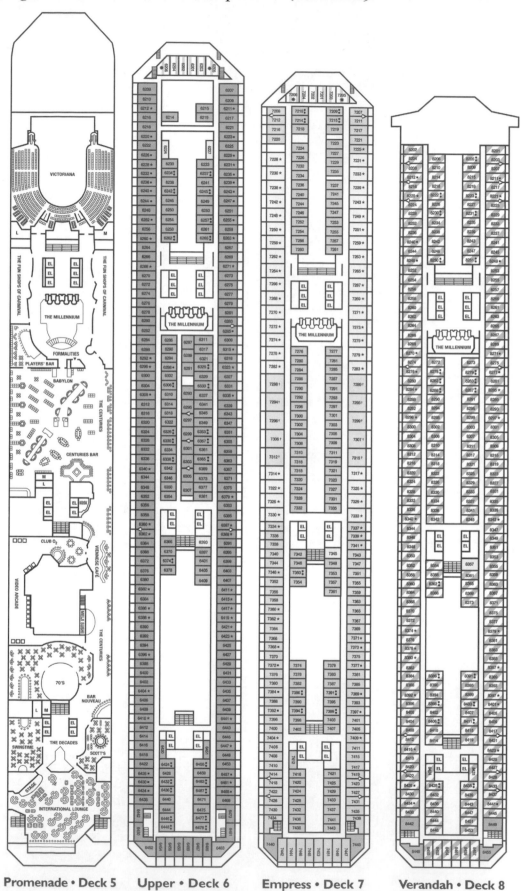

Promenade • Deck 5   Upper • Deck 6   Empress • Deck 7   Verandah • Deck 8

Figure 29.3 Deck Plan and Ship Profile *(continued)*

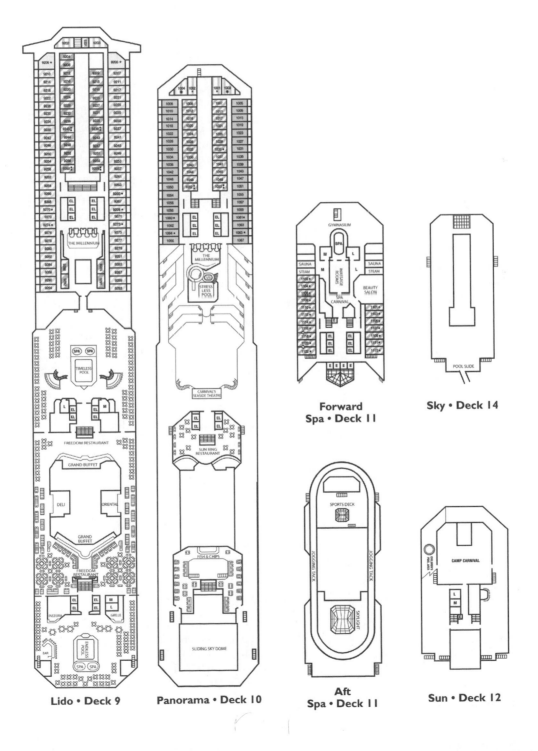

Lido • Deck 9

Panorama • Deck 10

Forward Spa • Deck 11

Sky • Deck 14

Aft Spa • Deck 11

Sun • Deck 12

Types of Cruise Lines

The Cruise Lines International Association (CLIA) is the world's premier cruise marketing and training association comprising 21 major cruise lines and 16,500 travel agencies. Its goal is promoting the desirability, diversity, and high value of the cruise vacation experience. CLIA divides the cruise lines into three types: contemporary, luxury, and premium depending on quality, service, amenities, and itineraries. Contemporary brands are geared to a mass market. Many of the contemporary brand cruise lines visit the same ports. Some distinctions between luxury and premium brands may have to do with the quality of food, level of service, and number of passengers on a ship. In comparing the passenger to crew ratio between two ships, one may get a rough estimate of the level of service. Another important factor for comparison would be the cruise itinerary. Premium cruise brands may visit more exotic ports.

The Major Cruise Lines

All of the larger cruise lines offer a well-packaged cruise that include a variety of itineraries, plenty of food, a variety of activities, and large scale Broadway production shows. The lines differ in the facilities, space, food, and service. Each cruise line has its own niche.

Cruising Areas

There are also more destinations to travel and more ports to depart from. There are over 30,000 different cruises to choose from each year, and about 2,000 cruise destinations in the world. Cruises can range from a 3-day getaway cruise from Miami to the Bahamas or an "Around the World 180 Day" cruise.

The Caribbean and Bahamas continues to be the number one destinations for cruises. Other leading cruising areas are Europe, Alaska, and Mexico and West Coast.

Most Caribbean 7-day cruises depart from Miami and usually visit 3 ports, including a private island (where clients can enjoy water sports and beach-side activities), and 2–3 days at sea. One has the option of visiting the Eastern Caribbean, Western Caribbean (which is geared toward beach lovers), or Southern Caribbean. A good choice for a first time Caribbean cruiser who is more concerned with the itinerary than the ship could be port-intensive cruise departing from San Juan, Puerto Rico, and visiting 6 islands. The ship is already in the Caribbean so it is easy to visit so many islands.

Cruises to Europe have become popular because a client only has to unpack once. Clients also like the fact that they go back each night to the familiar surroundings of their cabin and cruise ship. Alaskan cruises became very popular following 9/11 because passengers felt safer cruising in U.S. waters. Clients also have the option of taking "theme cruises." Some popular themes for cruises might be sports, music, food, wine tasting, and murder mystery. Other options include adventure cruises or expeditions to such places as the Galapagos Island, "around the world" cruises, and river cruises on such rivers as The Danube, the Rhine, and the Nile. On the Danube River tours, people can board a medium size boat of 100 to wander through the beautiful canyons and scenic splendor through 5 or 6 different countries. One possibility is to spend 3 days in Budapest exploring the city split into two parts by the river. Then board the boat to explore castles, abbies, or medieval cities that are difficult to reach except by boat, biking, or hiking. The river winds past Slovakia, the Czech Republic, Vienna

Table 29.1 **Big Eight Cruise Lines**

LINES	NO. OF SHIPS (MAY CHANGE BY PUBLICATION DATE)	BRIEF PROFILE
Carnival Cruises	23	Largest, most popular cruise line
Celebrity Cruises	8	Most elegant ships and spas
Costa Cruises	12	"Cruising Italian Style"
Cunard Cruises	3	Ocean liners—regularly scheduled transatlantic sailings
Holland America	13	Preserves many traditions of the past—good cooking demonstrations
Norwegian Cruise Line	11	Free-style cruising, Hawaii cruising
Princess Cruises	16	Best-known name the "Love Boats"
Royal Caribbean International	22	Good for the Caribbean and first time cruisers

(where you can do a Viennese waltz to a live orchestra), ending in Prague, the current European party capital.

Trends

Other trends in cruising include:

- Voyages to Antarctica
- Flexible and alternative dining options
- More large resort ships
- Multi-generational cruising aboard the resort-style ships
- Single parent cruising
- Widest ever variety of adventures ashore for active adults

Growth of Drive Market Cruising

In the past most cruise ships departed from Miami and Los Angeles. Now clients have the option of departing from ports that are within driving distance of their home. Now it is possible for passengers to start their cruise from such cities as Galveston, Boston, Mobile, and Philadelphia on designated sailings.

New Types of Pool Decks

Royal Caribbean is changing the concept of the pool deck when it introduces a pool deck that will emulate many of the features of a water park. On its ship, *The Freedom of the Seas*, the coolest spot aboard the ship will be the H_2O zone which will be a fabulous interactive water park that will offer surfing at sea. Other water-spouting attractions will be a waterfall, umbrella jets, and spray cannons.

A modern cruise ship is a restaurant, hotel, resort, and activities center.

Courtesy of Carnival Cruise Lines.

Career Opportunities

When one thinks of working for a cruise line there are two options: working on the ship or on land. The cruise industry generated almost 295,077 American jobs in 2003. This is expected to grow due to the increased popularity of cruising and the number of newer and larger ships that are being built. When one thinks about positions on a ship one must realize that a modern cruise ship is a restaurant, hotel, resort, and activities center. Many of the positions offered at those land-based establishments are offered on a cruise ship.

All the cruise ships except one are registered in other countries such as Panama and Liberia. This is referred to as a "flag of convenience." When flying a "flag of convenience" of another country, the cruise line does not have to follow United States' standards in regard to taxes and minimum wage requirements. Traditionally cruise lines tend to hire residents from less-developed countries for positions such as waiters, cabin stewards, and bartenders because residents from those countries are willing to work for less pay than Americans. Things changed in 2005 when Norwegian Caribbean Line's ship *The Pride of America* was the first ocean-going passenger vessel in nearly 50 years to sail under the American flag. As such, NCL was required to hire an all-American crew. NCL fully touts its NCL American brand.

Hospitality students with a degree can aspire to some of the better positions on a cruise ship. The top position in the rooms department is the hotel manager. The chief purser is responsible for personnel services and accounting. The cruise director is responsible for ensuring that guests are enjoying themselves. He/she is in charge of arranging activities and procuring entertainment for the ship. The chief steward is in charge of guest accommodations. These positions are similar to those in land-based operations.

The top position in the restaurant side of the cruise ship is the executive chef. The food and beverage director and the maitre d' report to him. Many cruise lines promote from within so an employee may start as a child's activities director and work their way up to cruise director. Many workers sign contracts for 6 months.

Each cruise line has policies concerning crewmembers fraternizing with guests. Some lines will allow its officers to mingle with the guests in selected areas. The crew does have its own deck which consists of cabins and shared space for activities. Often times the crew shares living accommodations. Working on a ship might seem glamorous but it does involve many hours of work per day. Members of the crew may get some time off when the ship is in port. At that time they may attend to their personal needs or take some time off at the beach. There are advantages to working on a ship. First of all, one gets to meet people from all parts of the world. Since the crew's accommodations and meals are taken cared of, one does not have to spend a great deal of money while on the ship so one has the opportunity to save money. The downside is that the crew is away from their family and friends for long periods of time. Since life aboard a cruise ship may not be for everyone, it may be good idea for a college-age student to seek summer employment on a cruise ship. Some larger cruise lines may hire youth activity directors for the summer. Other smaller cruise lines may hire one to act as both a steward and a waiter. Some cruise lines may have opportunities for internships during college.

On shore one can work at the company's headquarters in the areas of marketing and sales, reservations, and finance and accounting. There are also limited amount of positions working as a sales representative in major cities across the country. This position would entail visiting travel agents and groups highlighting the features and benefits of your product.

Summary

So if you like value, fun, pampering, variety of activities, and interesting itineraries, come join "the wonderful world of cruising."

≈ *Resources*

Internet Sites

Carnival Cruises: www.carnivalcruiselines.com
CLIA: www.cruisingorg/
Royal Caribbean International: www.royalcaribbean.com

≈ *Contributor*

Christopher De Sessa is an associate professor at Johnson & Wales' Hospitality College. In 1999 he won the National Tourism Foundation's Teacher of the Year Award. He has worked as a reservations agent for an airline, tour escort, and training director for a travel agency. For 23 years, he also worked for one of nation's oldest travel agencies.

Chapter 29
Review Questions

1. What are the major departments of a ship?

2. What are the different career opportunities in the cruise industry?

3. What are the major trends in the cruise industry?

4. Please list the names of at least five cruise lines.

5. Where are the major cruise areas of the world?

6. What is the name of the organization that promotes the cruise industry?

7. What is included in the price of a cruise?

Distribution Services

30

Donna Albano and Michael Scales,
The Richard Stockton College of New Jersey

© 2008, JupiterImages Corporation.

≈ Learning Objectives

- ☑ Describe career possibilities in the hospitality distribution services industry
- ☑ Identify and explain trends affecting the hospitality distribution services industry
- ☑ Describe elements unique to each segment of the hospitality distribution services industry
- ☑ Describe the role of a distributor sales representative in the hospitality distribution services industry
- ☑ Explain the purpose of hospitality industry trade shows and expositions
- ☑ Identify the size and scope of the hospitality industry's linen needs

≈ Chapter Outline

Introduction
Food and Beverage
Technology
Trends in Distribution Services

≈ Key Terms

Distribution services
Furniture, fixtures, and equipment
Purchasing
POS
PMS
Peripheral careers

Introduction

The distribution services industry is the vast network of peripheral companies that help hospitality enterprises get their products and services from creation to consumption. Some of the careers in distribution services include purchasing agents, information technology, accountants, human resources, warehouse managers, delivery drivers, food inspectors, and street sales. Many of these positions require sales people to meet face to face with hospitality operators weekly or more often. The sales representatives also provide information on cost cutting ideas, introduce new or improved products, and assist in menu development. It is typically the personal interaction that creates a working relationship between the hospitality industry and its vendors.

As you can see, there are many career possibilities in distribution services. The hospitality industry utilizes thousands of goods and services in daily operations. Distribution services are the backbone of the hospitality industry. Career choices and opportunities in the hospitality industry are many and expand beyond the popular segments of lodging and food and beverage. This chapter can help you answer some important career questions like what segment(s) is/are of most interest. How do I discover career opportunities? How do I plan a long-term career? Do I want to work for myself or for someone else? Do I want to work domestically or in a position elsewhere in the global hospitality industry (or both)?

Food and Beverage

Food Distribution

Food items are delivered daily to operations throughout the world. Price, quality, and quantity of food products are determined by chefs and kitchen managers each day. From the hotdog vendor at the ball game, to the fine dining restaurant, to hospitals and schools, all of these operations must purchase food products for mass production. Many food vendors seek out former restaurant managers and employees with knowledge of food products and operations to fill positions in this industry. Food distributors (also known as vendors or purveyors) supply fruits and vegetables, meats and poultry, seafood, dairy products, coffee and beverages, bread and baked goods, dry, canned, and frozen products,

and everything else needed for the food service operator.

Food product suppliers work directly with farmers, meat and poultry packaging plants, fish and seafood houses, dairies, and food processing plants. Many are small businesses that may carry a certain type of food. Dairy products and fresh baked goods and breads are normally delivered to restaurants and food service operations every day. These are sometimes considered standing orders in which the operators receive the same quantity of food products each day. Fresh produce (fruits and vegetables) distributors typically purchase products daily from a central distributor and act as an intermediary delivery directly to the food service operators for a profit. Some seafood distributors operate the same way, while many purchase large amounts of fish and butcher or fillet the fish on premise to be delivered daily. Meats and poultry are also often butchered on premise according to the food service operators' specifications. Meats and poultry products are generally delivered 3 to 4 days a week. Dry, canned, and frozen food products as well as coffee and beverages can be delivered once or twice a week.

Some food distributors carry a full line of food products including produce, meats and poultry, seafood, dairy products, coffee and beverages, bread and baked goods, dry, canned, and frozen products. Sysco, one the largest food service distributors in the United States, provides a full line of food products along with food service equipment, paper products, and cleaning supplies. Sysco also provides services to food service operators in kitchen design and cost cutting consultation. U.S. Foodservice and Sysco are two companies that employ sales representatives and are considered "total suppliers."[1] These companies supply everything from brand name products to equipment and supplies.

Many chain food service operations and multi-unit operations purchase products exclusively from system distributors. System distributors are commonly owned by the same corporations that own the chain food service operations. This allows the chain operation to control the quality and consistency of products and also enables the organization to purchase in large volume at reduced prices.

Foodservice Design

Another emerging peripheral career opportunity under the food and beverage sector of the hospitality industry is foodservice design. Because the food-

Corporate Profile
U.S. FOODSERVICE™

U.S. Foodservice™ is one of the leading broad line foodservice distributors in the United States, with yearly revenues exceeding $17 billion. The company distributes food and related products to over 250,000 customers, including independent and multi-unit restaurants, health care facilities, lodging establishments, gaming, cafeterias, schools and colleges, and government. U.S. Foodservice™ markets and distributes more than 43,000 national, private label, and signature brand items and employs more than 27,000 foodservice professionals.

Today, as the 21st century unfolds, U.S. Foodservice™

- Markets and distributes more than 43,000 national, private label, and signature brand items across America;
- Supports over 250,000 foodservice customers, including restaurants, hotels, health care facilities, cafeterias, and schools;
- Employs more than 27,000 foodservice professionals; and
- Embraces a customer base of independent and chain businesses.[2]

service industry is unique, an integral relationship exists between equipment, planning, productivity, and presentation of the final product. This relationship has the capacity to affect the interior and architectural design of the project. To provide effective services, a foodservice consultant must be prepared to participate in all aspects of the project.

Consulting firms like JEM Associates in New Jersey provide successful conceptualization and implementation of food preparation projects. They provide a full range of services from menu development through staff education, assuring a successful turn-key product for new or retrofit installation. Their clients include large and small corporate and private clients in casino resorts, schools, correctional facilities, retirement communities, health care, industrial food procession, and mass production facilities. A foodservice consultant provides services through the design and construction phases until the business is on stable footing.

Liquor Distribution

Many restaurants sell alcoholic beverages in addition to food. Wine, beer, and spirits are typically purchased on a weekly basis. From fine wines to kegs of beer the distribution of alcoholic beverages starts with the producers and ends on the guests' palates. The liquor distribution industry supplies these products to the hospitality industry. While state, county, and local laws dictate sales of alcoholic beverages, most liquor distributors operate the same way.

Liquor distribution sales representatives work closely with wine producers and distributors. A liquor sales representative typically attends wine tasting and training seminars in order to properly represent the products they sell. These sales representatives often pass along this knowledge to restaurant, club, bar, and catering operators with the hopes of getting the wines they represent included on the operations wine list. It can be a very competitive industry.

Wine pairing is another very important way liquor distributors provide a service to the hospitality industry. Many sales representatives work with restaurateurs to pair wines with food menu items. For this position a sales representative must be familiar with not only domestic and international wines, but liqueurs, beers, and spirits. This segment of the industry offers other positions in purchasing, accounting and finance, warehouse management, and marketing.

Promotions are also a big part of liquor distribution. A huge part of selling these products is getting guests to try them. Many bars and restaurants will work with sales representatives and the marketing department to promote certain alcoholic beverages on specific nights, giving away free or reduced price samples just as the food industry does in grocery stores. These promotions may also include entertainment, product logo giveaways (such as tee shirts, caps, and key chains), and interactive games.

Equipment and Supplies

All foodservice operations purchase non-food products from vendors. Everything from a broiler oven to a mop handle to paper towel rolls must be purchased for the efficient operation of a foodservice operation. This industry offers thousands of products that help operators maintain their workplaces. The equipment and supply industry works directly with foodservice operations, from supplying kitchen equipment to new businesses to providing paper and cleaning products to existing hospitality enterprises. Many suppliers also offer consulting advice in areas such as kitchen design and layout, equipment, menu design, and sanitation needs. How many juice glasses will a new restaurant with 300 seats need? How can I budget for dishwashing detergent next year? Should I purchase a conventional or convection oven? This industry provides expertise in answering these questions.

One company that specializes in providing equipment and supplies is Edward Don & Company. Edward Don & Company is a leader in foodservice equipment distribution. The company provides foodservice equipment and supplies to restaurants, government institutions, hospitals, hotels, and schools. Edward Don & Company also offers bar and fountain supplies, catering and cooking equipment, tableware, tables and chairs, paper goods, cleaning products, sanitation supplies, and 12,000 other products. The company distributes its products nationwide. Edward Don also designs and builds full-service kitchens for the foodservice industry. The company, owned by the Don family, was founded in Chicago in 1921.[3]

Another organization in the foodservice equipment industry is Restaurant Equipment World, Inc. Restaurant Equipment World, Inc. is a world leader of online restaurant equipment sales, installation, design, and export. The company owns and operates a network of 175+ product specific Websites with a database of more than 20,000 catalog items with photos. Restaurant Equipment World, Inc. has been in business for over 28 years and their site features REX—the restaurant equipment search engine.

Foodservice equipment distributors also provide products for daily use. Particularly paper goods such as take-out cups and containers, tooth picks, lobster bibs, aluminum foil, cocktail napkins, and toilet tissue, to name a few. These sales representatives also sell cleaning products including dishwashing detergent, bleach, hand soap, and degreasing products. Career opportunities in this industry include accounting/finance, administration, customer service, human resources, marketing, operations, information technology, and sales. Sales positions include management and nonmanagement positions in street sales, national accounts, and project managers for foodservice equipment division.[4]

The vast majority of distributor sales representatives earn income based on some combination of total sales collected and percent of gross margin on products sold. Like other sales position in and outside the hospitality industry, the more they sell, the more they earn. Many distributor sales representatives receive additional financial incentives if they achieve certain company goals: increasing average order sizes or sales of a particular product, maybe upping sales of private-label items. In order to create ongoing relationships with distributor sales representatives are expected to provide useful information and present products to hospitality managers while letting the managers make decisions. It is the steady long-term customers that will make distributor sales representatives successful.[5] Distributor sales representatives are generally provided a geographical area in which to sell their wares. These areas are typically referred to as territories. The sales representatives provide service to existing customers while constantly trying to acquire new customers in their territories. This is an extremely competitive industry that requires skilled professionals with impeccable personal and organizational skills. These individuals must also be self-motivated and driven. Much of their time is spent alone traveling the territory and working with technology, specifically email and cell phones, taking and placing orders to meet daily deadlines.

Linens

With the demand for upscale services growing at a rapid pace the purchasing, receiving, issuing, storing, and cleaning of linens, towels, tablecloths, and uniforms has become an intricate component of creating a favorable guest experience. Linen, ranging from very luxurious to normal, is used by various hospitality operations depending upon their requirements. In addition to purchasing laundry, hospitality operations have several choices when it comes to how they handle the laundry as well. Many peripheral industries are related to the rental and cleaning of hospitality laundry. Guestrooms, restaurants, banquets, fitness centers, and employees all create soiled linens, towels, tablecloths, and uniforms. Although many lodging properties in the United States operate an on-premise laundry, many others have their laundry cleaned and processed by outside contractors. Linen is a very important part of a hotel's image. Lodging customers measure quality as the sum of many little things, all of which are important.

Career opportunities in this peripheral hospitality segment of the industry could include working

Company Profile
AC LINEN

Located in the heart of "Always Turned On" Atlantic City, AC Linen is the current name of a laundry operation that has been around since the late 1890s. This facility now does some work for each of the city's 12 gaming halls in the Atlantic City casino properties. It is one of the largest commercial laundries on the Eastern seaboard. The ACLS also operations state of the art laundries in Norwich, Connecticut.

In addition, Atlantic City Linen Services (ACLS) Management Group consults other commercial plants and various industries (hotel chains, health care facilities, etc.) on design and operation of laundry facilities.

This operation is housed in a 14 million, 63,000 square foot complex that is energy efficient, computerized, and fully automated. As the casino gaming and nongaming hospitality industry continues to grow in the Atlantic City region, AC Linen plans on continued growth to service the marketplace.

AC Linen washes and dries about 100,000 pounds of laundry each day and its daily load includes about 25,000 sheets and 30,000 bath towels. Laundry is processed around the clock guaranteeing a 1 day turnaround for the casino hotels. The facility is open 24 hours a day, 7 days a week.

The current facility operates at about 40–50 percent of its capacity and the company has the ability to add more washers and dryers as its customer base grows. The company employs more than 200 workers and boasts annual revenues of $12 million.

for a company that sells apparel and uniforms, restaurant and foodservice related linens, lodging and bathroom related linens, or an off premise laundry company.

Furniture, Fixtures, and Equipment (FF&E)

Purchasing furnishings, supplies, and equipment is a function that can be performed by a corporate level purchasing department, a purchasing manager or agent at a hotel, or performed by a third party purchasing agent. The Internet has made the job of purchasing easier and faster but someone or some team must still ensure that the materials purchased are the right quality and quantity. In hospitality, there are three distinct types of purchasing. Two areas—operating supplies and disposables and food and beverage items—are purchases that can be performed through computerized programs. Purchasing these standardized products is migrating toward business-to-business Internet purchasing. Purchasing furniture, fixtures, and equipment requires a different process. Since almost every item is nonstandard or custom-made, cost-effective FF&E purchasing demands professionals who fully comprehend the variables and use expertise to create the best value.

There are other intangibles that a purchasing professional addresses. Verifying that the manufacturer has liability insurance can save the hotel owner millions of dollars in potential liability claims. Coordinating time and routing of freight by balancing cost, construction and installation schedules, and packaging can save money. Purchasing is an administrative function requiring technical knowledge about the products being purchased and the market dynamics that affect prices and supply.[6] A career in purchasing food and beverage for a hotel or restaurant would require some experience in food production and management as well as knowledge of how a kitchen operates. Keeping aware of market trends and new products is also important. Knowledge of grading criteria, labeling, and standards of quality is also important. A purchasing agent is required to judge if a fair price is being quoted by a distributor and match orders to purchase specifications. Learning how to deal effectively with suppli-

Purchasing requires technical knowledge of products and market dynamics that affect prices and supply.

© 2008, JupiterImages Corporation.

ers and master the managerial aspects of purchasing is necessary if you are interested in a career in the purchasing department of hospitality company. A skilled purchasing agent knows how innovative purchasing techniques can contribute to profits, efficient operations, and guest satisfaction.

The FF&E industries that students can consider include audiovisual and entertainment equipment, exercise equipment, badges, foodservice and preparation equipment, banquet equipment, bar equipment, electronic message displays, flooring supplies, luggage carts, housekeeping carts, guestroom case goods, chinaware, cleaners, decorative accessories, energy conservation equipment, Internet services, key control systems, maintenance equipment, safety products, vending machines, and much more.

Technology

The hospitality industry utilizes many systems and technologies in order to serve guests more efficiently and effectively. Information technology helps hospitality businesses reach their goals of delivering exceptional guest satisfaction. Hospitality information technology can range from computers and hardware to telephone systems and software. Hospitality industry technology systems range from electronic mail to global or international information systems, hotel information technology systems, energy management systems, call accounting systems, guest reservation systems, security systems, sales and marketing systems, and restaurant and foodservice information technology systems. More emerging technological trends being utilized by the hospitality industry is applicant tracking systems, key control, and yield management software. This automation helps make hospitality operations as efficient as possible while enhancing the guest's experience.

The links between point of sale (POS), property management (PMS), inventory and purchasing, sales and catering (S&C), and business intelligence (BI) systems are both tighter and more flexible. The PMS is the center of information processing in a hotel. It is a computer-based lodging information system that connects both the front of the house and back of the house activities. Computerized property management systems can simplify check in, track the status of rooms, and manage guest accounts. The PMS can also interface with electronic locking sys-

tems, energy management systems, and call accounting systems. The POS systems are computerized systems used to track food and beverage and other retail charges that may occur in a hospitality facility. The POS can provide software for food/beverage management, inventory control, labor tasks, and time and attendance. The POS equipment can include time clocks, hand-held terminals, and credit card authorization/settlement readers. As technology becomes less of a limiting factor, the challenge is relying on hospitality managers to make the best use of these tools for a more effective operation.

If you have an interest in a career in technology in the hospitality industry there are a number of jobs that are available in implementation of systems, product development, and web design. Companies that specialize in hospitality technology are generally looking for those candidates that have hospitality industry experience and a background or training in technology. Some companies specializing in sales and service of property management systems look for a hospitality and/or computer support background, knowledge of computers by training clients, troubleshooting/resolving problems, and team work skills. Two sample jobs are:

Corporate Trainer

This job requires a self-motivated individual with hotel management experience. This job also includes travel all over the country, meeting new people, and seeing new sites.

Client Support Representative

This job requires prior hotel experience and working with people and providing help.

Jobs that are available in companies that specialize in sales and service of point of sales systems are Administration, Customer Service, Database Administration, Implementation Specialist, Product Specialist, Service Technicians, Research and Development, Sales and Marketing, and Software Development. Many of the qualifications include prior experience with installation or support of POS/PMS or computer software and hardware and customer service. Additional skills include excellent verbal and written communication skills and excellent customer service skills.

Another category of peripheral hospitality careers are professionals that do nothing but design, promote, and manage exhibits and trade shows.

Professional Profile
DAVID KASINETZ

"I would not have the success I have today if it were not for my restaurant management background."

David Kasinetz is a Sales Manager for Advanced Hospitality Systems. He first worked for Darden Restaurants as a manager for Red Lobster upon completing his Bachelor of Science degree in Hotel and Restaurant Management from Widener University. David also studied Business Administration at The Pennsylvania State University. After several years he went to work for Pepperidge Tree Restaurants in Philadelphia. As technological changes began to occur in the restaurant industry, David followed his long time interest in computers and made a career change to Comtrex Systems Corporation as a sales consultant. David excelled in selling point of sales (POS) systems to food and beverage establishments. He left Comtrex for Advanced Hospitality Systems in 1997 where he has continued to be on the forefront of food and beverage technology. David admits, "I would not have the success I have today if it were not for my restaurant management background." His experience gives him the unique ability to work with clients on issues and concerns adapting and customizing POS systems for food and beverage operations. Mr. Kasinetz says his daily activities involve traveling, attending trade shows, conducting software demonstrations, preparing return on investments analyses, hiring, training, and managing a sales and administrative staff, and creating innovative marketing materials.

Required Skills—Excellent Communication Skills, Enjoy Public Speaking, Computer Skills, MS Office Applications, must be a great listener, salesmanship.

Required Knowledge—Understanding of Hotel and Restaurant Operations, Basic Computer Networking Concepts.

Highlights of Job—I enjoy travel and attending trade shows and every day meeting new and interesting people and helping them increase their profits.

Recommendations—Most high paying sales jobs are commission based. Do not expect to have great success immediately. It takes a few years to build a pipeline of prospects, but eventually you will reap the rewards. Learn as much as you can while working in operations. Pay attention to food and beverage cost/labor cost, be detail oriented, and enjoy the hard work. Restaurant management will prepare you for different opportunities down the road. It's invaluable experience.

Trade shows and expositions can be held in hotels, convention centers, or larger public venues. They are usually sponsored by companies or associations and can be public, professional, or retail oriented. Two of the most popular in the United States are The International Hotel/Motel & Restaurant Show and The National Restaurant Association Hotel Motel Show. The International Hotel/Motel & Restaurant Show, the world's largest showcase and exchange of industry products, trends, and developments, attracts every segment and facet of the industry. This show unveils more than 1,250 products and services and draws more than 35,000 attendees each year.[7] The International Hotel/Motel & Restaurant Show also highlights the many peripheral career opportunities that are available in the hospitality industry. It just takes one glance through the show directory to realize just how many peripheral industries it takes to support and supply the hospitality industry.

The annual National Restaurant Association Restaurant, Hotel-Motel Show is the largest single gathering of restaurant, foodservice, and lodging professionals in North and South America. As the industry's premier business venue, it offers attendees the best opportunities of the year for networking and exploring new trends, as well as insight on myriad industry issues via seminars and special events.[8] Professional exhibitors and designers belong to an organization called the Trade Show Exhibitors Association (TSEA). This association acts as the industry voice for exhibit and event marketing professionals. For over 30 years, TSEA has provided knowledge to marketing and management profes-

The beer industry has become extremely competitive within the past few years.

sionals who use exhibits to promote and sell their products, as well as to those who supply them with products and service.[9] Additional careers in this field include tradeshow marketing, tradeshow sales, and meetings and exhibits coordinator.

Trends in Distribution Services

When working as part of the distribution systems industry, it is important that professionals stay abreast of the many trends that impact the hospitality industry. The following trends will no doubt impact hospitality operations in the near future.

More than half the nation's restaurants and bars are now smoke-free by law, and as many as 70% are estimated to be that way by the year's end.[10] These laws are passing whether restaurants and bars want them to or not. The best course of action is to become actively involved in the legislative process so that all businesses in the industry are treated equally, and implementation and enforcement is reasonable. Students studying hospitality management should be aware of their local and national associations that take part in the legislative processes that will impact their business and industry. Membership and involvement in organizations like the National Restaurant Association and the American Hotel and Lodging Associations help keep you on top of public policy and legal matters that affect the hospitality industry. National issues in the hospitality industry include ADA, minimum wage, terrorism risk insurance, credit card acceptance, food safety, immigration reform, and the smoking ban.

In 2005 the New York City health department began a campaign against transfats. Restaurant inspectors determined that 30% of the city's 30,000 eateries used oils that contained transfats which has been linked to cholesterol problems and increased risk of heart disease. This campaign could develop in foodservice industry changes across the United States, much in the same way no-smoking bans are changing the industry through legislation.

Menu trends will include an increase in ethnic cuisines such as Thai, Mexican, and Caribbean. There will also be an emphasis in displaying ingredients such as whole grains, antioxidants, and other healthful aspects of food. Antioxidant-rich white tea will become an ingredient in many desserts, while other desserts will be based on single-origin chocolates from Ecuador, Venezuela, and Madagascar. Exotic tropical fruits will also be prominently featured on many menus.

Restaurant patrons wish to become more educated while dining out. This will require menus to include more information about nutritional content, origins of food products, and unique and innovative ingredients.[11]

Some restaurant operations, including Subway, are experimenting with more "eco" friendly stores. This includes adding recycling bins, utilizing recycled paper goods, and switching to cutlery and plastic drinking cups made of polypropylene instead of polystyrene, which uses less oil in its production. Subway estimates that that change alone will save 13,000 barrels of oil annually.[12]

The beer industry has changed in the past few years as new products and market placement have become extremely competitive within the industry. The beer industry markets their products directly against their competitors. Many producers have also expanded their product lines by creating products to increase the market of beer drinkers such as low carbohydrate beer, low alcohol and no alcohol beers, flavored beers, and alcoholic ciders, lemonade, and iced teas known as "hard" beverages. Imported beers have always been popular in the United States; today many of the most popular imported beers have increased their television marketing. Microbreweries have also become more prominent and appealing to the market as an upscale beverage as compared to the mass production breweries, taking marketshares away from the large breweries. One mass producer of beer is attempting to emphasize beer's social value by marketing the art of the brewing process, and the selection and use of natural ingredients much as wine makers do.[13]

The National Restaurant Association announced award winning kitchen innovations in 2006 including the MooBella Ice Cream System. A new creation that utilizes the space of a typical vending machine and produces real ice cream in 96 varieties, made to order in 45 seconds, as well as a refrigerator that improves food safety management by combining a thermometer and a programmable timer that emits a 70 decibel alarm when the current temperature of the food drops below 41°F/°C or time expires. The timer retains data for proof of HACCP compliance.[14]

Keeping abreast of trends in Hospitality Information Technology is important for managers and businesses in order to stay competitive and in order to deliver the best service product possible. For example, signature capture is more common, but mostly in cashier-desk operations (where the guest can sign on a small counter-top unit) and in hand-held terminal environments. It's becoming more common to have F&B and retail operations on the same POS software, especially for casinos and sports stadiums. This more accurately reflects the wide-ranging nature of guests' transactions at these locations, requires fewer different systems to buy and manage, and makes it easier to transfer staff and stock between outlets.[15]

iConnect employs thin technology, desktop applications, a 15-inch flat screen monitor, multi-media sound, and a full-size mouse and keyboard making it familiar and easy to use. Guests can surf the Internet and access email accounts, but there are plenty of mind-blowing benefits as well. Installed in all 1,406 guestrooms, Gaylord Palms Resort & Convention Center, located near Walt Disney World theme parks in Kissimmee, Florida, is the first to offer this complimentary technology. With a click of a mouse, guests can send requests for fluffy pillows, arrange for valet services, peruse restaurant menus, or send an intra-hotel message 24/7. Technologically delivered services are not a value added amenity but a necessary attribute of today's core hotel product.[16]

Summary

From this brief summary, you can see that the distribution services industry is a vast network of companies that offer services and product that keep lodging, restaurants, and attractions profitable and efficiently running. As an aspiring hospitality management professional, it is critical that you understand and appreciate the role that the distribution services industry plays in the big picture of the hospitality industry.

≈ Resources

Internet Sites

www.usfoodservice.com
www.don.com
www.ihmrs.com
www.aclinen.com
www.apics.org
www.restaurant.org
www.tsea.org
www.posamerica.com

References

JEM Associates at http://www.jemassociates.com
Mcyntyre, P. (2007). Industry should clean the air, reconsider its opposition to smoking ban legislation at http://www.nrn.com/article.aspx?id=346564

≈ Endnotes

1. Pavesic, D. V., and Magnant, P. F. (2005). *Fundamental Principles of Restaurant Cost Control.* Upper Saddle River, NJ: Pearson Prentice Hall.
2. U.S. Foodservice at http://www.usfoodservice.com/html/index.html
3. Edward, D. at http://hoovers.com/Edward-don/--ID_44487--/free-co-factsheet.xhtml
4. Edward, D. at http://www.don.com/aboutdon/joblistings.aspx
5. Restaurant Biz at http://restaurantbiz.com/index.php?option=com_content&tast=view&id=13282&itemid=93

6. Pavesic, D. V., and Magnant, P. F. (2005). *Fundamental Principles of Restaurant Cost Control.* Upper Saddle River, NJ: Pearson Prentice Hall.
7. International Hotel and Motel Show at http://www.ihmrs.com/content/home.htm
8. National Restaurant Association at http://www.restaurant.org/show
9. Trade Show Exhibitors Association at http://www.tsea.org/page_1.php
10. *Nation's Restaurant News,* 2007.
11. *Sun Times* at http://www.suntimes.com/output/news/cst-nws-eattrends16.html
12. *Wall Street Journal* at http://online.wsj.com/article/SB119560391050099871.html?mod=dist_smartbrief&mod=dist_smartbrief
13. Wharton School of Business http://knowledge.wharton.upenn.edu/article/1363.cfm
14. National Restaurant Association at http://www.restaurant.org/show
15. Inge, J. (2005). Technology Trends in F&B Refining the Recipe at http://www.joninge.com/art_recipe.pdf
16. Angelucci, P. (2005). How Can I Serve You? The Delicate Balance of Hotel Staff and Technology Working Together at http://www.hospitalityupgrade.com/hospitality/client/hu/articles.Nsf/77b53cfa89355b148525688c00608311/30fc24a37ebc03278525703600690a29?OpenDocument

≈ *Contributors*

Michael Scales, Ed.D., is currently an Associate Professor at The Richard Stockton College of New Jersey in the Hospitality Tourism Management Program. Prior to joining the college he had worked in the Hospitality Industry for over 20 years. Michael worked for Embassy Suites, Boca Raton; and Doubletree Hotel, Fort Lauderdale, Florida; the DuPont Country Club in Wilmington, Delaware; Solitude Ski Resort in Salt Lake City, Utah; and has been involved in opening new food and beverage operations in Key West, Florida; Philadelphia, Pennsylvania; and several towns along the New Jersey shoreline.

Donna Albano, Ed.D., is currently an Associate Professor of Hospitality and Tourism Management Studies at The Richard Stockton College in Pomona, NJ. She joined the Stockton Hospitality Management Program in the fall of 2003. Prior to joining Stockton, Donna taught at Atlantic Cape Community College in 1993 as an Adjunct Faculty member and held that position for 3 years before being promoted to Full Time Faculty in 1996. Prior to being an educator, Donna worked in the Hospitality Industry for 15 years with experience in food and beverage operations, franchise operations, and casino hotel operations.

Chapter 30
Review Questions

1. How would you define distribution services in the hospitality industry?

2. What is meant by "peripheral career opportunities"?

3. Liquor distribution includes beer, wine, and _____.

4. What is wine pairing?

5. Edward Don & Company is a leader in what industry?

6. Why are breweries adding new products such as low carbohydrate beer, nonalcohol beer, and hard cider?

7. With restaurant patrons wishing to be more educated during their dining experiences, restaurants will be pressured to provide menus offering information about _____, _____, and _____.

8. Equipment distributors play a role in the daily operations of food service operations. True or False?

9. What is the career opportunities outlined in this chapter?

10. What are some trends that will impact hospitality operations?

Meetings and Events Industry

31

B.J. Reed, University of Wisconsin—Platteville

© 2008, JupiterImages Corporation.

≈ Learning Objectives

☑ Describe the meetings and events industry
☑ Identify key industry-related terms, phrases, and acronyms
☑ List the most common hosts and venues for meetings and events
☑ Specify common services and supplies for meetings and events
☑ Discuss the economic impact of meetings and events
☑ Explore some of the support groups for meeting and event planners

≈ Chapter Outline

Overview of the Meetings and Events Industry
Types of Meetings and Events

≈ Key Terms

APEX
ASAE
ABC
Celebration(s)
CMP
CIC
Conference(s)
CSM
Convention(s)
Destination
DMAI
Exposition(s)
Exhibition(s)
Event(s)
ESG
FAM trip(s)
IAEE (formerly IAEM)
ISES

Meeting management
Meeting planning
MPI
Meeting(s)
PCMA
RCMA
RFP
Site
Site inspection(s)
Site selection
SGMP
Special event(s)
Sport(s) event(s)
Tradeshow(s)
Venue
Virtual conferencing
Virtual meeting(s)

Overview of the Meetings and Events Industry

*P*eople appear to have an intrinsic need for interaction. This need, whether expressed for survival or for entertainment, has been the underlying foundation of an industry that is so common, it is often overlooked as an actual industry. George Fenich, a respected author and hospitality educator, explains that while meetings and events have been part of people's lives throughout recorded history, ". . . the government did not even list 'meeting planner' as a recognized profession [in the Standard Industry Classification codes] until the late 1980s."[1] However, the meetings and events industry satisfies the basic need for human interaction and has become a leading facet of economies throughout the world. Defining and describing the meetings and events industry, though, has proven to be quite difficult.

The meetings and events industry is very complex. Numerous professional organizations exist to organize and promote various functions within the meetings and events industry; in fact, the Convention Industry Council (CIC), which is made up of representatives of many of these organizations, currently consists of 32 organizational members, representing more than 100,000 individuals.[2] The CIC membership list isn't an exhaustive list of industry-specific organizations, but it does provide a glimpse of the industry's complexity.

The meetings and events industry tends to be defined in terms of two "sides": meeting planners and meeting suppliers. The planning side consists of numerous organizations (associations, corporations, and government agencies throughout the world) and the people who make meetings and events happen. The supply side consists of many more organizations that provide products, services, or ideas for meeting and event planners. The division of planners and suppliers is a false dichotomy in that some suppliers are also planners. Some organizations provide services for meetings and events, while hosting their own meetings and events. Some venues (convention centers, for instance) provide in-house meeting planning services for their customers, the hosts of meetings held in their facilities. Who is the planner and who is the supplier? The division is not clear in many cases. The approach to two sides within the industry, though, has been a foundational concept in the industry and has led to membership categories within such organizations as

Meeting Professionals International (MPI). The following membership categories were updated by MPI in 2006: corporate meeting professional, association/nonprofit meeting professional, government meeting professional, supplier meeting professional, and meeting management professional. In addition, MPI states, ". . . we remain committed to maintaining our philosophy of a 50/50 balance between our planner and supplier members."[3]

Of course, another "side" exists within the meetings and events industry: attendees. Without the people who attend our meetings and events, the industry would become bankrupt. The most common objective for a meeting or event is to reach an established number of attendees. Meetings and events may be open to the public, or exclusive to employees or members, and may be used to reach potential members, employees, and other support groups.

Types of Meetings and Events

Meetings and events can be categorized by types; however, the definitions of terms used to categorize meetings and events vary throughout the industry. The Convention Industry Council has attempted to clarify industry terminology through an initiative known as the "Accepted Practices Exchange," or APEX. This initiative, begun in the 1990s, provides an online glossary of terms and phrases, as well as other benefits.[4] Since many professionals in the industry do not join professional development organizations, like MPI, and since only some of the professional development organizations in the industry are members of CIC, the definitions and phrases proposed by APEX are not used by every practitioner in the meetings industry. Generally, though, meetings and events consist of the following types: meetings, conferences, conventions, tradeshows, special events, sport-related events, celebrations, and other types.

As a general term, "meeting" includes virtually any occasion when two or more people get together in a particular spot, at the same time. Some meetings are held to conduct business; some are held to perform a specified, social ritual; some meetings are held to provide training or educational opportunities; while others may be held to raise funds for a cause. With current technology, the term "meeting" has expanded to include those occasions when two or more people meet synchronously, while being in different locations; we usually refer to these as "virtual meetings." This has given rise to software and a process known as "virtual conferencing." Meetings may be held in a variety of venues, as well. They are held indoors and out, in any country, on the seas, and in the air. Meetings cannot be defined in terms of duration, as they may last minutes, hours, or days. Meetings cannot be defined in terms of frequency or how often they happen. "Meeting" is defined in the APEX glossary as, "An event where the primary activity of the attendees is to attend educational sessions, participate in meetings/discussions, socialize, or attend other organized events. There is no exhibit component to this event."[5]

While the APEX glossary uses a very broad definition, in common usage, "events" are usually held for entertainment purposes. They may provide a variety of activities and could include educational opportunities, although that is less common. Events that are held for special occasions, rather than being held on a regular, often annual basis, are known as "special events." Events may be hours, days, or even weeks in duration. Events tend to be very large, often much larger than meetings, but the attendees come for various lengths of time (rather than attending the event from beginning to end). Large events often utilize multiple venues, and may include more than one city. A presidential inauguration is a special event, while a city festival is an annual event. A wedding is an event with a specific purpose (a ceremony) and a sporting event also has a specific, though quite different, purpose. Some sporting events, though, offer multiple sports, such as the Olympics. Many events charge admission fees to help cover expenses, while others, like weddings, are offered free to all participants with expenses being covered by the host.

"Conventions" are a specific kind of meeting. In this case, the meeting is typically held for many people, at one site, for a specific length of time (usually more than 1 day), and the meeting has at least two components. The first necessary component is the meeting, where business is conducted and/or educational opportunities are provided. The second component is a tradeshow or exposition, where several exhibitors provide samples of their service or products and may sell that product (although, selling is not a requirement) and the show is open only to convention attendees.[6] When the second component is provided to sell products on site, the component is known as a "tradeshow." When the second component is set up to provide information and samples of the product, particularly in business-to-business marketing, the component is often known as an "exhibition." This second component may stand alone—where no business meeting or educational opportunity is provided. In that case, the term used is "exposition." However, other definitions for exhibition, exposition, and tradeshow can be found throughout the industry.

When a meeting is used to conduct business and to provide educational opportunities, but no exhibition or tradeshow is available, that meeting is often known as a "conference." Conferences may be held for a single day or multiple days, but generally are held at one specific venue. They may be annual, periodic, or convened once for a specific purpose. "Virtual conferencing" is held online, typically using dedicated software and a phone line so that all members can hear speakers and they may be able to join in open conversations with other participants.

As these definitions indicate, meetings and events are elusive occurrences that defy easy description. To explore the meetings and events industry, we look beyond types or categories and examine who hosts the meeting or event, where the meeting or event is held, what services must be utilized for a successful meeting or event, what supplies must be utilized for the meeting or event, how these factors (hosts, venues, services, and supplies) are coordinated, and the economic impact of the meeting or event.

Hosts for Meetings and Events

Meetings and events are held for many reasons and by many hosts. These hosts include several types of organizations, but the most commonly identified hosts are associations, corporations, government agencies, and religious organizations.

Associations are formed for specific purposes and are not focused on profit. In the United States, this not-for-profit distinction is the basis for incorporation and allows the association to avoid paying income taxes on funds received as a part of doing business. Associations can be organized as charities, fraternal groups, or for a common interest. Besides satisfying the mission statement, bringing members together to explore and discuss their mutual interests is a common goal of associations. They hold board meetings, special interest group meetings, and annual meetings for the benefit of members and to attract new members. Many associations hold meetings or events that must make a profit; that profit is used to support the association's activities. Associations may hold meetings in the city where the association is headquartered, especially when the membership of the organization tends to be local, or their meetings may be on foreign soil, when the membership of the organization is international.

Corporations hold numerous meetings for employees, customers, and independent sales representatives. While many corporate meetings are smaller than their association counterparts, some corporate events are open to the public and may involve thousands of attendees. Corporations are organized for profit, but their meetings are rarely held for that purpose. Corporate meetings and events tend to promote products, services, or ideas and increase employee motivation and productivity. Corporations are increasingly international and so are their meetings.

Government agencies host numerous meetings and events, from training sessions for firefighters to public school festivals. Government agencies may have meetings specifically for their employees, but also host events that attract the public they serve. While government meetings and events tend to have limited budgets and a tightly focused purpose, some government meetings, like a presidential inauguration and ball, are elaborate affairs with international interest.

Religious organizations also have meetings and events, and some of these events are among the largest held anywhere in the world. Often, religious organizations can hold their meetings or events on properties held by the organization. When the organization, though, holds a general assembly for members of the organization, they may need numerous facilities across a destination; these are often called "city-wide" events. These meetings and events may be open to the general public, but are usually held for the purpose of developing strong relationships between the organization's members. Fundraising and member recruitment are also incentives for many religious meetings and events.

Many other organizations hold meetings, including military organizations (such as reunions of sailors who served on a specific ship within a certain timeframe), fraternal organizations, families, schools (such as high school reunions), and former employees. These groups tend to be so loosely organized, they are hard to define and to locate. They may not meet on a regular basis and get together only once every 5 or 10 years. Determining the size of these groups, the number of meetings and events they hold, and assessing their economic impact is impossible.

Venues of Meetings and Events

Meetings and events can be held on land or sea, or even in a well-equipped air carrier. They can be held indoors or out, in a matter of hours, or over several days. The location for meetings and events can be a park or within a complex of several buildings designed to host meetings and events. The most common venues for meetings and events are hotels, convention centers, and conference centers. Hotels have an advantage for meetings and events in that they provide sleeping accommodations as well as meeting space. They might also provide food and beverage services, shopping options, and entertainment. Convention centers may have attached hotels, but the main function of a convention center is to provide space for meetings that need large areas for tradeshows or expositions. They may need a ballroom, a dining hall, or an art exhibit area. Convention centers tend to have extremely versatile space that can be converted from a large, open room with 20,000 to 100,000 square feet of uninterrupted floor space, to several rooms separated by partitions or temporary walls. Convention centers generally have food and beverage service and may offer other amenities such as ushers, decorating services, and dedicated registration facilities. Providing state-of-the art communication technologies, such as wireless services throughout the facility, are also common in convention centers.

Conference centers are built to cater directly to corporate and association hosts who hold conferences for employees or members. These conferences may last hours or days, may be held for 15 or 1500 attendees, and may be planned weeks or years ahead. What they have in common is that the meeting takes place indoors, requires space with meeting-appropriate furniture (tables and chairs), and utilizes services involving audio/visual and other communication technologies. Conference centers tend to be very well equipped with the latest in computer, projection, and similar services. Hotels are typically conveniently located nearby, and the destination may have other attractions. Since the focus is on meeting, though, conference centers may not be located close to tourist venues.

Other facilities exist, of course. Meetings and events can be held on cruise ships, in parks, in historical sites, within corporate sites, at university and college campuses, and at facilities owned by religious organizations. These facilities usually have been built for customers other than meetings and events. They also tend to offer fewer options for services and supplies than dedicated convention and conference centers.

Services for Meetings and Events

In the process of setting up a meeting or event at a destination, the meeting host often contacts the locale's marketing representative. This person may work for the chamber of commerce, a convention and visitor's bureau, or a government agency in that area. These contacts are collectively known as destination marketing organizations (DMO) and they have a professional development organization known as Destination Marketing Associations International (DMAI). As representatives of their local hospitality industry, DMOs can provide information about hotels, convention and conference centers, restaurants, entertainment, speakers, tourism attractions, shopping, and other amenities in the area. They may represent only members of the DMO, but many represent the entire hospitality industry in that city, county, region, or state.

A destination management company (DMC) is usually a corporation established to help a distant host organization plan a meeting or event in the DMC's area. A contract is established between the DMC and the host of the meeting or event. As an independent contractor, the DMC is able to select services and suppliers from the local area on behalf of the host organization. While the DMC must know the area thoroughly, they are more flexible than the DMO in selecting sites, services, and suppliers in the area.

Most common venues (hotels and convention and conference centers) offer conference and convention planning services in the form of selecting, arranging, and monitoring services on site. The hotel's conference planner, though, rarely represents the convention center, and the conference center's planning services cannot represent the nearby restaurant. A disconnect would exist without the services of a DMC, unless the host organization keeps all planning duties "in-house" (the host organization's employees manage all of these details). Independent meeting or event planners may be utilized. Unlike a DMC, which is usually associated with a specific destination, an independent planner can help coordinate details at meetings and events held anywhere. An independent event planner located in a small town in southwest Wisconsin, for instance, plans special events in other states and cities like Los Angeles, Las Vegas, and Louisville. This independent planner might subcontract with a DMC in one of these locations. The independent planner develops a contract for services to be provided and is paid by the host organization.

Some services, such as volunteer recruitment and management, might be provided by the local DMO or DMC. Registration services can be provided by suppliers skilled in this function and will include online marketing materials, registration databases, online payments, on-site registration handling, and reports provided before, during, and after the meeting or event. Other services provided for meetings and events typically fall under the broader category known as "suppliers."

Supplies for Meetings and Events

In *Professional Event Coordination*, author Julia Rutherford Silvers wrote about the "six dimensions of an event experience."[7] These dimensions include marketing materials, transportation, the event's atmosphere, food and beverages, entertainment, and amenities. These six dimensions cover the main supply areas for meetings and events; we can also add one more category: technologies (audio and visual).

Marketing materials for meetings and events might include:

- brochures, fliers, and posters
- advertising (print and broadcast)
- Websites

Independent event planners can coordinate details of meetings and events held anywhere.

© 2008, JupiterImages Corporation.

- specialty items (name tags, t-shirts, wristbands, hats, bags, and many other items with printed logos)

Transportation providers include the following options:

- airlines (to provide transportation to and from the destination)
- established, local limousines, buses, and taxis (to provide transportation at the destination, to and from the airport, hotel, convention or conference center, and other venues)
- charter limousines, buses, planes, and ships/boats
- rental car agencies

Suppliers who have influence on the event's atmosphere might include a combination of the following options:

- venues (who may provide limited decorations)
- decorating companies (who may coordinate all atmosphere-related suppliers)
- florists
- audio/visual (A/V) companies
- artists

Food and beverages may be provided by the venue, but might also be provided by restaurants, caterers, and other licensed providers. Organizations may be tempted to provide their own food and beverages, but this task is subject to so many regulations and safety concerns that leaving it to experts is advisable. Besides providing nutritious, economical, and custom-based options, the food and beverages provider can influence the event's atmosphere.

For many meetings, the area of entertainment should include speakers (who might provide motivation, information, and education, as well as entertainment). Entertainment could also include area attractions or activities brought on-site by mobile providers, such as a carnival provider.

A/V supplies may be available in-house, as most meeting venues are equipped with basic projection and audio equipment, as well as some computers. However, communication technologies are evolving and facilities built 5 or more years ago may not be set up for emerging systems. Wireless capabilities are common, but aren't available at every facility. Over 200,000 cell phones are in use in the

U.S., but some destinations have unreliable connectivity, particularly in rural, ocean, and mountain settings. Elaborate meetings, like the annual meetings held by Meeting Professionals International and the Professional Convention Management Association, are dependent upon a world-class A/V provider. These events must have Internet connections, cutting-edge projection equipment, technology centers for speakers and attendees, in-house radios and temporary cell phones for staff members, as well as many other A/V options.

Coordinating Hosts, Venues, Services, and Supplies

In the June 2007 issue of *Convene* magazine, published by the Professional Convention Management Association, respondents indicated that meeting planners earned slightly more than $40,000 annually, while managers earned more than $56,000.[8] What are these meeting managers and planners doing to earn those salaries? Besides coordinating the efforts of a planning team, meeting and event planners are responsible for details. They develop the meeting or event specifications guide (ESG), which includes all of the details that collectively result in the successful meeting or event. The Convention Industry Council, through their APEX initiative, created a template for the ESG. This template can be found at http://www.conventionindustry.org/apex.

When the purpose, goals, objectives, and other preliminary details are in place, the meeting planner is instrumental in site selection, where the potential destination for the meeting or event is determined. This may be a foregone conclusion for meetings that can be held at facilities owned or managed by the host. When the destination, though, is more flexible, the meeting planner typically develops a document known as the "request for proposals" (RFP). This document specifies critical needs and wants for the meeting host, including projected purpose, goals, projected attendance figures, an agenda, hotel, dining, and other requirements for the meeting or event. The RFP is sent either to a DMO, a DMC, or directly to potential venues. The venues, DMC, and DMO respond with proposals, including projected costs and options for added value.

RFPs can be very specific and will include requirements, as well as preferences, that help the selection committee (or meeting planner) make an informed decision on where to hold the meeting or event. In an effort to select the best site for a meeting or event, planners provide RFPs that provide enough information to solicit detailed and thorough proposals. In *Convene* magazine, published by PCMA, Michelle Russell described a recent addition to RFPs from a government agency: "The U.S. Environmental Protection Agency (EPA) has given its procurement staff a list of questions that, as of last month, they must now ask hotels and convention centers that are bidding for EPA business. The questions run the gamut from recycling programs and energy efficiency to paperless billing and reused towels. Answers [in the proposals received] will be considered when evaluating bids."[9]

During the planning cycle, planners will often conduct site inspections. The site inspection may be held on an individual basis or may be conducted during a "FAM trip," an acronym for familiarization trip, where a destination showcases their facilities. FAM trips are often offered with all-expenses paid incentive, usually by the DMO, but some do not include transportation to and from the destination. Using FAM trips to conduct site inspections help control costs for the host organization. The timing, though, may not be ideal, so independent site inspections are common. During the site inspection, a meeting planner will determine where specific elements of the meeting can be held at the venue and which venues at this destination will be utilized.

Once the specific venues are selected, the meeting planner develops contracts with the selected facilities. In a classic text on hotel law, author Jack Jeffries wrote, "For many years, convention agreements were arrived at primarily by a handshake between the convention manager and the hotel manager. Because convention planning has become more difficult and complex over the years, the parties have now grown more accustomed to setting forth their understandings and agreements in written contract form."[10] While this was published 25 years ago, the words still have meaning for today's meeting and event planners. Since Jeffries described contract law, meeting and event planning, as well as the contracts that serve them, have continued to become more complex and difficult to execute successfully. Meeting planners need to be well informed about contract law and local regulations that may affect their meetings.

Planning a meeting or event may take only days, but frequently takes years. Associations tend to begin planning their annual events 5 or more years in advance. This long planning time requires a well-executed and written contract. Corporations tend to rely on months or weeks for planning corporate meetings, but contracts are still necessary. The meeting planner rarely works alone and may be responsible for coordinating the efforts of numerous contracts, and several committees who review those contracts, across various aspects of the meeting or event. The committees may be located in various international sites, as well, complicating the communication process and planning timeline.

The planner's task includes on-site management of the meeting or event, as well as personnel management. In addition, the planner is responsible for evaluation of the meeting or event and conducting all follow-up measures, such as financial management and contract review, acknowledging services rendered, and submitting reports and analyses to upper management.

Economic Impact of Meetings and Events

The economic impact of meetings and events is an elusive figure. As quickly as the information can be accumulated and published, the information is out of date. Many organizations have attempted to quantify the industry, but with ill-defined terms and roles, the industry remains difficult to describe with concrete figures and statistics. The impact though, is determined on the basis of expenditures by the following meeting or event stakeholders:

- hosts
- attendees and their guests
- service and supply providers

Besides the professional and psychological impact of a successful meeting or event on the stakeholders, the generated revenues from a specific meeting or event provide a positive economic impact on many entities, including the following:

- the venue(s)
- the destination's hospitality industry
- the host organization
- the supplier(s) outside the destination
- the attendees

Costs are associated with the meetings and events industry. These costs are difficult to track, and may be even more difficult to quantify. Some convention and conference centers are owned by public agencies, such as a city government, and may be operated at a loss. This loss is accepted as the cost of doing business for a thriving hospitality industry. Once the facility is built, though, how does the city government and local public determine an "acceptable loss" and how do they define a "thriving hospitality industry"?

In Canada, local chapters associated with MPI hold an annual conference to discuss meetings and events, their trends, and the potential economic impact on their cities. They forecast problems ahead for their growing hospitality industry. Those problems include challenges from technology innovations, a shrinking and trained workforce, and outside forces that impact global travel. For National Meetings Industry Day 2007, held in April, the participants learned that MPI Foundation Canada had "recently launched the country's first study of the economic impact of meetings and events." At that meeting, representatives from Edmonton reported an economic impact of $37 million in 2006 for that area, Winnipeg estimated $50 million in impact from 193 meetings held in their area in 2006, and they estimated that 54,000 conference participants spent approximately $880 per day in Winnipeg.[11]

The economic impact of meetings and events is a quantifiable way to describe the industry and to drive decisions and policies for cities, facilities, and groups. However, that economic impact is just a small indicator for the value of meetings and events. Glen Ramsborg, a leader in the meetings and events industry and senior director for education at PCMA, wrote:

> *Whether it is organized for a corporation, association, or government enterprise, a meeting or conference is a container for value. Regardless of a meeting's size or scope or who is responsible for its management, it is meant to make something positive occur for the participants whose interest and attention it targets. Increasingly, meeting logistics and operations that are well-organized and efficiently executed are becoming a minimum expectation, not a value-added attribute.[12]*

While most people think of costs as monetary or value added, a new cost is becoming a concern. Every meeting or event, for instance, leaves an environmental impact. In an effort to offset this negative impact, many meetings carefully consider measures to "green" the meeting and make it more environmentally friendly. Meeting planners, including those working for the EPA, select venues that take steps to lessen their demands for nonrenew-

A meeting is a gathering of two or more people at the same place and time. The purpose and venue of meetings vary. Attendees determine if the meeting was a success.

able energy sources and to increase their use and generation of recyclable materials.

Summary

The meetings and events industry is difficult to describe in concrete terms. The industry is complex, with planners and those who provide services and products for those planners, forming a core. In an effort to bring more cohesion and recognition to meetings and events, industry leaders, such as the members of the Convention Industry Council, have developed several initiatives. The Accepted Practices Exchange, or APEX, is one effort. Part of APEX is a glossary of terms, which encourages industry participants to communicate more clearly and effectively, using the same terms and acronyms with common definitions.

Meetings are divided into several types including conferences, conventions, tradeshows, special events, sports, and others. Generally, the term meetings can apply to a get-together of two or more people, at the same time, in the same place. Meetings or events may be held to entertain, educate, train, inform, practice, discuss, or to celebrate. Besides the various types of meetings and the variety of reasons to hold meetings, meetings can be differentiated by who serves as host of the meeting, with the three most common meeting hosts being associations, corporations, and government agencies.

Venues for meetings also vary, although the majority of meetings are held at hotels, convention centers, and conference centers. Meetings might also be held in the air, on sea, or in unique places on land. Parks, historical sites, college and university campuses, and facilities managed by religious organizations all serve as meeting venues. The services that are completely mobile can accommodate meetings at virtually any venue, but numerous services are tied to a specific venue or venue type. Some services are computer-based, such as application service providers, while others are provided by the facility itself. Services and suppliers to the meetings and events industry include several options, but generally involve these broad categories: marketing, transportation, audio/visual components, atmosphere, food and beverage, entertainment, and speakers.

The meeting planner is responsible for coordinating all of the people who provide facilities, services, or supplies to the meeting, as well as the planning committee members. The process most meeting planners follow is to determine the need and to identify a purpose, goals, objectives, and an appropriate venue. A request for proposals will be sent out to generate bids on all components for the meeting that are not handled in-house. Contracts are developed and key details are planned. This process may take weeks or several years, depending on the host and the need.

The economic impact of the meetings industry is difficult to determine, although numerous organizations attempt to quantify that impact annually. The monetary value of meetings is just a small part of the impact, though. Attendees determine if the meeting was a success, often based on how well that meeting met the attendee's needs.

≈ Resources

Internet Sites

Convention Industry Council (CIC): http://www.conventionindustry.org.

MPI—Meeting Professionals International is "the meetings and events industry's largest and most vibrant global community" and "is committed to delivering success for its nearly 23,000 worldwide members."
http://www.mpiwcb.org

PCMA—The Professional Convention Management Association is "a nonprofit international association of professionals in the meetings industry whose mission is to deliver breakthrough education and promote the value of professional convention management."
http://www.pcma.org/

ASAE—The American Society of Association Executives "is the membership organization and voice of the association profession. Founded in 1920, ASAE now has more than 22,000 association CEOs, staff professionals, industry partners, and consultant members."
http://www.asaecenter.org/

SGMP—The Society for Government Meeting Professionals "is a nonprofit professional organization of persons involved in planning government meetings, either on a full or part-time basis, and those individuals who supply services to government planners."
http://www.sgmp.org/

RCMA—The Religious Conference Management Association was founded in 1972 and their "ardent goal is to enable RCMA members achieve an unimaginable level of performance and creativity which will result in their designing events with greater spiritual impact, cost-savings, and increased attendance."
http://www.rcmaweb.org/

IAEE—The International Association of Exhibitions and Events was organized under a slightly different name in 1928. Now they are the "leading association for the global exhibition industry," and they represent over 6,000 professionals who manage exhibitions and events around the world.
http://www.iaem.org/

ISES—The International Special Events Society was founded in the late 1980s to "foster enlightened performance through education," to promote ethical professional behavior, and to help their 4,000 event planners in 41 chapters see the "event as a whole, rather than its individual parts."
http://www.ises.com/

ABC—The Association of Bridal Consultants "has been the professional organization for the wedding industry since 1981 and has over 4,000 members in 26 countries on six continents."
http://www.bridalassn.com/

≈ Endnotes

1. Fenich, G. C. (2008). *Meetings, Expositions, Events, and Conventions*, 2nd ed. Upper Saddle River, NJ: Pearson Prentice Hall, 15.

2. Convention Industry Council. About CIC at http://www.conventionindustry.org/aboutcic/about_cic.htm

3. Meeting Professionals International. New membership categories at http://www.mpiweb.org/CMS/mpiweb/mpicontent. aspx?id=650

4. Convention Industry Council. APEX facts at http://www.conventionindustry.org/apex/apex.htm

5. Convention Industry Council. APEX industry glossary—meeting at http://www.conventionindustry.org/apex/apex.htm

6. Convention Industry Council. APEX industry glossary—tradeshow at http://www.conventionindustry.org/apex/apex.htm

7. Silvers, J. R. (2004). *Professional Event Coordinator*. Hoboken, NJ: John Wiley and Sons.

8. Russell, M. (2007). Salaries hold steady in 2006. *Convene*, (June), 49.

9. Ibid.

10. Jeffries, J. P. (1983). *Understanding Hotel/Motel Law*. East Lansing, MI: Educational Institute of the American Hotel and Motel Association, 217.

11. National Meeting Industry Day 2007. *The Business of Meetings: An MPI Foundation Canada White Paper* at http://www. mpiweb.org/CMS/mpiweb/mpicontentadv.aspx?id=1131

12. Ramsborg, G. C. (2007). *Professional Meeting Management*, 5th ed. Dubuque, IA: Kendall Hunt, 12.

≈ *Contributor*

B. J. Reed, Ed.D., APR, CMP, is an associate professor in the Department of Communication Technologies at the University of Wisconsin—Platteville. Dr. Reed has been involved in planning meetings since 1978, when she began planning an annual conference and outdoor sporting events for the American Sighthound Field Association. She also spent 5 years as the executive director of a convention and visitor's bureau in the Midwest, ran an independent meeting planning company for 5 years, and then began teaching public relations and meeting management courses full-time. Reed holds two professional designations: APR (Accredited in Public Relations) from the Public Relations Society of America and CMP (Certified Meeting Professional) designations. She can be reached at <reedb@ uwplatt.edu>.

Chapter 31
Review Questions

1. What are meetings? What are events?

2. What is APEX?

3. Define "tradeshow" and provide an example.

4. What is the difference between an exhibition and an exposition?

5. Investigate one of the organizations mentioned in this chapter and answer the following questions:

   a. What is the address for the organization's Website?

   b. What benefits does this organization offer to members?

   c. What membership categories does the organization maintain?

   d. How many members does the organization have?

   e. What is the organization's purpose?

   f. Does this organization represent the "supply" or "planning" side of the meetings and events industry?

6. What are the common types of services provided for meetings and events?

7. What are the common types of supplies provided for meetings and events?

8. What does a meeting manager do?

9. What kinds of organizations host meetings and events?

10. What is "economic impact" and how is it determined for a specific city that attracts meetings and events?

Lodging and Restaurant Design

32

Ken Myers, University of Minnesota Crookston
Gail Myers, Suite Harmony Corporation

© Chad McDermott, 2008, Shutterstock.

≈ Learning Objectives

☑ Explain the role of the many professionals involved on a design team
☑ Describe what "universal design" is and how it impacts the planning and design of a hospitality establishment
☑ Explain the design considerations and how those considerations work together in creating the desired environment
☑ List organizations that rate hotels and restaurants on specific criteria and how hospitality establishments can use these criteria as they plan design projects

≈ Chapter Outline

Hospitality Design Fundamentals
Some of the Professionals Involved in the Design Team
Design Considerations
A Friendly Design Approach

≈ Key Terms

Acoustical engineers
Aesthetics
Architects
Color
Commercial kitchen designers
Contractors
Electrical engineers
Environmentally friendly
Flow

Function
Health inspectors
Hospitality managers
Interior designers
Interior plantscapers
Style
Sustainable design
Universal design

Hospitality Design Fundamentals

*I*t all begins with the concept. Every aspect of layout and design is driven by that central idea that will make your establishment an exciting place. Whether the concept is a southern style barbeque restaurant, a far eastern inspired spa, or a historical building turned hotel, every choice of lighting, piece of furniture, choice of linens, and even exterior signage will signal to potential guests who you are. The design and layout of the property also sets the stage for guest expectations and behaviors. Do you want guests to wear suits and ties? Do you want guests to stay a long time or move in and out quickly? Do you want your guests to have romantic memories of your establishment or do you want them to remember you as a hot, trendy new property? Elements like color, traffic flow, and music can all communicate strong messages to the guests. You control those messages by proper use of layout and design. Layout refers to the placement of furniture and equipment within spaces that guide the traffic patterns of both people and product. Design refers to the placement and selection of your building and the specifications for the colors, fixtures, walls, ceiling and floor treatments, furniture and equipment, lighting, and all of the accessories. The best interior designs will create a synergy through the combination of all the elements while adhering to applicable building codes. Creating ambience, providing for safety, buffering sound, and increasing efficiency and comfort for the guest—these are some of the goals of layout and design in the hospitality industry.

In this day of online restaurant reviews, hotel reservations, and general entertainment planning on the Internet, layout and design now plays a key role in consumer choice because it can be available to them before they ever take a step inside the establishment. Online tours and 360 degree exterior and interior room views allow the guest to make determinations before they venture outside. The décor creates an ambience or atmosphere that reflects the quality of the food, the pricing, and the level of service. Both the exterior and interior environments are important because they influence a patron's expectations, their mood, and their responses. If the planning has been successful the guest will pull out their credit card and book a reservation.

Many travelers today are influenced in their choice of lodging and restaurants by various rating systems. The two most highly regarded rating companies for hospitality establishments base a large portion of their criteria on layout and design elements. Mobile Travel Guide and AAA base their ratings for hotels on criteria they have established with layout and design specifics for the exterior, public areas, guestrooms, bathrooms, and hotel amenities in addition to service. Other rating services, such as American Express, examine restaurant quality with criteria covering ambiance, lighting, traffic flow, and general comfort, in addition to the quality of the food and service.

Whether the rating symbols are diamonds, keys, or stars; upscale hotels usually have some common characteristics. Some of the rating companies use words like "luxurious," "superior," and "well appointed" to describe the layout and design of a four star hotel. Yahoo travel ratings describes their four star hotel as having "upscale facilities, a well integrated design, stylized room décor, excellent restaurant facilities, and landscaped grounds." Some of the larger companies use very specific descriptions such as:

- a roomy registration area located away from the main traffic flow, with multiple conversation areas and several furniture groupings
- sheetrock as a ceiling material with trims or moldings
- decorative tissue boxes
- more luxurious guest room floor coverings such as marble, granite, carpet, or wood

Hotels must actually plan the rating they wish to achieve well in advance of construction because revisions in layout and design after the hotel is built can be costly. For example, one hotel chain saved money by installing vinyl bathroom flooring that resembled tile, only to find later that they met all of the four star criteria except for that flooring. Most highly rated hotels have wide corridors and spacious bathroom layouts. If not considered in the initial planning, these elements are difficult to impossible to change once the hotel is built.

Function, flow, and aesthetics are the important factors in making a decision about how a hospitality facility should be planned and maintained. Yes, guests need a comfortable bed to sleep on (function), but is the layout arranged so that they can get to the bathroom in the night without tripping on a chair, or escape to a nearby stairway in case of fire (flow)? In addition, is the bed well appointed with dust ruffle, extra pillows, and coordinating bed linens (aesthetics)? Guest perception is always the first consideration in function, flow, and beauty. Just any bed serves the function of a place to sleep but quality hotels are concerned about upgrading function to achieve a higher level of comfort. Radisson Hotels have been switching some of their conventional mattresses to the "Sleep Number Bed"; a specific brand name that consumers recognize and associate with increased comfort. Some luxury hotels are offering a more customized approach to function that allows guests to choose from a selection of pillows: goose down or foam, firm or soft. How a person sleeps directly impacts on their perception of the hotel in the morning. An appropriate traffic flow pattern is essential in a family dining establishment. For example, guests expect they will not have to take their kids through the bar to get to the restroom. Aesthetics or beauty plays a primary role in touching the emotions of people. A café seems a little more upscale . . . a little more pleasant if there are flowers on the table. A well-designed and aesthetically pleasing environment keeps the guests coming back.

It is hard to place an order of importance on function, flow, and aesthetics. Once again guest perception and expectations play a part in the layout and design choices. Great food served on picnic tables that are squeezed into a small space where elbows touch, where wait staff have a hard time

A well-designed and aesthetically pleasing environment keeps guests coming back.

maneuvering, and the noise of pots and pans blends in with loud music may be acceptable at an outdoor barbeque, but will leave a bad taste in the mouths of guests at most restaurants. Guests who walk in the door may expect adequate aisles, private space, and a low noise level so that they can hear conversation and enjoy comfortable seating.

Interior design is much more than selecting carpet or wall coverings to meet fire codes. The elements of interior design can be used to imaginatively create theatrics, special effects, or historic restoration. When you walk into a restaurant, whether it is freestanding, at the casino, or on a cruise ship, interior excitement is created by the materials on the wall, ceilings and floors, the psychological effect of color, and the level and type of lighting. A jazz club may use bold and unique color combinations, small halogen track lighting, and contemporary furniture to promote its "on the edge" feel. The flow-through of the concept should enter into every design detail including the furniture, menu, and the centerpiece. Even the switch plate covers are preplanned to become part of a total design concept.

Hospitality facilities are known to remodel every 5 to 7 years. No matter how old or new, the design of the inside of the building affects every aspect of the comfort and enjoyment of guests. In fact, design involves the stimulation of the five senses. How does the food smell in conjunction with the flowers on the table, the aromatherapy, and the smell of wood or leather? How does the texture of the carpet or the flooring work with the wall covering, the texture of the tablecloth and linens, and the ceiling materials? Is the room acoustically balanced so that guests can hear the music playing and hear the conversation of the partner next to them, without hearing the conversation of the next table? Do the guests feel soothed by the colors so that they are encouraged to linger over many courses, or are the colors passionate and brash encouraging a fast food approach? We will leave the sense of taste and the blend of exquisite flavors to the chef, but when it comes to artistic taste for the environment, the interior designer reigns. Do the styles mix: the furniture, the waiter's uniform, the china, glass, and silver? When one of these factors is different from the rest, a discord is created which results in guests feeling that something is not quite right. It may not be enough to make them leave, but it can be a reason to select another restaurant next time without them even being aware of why. Can a remodel of the layout increase business by adding more seats? Will a new layout train customers to stand in line, to order at a particular place, to become part of the flow of service? A green carpet creates a pathway to the registration desk when bordered by a contrasting color such as white marble. A key ingredient in making design decisions is whether all of these aspects of the décor blend together into a consistent whole.

These questions are answered with careful planning and a project design team that follows through from developing the very concept of the hospitality establishment to making that concept a physical reality. Add to that the responsibilities of health and safety standards required by building codes, analyzing specifications of products for use and wear, planning for the efficiency necessary for any services that are provided, and, of course, close attention to a budget, and you can begin to understand the knowledge required by a design team.

Some of the Professionals Involved in the Design Team

Architects: These professionals prepare and review plans for the overall construction. Qualified architects will have an AIA (American Institute of Architects) appellation.

Interior Designers: These professionals design interior spaces involving materials, finishes, colors, space planning, and layout. This person may be employed by the architects or may have their own design firm. The interior designer in this case should be a commercial interior designer as residential design is very different. A qualified applicant will have an ASID appellation. See American Society of Interior Designers Website.

Electrical Engineers: They design all of the electrical systems. They may have to prepare and stamp electrical plans to obtain building permits and are usually employed by the architects.

Contractors: They are the builders of the project. The general contractor will appoint a construction manager who will oversee specialty subcontractors needed for the project. Specialty contractors include trades people like cabinetmakers, carpet and tile installers, and painters. Contractors are hired by bid and recommendation and are licensed by the state.

Acoustical Engineers: They offer advice and planning for acoustic or sound issues and suggest materials to solve noise problems or enhance sound. They are usually employed by the architects.

Interior Plantscapers: They advise on the proper selection and positioning of plants as well as their maintenance, and are generally hired by recommendation.

Commercial Kitchen Designers: They provide planning and drawings for commercial kitchens as well as specifying equipment. They will begin with the menu and the number of seats to make appropriate determinations of the kitchen layout and design. Often these kitchen designers are freelance or are employed by equipment sales companies. There is no professional appellation here so check for appropriate hospitality background and equipment knowledge.

Health Inspector: Inspectors are employed by the state and interpret state codes. They will inspect existing facilities and must review and approve plans for new or remodeled food preparation areas, service areas, and restrooms. In addition, they will want to approve selections of interior finishes and equipment.

Hospitality Manager: This essential part of the team represents the owners of the facilities. They coordinate the design team and keep them on track with the concept and budget. They will be the final decision maker and/or represent investors, developers, or board members of the company. The manager will follow every detail of the plan. The manager may involve other company personnel including the purchasing agent.

Once you have a well-defined concept and you have selected your design team, you can begin on the new or remodel project. Every project is different and will require a different combination of members depending on what is to be accomplished.

Design Considerations

Each area in the hospitality establishment has different design considerations and priorities. In some areas safety and function come before beauty. In some areas pure drama is the most important element. The right interior design for your concept can allow guests to perceive the value of your services as much greater than the competition. A hotel lobby that uses plush carpet, incandescent lighting, and a fireplace may be perceived as a better value than a similar hotel lobby down the street that uses a loop carpet, cool fluorescent lights, and vending machines, even though the room prices of both hotels are comparable.

Some specific design considerations are as follows.

The Guest Room

The design of the guest room influences the perception of all of the hotel's facilities. Guests spend more time in their room than anywhere in the hotel. Rooms should accommodate the physical needs and comfort of a diverse group of people. Layout considerations include planned spaces to accommodate the five functions of a guest room: sleeping, bathing, grooming, dressing, and entertainment activities. Some guest rooms also become a workspace. Trends for guest room design include increased comfort and spa like details such as elaborate showerheads and featherbeds. More options for work and play include universal adaptors and docking devices for PDAs, MP3s, portable DVD players and phones, which many guests bring with them. Room design can be more fluid than other areas in a hotel as accessories can be changed frequently.

Food/Beverage Service Areas
(includes dining areas, bars, and meeting rooms/banquet areas)

Design concepts in these areas portray to guests the type of service offered and even the pricing. Crystal chandeliers may cue guests as to menu prices and even their attire in this setting. Design characteristics for fast food include easy maintenance, elements that encourage fast turnover, and lots of energy (see chart below). Some restaurants soften the hard edge of fast food design by adding plants, skylights, and play areas. Contrast this environment with tableside dining where there are often barriers for privacy and a high-level of comfort that makes guests want to stay. Theme restaurants are not just about food but also about creating an experience. Theatrical food and beverage areas allow guests to "see the show" from all areas. Open kitchens may be part of the show as are animatronics, displays, actors and acrobats, or plasma screens. Trends for food and beverage areas run from casual and trendy European styling to the nostalgic craze from the '40s and '50s. Lots of props add to the ambiance. Multitasking in a restaurant, including eating, drinking, and socializing has now expanded to include entertainment, games, and internet surfing all while you're still at the table or bar.

Kitchen/Food Production Areas

The kitchen square footage is planned at 1/3 to 1/2 of the dining area square footage. Ignoring this rule can cause a restaurant to fail as adequate space is needed for the manufacturing processes surrounding food. Workstations are established based on the menu, salad station, grilling station, etc. Tasks are analyzed and placed in efficient adjacencies. For example, baking areas can be next to roasting areas so that ovens are accessible to both. Areas to be considered are hot foods, cold foods, beverage, service, warewashing, storing and receiving, offices, and employee areas. Health and sanitation requirements will dictate some of the placement and the materials used for walls, floors, etc. Equipment selection and traffic patterns in the kitchen and to the dining room are important decisions that will affect

Table 32.1   Fast Service Design versus Table Service Design

FAST SERVICE RESTAURANT	TABLE SERVICE RESTAURANT
Bright warm colors	Soft peaceful colors/trendy special effects
Bright overhead lighting	Low level lighting with some lighting specifically for mood or atmosphere
Short seat depth and upright back on chairs	Long seat depth/angled back
Nonpadded or partially padded seating	Thickly cushioned seats and back
Hard surface low-cost floors	Multi-surface flooring including carpeting, tile, wood
Limited noise reduction	Finishes chosen to reduce noise including wall fabrics, linens, carpets, ceiling treatments
Line stanchions, condiments stations, open beverage dispensers for self-service	Wide aisles to accommodate waitstaff, tableside cooking, tray stands

A restaurant's design conveys to guests the type of service offered and even the pricing.

success. Management in the hospitality field is well aware that even service and food quality are largely affected by the layout and design of the kitchen and related production and storage areas. Trends include more color and design attention being paid to these areas as guests can often see them from dining rooms or actually dine in the kitchen on special VIP tables.

Common Areas (including corridors, elevators, stairways, lobbies, public restrooms)

The hallways in any hospitality establishment are not only the primary circulation areas, but also the escape system. The design should actually point the way to an exit, a cashier station, or a restroom, in the form of directional cues including wallpaper patterns, handrails, colors, and signage. Illumination of the walls and floors is also of primary importance as long, narrow dark hallways trigger negative emotional responses. Trends include hallways wide enough to provide niche seating areas as accommodation for those guests with reduced strength and endurance.

The number of seats in a restaurant will dictate the number of restrooms that are needed. Good restroom design is a way to communicate goodwill to guests by adding colorful tiles, easy to clean wall-coverings that are aesthetically appealing, flowers and makeup areas. Certainly, the appearance of cleanliness is part of good design. Some restrooms offer cloth hand towels as part of a luxury appeal.

Lobbies communicate the identity of the establishment to guests as well as provide adjacencies to all other public areas. Guests are encouraged to socialize, transact business, and linger. Typically there are changes in materials, lighting, and signage in lobby areas as directional cues to other main areas of the hotel. Trends for design include mixing a multitude of textures such as glass, wood, and even concrete with fabrics, leathers, and metal. Custom designs are often used in flooring such as logos created with tile or carpet, exotic lighting, and high ceilings. Lobby areas are often opened up to bar areas or entertainment areas to draw guests into the establishment.

Mechanical Equipment and Special Systems

The internal workings of the facility are usually unseen by the guests but are essential to their needs and comfort. Architects and technicians are involved in planning security systems, audio visual equipment and use, as well as telephone and computer accessibility for the guests and for the business of the hotel. Mechanical equipment planning and maintenance is also essential. Plumbing, electrical, and HV/AC systems (heating, ventilation, and air conditioning) must be efficient and meet environmental standards for the health and safety of everyone. Sprinkler systems, elevators, and fire extinguishers are inspected periodically to make sure they are working correctly.

Air quality in a hotel or restaurant can make or break what should be a pleasant experience even if the food and furnishings are of the highest standards; sewer smells, kitchen grease, or mildew would be offensive and would ruin the occasion. One new restaurant was constantly filled with smoke as their hood system in the kitchen was inadequate. Potential diners, enticed by a unique concept and a great menu, were uncomfortable with an atmosphere that was environmentally unfriendly and left guests smelling badly when they left. Hood systems, air exchange systems, and exhaust fans must be properly sized, installed, and maintained to create the desired environment.

A Friendly Design Approach

The design industry is moving in a friendly direction: people friendly and plant friendly. As professionals in the hospitality industry, we have the opportunity to make every guest comfortable and preserve our environment at the same time.

Universal Design

The importance of access to the environment for all physically challenged people began to be regulated in 1990 with the American Disabilities Act. The Act listed specific regulations that affected building codes and new construction all over the country which, as a result, affects the design of every hospitality establishment. Increased awareness of the growing aging population of the baby boomers and the variety of physical challenges affecting the entire population caused those in the design industry to develop products that would allow accessibility to all kinds of people, including adults, children, and the elderly. The term "Universal Design" was used to convey the idea that products (furnishings, hardware, etc.) and architectural changes could be made to make life easier for all people whether or not they have a disability. Some of those design changes today include barrier free/accessible rooms and lobbies, lever faucets and door handles, 34–36 inch door openings, grab bars in restroom stalls and shower areas, water fountains at different height levels, and self flushing toilets. Although hotels are required to have a certain percentage of handicapped rooms in order to be ADA compliant, the concept of Universal Design is that of inclusion so as to have all rooms are as barrier free and accessible as possible. Some efforts to create universal accessibility are as simple as wider aisles in a restaurant or full size mirrors in restrooms.

Sustainable Design

Strategies for reducing consumption involve design practices that are environmentally friendly. Governments, other businesses, and guests expect the hospitality industry to be environmentally conscious yet the competitive environment requires us to be luxury conscious. How do we accommodate both worlds and still be accountable for our planet? Luxury says no to low pressure shower heads but environmentally friendly design says yes to duel flush toilets. Guests still dictate what amenities they are willing to leave home for. Some environmentally friendly design aspects include using eco-friendly fabrics and organic bedding and regional building materials and resources including local artists, local stone, etc. Green design can be as simple as installing windows that open to let in the fresh air and durable goods like glass and porcelain instead of paper. Major recycling methods involve using dishwater and shower water to water gardens and landscaping (assuming soaps are biodegradable), or minor methods like putting recycling bins in restaurants or guest rooms. There are organizations that rate hospitality establishments on their "green" efforts. Two such organizations are the Audubon Green Leaf™ Eco-Rating Program, which advises and rates hospitality establishments on their sustainable design efforts and Environmentally Friendly Hotels organization that allows the guest to be involved in the rating.

Summary

The entire interior design industry is committed to making the hospitality experience more efficient, more beautiful, more exciting, and more profitable. Your layout and design choices communicate to the guest your commitment to their enjoyment and pleasure. Good design will keep guests coming back.

≈ *Resources*

Internet Sites

American Institute of Architects (AIA): www.AIA-online.org

American Society of Interior Designers (ASID): www.asid.org

The International Facility Management Association (IFMA): www.ifma.org

Three links for AAA Diamond Criteria: http://www.aaanewsroom.net/Main.asp?SectionID=&SubCategoryID=22&CategoryID=9&

http://www.aaanewsroom.net/Main.asp?CategoryID=9&SubCategoryID=22&ContentID=62&

http://www.aaanewsroom.net/Main.asp?CategoryID=9&SubCategoryID=22&ContentID=63&

Mobil Stars Criteria: http://www.mobiltravelguide.com/mtg/

Travelocity: http://svc.travelocity.com/info/info_popup/0,,YHOE:EN%7CRATINGS,00.html

Yahoo Travel: http://travel.yahoo.com/

Audubon Green Leaf™ Eco-Rating Program: http://www.auduboninternational.org/programs/greenleaf/?gclid=CKHm1bj-0I8CFSXOIgodQyjFzw

Environmentally Friendly Hotels: http://www.environmentallyfriendlyhotels.com

≈ *Contributors*

Ken W. Myers

Associate Professor & Program Leader of Hotel, Restaurant, & Institutional Management with the University of Minnesota Crookston. Professor Myers teaches several courses in hospitality management including Facility Layout & Design plus consults on design projects with the Suite Harmony Corporation.

Gail J. Myers, Allied ASID

Senior Interior Designer with the Suite Harmony Corp. and adjunct professor at the University of Minnesota Crookston. Ms. Myers consults on commercial and residential designs, has taught Facility Layout and Design, and is a noted speaker.

Chapter 32
Review Questions

1. What is the role of the Architect, Interior Designer, Electrical Engineer, Contractor, Acoustical Engineers, Interior Plantscapers, the Commercial Kitchen Designer, the Health Inspector, and the Hospitality Manager in a design project?

2. List the five functions of a hotel guest room?

3. Why is the design of a guest room considered more fluid than other areas in a hotel?

4. If the size of a restaurants dining room were 2,500 square foot, how many square feet would you expect the kitchen to be?

5. What term is used to convey the idea that product and architectural changes can make life easier for all individuals?

6. What are two organizations that rate hotels and restaurants on specific criteria?

7. How frequently do many hospitality establishments remodel?

8. How can design impact the guest room, food and beverage areas, and common areas of a hospitality establishment?

9. Compare and contrast how design considerations may impact guests at a fast service vs. a table service restaurant?

10. What are environmentally friendly methods that can be used by the hospitality establishments in their design?

11. What are ways that we can satisfy the desire for both luxury design and sustainable design?

International Tourism

33

Ernest P. Boger, University of Maryland, Eastern Shore

© Neale Cousland, 2008, Shutterstock.

≈ Learning Objectives

☑ To provide an introductory acquaintance with the landscape of tourism across national borders
☑ To emphasize breadth of coverage at the expense of depth in any particular area
☑ To lead/stimulate investigation of one or more of these areas as a prelude to lucrative and fulfilling career pursuit
☑ To articulate the definitional parameters of international tourism
☑ To summarize historical evolution
☑ To discuss size and scope
☑ To reference the marketing/regulatory organizations
☑ To explain approaches to the study of, debate the challenges, and assess career opportunities

≈ Chapter Outline

Background and Definition
Historical Evolution/Development of International Tourism
Size and Scope of International Tourism Today
Organizations for Regulation and Marketing of International Tourism
Dimensional Approaches to the Study of International Tourism
International Tourism Challenges
Career Opportunities

≈ Key Terms

Concorde
Cruise line
Grand tour
Jet age
Offshore
Passport

Supersonic flight
Sustainable tourism
Tourism
Travel
WTO

Background and Definition

*T*he working definition of tourism, historically advanced by the author, is "Voluntary and temporary alternate environment encounter for the purpose of enrichment." The tourist is necessarily, then, a "traveler" and a "visitor." By extension, international tourism refers to the visitor's movement or "travel" across sovereign national borders. Many definitions of tourism abound, but all have common components. First, they are always voluntary movements. Second, they require going beyond the traveler's every day surroundings. Third, they are focused on some form of experiential growth (i.e., enrichment). And finally, the traveler must return home, usually within a year. The World Tourism Organization (WTO)[1] provides detailed recommendations on definitions of tourism, tourists, and travelers that permit standardization for research, measurement, and application in varying jurisdictions.

Historical Evolution/ Development of International Tourism

Ancient Times—Heroic Figures

Human wanderlust is well documented in the archeological record, which stretches back at least 150,000 years to the African continent. However, the continental shifts of humanoids from Africa to Europe to Asia were motivated by a search for more accommodating surroundings for survival, rather than enrichment as we know it today. Also, going back (i.e., returning home), was not an option. As such, those movements would be classified as migration. No doubt, the seeds of exploration were planted in the human psyche as individuals reached out to define the "cutting edge" of their existence.

The invention of money as a medium of representational exchange by the Sumerians (Babylonians) around 4000 BC is recognized as a benchmark in international travel/tourism in that "value" became portable. Thus money represented a quantum leap from the barter system, which limited mobility and distance, because actual goods or services had to be present and/or performed. An updated, albeit substantially less revolutionary, comparison would be the substitution of credit cards, which eliminates the need to carry large quantities of cash.

Early travelers who we recognize as "heroic figures" today include the journey of the Sumerian King set forth in the Epic of Gilgamesh (ca. 2000 BCE) and Egyptian Queen Hatshepsut, whose journey in 1480 BCE to the land of Punt is well documented on the walls of temple Deir el-Bahri at Luxor. The Nile Valley burial tombs of the pharaohs punctuated by the great pyramids and the Sphinx were built between 2700 BCE and 1700 BCE and were well established as major attractions by 1200 BCE. Around the same time, 1760 BCE–1027 BCE, the Shang Dynasty pioneered trade routes to far-flung locales throughout what is present-day China. The jungles of Mexico and South America continue to reveal the ancient travel routes of Mayan and other ancient civilizations. The thirteenth century CE journey of Marco Polo from Italy to China and back must certainly be included in chronological benchmarking for international tourism.

The Roman Era—Order, Roads

Beginning around 150 BCE and by 117 CE, "Roman roads comprised a network of some 50,000 miles. They girdled the Roman Empire, extending from near (what is now) Scotland and Germany in the North, to the south well within Egypt and along the southern shores of the Mediterranean Sea. To the east, roads extended to the Persian Gulf in (what is now) Iraqi and Kuwait."[2] At that time, movement throughout that vast network would not have been considered "international" travel, as all fell within the Roman empire. A glance at the map of 2006 reveals a staggering conflagration of national boundaries and barriers as well as historical and contemporary animosities that severely restrict international travel in a region that was once united, albeit by force of arms.

The Grand Tour, Sixteenth through Nineteenth Centuries

The phrase "Grand Tour" entered the lexicon of travel as the sons of English nobility and wealthy aristocracy were escorted or sent abroad to the "finishing school" of the European continent to be enriched by the arts, science, language, and culture of the so-called civilized world. These tours often spread over several years, thereby overlapping into the time period usually associated with migration. However, the "must return home" caveat overrules in this case and clearly stamps this historical movement as international tourism. The most ambitious itinerary began with France including a heavy infusion of Paris. Italy, including Florence, Genoa, Ven-

The modern American version of the "Grand Tour" of Europe is typically a 21-day experience.

ice, and hopefully Rome, came next. Return to England was through Germany and the Low Countries via Switzerland, should the Alps not prove too daunting. Today, variations of this itinerary are popular among U.S. international travelers, generally presented as a 21-day experience. It is not, however, uncommon for some to attempt this journey over a "long weekend" and report back that, "I've done Europe!" Serious travel professionals lament the disingenuousness of such claims.

Thomas Cook—1841

Any discussion of international travel must recognize Thomas Cook, generally regarded as the father of the packaged tour or excursion. His prominence began with a 1-shilling, 12-mile, round-trip rail excursion from Leicester to Loughborough, England. Amenities included a picnic lunch and a brass band. He moved on to develop escorted tours to the European continent, to the Americas, and beyond. Like all good ideas, imitation becomes the sincerest form of flattery, and so his pioneering techniques and styles of international tourism servicing were emulated worldwide. Today the company continues to be a major player in the international travel/tourism marketplace. Indeed, the *Thomas Cook European Timetable* is still today considered the definitive source of information about European rail service.[3]

World War II—National and International Mobility

World War II fueled the largest people movement across the United States and the Americas on to Europe and related theaters of war. Travel was mostly by troopship, although airlift became increasingly reliable and available as the war wore on. This was not tourism as it was neither voluntary nor for enrichment. Survival was at the high stakes table in this case, and return home was not guaranteed. By the end of the war, however, more than 17 million U.S. and Canadian citizens had been exposed to Europe, Asia, and Africa via military assignments and were anxious to share these experiences with relatives and friends in the relative affluence of peacetime that ensued. Thus, 1945, the end of the war, represents a benchmark in the explosion of mass tourism on the international scene.

The Jet Age—1960

The most extraordinary quantum leap in international tourism occurred with the initiation of intercontinental jet passenger air service by American Airlines on January 25, 1959. The Boeing 707, utilizing jet engines proven in military aircraft of WWII, made the trip from Los Angeles to New York City in about four hours. A decade later, Pan American World Airways debuted the Boeing 747 whiffing 352 passengers from New York City to London in about seven hours, giving birth to the jumbo jet era. Now international tourists could think in terms of hours versus days or months of travel via steamship to foreign lands.

The Twenty-First Millennium

The introduction of supersonic flight, via the Concorde collaboration between British Airways and Air France, provided a glimpse of what the international traveler/tourism can expect as the twenty-first century gets underway. A Concorde flight including a mixture of subsonic and supersonic flight reduced the travel time from London to New York to three and one-half hours. With the time zone changes, one popular trick was the ability to ring in the New Year in London, board Concorde. Ring the New Year in again while crossing the international dateline (Greenwich meridian), and then pop the final champagne cork upon landing in New York City. Unfortunately for the intrepid and relatively well-heeled international traveler, all Concorde service, and with it all supersonic passenger flight, was retired in 2000 after a fatal crash on takeoff from Orly Airport in Paris. This was the only serious accident in the history of the aircraft and resulted from a combination of once-in-a-lifetime circumstances. In reality, the Concorde was an extremely unprofitable program for the airlines to maintain, given the economics and technology of the times.

It is relatively certain that the resumption of supersonic flight awaits only a matter of time and cost-effective technology. This will be followed in a geometrically reduced time frame by full space-based passenger flight. This will represent a quantum leap in international travel where transcontinental travel will be reduced from hours to minutes.

Size and Scope of International Tourism Today

The all-encompassing pervasiveness of tourism is a classic case of the forest being obscured by the trees. When international and domestic tourism are taken together, they represent the largest industry in the world, both in terms of income dollar volume and people employed.

Some 808 million international tourist arrivals were recorded for the 2005 calendar year. The WTO Website (www.world-tourism.org) has the most current and extensive data.[4] *Tourism 2020 Vision* is the WTO's long-term forecast and assessment of the development of tourism up to the first 20 years of the new millennium, or the year 2020. That report projects world tourist arrivals to grow from 3.2 percent per annum to 4.5 percent by 2020. This translates into 1.56 billion international arrivals worldwide, with 1.2 billion intraregional and .4 billion long haul (between regions). The top three recipient destinations are outlined in Figure 33.1.

Figure 33.1 Top 3 International Recipient Destinations—2020 (WTO)

	(MILLIONS)	
REGION	PROJECTED ARRIVALS	MARKET SHARE %
Europe	717	46
East Asia/Pacific	397	25
Americas	282	18
Africa	<164	<11
Middle East	<164	<11
South Asia	<164	<11
All Regions	1560	100

WTO data further indicates uneven distribution in regional arrivals. In 2000, Africa received 1 percent of international arrivals, the Middle East followed with 3 percent, East Asia/Pacific 16 percent,

the Americas 19 percent, and a whopping 57 percent to Europe. WTO estimates that these shares will equalize over the next two decades with Europe settling to about 45 percent of the total.

Figure 33.2 2006 International Tourist Receipts—(WTO)

	(US$ BILLION)	
REGION	INTERNATIONAL TOURIST RECEIPTS	% WORLD MARKET SHARE
Europe	374.5	51
Americas	154.0	21
Asia/Pacific	152.6	21
Middle East	27.3	4
Africa	24.3	3
Total	732.7	100

In addition to regional receipts as shown (Figure 33.2), WTO data are available for individual countries within those regions. From that data one can make interesting comparisons. For example, tourism receipts for the entire continent of Africa are approximately the same as the Caribbean.

Figure 33.3 Primary Originating Destinations 2006—Outbound Tourism—(WTO)

	(MILLIONS)	
REGION	TOURIST DEPARTURES	MARKET SHARE %
Europe	473.7	57
Asia/Pacific	166.5	20
Americas	142.2	17
Middle East	24.8	03
Africa	24.5	03
All Regions	831.7	100

As the data in Figures 33.1–33.3 illustrate, any way one wants to track it, international tourism continues to live up to top billing as "the world's largest industry."

Organizations for Regulation and Marketing of International Tourism

World Tourism Organization (WTO)

The World Tourism Organization has been cited several times in previous parts of the chapter. Now it is

---

TOURISM AS INSTRUMENT OF GLOBAL TOLERANCE, PEACE, AND UNDERSTANDING— WORLD TOURISM ORGANIZATION

Tourism for Prosperity and Peace

At the start of the new millennium, tourism is firmly established as the number one industry in many countries and the fastest-growing economic sector in terms of foreign exchange earnings and job creation.

International tourism is the world's largest export earner and an important factor in the balance of payments of most nations.

Tourism has become one of the world's most important sources of employment. It stimulates enormous investment in infrastructure, most of which also helps to improve the living conditions of local people. It provides governments with substantial tax revenues. Most new tourism jobs and businesses are created in developing countries, helping to equalize economic opportunities and keep rural residents from moving to overcrowded cities.

Intercultural awareness and personal friendships fostered through tourism are a powerful force for improving international understanding and contributing to peace among all the nations of the world.

The UNWTO recognizes that tourism can have a negative cultural, environmental and social impact if it is not responsibly planned, managed and monitored. The UNWTO thus encourages governments to play a vital role in tourism, in partnership with the private sector, local authorities and non-governmental organizations.

In its belief that tourism can be effectively used to address the problems of poverty, UNWTO made a commitment to contribute to the United Nations Millennium Development Goals through a new initiative to develop sustainable tourism as a force for poverty elimination. The programme, known as ST-EP (Sustainable Tourism-Eliminating Poverty), focuses the longstanding work of both organizations on encouraging sustainable tourism with a view to alleviating poverty and was implemented in 2003.

---

time for a fuller understanding of its functions. The World Tourism Organization (WTO), or sometimes (UNWTO), is an international intergovernmental body hosted by the United Nations as a special agency and is entrusted with the promotion and development of responsible and sustainable tourism worldwide. It is headquartered in Madrid, Spain. Perusal of the Website (www.world-tourism.org) reveals some of the vehicles available for accomplishing that mission. They include business council, a Global Code of Ethics for Tourism, market intelligence, statistics, and publications. In 2005, membership included 145 countries, seven territories, and more than 300 affiliate members representing the private sector, educational institutions, tourism associations, and local tourism authorities. WTO is the unquestioned leading organization in fostering international tourism.

World Travel & Tourism Council (WTTC)

Unlike WTO, whose core membership group consists of sovereign governments, the World Travel & Tourism Council (WTTC) is more private-sector focused.

As reproduced from the WTTC Website:

The World Travel & Tourism Council (WTTC) is the forum for global business leaders comprising the presidents, chairs and CEOs of 100 of the world's foremost companies. It is the only body representing the private sector in all parts of the Travel & Tourism industry worldwide.

WTTC's mission is to raise awareness of the full economic impact of the world's largest generator of wealth and jobs—Travel & Tourism. Governments are encouraged to unlock the industry's potential by adopting the Council's policy framework for sustainable tourism development—Blueprint for New Tourism.[5]

In addition to publications and logistical support from the Website, WTTC activities include hosting a lodging investment summit, a world tourism forum, and a time share/resort investment conference.

International Air Transport Association (IATA)

The International Air Transport Association, or IATA, is the trade association for the world's largest airlines. Like all trade associations, they provide opportunities for their member organizations to collaborate and achieve high standards of operations, marketing, and cost control. For the international traveler/tourist, the two passages from their website are instructive:

Continual efforts by IATA ensure that people, freight and mail can move around the vast global airline network as easily as if they were on a single airline in a single country. In addition, IATA helps to ensure that members' aircraft can operate safely, securely, efficiently, and economically under clearly defined and understood rules.

For **consumers***, IATA simplifies the travel and shipping process. By helping to control airline costs, IATA contributes to cheaper tickets and shipping costs. Thanks to airline cooperation through IATA, individual passengers can make one telephone call to reserve a ticket, pay in one currency, and then use the ticket on several airlines in several countries—or even return it for a cash refund.*

Cruise Line International Association (CLIA)

Today's cruise ship excursions present an excellent multi-dimensional opportunity to observe international tourism in action. The ship itself as a floating destination hotel and resort[6] provides an instantaneous "alternative environment encounter" the minute one steps onboard. More alternate environments are encountered as the ship moves in and out of the various ports comprising its itinerary. "Enrichment" can range from touring an archeological dig to swimming with sharks to attending a service in a 500-year-old church and everything in between. Since 1980, nearly 100 million persons have taken a deep-water cruise of 2+ days. However, this represents only 16 percent of the U.S. population. Thus, the market potential remains strong.

It is therefore expected that there would be a strong trade association. The Cruise Line International Association (CLIA) is that body. It is the official trade organization of the North American cruise industry. As announced on the CLIA Website www. cruising.org.[7]

Cruise Lines International Association is a marketing and training organization composed of 19 of the major cruise lines serving North America. CLIA was formed in 1975 in response to a need for an association to promote the special benefits of cruising. CLIA exists to educate, train, promote and explain the value, desirability and affordability of the cruise vacation experience.[8]

In addition, CLIA offers support and training for the travel agent professional community and administers the Cruise Counselor Certification Program.

Dimensional Approaches to the Study of International Tourism

The great fascination and challenge in studying tourism is the many points of departure from which study can be launched. Goeldner[9] proposed eight approaches, as follows.

Geographical

From prehistoric times to present, "alternative environment enrichment" provided by the magnetic attraction of topography continues to be a compelling reason for crossing national borders. As Goeldner[10] elaborated, "The geographer's approach to tourism sheds light on the location of tourist areas, the movements of peoples created by tourism locales, the changes that tourism brings to the landscape in the form of tourism facilities, the dispersion of tourism development, physical planning, and economic, social and cultural problems." An illustration of the marketing value of geographical analysis lies in a promotional slogan from the island country of Jamaica, which promises the opportunity to experience the topography of a continent in an area the size of Rhode Island.[11] This is indeed the case, because one can go from a 7,400-ft. mountaintop to sea level in a few hours.

Sociological

Sociology is the study of people in groups and group behavior. Tourism movements frequently

Cruise ship excursions present an excellent opportunity to observe international tourism.

© Bryan Busovicki, 2008, Shutterstock.

take place with affinity groups. International tourism invariably brings unfamiliar nationalities in contact with each other. Such international encounters are generally pleasant and without friction, given proper preparation on both sides. Occasionally, diplomatic and social conditions are such that international travel is a non-starter. Currently, regular Americans cannot vacation in the ancient city of Baghdad, due to the existence of wartime conditions and dangerous pockets of anti-U.S. sentiment.

Economic

International tourism revenue streams are highly desirable for their ability to "multiply" as their flow infuses throughout international destination communities. Indeed, tourism revenues often represent the only, or major, opportunity for nations to acquire hard or key currency, which is necessary to purchase goods and services not produced in that particular country. The Caribbean/Atlantic country of Cuba continues at this writing to be off limits for regular U.S. travel. However, special licenses are available and special exceptions are made. Upon arrival, travelers find a warm welcome for the U.S. dollars and the tourists who will leave them behind.

Historical

This approach to the study of international tourism relies on making comparisons of tourism movements as they have evolved over time. The State of Florida, for example, enjoys a healthy influx of international tourists going to and from the various cruise ships that depart from the state. This target population grows in direct proportion to the annual increase in ships calling Florida homeport.

Institutional

In this instance, focus is on the facilities such as hotels, ground transportation, restaurants, travel agencies, and other intermediaries that facilitate the experience of the international traveler. These also include governmental agencies like customs and immigration and their role in managing entry to the country's frontier. A few countries are authorized to operate U.S. pre-clearance facilities on their soil, thereby enabling visitors returning to the U.S. to immediately depart the airport as easily as when traveling domestically. The Bahamas is one such favored nation.

Product

The step-by-step design, creation, and distribution of tourism products are at the heart of the product approach to international tourism study. These include airline seats and guided tours, and well as native crafts and deep-sea fishing.

Managerial

Management by definition involves planning, organizing, staffing, directing, and controlling. These functions are constantly under scrutiny as professionals strive to provide positive, profitable, and sustainable experiences for the international traveler.

Interdisciplinary and Systems Approaches

Because tourism in general and international tourism in particular cuts across all aspects of society as noted earlier, tourism philosophers are calling for a systems approach that coordinates all the approaches and derives a unified whole.[12]

International Tourism Challenges

The multidimensional nature of tourism as detailed in the foregoing section presents distinct challenges that are exacerbated significantly when international boundaries are crossed as the tourists seek that alternative environment encounter and attendant enrichment. Some of the more challenging aspects follow.

Language

Naturally, communication is vital for the full absorption of new experience. Tourists who would seek out an international adventure are sometimes shocked when they experience difficulty or are unable to communicate altogether with individuals in countries that speak the same language, for example, the U.S. traveler's encounter with the Irish brogue, British Cockney, or Virgin Islands word inflections and rhythms. Completely "foreign" languages create even more challenges but are sometimes welcome as a part of the "exotic" experience. Traveling in guided tour groups admirably solves each of these potentially troublesome scenarios.

Customs/Culture

To prevent embarrassment, disgust, or even hostility, it is always essential to study the "do's and taboos" of the receiving culture. Over the millennia, human societies have evolved meaning and substance for an incredible variety of dress patterns, hand gestures, seating arrangements, body language, and hygienic practices. Nothing could be worse than unintentionally offending a gracious international host with a mistaken act or hand motion that would seem perfectly natural at home. The ancient adage, "When in Rome, do as the Romans do," continues to serve as a practical mantra for international travel. It is also important to resist the urge to force one's culture on the visiting culture. This is illustrated by the requirement of women to walk behind men when in the presence of a certain king in the African country of Ghana.

Currency

Currency in recent years has become less of a challenge in international travel due to the worldwide use of the credit card. Charges encountered in the currency of the realm are instantly or eventually translated into one's home currency, and the bill is paid accordingly at some future date. Also, the introduction of the euro as the standard currency of the major countries on the European continent has mitigated some historical traveler dismay in constantly needing different local currencies to function in countries that are in close proximity. A standard practice has been to "convert at the border" and start the recalculation. The introduction of the euro has eliminated that process.

Politics

In all countries politics create passion and polarization sometimes spilling over into internal hostility that creates unsafe conditions for international travel. Governments of the world usually issue "Travel Advisories" to alert its nationals that travel is unsafe to certain destinations. In some cases, travel is forbidden to such areas until further notice.

Security

Although adventure travel is more popular than ever, the threat to personal safety is the fastest way to kill international travel. This begins with the transportation mode, particularly aircraft, which were proven vulnerable to highly motivated terrorists in the 2001 attacks of 9-11 on New York City and Washington, D.C. Occasionally, hotels catering to international travelers are singled out as targets of terrorists who want to "make a point" against a particular country's citizens. Happily, these are rare expectations, and tourists taking reasonable precautions specific to the destination are unlikely to experience tragic unpleasantries.

Sustainable Development and Ecotourism

One dilemma of international tourism is that the uniqueness of the destination that attracts the tourist can be destroyed by these same tourists if proper management of the environmental encounter is not in place. This is particularly acute for nature-based or natural attraction tourism. International destinations sometimes in lesser-developed countries eager for the hard currency of the tourist fail to provide the safeguards that will protect and sustain the environment and experience. Ecotourism places emphasis on embracing a tourism experience that is also benevolent to the host environment. Sustainable development is a concept that requires the design and developmental pacing of infrastructure and superstructure to enhance the carrying capacity of the supporting area but not at the expense of the environmental attraction that fuels development in the first place. The requirement that no structure can be built higher than the tallest palm tree in Negril, Jamaica, is a case in point.

Career Opportunities

Following are some institutions that provide excellent opportunities for careers in international tourism.

- Travel agencies
- Tour companies
- Hospitality service institutions (airlines, hotels, foodservice)
- Umbrella marketing agencies (CVB, national tourism offices)
- Immigration, customs, embassy postings

The actual job responsibilities are as diverse as the phenomenon of tourism itself. An excellent source of related career information is *Travel Perspectives: A Guide to Becoming a Travel Professional*, written by two seasoned professionals who also operate a specialized school and training program.[13]

Summary

This chapter set out to present broad and reasonably comprehensive introductory exposure to the subject of international tourism. Discussion opens with a working definition of tourism that contains all the elements critical to any definition of tourism and travelers. The historical perspective follows, with a listing of benchmark international travels and travelers. Recent statistical data establishing the legitimacy of tourism's claim to be the "world's largest industry" appears in the third section. Regulatory and marketing agencies facilitating international tourism are introduced with Websites for further study. A popular academic listing of approaches to the study of tourism are referenced and comments offered to heighten their importance as components of international tourism. International tourism challenges including language and security lead into a final section on international careers. An essay on prospects for world peace via tourism reproduced from the World Tourism Organization Website is shared.

Accordingly, it is the author's expectation that the reader has gained substantial insight and awareness of the exciting journeys, both personal and professional, that lie along the pathways, seaways, and airways of international tourism.

≈ *Resources*

Internet Sites

Cruise Line International Association (CLIA): www.cruise.org
International Air Transport Association: www.iata.org
U.S. Treasury, Customs Division, "Know before You Go": www.customs.tres.gov/travel/know/htm
World Tourism Organization (WTO): www.world-tourism.org
World Travel and Tourism Council (WTTC): www.wttc.org

≈ *Endnotes*

1. World Tourism Organization (WTO). www.world-tourism.org
2. Goeldner, C., and Brent Ritchie, J. R. *Tourism. Principles, Practices, Philosophies,* 9th ed. Hoboken, NJ: John Wiley, 2003, p. 45.
3. *Thomas Cook European Timetable.* Timetable publishing office, Peterborough England, 2006.
4. World Tourism Organization (WTO). www.world-tourism.org
5. World Travel and Tourism Council (WTTC). www.wttc.org
6. International Air Transport Association. www.iata.org
7. Boger, E. P. "Conflict or Compliment? Marketing Strategies of Caribbean Tourist Boards vs. Cruise Ship Lines." In *The Practice of Hospitality Management*, edited by A. Pizam, R. C. Lewis, and P. Manning, Westport, CT: AVI Press, 1983, Chapter 42, pp. 413–426.
8. Cruise Line International Association (CLIA). www.cruise.org
9. Goeldner, C., and Brent Ritchie, J. R. *Tourism,* p. 45.
10. Ibid.
11. *Destination Jamaica (Official Visitor's Guide).* Kingston, JA: 2005. Jamaica Hotel & Tourist Association.
12. Todd, G., and Rice, S. *Travel Perspectives: A guide to becoming a travel professional,* 3rd ed. Albany, NY: Delmar, 2002, pp. 1–16.
13. Ibid.

≈ *Contributor*

epboger@umes.edu

Ernest P. Boger, II (CHA, FMP, CHE, MHCIMA), a native of Tampa, Florida, is the University of South Florida's first Black graduate. Dr. Boger is CEO of the consulting company VIP Hosts Internationale, Inc. and is associate professor in Hospitality Management with (IMCA)-Revans University, serving as advisor to the Caribbean Doctoral Set. He is widely published on Hospitality Education, Marketing, and Tourism, including an anthology (1975–2004), *Selected Readings in Hotel, Restaurant and Tourism Administration*. He was appointed by the Governor of Florida to the Citizens Advisory Committee on Coastal Resource Management. He is a founding board member of the Multicultural Food Service & Hospitality Alliance (MFHA). For the past five consecutive years, he has been named "One of the most influential African/Americans in Travel/Tourism" by *Black Meetings & Tourism Magazine*. The National Coalition of Black Meeting Planners bestowed its "Pioneer" award on him in 1996. In 2002 he was presented with the "Steve Fletcher Achievement Award." It is the second-highest award established by International CHRIE.

Chapter 33
Review Questions

1. Discuss the three common components of the definition of tourism.

2. How did the invention of "money" stimulate the growth of international tourism?

3. Compare the original "Grand Tour" with the Grand Tour of today.

4. Identify three benchmarks in the evolution of international air travel.

5. Select five pieces of statistical evidence indicators to make the case for tourism.

6. Visit the Web sites of WTO, WTTC, and IATA. Compare and contrast.

7. Explain the ease of multinational travel via a cruise.

8. Identify and interview an individual actually holding one of the positions noted in the career opportunities section.

Private Clubs

34

Denis P. Rudd and Richard J. Mills, Jr., Robert Morris University

© Brian Chase, 2008, Shutterstock.

≈ Learning Objectives

☑ Understand the components of the club management industry
☑ Identify the function that private clubs play in the hospitality industry
☑ Explain the significance and economic impact made by clubs
☑ Identify future employment opportunities in the club industry

≈ Chapter Outline

Economic Impact
Modern Environment
Variety of Clubs
Legal Form of Business
Management Styles
Technology
Club Managers Association of America (CMAA)
National Club Association (NCA)

≈ Key Terms

Club
Member
Country clubs
Full membership
Social membership
Yacht club
Military clubs
City clubs
Equity clubs
Proprietary clubs
CMAA
NCA
Service

WE SERVE THE WORLD

"America has a Club for everyone."

Joseph Donahue
General Manager Westchester Country Club

Since the beginning of civilized man, archaeologists have found evidence of clubs throughout the world. Once man changed his wandering ways and started settlements, there was a need for people with common interests to associate with each other, despite having no ties of kinship. The ancient Egyptians had clubs that fulfilled religious, business, and social needs of the Pharaoh, religious leaders, and their people. The Greeks had their Hetairai, a loose association of likeminded individuals who gathered together for religious, political, commercial, and athletic reasons and developed clubs specifically for dining. And, the Romans developed a more formal club and were the first to integrate social gatherings into the Roman baths.

While the roots of the ancient club can be traced back thousands of years, the beginning of the modern club surfaced in London during the 1700s with the introduction, growth, and development of the London coffee houses. These coffee-house clubs soon became hotbeds of political scandal-mongering and intrigue, and in 1675 King Charles II issued a proclamation saying that coffee houses should be suppressed because they were places that bred scandal and malicious gossip that was against the King and country. This proclamation was so unpopular it was almost instantly withdrawn. By Anne's reign the coffee-house club was a feature of England's social life.

These clubs were actually special rooms in taverns that operated on an invitation only basis for their members. One of the most famous clubs of the time was the Bread Street Club. Members met at a tavern and individuals such as William Shakespeare and other literary notables of the Elizabethan time frequented these establishments. The Royal and Ancient Golf Club of St. Andrews, Scotland, founded in 1758, said to be the birthplace of golf, is the forerunner of the modern country club. During Queen Victoria's reign, clubs were only for members of the upper class, but that changed. The notion of clubbing, mentioned as early as the 1600s in the Diary of Samuel Pips, developed in England when groups who regularly met in taverns began to assume a more permanent character. By the middle of the 19th century, the middle class was able to join clubs. Clubs were developed for the working man, allowing them to escape from their tiring days, their wives, children, and from the gin palaces and public houses. The working men's club movement was a way to keep the middle class man sober. Many of these clubs provided amusement and refreshments as well as newspapers and books and aimed to morally and socially improve the working man by educating him.

In America the earliest known social club was the Fish House in Philadelphia. This club emphasized drinking and socializing. The concept was very popular and, by the mid 1700s, clubs had been established in Annapolis, Boston, Charleston, New Orleans, Philadelphia, and New York. Many of these American clubs used the British model. During the 1800s one of the most famous clubs formed was the first women's club called Sorosis. This club was for actresses, artisans, supporters of the union's causes, and those interested in the arts. In most cases these women's clubs focused on social services and promoted women that were in the business and professional fields.

Within the heady industrial development that so profoundly transformed the American economy and American society in the decades following the Civil War, the proliferation of the new American clubs revealed the strength and social stature of their founders, most of whom were newly wealthy entrepreneurs. The new clubs provided a place where peers could meet and discuss mutual problems and solutions. As American urban centers expanded and became more industrial, the desirable residential districts were located farther and farther from the business and industrial centers. Busy businessmen could no longer go home for lunch. A downtown club could provide a pleasant environment and excellent noontime meal that later became an important part of the American club. Once considered the playground of the rich and famous, the club became a center for the American family and its recreational activities.

Currently, a **club** is defined as a group of persons organized or united for social, literary, athletic, political, or other purposes. There are ever increasing markets for private clubs as people join clubs to engage in social discourses and to surround themselves with others who have similar interests. With over 14,000 private clubs in the United States alone, clubs have created an atmosphere conducive to friendliness and comfort while catering to a multitude of clientele.

Economic Impact

The Club Managers Association of America (CMAA), the premier industry professional association of 7,000 managers for approximately 3,000 membership clubs, compiled the 2006 Economic Impact Survey. The survey reported CMAA member managed clubs generating annual gross revenues of over $14 billion per year with food and beverage revenue contributing $4.5 billion. Average CMAA-managed club income is approximately $5.18 million dollars. The average club spends $1.2 million within the state as a whole; overall club operations generate $6.21 billion for state economies around the country. A typical club pays over $150,000 in property taxes, provide over $367 million for charities with approximately 83% of this money moved into local community charities, and report an excess of $6.4 million in student scholarships.[1]

Modern Environment

The competitive landscape has increased significantly over the past several years placing never before experienced pressure on membership at private clubs. Specifically, industry experts have drawn a general consensus identifying the changing golf course marketplace and population demographics as key culprits. Frank Vain, president of The McMahon Group, a consulting firm to the private club industry, says the biggest challenge is the evolving golf marketplace that "has experienced a total reversal in market composition. Going back to the 1920s, about 80% of the golf courses were private. Public golf was almost unheard of, and up until the 1990s, most of the existing public courses were not comparable to private courses."[2] Vain's group now estimates that currently about 75% of U.S. golf courses are public and is projected to plateau at 80% around 2010.

Furthermore, these public facilities have grown in quality commensurate with its numeric growth. Steve Graves, president of Creative Golf Marketing, a membership-marketing firm, comments that private clubs today are in direct competition with upscale daily fee courses.

These clubs are not your typical municipal courses that we all grew up around, suggested Graves, these courses are being built and designed by the best in the industry and offer equal and many times better golf courses than a typical private club. [Therefore] the upscale daily fee courses present an adequate golf experience without the high monthly cost associated with being a member of a private club.[3]

Vain further accentuates the point, "Most of the new course construction has been in the high-end arena with the conditions, accessibility, and slope rating that can rival the private club experience, except there are no initiation fees, dues, or assessments. There is a whole generation of people growing up not having or needing a private club still able to call themselves golfers. This was simply not possible 20 years ago."[4]

Additionally, the influence of technology, ease of travel, and the transient lifestyle produced by the corporate career ladder has created a different societal need and, hence, a change in the population demographics. Leesa Mitchell, CMP, operator of Members Solutions, a consulting firm that has been involved in marketing high-end daily fee operative clubs, states,

Many clubs have failed to change in correlation to the changing needs of our society. Many clubs are looking for the 'tried and true' program to recruit and retain members. In my opinion, the fact of the matter is, those programs do not exist. Every club has a different situation, different demographic, and different trend line. In recruiting and retaining members, those are the areas that many clubs have been failing to recognize and utilize in their planning. Turning a deaf ear to demographics and related trending is not the route to go and creates a challenge in recruitment and retention, as well as maintaining a positive satisfaction level of existing members.[5]

In crisis situations, short cuts often abound and glow with appeal. The private club industry is not immune. Graves articulates that one of the most disturbing national trends within the industry are clubs resorting to the "path of least resistance" by drastically reducing initiation fees or completely waiving initiation fees in order to compete. The harder path, and ultimately more fruitful, is to set member retention, recruitment, and satisfaction as the club's highest priorities. Gregg Patterson, general manager of The Beach Club of Santa Monica, CA, states that since members have options with their leisure time and money then a key realization for the club manager becomes that this is a "consumer oriented world." Patterson states, "All clubs need to find out what their members want and go after it aggressively. Every member has similar wants, goods, services, programs, facility and a sense of community but the expression of those wants change with time."[6]

Therefore, it is of critical import for the club manager to stay abreast of the consumers need and want continuum. Case in point is the busier American lifestyle with children's athletic events, community functions, and alternative entertainment activities that serve to place more scrutiny on a family's discretionary dollars. Thus, a main reason for problematic retention and recruitment is lack of use of the facilities. Vain concluded that in light of this scenario too many clubs "have failed to update their product to appeal with the growing age brackets of baby boomers."[7] Given the above discussion, a consensus is again drawn as to the options available to success. A club manager may take a more formal route such as hiring a membership director focused specifically on retention and recruitment. Utilizing third party firms in the consultation arena, drawing upon survey information cultivated in-house, or

In addition to golf, many clubs offer facilities for swimming, tennis, horseback riding, and more.

© Nick Stubbs, 2008, Shutterstock.

from broader industry outlets. Using this information to tweak or remodel the product to fit the niche that is unique to each club situation.

Variety of Clubs

Although all clubs share a common bond being the fee/due paying member, the private club industry has evolved into a vast landscape of variety. Listed and described below are some of the most common clubs in existence today.

Country Clubs

Around 80% of all private clubs are country clubs and they often provide elaborate social amenities along with their outdoor recreational facilities. Activities in a typical country club usually center on

Profile
A CLUB MANAGER'S PERSPECTIVE: *DAN BRENNAN, EDGEWORTH CLUB*

The Edgeworth Club[8] was formed in 1893. Under the bylaws its purpose was to promote interaction and friendship among its members and their social enjoyment, and for the purpose of furnishing facilities for athletics and other innocent sports, and the erection and maintenance of a building or buildings thereafter. Sports that were emphasized at the club were tennis, bowling, and golf. The architectural style of the Edgeworth Club is decidedly Elizabethan, which lends itself particularly to the ground on which it was built and the uses for which it was designed. The Edgeworth Club hosted the Wightman Tennis Cup matches, a prestigious international  tennis event. Since then its emphasis has been on tennis and paddle tennis. The club is the principal location for charity events in the raising of funds for health associations and other organizations, as this is an important part of the club personality. Similarly, the century-long tradition of the ventricle presentations involves club members in all phases of the writing, directing, and acting in these entertainments.

the golf course; yet, many clubs also provide members with outdoor facilities for swimming, tennis, horseback riding, and other interests. Members might hold weddings, reunions, or other social events there. Recently many upscale housing projects have encouraged the building and growth of country clubs: to attract neighboring communities and new residents. There are two types of memberships at country clubs: full memberships which entitles the club member to the full use of the facilities the club offers, and social membership which permits the member to use specific facilities, such as the restaurant, lounge, bar, tennis courts, etc. Social membership sometimes requires that club members use the club's facilities at certain times or days. Equinox Country club in Manchester, Vermont, and the California Country club in Whittier, California, are two examples of country clubs. In the past country clubs were seen as the last bastions of the upper class elite. In some cases this is still true; however, in most instances the stuffy cigar smoke and the Mayflower context are no longer used to determine whether an individual should be qualified for membership.

Yacht Clubs

Yacht clubs are 4% of the total clubs. These clubs are designated for establishments near or on the water, and generally promote and regulate boating and yachting. The Montauk and Rochester yacht clubs are examples of this type of organization. Most yacht clubs own and operate a marina for their members, which may include the operation of a clubhouse with dining and recreation facilities.

Military Clubs

Military clubs cater to the enlisted man, the non-commissioned officer, and the officer. Military bases in the United States and overseas provide these clubs for the welfare and the benefit of the soldiers. They provide extended amenities for their club members, such as guest quarters, recreational activities, food and beverage operations, and entertainment. In the past the clubs have been run by military personnel, but recent changes in resource allocation have required the military to contract civilian firms to provide services. These facilities are located around the world and include the Bamberg officer's club in Bamberg, Germany; the Fort Benning officer's club in Fort Benning, Georgia; and the 911th Airlift Wing of the United States Air Force.

Before 1974 they had two military clubs on base. The NCO Club was for the enlisted members of the base and the Officer's Club was designated for the officers of the base. Due to the down sizing in the military and the costs of running two clubs, the 911th NCO and Officer's Club became a Consolidated Open Mess (Club) in February 1974. Today's Club is open to officer and enlisted members of all branches of the Armed Forces—Air Force, Army, Navy, Marines, and Coast Guard and is currently 1,133 members strong. Being a member of the Club is a tradition at the 911th Airlift Wing. Members join the Club for several reasons but the biggest include camaraderie and a place to share military experiences with other armed services members. It is also a gathering place for the numerous retirees in the area. The 911th Club hosts several events each month for its members ranging from official functions to holiday celebrations, as well as membership nights, sports parties, meet-and-greets, birthday parties, wedding receptions, and other functions. The Club offers excellent dining opportunities and does promotions with giveaways.

Professional clubs are for people in the same profession for social and business interaction. The Engineer's Club of St. Louis is a professional club that appeals to engineers from the St. Louis area.

Social clubs, similar to the Everglades Club in Palm Beach, Florida, concentrate on serving the social needs of member who are normally from similar social-economic backgrounds.

City clubs, as the name implies, are usually located in urban communities and range from luncheon-only clubs that serve segments of the business population to fully integrated dining and athletic clubs make up about 11% of its clubs. Unlike most private clubs, city clubs may rent out guest rooms, organize themselves around a specialized profession, or associate with a particular college or university. City clubs fall into the following categories: professional, social, athletic, dining, fraternal, and university. The Duquesne Club has achieved the number one ranking among America's 10,000 private clubs according to a national survey conducted by the Club Managers Association of America.

Athletic clubs, such as the Palm Beach Bath and Tennis Club and the Toronto Cricket and Skating Club provide an outlet for working out, athletic activities, dining, and meeting.

Dining clubs are usually located in large office buildings offering their members top-quality food-service in urban surroundings. Examples include the Toronto Hunt Club and the Union Club of British Columbia.

Fraternal clubs, like the Elks Club and the Veterans of Foreign War, provide fraternal organizations with a central location for meetings, dining, and social activities.

University clubs are reserved for the activities of faculty, alumni, and guests. The Harvard, Yale, Princeton Club of Pittsburgh, and the University of Toronto Faculty Club are perfect examples.

Club Personnel

As club types, country clubs are the largest employers, followed by golf clubs and city clubs. Taken together, the total employment in country clubs is 4 times the number employed in golf clubs, and almost 10 times the number of those employed by city clubs. The ratio of full-time and part-time nonseasonal employees is almost exactly the same for both golf clubs and country clubs. Approximately 43% of all employees in these clubs are full-time and nonseasonal. This contrasts sharply with city clubs, where 74% of the employees are full-time nonseasonal employees. Similar ratios were found among full-time and part-time seasonal employees in both golf and country clubs. However, among city clubs, only one-third of the seasonal employees are part-time.

Legal Form of Business

Club ownership includes two categories: equity clubs and proprietary clubs. **Equity clubs** are non-profit clubs and are the oldest form of club management; yet, they are still the most common form of ownership today. These clubs are owned and organized by the members for their own enjoyment. The board of directors then establishes the policies, budget, and does the hiring and firing of executives, such as the club manager. Any profits that are generated from the dues or club operations must be reinvested in the clubs services and facilities and cannot be returned to the members.

Proprietary clubs are operated for profit and are owned by a corporation, company, business, or individual. These clubs became popular in the 1970s and 1980s and provided an expansion of club membership and stringent admission requirements. Club members purchase a membership from the club's owner(s) and have limited input and control over the activities or management of the daily operations

of the club. In some cases contract organizations run the facility for the owner. The club manager reports to this organization or the owner of the facility. Depending on the type, interest, and development of all clubs, the category of ownership may vary.

Management Styles

As a student one of the most challenging experiences in life will be to choose a career. If you're looking for a career that is creative and combines business skills, human resource management, marketing, and public relations, welcome to the world of club management. It is one of the fastest-growing industries and hospitality fields and will provide you with outstanding career opportunities in the future. Club management is similar to that of hospitality management because it offers similar facilities. The largest difference is that the club, unlike a hotel or restaurant, is actually looked at as being owned by the members. The member pays a fee each year, which can vary drastically depending on the nature of the club. In turn, the members feel that they are the owners of the facility. Having one boss may be difficult, but imagine having thousands! This sometimes can put the manager in a difficult situation.

The manager of a club is actually governed by a constitution and the by-laws of the club. The board of directors and club president are elected by their peers to insure the goals and mission of the club are carried out effectively, and they create the constitution and by-laws that govern members' policies and standards. Club management structure is similar to that of company structure. There is a president, vice president, treasurer, secretary, and different committees. The manager of a club, usually referred to as the Chief Operating Officer or the General Manager, has to answer to and abide by the rules set forth by the governing body and is responsible for all areas of club operation. While the board of directors and president may be responsible for the policy setting and implementation, it is the club manager's job to hire personnel to run the day-to-day operations of the club.

Technology

Club managers ranked the important technologies of the future, in a recent study by Dr. Kasavana from Michigan State University.[9] (1) Convert the club to a wireless environment. (2) Utilize e-procurement in order to lower transaction costs improved pricing and enhance productivity, leveraged purchasing, reduce inventory, and improve communications. (3) POS technology touch input and handheld terminals; handheld technology eliminates the duplication by recording the order directly into the POS device right at the table thus saving significant time. (4) MRM data mining capturing and storing member data forming a club's central focal point of its information systems. (5) ASP subscription outsourcing provides a third-party agency that manages and use and distribute Internet-based services. Future technologies will provide clubs with a competitive advantage through product differentiation, unique service, cost reduction and market segmentation.

Club Continuing Education

The sprawl of the club industry, in all its variety, onto the cultural and business landscapes has served, as Perdue, Ninemeier, & Woods[10] astutely observe, to increase the industry's sophistication thereby prompting managers to utilize new technologies and products in order to offer improved services all the while operating in an extremely competitive environment and labor market. As a result of these changing dynamics, the need for lifelong learning has emerged as a key element for individuals, organizations, and societies in maintaining their competitive position.[11]

It is to this end that the CMAA and its Canadian counterpart, the Canadian Society of Club Managers, have been instrumental in keeping its members, and, thus, the industry as a whole, in a learning mode. These organizations have served as a bridge to bring academia and club management together producing collaborative efforts in the valuable forms of management development/professional credentialing programs, teaching, conference participation, and applied research.

Club Managers Association of America (CMAA)

Many club managers belong to the Club Managers Association of America (CMAA). This organization is the oldest and most widely respected association representing the club management professional and is comprised of more than 7,000 professional managers from the most prestigious private country, city, yacht, and military clubs in the United States and around the world. In the early 1920s professional club managers recognized the impact clubs had on the American way of life and the need for a professional association of these clubs. In February of 1927 the first annual meeting of the CMAA took place.

CMAA actively promotes and advances cooperation among individuals directly engaged in the club management profession, as well as other associations in the hospitality industry. In addition CMAA encourages the education and professional advancement of it members and assists club officers and managers throughs their management to secure the utmost in efficient and successful operations. The organization recognizes its responsibility to assist students in gaining a better understanding of the private club management profession and in selecting a career in this sector of the hospitality industry. The Club Managers Association of America adheres to a strict code.

CMAA Code of Ethics*

We believe the management of clubs is an honorable calling. It shall be incumbent upon club managers to be knowledgeable in the application of sound principles in the management of clubs, with ample opportunity to keep abreast of current practices and procedures. We are convinced that the Club Managers Association of America best represents these interests, and as members thereof, subscribe to the following CODE OF ETHICS:

We will uphold the best traditions of club management through adherence to sound business principles. By our behavior and demeanor, we shall set an example for our employees and will assist our club officers to secure the utmost in efficient and successful club operations.

We will consistently promote the recognition and esteem of club management as a profession and conduct our personal and business affairs in a manner to reflect capability and integrity. We will always honor our contractual employment obligations.

We shall promote community and civic affairs by maintaining good relations with the public sector to the extent possible within the limits of our club's demands.

We will strive to advance our knowledge and abilities as club managers, and willingly share with oth-

*WWW.CMAA.org

er Association members the lessons of our experience and knowledge gained by supporting and participating in our local chapter and the National Association's educational meetings and seminars.

We will not permit ourselves to be subsidized or compromised by any interest doing business with our clubs.

We will refrain from initiating, directly or through an agent, any communications with a director, member or employee of another club regarding its affairs without the prior knowledge of the manager thereof, if it has a manager. We will advise the National Headquarters, whenever possible, regarding managerial openings at clubs that come to our attention. We will do all within our power to assist our fellow club managers in pursuit of their professional goals.

We shall not be deterred from compliance with the law, as it applies to our clubs. We shall provide our club officers and trustees with specifics of Federal, State and Local laws, statutes and regulations, to avoid punitive action and costly litigation.

We deem it our duty to report to local or national officers any willful violations of the CMAA CODE OF ETHICS."[12]

Club Type and Location

- 80% of CMAA members' clubs are golf and country clubs.
- 13% of CMAA members' clubs are city clubs.
- 4% of CMAA members are yacht clubs.
- 65% are IRS classified tax-exempt 501(c)(7) organizations.

Club Income

- Gross revenues equaled $14 billion for all clubs in 2006.
- Food and beverage revenues equal $4.5 billion.
- The average club income is $5.18 million.

Club Employees

- Clubs employ more than 289,821 employees.
- Club payrolls over $4 billion.

Club Outreach Programs

- Clubs raised $367 million for charities in 2006.
- In 2006, most of CMAA's 50 chapters sponsor scholarship funds.

Economic Impact of Clubs

- The average club spends $1.05 million in the local community.
- The average club spends $1.2 million within the state as a whole.
- Overall, club operations generate $6.21 billion for state economies around the country.
- A typical club pays $150,773 in property taxes.

A student chapter of CMAA can be offered at any school that offers an undergraduate or graduate program in hospitality. As chapter members students participate in professional development programs, site-visitation at local clubs, hands-on club operations and demonstrations, and leadership development programs. The CMAA provides its student chapters with an internship directory, which provides more than 200 internships at private clubs around the world.

National Club Association (NCA)

The National Club Association has served as an invaluable resource for thousands of club leaders across the country for more than 45 years. Although noted for their influence on Capitol Hill, NCA's staff of professionals is also readily available to answer members' questions and concerns about compliance, governance, and federal and state tax issues. In addition, their team constantly gathers industry-specific news and trends data and disseminates pertinent information so that club leaders can focus on giving their members that unparalleled club experience.

Specifically NCA strives to:

- Provide support and information to assist club leaders in addressing legal, governance, and business concerns.
- Help clubs strengthen their financial health and protect their assets.
- Ensure recognition and advancement of club interests through lobbying and other government relation's activities, seeking to preserve the independence of clubs to operate.
- Assist clubs in complying with laws and regulations.

Summary

Clubs provide a unique managing experience that combines many elements of the hospitality and tourism industries. Club managers must be versatile and open to the changing needs of the club members and the world around them. The most important job of a club manager is to provide club members with a positive experience every time they attend a function at the club. If managers fail to do this, attendance and membership will drop off and the club will cease to exist. Service is the key to a club manager's success and service is the core of the business. Club managers must remember that they "serve the world."

≈ Resources

Internet Sites

Algonquin Club of Boston: http://algonquinclub.memfirst.net/Club/Scripts/Home/home.asp
American Club in Singapore: http://www.amclub.org.sg/
American Society of Golf Course Architects: http://www.golfdesign.org/
Ariel Sands Beach Club: http://www.arielsands.com/
Army Navy Country Club: http://ancc.org/
Association of College and University Clubs: http://www.collegeanduniversityclubs.org/
Atlanta Athletic Club: http://www.atlantaathleticclub.org/
Ballantyne Country Club: http://www.crescent-resources.com/communit/charlott/ballanty/default.asp
Bear Creek Golf Club: http://www.bearcreekgc.com/Club/Scripts/Home/home.asp
Belmont Country Club: http://www.belmontcc.org/Club/Scripts/Splash/splash.asp
Boca Raton Resort & Club: http://www.bocaresort.com/
California Yacht Club: http://calyachtclub.com/cms/index2.htm
Capitol Hill Club: http://www.capitolhillclub.com/
Cedar Rapids Country Club: http://www.thecrcc.com/
Club Managers Association of America: www.cmaa.org
Club Services: http://www.clubservices.com
ClubCorp: http://www.clubcorp.com
Country Club of Lansing: http://www.cclansing.org/
Country Club of St. Albans: http://www.stalbans.com/
Golf Course Builders Association of America: http://www.gcbaa.org/
Golf Course Superintendents Association of America: http://www.gcsaa.org/
International Association of Golf Administrators: http://www.iaga.org/
International Club Network: http://www.privaccess.com/
International Health, Racquet, & Sportsclub Association: http://csdemo12.citysoft.com/IHRSA/viewPage.cfm?pageId=2
International Military Community Executives Association: http://www.imcea.com/
Ladies Professional Golf Association: http://www.lpga.com/
Lighthouse Point Yacht and Racquet Club: http://www.lpyrc.com/
National Association of Club Athletic Directors: http://www.nacad.org/
National Club Association: http://www.natlclub.org/
Professional Golfers Association of America: http://www.pga.com/
Sanctuary Golf Club: http://www.sanctuary-sanibel.com/
The ACE Club: http://www.theaceclubonline.com/
The Virtual Clubhouse/Club Management Magazine: www.club-mgmt.com

References

Barnhart, C. L., ed. (1990). *The American College Dictionary.* New York: Random House.

Brown, M. M., Donnelly, L., and Wilkins, D. G. (1989). *The History of the Duquesne Club.* Pittsburgh, PA: Art and Library Committee.

Club Managers Association of America. (1999). The CMAA Student Advantage: A Commitment to Your Future at http://www.cmaa.org/student/adv_bro/index.htm

Crossley, J. C., and Jamieson, L. M. (1997). Introduction to Commercial and Entrepreneurial Recreation. Champaign, IL: Sagamore Publishing.

Membership issues: Opinions on what works in today's private club industry at http://www.boardroommagazine.com/fa59.cfm

Perfect storm: What does it mean for private clubs? at http://www.boardroommagazine.com/fa58.cfm

Singerling, J., Wood, R., Nimemeier, J., and Purdue, J. (1997). Success factors in private clubs. *Cornell HRA Quarterly, 38.5.*
Walker, J. R. (2001). *Introduction to Hospitality,* 3rd ed. Upper Saddle River, NJ: Prentice-Hall.

≈ *Endnotes*

1. Club Managers Association of America. Economic impact survey 2006 at http://www.cmaa.org/EconImpactSurvey/2006EconImpactSurvey.doc
2. Perdue, J., ed. (2007). *Contemporary Club Management.* Virginia: Club Managers Association of America.
3. Ibid.
4. Ibid.
5. Club Managers Association of America. Club management forum at http://www.cmaa.org/conf/conf2000/time.htm
6. Ibid.
7. Ibid.
8. Edgewood Club Home Page at http://www.edgewoodclub.com
9. Perdue, J., Ninemeier, J. D., and Woods, R. H. (2002). Comparison of present and future competencies required for club managers. *International Journal of Contemporary Hospitality Management, 14(3),* 142–146.
10. Barrows, C. W., and Walsh, J. (2002). Bridging the gap between hospitality management programmes and the private club industry. *International Journal of Contemporary Hospitality Management, 14(3),* 120–127.
11. Club Managers Association of America at http://www.cmaa.org

≈ *Contributors*

Denis P. Rudd, Ed.D., CHA, FMP, CTP

University Professor and Director of Hospitality and Tourism Management
Robert Morris University
VOICE: 412-262-8636; FAX: 412-262-8494; E-mail: rudd@robert-morris.edu

Denis P. Rudd, Ed.D., CHA, FMP, is The University Professor and Director of Hospitality and Tourism Management at Robert Morris University Pennsylvania at both the Coraopolis and Pittsburgh campuses. Dr. Rudd received his Bachelor's Degree in Finance and Commerce from Rider College, Lawerenceville, New Jersey, a Master's in Business Administration, a Masters in Education Counseling, Specialist in Higher Education Administration, and a Doctorate in Educational Counseling from the University of Nevada, Las Vegas. In 1995 he accepted the position as Professor and Director of Hospitality and Tourism Management for Robert Morris College Coraopolis and Pittsburgh, Pennsylvania. Dr Rudd has recently published three texts entitled *Introduction to Casino and Gaming, Club Operations,* and *Convention Technology.* In addition Dr. Rudd has received certification as a CHA and FMP from the National Restaurant Association and the Educational Institute of the American Hotel Motel Association and PTC, from the International Meeting Planners Association. In 2005 Dr. Rudd was honored by being appointed the first University Professor of Robert Morris University.

Richard J. Mills, Jr., Ph.D.

Assistant Professor, Hospitality and Tourism
Robert Morris University
VOICE: 412-262-8636; FAX: 412-262-8494; E-mail: mills@robert-morris.edu

Dr. Richard J. Mills, Jr., has many years of both professional and academic experience. He is currently a certified Sous Chef through the American Culinary Federation and has worked in the industry as a professional cook, chef, and foodservice director for more than 12 years. Dr. Mills is currently an Assistant Professor teaching in the Hospitality and Tourism department at Robert Morris University, Moon Township, PA. In addition Dr. Richard J. Mills, Jr. holds two Master's degrees, an MLS and MA, and has taught, researched, and published several books and publications in the areas of food and communication. While teaching at various universities throughout his career Dr. Mills has had the opportunity to implement various courses at the undergraduate level, in food production management and quantity food production. Dr. Mills received his Doctorate Degree in the Communication and Rhetorical Studies from Duquesne University in Pittsburgh, PA, with an emphasis on food and culture.

Chapter 34
Review Questions

1. What types of services are likely to be offered at a city club?

2. Describe the types of military clubs and the purposes they serve.

3. What is the mix of full-time to part-time staff at country clubs?

4. What is the mix of full-time to part-time staff at city clubs?

5. What is the mix of year round to seasonal staff in country clubs?

6. What is the mix of year round to seasonal staff in city clubs?

7. What types of facilities are likely to be found at a country club?

8. Define an equity club.

9. Define a proprietary club.

10. Sketch an organization chart that shows which positions report to whom.

11. What is CMAA? Visit their Website at www.cmaa.org.

12. What is NCA, and what are the goals of NCA?

Assignment 1

Visit Club Managers Association of America's Website, ClubNet (www.cmaa.org). This Website offers links to homepages for numerous private clubs throughout the United States. Visit as many of these homepages as possible to gain an understanding of the variety of private clubs available as well as the quality facilities that are provided for members and their guests.

ClubNet also describes the numerous professional development opportunities available for club managers through CMAA. Peruse this section of ClubNet to better understand how professional development and learning is a life-long pursuit.

As you look ahead and plan your career, how will you pursue professional development and continuous educational opportunities?

Assignment 2

According to an article in *Club Management* by Chris White (December 2000), the growth of the spa industry can provide opportunities for the private club sector. The spa industry has grown across the United States due to a number of reasons delineated by White (p. 94):

- Baby boomers' desire to slow the effects of aging

- The high costs of conventional, remedial health care as compared to preventive health care

- The increasing concern for the quality of the lengthening average lifespan

- Increasing amounts of personal disposable income

The variety of types of spas is also expanding. Spas no longer have to be the destination, resort or cruise line spas also known as vacation spas. Day spas, which tend to cater to local clientele and offer hair salons, skin care, body treatments, and massage, are a growing segment. White emphasized in this article that the day spa market may provide enormous opportunities for private clubs particularly involving massage, body treatments, and possibly skin care.

What is your opinion of these expanded services for private clubs? What other types of amenities might be added that would be popular with private club members? How could these services be effectively marketed to the membership? What are potential disadvantages of offering "day spa" types of services?

Assignment 3

Many clubs are increasingly experiencing quite varied demographics among their membership resulting in contrasting membership expectations and demands. For example, while clubs may still have a population of older members who have perhaps been with the club for many decades, younger members, often with children, are also a growing segment. While the older members may still enjoy dressing up for an evening of fine dining, this may not be realistic or pleasurable for a family with three young children. How does a club cater to differing member preferences? The solution of operating different facilities to cater to the preferences of all members may work for some clubs but would be too costly and unrealistic for many operations.

If you were the new General Manager of a club with these dilemmas (varied member preferences/limited budget and the membership resistant to increases in dues), what would you suggest? Think of going before the club's board with at least three options to possibly increase member usage of the food and beverage facilities. What will you propose?

Senior Living Centers

35

Brad Beran, Johnson & Wales University, Charlotte

© Jennifer A. Walz, 2008, Shutterstock.

≈ Learning Objectives

- ☑ Define and identify the different types of senior assisted living centers
- ☑ Identify job requirements that are similar to other segments within the hospitality industry
- ☑ Identify job requirements that are unique to senior assisted living centers
- ☑ Understand and identify define the career positions, scope, and growth potential of careers within senior assisted living centers
- ☑ Understand the market needs and trends of senior assisted living centers
- ☑ Identify specific guest needs, demands, services, and requirements and the types of centers that fill these needs

≈ Chapter Outline

Introduction
Independent, Assisted, Full Care, and Respite Care Living Centers
Market Outlook and Cost Support
Development and Ownership of Senior Living Centers
Work, Jobs, and Positions in Living Centers

≈ Key Terms

At-home assisted living
Assisted living communities
Full care centers/nursing homes
Respite care
Growth and demand for living centers
Support services
Forms of ownership
Costs and reimbursement

Introduction

*B*aby boomers are beginning to retire and will continue to retire in large numbers over the next two decades. This group of retirees will be the healthiest, most financially well off, most independent and mobile, and longest living of any group to date. Census data from the U.S. Department of Commerce[1] shows that 35 million people, or 12.4% of the population, are 65 years old or older; 60 million people, or 21% of the population, are 55 years old or older; and about 97 million people, just over a third of the total population of the United States, 34.4%, are 45 years old or older.

Where are these people retiring? Of the 100 fastest growing counties in the United States, only eight are in the northern part of the country, above the Mason-Dixon line. All other counties are in the south spanning from the Atlantic to the Pacific oceans and all points in between.[2] Not all of the growth can be attributed to retiring seniors, but much of it is from retirees.

Who are these people? Demographic data indicates that as of the 2004 projections of the total population, of those 65 years and older, 14.3% are women and 10.4% are men. By 2010 the split should be 14.8% women and 12.2% men. By 2030, the expectations are 20.7% women and 17.6% men. Put another way, by 2030, 38.3% of the population of the United States should be retired.[3]

The potential market for Senior Living Centers is enormous. Senior living centers provide many services to attract and support the needs of this population. The potential clientele has many different needs and goals for their retired years including people who no longer have the ability and/or desire to maintain a private residence, want greater flexibility and/or fewer responsibilities during their retirement, and are looking to senior living centers to meet their residential and personal needs.

Senior living centers are filling the need of retirees by offering a multitude of services and conveniences. The services and conveniences are as minimal or as extensive as retirees' desire depending on needs, demands, health, family and support, and financial situation. Minimal services can be limited to living space and basic interior and exterior maintenance at one end of the spectrum to full service living centers offering restaurants and meal plans, laundry, cleaning, pharmacy and basic medical services, transportation, activities and entertainment, and more. As the level and amount of service increases, so does the cost to the living center resident.

Senior living centers can be categorized by the amount and level of service they provide ranging from at-home and independent living centers to full care living centers.

Independent, Assisted, Full Care, and Respite Care Living Centers

Independent Living Communities

Independent living communities are for the most healthy and independent residents. These residents typically own a car, are in good health, drive often, are quite independent, and come and go as they please. If they require any medical support at all, it is minimal and usually not much more than pharmacy support for medications.

Independent living communities for independent residents like these offer the fewest services and are the lowest cost. Sometimes seniors do not want the responsibility of house maintenance so they look for this type of housing. Typical services at this level are lawn care, snow removal, and similar outdoor maintenance. There are some communities where one can buy a small house to live in with all the maintenance included, then when they need more care, the house is sold to provide the money to move to additional care facilities on premise. Other services often include a community center and/or recreation center and may include food services (restaurant or catered meals) and/or home replacement meals and laundry services. These centers often resemble apartment complexes. Newly built facilities are usually no more than two stories high and often look more like a small community of duplex or multiplex housing.

One example of high-level services at the independent level is Sunrise Independent Living Communities. Services for residents include exercise and wellness programs, outings to local events and attractions, on-site entertainment, programs and activities, fine dining, landscaped grounds, barber and beauty shops, housekeeping, linen, and transportation services and more.[4] The price for independent living communities ranges from about $1300 per month to upward of $6000 per month depending on location and the number and type of services offered and selected by the resident. The resident pays for the fees with possibly some government assistance.[5]

At-Home Assisted Living

For some seniors who are healthy and relatively independent, the prospect of giving up their home is unacceptable, yet they need assistance in certain tasks. A small but growing area known as At-Home Assisted Living fills this need. This service provides support for a multitude of needs such as light housekeeping, meal preparation and planning, bathing and grooming assistance, medication management, errands and shopping services, and more.[6] These can work in conjunction with governmental agencies and churches.

Assisted Living Centers

The typical resident of assisted living centers either drive minimally, or do not drive at all. As a result, it is difficult to live in their own homes. Often they need varying degrees of assistance due to limitations such as medical, physical, or mental conditions. It can be something as simple as regularly forgetting to turn off the stove or to eat or to take their medication. They are not as healthy or independent as residents of independent living centers and may be in declining health. These residents value their independence, but are not capable or comfortable living completely independently. Typically, the longer these residents stay at a center, the more services they require as they age. These centers are often set up as smaller, efficiency apartments, or as group units with a central common area and bedrooms for 8 to 20 residents with several units per center. Some of the assisted living centers offer two room suites so that two women or men can share to cut expenses. However, another option is when a married couple wants to stay together but one needs more care than the other.

Assisted living centers offer more services at a greater cost to their residents. In addition to the services offered at independent centers, assisted centers generally add or offer assistance with medications, meal preparation and/or feeding, personal care (shaving, showering, dressing, etc.), ambulatory care, and transportation services. Medical care may be onsite, but is minimal, usually provided by a Licensed Practical Nurse (LPN) or Registered Nurse (RN), is often not available 24 hours per day, and is generally for minor injuries, consulting, and referrals. Some assisted living centers provide specialty care for residents with Alzheimer's and other debilitating, noncommunicable disease. Coordination with external physician and pharmacy services are provided as the medical needs of this group are much greater than in independent living centers.[7] Living center administration must be aware of special medical requests, such as Do Not Resuscitate orders, visitation restrictions, hospital preference in case of emergency transport, personal physician information, and the like.

Services available for assisted living are usually offered in one of three ways. A resident may select from a menu of services and pay a fee based on the number and type of services selected. Another option allows a resident to select one of several service programs or packages, each offering more services at different price points. In these cases, as a person needs more care over time, they can stay in the same facility longer. Finally, an assisted living center may offer only one set of services at one price. In this instance, if a resident requires more services than are available, they must move to another center to have their needs met which is usually a transfer to a full service center/nursing home.

At Sunrise Assisted Living Centers, services include three meals per day served in a restaurant style setting, health and wellness assessments, scheduled transportation, activities programs, weekly housekeeping and linen service, and personalized levels of care based on each resident's needs.[8] The price for assisted living centers ranges from about $1800 per month to upwards of $3500 per month depending on services used. Alzheimer's care is more expensive, from nearly $3000 per month to around $4000 per month. The resident most often pays for these costs with possibly some assistance from Medicaid.[9] In other facilities, depending on the ratio of caregivers to residents, the size of the rooms, or the availability facilities, pricing can be daily or monthly, sometimes reaching over $6000 a month, while others may require a one time admittance fee that can be over $150,000.

Full Care Living Centers

Full care living centers are most commonly known as nursing homes. Residents are unable to live by themselves and, at best, can only provide minimal care for themselves. These residents may require feeding assistance, may be bedridden, and may need continual observation and care. These centers provide full service for those seniors least able to care for themselves. All services are provided for these residents, which includes all meals, housekeeping, laundry, eating, personal care, medication, and other services. Medical personnel are on staff 24 hours each day, including Registered Nurses (RNs), Licensed Practical Nurses (LPNs), and Certified Nursing Assistants (CNAs). Doctors are on call and often maintain a regular schedule. Pharmacy services are provided and some medical testing is often available on-site.

Sunrise Senior Living nursing homes offer 24 hour nursing, post-hospital care, post-surgical care, physician and pharmacy coordination, family counseling and other support services, and emotional and physical health and wellbeing.[10] Nursing home prices will range from around $3000 per month to around $6000 per month depending on services needed by the resident. Residents pay these costs themselves and Medicare or Medicaid can supplement the costs.[11]

Respite Care

Many assisted living centers and full service centers offer respite care as an option if there is space available. Respite care is a short term, temporary use of assisted living center resources and services. This care is designed to fill the needs of an individual who may need assistance in recovery from surgery, injury, or other ailment and only needs temporary assistance during recovery and rehabilitation. Re-

spite care generally lasts from one week to a few months and is usually billed by the day and/or week. Typical services for respite care can include medical and pharmacy services, physical therapy, meals, laundry and housekeeping services and other services, as needed depending on each situation.[12] Costs for respite care vary from about $100 to $185 depending on location and level of care and services needed.[13] Respite care fees are usually paid for through some combination of insurance, Medicare, Medicaid, and personal funds.[14]

Some facilities are a one stop place. A person can start in independent living and then move to a new wing for more care until they reach the skilled nursing level. This is especially good as seniors settle in and get to know the facility. They can continue to be near their friends and nurses even though they have to move to a different wing. In addition, as they lose their short term memory, guests can have time to develop comfort zones. To create better comfort zones, some facilities are designed for specialty interests. For example, there are facilities that specialize in people who love to grow wines and they all work in the wine making. Other facilities cater to ethnicities or religious preferences. One place has special programs in flower arranging, bonsai, and other Japanese cultural skills for their residents.

Market Outlook and Cost Support

Expected Demand

The 2000 census lists 1,720,500 residents in nursing homes. By 2010 it is projected that there will be 36,818,000 Americans aged 65 or older and by 2020 the estimate increases to 47,338,000 and to 81,999,000 by 2050.[15] In order to meet the expected demand for senior living centers, an additional 1.25 million units will need to be built. Put another way, the construction of one unit capable of housing 600 residents must be built each week for the next 40 years to fill the expected demand. Private companies are building and/or completely renovating apartments and other buildings into senior living centers to begin to meet the demand through private investment and federal programs. To put these figures into dollars, in 2000, long term care for those 65 and older was $123 billion and expected to double in 30 years.[16]

© 2008, JupiterImages Corporation.

To increase guest comfort, some care facilities are designed for, or offer programs in, areas of special interest.

Government Support

Medical costs have risen drastically over the last several years with costs for seniors accounting for a significant portion. In order to address and try to contain these costs and to help improve the quality of life for seniors, the federal government is also expanding the market for living centers. In order to reduce costs while still providing services, seniors who meet certain eligibility criteria are encouraged to consider assisted living centers instead of more expensive nursing home care. To accomplish this, two programs have been developed. First, Medicare has developed the PACE program. PACE has options that allow qualified seniors to receive assistance while remaining in their own homes, adult day health centers, and inpatient facilities.

From the Medicare Website:

Program of All Inclusive Care for the Elderly (PACE)

PACE is unique. It is an optional benefit under both Medicare and Medicaid that focuses entirely on older people, who are frail enough to meet their State's standards for nursing home care. It features comprehensive medical and social services that can be provided at an adult day health center, home, and/or inpatient facilities. For most patients, the comprehensive service package permits them to continue living at home while receiving services, rather than be institutionalized. A team of doctors, nurses and other health professionals assess participant needs, develop care plans, and deliver all services, which are integrated into a complete health care plan. PACE is available only in States, which have chosen to offer PACE under Medicaid.[17]

A second program is matching government funding under the HUD Section 202 grants program.[18] This program provides matching funds at an assortment of levels to individuals and companies for supportive housing for the elderly and persons with disabilities. Eligibility requirements apply based primarily on income level.

Several Websites and other forms of assistance in defining, identifying, and selecting a senior living center and/or determining the levels of service needed are available. One site, A Place for Mom, offers a complete and free consulting and advice to families considering senior living center alternatives.

Development and Ownership of Senior Living Centers

Religious Groups

Senior living center residents do not own their apartments. They are tenants who contract for the space and services they receive. Senior living centers have several types of ownership. Some are owned by religious orders, such as Menorah Park, which is owned by the Jewish Orthodox. Religious based living centers are operated for members of their religion and costs can be subsidized by the religion.[19]

Charities and Foundations

Charities and foundations, such as the Bethesda Living Centers are owned by the Bethesda Foundation, and operate the living centers. Like religious owned living centers, resident fees are often subsidized to some degree. Residents generally must meet certain criteria to belong to these living centers, such as income guidelines, specific medical needs, etc.

Private Businesses and Corporations

Private companies and corporations, such as Sunrise Assisted Living, Inc. and Southern Manor Living Centers, LLC, provide a third type of ownership. These are usually for profit companies supported by private investment, returning dividends or tax deductions to investors, often through Real Estate Investment Trusts or REITs.[20] Government agencies also own retirement centers, however, this type of ownership is declining and most often was limited to nursing homes. As local and state governments cut costs and move toward the privatization of services, many community/government owned senior centers are being sold to private concerns or closed.

Individually Owned with Contracted Management and Services

All prior forms of living centers involve private groups, investors, and nonprofits as the owners and providers of services. In each of those cases, all services are contracted for including living quarters, which are leased spaces. In individually owned living centers, private individuals own their living space which can be anything from a free standing bungalow, to an apartment, called apartment homes. Think of the latter as a condominium form of ownership. In these examples, the owners have all of the benefits of ownership, such as complete freedom to remodel, renovate, and the like, with the tax benefits of ownership.

Purchasing a property within an assisted living community may have barriers. Due to the current sub-prime lending problems and tightening of credit, some people may have difficulty obtaining a mortgage. This is not the usual case, however, as many community members have sold other homes, used the income from the sale to purchase within the assisted living community, and often purchase for less money than their prior home sold for, saving the difference. Purchasing in an assisted living community may require an application and acceptance by an association who will often have covenants, or restrictions, on what is allowed in the community. It then falls to the owner to maintain the rest of the property in accordance with community requirements. Assisted living communities contract with, or are operated by, management companies to maintain grounds, operate a club house and recreation area, coordinate activities, and more.

Most of the living communities offer many of the same amenities provided by other senior living centers, such as a clubhouse, recreation center and support, medical assistance, full service restaurant with or without a meal plan, and more. Larger operations offer the opportunity to trade or move into higher care and more services as they are needed by the resident.

Work, Jobs, and Positions in Living Centers

The Nature of Work in Assisted Living Centers

By their needs, characteristics, and service to residents, assisted living centers have career tracks that share many similarities to other hospitality venues. Private clubs have a consistent, semi-captive crowd. One challenge is to create interesting and creative opportunities for members from menus to activities. Assisted living centers have this same challenge, a consistent clientele.

Hotels and hospitals are 24 hour a day, 7 day per week operations with on site residents who may need services at any time. Assisted living centers are in the same situation whether it's basic needs such as heat, light, and power, security, or a medical emergency.

Event planning, activities, and recreation services are part of the services to meet guest needs, along with special events, catering, and nutrition/dietetics services (e.g., nutrition counseling, menu and recipe analysis, food service consulting).

Restaurant operations and management are part of assisted living centers, from menu planning, dining room set up, to servers, chefs, product and inventory management, food safety and sanitation, and more.

Resort operations tasks are also part of assisted living centers including recreation services and maintenance, grounds maintenance (e.g., golf course, swimming pools), snow removal, mowing, gardens, and walkways.

Assisted living centers are diverse places to work. Some centers have residency requirements for managers who may receive living quarters for themselves and their families as part of their job compensation.

Service Coordination

Part of the manager's job is to coordinate multiple services from external providers for the residents. This often includes medical scheduling and doctor visits, pharmacy services, transportation (through self operated or contracted services), nursing and other medical care, grounds and maintenance issues, ambulatory services, emergency services, including medical emergencies, natural disasters, security issues, and physical plant maintenance and repair. All of this involves good planning and scheduling, contacts with different vendors, contract analysis, bidding and procurement systems, a high level of organization, and more.

Positions in Living Centers

Positions in living centers are as varied as the nature of the work. Living centers can provide jobs in many different areas of interest, of which many are hospitality related. Some positions include:

- **Administrative**
  Executive Director
  General Manager
  Regional Director (for multi-unit operations)
  Purchasing Director
  Information Systems

Business Director
Marketing

- **Food Service**
  Food and Beverage Director
  Catering Manager
  Nutritionist
  Executive Chef
  Station Chef
  Cook
  Dining Room Manager
  Host/Hostess
  Server

- **Residence**
  Director of Residence Services
  Activities Director

Housekeeping Manager
Housekeeper
Facility Maintenance
Grounds Keeper

Summary

In closing, Senior Assisted Living centers offer stable careers in a growing and high demand field with jobs similar to those found in a broad assortment of hospitality venues. These positions tend to not have the stress and pressure of other operations, like restaurants, offer good pay and benefits, and are often overlooked by hospitality professionals as solid and stable career choices.

≈ *Resources*

Internet Sites

Medicare Nursing Homes: http://www.medicare.gov/Nursing/Overview.asp
Medicare Nursing Home Alternatives: http://www.medicare.gov/nursing/alternatives/PaceSites.asp
Saint Barnabas Health Care Systems: http://www.saintbarnabas.com/locator/index.html
Menorah Park Center for Senior Living: http://www.menorahpark.org/
Life Care Centers of America: http://www.lcca.com/
American Senior Living Centers: http://www.aslc.net/
Bethesda Adult Communities: http://www.bethesdalivingcenters.org/home/index.cfm?flash=1
Southern Living Centers: http://www.southernlivingcenters.com/
Sunrise Senior Living Centers: http://www.sunriseseniorliving.com
Senior Living Centers, Inc.: http://www.senior-living-communities.com/

≈ *Endnotes*

1. U.S. Department of Commerce, Census Bureau at http://www.census.gov
2. Ibid.
3. Ibid.
4. Sunrise Senior Living, Inc. at http://www.sunriseseniorliving.com
5. A Place for Mom. The search for senior care at http://www.aplaceformom.com/default
6. Sunrise Senior Living, Inc. at http://www.sunriseseniorliving.com
7. Saint Barnabas Health Care Systems, Inc. at http://www.saintbarnabas.com/locator/index.html
8. Sunrise Senior Living, Inc. at http://www.sunriseseniorliving.com
9. A Place for Mom. The search for senior care at http://www.aplaceformom.com/default
10. Sunrise Senior Living, Inc. at http://www.sunriseseniorliving.com
11. A Place for Mom. The search for senior care at http://www.aplaceformom.com/default
12. Bethesda Adult Communities. Where life blooms again at http://www.bethesdalivingcenters.org/home/index.cfm?flash=1
13. Respite care programs and costs. (2001). *Senior Journal* at http://seniorjournal.com
14. A Place for Mom. The search for senior care at http://www.aplaceformom.com/default
15. U.S. Department of Health, Education and Welfare. Medicare online at http://www.medicare.gov
16. Reverse mortgages can help with long-term care costs. (2004). *Senior Journal* at http://www.seniorjournal.com/NEWS/ReverseMortgage/4-04-15LTC.htm
17. U.S. Department of Health, Education and Welfare. Medicare online at http://www.medicare.gov

18. U.S. Department of Housing and Urban Development. Section 202 grants at http://www.hud.gov/news/release.cfm?content=pr06-003.cfm
19. Menorah Park Center for Senior Living at http://www.menorahpark.org
20. Harper, D. (2004). What are real estate investment trusts (REITs)? at http://www.investopedia.com/articles/04/030304.asp

≈ *Contributor*

e-mail bradley.beran@jwu.edu

Dr. Bradley Beran is an Associate Professor in The Hospitality College at Johnson & Wales University-Charlotte Campus. His background includes a Ph.D. from Syracuse University, an MBA from Northern Michigan University, a BA in Hotel, Restaurant, and Institutional Management from Michigan State University, and a Certificate in Culinary Arts from the Culinary Institute of America. Dr. Beran's experience includes country club management, resort management, catering, food sales and marketing, product research, development, and testing, and consulting in the areas of cost control, finance, menu analysis, product development and marketing, hotel development, design, and operations, equipment design and testing, restaurant planning and operations. He has worked with assisted living centers, purveyors, hotels, restaurants, caterers, sports arenas, and other hospitality venues.

Chapter 35
Review Questions

1. What are the characteristics of a senior for:

    - At-Home Assisted Living
    - Assisted Living Communities
    - Full Care Living Centers
    - Respite Care

2. Describe the type of services offered at each of the following:

    - At-Home Assisted Living
    - Assisted Living Communities
    - Full Care Living Centers
    - Respite Care

3. What is the PACE program and why is it important to seniors?

4. Describe the expected assisted living potential market and explain what factors contribute to this market.

5. What job characteristics at Assisted Living Centers are similar to:

    - Private Clubs
    - Hotels
    - Restaurants
    - Resorts

Travel Management Companies and Tour Operators

36

Patrick T. Tierney, San Francisco State University

© Lee Torrens, 2008, Shutterstock.

≈ Learning Objectives

☑ To introduce services provided by travel management companies and tour operators
☑ To know differences in traditional, contemporary, and electronic travel and tour agencies
☑ To learn about consumer trends related to travel bookings and tours
☑ To gain insights into management issues and techniques
☑ To learn types of jobs in travel management companies and tour operators

≈ Chapter Outline

Travel Management Company Operation
Tour Operators
Future of Travel Management Companies and Tour Operators

≈ Key Terms

Airlines reporting corporation
Consolidators
Electronic travel agencies
Foreign independent tour (FIT)
Global destination systems
Incentive travel houses
Outside sales agents
Preferred providers
Receptive operator
Sales commission
Ticketing fee
Tour escort
Tour operators
Travel agent
Travel management company

*E*xpanding demand from the domestic and international tourist and the travel industry complexity have led to an increasing desire by many travelers for highly specific travel information and a unique travel experience, help in making their travel plans, and convenient packages of travel services. Out of these needs have evolved *travel management companies*, including *electronic travel agencies*, and *tour operators*. *Travel management company* (TMC) is a more contemporary and accurate term for the new travel agency because it reflects less of a ticketing role and more consulting and management functions that successful agencies now provide. According to a leading travel industry research group Yesawich, Pepperdine, Brown & Russell[1] travel management companies are shifting into sellers of "complex" and "high risk" travel products and services, such as cruises, all-inclusive vacations, multi-stops tours, and group packages and away from selling airline tickets. *Travel agents* within a travel management company act to match the travel desires of leisure and business travelers with the most appropriate suppliers of tourist services. Agencies do not normally own the means of production, that is the lodging facilities, restaurants, or attractions that will be used by travelers, but act as agents for the suppliers. So what do travel management companies provide? They provide information to plan an optimal trip, arrange individualized coordinated itineraries, and secure tickets for transportation, lodging, receptive services, resorts and cruise lines, and recreation attractions. TMCs still play a key role in the travel industry representing about 70% of the U.S. travel market sales.[2]

Electronic travel agencies, such as Travelocity.com, have developed from the Internet revolution and communicate entirely via Websites and email. They do not have physical locations where clients can go, but they employ extensive databases, online booking technology, and are open 7 days a week and 24 hours per day. They have taken away a significant amount of travel industry sales, especially domestic airline ticketing, and are projected to reach 40% of the U.S. travel market by 2007, according to PhoCusWright, a leading internet research firm.[3]

Tour operators organize complete travel programs for groups or individuals to every continent, by all kinds of transportation modes. Perish the thought of tour operators only offering sedate sightseeing to groups of senior citizens in busses, today there are a vast array of tour itineraries and formats that appeal to youthful and mature audiences alike.

Tour operators are different from travel agents and individual suppliers in that they plan, arrange, and market preestablished *packages* at a *set price* that include, to varying degrees, transportation, lodging, educational opportunities, recreation, meals, and entertainment. Many, but not all, tour companies operate substantial portions of the tour package. They make their profit from operations, markup, and/or buying other accommodations, meals, and necessary services at discount rates. They can offer competitive rates through volume buying power. The importance of the tour industry is underscored by the fact that residents of the United States and Canada spent a total of approximately $166 billion on packaged tours worldwide.[4]

Travel Management Company Operation

In 1867 Thomas Cook introduced the first hotel coupon and started the travel agency business. The modern travel agency era really began with the advent of the airline industry in the 1960s. Since that time the number, roles, and types of travel agencies have mushroomed. Some travel agencies specialize in one type of travel service, while others, as exemplified by the country's largest travel agency conglomerate American Express, are active in multiple markets. Over 85% of travel agencies today are considered small independently owned businesses. Most (57%) TMCs are single-location businesses but over half (73%) are affiliated with or buy the services of a consortium or association. The average independent TMC receives 68% of their revenue from leisure sales (see Figure 36.1), 25% from business and 7% from combination business and leisure buyers.[5]

Figure 36.1 **Sources of Travel Management Company Revenue, 2005**

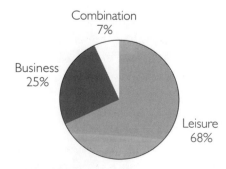

Source: Travel Weekly.com. October 27, 2005

Types of Travel Management Companies

Corporate Agencies

Those agencies who specialize in serving business clients, often with little or no walk-in clientele. They cater to corporations on the telephone or through email, often working under contracts which provide for exclusivity but also require the return of a portion of the normal travel agent commission, or on a fee-based arrangement. They rely heavily on revenue from airline tickets, hotel rooms, and rental cars.

Leisure Agencies

Tourists going on vacation are the primary clients of this agency. Clients have traditionally gone to the agency office to discuss options and to look at brochures and videos. This business relies heavily on cruise sales, resort packages, airline tickets, rental cars, tours, and hotel room sales.

Wholesalers

These organizations sell primarily to travel agents and not to the general public. They organize and promote specific types of travel services, but do not operate the tours or facilities. Wholesalers contract with suppliers for blocks of tickets or rooms in anticipation of future sales.

Specialized Leisure Agencies

A growing trend in the travel agency business are shops that specialize in one category of leisure product, such as cruise or dive agencies, or in one region of the world. By limiting what they sell these agents can become experts on unique products, services, and destinations.

Incentive Travel Houses

These agencies develop customized programs for corporations who offer incentives for high employee productivity by providing deluxe travel rewards. They setup and administer reward contests, inform eligible staff and contract with suppliers. Incentive agencies earn their profits from supplier commissions and management fees.

Consolidators

These are businesses that purchase large blocks of airline seats or cruise berths at a substantial discount and resell them to travel agents or the general public for a lower than normal fare. They may also have contracts with certain airlines for larger commissions on certain routes. Consolidators, also known as "Bucket Shops," advertise to the public in the travel sections of metropolitan newspapers, while others deal exclusively with travel agents.

Electronic Travel Agencies

As a result of the Internet revolution and communication advances, a growing number of companies sell travel products entirely via Websites. There are no human travel agents to talk with and they do not have physical locations where clients can go, but they employ extensive databases and online booking technology. Some electronic travel agencies are independently owed, like Travelocity,[6] while others are owned and/or controlled by the airlines, such as Orbitz.[7] Initially these businesses only offered airline tickets, but now they offer a wide range of travel services and have moved aggressively into booking hotel rooms and rental cars.

How Travel Management Companies Get Paid

Since TMCs do not own the facilities or equipment used to operate destination services they are paid only when they make a sale. Payment is in the form of a commission, based on a percentage of the sale price, or increasingly payment is by an additional ticketing charge. The cost of the agent commission was built into the sales price so in the past it did not cost the consumer more to use the travel agent than if they went direct to the supplier. Commissions historically have been about 10% for airline tickets and other services, but on February 9, 1995, Delta Airlines announced it would pay travel agents no more than $25 on any one-way domestic ticket. Since then all major U.S. airlines have discontinued paying commissions on domestic flights altogether. The main exception to this no commission policy is where the airlines and large travel agencies have a preferred-provider contract that allows for a small commission. In contrast to the airlines, other segments of the travel industry, such as cruise lines announced at the same time it would increase its travel agent commission from 10 to 12%. The end result has been that more travel agencies are seeking other sources of revenue besides the sales of airline tickets, such as commissions from cruise lines, tours, resorts, and international air carriers. In fact, many travel suppliers offer agents *over-ride commissions* of an additional 2–5% to encourage group sales or introduce new travel products or services. A large number of agencies have diversified and are starting to develop and market their own tour packages, others like Corniche Travel has also started an event planning company.[8] Still other experienced agents charge *hourly fees* for the time they spend developing complex customized vacation packages. A *ticketing fee* of from $15–$40 in addition to airline ticket price is being charged customers by an increasing number of agencies. Even electronic travel agencies are charging a ticketing fee. For example, Expedia.com has a $5 ticketing fee, but they show it in the ticket price, rather than as a separate charge. Another way to increase profits has been by reducing their operational costs through increased automation. TMCs offer their own online booking and many use "robotics" software programs that handle automated ticketing, check for compliance with corporate travel policies, and email a complete itinerary. Lastly, more travel agents are quoting lower fares to consumers than the public can be found on the Internet by becoming or using consolidators.

Certainly one of most desired benefits of being a travel agent is discount travel to destinations worldwide. Suppliers wanting to promote new travel services are often willing to provide familiarization trips at little or no cost to agents. Airlines, cruise lines, and resorts provide very low cost tickets or ticket class upgrades. An inclusive 5 day stay at a new resort in Brazil for only the cost of taxes, for example, is a unique opportunity available to travel agents. These benefits tend to make up for the rather low wages that travel agents receive, which average about $45,000 per year for an agent with 3 years of experience. Some agents are paid a monthly salary, some only commission, others a combination of these. So persons considering becoming a travel agent must weigh their financial goals against the excitement and low cost of travel that are available to agents.

From the outside a travel agency in your neighborhood appears to be a lucrative, if not glamorous, business. But increasing competition from larger agencies with volume discounts and lower overhead, electronic travel agencies, the Internet elimination of airline commissions and generally increasing costs of doing business have resulted in low profitability, distressed sales and business failures, especially small independent neighborhood compa-

nies. To increase profitability three-quarters of TMCs have joined consortiums, groups of agencies that combine strength to negotiate lower rates for clients and higher commissions for their agencies. A member agency is often required to use a limited number of *preferred providers* who have contracts with the consortium. With such contracts the agency must offer a fare quote from their preferred supplier first, but can sell to any supplier the consumer wishes.

Automation and Certification

Precise accurate information on schedules, availability, and rates is critical for a travel consultant to know, but the scope and amount of information on the global travel industry is overwhelming. Therefore, computerized databases are a basic tool of the travel agent. *Global Destination Systems* (GDS) such as Apollo, Sabre, World Span, and Amadeus, list over 15 million fares, a quarter of which are updated daily. These systems were started by airlines and at one time carried just airline schedules and inventory, but today they have become full scale travel information systems that also contain lodging, tours, and attraction information. Effective data search and ticketing with a GDS are critical skills for agents.

In order to be able to issue domestic tickets, an agency must be approved by the *Airlines Reporting Corporation* (ARC). This organization is an association of U.S. airlines who facilitate funds transfer and ensure that travel agencies have experienced management. For sale of international airline tickets, a travel agency may also be approved by the *International Airlines Travel Agent Network* (IATAN), who has similar responsibilities to the ARC. These licensing agreements limit companies who can sell travel to legitimate businesses and help protect the consumer from fraud. Individual travel agents must show proper identification in order to receive travel discounts and promotions. The most accepted form of credential is a photo identification card issued by IATAN. Some travel agencies, but not all, require that their senior agents be a *Certified Travel Counselor* (CTC). The later credential, issued by the Institute of Certified Travel Agents, is awarded to persons who pass rigorous examinations and have 5 years full-time experience in a travel agency.

Although the full-time in-office travel agent will continue to be the backbone of any TMC, there are a growing number of *Outside Sales Agents* (OSA) who are affiliated with the company, but are independent contractors, not employees. The OSA work at their home and provide their own telephone and pay employment taxes, but share commissions with their affiliated agency.

Information Revolution and Travel Management Companies

Travel agencies no longer have exclusive access to the myriad schedules, fares, and destination information that are found in a GDS. One of the most popular types of sites on the world wide web provide travel ticketing. The electronic travel agency Travelocity, for example, allows booking reservations on most domestic and international flights, for a $5 booking fee. It also has content on destinations, an area where viewers can ask questions about travel providers, and a shopping "mall" with specialized travel merchandise for sale. Suppliers have also embraced the Internet as a way to lower their travel sales distribution costs. Hilton Hotels, for instance, was one of the first lodging chains to place all of its properties worldwide on the Internet. Travelers themselves, especially business travelers, have gone directly to supplier Websites, by-passing the middle organization. Obviously, this type of lower cost service is in direct competition with some of the services that both traditional and electronic travel agencies have provided. The travel management business has been undergoing a radical transformation due to changes brought on by the Internet and air carrier payment policies.

But the Internet revolution is also threatening other "middle men" and it is leading the push toward a more direct consumer-supplier link. For example, in January 1999, Delta Airlines announced that it will require anyone not booking directly with only the Delta Website to pay a $2.00 per ticket surcharge. Subsequently, Delta and other airlines have backed off requiring surcharges, but instead are offering lower priced "internet only" fares to drive traffic to their Websites. Online booking of airline tickets has grown at a rapid rate, until 2006. For the first time, the number of persons booking travel online declined in 2006 but online sales volume continued to increase.[9] The reason for this decline is attributed to current search engines not taking other factors beside price and travel times into consideration when a client wants to plan a trip. In 2007 Travelocity introduced a personalized search engine product for road travelers called the "Road Trip Wizard." It asks users to identify their interests and trip preferences, and it provides maps and driving directions and suggests tourist attractions and hotels, which can be booked at that time. This and other technological innovation is expected to again lead to increases in the percentage of travelers booking through the Internet. However, recent research suggests that the majority of travel management companies that were able to survive the increased use of the Internet over the last 5 years will remain profitable in the longer run, even as use of Internet for airline ticket sales increase further.[10]

Tour Operators

The most basic functions of a tour operator are to bundle together a *package* of travel services, offer it at a fixed price and provide some or all of the services during a tour itinerary. In order to develop and operate exciting and safe tour programs the tour operator staff must have a very good understanding of what consumers desire, outstanding knowledge of destinations, keen negotiating skills to secure reasonable supplier prices, sophisticated marketing skills, exceptional guides, a strict trip budget, and a well constructed risk management plan for each tour. They usually provide and operate transportation equipment, such as a motorcoach, van, raft, or ship. A strong consumer trend in tours is more active healthy programming, with convenience and safety. Describing exactly what a tour operator offers can be tricky because there are many types of tours. Below is a listing of the most common tour formats.

Rafting tour, Green River, Dinosaur National Monument, Utah.

In a *group tour* clients travel with a number of individuals sharing similar interests and have the potential for substantial savings and unique opportunities. *Escorted tours* offer a professional guide who remains with a tour group for the entire package. This escort takes care of travel problems that may arise and usually is knowledgeable about the culture and natural history of the area being traversed. A fully *inclusive tour* provides everything that a traveler will need for a set price, except for shopping, gambling, and personal needs. This type of tour is the most convenient since the escort facilitates and pays for all included services.

A *foreign independent tour* or *FIT* is a travel package which normally includes some lodging and a rental car or train pass, but they are not just to foreign countries. It can also include airline tickets and specialty recreation activities, like rafting trips or attraction admissions. The traveler is independent when it comes to travel and must get from destination to destination on their own by driving a rental car or catching trains and busses.

A *fly-drive package* is a common tour in the U.S. and includes flights, motels, and a rental car. Mass marketing companies, such as Pleasant Hawaiian Holidays, specialize in this type of tour. Such a package allows the traveler to enjoy volume discounts but have the freedom to travel where they wish in between specific meeting dates.

Types of Tour Operators

The escalating demands of sophisticated travelers and the competitive nature of the travel industry has resulted in the tour operator business becoming more specialized with many types of tour services. Some companies engage in only a narrow niche in the tour market, such as Adrift Adventures, a whitewater rafting outfitter in Jensen, Utah,[11] while other large organizations, such as Maupintour,[12] operate tours throughout the world via multiple transportation modes. To further confuse things some air carriers and travel management companies also act as tour operators. Described below are the most well recognized types of tour operators.

Wholesale Tour Company

Arranges and promotes tour packages, but sells them primarily to travel agents or international tour operators, and not the general public. They often do not operate any portion of the tour. Marketing to

Specialty travel tours may be geared toward sightseeing in unique settings.

the travel trade is one of the strengths of this type of firm. Revenues come primarily from markup of tours they represent.

Receptive Operator

This type of company, also called a ground operator, may meet and greet groups at airports, make arrangements for lodging, and shuttle them to the lodging at one particular destination. They also frequently offer foreign language interpreters, sightseeing tours, or step-on guides.

Specialty Travel Tour Operators

Organizations who possess highly specialized equipment and guides for unique tours, such as diving, rafting, biking, and photography programs. Tours may be geared toward adventure and risk activities, nature or eco-tourism, skills development, or simply sightseeing in unique settings. Clients are often younger than for other tours, averaging 40 years old.

Motorcoach Tour Operators

These companies own and operate deluxe motorcoaches holding up to 52 passengers, with some costing over $250,000. Sightseeing via a motorcoach is still the most popular and economical tour both domestically and internationally. Operators may provide long distance or local tours, with and without narration. Some motorcoaches have two levels for sightseeing and sleeping onboard, others have bars, and gambling tables.

Types of Jobs with a Tour Operator

Tour Escort/Guide

The tour guide job provides exciting opportunities to enter the travel profession and for a career traveling the globe. This occupation can require the skills of a teacher, entertainer, accountant, doctor, and psychologist. Tour conductor and guide schools provide training and certification to get a start in the field. Guides lead everything from adventure travel, like rowing a raft through the Grand Canyon, to sightseeing tours in the wine country of Italy.

Operations Manager

This professional manages the logistics of equipment and staff scheduling, as well as coordination with other suppliers. This person must also be proficient in budgeting. He or she works primarily in the office and not on the road.

Tour Planner

Designing a new tour, contracting with appropriate suppliers, testing the itinerary, and costing the program are the duties of a tour planner. This person must be in touch with changing client wants and supplier status. Such a position usually involves a balance between business travel and office work.

Sales and Marketing Manager

He or she works with key trade industry and client accounts, and develops promotions directed at consumers. They must be very familiar with company services and the competition. Personal sales skills are very important in this position.

Future of Travel Management Companies and Tour Operators

Despite being battered by global changes in the marketplace, travel management companies and tour operators will continue to provide needed services to business and leisure clients in the future. Undoubtedly, there will be consolidation through attrition and independent agencies joining consortiums. Travel agencies have shifted away from their traditional dependence on domestic airline ticket sales and are looking for more profitable opportunities as consumers are better able to book flights directly and revenues from commissions decline. More agencies will rely on outside sales associates to reduce employment costs and enlarge their reach in the marketplace. The shear magnitude of travel services available and the need for expert advice will continue to push small agencies to specialize and large firms to hire agents who are experts in a segment of the industry.

The rebound in U.S. and global economies in 2004–2006, the lack of other highly publicized airplane hijackings after the tragic events of September 11, 2001, at the World Trade Center in New York, more sophisticated marketing and the increasing use of technology to lower costs has resulted in growth for many larger TMC organizations. Most industry analysts agree that there will be continued consolidation in the industry, but TMCs and tour operators will not disappear because they add value through personalized service and are increasingly savvy businesses. Many people with Internet hook-ups, simply do not have the time or desire to conduct an extensive search of the Internet, and these folks will continue to look to travel consultants for assistance with lengthy and expensive travel plans. Others will still value the specialized expertise and time savings that experienced consultants possess. The days of agents simply being "order takers" are nearly gone and they are being quickly replaced by true *travel consultants*. Revenue growth in electronic travel agencies will continue and this will provide exciting opportunities for sales, programming, and operations jobs with these companies.

Tour operators will need to design tours that cater to changing customer demands such as family travel.

Tour operators will need to design new tours that cater to changing customer demands, such as family travel, more independence, and participation. Aging of the population will provide expanding opportunities for senior travel, served by new and more active tour programs. Demand for ecotourism and other specialty travel tours are predicted to experience rapid growth. But managers will need to contend with increased access restrictions and regulations. They must develop ways to assure clients their deposits are secure and satisfaction guaranteed.

Summary

Travel by U.S. and international residents has recovered from the September 11, 2001, events in New York and by 2007 it is booming. Travel management companies and tour operators provide needed services and are well positioned to increase sales. But both will have to reduce overhead and increase profitability. Enlightened TMC and tour operator managers see substantial future business opportunities, although the way they conduct their affairs will need to evolve to keep pace with changing consumer demands and technological changes.

≈ Resources

Internet Sites

Adrift Adventures: www.adrift.com
American Society of Travel Agents: www.asta.org
PhoCusWright Travel Research: www.phocuswright.com
National Tour Association: www.nta.org

≈ Endnotes

1. Yesawich, P. Ten trends to watch in the year ahead at http://ehotier.com/browse/news_more_.pdp?id=D721301100M
2. PhoCusWright. U.S. online travel market fueled by supplier sites, though growth slows at http://www.phocuswright.com/press/releases.php
3. Ibid.
4. *2001 Packaged Travel in North America.* (2001). Lexington, KY: National Tour Association.
5. *Travel Weekly.* Travel agencies are solo, small and selling hard at http://www.travelweekly.com
6. Travelocity at http://www.travelocity.com
7. Orbitz at http://www.orbitz.com
8. Terro, R. (2005). Anastasia's way: Corniche travel carves an artful path through the world of luxury. *Luxury Travel Advisor*, (October).
9. Tedeschi, B. (2007). Travel sales still growing, but numbers of customers are declining. *New York Times*, (October 29).
10. Gulker, M. (2006). *Reshuffling the Retail Deck: Internet Adoption and the Profitability of Brick and Mortar Travel Agents.* Stanford, CA: Stanford Institute for Economic Policy Research.
11. at http://www.adrift.com
12. at http://www.maupintour.com

≈ Contributor

Patrick T. Tierney, Ph.D.
Former Owner, Adrift Adventures
Professor, Departments of Hospitality Management and Recreation
San Francisco State University

Patrick Tierney received a Ph.D. in Recreation Resources with a concentration in Tourism from Colorado State University in 1991. Currently he has a joint appointment in the Departments of Hospitality Management and Recreation-Leisure Studies at San Francisco State University, where he is a professor teaching classes in recreation, tourism, travel management, resort management, and eco-tourism. Dr. Tierney is also actively involved in tourism research. He is recipient of the 1997 Best Tourism Research Award from the California Division of Tourism, the 1991 Excellence In Research Award from the Commercial Recreation and Resort Association, as well as co-recipient of the 1990 Colorado Rural Tourism Achievement Award.

In addition to his academic pursuits he is actively involved in tourism, through being co-owner, for 25 years, of Adrift Adventures, an ecotourism adventure recreation business offering summer whitewater learning adventure vacations in Colorado, Utah, and Alaska. Pat serves on the Board of Directors of the California Travel Industry Association and the Board of the Bay Area Partners In Responsible Tourism.

Chapter 36
Review Questions

1. What is the name of the privately-operated global ticketing system used extensively by travel agents for airline tickets? Why are these organizations so important to travel management companies?

2. An FIT package usually includes what services and products?

3. Can anyone sell airline tickets? What are two organizations that have a licensing requirement for a company to be able to sell domestic and international airline tickets?

4. What is the difference between travel agencies who are primarily order takers, in comparison to travel consultants?

5. Why have travel management companies shifted from "order takers" to travel consultants and managers?

6. Are tours just for seniors on motorcoach based siteseeing trips? What types of tours are available in major tourist destinations?

Real Estate Opportunities in the Hospitality Industry

37

Karl J. Mayer and John M. Stefanelli,
University of Nevada, Las Vegas

© Paul Cowan, 2008, Shutterstock.

≈ Learning Objectives

☑ To familiarize the student with an important and dynamic sector of the hospitality industry—the real estate area
☑ To understand the importance of real estate
☑ To understand the variety of career choices that are available for those students who wish to focus on hospitality real estate
☑ To identify the skills, background, and experience required to effectively engage in the real estate field
☑ To distinguish which hospitality programs offer specific classes in real estate at the present time

≈ Chapter Outline

Typical Hospitality Real Estate Positions
Desirable Background for Hospitality Real Estate Positions
Hospitality Programs Offering Real Estate Courses
Your Future in Hospitality Real Estate

≈ Key Terms

Appraisers
Broker
Real estate representative
Support staff
Vacation-ownership firm

One of the advantages of working in the hospitality industry is the availability of a wide array of career options. Although most of the jobs are in operations management (that is, production and service positions), several support staff positions are available for persons who want to be in the hospitality industry, but who are not interested in working in an operations role. For example, support staff positions exist in hospitality accounting, purchasing, inventory control, human resources, data processing, and real estate.

Many avenues can lead to working in a staff role. Some people enter these positions while going to school. Some move into them upon graduation. Others move into them only after working in several operations positions. A few find themselves thrust into these jobs through a combination of circumstances. An internship, if your program of study offers one, is often an excellent way to explore whether working in a staff position, such as hospitality real estate, would be a feasible career option for you.

Hospitality real estate offers a number of interesting and worthwhile career opportunities. Several hospitality firms employ real estate specialists, including market analysts, location analysts, and lease negotiators. However, you do not have to be employed by a hospitality company in order to work in this field. For instance, you could be an independent appraiser or work for a lender, private investor, or real estate brokerage firm. The next section of this chapter will discuss the typical positions that are available for those who are interested in a real estate career in the hospitality industry.

Typical Hospitality Real Estate Positions

Several career options in real estate relate directly or indirectly to the hospitality industry. Persons wishing to work in this area may find employment with real estate departments in multi-unit hospitality corporations, appraisal firms, real estate brokerages, vacation-ownership firms, business brokerages, site selection firms, and lending institutions. The skills needed to perform well in hospitality real estate are very diverse and depend on the specific area of emphasis that a person chooses. These skills are identified and discussed later in this chapter, but first, the wide variety of positions that are available in hospitality real estate will be considered.

Company Real Estate Representatives

Many large multi-unit hospitality corporations employ a real estate director and one or more real estate representatives. These persons are usually responsible for the following activities:

1. Performing location analyses; i.e., evaluating real estate sites to determine whether the company should construct new businesses in these locations;
2. Evaluating existing business locations from the perspective of acquiring and managing the business that is situated there;
3. Working with a hospitality company's franchisees (if the firm franchises its business) to assist with site selection decisions, provide design advice, or help coordinate the activities of the company's internal resources with the franchisees;
4. Working with a variety of external agents; for example, negotiating lease or purchase agreements with brokers and/or owners; and
5. Interfacing with the company's legal, construction, operations, and financial personnel.

Although the Internet has allowed company real estate representatives to perform more efficiently from the corporate office, these representatives nevertheless typically travel a great deal. It is not unusual for them to be on the road 4 days a week. Such extended travel, however, is necessary in order to evaluate a site properly. Real estate, by its very nature, is a highly localized business opportunity, even for very large national or international firms. If insufficient time is spent researching a location, the company may make a rash decision. Since location is a critical factor influencing a hospitality property's success, it is very important to make solid, well-informed site-selection decisions.

Appraisers

Real estate appraisers are employed to render estimates of value. They are trained to value various assets, including real estate (i.e., land and buildings); furniture, fixtures, and equipment (FFE); collectibles and artifacts; and going-concern businesses.

Commercial lenders, investors, sellers, insurance companies, contractors, attorneys, accountants, pension funds, and other entities having a financial stake in a hospitality project engage appraisers. For example, before a commercial lender, such as a bank or savings and loan, can lend money, it must have the collateral (i.e., assets) appraised by an independent appraiser it selects. A hospitality firm that needs to borrow money to build a new property must pay the cost of the appraisal needed to satisfy this regulatory requirement.

Some appraisers specialize exclusively in the hospitality industry. The major one, *Hospitality Valuation Services* (HVS), was founded in 1980. Currently, HVS has 11 offices in the United States, including New York, San Francisco, Miami, Dallas, Chicago, Atlanta, and Denver, as well as offices in Mexico, Canada, London, Hong Kong, China, Brazil, and five other countries. Although its array of client services has expanded in recent years, HVS's major focus is the appraisal of lodging properties.

It is unusual, however, for individual appraisers to specialize in hospitality because there may be insufficient work available to make it a full-time job. Generally speaking, appraisers tend to specialize in a particular category and not in a particular industry. For instance, a business valuation specialist who appraises restaurants will also typically appraise related businesses, such as taverns, liquor stores, bakeries, and food marts.

In other cases, appraisers may be part of a larger consulting practice. The firm *Ernst & Young* is representative of these types of appraisers, and has consultants who are specifically designated to serve the hospitality industry through its Real Estate, Hospitality and Construction Services Group. Besides their appraisal work, these firms also conduct a wide variety of other assignments designed to assist their client companies.

In addition to appraisal assignments, appraisers usually counsel clients. For example, a motel owner may hire an appraiser to estimate the most likely sales price for the property. He or she may also ask the appraiser to suggest things the owner could do to make the motel more attractive to potential buyers. In this role, the appraiser is required to draw upon his/her considerable expertise in the real estate field to make sound recommendations to the property owner.

Lastly, over and above an appraising or counseling role, some appraisers also get involved with real estate sales, property management (such as overseeing a shopping center complex), and loan brokerage (such as helping clients search for and secure the most favorable debt financing available). It is important to note, however, that in all aspects

The role of real estate agent continues to evolve with the impact of technology and the growth of the Internet.

of appraisal work, it is essential for appraisers to render objective, unbiased advice and to avoid any situations that might be possible conflicts of interest between themselves and their clients. To do otherwise would severely impair their reputations.

Real Estate Sales

While property owners are free to sell their properties without help from other professionals, most prefer using a third party to represent their interests. The same is true for potential buyers. Thus, brokers play a valuable role by serving as an intermediary in a real estate sales transaction.

Several brokerages specialize in the sale of lodging properties. For example, there are consortiums of brokerages in the United States that account for a majority of all lodging properties sold nationwide.

A brokerage office may also specialize in the sale of restaurants, taverns, liquor stores, and other similar hospitality businesses. In large cities, it is not unusual to find offices that deal exclusively with the sale and purchase of restaurants, or with tavern operations.

Persons working in a sales office generally are in business for themselves; that is, they are independent contractors. Their livelihood depends on the amount of property sold, in that their main (and most often, only) source of income is sales commissions which are generated when deals are concluded. Some sales associates represent sellers and some represent buyers. Few represent both parties in a transaction because doing so may be a conflict of interest.

While sales commissions are their primary source of income, some sales associates prefer to operate as independent consultants. In the typical sales transaction, the seller pays the commission, which is then divided among the relevant sales offices that helped consummate the deal. However, some salespersons work strictly for hourly fees and are paid regardless of the outcome of a transaction. In effect, they sell their time and are compensated accordingly.

A day in the life of the typical real estate sales associate finds him or her showing property to potential buyers, shopping and analyzing other properties in the market, gathering pertinent data, suggesting appropriate sales and purchase strategies, recommending alternative financing arrangements, estimating the most likely sales prices, organizing and completing deal-related paperwork, negotiating contract terms and conditions, and shepherding the deal to ensure that it stays on track and is finalized.

The role of a real estate sales associate is continuing to evolve due to the impact of technology and growth of the Internet. The Internet is making it possible for companies to circumvent intermediaries and "go direct" to potential buyers and sellers on a worldwide basis. Although many aspects of being a real estate sales associate will not be affected by these developments, students who are interested in this area should carefully explore the impact of these trends on the future of working in a real estate sales position.

Vacation Ownership Sales

A vacation-ownership firm is in business to sell long-term vacation packages to guests. They sell "slices of time," in that they normally sell a guest the right to use a vacation apartment, hotel room, or condominium for a specified time period per year (usually 2 weeks) for several years (usually 7 to 20 years) at a specific property in a specific location. Alternatively, they can also purchase "points" from a vacation-ownership firm that allow them to take future vacations in various locations in exchange for using a specified number of the "points" that they own each year.

Guests who prepay for these vacations usually have the option of swapping their time at one location for comparable time at other vacation locations that are part of a time-share exchange network. Normally the guest pays a small fee for this exchange privilege.

In most cases, the prepaid vacation is an economical alternative to paying for vacations every year. Usually the guest needs to pay only a rela-

tively modest maintenance fee each year in order to defray the cost of routine repairs, necessary remodeling, and so forth. In addition, the guest will pay local property taxes on a proportionate basis—normally, these annual tax payments are also fairly modest amounts.

At one time these "time-share operations" had a seedy reputation. Most of them were high-pressure sales operations that generated numerous consumer complaints. However, while a few of these boiler-room operations probably still exist, the industry is now generally considered to be quite legitimate. This is due primarily to the involvement of major lodging firms in the field such as Disney, Hilton, Marriott, Carlson, and Starwood. Their participation has legitimized the industry. In addition, other large firms, such as Fairfield Resorts, Bluegreen, and Royal Resorts, have specialized in providing high-quality time-share properties for guests. Today, this sector represents a major growth area in the hospitality field. It offers excellent opportunities for hospitality students who are interested in the variety of careers available in vacation ownership sales. For those uninterested in sales, there are also many positions available in vacation-ownership operations, such as housekeeping, maintenance and engineering, and property management.

Business Opportunity Sales

A business opportunity is an ongoing business located in leased real estate facilities. The owner typically sells the business's furniture, fixtures, and equipment (FFE), its leasehold improvements (i.e., interior finishing of the leased premises), the business name and reputation, and perhaps some other types of assets, such as inventory or a valuable liquor license. The business opportunity purchase usually includes everything except the real estate.

A business opportunity brokerage is very similar to the typical real estate brokerage. While business brokers do not normally sell real estate, they do sell businesses that must be transferred to buyers. In effect, the work performed by business sales associates parallels almost exactly that performed by most real estate sales associates. However, like the role of the real estate sales associate, this intermediary role will likely continue to evolve due to the development of new technology and the growth of the Internet, so students should be mindful of the potential impact of these trends on future careers in this area.

Site Analysts

Some research firms, real estate brokerages, and business brokerages provide location analysis for persons or firms unable or unwilling to do the work themselves. These companies typically maintain computerized databases that can be adapted to suit any need or answer any question. Their reports help clients make sound real estate and business decisions.

Some hospitality firms prefer to contract out this type of work to independent firms because it is more economical than maintaining their own real estate divisions. This concept is known as outsourcing. However, even those large hospitality companies that have real estate divisions are apt to use an outside firm on occasion because it is not always feasible for them to study every potential site, especially if a site is in a market where the firm does not have any existing properties under management.

Financial Positions

Many lending institutions are active in hospitality finance. These lenders provide the discretionary capital that allows new properties to be conceived and developed, or existing properties to be refinanced. The major players include the following organizations:

1. Life insurance companies that specialize in financing lodging properties;
2. Pension funds that invest in lodging properties or lend to them;
3. Banks and savings and loans that make real estate and business loans to qualified hospitality operators;

Hospitality real estate positions are academically-oriented; requiring research, writing, and computer skills.

4. Government agencies (such as the Small Business Administration) that make direct loans or guarantee loans made by a third party; and
5. Leasing companies that will construct a property and/or provide all necessary equipment and lease these assets to a manager/operator (especially in the gaming or restaurant sector of the hospitality industry) on a rent-to-use or a rent-to-own plan.

Lenders must qualify potential borrowers. Before recommending a loan, the lender must ensure that there is a high probability that the money will be repaid in a timely manner. Lenders must perform "due diligence," which means that they must evaluate a borrower's credit worthiness, character, reputation, capacity to repay, business skill, and collateral. These evaluations require that a skilled financial professional is involved in the decision to extend credit to a borrower.

Lenders who are heavily involved in hospitality finance may employ real estate experts on their own staffs to perform these functions. For example, DePfa Bank AG (Deutsche Pfandbriefbank) is a German-based institution that has a specialized hotel financing team. This team has financed first class hotels all over Europe and the United States, including properties such as the Plaza Hotel in New York City and the Adam's Mark Hotel in Dallas. In other cases, a lending institution may outsource these tasks to appraisers or consulting firms on an as-needed basis. Whichever approach is taken, it creates an opportunity for you to build a hospitality real estate career in a financial position.

Desirable Background for Hospitality Real Estate Positions

If these career opportunities seem exciting, you should begin to prepare for them now. It is never too early to select the right college courses and work experiences most likely to give you an edge when applying for this type of work.

These positions are very academically-oriented, in that a great deal of research, writing, and computer skills is needed to be successful in a hospitality real estate position. You should take college courses designed to develop and enhance these skills.

You should also take a basic real estate course, real estate investments course, and real estate appraisal course. These classes will give you the best perspective of the industry, as well as highlight the various career opportunities that may exist in your local area. The next section of this chapter discusses which hospitality programs presently offer such courses.

Accounting and finance courses are also necessary for success. At the very least you should take the basic accounting and financial principles classes. Generally, however, additional finance courses are necessary to acquire the techniques needed to prepare the types of research projects that you will encounter.

Computer literacy is a must. You should be very familiar with word processing, database, and spreadsheet software. In addition to working with your own computer files, you must be able to use the computerized databases most offices subscribe to. For instance, a real estate sales office usually subscribes to a computerized multiple listing service (MLS). Sales offices also typically use services that provide demographic data and updated lists of lenders and their current loan terms and conditions. The number of service firms offering these data has expanded significantly in recent years in order to meet the industry's ever-increasing demand for information. Also, geographic mapping software is now available, offering detail that can be used to examine a potential site on-screen before ever leaving the office for a site inspection.

Computer literacy is also needed to efficiently access information available on the Internet. In recent years, there has been an explosion of real estate information that can be downloaded from Internet sources. This information could include local market data and reports, national economic trends and conditions, financing availability and terms, or federal and state guidelines for site development activity. Thus, a broker, appraiser, or real estate director can now obtain a great deal of pertinent information without ever leaving the office. However, since real estate is inherently a localized business opportunity, there is no substitute for on-site visits by a trained real estate professional.

Many real estate positions require licensing or certification, or both. For instance, if you want to be an appraiser, you will likely need a state license as well as certification from a nationally-recognized appraisal association.

Finally, you should acquire a reasonable amount of operations experience before tackling one of these staff positions. If you want to work in a hospitality company's real estate division, you should have a basic understanding of how the firm's food, lodging, or gaming units are operated and managed. This provides the perspective needed when wrestling with decisions that can make or break your employer's bottom line.

Hospitality Programs Offering Real Estate Courses

The authors of this chapter recently surveyed the top 25 hospitality programs in the United States in order to determine whether they offered specific real estate courses, or a concentration (specialization) in the real estate area. As of the latest edition of this textbook, only six of these leading programs offered at least one real estate course (Cornell, Michigan State, UNLV, Penn State, University of Central Florida, and Florida International University) as a part of their hospitality programs. Further, Cornell and Michigan State appear to be the only two hospitality programs that also offer a specialization, or concentration, in this area. Other schools, such as Virginia Tech and Florida State, have real estate courses available through the university's College of Business, but do not currently offer them within their hospitality programs.

The results of this survey were very comparable to a similar research study that was conducted in 2001, so not much has improved in terms of the availability of specific real estate coursework in most hospitality programs in the United States. Thus, students who are serious about a career in hospitality real estate may want to carefully consider their choice of a program and select one that offers a real estate curriculum, either in the hospitality program itself, or in a related business program at the university.

Your Future in Hospitality Real Estate

Research and experience have shown that for every four people graduating with a degree in hospitality administration, one of them leaves operations, or leaves the industry entirely, after working for only 1 year. Interestingly enough, for every four people who leave operations, or exit from the hospitality industry, one of them ends up in some type of financial management career. In a nutshell, then, the odds are about one in eight that you will end up in one of the careers discussed in this chapter.

Hospitality is a people industry, and so is real estate. The skills, education, and work experience you have already earned and will earn in the future will qualify you for many types of careers. Take the time to explore the many options that are available. Hospitality is a field that can accommodate many career interests and many different backgrounds. If you choose a career in hospitality real estate, you can be assured that many exciting challenges and new opportunities will lie ahead.

Summary

This chapter introduced you to the opportunities that are available for hospitality students who have an interest in real estate. Real estate is a vitally important aspect of most sectors of the hospitality industry, and those students who decide to pursue a career in this area will find it to be a rewarding and challenging career option. They would be well advised to take full advantage of the quantitative courses that are available in the hospitality school in which they are already enrolled. Alternatively, they may choose to attend one of the hospitality programs that offer either specific real estate courses or a concentration in this unique and exciting area.

≈ Resources

Internet Sites

Hospitality Valuation Services: www.hvsinternational.com
Ernst & Young: www.ey.com/global/content.nsf/International/Industries_-_REHC
Fairfield Resorts vacation ownership: www.fairfieldresorts.com
Real estate terms and definitions: www.realestateabc.com/glossary

≈ Contributors

John Stefanelli, 61, is a Professor in the Department of Food and Beverage Management, William F. Harrah College of Hotel Administration, at the University of Nevada Las Vegas (UNLV). He earned his PhD from the University of Denver, the MBA from Michigan State University, a BS from the University of Illinois, and an AAS from the College of DuPage. He has been at UNLV since 1978, serving in teaching and administrative positions, including Chair of the Department of Food & Beverage Management and Associate Dean of the College. Over the years he has authored or coauthored several publications, among them many textbooks that are widely used in hospitality education. In addition to his academic responsibilities, Stefanelli has consulted for many restaurant companies and individuals. He recently completed his duties as Department Chair and has returned to full-time teaching status, with a special focus on developing distance education classes. A Vietnam veteran, Stefanelli and his wife of 35 years, Deanna, have two children and four grandchildren. They live in Henderson, NV. e-mail: john.stefanelli@unlv.edu

Karl J. Mayer, 53, is an accomplished academic researcher and a skilled business practitioner with more than 20 years of experience in various sectors of the economy. Dr. Mayer is an Associate Professor at the William F. Harrah College of Hotel Administration at the University of Nevada, Las Vegas, where he teaches graduate and undergraduate hospitality accounting, finance, and marketing courses. During 2000–2001, he served as Assistant Professor with Temple University's School of Tourism and Hospitality Management. He received his PhD in Hotel Administration from UNLV in 1999, where he was the recipient of the Ace Denken fellowship award. Dr. Mayer holds an MBA in Business Administration from Harvard University in 1984. He also earned a MS in Engineering from Columbia University in 1976 and a BS in Engineering from the University of Wisconsin in 1974. Dr. Mayer has published in a wide variety of academic and trade journals, including the *Journal of Services Marketing* and the *Cornell HRA Quarterly*. Dr. Mayer's research interest areas include hospitality real estate and finance, casino gaming, and services marketing and management. e-mail: karl.mayer@unlv.edu

Chapter 37
Review Questions

1. List the typical hospitality-related real estate positions that are available to you.

2. What are the functions of a real estate director and the real estate representatives who work for large, multi-unit hospitality corporations?

3. Discuss the importance of having real estate representatives make well-informed site selection decisions when working with hospitality companies.

4. What functions are performed by real estate appraisers? Who would typically hire an appraiser? How do most appraisers handle areas of specialization?

5. Explain the concept of "independent contractor" as applied to persons working in real estate sales. How are these people usually compensated?

6. List what is typically included in a business opportunity purchase. What is the function of the business opportunity brokerage?

7. What types of businesses may be involved in conducting a site analysis?

8. What is a vacation ownership firm? How has the vacation ownership industry been legitimized?

9. List the types of organizations that are most active in hospitality finance and are major lenders in this industry.

10. Discuss the impact that the Internet is having on the careers of people working in hospitality real estate positions.

11. Describe the type of skills and experience that would be beneficial for someone seeking a career in hospitality real estate.

Teaching in Hospitality, Foodservice, and Tourism Management

38

John Wolper and Paula Wolper, University of Findlay

© Dmitriy Shironosov, 2008, Shutterstock.

≈ *Learning Objectives*

☑ Identify the different types of schools and institutions where one could teach hospitality
☑ Describe requirements necessary to teach hospitality
☑ Identify the rewards related to teaching

≈ *Chapter Outline*

Overview of Teaching in Hospitality, Foodservice, and Tourism Management
Why Consider Teaching Hospitality as a Career?
How to Get A Job as an Academic

≈ *Key Terms*

Adjunct professor
College
Culinary programs
Master's degree
Resume
Tenure
University
Vitea
Vocational programs

Overview of Teaching in Hospitality, Foodservice, and Tourism Management

*T*here are many challenges faced by educational service providers in that many segments of the hospitality and tourism business are imbued with a relatively high degree of turnover, both within hourly and managerial ranks. Many organizations cannot afford to sustain a training department so they turn to educational institutions to help keep them supplied with competent individuals with great attitudes and work ethics. While ultimately, that is the most desired outcome, many organizations know and understand the need to keep educating and training their workforce in order to remain competitive and healthy. J. W. Marriott, Jr., has been quoted as saying "For us, this is not a new proposition. For more than 70 years, we've lived by a simple motto. If we take care of our associates, they'll take care of the guest."[1] There is complete truth in that statement and companies must find ways to sustain a viable labor force capable of providing the kind and type of service each business requires. In a speech given by J. W. Marriott, he states that one of their company's greatest resources is human capital and they have pledged to train that workforce for the needs of the future. All hospitality companies are concerned about training and maintaining their workforce to meet the needs of the industry.

To begin, the profession of teaching is a very rewarding and demanding career. Seeking a teaching career within the broad scope of the hospitality industry requires a working knowledge of technical, human, and conceptual skills. It has often been said that a career in the hospitality industry is recession proof. Think about that statement for a moment and you will find a great truth in that. People must eat and sleep and that encompasses a vast proportion of the components that teachers seek to train, educate, and mentor within the scope of the hospitality/service industry.

To explore this matter further, those who seek a career in hospitality/culinary education must bring more than an appropriate degree to the job. Experience in several aspects of this industry are expected, no matter what level you teach at, be it a high school program, a community/2-year college, a 4-year college/university, or even a certificate program. Today institutions are seeking individuals who possess extensive working knowledge, coupled with an appropriate degree or highly specialized certificate.

High School Programs

Most high school programs provide students with training that will enable them to work entry-level positions in foodservice, lodging, or tourism. These skills can include how to clean a room properly to check in procedures at the front desk to preparing food in the kitchen. In these programs, students participate in hands-on, practical, skill-building exercises.

The Academy of Travel & Tourism® and ProStart® are two programs designed to introduce high school students to the hospitality and tourism industry. These programs benefit high school teachers by providing a well-designed curriculum appropriate for an introduction to the industry. Students in these programs obtain knowledge, skills, and experience that enable them to become superior candidates for jobs in the industry. Students who complete a program and choose to continue with their education in hospitality and tourism may be awarded college credits towards an Associate's or Bachelor's degree.

Teaching at the high school level requires specialized teaching certificates as mandated by each specific state. Students interested in teaching on this level should consult with their state department of education to determine the level of education and certifications necessary to start teaching in a high school vocational program. One could also check with a college offering education degrees for guidance regarding what certifications are necessary. High school programs have many different types of opportunities from culinary programs to hospitality management programs. These programs are generally seated in a vocational venue that is part of or affiliated with school districts. Teachers on this level have the unique opportunity to touch the life of a young person and start them on either a promising career path or the chance for higher education.

Post-Secondary Programs: Vocational/Technical Schools, Training Institutes

Much like high school programs, the emphasis here is on training. It's likely that the facilities will be more elaborate (commercial kitchens, front desk simulations, even small travel agencies) and allow

Profile
JULIE LANE, HIGH SCHOOL VOCATIONAL TEACHER

I have always worked in the hospitality industry even when I was in high school I worked at a Holiday Inn. For 6 years I owned my own restaurant and dinner theatre, it was a blending of things I love to do: restaurant, singing, and performance. After working in the kitchen of another restaurant, I went on to gain vocational certification to teach high school.

Teaching is an extremely rewarding career. The opportunity to see the student's progress as they learn is amazing. While in school I see the growth of both their cognitive and hands on learning skills, skills that prepare them for a career in the hospitality industry. Often they start in entry level positions and as their ability grows they progress in their career path. In addition to the hands on opportunities in the classroom, many of the students work in the field, which even allows them to be proficient that much sooner.

Teaching at the vocational level is very active and interesting. On one hand you need to keep up with industry standards while teaching every day. It is a challenge to keep up with the changing world, because this change must be reflected in everything I do as a teacher.

Julie Lane
Instructor, Hospitality and Restaurant Services
Millstream Career and Technology Center
Findlay, Ohio

the students to focus more narrowly on a particular area of interest. Therefore topics for certificates might be how to be a travel agent or tour guide. Many trade associations will offer certificates in their areas to help their members become more knowledgeable and demonstrate their expertise.

This means that the instructor, likewise, will need an appropriate background in a specific area. Typically, the instructor will be someone from industry with years of experience who has a special expertise in the certificate area. Students, who complete a course of study, typically 1 year, are awarded a diploma or a certificate.

Two-Year Programs: Community Colleges, Culinary Arts Academies

Most 2-year programs award the graduate an associate's degree. However unlike 4-year institutions, courses will be more focused on gaining information that is necessary to get an entry level job in the field. Many 2-year programs have a culinary and/or foodservice management option for students. Many programs have a commercial kitchen, and students are responsible for planning, preparing, and serving meals to the public in a restaurant setting. However, there are very famous programs like CIA or the Cordon Bleu in Paris that develop high quality chefs. Typically, a 4-year institution will accept transfer credits from a 2-year program, thereby reducing the

amount of time it will take for a student to obtain a Bachelor's degree, if a student wants to pursue a higher degree.

An instructor at a community college needs industry experiences in their teaching area and usually at least a Bachelor's degree with a very specialized background containing a high degree of knowledge in a specific content area often unique to our industry. However, years of experience and reputation can sometimes offset a degree. Having said that, a Master's degree is often a requirement.

Four-Year Programs: Colleges, Universities

At a 4-year institution, a hospitality and tourism program may be a "college," a "school," or a "department" functioning within a university (e.g., the College of Hospitality, Retail, and Sport Management at the University of South Carolina). Hospitality programs can also be located within other large academic units, such as business (e.g., the Lester E. Kabacoff School of Hotel, Restaurant and Tourism Administration College of Business Administration, University of New Orleans), consumer and family services, human ecology, health and human development, food and agriculture, or applied science and technology.

Graduates of a 4-year program obtain a Bachelor's degree. This combines 2 years of developing a

Profile
WILLIAM POWELL

My culinary career began in a manner familiar to many working chefs, I opted to develop my skills through working my way up the ranks of the professional kitchen. I worked in a variety of fine dining restaurants throughout the United States, but had a hunger for a deeper understanding of the culinary arts. I decided to return to culinary school as a nontraditional student after working in the industry for 15 years. My interest in teaching was piqued as I attended a local community college in West Texas and came to know a diverse set of chef instructors and students. I was attracted to the diverse population of learners that ranged from post-secondary high school students to the retirees pursuing a lifelong dream of becoming a chef. I knew from my experience as a nontraditional culinary student at Odessa College that I wanted to work in a community college setting that embraces diversity, strong academics, and is truly concerned with student success.

My transition from industry to higher education is similar to many of my chef instructor contemporaries. The path included both formal and "real world" educations by combining 24 years of culinary industry experience with undergraduate and graduate level degrees. The formal educational experience provided solid academic preparation in culinary arts, business, and education, while the years of industry experience afforded me the opportunity to gain in depth knowledge of the culinary arts field that cannot be gained solely through textbooks. My students often comment on how the integration of my personal experiences into classes provided great illustrations that make the course content come alive.

My responsibilities as a community college educator encompass many of the appealing characteristics of a traditional culinary arts career. The contemporary chef instructor still has the opportunity to work with food through lab classes and department food operations. These responsibilities are coupled with the opportunity to develop new courses, serve on academic committees, become involved in student organizations, and provide academic advising to students. While my job is fast paced and demanding, I truly consider it the most rewarding professional experience of my 24-year career in the culinary arts field. While I still get a great deal of satisfaction from creating a great meal for guests, it does not come close to the feeling of pride as I watch my students walk across the stage at graduation and begin their professional journey.

Chef Bill Powell, MAE, CCC
Coordinator, Department of Food, Nutrient and Hospitality
Owens Community College
Toledo, OH

broad liberal arts background with 2 years of specific hospitality courses. A person should know about the world around them because we don't live in a vacuum. When a manager interacts with other people, he/she is expected to be able to talk intelligently on many different topics outside the realm of the operations. Although the industry used to be known for promoting from within—the bellboy who ended up owning a hotel chain with 84 properties—the industry has matured considerably. A Bachelor's has become the minimum credential for middle and upper management. We will always have the Rich Melmans—an entrepreneur with no college degree—but more and more, the industry demands a college degree.

At the 4-year degree granting institutions, where programs exist, an added dimension is now re-quired, and that often includes an earned doctorate or in rare instances, at least a Master's degree, all with highly specialized knowledge, and the ability and demonstrated record of research and publishing in the field. Institutions with accredited programs do not waiver on what they expect from their faculty regarding their credentials. Each institution establishes those key indicators as minimums for even considering a full-time faculty hire. There are exceptions, but they are becoming rare at the 4-year degree and higher granting institutions.

Graduate Programs: Universities

Some universities provide the graduate student with a choice. A student may choose a degree in hospitality management, often referred to as a Professional-degree program, with the emphasis on coursework and a major project, which is most beneficial for returning to industry; or a research-oriented degree (i.e., Master of Science) that concludes with a thesis, which is better for anyone in education or research.

Usually, doctoral programs are designed for people who wish to teach and conduct research at the college or university level. Here, students also have choices. Some universities offer a doctorate in hospitality and tourism management, e.g., Ph.D. in Hospitality Administration at Texas Tech University, while others offer a doctorate in a related area with an emphasis in hospitality and tourism management (e.g., Ph.D. in Nutrition and Food Science with an emphasis in Hotel and Restaurant Management at Auburn University). Doctoral programs conclude with a dissertation.

Most universities that have graduate programs have graduate student assistantships at both the teaching and research levels. If you plan to pursue a career in education, seek out this opportunity to teach a class or work with a leading researcher in the program. Some universities have support programs for first-time teachers/researchers, or for faculty who want to become more effective teachers and researchers. An assistantship, and a course in "how to be the best teacher/researcher you can be," will provide you with additional qualifications for obtaining the position you would most like to have.

Professors who teach at this level must not only have a doctorate but also a stream of research that continually improves their knowledge base. Major research universities require a faculty member to have a track record of research and publication, and what is known as a "terminal degree." A terminal degree means the highest degree in that field; it is the end of the line in obtaining degrees. Typically, in a university hospitality and tourism program, you'll find faculty with Ph.D.s (doctorates in philosophy), Ed.D.s (doctorates in education), or J.D.s (doctorates in law). Some universities are willing to hire a candidate who is "ABD" (all but dissertation) with the stipulation that he/she must complete the terminal degree within a specified time. Universities that hire an ABD candidate will probably give that teacher the academic rank of Instructor. Once the terminal degree is earned, the rank will be changed to Assistant Professor. It is customary to request promotion to Associate Professor when tenure is earned. For promotion to full Professor, an academic must be considered outstanding in the field, especially in the areas of teaching and research, and to have established a national, if not international, reputation as a leading scholar.

Adjuncts

Another growing and somewhat necessary trend may be that all types of institutions will hire adjunct or part-time instructors who possess a high degree of experience and knowledge in a particular content area where it is difficult to find a full-time faculty member. This trend is becoming commonplace and is expected to continue to grow as this alleviates the academic need hire a full-time faculty member who may not possess this knowledge. Many of these part-time hires are coming from careers where they performed tasks and duties particular to the content area. Often hires are current full-time employees or retired executives who can fill this void. A good way to test one's desire and aptitude to teach is to find an adjunct opportunity. Another trend appears to be that senior administrators are seeking several part-timers with experience in all aspects of their field, thereby reducing their labor and long-term commitment costs to execute specialized programs. May we submit that this trend is not relegated just to hospitality/tourism management, but a wider spectrum across all types of institutions defined earlier in this segment.

Why Consider Teaching Hospitality as a Career?

First and foremost it is the opportunity to work with people who are enthusiastic about the industry. We work in a very exciting industry and it is rewarding to be able to share our experiences and outlooks with those people planning on making hospitality their career. It is personally rewarding to see students grow and mature. If you ask most teachers they will list the opportunity to play a role in shaping a person's career and life as the primary reason they teach. This is even more evident in hospitality education as we have the opportunity to work one-on-one with students in labs and experiential based classes.

In addition, as highly experienced professionals seek to change careers or enter early retirement, they are also valuable resources for many of these hospitality programs. Teaching provides them with a new and fresh perspective of what our future workforce and leaders think and look like. Having an opportunity to influence a young mind into a career field of almost unlimited potential, is a very attractive and compelling reason to enter the highly respected field of teaching.

While teaching is enjoyable it also takes hard work to educate and train young and not so young minds. Many individuals are returning to these programs (especially at the 2 and 4 year levels) to obtain the necessary credentials and skills needed to work successfully in this industry. This trend is expected to continue given the growth of the service industries and the portability of the work. Education will continue to play a critical role in the growing demand that is anticipated over the next several years. Many companies are partnering with educational institutions and training/career centers to assist them with delivering service training. This training encompasses a broad spectrum of needs as defined by the organization to which many educational institutions (both nonprofit and for profit) are delivering to meet a myriad of needs.

How to Get a Job as an Academic

Requirements

To apply for a position within the industry, you should have an excellent resume; for education, you will want an outstanding curriculum vitae. As in a resume, a vitae must be continually updated as you acquire important job-related accomplishments. For an educator, these will fall under three major headings: teaching, research, and service. A different emphasis will be placed on each of these depending on the institution. Furthermore, different institutions define these categories each using its own specifications. Therefore, what is acceptable at one institution may not be acceptable at another.

Student and peer evaluations are an important part of assessing a teacher's performance. High schools, post-secondary programs, and community colleges generally place the greatest emphasis on this aspect of a professional's career.

Research includes the completion of a unique project designed to add knowledge to the field and disseminating the results through publication and/or conference presentation. Demonstrating mastery in this category is very important for faculty at research-oriented universities.

Service is a priority to the department/school/college/university, to the profession, and to the community. These activities include being a faculty advisor to student organizations, serving on professional association committees, and donating professional expertise to charitable institutions.

Tenure and Teaching Load

Colleges and universities will place new faculty in "tenure track lines." Some community colleges offer tenure, some do not. This means that a faculty member must show development and progress in the three areas of teaching, research, and service in order to continue in that position. A faculty member will have a periodic review, typically annually, and after the fifth year of employment, a university committee will examine that faculty member's record for a tenure decision. When tenure is granted, this means a faculty member has employment in that department on a continuing basis. Some universities have instituted periodic post-tenure reviews for faculty, to ensure those faculties who continue to develop are rewarded appropriately. Faculty who are expected to conduct research and remain active as scholars will normally be given reduced teaching loads.

Lifestyle and Compensation

Hospitality and tourism educators tend to be like their counterparts in the industry: outgoing, enthusiastic, and very busy. For each class taught, it is expected that about 2 to 4 hours of preparation are needed. However, when you first start teaching, that time dramatically increases as you select textbooks, outline the chapters, develop classnotes, decide how you want to teach the information, find outside materials including video/dvd selections and guest speakers, and create assignments that help students apply what they learn. That is just the teaching side.

Then, many professors are expected to write and get published. Depending on the type of publication, it must be accepted by an editorial board which might take from 6 months to 1 or 2 years. Oh, and did I mention, the public service side . . . be on department, school, and university committees; attend/present at local, national, and international industry meetings and functions; and be involved in the regional hospitality education chapters. But, one advantage to the profession is that, when not in the classroom or attending a meeting, a professor can arrange their schedule to suit themselves. Educators must be able to work autonomously, both inside and outside the classroom. Most educators appreciate this independent aspect of their work. They also value academic freedom. This gives an educator the right to teach as they see fit.

The general public holds the notion that educators have 3 months of vacation during the summer. This is certainly a misconception. Professional development activities—research, writing, conferences, updating, and revising class material—are time-consuming and there is scant opportunity during the academic year to pursue these. If an educator wants to remain employed, they must be making adequate progress in professional development.

If your goal is to become wealthy, education is probably not the career for you. However, if your goal is to be enriched by lifelong learning, you will be immensely rewarded. If you are fortunate, when alumni return to campus, you will be seated at a table with your former students who are now making far more money than you are. This is an excellent opportunity to convince them of the value of their education and the benefits of helping other students. Salaries are good; however, depending upon your level of academic achievement and research, they vary. This is true in the world of business, and we must think of institutions of learning as businesses. While senior administrators must meet a variety of state, federal, and often accrediting standards in the academic programs they oversee, they must also deliver that education in the most cost effective way possible. Salaries are often commensurate with degrees achieved, documented research, and experience both in teaching and in the field.

Summary

Education is the foundation, the cornerstone, and very often the bridge that keeps our hospitality businesses vibrant and successful. We would be remiss if we did not acknowledge the pivotal role that technology has and will continue to play in educating and enhancing the ways in which we conduct our businesses and train and educate our workforce. The ways in which we are able to communicate have proliferated and dramatically enhanced our opportunities in the field of education and training. Savvy young people, and in fact all ages, are deluged with a variety of ways to both receive and send a variety of messages. To this end, we as educators must keep pace with our need to utilize these ever changing technologies in educating and training our labor force. The ability to use global resources in a cost efficient manner has reached unprecedented heights for those educators who have connected to how multi-generational populations both communicate and learn.

To sum up, we have many opportunities to work with our constituents globally in the training and educational preparation of our present and future labor supply. Educations must keep pace with both the organizations and businesses and their needs, while maintaining a balance that will satisfy the employee's need to see their future while providing an education that will prepare them for a stable future. We, as Peter Senge best said it, are "lifelong learners" who must continue to learn if we are to continue to grow.

≈ *Resources*

Internet Sites

The Council on Hotel, Restaurant, and Institutional Education: www.chrie.org
The International Council on Hotel, Restaurant, and Institutional Education: www.chrie.org
National Academy Foundation (NAF) The Academy of Travel & Tourism: www.naf-education.org
The National Restaurant Association Educational Foundation (NRAEF) Prostart program: www.nraef.org/prostart/

≈ *Endnote*

1. Marriott, J. W. Jr., 2000. "J.W. Marriott, Jr. Outlines the Company's Five-point Strategy to Attract and Retain Employees." Hotel Online, special report. www.hotel-online.com/News/Pressreleases2000_4th/Oct

≈ *Contributors*

Dr. John M. Wolper
Associate Professor of Business
Director of Hospitality Management
The College of Business
The University of Findlay
1000 North Main Street
Findlay, Ohio 45840
wolper@findlay.edu

Prof. John Wolper, area director of the Hospitality Management Program and associate professor of business at The University of Findlay. Wolper holds a Ed.D. in leadership administration from Indiana University of Pennsylvania and a B.S. and a M.S. in hotel, restaurant, and travel administration from the University of Massachusetts. His current research is in the area of leadership styles and curriculum management.

Paula J. Wolper
Assistant Professor of Business
Hospitality Management
The College of Business
The University of Findlay
1000 North Main Street
Findlay, Ohio 45840
pwolper@findlay.edu

Paula Wolper is an assistant professor in the hospitality program at The University of Findlay in Findlay, Ohio. Wolper holds a MBA from The Pennsylvania State University, The Behrend College and her B.A. was in Hotel, Restaurant, and Institutional Management at Michigan State University.

Chapter 38
Review Questions

1. If you decided that you wanted to teach hospitality, what are different types of schools in which you could teach?

2. Name at least two things necessary that would enable you to teach?

3. Please name two programs listed in the book designed to introduce students to the world of hospitality and tourism on the high school level.

4. What is the difference between the type of education offered in Vocational/Technical schools as opposed to a college education?

5. Why does someone generally decide to pursue a doctorate?

6. What could you do if you wanted to try teaching before pursuing it as a full-time career?

7. What is one reason to become a hospitality teacher?

8. What do professors usually do in the summer months?

9. Interview one of your teachers or professors. What do they say is the most rewarding aspect of their profession? What is involved in preparing to teach a class? What work do they need to do to prepare themselves to teach a class? What advice would they give someone who is thinking about teaching hospitality as a career?

Management Consulting

39

Joe Hutchinson, University of Central Florida

© Yuri Arcurs, 2008, Shutterstock.

≈ Learning Objectives

- ☑ To learn about different types of consulting firms
- ☑ To understand what it means to be a management consultant
- ☑ To know skills requirements and personality traits
- ☑ To understand the ethics
- ☑ To learn how to develop a career path

≈ Chapter Outline

Types of Management Consulting Firms
The Nature of the Work
The Consultant's Lifestyle
Consulting Skill Requirements
Personality Traits
Ethics, Certification, and Professional Development

≈ Key Terms

Consultant
Consulting careers
Consulting firms
Consulting qualifications
Consulting skills
Hospitality consultant
Management consultant

A person with years of experience, a talent for identifying problems, and the ability to find creative solutions may want to become a consultant. The consulting industry is a rapidly growing segment in the service sector of the U.S. economy. Consultants offer a wide range of professional services to clients in many different fields.

A consultant may be any individual who has a specific area of expertise and is compensated for providing advice or other services to a client. Sometimes people are hired as consultants after firms downsize and then hire them back as independent contractors. This allows the firm the advantage of retaining the expertise without the former budgetary constraints or expenses. Other times, a firm may be looking for an objective viewpoint to convince the board of directors or upper-level management that their plans and strategies are sound and feasible.

There is a saying that experts are people who live more than 50 miles away. Sometimes we tend to give consultants more credibility if they are not part of the company or community. In any case, a consultant can work independently or they can join a firm. Correspondingly, a client may be served by an individual, a group of persons, or an organization that compensates the consultant in exchange for the advice or other services received.

Hospitality management consulting is an industry-specific form of consulting that may be included under the broader umbrella of business or management consulting. Management consultants often focus their services in specific functional areas, such as general management, human resources, marketing, management information systems, operations, administration, and finance/accounting. Most management consultants who serve clients in the hospitality industry also serve clients in numerous other industries. A hospitality management consultant would be a consultant who serves only hospitality industry clients and provides services in one or more functional areas.

Hospitality organizations may hire an external consultant because specialized expertise may be unavailable within their organizations to complete the specific tasks within the necessary time frame. For example, consultants may be hired to design a foodservice facility or to conduct a hotel feasibility study. Even when an organization has adequate internal expertise to complete the necessary tasks, an outside consultant may be hired because of the sensitive nature of the issues involved, the objectivity provided by an outsider, and/or the reputation and credibility of the consultant or the firm that he or she represents.

This chapter provides an overview of the management consulting profession. Topics discussed include the types of management consulting firms, the nature of the work, the consultant's lifestyle, consulting skill requirements and personality traits, ethics and professional development, and the consulting career.

Types of Management Consulting Firms

Management consulting firms may be classified according to a number of characteristics, such as their size, level of specialization, industries served, geographical location, or types of clients/industries that they serve. Consultants who provide services to clients in hospitality organizations are often found in the following types of firms.

General Management Firms

These firms provide general management consulting services to international clients in many different industries. Consultants in these firms may be referred to as generalists who provide a broad range of services to their clients and tailor their services to the specific needs of each client. In some cases, they can assess an organization's structure and recommend restructuring and position cuts and/or additions. Other times, they can examine management practices or organizational efficiencies. With today's prevalence of corporate mergers, consultants provide an objective approach to blending companies together with services that may include strategic planning, psychological testing for compatibility, skill assessments, or recommendations for department restructuring. The better-known international firms that provide general management consulting services to a diverse base of clients include McKinsey and Company, Boston Consulting Group, and Booz Allen Hamilton.

Management Consulting Divisions of Certified Public Accounting (CPA) Firms

Large international CPA firms may have a consulting presence in the hospitality industry. These firms are staffed with consulting professionals who have backgrounds, experiences, and education in the hospitality industry. These firms often perform project feasibility studies or recommend improvements in areas such as strategic planning, operating efficiencics, product/service quality, or customer service. PricewaterhouseCoopers is an example of a larger international accounting/consulting firm that includes a consulting division specializing in the hospitality industry. Hospitality consultants in these larger firms often focus on the lodging industry, particularly with respect to hotel development.

Functionally Specialized Firms

A number of consulting firms may serve clients in the hospitality industry and many other industries by providing their expertise in a specific functional area. Specialists in these firms focus on their narrow area of expertise. For example, a firm that specializes in management information systems may develop the system requirements for a large hotel. Another consultant may be the advertising agency that creates the media campaign for the company.

Industry-Specific Firms

Some firms serve only the management of organizations in the hospitality industry. These firms often provide specialized consulting services to their clients by focusing on a specific industry segment (i.e., foodservice industry), an industry subsegment (i.e., full-service restaurants), and/or a specific functional arca in certain industry organizations (i.e., facilities/equipment layout and design in foodservice operations). PKF Consulting is a national consulting firm that specializes in the lodging industry. Some of you may have seen their reports on salaries for different positions in different segments of the hotel industry across the nation. They also track and report various lodging statistics for various regions of the United States. On the other hand, Cini-Little International serves clients in a wide variety of foodservice operations. A large number of small firms and sole practitioners also specialize in the layout and design of kitchen facilities. In fact, most consultants specialize in hospitality industry consulting do work for either small firms (2 to 10 employees) or operate as sole practitioners (one-person firms).

Internal Consultants

External consultants serve clients of different hospitality firms, whereas internal consultants serve only one hospitality organization. These consultants may be on the payroll of the organization or they may serve on a contract basis exclusively with that one organization. These individuals are often referred to as "troubleshooters" or "field consultants" and perform many of the functions that external consultants perform. Most large restaurant and lodging chains have in-house personnel who provide operational support and assistance to both company-owned and franchised units of those organizations. For example, chain hotels or restaurants often have in-house consultants or troubleshooters who conduct on-site visits to specific units or properties in the chain to identify problems and develop solutions for implementation. Others might locate sites for new development and evaluate their feasibility for success.

The Nature of the Work

Although the work of a consultant varies significantly among individuals and firms, there are three major steps in the consulting cycle that are common to most consultants: marketing, the consulting engagement, and administration.

Marketing

The marketing of consulting services is usually designed to build the reputation of an individual or a firm as a leading expert in a specific area. Every consulting firm, irrespective of size, must generate and sustain enough work to stay in business. Marketing in consulting involves the direct or indirect solicitation of new clients and/or efforts to generate additional business from existing or previous clients. Forms of indirect marketing include active membership in trade associations, serving on industry boards and panels, writing books and articles, making conference presentations, or conducting workshops and seminars. More direct forms of marketing would include advertising, direct mail, and meetings with potential clients.

The Consulting Engagement

Each new consulting project is typically referred to as a consulting engagement. Most engagements begin with an initial client meeting to discuss the scope and nature of the client's needs. The consultant may have responded to a phone call or a request for proposal (RFP). An RFP is a document, frequently used by government organizations, that outlines the nature of the work requested and other

The final report to the client usually includes an oral presentation of findings and recommendations.

project details. Following an initial client meeting or the receipt of an RFP, the consultant often prepares a formal proposal. This proposal will clarify the details of the engagement by outlining the project background and objectives, the approach and work plan that will be used to complete the engagement, the final deliverables that will be provided to the client (i.e., oral presentations and written reports), and other project details (i.e., project fees, billing procedures, timing, and qualifications of consultants). After completing all the work steps outlined in the proposal, the consultant usually presents a final report to the client, in addition to an oral presentation discussing the findings and recommendations outlined in the report.

Administration

Consultants must perform other duties in addition to soliciting clients, writing proposals, meeting with clients, and completing consulting engagements. A number of administrative tasks must be completed in every consulting firm. In large firms, there usually will be a project manager who directs the work of the consultants on the project, maintains an ongoing dialogue with the client, and ensures that payments for services are received in a timely manner. These consultants may also be responsible for establishing a project budget and ensuring that each consulting engagement is completed within the allocated amount of time and dollars. Larger firms have support staff to perform necessary administrative and clerical tasks within the firm (report production, telephone calls, graphics, copy services, payroll, benefits, professional development, taxes, etc.). In small firms or sole proprietorships, consul-

tants typically will be responsible for completing all relevant administrative tasks required to operate the business.

The Consultant's Lifestyle

There is no common lifestyle shared by all individuals in the consulting profession. The lifestyle of a consultant may differ significantly from one firm to another. Factors that may influence a consultant's lifestyle include the size of the firm, the type of services provided, the geographical area covered, and the industries served. For example, sole practitioners may shape their own working conditions to match their desired lifestyle by limiting travel, selecting only certain clients to serve, determining their own work hours, setting their own fees, working out of their own home, or working part-time. Conversely, consultants in large firms usually have little input into the services they provide, the hours they work, the type of clients they serve, the fees they charge, or the geographical locations where they work.

The consulting profession may be very rewarding for certain individuals. Consultants have the opportunity to help and influence others and may derive a great deal of satisfaction from making a positive contribution to both clients and society. There is also the potential of high earnings, status, and respect. Many consultants thrive on the constant new challenges they are faced with and the opportunities to learn so much in a short period of time.

Despite the many rewards of consulting, there are lifestyle trade-offs involved. Although these job benefits are enjoyed by some consultants, the actual working conditions are usually much different from what they appear to outsiders. Most consultants are required to meet difficult project deadlines by working long hours under intense pressure to complete their tasks. The consultant must become absorbed in these projects and may be required to spend days, weeks, or months of sustained focus on a project until problems are diagnosed and appropriate solutions are generated. This lifestyle can be physically and mentally fatiguing.

Travel demands and uncertain living conditions also present a challenge for most consultants. Significant amounts of a consultant's time may be spent in travel. This often requires an individual to spend weeks at a time away from home. Although a sole practitioner may have greater control over travel demands, most successful independent consultants will be required to travel frequently over a wide geographic area.

Consulting Skill Requirements

The skill requirements of a consultant will vary according to the nature of services provided, the industries served, or size of the firm. However, a number of skills are required for all consultants. These skills are discussed next.

Technical Skills

All consultants must have a certain level of expertise in a particular industry, function, or technique. However, it takes more than just experience, education, and skills to be a successful consultant. All consultants must have the unique ability to translate their knowledge base into applications that provide value to their clients.

Communication Skills

The ability to communicate both orally and in writing is one of the most critical skills needed to be a successful consultant. All consultants must communicate with other individuals on a regular basis. This communication may take the form of telephone conversations, meetings, interviews, presentations, or written proposals and reports. Consultants must have the ability to convey information clearly and professionally through every step of a consulting engagement.

Interpersonal Skills

The relationship between the client and the consultant is critical to the successful completion of all consulting engagements. The consultant must have strong interpersonal skills that create a mutual sense of trust and openness with clients. This requires that the consultant remain sensitive to the client's needs and feelings.

Administrative Skills

In addition to performing the tasks of a consulting engagement, a consultant may be required to maintain regular communication with clients, review the work quality of other consultants, keep projects within budgeted hours and costs, and manage the client billing and collection process. As a sole prac-

titioner, these responsibilities are magnified, because one individual is responsible for completing all project tasks and managing the business.

Marketing and Selling Skills

A consultant's ability to market and sell a firm's consulting services is essential to the promotion to upper-level positions in a large firm. To build and sustain a viable consulting business, a firm must maintain a strong relationship with existing and previous clients, while continually adding new clients.

In large firms, a progression usually occurs in terms of a consultant's skills development. New consultants are typically hired on the basis of their technical expertise. An individual will usually first work on technical-related tasks relevant to his or her expertise. After this stage is mastered, the consultant will progress into a supervisory role. In this capacity, more emphasis will be placed on communication, administration skills, and interpersonal skills. As the consultant advances in the firm, he or she will become more involved in marketing and sales.

Personality Traits

Although a consultant may meet the skill requirements to complete all necessary tasks effectively, certain personality traits are necessary to pursue a career in the consulting profession. The following personality traits are usually required for all consultants, irrespective of the work settings.

Ambition and Self-Motivation

A consultant must have a high desire for personal success and must be internally driven, as there is often little outside motivation or direction. This requires an individual to have the initiative to start and complete tasks in an effective and efficient manner with little oversight and guidance.

Ability to Work with Others

A consultant is required to work with other consultants, clients, and employees of a client's organization on an ongoing basis. Thus, the individual must be able to get along with others and enjoy participating in a team-oriented process. Quite often, this includes active listening to hear what the other person is saying. Once you understand the other person's point of view, you can discuss some creative intermediary step. Along with active listening comes the skill to mediate different viewpoints so that consensus of opinion for new directions can be implemented.

A consultant is also a marketer who must both create and sell the product to the client. Like any good salesman, they must be able to adapt and modify proposals to address specific client concerns and to know when the sales job is finished.

Self-Fulfillment

Despite the many benefits that a consultant may provide to his or her clients, their contributions often are unrecognized. Consultants usually receive few tangible forms of personal recognition (i.e., certificates and awards) for their accomplishments. This requires the individual to have a strong sense of self-fulfillment.

Mobility, Flexibility, and Tolerance for Ambiguity

Because most successful consultants serve clients dispersed across wide geographic regions, the traveling demands can be rigorous. Further, the nature of projects and the work settings may change on a regular basis, with roles and client problems not well defined. An individual who does not have the mobility to travel extensively, the flexibility to shift directions on short notice, or the tolerance to work in ambiguous situations may have difficulty coping with the challenges of consulting.

High Energy and the Ability to Work under Pressure

The numerous demands and challenges of the consulting profession provide a great deal of excitement but also require high and sustained levels of energy. Most consultants must be able to work long hours on a regular basis. Projects often must be completed under significant pressure to meet multiple deadlines and to satisfy prior commitments made to clients. Although individuals may enjoy the challenges of consulting, it is difficult to maintain such a demanding pace over a sustained period of time.

Self-Confidence

Consultants must be confident in themselves, and they must be able to instill in their clients a strong sense of confidence in them. This often requires an ability to deal with rejection and failure due to lost proposals, mistakes, or a client's unwillingness to accept their recommendations. A consultant must overcome these barriers and continue to move on confidently to each new engagement with a fresh start. A consultant also must have enough self-confidence to think outside the box and be creative in recommending the best possible solutions to a problem or issue, even when those recommendations are not popular.

Ethics, Certification, and Professional Development

Unlike many other professions, there are no government regulations, certification requirements, or codes of ethics that universally apply to all consultants. Because consulting applies to all fields, it is not possible to have one general licensing procedure. However, most major professional consulting associations and large consulting organizations have a code of ethics that outlines the consultant's responsibilities to the client and to the public.

Consultants are often faced with a number of ethical dilemmas that are not regulated by law and are not that obvious. Some ethical issues common to the consulting profession include confidentiality, conflict of interest, objectivity, and professional involvement. Specific examples of the type of ethical dilemmas consultants are often faced with include:

- The client seeks assistance for services outside the consultant's scope of competence.
- The consultant has an existing relationship or other interests with the client that would influence his or her objectivity in completing the work.
- The client requests the consultant to manipulate the results to favor the client's position.
- The client requests that the consultant omit, conceal, or revise certain information.
- The client requests that the consultant obtain proprietary information from a former client.

Professional development opportunities are available to enhance and refine an individual's technical expertise and consulting skills. Because technical skills can become obsolete quickly, successful consultants stay current by attending workshops, seminars, lectures, and professional meetings. These skills are further updated by reading current books, periodicals, and newspapers. To improve their consulting skills, consultants may attend professional association consulting skills workshops. Large consulting firms usually conduct their own in-house training to further enhance the consulting skills of their professionals.

Summary

The consulting industry is anticipated to continue to outpace the growth of the U.S. economy by a wide margin. This provides a bright outlook for those individuals who desire to pursue a career in management consulting. Consulting can be a rewarding profession for individuals at all ages and career stages, such as recent MBA graduates, individuals in midcareer, retirees, or part-time consultants searching for other outlets to use their skills. The appeal of a career in consulting has continued to grow, as an increasing number of individuals enters the field to utilize their knowledge, skills, and experience.

Individuals who are considering a career in management consulting should take a personal inventory of their interests, skills, and personality traits. Although a person may desire a career in consulting initially, a more thorough examination of the skill requirements, lifestyle, and personality traits of successful consultants may reveal a lack of compatibility with a person's actual needs and desires. However, an individual's talents, interests, and personal situation may change a number of times during his or her career. As these changes occur, each individual should reevaluate his or her fit with a consulting career.

There are many different career paths that people take to become a consultant. These paths depend on a number of factors, such as age, education, experience, interests, and skills. Many sole practitioners have begun consulting careers after being laid off as part of company downsizings, restructurings, or mergers. Conversely, MBA graduates who lack the experience, skills, or capital to start their own firm often seek positions with national or regional consulting firms or as internal consultants to large companies. Even in these situations, it is usually desirable to have at least five years of management experience to establish credibility among clients. The expertise demonstrated through business management experience and the knowledge gained through education and other professional development opportunities should serve as assets for those interested in pursuing a career in management consulting.

≈ Contributor

Dr. Joe Hutchinson is currently an associate professor in the Rosen College of Hospitality Management at the University of Central Florida. Prior to that, he was an associate professor in the Department of Tourim Mamagement at the University of Southern Mississippi, and a faculty member in the Department of Hotel, Restaurant, and Institution Management at Iowa State University. Dr. Hutchinson received a BS degree in Hotel and Restaurant Management from the University of Houston, an MBA degree from Southwest Texas State University, and a PhD degree in Hospitality and Tourism Management from Virginia Polytechnic Institute and State University.

Dr. Hutchinson has taught courses in the introduction to hospitality and tourism management, human resources management, financial management, strategic management, quality service management, hospitality law, gaming law, casino operations management, and strategic planning for public and nonprofit organizations. He has conducted research in the areas of customer satisfaction and service quality. Prior to his academic background, Dr. Hutchinson served as a management consultant with KPMG Consulting and two other international accounting/consulting firms. He continues to provide management consulting services to public- and private-sector clients throughout the United States. Prior to his management consulting career, Dr. Hutchinson served for seven years as a general manager of independent and chain-operated casual-themed restaurants.

C h a p t e r 39
Review Questions

1. Define "consultant."

2. Describe the profile of a "management consultant."

3. Describe the profile of a "hospitality consultant."

4. When is it most likely for a hospitality business to hire a consultant? List three situations.

5. How are management consultant firms classified?

6. Define "generalist."

7. In which hospitality segment is one most likely to find a CPA consultant?

8. Describe the role of an internal consultant.

9. For whom does an internal consultant most likely work?

10. What are the three major steps in the consulting cycle?

11. What is the goal of the marketing phase?

12. What are several forms of direct marketing?

13. What are several forms of indirect marketing?

14. What is an RFP?

15. What are some of the administrative duties of a consultant?

16. Who performs the administrative duties in a large consulting business? In a sole practitioner's business?

17. What are five of the factors that influence a consultant's lifestyle?

18. How does the lifestyle/workstyle vary between the sole practitioner and the consultant who works for a large firm?

19. What are the rewards associated with a consulting career?

20. What are the drawbacks associated with a consulting career?

21. List the skills required for working as a consultant. What is the progression of skills from the newly hired consultant stage to that of being more experienced?

22. What types of communication skills do consultants need?

23. Why are communication skills particularly important?

24. How do interpersonal skills influence the building of trust with the client?

25. What personality traits are important for success as a consultant?

26. Why is "tolerance for ambiguity" important to a consultant's success?

27. What are some ethical dilemmas common to consultants?

28. What are the projections for careers as consultants?

29. How do consultants stay current in their area of expertise?

30. How many years of work experience does one need before embarking on a career as a consultant?

Glossary

ABC—Association of Bridal Consultants

Adjunct Professor—A professor employed by a college or university on a part-time basis

Adjusted Gross Income—Gross income adjusted by business and other specified expenses

ADR (Average Daily Rate)—This is computed by dividing room revenue by the number of rooms occupied

AIDA (Awareness, Interest, Desire, Action)—The catalysts on behalf of customers to pay and experience once (or the motivation to repeat visit) a hospitality product or service

Airlines Reporting Corporation—A nonprofit organization representing U.S. airlines that facilitate funds transfer between suppliers and agents, and ensures that travel agencies have experienced management through licensing

Ambience or **Servicescape**—The landscape within which service is experienced has been used to describe the physical aspects of the setting that contribute to the guests' overall physical "feel" of the experience

American Culinary Federation, Inc. (ACF)—The premier professional chefs' organization in North America, with more than 230 chapters nationwide and 20,000 members. ACF offers culinarians of all ages, skill levels, and specialties the opportunity to further their career, as well as enhance their life

Amusement Parks—Commercially operated enterprise that offers rides, games, and other forms of entertainment

Angel Investor—An investor who provides lower levels capital to entrepreneurial projects in the early stages. Many times a former entrepreneur who has harvested their business

AP (As Purchased)—Before a menu item is prepared and any waste has been removed

APEX—Accepted Practices Exchange; see Convention Industry Council

Appraisers—A professional who is trained to value land and buildings, and is hired to render estimates of value

Apprenticeship—Apprenticeship is an on-the-job training program combined with technical classroom instruction. The American Culinary Federation Foundation (ACFF) operates both 2- and 3-year apprenticeship programs. Currently, there are nearly 2,000 apprentices learning in approximately 80 American Culinary Federation Foundation (ACFF) sponsored culinary apprenticeship programs in the United States

Appropriation—The use of the name or likeness of an ordinary, uncelebrated person for commercial purposes

ASAE—American Society of Association Executives

Assisted Living Communities—Communities dedicated to seniors, providing support, maintenance, and living assistance in a community environment. These communities often offer a multitude of residency choices including houses, condominiums, and apartments

At-Home Assisted Living—A service that provides support for a multitude of needs such as: light housekeeping, meal preparation and planning, bathing and grooming assistance, medication management, errands and shopping services, to seniors at their private homes

Attractions—Places we visit and the things we do while we are traveling or visiting

Bar—Specialized counter on which drinks are served and is the name generally applied to the whole of the drinking establishment

Base Fees—These are the basic management fees that contract management companies receive for operating a foodservice or lodging property. These fees are typically a percentage of gross revenues

Bed and Breakfast—Lodging facilities with 2–12 rooms, which are either current or former private residences converted by the owner to accommodate guests

Berth—A bed on a ship

Beverage Cost Ratio—Found by dividing beverage cost by beverage sales

Board Plan—This is a type of meal plan offered on college and university campuses. The board plan allows students to pre-purchase a certain number of meals in the dining halls

Bow—The front of the ship

Brand—In a brand management form a mega-corporation owns multiple chain operations under the same parent umbrella structure. A mega-corporation that owns multiple chains under the same umbrella would prefer to refer to treat each of the chains as a separate brand to emphasize the different images projected by the chains

Branding—This term refers to the foodservice products offered in on-site foodservice locations. There are national brands like Quiznos or Pizza Hut, as well as regional brands, which are specific to a region of the country. On-site foodservice operators also have their own brands

Breakeven—The level of sales at which the business will make neither an income nor a loss

Bridge—The navigational and control center of the ship

Broker—A professional who serves as an intermediary in a real estate sales transaction

Business Model—Hospitality chain business models can be of four types—simple form, mixed franchise form, management/franchise form, and brand management form. In a simple form, a chain can consist of a single owner/investor that has full equity stake in all the units owned by company. In a mixed franchise form chain, there is a mix of ownership with some units being owned and operated by the parent company (known as the franchisor) and the rest owned and operated by many other owners/investors (known as franchisees). If a management/franchise form the parent company (franchisor) also engages in offering professional management services for its non-company-owned (franchised) units, the company can be said to be using the management/franchise form of chain operations

Business Plan—A detailed plan that identifies the opportunity, the resources needed, the team make-up, the market, the operating plan, the risks, required finances, and an exit plan for a specific proposed business venture

By-Laws—Governing rules for an organization

Cabin—A room on a ship; also called a stateroom

Career Fair—An event where many recruiters come together on-campus or at a local convention center to meet and interview potential employees for employment opportunities

Cash Flow—Cash receipts minus cash payments over a period of time

Casino Manager—The highest ranking person in the casino

Casual Dining Restaurant—A foodservice establishment that offers food and beverages at moderate prices and offer a level of service below that of an upscale property

Cause of Action—The legal theory under which the injured party believes that someone else should be held responsible for their injuries

Celebration(s)—A type of meeting; see APEX glossary

Chain Advantages—The advantages of a chain operation include market reach, economies of scale, more streamlined operations, greater marketing power, more service options, greater access to financing, and more professional management

Chain Disadvantages—The disadvantages of chain operations include greater operational constraints, higher financial strain, and more legal woes

Chain Operations—Chain-operated hotels, restaurants, and other similar businesses are owned by the same company and offer similar goods and services, but are found in different geographic locations

Check(s)—Casino chips that are nonmetallic gaming tokens used in place of currency in the casino and come in various denominations ranging from 1 to 5 thousand dollars

Chef—A chef is leader in charge of a kitchen and term comes from the French for "chief" or "director." Today we use this term to describe the chief cook in the kitchen

Chips—(1) Token used instead of cash on all gaming tables and used to mark a bet. (2) A gambler with a lot of money. (3) The small electronic device that contains the computer program found in a slot machine; made of etched silicon

CIC—Convention Industry Council

City Clubs—Establishments that are in urban areas and cater to the businessman or woman, provides dining services and occasionally athletics

CLIA—Cruise Line International Association

Client—This is the specific individual within the host organization that is responsible for monitoring the foodservice operator's performance

Club—A group of persons organized for social, literary, athletic, political, recreational, or other purposes

CMAA—Club Managers Association of America formed in 1920

CMP—Certified Meeting Professional

Coffee Shop Restaurant—Establishments that serve breakfast, lunch, and dinner in an informal manner. Many are open 24 hours per day

College—An institution of higher learning furnishing courses that lead to a Bachelor's degree

Comfortable Carrying Capacity—The maximum number of participants who can utilize the facility at one time

Commercial Foodservice—A foodservice operation where the primary function of the establishment is the sale of food for profit

Comp(s)—Short for complimentary goods or services to players and can apply to things as low cost as drinks to full room, beverage, and transportation costs. They are a marketing tool used to attract players to a certain casino and are called full comps (room, food, beverage)

Conceptual Skills—The ability to see the company or department as a whole and understand how the different parts work together

Conference(s)—A type of meeting; see APEX glossary

Condo-Hotel (Condominium Hotel)—A lodging property where all or part of the "rooms" or suites are owned by independent entities, either for the owners' personal use or for rental purposes. The day-to-day "hotel" operations are run by a management company for a fee, on behalf of all the owners

Consolidators—Businesses that purchase large blocks of airline seats or cruise berths at a substantial discount and resell them to travel agents or the public at lower than normal fare

Contract Services Management—The term used to describe the segment of the hospitality industry dedicated to operating foodservice locations and lodging properties that are owned by another individual or corporation. Owners contract with organizations in this segment to manage their properties

Control—Comparing the performance of employees in a workforce against the objectives and goals that have been set by the company

Convention(s)—A type of meeting; see APEX glossary

Conversational Currency—"Bragging rights" to the latest resort/vacation experience

Copyright—A form of protection provided to the authors of "original works of authorship" including literary, dramatic, musical, and artistic works both published and unpublished

Cost Control—The management concept of controlling costs through effective management practices

Cost Control—The ability to maintain a profit based on proper ordering and securing inventories before, during, and after their sale

Costs and Reimbursement—The cost of various services provided by living centers and what costs are reimbursed through insurance or other compensation programs

Country Clubs—Hospitality establishments that provide elaborate social events, offer dining, pool, tennis, and golf

CRM (Customer Relationship Management)— The process by which companies track detailed requests and personal information about their clientele to customize the sales process and enhance the guest's experience

CSM—Convention services manager

Culinary Programs—Educational programs focused on giving students the skills necessary to work in a commercial kitchen

Culinology®—An approach to food that blends the culinary arts and food technology. One type of culinologists® are research chefs developing recipes and products for food manufacturers, restaurants, food suppliers, or on-site operators

Cultural Tourism—Travel directed toward experiencing the arts, the heritage, the special character of people and place

Dealer—Casino employee who conducts a table game but does not necessarily deal cards; also called the croupier

Deck Plan—Diagram that shows the locations and public spaces on a cruise ship

Defamation—An untrue statement about another that is published or communicated to a third party who understood it which resulted in damages

Defendant—The person against whom a lawsuit has been filed

Democratization of Travel—The concept that travel, leisure travel in particular, is no longer the sole province of the wealthy and that the practice of traveling for leisure has permeated through all levels or strata within society

Destination—A city or region where a meeting will be held

Destination Resort—Self contained, often in remote locations and the recreational amenities offered are the motivating factors to travel to the destination

Detour—A minor deviation from the employer's work for the employee's own personal reasons

Dinner House Restaurants—Open for dinner and sometimes lunch. They have a varied menu selection and offer alcoholic beverages

Discounting—The method of reducing an item from the regular price

Distillation—The process where the alcohol of a fermented beverage is "separated" from the remainder of the liquid

Distilled Beverage—Common distilled beverages (spirits) are vodka, gin, whisky, tequila, etc.

Distribution Channels—Manners through which travel providers advertise, sell, or confirm purchase of their products to clientele

Distribution Services—The vast network of peripheral companies that help hospitality enterprises get their products and services from creation to consumption

DMAI—Destination Marketing Association International

DMC (Destination Management Company)— An organization that collectively assists with all travel planning, including accommodations, transportation, events, and excursions, for groups of visitors arriving from outside the local market

Dram Shop Laws—Makes a business which sells alcoholic drinks or a host who serves liquor to a drinker who is obviously intoxicated or close to it, strictly liable to anyone injured by the drunken patron or guest

Drop—During a given time frame, total amount of cash plus markers at a table, on a shift, or in an entire casino

DUI—Driving under the influence

E-Generation—Refers to the generation of new entrepreneurs who are accumulating their future wealth through the development of equity in a business venture

Economic Growth—The increase over time in the capacity of an economy to produce goods and services and (ideally) to improve the wellbeing of its citizens

Elasticity of Demand—A measurement of whether an increase in price results in a decrease in demand

Electronic Travel Agencies—Providing extensive information and online ticketing via the Internet

Employment Brand—The image of the business as viewed through the eyes of prospective employees. It can also be defined as the image of the applicant as viewed through the eyes of the business

Empowering—Where a contemporary leader has created the organizational work environment in which staff members are trained in necessary skills, enabling them to handle most customer service encounters; management must support the decisions made by the staff members

Energy Management—The management and control of heat, air conditioning, water usage, electric usage, and gas usage

Entrepreneur—A term often used to define risk taking behavior that results in the creation of new opportunities for individuals and organizations

Entrepreneurial Team—A mix of individuals with relevant experience and expertise necessary to pursue a defined business opportunity

Environmental Scanning—The acquisition and use of information about trend changes in technology, politics, culture, economics, competition, and social concerns; the knowledge of which would assist management in taking advantage of opportunities and minimizing risks when planning the organization's strategic plan for the future

EP (Edible Portion)—After a menu item has been prepared and all waste has been discarded

Equity Clubs—Those facilities owned by their membership, are nonprofit; oldest form of clubs

ESG—Event specifications guide; see APEX and Convention Industry Council

ESOP—Employee stock option plan administered through a trust established by the company to distribute stock to its employees

Ethics—A set of principles that managers apply when interacting with people and their organizations; fair and equal treatment, truth, lack of bias, consistency, and respect of others

Event(s)—A type of meeting or a function within a meeting; see APEX glossary; temporary attractions

Exhibition(s)—A type of meeting, often used interchangeably with "exposition"; see APEX glossary

Exposition(s)—A type of meeting, often used interchangeably with "exhibition"; see APEX glossary

Eye (Eye in the Sky)—Electronic surveillance equipment suspended from the ceiling and tied into a central observation point

False Light—A misrepresentation of one's character, beliefs, history, or activities that would hold the person in "false light" to the public

FAM Trip(s)—Familiarization trip

Fermentation—The biological process by which sugars are converted into ethanol and carbon dioxide

Fermented Beverage—Common fermented beverages are beer, wine, sake, and mead

Fill—Bringing additional checks from the cage to the table to replenish the dealer's bankroll

Fixed Expenses—Expenses that, over the short run (a year or less), do not vary with revenue

Flag of Convenience—When a ship is registered in a foreign country for purposes of reducing operating costs and avoiding government regulations

Floor Person—Supervisor of the gaming tables who is responsible for keeping the racks full, attending to any problems at the tables, supervising the dealers, and watching for irregularities

Food Cost—The cost to produce a food item for sale; this includes actual cost of the food, labor costs, and energy costs

Foreign Independent Tour (FIT)—A travel package which normally includes airfare, lodging, and some recreational activities, but is not necessarily just in foreign countries. The traveler is independent when it comes to travel and must get from destination to destination on their own by driving a rental car or catching trains and busses

Forms of Ownership—Senior living centers can be owned by private groups, religious orders, corporations, and trusts (REITs)

Franchise—A form of business organization in which a firm that has a successful product or service (the franchisor) enters into a contractual relationship with other businesses (franchisees), operate under the franchisor's trade name, and use the franchisors methods and expertise in exchange for a fee

Franchise Advisory Board—Franchise advisory boards address issues of both the franchisor and franchisees or referral organization and its members. Franchisee advisory groups can be a valuable source of marketing, operations, and product/service development ideas

Franchisee—A person or organization that contracts with a franchisor to use their business name and/or licensing of trademarks and methods of doing business

Franchisor—Organization granting a franchise and providing business name and/or the licensing of trademarks and methods of doing business

Frolic—A substantial deviation from the employer's work for the employee's own personal reasons

Full Care Centers/Nursing Homes—Residency centers for seniors who need the most care. These facilities offer the full array of support including medical, pharmacy, and personal services

Full Membership—Entitles a member to full use of the club, all amenities during any hour of operation

Furniture, Fixtures, and Equipment—A major portion of hospitality capital expenditures

Galley—A kitchen on a cruise ship

Game Show—Involves members of the public or celebrities, sometimes as part of a team, competing for points or prizes

Gaming/Gambling—Casino style activities offered on a cruise ship or at a resort

Global Destination Systems—Powerful database systems, such as Apollo, Sabre, and Amadeus, that list and offer ticketing for millions of air, hotel, and rental car services and provide worldwide attraction information

Grand Tour—A kind of education for wealthy noblemen. It was a period of European travel which could last from a few months to 8 years

Gross Profit—Sales revenue minus sales cost

Gross Registered Tonnage—A measurement of a ship's enclosed space

Growth and Demand for Living Centers—Senior Living Centers have an extremely high potential for growth with the number of senior citizens expected to be 36,818,000 by 2010 and 81,999,000 by 2050

Handle—Total amount of money that continually changes hands through a series of bets before it is actually won or lost

Harvest the Business—The entrepreneur makes the determination to sell their business

Heritage Tourism—The practice of people traveling outside of their home community to visit historic sites, to participate in local festivals, to enjoy local arts and crafts, sightseeing, and recreation

High Roller—A premium player; anyone able and willing to spend $5,000 or more in a weekend of gambling

High Season—Typically a 3- or 4-month period when demand for the hospitality service, product, or amenities are at its highest

Host—This is the organization that hires the foodservice operator to manage their foodservice locations

Hotel Ratings System—The system or process by which hotels are evaluated, usually by independent auditors

House—The casino, casino employees, casino's funds or bank

IAEE (formerly IAEM)—International Association of Exhibitions and Events

Incentive Fees—These are additional fees given by owners to contract management companies to encourage them to manage the lodging or foodservice property in a way that increases the property's overall profit

Incentive Travel Houses—These agencies develop customized programs for corporations who offer incentives to induce high employee productivity by providing deluxe travel rewards

Independent Business Owner—Similar to the entrepreneur with the distinction that they prefer operating a single business operation on a smaller scale than a entrepreneur

Industrial Attractions—Consist of operating concerns, manufacturing, and agricultural, whose processes and products are of interest to visitors

Industry Association—An association or organization that represents the needs of members of a certain profession

Information Resources—Places in which information can be placed. Here, information refers to any text, graphics, pictures, narratives, and opinions related to hospitality and tourism

Intangibility—Not perceived by touch, cannot be visualized. Service would be an example of an intangible in the hospitality industry

Internship—A paid or unpaid temporary employment experience designed to acquaint the student to business operations by providing them an opportunity to shadow managers in various positions within a foodservice or lodging facility

Interpersonal Skills—The ability to understand people and work well with them on an individual basis and in groups

Interview—A formal meeting between two or more individuals

Interviewee—Person being interviewed

Interviewer—Person conducting the interview

Intrusion—An intentional intrusion, physical or otherwise, upon the solitude or seclusion of another that would be highly offensive to a reasonable person

IPO—Initial public stock offering. Stock sales registered through the Securities and Exchange Commission for typically younger companies

ISES—International Special Events Society

Journals—Academic research publications done by educators and industry practitioners

Labor Cost—The cost of labor in running your operation; this includes wages and benefit costs

Labor Intensive—The business or industry that employs a large number of employees to provide customers with a product or service

Labor-Intensive Business—Many of the services provided by the industry require high levels of personal service and attention to detail. This is a key element of the hospitality industry

Leadership—The influencing of others to channel their activities toward reaching the goals of the business

Lifespan—An attraction classification according to their lifespan or time-related criteria based upon their duration

Limited-Service—Lodging facilities that provide a limited number of services to the guests

Liqueur—A distilled beverage with a higher sugar content

Long-Term Stay—Lodging facilities where all guestrooms include a kitchenette and provide clean, comfortable, inexpensive rooms that meet the basic needs of the guests

Look-to-Book Ratio—Number of requests to a booking engine per reservation made

Low Roller—A person who makes $1 and $2 bets; also known as *grinds*, *suckers*, or *tinhorns*

Low Season—Typically a 3- or 4-month period where demand for the hospitality service, product, or amenities is at its lowest

Macro Environment—The external, global factors exerting pressure on the hospitality organization, typically categorized by identifying the STEEP criteria

Man-Made Attractions—Owe their very existence to the intervention of humans

Management—The process of getting tasks accomplished through people.

Marker—An IOU or credit extended to a player

Market Share—The portion of the overall market that a company can quantify as recurring sales on a consistent basis. Divide actual product sales by total available product in a particular product market

Master's Degree—A degree awarded by a graduate school or department, usually to a person who has completed the necessary coursework

Meeting(s)—When two or more people get together at the same time and same place for a common purpose

Meeting Management—Strategic decision-making and coordination to host a meeting

Meeting Planning—Making logistical arrangements to host a meeting

Mega Resort—A final or primary destination where one can find all aspects of the hospitality industry either in a highly compact region or within the confines of a specific hospitality property

Member—Regardless of type of club, each is made up of members, who have applied for and been accepted into membership

Member Benefits—Products, services, or perks available to an individual as part of an organizational membership

Micro Environment—The immediate, internal surroundings within a hotel (or other hospitality entity), including multiple departments and their standard operating procedures

Military Clubs—Cater to enlisted men and women and the noncommissioned officer; provides a social outlet, often has golf

Mission Statement—A statement of purpose that defines an organization. A mission statement is usually one to two sentences long and outlines the values and identity of the organization

Mom and Pop—An independent restaurant or hotel usually owned by one person, a group of people, or a family without any franchise affiliation

Moment of Truth—Actual person-to-person interactions between the customer and the person delivering the service experience

Moral Development Theory—Lawrence Kohlberg's conception of the three components for morality and leadership: preconventional; conventional; and postconventional

MPI—Meeting Professionals International

Multi-Use Resorts—Combination of recreational facilities, resort hotels, timeshare units, residential single or multi-family homes that make up the resort offerings

Museum—Typically a nonprofit, permanent institution in the service of society and of its development and open to the public, that acquires, conserves, researches, communicates, and exhibits for purposes of study, and education enjoyment, the tangible and intangible evidence of people and their environment

Myth—A false belief

Natural Attractions—Those that occur in nature without human intervention

NCA—National Club Association

Negligence—The cause of action that arises when a duty owed to someone on the property is breached, resulting in injury or damages to the individual

Networking—The process of connecting with people of like interests who may be of help to you and you a help to them

Non-Destination Resort—The nearby man-made or natural attraction is the primary reason for travel and stay at the resort, not the resort itself

Noncommercial/Institutional Foodservice—Foodservice operations where the service of food is not the primary function of the operation where food is being served

Nonprofit Organization—An economic institution that operates like a business but does not seek financial gain

Occupancy Percentage—The ratio relating the number of rooms sold to the number of rooms available

Offline Resources—Hardcopy of periodicals (i.e., magazines, newspapers, journals, newsletters)

Online Resources—Information can be retrieved from a Website

On-Site Foodservice—Noncommercial foodservice usually thought of as institutional that serves the dining needs in areas such as healthcare, schools and universities, corporate and manufacturing operations, military, children and adult communities, and correctional facilities

On-Site Foodservice Management—This is the term used to describe the contract foodservice segment of the hospitality industry

Operator—The individual or organization that manages the day-to-day operations of the lodging property or foodservice location

Operator Loan and Equity Contributions—This is a way for contract management companies to contribute to reducing the debt incurred by the owners. It is also a method of gaining some ownership (equity) in the property. Operators may offer loans to the owners the help offset start-up costs or cover initial cash flow losses. Operators may also offer funding or equity in the property. These equity contributions are typically 5 to 15% of the total equity investment

Operator System Reimbursable Expenses—These are the funds paid to the operator by the owner for property management systems, marketing programs, management information systems, foodservice management systems, etc

Opportunity—The premise of a business proposition that has gone beyond a good idea and shows a viable market with income potential

Organization Chart—A diagram that describes the basic arrangement of work in a business

Organization's Culture—A system of shared meaning held by members that distinguishes the organization from other organizations

Organizing—The efforts involved with determining what activities are to be done and how employees are grouped together to accomplish specific tasks

Origin—Classifies if the attraction is natural or man-made

Outside Sales Agents—Individual who is affiliated with the travel agency, acting as an independent contractor, not employee, who sells travel products and shares commissions with their affiliated agency

Owner—The individuals or corporations that legally own the lodging property or foodservice location

Patent—The grant of a property right to an inventor issued by the United States Patent and Trademark Office

PCMA—Professional Convention Management Association

Periodicals—Publications such as magazines, newspapers, and journals that are published on a regular basis such as daily, weekly, monthly, or quarterly

Peripheral Careers—The employment opportunities that help hospitality enterprises get their products and services from creation to consumption

Perishability—A product with a determined shelf life. Food would be an example of a perishable product in the hospitality industry

Pit—In the casino layout, a single grouping of adjacent table games

Pit Manager—In the casino management hierarchy, the most senior gaming supervisor in the pit who supervises play and the activities of several floor persons. Also known as the *Pit Boss*

Plaintiff—The alleged aggrieved person who commences the lawsuit

Planned Play Environments—These provide recreation and entertainment sporting facilities, such as ski and golf resorts; commercial attractions which include theme and amusement

Planning—The establishment of goals and objectives and deciding how to accomplish these goals

PMS—The computerized systems used by hotels to manage its rooms revenue, room rates, reservations and room assignments, guest histories, and accounting information, as well as other guest service and management information functions

Portion Control—The designation of specific portion size as a means of controlling costs

POS (Point of Sale)—A network of electronic cash registers and pre-check terminals that interface with a remote central processing unit

POS—A location at which goods and services are purchased

Preferred Providers—Agencies sign contracts with specific suppliers to try and sell their services first and in return receive a large sales commission

Proactive Management—The technique of forecasting problems and creating a plan for their resolution

Profit Sharing Plan—A benefit given employees, in addition to salary and wages, that permits them to share in a percentage of the profits of the company, distributed to them in either dollars or shares of ownership in the company. Profit sharing motivates employees to be more productive

Proprietary Clubs—Those owned by a corporation, company, business, or individual; they are for profit businesses

Purchasing—The job of procuring general and specialized equipment, materials, and business services for use by an establishment

Purser—The person on a ship responsible for the handling of money on board

Quick Service Restaurant (QSR)—Considered to be informal dining establishments that specialize in delivering food quickly

Rate Integrity—Maintaining confidence in rate tiers, financial strategies, and value of product to price

RCMA—Religious Conference Management Association

Reactive Management—The technique of resolving unexpected problems that ensures customer retention and satisfaction

Real Estate Representative—A person who works for the hospitality firm that specializes in real estate transactions, including site location and analysis

Recreational Amenities—Amenities such as golf, tennis, scuba diving, spa, fishing, and hiking activities that are provided to the guest at a resort

Receptive Operator—A company may meet and greet groups at airports, make arrangements for lodging, and shuttle them to the lodging at one particular destination and offer foreign language interpreters

Referral Organization—Referral organizations are comprised of member properties that are linked together for marketing purposes

Relocation—The act of moving from one place to another for employment advancement

Residential Resort Lifestyle Communities—Primarily second home developments that provide residents the comforts, activities, ambience and amenities found at resorts

Resort—Blending of food, beverage, and lodging offerings with recreational activities and amenities in an ambient environment

Resort Cruise Ships—Floating resorts that offer a wide range of recreation, entertainment, and programming activities for guests

Resort Hotel—Range in size from few to thousands of rooms and as self-contained environments appeal to business and leisure guests seeking relaxation, lodging, recreation activities, and meeting facilities on site

Resort Spa—Located on resort property, offering many spa treatments that are often available to both resort and outside guests

Resources—People, financial, and assets (such as physical plant and equipment) used by the entrepreneur to pursue opportunities and convert them into wealth

Respite Care—Short term care designed to fill the needs of an individual who may need assistance in recovery from surgery, injury, or other ailment and only needs temporary assistance during recovery and rehabilitation. Respite care generally lasts from one week to a few months

Respondeat Superior—The concept that an employer will be held liable (vicariously) for the acts or omissions of an employee which occur in the course and scope of employment

Restaurant—An establishment where meals are served to customers

Restaurant Ratings System—The system or process by which restaurants are evaluated, usually by independent auditors

Resume—A brief account of one's educational, professional, or work experiences and quantifications submitted for consideration of employment

Return on Investment—Measure of profits achieved calculating the ratio of net income to total assets (simplest version)

Revenue—Incoming money obtained from guests by the selling of food, drink, or hotel rooms

Revenue Forecast—An estimate of money earned from sales or in exchange for goods or services over a period of time (typically on a monthly or annual basis)

Revenue Per Guest Usage—Total resort revenue (includes all supporting recreation amenity activity) divided by the total number of guest visits

RFP (Request for Proposal)—Distributed by planners, this tool solicits availability of specific dates, rates, and entertainment options at various hotels within a specified geographic market

Right of Publicity—The use of the name or likeness of a celebrity for commercial purposes

Risk Management—The process of recognizing potential risks (physical and otherwise), assessing those risks, and developing strategic responses to manage and minimize those risks

Sales Commission—A percentage of the sales price paid by the supplier to the agent upon the purchase of a travel product or service

SBA (Small Business Administration)—Often underwrite loans through commercial lending institutions for small business financing

SBIC (Small Business Investment Companies)—Federally funded private venture capital firms funding primarily expansions of new or risky ventures

Scientific Management—The movement started by Frederick Taylor (Father of Scientific Management) in the early 1900s that involved creating efficiencies in the production process through time and motion studies. Taylor championed the idea that management, not workers, should control how "work" was done; therefore, every step of the process need be broken down into the most efficient steps for them to follow

Secondary Attraction—Of lesser importance to the traveler and might be considered simply a stop along the way to get to the primary attraction

Security Department—The department that controls and protects the casino from crimes, and provides the protection of all people who are legitimately on the firm's property from bodily harm caused by the deliberate behavior of another person

Self-Operators—These are organizations who manage their own foodservice locations, even though foodservice is not their area of expertise

Service—1) A type of product that is intangible, goods that are inseparable from the provider, variable in quality, and perishable. 2) The reason why private clubs exist; members receive high-end, personalized service at their club

Service Experience—Sum total of the experience that the customer has with the service provider on a given occasion

Service Product—Entire bundle of tangibles and intangibles in a transaction which has a significant service component

SGMP—Society for Government Meeting Professionals

Shift Manager—In the casino management hierarchy, the person who controls the entire casino on his shift and answers only to the casino manager

Shopping—Searching for or buying goods or services

Site—A particular facility or place for a meeting or event

Site Inspection(s)—Touring a particular facility or place to determine when, if, and how to use that site

Site Selection—Determining which site to use for a meeting or event

Slot Attendants—In general are the base line employees of the department and report to the slot supervisor

Slot Shift Managers—Responsible for overseeing the same responsibilities as the slot manager, but only during their assigned shift

Slot Manager—The person responsible for the direction and administration of controls with regard to personnel and operations within the department

Slots—An abbreviation for slot machines, which are the mechanical or computerized game machines

Slot Supervisor—Reports to the slot shift manager, and has duties including assigning the duties of all slot attendants, paying jackpots, filling machine hoppers, and completing related paperwork, as well as handling any complaints from the slot customers

SMERFE Market Segmentation (Social, Military (or Medical), Educational, Religious, Fraternal and Environmental)—Standardized industry categories of group clients targeted through sales and marketing initiatives

Social Membership—Entitles a member to limited use of a country club, typically dining, pool, and tennis, but not golf; reduced initiation fee and dues structure

Social Networking—Interacting with people who can impact your career options or advancement

Space Ratio—An approximation of how much space is on a cruise ship; divide the GRT by the number of passengers

Space Tourism—The commercial development by private enterprise for the public at large of earth orbital and sub-orbital flights, beyond earth orbit experiences, and earth-based simulations for both training and entertainment purposes

Special Event(s)—Typically, this is a one-time celebration

Spirits—Common distilled beverages (spirits) are vodka, gin, whisky, tequila, etc.

Sport(s) Event(s)—An activity for the purpose of sports competition

Stabilizer—Winglike projections on a cruise ship that is used to reduce and eliminate roll (side-to-side movement)

Staffing—Supplying the human requirements necessary to service guests

Status of Attraction—The importance or interest to the traveler

Statute of Limitations—The minimum timeframe during which a plaintiff must file their lawsuit in order to proceed with the litigation

Strategies—Long term operational goals and direction of a business

Student Organizations—These are groups of students that come together in their free time to organize activities to support their common vocational interests

Supply and Demand—Supply is the amount of product and/or service available in the market (e.g., hotel rooms, restaurant seats, cruise berths) while demand is the amount of desire from consumers to partake of that product and/or service

Support Services—Services provided in addition to basic living, such as transportation, housekeeping, laundry, pharmacy, and more

Support Staff—Professionals who work in hospitality and tourism but not in an operations management position

Surveillance Department—The department with the ability of the organization to observe all behaviors on the total area of the property

S.W.O.T. Analysis (Strengths, Weaknesses, Opportunities, Threats)—A traditional company's assessment of the status of their product and services, both internally (via strengths and weaknesses) and externally (via opportunities and threats) as they relate to the competition

Table Games—A game that uses a table as part of the action

Technical Skills—The skills involving knowledge of and the ability to perform a particular job or task

Tender—A boat that ferries passenger from the ship to the port when the cruise ship is too big to dock at the pier

Tenure—Status granted, usually after a probationary period, indicating that the position is permanent

Term—This is the length of the contract between the operator and owner

The 4 P's of the Marketing Mix (Product, Price, Place, Promotion)—Identifying the goods/services, sales amount, location for distribution, and manner of marketing within the outreach process

The Marriott Way—The management style that incorporates concern for all associates (employees), hands-on management, and an unrelenting commitment to customer service as articulated by Bill Marriott

Theme Parks—Offer escape; as a result of modern technology they replicate both real as well as "unreal" places that may or may not exist beyond the gates

Third Party Distribution System—These organizations do not own the products or services that they are selling; their role is to connect buyers with sellers

Third Party Liquor Liability—An expense incurred as the result of a lawsuit by an injured party, i.e., to bring suit for loss or injury as a result of being served alcoholic beverages to level of intoxication

Ticketing Fee—An additional charge above the base cost of the ticket that is charged by a TMC to cover their ticketing costs

Top Down Approach—Is a method of attempting to sell the most expensive item first and then offering a less expensive item next if there is continued sales resistance

Topography—Can be broadly subdivided into three areas of interest: *landforms*, *wildlife*, and *ecology*

Torts—A large classification of different types of civil wrongs that result in injury or damages to either people or property

Tour Escort—A person who travels with a group and acts as guide and business manager, using the skills of a teacher, entertainer, accountant, doctor, and psychologist

Tour Operators—Organize market and operate packages of travel services with a variety of themes, ranging from adventure to sightseeing, for groups or individuals

Trademark—Is a word, name, symbol, or device that is used in trade with goods to indicate the source of the goods and to distinguish them from the goods of others

Trade Secret—A formula, pattern, design, process, instrument, practice, or compilation of information used to obtain a competitive advantage over competitors

Tradeshow(s)—An exhibition of products or services for a specific trade or industry

Travel Agent—Individuals within a travel management company that match and ticket the travel desires of leisure and business travelers with most appropriate suppliers of tourist services

Travel Management Company—A contemporary term for travel agencies that provide consulting, ticketing, and management of travel products for leisure and business traveler

Trend—A general course of action, direction, or behavior pattern that can be identified as a focus of marketing efforts

U.S. Small Business Administration—Provides counseling, business plan assistance, and available financing for small business concerns in the U.S.

Units—A term used in the hotel industry that is more commonly referred to as a hotel room

University—An institution of learning at the highest level, authorized to confer both undergraduate and graduate degrees

Unreasonable Publication of Private Facts—The public disclosure of true, but private, information which would offend a reasonable person if released (such as the release of a persons' medical records to the local newspaper by that person's doctor)

Upscale Restaurant—A foodservice establishment that offers the best in food, beverages, and level of service

Up-Selling—A selling technique used to convince customers to purchase one of your more expensive items first

Vacation-Ownership Firm—A business focused on selling long-term vacation packages to guests; these "slices of time" may be hotel rooms or condominium units located at a specific property, or they may be sold as "points" which are used for future vacations

Vacation Ownership/Timeshare Resorts/Condo Hotels—In the most basic form it is the right to accommodations and use of recreational facilities at a vacation development for a specified time period for a defined number of years or into perpetuity, as defined in the purchase agreement or redeemable through purchased vacation club points

Variable Expense—An expense that varies on a linear basis with sales or revenue

Venture Capitalist—An investor who provides capital for medium- to high-risk entrepreneurial venture for a higher than normal rate of return

Venue—A specific location for a meeting or event, often refers to a facility

Virtual Conferencing—A business activity held via technology over a distance, rather than meeting face-to-face

Virtual Meeting(s)—A meeting that is held between two or more people at a distance, via technology, rather than meeting face-to-face

Vision—Leadership quality for creating the future. An essential quality for leadership; a successful vision is leader initiated, shared, and supported by followers

Vitea—A brief biographical resume of one's career and training often used in education

Vocational Programs—Programs focused on providing skills and education that prepares you for a job

Volume Purchasing—Purchasing in bulk volume in order to save money as most suppliers will offer a discount for volume purchasing

Win—The amount of each dollar wagered that is won or held by the house before operating expenses and other costs have been paid and does not represent profit

Wine—A fermented alcoholic beverage made from fruit

World's First National Park—Yellowstone was created in 1872

Yacht Club—Establishments near or on the water, activities center around sailing and boating, dining also available

Yield Management—A combination of occupancy percentage and the average daily rate

Index